CURRICULAR AND INSTRUCTIONAL APPROACHES FOR PERSONS WITH SEVERE DISABILITIES

edited by

ENNIO CIPANI

University of the Pacific

FRED SPOONER

University of North Carolina at Charlotte

ALLYN AND BACON

Boston   London   Toronto   Sydney   Tokyo   Singapore

ACKNOWLEDGMENTS

We would like to acknowledge the support and assistance of the reviewers who worked with us in shaping the content of the text: Michael P. Brady, University of Houston; Jacki L. Anderson, California State University, Hayward; David L. Westling, Florida State University; and Eileen M. Furey, University of Connecticut. The authors who have contributed to the content also deserve a special thank you for their persistence, perseverance, and patience in the completion of their respective chapters. Melba Spooner, Paul Fleischer, Peggy Ingram, and Phyllis Griffin, University of North Carolina at Charlotte, played important editorial roles and assisted in facilitating communication between the staff at Allyn and Bacon and the contributing authors. We appreciate the efforts of Paul and Nancy Fleischer, Charlotte, North Carolina, Jim Morgan, Albuquerque, New Mexico, and Edie-Jo Lane Hood for their assistance in preparing the Instructor's guide. Finally, we would like to thank the support staff at Allyn and Bacon, including Ray Short, Christine Shaw, and other assistants.

Series Editor: Ray Short
Editorial Assistant: Christine Shaw
Cover Administrator: Linda Dickinson
Manufacturing Buyer: Louise Richardson
Editorial-Production Service: Spectrum Publisher Services
Cover Designer: Suzanne Harbison

Copyright © 1994 by Allyn and Bacon
A Division of Paramount Publishing
160 Gould Street
Needham Heights, Massachusetts 02194

Library of Congress Cataloging-in-Publication Data

Cipani, Ennio.
    Curricular and instructional approaches for persons with severe disabilities / Ennio Cipani, Fred Spooner.
        p.   cm.
    Includes bibliographical references (p.   ) and index.
    ISBN 0-205-14090-4
    1. Handicapped students—Education—United States. 2. Handicapped students—Education—United States—Curricula. I. Spooner, Fred. II. Title.
LC4031.C56   1993
371.91'0973—dc20   93-38165
                                            CIP

Printed in the United States of America

10 9 8 7 6 5 4 3 2 1   98 97 96 95 94 93

This book is dedicated to our families and mentors: the Cipani family, Lucinda, Lorenzo, Vanessa, and Alessandra; the Spooner family, Melba, Travis, and Jason; Jon S. Bailey, Florida State University; and H. William Heller, University of South Florida, St. Petersburg Campus.

CONTENTS

James E. Martin
School of Education, University of Colorado–Colorado Springs

Linda A. Heyne and Stuart J. Schleien
University of Minnesota–Minneapolis

Joe Reichle
University of Minnesota

Jeff Sigafoos
University of Queensland

Lori Goetz and Pam Hunt
*San Francisco State University and The California
Research Institute*

**CHAPTER 11   STRATEGIES AND INSTRUCTIONAL PROCEDURES
TO PROMOTE SOCIAL INTERACTIONS
AND RELATIONSHIPS   289**

Thomas G. Haring
University of California–Santa Barbara

Diane Ryndak
State University College at Buffalo

**CHAPTER 12   A FUNCTIONAL APPROACH TO ACADEMICS
INSTRUCTION   322**

Deborah Bott Slaton, John Schuster, and Belva Collins
University of Kentucky

Douglas Carnine
University of Oregon

CHAPTER 13   ASSISTIVE TECHNOLOGY   351

Mary K. Dykes
University of Florida–Gainesville

Julia M. Lee
Valdosta State College

PART THREE
ISSUES IN SERVICE DELIVERY   365

FOREWORD

Sometime about 10 years ago, invitations to deliver a keynote address stopped coming to me and, instead, requests to do the history on the development of programs for students with disabilities came in their place. But as I reflect more on this, I have come to realize that there are certain advantages to longevity in any discipline of research and study. Beyond the obvious advantage of becoming "senior," it does place one who has "lived the history" in a position to discriminate and mark the critical issues, significant events, and contributions that have occurred and continue to occur in our profession. In the process, it calls attention to those changes that promise to make a difference in the way we serve people with disabilities.

The historical perspective provides a reference for evaluating change and determining whether current ideas are new or a recycling of ideas we have had before. If an idea is new, does it really represent an increment of progress, or is it possibly regressive? Obviously, progress in technologies and practices advances at different rates. New practices arise slowly in some disciplines, whereas in others advances occur so rapidly that by the time one is handily using the new technology, it is obsolete.

There is another contrast in educational practices that is clearly discernible. It is contrast, in the advancement of our policies and procedures, between those used with students with mild disabilities and those used with people with severe disabilities. For students with mild disabilities, contemporary educational thought is to implement a whole-language, experience-based curriculum and emphasize full-day placement in regular classrooms. When I was in elementary school, all of the students with mild disabilities and many with moderate disabilities were in the regular grades; learning through actual life experiences, à la John Dewey, was conventional practice. I do not mean to ignore the ground we have covered since my elementary experience, but there are many similarities between what was commonplace in the 1930s and the ideas that are being promoted today in educating students with mild disabilities.

By contrast, the functional education of persons with severe disabilities has shown a steady, straight-ahead, increment-by-increment line of progress toward extended, more effective services. There are good reasons for this. One crucial reason is that the education of students with severe disabilities has used a more empirical, scientific approach to strategy development and decision making. Behavioral change in the predicted direction has been used as the criterion for defining and accepting progress. In addition, educators of students with severe disabilities have seen that there is more to new learning than simply the acquisition of new behaviors. Teaching has been comprehensive, in that it continues until the student performs the behavior competently, in a variety of settings, under a host of conditions—until the skill is a functional addition to the student's response repertoire.

Beyond recognizing the complex nature of learning, we recognize that for students who have severe disabilities, very little incidental learning takes place. Often, when it does occur, incidental learning competes directly with what we have targeted to teach.

We have seen that these students do not easily forgive any faulty logic that may be reflected in our instructional programming, implementation, and consequation of responses. For greatest teaching effectiveness, the historian's perspective reveals the riches our efforts have gained from applying a few crucial rules and principles:

1. Possibly the most important rule is that the skills we teach must have functional value and be used frequently.

   Rule: Teach functional skills and develop skill routines using those skills.

2. The generalized performance of new skills is facilitated by teaching those skills in the setting in which they are used or in as close an approximation as possible, and by providing ample opportunity within those settings for using the skills.

   Rule: Provide natural opportunities to perform functional skills in natural settings to facilitate acquisition and generalization.

3. Because a single skill, such as crossing the street on a green light, is rarely useful in and of itself, teaching the cluster of skills that are necessary for purposeful, functional behavior can be facilitated greatly by teaching these steps in an appropriate sequence. Such a skill cluster might involve crossing several streets (with a variety of conditions and cues), walking several blocks, discriminating an appropriate store, finding the desired items, and making the complete transaction.

   Rule: Sequence skill routines with functional consequences to enhance useful learning.

4. Because there is a highly significant relationship between communication skills and all levels of social interactions, persons with severe communication deficits must develop a method of communication. Where augmentative or alternative communication is indicated, proper assessment and designs for facilitating communication are crucial.

   Rule: Communication (i.e., reciprocal exchange of information) is essential to social interaction.

5. Frequently, when one is teaching new behaviors, well-established "old" behaviors compete stubbornly with the new ones. In these cases it is important that only the new response be reinforced.

   Rule: Reinforce only the behaviors targeted for acquisition.

6. In cases in which inappropriate behaviors persist, conducting functional analyses of those behaviors is the most effective way to establish the events or conditions that systematically precede or follow the behavior. Once the consistent link between the behavior and its consequences is found, the intervention follows readily.

   Rule: Finding the immediate cause of behavior is essential to changing it.

7. Opportunities for a student to see appropriate behaviors and to imitate them can provide an efficient strategy for building desired skills, particularly social skills.

   Rule: Observation and modeling (i.e., vicarious learning) is an efficient strategy for teaching complex behaviors.

8. Continuous monitoring of the student's behavior during skill acquisition and fluency building is particularly critical because undesirable behavior often follows high error rates. High error rates reduce desired learning opportunities for positive consequences.

Rule: Use a data-based decision process when making interventional changes.

It delights me that these rules reverberate throughout this book's assertions on curricular and instructional procedures. These are the procedures that have made possible the gains we have shown through teaching students with severe disabilities. These gains, in turn, have demonstrated great value to the society in which these people are gradually being included. This book is the most comprehensive coverage of curriculum specifically targeted at children and youth with disabilities available at this time for university students. It is far-reaching because it includes vital information about the role of the support disciplines and contemporary instructional technologies.

Another remarkable aspect of this ambitious project is the gifted authors who were selected. Their contributions provide an up-to-date view of the application of behavior principles and the comprehensive management of students with severe disabilities.

Cipani and Spooner, it is clear, knew exactly what they wanted to achieve with this project and accomplished their ideas with style and effectiveness. Historical perspective reveals no shortcuts to effective teaching—the hard work involved in the systematic application of behavior principles embraced in applied behavior analysis provides the most productive basis. The editors and authors punctuate this point clearly throughout. Those who seek shortcuts ultimately shortchange their students. Behaviorism does not attract professionals who like easy practices laced with mentalistic ideas. The paradox is much as Don Baer has put it: "The vast majority of us think of ourselves mentalistically, not behaviorally. Indeed, our stereotype of something called 'behaviorism' is that it denies that we do anything resembling thinking, and so we prove that stereotype wrong every time we think about it."[1]

Norris G. Haring

---

[1]Baer, D. M. (1991). The future of applied behavior analysis for people with severe disabilities. In L. H. Meyer, C. A. Peck, & L. Brown (Eds.), *Critical issues in the lives of people with severe disabilities* (p. 614). Baltimore: Paul Brookes Publishing Co.

PART ONE

BASIC PRINCIPLES OF ASSESSMENT, INSTRUCTION, AND MANAGEMENT

A textbook on curriculum and instruction might begin by asking what the educational system has to offer the learner clientele. Unlike other fields of education in which current service delivery models have existed for decades, educational service for persons with severe disabilities is a relatively recent development (Haring, 1977, 1978; Public Law 94-142). The special education field has seen drastic alterations in the types of service provided and subsequent benefits to the consumer (i.e., persons with severe disabilities). In the 1990s, the potential benefits to the consumer are vastly different than those that were expected as potential outcomes several decades earlier. The following two hypothetical scenarios illustrate potential differences for persons with severe disabilities who were receiving services available in the early 1960s compared with services that are available in the 1990s. The differences include: (1) the educational service delivery system; (2) the development of skills in the learner; (3) the teaching competencies of the teacher; and (4) ultimately, the quality of life.

1960

Bobby is a 6-year-old child who lives at home with his parents. His mental retardation was diagnosed early in life, cause unknown. After his third birthday, his parents were told by their physician that the best alternative for Bobby, given his condition, would be to place him in a state facility for the developmentally disabled. However, Bobby's parents decided to raise their child in their own home, against the advice of their physician and many of their friends who claimed that institutionalization would be in the best interests of all. (The decision to keep their child, rather than put him in an institution, was uncommon. Many other parents "heeded" the advice of professionals and institutionalized their child early in life.) When Bobby reached school age, his parents went to the local public school to see if Bobby could enter kindergarten. He was tested by the school psychologist and found to have a mental age that was less than that of a child 5 years of age. On the basis of this information, the school district indicated that it did not have a program for Bobby since it was obvious that his mental capability was not at a level at which he could profit from such education. His parents were told that it was in Bobby's best interest to not come to school at that point, because it might be "too frustrating for him," given his limited ability. Now, Bobby sits at home where his parents try to do their best to raise him, but without any educational services or technical resources regarding methods to teach him new skills and effectively manage some inappropriate

1

behaviors that are on the increase, it is very likely that Bobby will eventually be institutionalized before the age of 10.

Chris is a 14-year-old female who is more fortunate than Bobby because her skill development at 6 years of age allowed her to receive public educational services. However, after entering the school system, she was immediately placed in a classroom for trainable children who had mental retardation. Her teacher, Mr. Smyth, had taught for 10 years at the junior high school level and felt that he needed a "rest" from the pressures of teaching adolescent boys and girls. He decided on teaching special education because he heard from some fellow teachers that the student–teacher ratio was considerably less compared with a regular class and that most of the time you "just watch the kids to make sure they do not hurt themselves." Mr. Smyth was told by other colleagues that there was no need for daily lesson plans because the students would probably work on the same tasks throughout the year. Chris's educational program consists of a number of tasks designed to teach basic prerequisite skills; for example, stringing beads in a pattern, color-sorting tasks, painting, arts and crafts activities, as well as playing with age-inappropriate games and puzzles. Mr. Smyth gives the students a nap after lunch, because he says, "Most people know that persons with mental retardation need more rest!" The materials, as well as the music, the records, and the games are certainly appropriate for children of 5- to 6-years-of-age, but not appropriate for adolescents! Upon questioning, Mr. Smyth indicated that such materials are designed at a level congruent with the student's mental age. He said he would worry about presenting age-appropriate functional material because these types of tasks might "overload" the students' capacity.

1990

Jane is a 4-year-old girl with severe mental retardation who lives at home with her parents. Her parents receive technical assistance from a trained certified special education teacher for a range of care and education issues, including techniques designed to let Jane become more independent in everyday activities. The teacher, Mrs. Jones, sets up programs for use by the parents in their home. Jane's parents collect data on specific learning objectives and review it with Mrs. Jones biweekly. Three days a week, Jane also attends a preschool program funded by the public schools at a special site. For the other 2 days of the week, she attends a regular preschool with nondisabled children. The teacher at the special site teaches skills that Jane will need to successfully integrate into kindergarten and first grade. At the preschool program with same-age peers Jane works on the same activities as the other children. The preschool teacher at this setting also receives assistance from the special education teacher with effective teaching strategies and task adaptations. This collaboration allows Jane to acquire the new skills.

Manuel is a 16-year-old adolescent with severe mental retardation. He is currently placed in an educational transition program. This program has a number of components designed to teach Manuel critical skills needed for adult life. He spends 3 days a week at a local fast-food restaurant working as a supported employee and learning janitorial skills. The teacher/job coach initially trained him to competently perform the technical aspects of the janitorial position. Now that Manuel is competent in the duties of a janitor, he only requires intermittent monitoring of his performance from the job coach, who collaborates with supervisory staff at the restaurant site. Manuel is now working on developing appropriate social and conversational skills with fellow employees and supervisors. He is also learning relevant domestic and community skills that will allow him to eventually live in a supervised apartment with one other person. He will be taught to meet his needs while living in his apartment by accessing relevant community activities. He will learn to choose what he would like to eat, how to plan daily meals, and how to choose from a variety of leisure activities during the weekend.

The scenarios of the 1960s and the 1990s present quite a contrast. The 1990 scenario does not imply that all persons with severe disabilities currently receive the kind of services just described. Rather, it is the *exceptional* programs that provide a wide range of services, similar to those depicted through Jane and Manuel. However, there are proven methods and technologies to provide such services, given well-trained teachers and other educational personnel. This textbook is about those methods and technologies.

Before presenting our philosophy of the education and treatment of persons with severe disabilities, it is imperative to give a brief glimpse of the characteristics and definitional criteria of learners who have severe disabilities. The definitions and characteristics of such a diagnosis have evolved during the years (Brimer, 1990). Most definitions refer to a functioning level of one half (or less) compared with the expected level that is based on chronological age (Justen, 1976). Later definitions tried to involve a functional aspect by requiring that an assessment of an individual not just be restricted to typical academic, intelligence, and/or achievement tests, but also include an analysis of the functional capability of the individual in everyday environments (Grossman, 1983). The American Psychiatric Association's (APA) Diagnostic and Statistical Manual of Mental Disorders (DSM III-R) identifies several levels of mental retardation. A diagnosis of 318.1, severe mental retardation, is made on the basis of severe mental subnormality, with intelligence quotients (IQs) between 20–34; a diagnosis of 318.2, profound mental retardation, is made on the basis of profound mental subnormality, with IQs under 20 or commonly identified as unmeasurable by a professional psychologist (American Psychiatric Association, 1980). Many states, including California, classify students as having mild disabilities or severe disabilities, with a subsequent placement in classes designated for such persons (Abramowicz & Richardson, 1975; Brown et al., 1977). Often, persons with severe disabilities have severe levels of impaired functioning across all domains and con-

texts, with severe deficiencies in communicative capabilities (Gaylord-Ross & Holvoet, 1985). These deficits can be in addition to other disabilities, including cerebral palsy, physical impairments, and/or behavior disorders.

The classification of persons with severe disabilities includes a variety of problems, skill deficits, and learning styles and capabilities, as well as additional physical and emotional problems that could be quite similar to those found in the general population. The major characteristics of nondisabled persons are difficult to identify in a few sentences. Persons classified as having severe disabilities cannot be described in several sentences either, unless an understanding of the individual differences among people is discounted. In our opinion, there are too many differences to forgo such an analysis.

All of the previous definitions do not take into account the potential differences in learning styles and learning rates of persons with severe disabilities. Perhaps the best definition is a functional one made on the basis of the child's needs in academic and/or basic skills areas (Sailor & Haring, 1977), as well as a possible analysis and understanding of the child's learning rate and potential for skill acquisition, documented via previous history with certain instructional procedures.

The definitions and characteristics of persons with severe disabilities are quite varied. Therefore, the important question is: "What do teachers need to know in order to work with them?" To this question, we offer this textbook!

Curricular and Instructional Approaches for Persons with Severe Disabilities is a compilation of chapters, which encompasses three major areas: (1) basic principles for teaching persons with severe disabilities, (2) curricular and domain areas, and (3) trends and issues in service delivery. All chapters present information that is supported by a strong empirical basis. The editors present a strong advocacy for the empirical approach as a foundation for treatment and educational procedures for teacher training. It is our contention that people who wish to teach individuals with severe disabilities should possess the following qualities upon completion of a preservice university training program: (1) be a solid technician of teaching and management strategies, capable of utilizing current state-of-the-art techniques found to be effective in the research and/or clinical literature; (2) be a scientist practitioner (Barlow, Hayes, & Nelson, 1984), capable of evaluating instructional and management programs and revising such programs as a function of collected data; and (3) be a humanist, capable of feeling empathy and concern for the quality of the lives of the individuals we serve. It is hard to determine whether a textbook (or a college course) can teach and evaluate the latter quality (although we hope that the material presented in this text conveys each author's genuine concern for enhancing the quality of life for individuals with severe disabilities). However, it is imperative that an instructional text be capable of providing skills relevant to the first two qualities, and this book is offered to that end.

Authors of the individual chapters bring nationally recognized expertise to their material. We are fortunate to have assembled such a distinguished group of professionals, all of whom are at the forefront of research and practice in the field of education and in the treatment of persons with severe disabilities. Their expertise provides information on the current methods and techniques for working effectively with this population.

It is our hope that teachers in the disability field are no longer viewed as persons who entered the field because they either failed or did not care to work with nondisabled children (as depicted in the earlier scenario). Rather, we hope the choice to enter this profession was made on the basis of their ability to be an effective teacher, their ability to change the behavior of persons with severe disabilities, and their care and willingness to work with this special population. It was not long ago that teachers in special education and, in particular, those working with students with more severe disabilities, were sometimes teachers who were deemed to be unsuccessful with regular class elementary and secondary students. It is our conten-

tion that an individual who wishes to work in our field needs to be as well trained as other teachers (Sontag, Burke, & York, 1973). A teacher's repertoire of instruction and management strategies critical for success in our field represents a much greater basis of a teaching technology than those repertoires needed for success in working with nondisabled learners. Such a technology base was developed from research literature that makes available a powerful instructional and behavioral technology for practitioners in this field.

In the 1990s, the state of affairs for persons with severe disabilities is drastically improved from that available to this clientele just several decades ago, given this technological base. Examine the two scenarios presented earlier and contrast the differences in the training techniques, skills, and instruction of the teachers; the skills being taught to the learner (as well as *where* the skills were taught); and the ability to acquire such skills, given a solid instructional program. One can quickly identify that we have come a long way in the past several decades! The multitude of studies conducted in applied settings across the country have built an empirical basis for sound practice at the local level (Matson, 1990; Spooner & Test, 1991). This immediate applicability to problems and issues that affect the lives of persons with severe disabilities has allowed these people, and their loved ones, to hope for a more fruitful and useful life in the mainstream of society. It is to this end that the current book promotes useful, empirically derived strategies for classroom and community environments.

The chapters contained in Part I involve basic principles for working with persons with severe disabilities. One must be able to learn to walk before one can run; in a similar vein, before the reader begins to acquire specific skills in teaching relevant behaviors and skills in a variety of contexts to persons with severe disabilities, he or she must have some general overriding principles that guide everyday teaching and management behaviors. The first five chapters cover the basic principles that one must have in order to be an effective teacher of persons with severe disabilities.

In the first chapter, the authors describe basic principles of behavior change. The research conducted during the last several decades in the disability field is well-grounded in the basic principles of operant behavior, beginning with an early study in 1949 to increase arm movement in a person with profound mental retardation (Fuller, 1949). It is the editors' contention that current and future teachers must have a thorough grounding in such principles in order to effectively utilize the teaching techniques and procedures discussed in Part II. An understanding of basic principles of behavior forms is the "skeleton" of the skills to be acquired by the teacher. Once the skeleton is in place, the individual will be able to comprehend, utilize, adapt, and generalize the methods and techniques offered in later chapters. Behavior analysis is seen as an enabling methodology for the application of the principles and philosophy of normalization to include people with more severe disabilities by providing a powerful teaching and behavioral technology.

The second chapter provides specific information on functional assessment. Assessment is the cornerstone to effective instructional practice. Chapter 2 takes a strong stand in requiring assessment of children, adolescents, and young adults to be functional (i.e., address the child's needs and requirements to live a life with nondisabled peers) as much as possible. It is not enough for an assessment to determine that a child has a disability. That information is not useful in determining what can be done about the disability and often provides information apparent to nonprofessionals. This chapter provides information on purposes and processes of functional assessment, as well as methods for involving family members in the assessment process and subsequent individualized education plans (IEPs).

Chapter 3 provides information that is utilized as a direct result of the data obtained in the assessment process. At this point, the teacher needs to have skills in identifying a functional model for program and curriculum development. This chapter complements the information provided in the second chapter. An assessment of the person's needs in current and future settings dictates the nature of the educational program components and related curriculum. Functional assessment leads to effective instruction. This link between assessment, program development, and instruction will dominate the discussion of material in the curriculum and domain chapters found in Part II. The stress on teaching skills to a mastery level and fluent criterion, that maintain over time and generalize to relevant environments, is a critical requirement of all IEPs.

In summary, the latter two chapters teach competence in one important aspect: identifying *what to teach*. Once the teacher has identified what to teach (that being relevant functional useful skills), the question then becomes *how to teach*.

Chapter 4 presents the principles of an instructional technology and its application to everyday teaching situations in classrooms, home, and community settings. This chapter presents basic methods and teachings that form the basis of the instructional program described in Part II. From a behavioral perspective, the field of instructional technology comprises a set of procedures based on operant conditioning principles. After several decades of research, such procedures have been empirically verified with persons who have severe disabilities and have been refined in the 1990s to allow a teacher to develop a wide variety of skills needed for community and domestic environments. For those readers coming from a nonbehavioral background, the procedures delineated in Chapter 3 could appear quite novel. However, in keeping with our earlier contention regarding effective teaching behaviors, such systematic procedures, which teach targeted skills in a precise fashion, are the mainstay of educational practice for teachers in this field.

Finally, the basic principles section would be incomplete if the state-of-the-art techniques available for intervening with possible behavior and management problems sometimes exhibited by persons with severe disabilities were not addressed. Chapter 5 provides an introduction and description of behavior problems found in persons with severe disabilities and approaches them with an inclination to use techniques developed from operant principles, which are based on a nonaversive approach to intervention. This type of knowledge is necessary when designing interventions that are both powerful in terms of their effect on the child's behavior as well as acceptable to the members of society (deemed nonaversive). This chapter provides a historical look at "where we've been" and also examines the current persuasion of professionals to utilize a functional analysis of behavior in determining the relevant treatment of choice.

REFERENCES

Abramowicz, H., & Richardson, S. (1975). Epidemiology of severe mental retardation in children: Community studies. *American Journal of Mental Deficiency, 80,* 18–39.

American Psychiatric Association. (1980). *Diagnostic and Statistical Manual (DSM-III-R).* Washington, DC: American Psychiatric Association.

Barlow, D. H., Hayes, S. C., & Nelson, R. O. (1984). *The scientist practitioner: Research accountability in clinical and education setting.* New York: Pergamon Press.

Brimer, R. W. (1990). *Students with severe disabilities: Current perspectives and practices.* Mountain View, CA: Mayfield.

Brown, L., Wilcox, B., Sontag, E., Vincent, B., Dodd, N., & Gruenwald, L. (1977). Toward the realization of the least restrictive educational environments for severe handicapped students. *AAESPH Review, 2,* 195–201.

Fuller, P. (1949). Operant conditioning of a vegetative organism. *American Journal of Psychology, 62,* 587–590.

Gaylord-Ross, R., & Holvoet, J. F. (1985). *Strategies for educating students with severe handicaps.* Boston: Little, Brown & Company.

Grossman, H., (Ed.). (1983). *Classification in mental retardation.* Washington, DC: American Association on Mental Deficiency.

Haring, N. G. (1977). Welcome address to the second annual AAESPH Conference, Kansas City, Missouri, November 12–14, 1975. In N. G. Haring & L. J. Brown (Eds.), *Teaching the severely handicapped, Volume II.* New York: Grune & Stratton.

Haring, N. G. (1978). Progress and Perspectives. In N. G. Haring and D. D. Bricker, (Eds.), *Teaching the severely handicapped: Volume III.* Columbus, OH: Special Press.

Justen, J. (1976). Who are the severely handicapped? A problem in definition. *AAESPH Review, 1*(5), 1–11.

Matson, J. (1990). *Handbook on behavior modification with the mentally retarded* (2nd ed.). New York: Plenum Press.

Sailor, W., & Haring, N. G. (1977). Some current dimensions in the education of the severely/multiply handicapped. *AAESPH Review, 2,* 3–23.

Sontag, E., Burke, P., & York, R. (1973). Considerations for saving the severely handicapped in the public schools. *Education and Training of the Mentally Retarded, 8,* 20–26.

Spooner, F., & Test, D. W. (1991). *TASH monograph on instruction.* Seattle: The Association for Persons with Severe Handicaps.

CHAPTER 1

BASIC PRINCIPLES OF LEARNING

RANDY LEE WILLIAMS
VIKKI F. HOWARD
BETTY FRY WILLIAMS
T. F. MCLAUGHLIN
Department of Special Education, Gonzaga University

In their seminal article, Baer, Wolf, and Risley (1968) stated,

> *Analytic behavioral application is the process of applying sometimes tentative principles of behavior to the improvement of specific behaviors, and simultaneously evaluating whether or not any changes noted are indeed attributable to the process of application—and if so, to what parts of that process. (p. 91)*

In other words, applied behavior analysis is concerned with objectively *analyzing* the causes of socially significant and observable *behavior* in *applied* or natural settings. In regard to persons with severe disabilities, the scientific study of human behavior involves the attempt to determine the causes of behavior and effective means to change behavior. Although applied behavior analysts do not minimize the effects of genetics or other biophysical factors, these factors usually cannot, and perhaps should not, be manipulated. Thus, applied behavior analysts focus on the environmental variables that can be altered to improve individuals' behaviors and, consequently, their lives. The term *applied behavior analysis* came into widespread use with the publication of the *Journal of Applied Behavior Analysis* in 1968, replacing the formerly used, and less accurate, terms *operant conditioning* and *behavior modification*.

Applied technology has evolved from a rich history of early laboratory research. Very tightly controlled laboratory studies were conducted initially with animals, and later with people. These studies were critical in determining the basic principles that control behavior. Skinner (1953) described the science of human behavior as moving systematically (1) from determining lawful relationships between environmental events and behavior, (2) to predicting under what circumstances particular behavior would occur, and, finally, (3) to utilizing learning principles to establish control over behavior, such as in effective treatments for persons with severe handicaps. Wolf (1978) later added that the key consumers of the behavior change programs (e.g., parents, teachers, employers, etc.) needed to evaluate whether the procedures were socially acceptable to them and whether the changes in targeted behaviors were perceived as being important changes.

Applied behavior analysis consists of applying the findings of basic research regarding the basic principles of learning for the purpose of changing behavior (Kazdin, 1978). This application is directed at increasing and maintaining socially sig-

The authors would like to dedicate this chapter to the memory of B. F. Skinner (1904–1990) whose lifetime achievements have brought about countless significant improvements to the technology of teaching persons with severe disabilities and to the quality of their lives.

nificant appropriate and adaptive behaviors and eliminating inappropriate or maladaptive behaviors. This approach is in contrast to the prevalent medical model, which views abnormal and maladaptive behavior as symptomatic of some underlying physical, psychological, or processing disorder. The medical model views the correction of these underlying processes as the key to eliminating current and future symptoms (Ross, 1977). On the other hand, applied behavior analysis focuses attention on directly changing the unwanted behaviors, without assuming that underlying factors are the key to improvement (although physiological processes may play a part). Before describing the basic principles of learning, it will be useful to one's understanding of the field to provide a brief history of applied behavior analysis and its initial application to persons with severe disabilities.

HISTORY OF APPLIED BEHAVIOR ANALYSIS

A behavioral approach to analyzing behavior began with the pioneering work of three Russian physiologists in the late nineteenth century: Ivan Sechenov, Ivan Pavlov, and Vladimer Bechterev (Kazdin, 1978). Unlike most professionals of their day, these researchers brought objective methodologies to the study of behavior. As a result, their work helped to move psychology under the umbrella of science and away from unsubstantiated and metaphysical explanations of behavior. The Russian researchers interpreted and evaluated behavior in terms of responses occurring as the result of preceding or antecedent stimuli. Pavlov's research into conditioned reflexes was particularly rigorous and influential in the interpretation of the causes of behavior (Pavlov, 1927). One of Pavlov's classic studies still illustrates clearly one of the two major categories of behavior, *respondent behavior,* and how that behavior may be conditioned to occur in the presence of a previously neutral stimulus.

Pavlov noted that food, coming into contact with the tongue of a dog, inherently and reliably resulted in the reflex of salivation. The food was known as an unconditioned stimulus (UCS), which elicited the unconditioned response (UCR) of salivation. Pavlov found that the sight of food also elicited salivation, and yet the sight of food, he reasoned, could not physiologically cause the salivation. Apparently, the sight of food elicited salivation because it was always paired with the food that was then put in the dog's mouth. To test this idea, he took a formerly neutral stimulus (NS), a tone ("neutral" in that it did not cause salivation), and immediately preceded the presentation of food with the tone. After a number of pairings of the tone (NS) and the food (UCS), the tone alone elicited salivation. The tone then was known as a conditioned stimulus (CS) that elicited the conditioned response (CR) of salivation. Figure 1.1 outlines the major steps of this study in respondent conditioning.

Pavlov's research greatly influenced the work

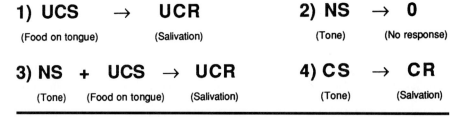

FIGURE 1.1   A diagram of the classic study by Pavlov in which he respondently conditioned a dog to salivate to the sound of a tone.

of the American behaviorist John B. Watson (1878–1958). Watson led a "behavioristic revolt" against the study of consciousness as the focus of psychology and insisted that introspection as the method of observation was inappropriate (Kazdin, 1978). Watson (1919) applied the work of behavioral psychology with animals to human behavior and interpreted all behavior, from instincts to verbal behavior, as developing and changing through the respondent conditioning processes reported by Pavlov.

A brief summary of a classic study by Watson and Rayner (1920) should help clarify Watson's interpretation and application of respondent behavior and respondent conditioning to human behavior. Watson and Rayner's subject was a healthy 11-month-old boy named Albert. Like most normal infants, Albert showed a startle response (UCR) to loud noise (UCS) and cried (UCR) after two or three successive repetitions of metal being struck by a hammer. Moreover, Albert showed no fear of a variety of objects and animals that were presented to him, for example, a white rat, rabbit, dog, monkey, and various toys. These objects were initially neutral stimuli in terms of eliciting crying and a startle response. Watson and Rayner attempted to determine whether they could condition fear or phobic reaction by Albert to the white rat. Each time Albert approached or tried to touch the rat (NS) the experimenters would hit metal with a hammer (UCS) behind Albert's head. After only a few

such pairings, the presentation of the rat alone (CS) elicited crying (CR) in Albert. Figure 1.2 shows how this phobic reaction to a rat was respondently conditioned in Albert.

Although Watson's work was clearly important to the later development of applied behavior analysis, the principles and procedures with which he tried to explain and change human behavior bore little resemblance to a contemporary understanding of human behavior. Following Watson's pioneering work, a variety of learning theories were developed, but it is clearly B. F. Skinner (1904–1990) who is considered the "founding father" of applied behavior analysis. In the late 1930s Skinner distinguished between two distinct categories of responses: *respondent behavior,* as identified by Pavlov, and another category of learned behavior that Skinner referred to as *operant behavior* (Skinner, 1938, 1953).

Skinner described operant behavior as being evoked by discriminative stimuli, which had been previously associated with the reinforcement of particular behaviors of the individual. Operant behavior "operated" on the environment, which, in turn, generated consequences. These consequences made the operant behavior more or less likely to occur again in the future.

This category of operant behavior and operant conditioning seemed to be that which Thorndike had identified in 1911, which was based on his research of escape and positive reinforcement

1) **UCS** → **UCR**
(Loud noise)   (Crying)

2) **NS** → **0**
(Rat)   (No response)

3) **NS** + **UCS** → **UCR**
(Rat)   (Loud noise)   (Crying)

4) **CS** → **CR**
(Rat)   (Crying)

FIGURE 1.2 A diagram of the classic study by Watson and Rayner in which a child was respondently conditioned to fear a white rat.

with various animals, and the "law of effect" that he identified (Kazdin, 1978; Keller & Schoenfeld, 1950). Thorndike found that a hungry cat placed in a box learned to escape by pulling a string, pushing a lever, and so forth, to reach a small piece of food outside the box and could do so in progressively less time in successive trials. Thorndike noted that the decreases in escape time were associated with fewer random errors by his subjects, while the behaviors emitted by the subjects that were "instrumental" in their escape seemed to be strengthened. Skinner induced the basic principles of human behavior from the existing basic and applied research of his time. The technology based on these principles of learning had an immediate and dramatic effect on improving the behavior and lives of persons with severe handicaps.

Some behavior analysts (Whaley & Malott, 1971) attribute the first "applied" use of the principles of learning to Fuller's (1949) study involving an 18-year-old man with profound mental retardation residing at a state institution. His few overt behaviors consisted of opening his mouth, blinking his eyes, and making very limited movement of his arms, head, and shoulders. The institution's professional staff believed that he had learned nothing in 18 years and, furthermore, could be taught nothing. In two experiments of four sessions each, Fuller systematically followed each movement of the young man's right arm alone with the presentation of a milk-sugar solution into his mouth. The rate of right arm movement increased from .67 movements per minute during baseline observations to a rate of 3 per minute during the last session of conditioning through positive reinforcement. Increased movements of the left arm, head, and shoulders were initially noted during conditioning, but these generalizations went unreinforced and eventually decreased to baseline levels. This differentiated change in the man's repertoire indicated to Fuller that other behaviors and discriminations by this man ought to improve with training.

By the late 1950s and early 1960s, operant conditioning methods were extended from laboratory research with animals, and to a limited degree with human clinical populations, to applied settings with persons having various disabling conditions (Kazdin, 1978). The rest of this section briefly summarizes a few of the early applied operant conditioning studies that sought to remediate socially significant problems of persons with severe disabilities. The studies chosen exemplify some of the most effective and practical procedures based on the basic principles of learning.

1950s

A good example of the early application of behavioral principles is found in the comprehensive research of Ayllon and Michael (1959). Ayllon and Michael developed procedures to be used by psychiatric nurses to improve a variety of behaviors exhibited by 14 patients diagnosed as "schizophrenic" and 5 patients diagnosed as "mentally defective." All targeted behaviors were those that had previously been targeted for change, but for which no improvements had ever been documented. Through several applications of behavior analytic procedures, clinically significant improvements in a variety of important behaviors were observed within 6 to 11 weeks. For example, an extinction procedure was used with one patient who frequently and inappropriately entered the nurses' station. Social attention by the nurses was withheld whenever the patient entered, and the rate of entering the office decreased from about 15 times a day to twice a day. With another patient, a differential reinforcement procedure was used, in which the patient received attention for behavior that was incompatible with violent attacks on others. With two other patients, negative reinforcement (escape/avoidance) procedures were used to decrease refusals to self-feed. While feeding these two noncompliant patients, the nurses "accidentally" spilled food. The patients escaped the "accidents" by taking over self-feeding or avoided "accidents" by self-feeding the entire meal. A satiation procedure combined with extinction was implemented to decrease a patient's hoarding of magazines. In this procedure, the ward was flooded with magazines and attention was withheld from the patient for hoarding, resulting in the cessation of hoarding. This study by Ayllon and Michael is considered a classic, in part because of the improvements in socially significant behaviors. In addition, the change agent in each case was the staff, dealing directly with the patients, rather than a psychologist or psychiatrist, and these changes were brought about in the patients' daily environment, rather than in an office or lab setting.

1960s

In the 1960s Azrin joined Ayllon, and their collaboration resulted in the development and refinement of the token economy (Ayllon & Azrin, 1965, 1968), the most effective and one of the most practical motivation systems devised for working with diverse populations (Kazdin, 1977), particularly with persons having developmental disabilities (B. F. Williams, R. L. Williams, & McLaughlin, 1989). Ayllon and Azrin established the token economy in a hospital setting for psychiatric patients. Tokens were given to patients contingent upon the occurrence of various targeted appropriate behaviors. Tokens could later be exchanged for a variety of backup reinforcers selected by individual patients from the hospital commissary.

Other research during this period investigated the effects of behavioral bases for teaching procedures, such as shaping and fading, on the development of appropriate skills and behaviors. An excellent example of the use of a fading procedure with a socially significant problem was that provided by Meyerson and Michael (1964). In working with children with severe mental retardation and/or hearing impairments, Meyerson and Michael (1964) developed a method for assessing their auditory capability. Assessment had been particularly difficult, because none of the children possessed an effective means of communication. A simple discrimination task was designed. A light would come on over one of two levers and the children were reinforced for pressing the lever

that had the light above. Next, headsets were put on the children and sound was delivered to one side, while simultaneously, the light over the lever on that same side was lit. The light associated with sound was systematically and gradually dimmed when the sound came on, until eventually sound came in on one side of the headsets unaccompanied by any light. The children who were not deaf continued to press the lever on the side of the source of sound. At this point, for those children who were responding correctly (i.e., could hear), the sound intensity and frequency were varied, so that a hearing test was successfully completed and appropriate corrective measures could be taken.

Wolf, Risley, and Mees (1964) used a shaping procedure to teach a boy diagnosed as having autism to wear corrective lenses. Although adult attention was not found to be reinforcing, food was. Small pieces of candy and fruit were given contingently for approaching the glasses, then for touching them, and finally, only for wearing them. Unfortunately, food was only mildly reinforcing until breakfast was withheld prior to sessions; then progress became very rapid when ice cream was used as the reinforcer. Once the boy wore his glasses regularly, more naturally occurring reinforcers, such as going for a walk and receiving favors, were effective in maintaining his wearing the glasses.

1970s

Researchers and practitioners in the 1970s continued to use positive techniques to establish and/or increase appropriate behaviors of persons with severe disabilities. For instance, the very effective technology for teaching language to persons with severe disabilities, begun in the late 1960s (Risley & Wolf, 1967) was extended in the 1970s (Guess, Sailor, & Baer, 1974). Applied behavior analysts also investigated procedures for reducing inappropriate behaviors. For instance, Repp and Deitz (1974) used various versions of a procedure termed differential reinforcement of other behavior to reduce substantially serious aggressive and self-injurious behavior by institutionalized children with moderate to severe mental retardation. Behavior other than aggression or self-injury earned the children various types of rewards, whereas aggressive or self-injurious behavior resulted in no consequences, a firm "no," loss of tokens, or a brief time-out.

As the decade continued there was increasing interest in reducing serious inappropriate behavior as humanely and effectively as possible. For example, Foxx and Shapiro (1978) developed a "time-out ribbon" as an effective alternative to more exclusionary forms of time-out for reducing the disruptive behavior of five boys with severe mental retardation. The boys in this study received praise, smiles, and edibles contingent upon appropriate behavior; yet the level of disruptive behavior remained quite high. Next, the children were given ribbons to wear around their necks. As long as they had their ribbons on they would receive rewards contingent upon appropriate behavior. If a child misbehaved, he would lose the ribbon for three minutes and could not earn rewards or participate in classroom activities for that brief period of time. Misbehavior dramatically dropped from 32 percent to 42 percent of the time to only 6 percent of the time.

1980s

As in the previous decades, effective technology for increasing various appropriate behaviors and decreasing various inappropriate behaviors continued to be refined in the 1980s. One important shift in the technology being developed by applied behavior analysts was increased emphasis on antecedent stimuli, rather than the disproportionate emphasis that had been placed on consequent stimuli in the previous decades. For example, Egel, Richman, and Koegel (1981) found that students with autism greatly improved their mastery of various discrimination tasks (e.g., color, shape, etc.) when nondisabled peers modeled correct responses. Another impressive example of manipulating the antecedent stimuli to target behaviors was the study by

Halle, Baer, and Spradlin (1981). They taught teachers to delay their assistance to six children with moderate mental retardation to provide the children with more opportunities to use language. This relatively simple technique was easy to implement and resulted in substantial increases in verbal initiations by the children.

The behavioral research sketched in this brief history touches only a very small portion of the research that has been conducted. An extensive body of literature (e.g., *Journal of the Experimental Analysis of Behavior,* 1957–present; *Journal of Applied Behavior Analysis,* 1968–present) corroborates the basic principles of learning and the success of applied behavior analysis in improving the social, cognitive, physical, self-help, and other independent living skills of persons with severe disabilities. Effective and practical procedures based on the principles of behavior have continued to be refined, and new procedures developed; yet the principles of behavior have not changed. Skinner's analysis of the principles of behavior and learning, which he described in *Science and Human Behavior* in 1953, was so accurate that these principles are basically the same today and have been verified by thousands of basic and applied research studies. The following section briefly summarizes those principles of learning that are of paramount importance for change agents to understand thoroughly if they are to be maximally effective in helping persons with severe disabilities.

PRINCIPLES OF LEARNING

By understanding the basic principles of learning and their interactions, a teacher will have the theoretical framework to explain and understand diverse and complex aspects of human behavior. In turn, this understanding should lead to more effective and practical implementation of procedures based on those principles. An understanding of these principles is also essential for understanding the information, procedures, and findings contained in this book.

Operant Versus Respondent Behaviors

As mentioned earlier, Skinner (1953) carefully differentiated between (1) two categories of behavior: respondent and operant behavior, and (2) two distinct processes of conditioning: respondent conditioning and operant conditioning. Respondent behavior is controlled by antecedent stimuli, which immediately precede the behavior. True reflexes are examples of respondent behavior, because they are controlled by preceding stimuli, for example, the patellar or knee jerk reflex (UCR) in response to a blow just below the kneecap (UCS). Other examples are a rapid pulling away of the hand (UCR) when it comes into contact with a burning stove (UCS) and pupil constriction (UCR) when bright light is presented to the eye (UCS). Humans are born with certain unconditioned responses to specific unconditioned stimuli. In addition, when certain formerly neutral stimuli immediately precede or are simultaneously presented with unconditioned stimuli (e.g., Albert in the Watson and Rayner [1920] study), these previously neutral stimuli become conditioned stimuli that elicit conditioned responses (e.g., Albert's crying, which was elicited by the white rat).

The closer an object or event resembles an unconditioned or conditioned stimulus, the more likely that stimulus is to elicit an unconditioned or conditioned response. Watson and Rayner found that when they presented other objects to the child, the closer the object was in similarity to the white rat (e.g., the white rabbit versus woolen fabric), the more likely the object was to elicit crying in Albert. This effect on responding is referred to as *stimulus generalization.* Conversely, the more dissimilar the object was to the white rat, the less likely it was to elicit crying.

A form of extinction, or lessening of reaction, occurs with respondent conditioning. If a conditioned stimulus is presented repeatedly without being paired with the unconditioned stimulus, then the conditioned stimulus is progressively less likely to elicit a conditioned response. If Watson and Rayner had continued to present the white rat without presenting the loud noise, the rat would have eventually become a neutral stimulus again (unfortunately for Albert, this was not done). A sophisticated form of this procedure has been used to decrease phobias in people (Wolpe, 1958).

Consequences have no effect on the probability that a respondent behavior will or will not occur again. Operant behavior, on the other hand, is controlled by both antecedent stimuli that immediately precede *and* consequent stimuli that immediately follow the behavior. In the example diagrammed in Figure 1.3, a child is learning to make requests.

The parent asks the child if she wants a drink (S^D), which sets the occasion for the response, "I want a drink" (R), which is followed by receiving the drink (S^{R+}), which in this case increases the future probability or rate ($R\uparrow$) that the child will make similar requests in the future. Table 1.1 compares some of the functional variables for respondent versus operant behaviors.

Operant Principles

The vast majority of human behaviors are operant and are controlled by the principles of operant conditioning. Thus, the rest of this chapter focuses

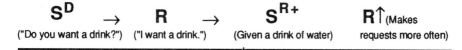

S^D → R → S^{R+} $R\uparrow$ (Makes
("Do you want a drink?") ("I want a drink.") (Given a drink of water) requests more often)

FIGURE 1.3   A diagram of an example of operantly controlled behavior to illustrate the two major controlling factors.

TABLE 1.1   A Comparison of Some of the Functional Variables That Control Operant and Respondent Behaviors

RESPONDENT BEHAVIOR	OPERANT BEHAVIOR
Behavior is elicited by UCS or CS.	Behavior is evoked by S^D.
Consequences have no effect on the future probability of the response.	Consequences control the future probability of the response.
Extinction in CR occurs when CS is no longer paired with the UCS.	Extinction occurs when the response is no longer reinforced.
Stimulus generalization is more likely to occur the more similar a new stimulus is to the UCS or original CS.	Stimulus generalization is more likely to occur the more similar a new stimulus is to the S^D.

on the application of operant principles to persons with severe disabilities. As mentioned earlier, any given operant behavior is controlled by both antecedents and consequences. The following section defines the principles of operant conditioning and clarifies each through example and/or diagram. The basic principles of learning, as opposed to the procedures based on those principles, are defined by their *effect on behavior*, and not by the intention of the person using the procedures to try to change behavior. This is true whether or not the procedures are based on the principles of learning.

Positive Reinforcement.   Positive reinforcement is (1) the presentation of a stimulus (2) contingent upon a response (3), which *increases* the future probability of the response. A stimulus is an object or event that is observable through one's senses, that is, can be seen, heard, felt, tasted, or smelled. A stimulus can be very simple, such as the color of an object, or very complex, such as a person's "best friend." *Contingent* refers to the relationship between the response and the stimulus immediately following the response. This contingent stimulus is dependent upon the response occurring (although the consequence can sometimes simply be due to chance). A response is an observable behavior, and the terms *response* and *behavior* are synonymous. The increase in the future probabil-

ity of the response is objectively verified by an increase in the rate of the response as measured later, typically across several days. A consequent stimulus is defined as a positive reinforcer by its actual effect of increasing the future probability or rate of a behavior, not by the intentions of the person presenting the consequent stimulus.

For example, a girl with autism is praised each time she makes eye contact with her mother. If during the next few hours or days there is an increase in eye contact, then praise did function as a positive reinforcer. However, if during the next few hours or days there is not an increase in eye contact, then praise did *not* function as a positive reinforcer, even though it was the intention of the mother to increase eye contact by the child.

Another example illustrating the difference between intention and effect in defining positive reinforcement is the following. A boy with mental retardation has a serious behavior problem. He is spanked by his father each time he hits another child or throws rocks, pencils, or other objects at other children, and the rate of his aggressive behavior actually increases from an average of 5 times per day to 15 times per day. In this case spanking acted as a positive reinforcer, even though the intention of the father was to "punish" (decrease) his son's aggression.

Typically, rewards in the form of praise, smiles,

$$S^D \quad \rightarrow \quad R \quad \rightarrow \quad S^{r+} \qquad R\uparrow$$

(Sister walks by brother) (Brother teases sister)   (Sister cries)   (Brother teases more often)

FIGURE 1.4   A diagram of an example of positive reinforcement.

and material things are given to persons with the intention of positively reinforcing a certain behavior, but it is effect, not intention, that is the defining characteristic of positive reinforcement and the other principles of learning. Although many positive reinforcers are "pleasant," this is not the defining characteristic of the principle, and the idea that positive reinforcers are always "pleasant" is both incorrect and misleading. The diagram in Figure 1.4 illustrates the principle of positive reinforcement.

The sister's walking into the room acts as a discriminative stimulus (S^D, described in detail later) in setting the occasion for the brother's behavior (R). The brother teases his sister and, as a consequence, she cries (S). It is found that later her brother's rate of teasing increases; that is, he actually teases her more often (R↑) during the next few days. The fact that the sister's crying increased her brother's response of teasing means that her crying acted as a positive reinforcer (S^{r+}) for teasing even though she had no intention of trying to reinforce teasing (the "r" in "S^{r+}" indicates that the stimulus acted as a reinforcer and the "+" indicates that the stimulus was presented).

Negative Reinforcement.   Negative reinforcement is (1) the removal of a stimulus (2) contingent upon a response (3), which *increases* the future probability of the response. Note that the

effect on the response is exactly the same as that of positive reinforcement; that is, the response occurs more frequently in the future. The only difference between positive and negative reinforcement is that a stimulus is removed contingent upon a response in negative reinforcement; whereas the stimulus is presented contingent upon the response in positive reinforcement. It is important to see clearly that the frequent misuse of the term "negative reinforcement" to denote punishment is incorrect, and the effect of negative reinforcement is the exact opposite of punishment. Figure 1.5 is a diagram of an example of negative reinforcement. In this example the teacher had hoped to teach a 5-year-old boy with autism to tie his own shoe.

The teacher's request "Tie your shoes" sets the occasion (S^D) for the boy to hit himself (R). The teacher tries to stop the boy from hitting himself and, in so doing, removes the task of tying the shoes (Sr——the "−" indicates the stimulus was removed contingent upon the response). Since the effect on the response was found later to increase the rate of self-injury (R↑), removing the task acts as a negative reinforcer (S^{r-}), although the teacher had no intention of producing this effect.

Natural consequences may also serve as negative reinforcers, and as with positive reinforcers, the behaviors increased may be appropriate or inappropriate, depending on what behaviors were followed by the reinforcers. For example, suppose

$$S^D \quad \rightarrow \quad R \quad \rightarrow \quad S^{r-} \qquad R\uparrow$$

(Boy asked to tie shoe)   (Boy hits self in head)   (Task removed)   (Boy hits self more often)

FIGURE 1.5   A diagram of an example of negative reinforcement.

$$S^D \qquad \rightarrow \quad R \qquad \rightarrow \quad S^{p+} \qquad R\!\downarrow\!\text{(Child makes eye}$$

(Teacher says,"Look at me) (Girl makes eye contact) (Teacher hugs child)   contact less often)

FIGURE 1.6   A diagram of an example of punishment in which a stimulus is presented contingent upon a response.

one is trying to teach an adolescent girl who has moderate to severe mental retardation to get to the correct bus at the correct time in order to reach a work site on time. On several occasions, getting to the bus stop too late means the unpleasant consequence of having to walk to work. Eventually, this person gets to the correct bus stop early, thus removing the threat of having to walk and being late to work. In the future, this adolescent girl gets to the correct bus stop punctually more often.

Punishment Involving the Contingent Presentation of a Stimulus.   One form of punishment is the (1) presentation of a stimulus (2) contingent upon a response (3), which *decreases* the future probability of the response. This category of punishment is analogous to positive reinforcement in that a stimulus is presented contingent upon a response, but has the opposite effect of positive reinforcement in that the future probability of the response is decreased. Figure 1.6 is an example of this principle of punishment.

In the example presented in Figure 1.6, the teacher was trying to increase the eye contact made by a young girl with severe multiple handicaps. Each time the girl made eye contact (R) with her, the teacher gave her a hug (S^+) to try to reinforce this behavior. It was found that the actual

effect of hugs on this child was punishment (S^{p+}). There was a decrease in the child's rate of eye contacts ($R\!\downarrow$) while this intended "positive reinforcement" procedure was in effect.

Punishment Involving the Contingent Removal of a Stimulus.   The second form of punishment is (1) the removal of a stimulus (2) contingent upon a response (3), which *decreases* the future probability of the response. This category of punishment is analogous to negative reinforcement in that a stimulus is removed contingent upon a response, but has the opposite effect of negative reinforcement, in that the effect on the response is that of decreasing the future probability of the response. Figure 1.7 is a diagram of an example of this principle of punishment.

In the example in Figure 1.7 the teacher removed the toy from the child to try to punish the child. This is a punishment *procedure*. The fact that the child's behavior actually decreased in rate as a result of the procedure indicates that the entire process diagrammed in Figure 1.7 is also an example of the principle of punishment. However, a minimally different second diagram should illustrate the difference between a punishment procedure and actual punishment by showing the differences in effect produced by the consequent

$$S^D \qquad \rightarrow \quad R \qquad \rightarrow \quad S^{p-} \qquad R\!\downarrow \text{ (Child breaks toys}$$

(Teacher gives child a toy)   (Child breaks toy)   (Toy is taken away)   **less often**)

FIGURE 1.7   A diagram of an example of punishment in which a stimulus is removed contingent upon a response.

$$S^D \quad \rightarrow \quad R \quad \rightarrow \quad S^{r-} \qquad R\uparrow \text{(Child breaks toys}$$

(Teacher gives child a toy)   (Child breaks toy)   (Toy is taken away)   **more often)**

FIGURE 1.8   A diagram of an example of positive reinforcement, illustrating that it is the effect on behavior that is the key defining characteristic of positive reinforcement.

stimulus. In this second case, diagrammed in Figure 1.8, the circumstances are exactly the same, but the effect is the opposite, that is, reinforcing.

The two-by-two diagram in Table 1.2 shows generically the two forms of both reinforcement and punishment clearly and concisely. However, one other major principle of operant learning that involves consequent stimuli is not taken into account in this diagram: the principle of extinction.

Extinction.   Extinction is (1) the withholding of a reinforcer (2) for a previously reinforced response (3), which decreases the future probability of the response. Unlike the principles of reinforcement and punishment, the principle of extinction does not involve the presentation or removal of a stimulus immediately contingent upon the emission of the response. In the example diagrammed in Figure 1.9, the situation before the extinction procedure was implemented is the same as that in the example described and diagrammed in the previous section on negative reinforcement. Since the

self-injury increased in rate when the task was contingently removed, one might make the educated guess that removal of the task negatively reinforced the self-injury. In order to try to decrease self-injury, an extinction procedure is implemented, as shown in the second diagram labeled "After."

Once the extinction procedure is implemented, there is a temporary increase in the rate of self-injury, known as an *extinction burst,* but across several days the rate of self-injury gradually decreases. Note that there is no stimulus removed or presented immediately following the self-injury ("0" indicates no stimulus change immediately following the response). In this case, the task, which had been previously removed contingent upon self-injury, is no longer removed.

Although seldom mentioned, there is a form of extinction that involves the withholding of punishers. This form of extinction is defined as (1) the withholding of a punisher (2) for a previously punished response (3), which increases the future

TABLE 1.2   A Breakdown of the Critical Aspects of the Definitions for Both Forms of Reinforcement and Punishment

	STIMULUS PRESENTED CONTINGENT UPON A RESPONSE	STIMULUS REMOVED CONTINGENT UPON A RESPONSE
Response Rate Increases	Positive Reinforcement (S^{r+})	Negative Reinforcement (S^{r-})
Response Rate Decreases	Punishment (S^{p+})	Punishment (S^{p-})

Before:

$$S^D \quad \rightarrow \quad R \quad \rightarrow \quad S^{r-} \quad R\uparrow \text{(Boy hits self}$$

A boy is asked to tie shoe)   (Boy hits self in head)   (Task removed)   more often)

After:

$$S^D \quad \rightarrow \quad R \quad \rightarrow \quad 0 \quad R\downarrow \text{(Boy hits self}$$

(A boy is asked to tie shoe)   (Boy hits self in head)   (Task **not** removed)   **less often**)

FIGURE 1.9   A diagram of a previously reinforced behavior (the "Before" diagram) that is later extinguished (the "After" diagram).

probability of the response. For example, at recess a bully had consistently teased an 8-year-old boy who has Down syndrome whenever the boy tried to participate in a baseball game with other children. As a result, the child no longer attempted to play with the other children. However, the principal found out what was occurring during recess and spoke to the bully and his parents about the problem and what would happen if such behavior ever happened again. In a few days the 8-year-old boy participated with the other children without ridicule and was increasingly likely to participate with other children during recess.

Unconditioned Reinforcer.   An unconditioned reinforcer is a consequent stimulus that is inherently reinforcing. For whatever reasons, genetic, physiologic, or others, certain consequent stimuli inherently increase the probability or rate of whatever responses they follow. For most people, food, water, and sex are unconditioned or "primary" reinforcers.

Conditioned Reinforcer.   A conditioned reinforcer is a stimulus that gains its reinforcing strength by being paired with one or more existing reinforcers (unconditioned or previously conditioned reinforcers). To function in our society, it is critical that praise, smiles, a job well done, grades, money, and so on become conditioned or "secondary" reinforcers.

Simple Conditioned Reinforcer.   A simple conditioned reinforcer is a stimulus that gains its reinforcing strength by being paired with a single reinforcer. Assuming that a teacher's praise *is not* a reinforcer and that music *is* a reinforcer for a particular boy with autism, then pairing praise with each presentation of music should gradually make praise a simple conditioned reinforcer. However, the number of such pairings needed to make praise a conditioned reinforcer will vary greatly among individuals. The problem with making praise a simple conditioned reinforcer is that as the child becomes satiated with music, not only does music lose its reinforcing strength, but praise—which had gained its reinforcing strength by being paired with music—also loses its reinforcing strength. To overcome this serious problem, one should develop praise into a generalized conditioned reinforcer.

Generalized Conditioned Reinforcer.   A generalized conditioned reinforcer gains its reinforcing strength by being paired with many reinforcers. As applied to the preceding example, if praise is paired frequently with a variety of already effective reinforcers for the child (e.g., varieties of music, drinks, physical stimulation, high-rate activities), then praise will become a generalized conditioned reinforcer. The major advantage of generalized conditioned reinforcers, such as praise and money, is that their reinforcing strength is affected by satiation to a much lesser extent than primary or simple conditioned reinforcers.

Discriminative Stimulus: S^D.   A discriminative stimulus known as an S^D (pronounced "S-Dee") sets the occasion for (or "evokes") a response because in the past the occurrence of a response has been reinforced in its presence. How a stimulus becomes an S^D is shown in the example of discrimination training in the section on stimulus control that follows.

Discriminative Stimulus: S^Δ   A discriminative stimulus known as an S^Δ (pronounced "S-Delta") inhibits or makes the occurrence of a response less likely because in the past the occurrence of the response was extinguished or punished in its presence. How a stimulus becomes an S^Δ is shown in the example of discrimination training in the following section, "Stimulus Control."

Stimulus Control.   Stimulus control refers to the fact that certain antecedent stimulus conditions increase or decrease the probability of certain responses. Stimulus control has been used in reference to and studied most frequently in the form of discriminative stimuli that set the occasion for responses (S^Ds) or suppress their occurrence (S^Δs). Discrimination training, whether used systematically or incidentally, develops the functioning of S^Ds and S^Δs. Discrimination training is (1) the differential reinforcement of a specific response in the presence of a particular stimulus (S^D) and (2) the withholding (extinction) of reinforcement for that same response in the presence of other stimuli (S^Δs). Figure 1.10 shows a diagram of an example of the successful use of discrimination training to develop stimulus control.

Assuming (in Figure 1.10) that receiving the ball and/or praise is reinforcing (S^{r+}), then the child will be more likely ($R_1\uparrow$) to imitate the word "ball" (R_1) when the teacher says, "Say 'ball'" (S^D) because saying "ball" is consistently reinforced in the presence of the S^D, "Say 'ball.'" Other responses (R_2) are extinguished (0) in the presence of the S^D for "ball"; therefore, these other responses are less likely to occur ($R_2\downarrow$) in the presence of this S^D. Moreover, the child will be less likely ($R_1\downarrow$) to say "ball" (R_1) when the teacher says, "Say 'mom'" (S^Δ), because the response

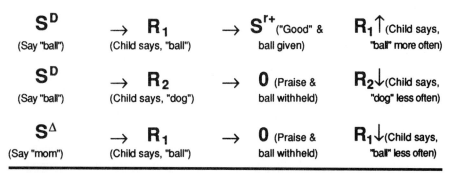

FIGURE 1.10   A diagram of an example of the use of discrimination training procedure to develop stimulus control of a behavior.

"ball" is consistently extinguished (0) when it occurs in the presence of the S^Δ. The fact that the presence of an S^D increases the probability that a given response will occur and that an S^Δ decreases the probability that a given response will occur is known as stimulus control. It should be noted that a stimulus, such as a basketball, may serve as an S^D for one response (e.g., "Ball, please") and concomitantly function as an S^Δ for thousands of other responses (e.g., saying, "I want cake"; hysterical laughter; hitting; saying, "my foot hurts"; etc.). Virtually all operant behaviors that teachers and parents want to teach require discrimination training procedures to establish stimulus control.

Setting Events.   Recently, applied behavior analysts have begun to focus more attention on setting events (Wahler & Fox, 1981) and establishing operations (Michael, 1988). The probability of a specific behavior's occurring is directly affected by discriminative stimuli (S^Ds and S^Δs), but other environmental variables, known as setting events, which precede and may overlap with responding, also affect the likelihood of responding, although in a less direct and obvious way than do discriminative stimuli (Wahler & Fox, 1981).

Bijou and Baer (1961) stated that:

setting events are more complicated than the simple presence, absence or change of a stimulus (such as turning on a light, sudden drop in temperature, or a smile from mother). Instead a setting event is a stimulus-response interaction, which simply because it has occurred will affect other stimulus-response relationships which follow it. (p. 21)

Bijou and Baer (1961) exemplified this by saying that an infant whose napping was interrupted by outside noise later cried and fussed when placed in a playroom, rather than appropriately playing as usual. The noise was a setting event that altered the probability of the responses of crying and playing. The noise was not a discriminative stimulus that immediately set the occasion for crying. Wahler and Fox (1981) also included other

complex antecedent conditions as setting events. A setting event could be a previous marital squabble, varying amounts of drugs or alcohol in the bloodstream, fatigue, lack of sleep, the presence or absence of a specific audience, various hormonal levels, financial poverty, and so forth, affecting the likelihood of later behavior in the presence of discriminative stimuli. Consider, for example, a girl who has an inner-ear infection resulting in earache during the night, which seriously disturbs her sleep. In school the next day the child is apt to become irritable with only slight provocation, may fail to respond consistently to verbal requests by her teacher, and speaks at a level much louder than usual when answering questions by the occupational therapist.

Setting events have less obvious and less immediate control over specific behaviors and have not often been the focus of functional analyses by applied behavior analysts. However, Wahler and Fox (1981), while admitting the difficulty of making functional analyses of setting events, still made a strong case for attempting to do so and offered practical suggestions for carrying out such analyses.

Establishing Operations.   Keller and Schoenfeld (1950) outlined one form of setting event known as an *establishing operation*. Later, Michael (1988) added to the Keller and Schoenfeld analysis and stated that:

an establishing operation (EO) is an environmental event, operation, or stimulus condition that (1) is correlated (either because of phylogeny or ontogeny) with the reinforcing or punishing effectiveness of other events; and (2) allows the effectiveness with which S^Ds for responses consequated by those events evoke those responses. (p. 39)

Michael (1988) viewed the first effect as *value-altering* (i.e., changing the strength of a reinforcer for the individual) and the second as *evocative* (i.e., changing the probability that certain responses will occur). For example, food deprivation is an establishing operation that (1) increases the reinforcing strength of food and (2) increases the probability of (evokes) the types of behavior that had been previously reinforced with food.

Deprivation.   When a reinforcer is withheld for a relatively long period of time, there is an increase in strength of that particular reinforcer. Furthermore, the longer the reinforcer is withheld, the greater its effect at increasing the future probability of a response when it is presented. If a piece of cereal is found to be a reinforcer for a child's attempts at imitation, then in a normal day the cereal would become increasingly effective, the longer the delay since the child's previous meal. Therefore, particularly effective teaching within a natural setting can occur during regular mealtimes.

Satiation.   When a reinforcer is presented frequently in a relatively short period of time, there is a decrease in reinforcer strength. Continuing the preceding example, cereal, as a reinforcer for the child's imitative responses, will be much less effective just after lunch than just before or during lunch. It should be stressed that both satiation and deprivation are descriptive of behavioral processes and are not explanations of these processes.

Stimulus Generalization.   When a response, which has been reinforced in the presence of one discriminative stimulus, occurs in the presence of a different discriminative stimulus, without explicit training or prompting, this is known as stimulus generalization. A child is praised for saying "blue" when shown a navy-blue ball and asked, "What color?" Later, the child says "blue" when shown a bright blue toy car (correct response) and also says "blue" when shown a black toy truck. Both uses of the response "blue" with the later objects are examples of stimulus generalization, although only the use of "blue" in the presence of a blue object is considered "correct." To promote "conceptual behavior" (e.g., the concept of blue) one would present the child with a wide variety of examples (various blue objects

and various shades and hues of blue) and nonexamples (various nonblue objects) of the concept (concept = stimulus class = a set of stimuli with at least one common characteristic). The child would demonstrate conceptual behavior (Whaley & Malott, 1971) if his or her behavior showed (1) stimulus generalization within a "concept" or stimulus class (e.g., identifies all blue objects as "blue") and (2) discrimination between "concepts" or stimulus classes (e.g., identifies nonblue objects as "not blue" or correctly identifies the colors of the nonblue objects. For instance, the child says that a red fire truck is "not blue" or that it is "red").

Response Generalization.   When a response has been reinforced in the presence of one discriminative stimulus, and, as a result, a different but related response occurs more frequently (not necessarily to the same S^D), this is known as response generalization. For example, a child is explicitly reinforced with praise and a hug for imitating certain behaviors modeled by the child's parent (e.g., touching nose, clapping hands, etc.). As a result, there is a concomitant increase in the rate at which the child imitates other persons' modeling of different physical movements. It is because of response generalization that a shaping procedure enables a teacher to differentially reinforce successive approximations to the target behavior. Since each response varies, a skillful teacher reinforces those attempts that are closer approximations to a target behavior and extinguishes those responses that are not so close to the target behavior. If every emission of a response to a discriminative stimulus were the same, a person would never acquire new skills.

Generalization Over Time.   The fact that an individual emits a response to a particular discriminative stimulus at one moment does not necessarily mean that it will occur an hour, a day, or a week later. Retention or maintenance of a learned response over time is considered a third form of generalization (Alberto & Troutman, 1990).

Conclusions

A clear understanding of the basic principles of learning has given applied behavior analysts a comprehensive and accurate framework, from which they have developed effective and practical procedures for changing human behavior. This theoretical framework, with stress placed on the evaluation of procedures' actual effects on behavior, has resulted in a refinement of technology unsurpassed by any other field in psychology or education. Applied behavior analysis is far more complex, dynamic, and effective than a "bag of tricks" or a "cookbook" approach to teaching and helping persons with severe disabilities.

These basic principles have been the foundation for the development of the most effective procedures in existence for persons with severe disabilities. Although the basic principles of operant learning have been known for several decades, their application to very complex problems (social, physical, academic, etc.) has evolved dramatically in recent years. Some of these advances in technology by applied behavior analysts include: (1) functional language development, (2) functional and generalizable skills, (3) self-management, (4) training for employment, and (5) improved instruction for the classroom and community. A brief summary of some of the most recent advances in technology developed and evaluated by applied behavior analysts follows.

CURRENT PRACTICES

Language

Advances in language training have continued in recent years with increased focus on functional language in more natural settings (Hunt, Alwell, & Goetz, 1988). Applied behavior analysts have developed strategies of intervention to replace inappropriate behaviors with functional communication behaviors (Carr & Durand, 1985; Horner & Budd, 1985). Adaptive communication devices are being used more frequently during naturally occurring activities and in natural settings, thus providing appropriate alternative behaviors for

securing reinforcers and assisting in learning other complex skills (Coots & Falvey, 1989). Behavior analysts have been able to teach the spontaneous use of requests by children with severe disabilities to earn access to reinforcing events and to develop functional choice-making skills. Behavior analysts have also reinforced the elaboration of simple movements or gestures made by persons with severe disabilities to increase their use of more complex forms of communication (Rogers-Warren & Warren, 1984).

Functional and Generalizable Skills

In earlier years, applied behavior analysts tended to focus on teaching specific skills within a particular setting. The problem with this approach was that it was often left to chance whether the individual would respond appropriately with later changes in the situation, in the setting, or over time. Currently, considerable effort is being devoted to developing a technology for teaching persons with severe disabilities ways of generalized behavioral responding (Stokes & Baer, 1977). The development of a technology for teaching generalized responding under varying conditions will substantially increase the functionality of persons with severe disabilities, decrease many of the practical problems normally associated with promoting generalization (Horner, Dunlap, & Koegel, 1988), and greatly reduce the overall time needed for instruction and training by professionals (Haring, Breen, Pitts-Conway, Lee, & Gaylord-Ross, 1987). Recently, persons with severe disabilities have been taught generalized language acquisition (Goldstein & Mousetis, 1989), generalized requesting (Doyle, Goldstein, Bourgeois, & Nakles, 1989), generalized responses to questions involving "who," "what," and so on (Secan, Egel, & Tilley, 1989), generalized naming of objects (Foxx, Faw, McMorrow, Kyle, & Bittle, 1988), generalized self-initiative in job related activities (McCuller, Salzberg, & Lignugaris-Kraft, 1987), and generalized play behavior (Haring & Lovinger, 1989).

In the last decade, Horner and his associates (Horner & McDonald, 1982) developed a technology of "general case training" based on "direct instruction," developed by Engelmann and his colleagues (Engelmann & Carnine, 1982). General case training includes systematic diversity of critical discriminative stimuli in training, thus increasing the probability that after instruction the person will perform skills correctly in various naturally occurring settings and situations, such as using the telephone (Horner, Williams, & Steveley, 1987), crossing streets (Horner, Jones, & Williams, 1985), purchasing groceries (McDonnell, Horner, & Williams, 1984), and selecting clothes (Haring & Breen, 1987).

Self-Management

A critical goal for behavior analysts who teach persons with severe disabilities is to establish maximal independence through self-management in community, personal, vocational, and social situations (Sailor, Gee, Goetz, & Graham,1988). Self-management strategies that have been taught successfully include: self-monitoring, self-evaluation, self-reinforcement (selection and presentation of reinforcers), and presenting verbal and nonverbal self-prompts (Alberto & Troutman, 1990). There are many areas in which self-management has been successfully taught to increase independence. For example, students with autism were taught to use self-management procedures to reduce stereotypic behavior (R. L. Koegel & L. K. Koegel, 1990). Effective procedures have also been developed in which (1) the student uses picture prompting (photos, drawings, or symbols) to "show" nonreaders how to complete behavioral chains that had been trained previously (Lignugaris-Kraft, McCuller, Exum, & Salzberg, 1988) and (2) nonreaders learn to read recombined picture symbols that constitute an instructional system for novel tasks (Howard, Spellman, Cress, Simmons, & See, 1989).

Employment

Until recently, persons with severe disabilities were, at best, given prevocational training in school and, later, training in segregated workshops (Wehman, Wood, Everson, Goodwyn, & Conley, 1988). There have been advances in teaching important functional skills, such as job initiative, within sheltered workshop environments (McCuller, Salzberg, & Lignugaris-Kraft, 1987). With recent advances in teaching technology, competitive and successful supportive employment opportunities and training have become available for persons with severe disabilities (Howard & Williams, 1991). Adults with severe mental retardation have been taught to use problem-solving skills, to use self-management and generalization training, and to solve work-related problems while on the job (Hughes & Rusch, 1989). Food preparation skills have been effectively taught to adults with moderate to severe mental retardation through the use of "coincidental" training (a procedure in which additional opportunities for interaction are planned and implemented by the instructor) combined with quality control checks (Likins, Salzberg, Stowitschek, Lignugaris-Kraft, & Curl, 1989). Job coaching, using a series of prompts, was responsible for the acquisition and maintenance of janitorial skills by one 19-year-old who was severely disabled (Test, Grossi, & Keul, 1988).

Instructional Technology in the Classroom and Community

Applied behavior analysis has typically emphasized systematic instruction, which utilized massed training trials and strict control over the training procedures. However, recent research has suggested that highly structured training situations may vary enough from the targeted natural settings that persons often do not generalize skills outside the training setting (Stokes & Osnes, 1988). Some practitioners have suggested training "diversely," that is, using systematic variability in prompts, trainers, settings, and reinforcers during training (Stokes & Osnes, 1988). Applied behavior analysts have also increased the implementation of strategies within naturally occurring settings and instructional opportunities; thus, trials tend to be more dispersed, rather than massed in a relatively short period of time (Goetz & Gee, 1987). Comparisons of interspersed and massed trial training have indicated that the use of naturally occurring moments can result in more efficient acquisition of functional skills (Goetz & Gee, 1987). Instruction for persons with severe disabilities has predominantly been completed through the use of one-on-one training. This procedure has been questioned as to its appropriateness and efficiency, even for students with the most severe disabilities (McCormick & Schiefelbusch, 1984). Some research has indicated that under certain circumstances students' learning rates can be increased in small group situations, rather than in strictly one-on-one situations (Frankel & Graham, 1976; Koegel & Rincover, 1974).

There are several recent areas of inquiry in the design and delivery of effective instruction. One area in which behavior analysts have substantially increased the body of knowledge is in how motivation is maximized for persons with severe disabilities. Recently, behavior analysts have found that varying the type of reinforcer every few trials (even though the different reinforcer is usually less effective) can increase the individual's rate of correct responding (Egel, 1981). It was also found that varying the tasks frequently can increase the rate of correct responding, as compared with continued performance on the same task for prolonged periods of time (Dunlap & Koegel, 1980). In addition, applied behavior analysts have made substantial advances in understanding how to reduce and delay reinforcement (Dunlap, Koegel, Johnson, & O'Neill, 1987) to promote generalization and maintenance of skills in more normal environments. The efficacy of child-preferred activities (Koegel, Dyer, & Bell, 1987) and the use of aberrant behaviors as reinforcers (Charlop, Kurtz, & Casey, 1990) has also been recently evaluated. Many clinicians have reported that naturally occurring reinforcers can be more effective than "contrived" reinforcers (Berkman & Meyer, 1988) and that naturally occurring reinforcers can result in greater generalization of skills (Wilcox & Bellamy, 1987).

A second area of progress has been the refinement of Skinner's "errorless" learning technology (Holland & Skinner, 1961; Skinner, 1954, 1961). Basic and applied research have shown that persons learned more rapidly when they made fewer errors during instruction than when they made many errors (Colvin & Horner, 1983; Sidman & Stoddard, 1967; Terrace, 1963). The absence of errors allows learners to practice repeatedly and to be reinforced for correct responses in the presence of discriminative stimuli. Errorless instruction usually entails a fading procedure, which transfers control from contrived prompts or cues to the original or targeted discriminative stimulus. Current applied behavior analytic research has refined this technology and has begun to determine the relative efficacy of its different forms, for example, physical prompting/fading, systems of least prompts, delayed prompting, graduated practice, simultaneous prompting, and task demonstration (Howard & Williams, 1991).

A third area of refinement is the utilization of technological hardware advancements of the 1980s in the behavioral approach to teaching new skills. Adaptive equipment has become very sophisticated, and persons with severe disabilities have been taught to use a variety of modalities to respond to and control their environment (Hofmeister & Friedman, 1986). For example, microswitches were used by Wacker, Wiggins, Fowler, and Berg (1988) to allow students with profound and multiple disabilities to make requests for activities. Videotaped modeling has recently been successfully used to teach students with autism conversational skills (Charlop & Milstein, 1989). As a result of substantial advancements in teaching technology, some functional academic training is an appropriate target for many persons with severe disabilities, particularly the basic academic skills of reading, mathematics, and writing. Although in its infant stage, computer technology, such as the interactive video disc, has been used to teach survival words, coin recognition, and time telling (Hofmeister & Friedman, 1986). Other technological advances include the use of artificial computer intelligence to enter data on the behavior of persons with severe disabilities and, in turn, to receive suggestions regarding appropriate instruction based on (1) the entered data and (2) principles of learning (West, Young, Johnson, & MacFarlane, 1986). This computer software was developed to be used by precision teachers (Lindsley, 1964). The data that are entered are automatically charted with celeration/deceleration lines and calculations of learning rates (West et al., 1986) and/or with intervention recommendations (White, 1986). Data collection and analysis have been improved most recently by the current bar code technology (Eiler, Nelson, Jensen, & Johnson, 1989). Behavior analysts may collect larger amounts of data more efficiently by sweeping a small "wand" across bar-coded forms. These data can then be downloaded into a microcomputer that can store, summarize, and graph the data. Various adaptive hardware and other computer advances for persons with serious physical disabilities give behavior analysts a new and exciting frontier in procedural development and applied research (Williams, 1990).

A fourth area involves the utilization of antecedent control and reinforcement contingencies as a primary method of changing inappropriate behavior. Current opinion within applied behavior analysis, and within society in general, is that persons with severe disabilities be treated with dignity and humaneness. Whenever possible, effective, practical, and nonaversive procedures should be used (Alberto & Troutman, 1990). Differential reinforcement procedures have been used in an effort to increase appropriate behavior and simultaneously reduce excessive inappropriate behavior (Corte, Wolf, & Locke, 1971). A recent strategy that shows promise for evoking appropriate behavior is to present tasks and requests that the student readily complies with prior to the student being assigned a task that he or she typically reacts to unfavorably (Singer, Singer, & Horner, 1987).

A recent alternative nonaversive approach that shows promise in reducing self-injury, developed by Iwata and his associates, is based on the principle of extinction (Iwata, Pace, Kalsher, Cowdery, & Cataldo, 1990). In many instances self-injury in a person with developmental disabilities appeared to be evoked by demands or requests. The demands were withdrawn in order to restrain and protect the individual from self-injury, but this appeared to have inadvertently negatively reinforced (increased) the self-injurious behavior (Iwata, Dorsey, Slifer, Bauman, & Richman, 1982). The extinction procedure involved making the request or demand (Iwata et al., 1990), but if self-injury occurred following the request, then trainers would physically, and nonpunitively, guide the individual through task completion, which was then positively reinforced. As a result, self-injury decreased and appropriate behavior increased. Another nonaversive procedure has recently been developed and shown to be successful with serious noncompliant behavior. Initially, noncompliant persons were given tasks that had a high probability of being compliantly completed (Mace et al., 1988). Those tasks that had previously elicited consistent noncompliant behavior were then gradually introduced, resulting in subsequent lower levels of noncompliance.

Some seriously inappropriate behaviors (e.g., self-injury, aggression, and excessive self-stimulation) may not be changed sufficiently or expediently in some individuals with the use of nonaversive procedures alone. Applied behavior analysts have developed effective procedures using contingencies for target behaviors to reduce or eliminate self-injury, aggression, and excessive self-stimulation. Procedures such as time-out (Wolf et al., 1967) and the contingent presentation of aversives, such as contingent mist (Dorsey, Iwata, Ong, & McSween, 1980), contingent loud noise (Sajwaj & Hedges, 1971), contingent lemon juice squirted into the mouth (Mayhew & Harris, 1979), contingent overcorrection (Sharenow, Fuqua, & Miltenberger, 1989), and contingent shock (Corte et al., 1971; Linscheid, Iwata, Ricketts, Williams, & Griffen, 1990) have substantially reduced dangerous, self-injurious behaviors. A detailed account of the issues involved with the use of aversive events is given in Chapter 5.

The Association of Behavior Analysis advocates the use of aversive procedures only when deemed necessary, only after all reasonable positive procedures have been found to be ineffective for the individual under consideration, when informed consent has been obtained, and when careful monitoring is ensured. The Association of Behavior Analysis has begun a task force advocating the prudent use of behavior reduction techniques for those individuals requiring them, but giving those individuals and their families "the right to effective behavioral treatment" (Van Houten et al., 1988).

SUMMARY

The recent trends and practices in working with persons with severe disabilities are many and var-ied. Yet these advances in technology have occurred because of the solid data-based approach of applied behavior analysis, which is based on the principles of learning (Skinner, 1957; Whaley & Malott, 1971), and the discarding of unsubstantiated theory, opinion, or fad. Politics and social values have steered technological advances in certain directions and away from others, yet today teachers, parents, and other professionals have much more effective and practical treatment procedures available to them to teach individuals with severe disabilities than ever before. With the scientific approach of applied behavior analysis, this effective technology will continue to expand and to be refined. The following chapters present the application of the basic principles to a variety of areas that represent the most effective and practical curriculum and methods for teachers working with persons with severe disabilities.

REFERENCES

Alberto, P. A., & Troutman, A. C. (1990). *Applied behavior analysis for teachers: Influencing student behavior* (3rd ed.). Columbus, OH: Charles E. Merrill.

Ayllon, T., & Azrin, N. H. (1965). The measurement and reinforcement of behavior of psychotics. *Journal of the Experimental Analysis of Behavior, 8,* 357–383.

Ayllon, T., & Azrin, N. H. (1968). *The token economy: A motivational system for therapy and rehabilitation.* New York: Appleton-Century-Crofts.

Ayllon T., & Michael, J. (1959). The psychiatric nurse as a behavioral engineer. *Journal of the Experimental Analysis of Behavior, 2,* 323–334.

Baer, D. M., Wolf, M.M., & Risley, T. R. (1968). Some current dimensions of applied behavior analysis. *Journal of Applied Behavior Analysis, 1,* 91–97.

Berkman, K. A., & Meyer, L. H. (1988). Alternative strategies and multiple outcomes in the remediation of severe self-injury: Going "all out" nonaversively. *The Journal of The Association for Persons with Severe Handicaps, 13,* 76–86.

Bijou, S. W., & Baer, D.M. (1961). *Child development, I: A systematic and empirical theory.* New York: Appleton-Century-Crofts.

Carr, E. G., & Durand, M. V. (1985). The social-communicative basis of severe behavior problems in children. In S. Reiss & R. Bootzin (Eds.), *Theoretical issues in behavior therapy* (pp. 219–254). New York: Academic Press.

Charlop, M. H., Kurtz, P. F., & Casey, F. G. (1990). Using aberrant behaviors as reinforcers for autistic children. *Journal of Applied Behavior Analysis, 23,* 163–181.

Charlop, M. H., & Milstein, J. P. (1989). Teaching autistic children conversational speech using video modeling. *Journal of Applied Behavior Analysis, 20,* 275–285.

Colvin, G. T., & Horner, R. H. (1983). Experimental analysis of generalization: An evaluation of a general case program for teaching motor skills to severely handicapped learners. In D. Hogg & P. Mittler (Eds.), *Advances in mental handicap research: Vol. II, Aspects of competence in mentally handicapped people* (pp. 309–345). Winchester, England: John Wiley & Sons, Limited.

Coots, J., & Falvey, M. A. (1989). Communication skills. In M. Falvey (Ed.), *Community based curriculum: Instructional strategies for students with severe handicaps.* (pp. 255–284). Baltimore: Paul H. Brooks Publishing Co.

Corte, H. E., Wolf, M. M., & Locke, B. J. (1971). A comparison of procedures for eliminating self-injurious behavior of retarded adolescents. *Journal of Behavior Analysis, 4,* 201–213.

Dorsey, M. F., Iwata, B. A., Ong, P., & McSween, T. E. (1980). Treatment of self-injurious behavior using a water mist: Initial response suppression and generalization. *Journal of Applied Behavior Analysis, 13,* 343–353.

Doyle, P. J., Goldstein, H., Bourgeois, M. S., & Nakles, K. O. (1989). Facilitating generalized requesting behavior in Broca's aphasia: An experimental analysis of a generalization training procedure. *Journal of Applied Behavior Analysis, 22,* 157–170.

Dunlap, G., & Koegel, R. L. (1980). Motivating autistic children through stimulus variation. *Journal of Applied Behavior Analysis, 13,* 619–627.

Dunlap, G., Koegel, R. L., Johnson, J., & O'Neill, R. E. (1987). Maintaining performance of autistic clients in community settings with delayed contingencies. *Journal of Applied Behavior Analysis, 2,* 185–191.

Egel, A. L. (1981). Reinforcer variation: Implications for motivating developmentally disabled children. *Journal of Applied Behavior Analysis, 14,* 345–350.

Egel, A. L. , Richman, G., & Koegel, R. L. (1981). Normal peer models and autistic children's learning. *Journal of Applied Behavior Analysis, 14,* 3–12.

Eiler, J. M., Nelson, W. W., Jensen, C. C., & Johnson, S. P. (1989). Automated data collection using bar code. *Behavior Research Methods, Instruments, and Computers, 21,* 53–58.

Engelmann, S., & Carnine, D. (1982). *Theory of instruction.* New York: Irvington.

Foxx, R. M., Faw, G. D., McMorrow, M. J., Kyle, M. S., & Bittle, R. G. (1988). Replacing maladaptive speech with verbal labeling responses: An analysis of generalized responding. *Journal of Applied Behavior Analysis, 21,* 411–417.

Foxx, R. M., & Shapiro, S. T. (1978). The timeout ribbon: A nonexclusionary timeout procedure. *Journal of Applied Behavior Analysis, 11,* 125–136.

Frankel, F., & Graham, V. (1976). Systematic observation of classroom behavior of retarded and autistic preschool children. *American Journal of Mental Deficiency, 81,* 169–176.

Fuller, P. (1949). Operant conditioning of a vegetative human organism. *American Journal of Psychology, 62,* 587–590.

Goetz, L., & Gee, K. (1987). Teaching visual attention in functional contexts: Acquisition, generalization, and maintenance of complex motor skills. *Journal of Vision Impairment and Blindness, 81,* 115–117.

Goldstein, H., & Mousetis, L. (1989). Generalized language learning by children with severe mental retardation: Effects of peers' expressive modeling. *Journal of Applied Behavior Analysis, 22,* 245–259.

Guess, D., Sailor, W., & Baer, D. (1974). To teach language to retarded children. In R. Schiefelbusch & L. Lloyd (Eds.), *Language perspectives: Acquisition, retardation, and intervention* (pp. 529–563). Baltimore: University Park Press.

Halle, J. W., Baer, D. M., & Spradlin, J. E. (1981). Teachers' generalized use of delay as a stimulus control procedure to increase language use in handicapped children. *Journal of Applied Behavior Analysis, 14,* 389–409.

Haring, T. G., & Breen, C. G. (1987). Teaching between-class generalization of social and other functional skills. Paper presented at the 14th Annual Conference for The Association for Severely Handicapped. Chicago, Illinois.

Haring, T. G., Breen, C. G., Pitts-Conway, V., Lee, M., & Gaylord-Ross, R.G. (1987). Adolescent peer tutoring and special friend experiences. *The Journal of The Association for Persons with Severe Handicaps, 12,* 280–286.

Haring, T. G., & Lovinger, L. (1989). Prompting social interaction through teaching generalized play initiation responses to preschool children with autism. *The Journal of The Association for Persons with Severe Handicaps, 14,* 58–67.

Hofmeister, A., & Friedman, S. (1986). The application of technology to the education of persons with severe handicaps. In R. Horner, L. Meyer, & H. D. Fredericks (Eds.), *Education of learners with severe handicaps: Exemplary service strategies* (pp. 351–368). Baltimore: Paul H. Brookes Publishing Co.

Holland, J. G., & Skinner, B. F. (1961). *The analysis of behavior: A self-instructional program.* New York: McGraw-Hill.

Horner, R. H., & Budd, C. M. (1985). Teaching manual sign language to a nonverbal student: Generalization of sign use and collateral reduction of maladaptive behavior. *Education and Training for the Mentally Retarded, 20,* 39–47.

Horner, R. H., Dunlap, G., & Koegel, R. L., (Eds.). (1988). *Generalization and maintenance: Life-style changes in applied settings.* Baltimore: Paul H. Brookes Publishing Co.

Horner, R. H., Jones, D. N., & Williams, J. A. (1985). A functional approach to teaching generalized street crossing. *The Journal of The Association for Persons with Severe Handicaps, 10,* 71–78.

Horner, R. H., & McDonald, R. S. (1982). Comparison of single instance and general case instruction in teaching a generalized vocational skill. *The Journal of the Association for the Severely Handicapped, 7,* 7–20.

Horner, R. H., Williams, J. A., & Steveley, J. D. (1987). Acquisition of generalized telephone use by students with moderate and severe mental retardation. *Research in Developmental Disabilities, 8,* 229–247.

Howard, V. F., Spellman, C. R., Cress, P. J., Simmons, R., & See, C. (1989). A picture symbol transitional instructional procedure for mentally handicapped and autistic students and adults. *Focus on Autistic Behavior, 4,* 2–20.

Howard, V. F., & Williams, R. L. (1991). Advances in education for persons with severe handicaps. *Psychology in the Schools, 28,* 123–138.

Hughes, C., & Rusch, F. R. (1989). Teaching supported employees with severe mental retardation to solve problems. *Journal of Applied Behavior Analysis, 22,* 365–372.

Hunt, P., Alwell, M., & Goetz, L. (1988). Acquisition of conversation skills and the reduction of inappropriate social interaction behaviors. *Journal of the Association for Persons with Severe Handicaps, 13,* 20–27.

Iwata, B. A., Dorsey, M. F., Slifer, K. J., Bauman, K. E., & Richman, G. S. (1982). Toward a functional analysis of self-injury. *Analysis and Intervention and Developmental Disabilities, 2,* 3–20.

Iwata, B. A., Pace, G. M., Kalsher, M. J., Cowdery, G. E., & Cataldo, M. F. (1990). Experimental analysis and extinction of self-injurious behavior. *Journal of Applied Behavior Analysis, 23,* 11–27.

Kazdin, A. E. (1977). *The token economy: A review and evaluation.* New York: Plenum Press.

Kazdin, A. E. (1978). *History of behavior modification: Experimental foundations of contemporary research.* Baltimore: University Park Press.

Keller, F. S., & Schoenfeld, W. N. (1950). *Principles of psychology: A systematic text in the science of behavior.* New York: Appleton-Century-Crofts.

Koegel, R. L., & Koegel, L. K. (1990). Extended reductions in stereotypic behavior of students with autism through a self-management treatment package. *Journal of Applied Behavior Analysis, 23,* 119–127.

Koegel, R. L., Dyer, K., & Bell, L. K. (1987). The influence of child-preferred activities on autistic children's social behavior. *Journal of Applied Behavior Analysis, 20,* 243–252.

Koegel, R. L., & Rincover, A. (1974). Treatment of psychotic children in a classroom environment: In learning in a large group. *Journal of Applied Behavior Analysis, 7,* 45–59.

Lignugaris-Kraft, B., McCuller, G. L., Exum, M., & Salzberg, C. L. (1988). A review of research on picture reading skills of developmentally disabled individuals. *The Journal of Special Education, 22,* 297–329.

Likins, M., Salzberg, C. L., Stowitschek, J. J., Lignugaris-Kraft, B., & Curl, R. (1989). Co-worker implemented job training: The use of coincidental training and quality-control checking in the food preparation skills of trainees with mental retardation. *Journal of Applied Behavior Analysis, 22,* 381–393.

Lindsley, O. R. (1964). Direct measurement and prosthesis of retarded behavior. *Journal of Education, 147,* 62–81.

Linscheid, T. R., Iwata, B. A., Ricketts, R. W., Williams, D. E., & Griffin, J. C. (1990). Clinical evaluation of the self-injurious behavior inhibiting system. *Journal of Applied Behavior Analysis, 23,* 53–78.

Mace, F. C., Hock, M. L., Lalli, J. S., West, B. J., Belfiore, P., Pinter, E., & Brown, D. K. (1988). Behavioral momentum in the treatment of noncompliance. *Journal of Applied Behavior Analysis, 21,* 123–141.

Mayhew, G., & Harris, F. (1979). Decreasing self-injurious behavior: Punishment with citric acid and reinforcement of alternative behaviors. *Behavior Modification, 3,* 322–336.

McCormick, L., & Schiefelbusch, R. L. (1984). *Early language intervention: An introduction.* Columbus, OH: Charles E. Merrill.

McCuller, G. L., Salzberg, C. L., & Lignugaris-Kraft, B. (1987). Producing generalized job initiative in severely mentally retarded sheltered workers. *Journal of Applied Behavior Analysis, 20,* 413–420.

McDonnell, J. J., Horner, R. H., & Williams, J. A. (1984). Comparison of three strategies for teaching generalized grocery purchasing to high school students with severe handicaps. *Journal of The Association for Persons with Severe Handicaps, 9,* 123–133.

Meyerson, L., & Michael, J. (1964). Hearing by operant conditioning procedures. Report of the proceedings of the International Congress on Education of the Deaf and of the 41st Meeting of the Convention of American Instructors of the Deaf. U.S. Government Printing Document #106. *Proceedings of the International Congress on Deaf Education* (pp. 238–242). Washington, DC: Gallaudet College.

Michael, J. (1988). *Concepts and principles of behavior analysis: A collection of papers by Jack Michael* (4th ed.). Kalamazoo: Western Michigan University.

Pavlov, I. P. (1927). *Conditioned reflexes.* (G. V. Anrep, Trans.) London: Oxford University Press.

Repp, A. C., & Deitz, S. M. (1974). Reducing aggressive and self-injurious behavior of institutionalized retarded children through reinforcement of other behaviors. *Journal of Applied Behavior Analysis, 7,* 313–325.

Risley, T., & Wolf, M. M. (1967). Establishing functional speech in echolalic children. *Behaviour Research and Therapy, 5,* 73–88.

Rogers-Warren, A., & Warren, S. (1984). The social basis of language and communication in severely handicapped preschoolers. *Topics in Early Childhood Special Education, 4*(2), 57–72.

Ross, A. O. (1977). *Learning disability: The unrealized potential.* New York: McGraw-Hill.

Sailor, W., Gee, K., Goetz, L., & Graham, N. (1988). Progress in educating students with the most severe disabilities: Is there any? *Journal of The Association for Persons with Severe Handicaps, 13,* 87–99.

Sajwaj, T., & Hedges, D. (1971). Functions of parental attention in an oppositional, retarded boy. *Proceedings of the Annual Convention of the American Psychological Association, 6,* 697–698.

Secan, K. E., Egel, A. L., & Tilley, C. S. (1989). Acquisition, generalization, and maintenance of question-answering skills in autistic children. *Journal of Applied Behavior Analysis, 22,* 181–196.

Sharenow, E. L., Fuqua, R. W., & Miltenberger, R. G. (1989). The treatment of muscle tics with dissimilar competing response practice. *Journal of Applied Behavior Analysis, 22,* 35–42.

Sidman, M., & Stoddard, L. T. (1967). The effectiveness of fading in programming a simultaneous form discrimination for retarded children. *Journal of the Experimental Analysis of Behavior, 10,* 3–15.

Singer, G. H. S., Singer, J., & Horner, R. H. (1987). Using pretask requests to increase the probability of compliance for students with severe disabilities. *Journal of The Association of Persons with Severe Handicaps, 12,* 287–291.

Skinner, B. F. (1938). *The behavior of organisms.* Englewood Cliffs, NJ : Prentice Hall.

Skinner, B. F. (1953). *Science and human behavior.* New York: The Free Press.

Skinner, B. F. (1954). The science of learning and the art of teaching. *Harvard Educational Review, 24,* 86–97.

Skinner, B. F. (1957). *Verbal behavior.* New York: Appleton-Century-Crofts.

Skinner, B. F. (1961). Why we need teaching machines. *Harvard Educational Review, 31,* 377–398.

Stokes, T. F., & Baer, D. M. (1977). An implicit technology of generalization. *Journal of Applied Behavior Analysis, 2,* 349–367.

Stokes, T. F., & Osnes, P. G. (1988). The developing applied technology of generalization and maintenance. In R. H. Horner, G. Dunlap, & R. L. Koegel (Eds.), *Generalization and maintenance* (pp. 5–19). Baltimore: Paul H. Brookes Publishing Co.

Terrace, H. S. (1963). Discrimination learning with and without "errors." *Journal of the Experimental Analysis of Behavior, 6,* 1–27.

Test, D. W., Grossi, T., & Keul, P. (1988). A functional analysis of the acquisition and maintenance of janitorial skills in a competitive work setting. *Journal of The Association of Persons with Severe Handicaps, 14,* 197–204.

Van Houten, R., Axelrod, S., Bailey, J. S., Favell, J. E., Foxx, R. M., Iwata, B. A., & Lovaas, O. I. (1988). The right to effective behavioral treatment. *Journal of Applied Behavior Analysis, 21,* 381–384.

Wacker, D. P., Wiggins, B., Fowler, M., & Berg, W. K. (1988). Training students with profound or multiple handicaps to make requests via microswitches. *Journal of Applied Behavior Analysis, 21,* 331–343.

Wahler, R. G., & Fox, J. J. (1981). Setting events in applied behavior analysis: Toward a conceptual and methodological expansion. *Journal of Applied Behavior Analysis, 14,* 327–338.

Watson, J. B. (1919). Psychology from the standpoint of a behaviorist. Philadelphia: Lippincott.

Watson, J. B., & Rayner, R. (1920). Conditional emotional reactions. *Journal of Experimental Psychology, 3,* 1–14.

Wehman, P., Wood, W., Everson, J. M., Goodwyn, R., & Conley, S. (1988). *Vocational education for multihandicapped youth with cerebral palsy.* Baltimore: Paul H. Brookes Publishing Co.

West, R. P., Young, K. R., Johnson, J. I., & MacFarlane, C. A. (1986). *Curriculum monitoring and instructional decision-making.* Logan: Utah State University.

Whaley, D., & Malott, R. (1971). *Elementary principles of behavior.* Englewood Cliffs, NJ: Prentice Hall.

White, O. R. (1986). Precision teaching—Precision learning. *Exceptional Children, 52,* 522–534

Williams, B. F. (1990). Computer applications in behavior analysis: A review of the literature. *Educational Technology, 30*(5), 34–38.

Williams, B. F., Williams, R. L., & McLaughlin, T. F. (1989). The use of token economies with individuals who have developmental disabilities. In E. Cipani (Ed.), *The treatment of severe behavior disorders: A monograph of the American Association of Mental Deficiency, 12,* 3–18.

Wilcox, B., & Bellamy, G. T. (1987). *A comprehensive guide to the activities catalog: An alternative curriculum for youth and adults with severe disabilities.* Baltimore: Paul H. Brookes Publishing Co.

Wolf, M. M. (1978). Social validity: The case for subjective measurement or how applied behavior analysis is finding its heart. *Journal of Applied Behavior Analysis, 11,* 203–214.

Wolf, M. M., Risley, T. R., & Mees, H. L. (1967). Application of operant conditioning procedures to the behavior problems of an autistic child. *Behaviour Research Therapy, 1,* 305–312.

Wolpe, J. (1958). *Psychotherapy by reciprocal inhibition.* Stanford: Stanford University Press.

CHAPTER 2

ASSESSMENT FOR A FUNCTIONAL CURRICULUM

BUD FREDERICKS
Teaching Research, Western Oregon State College

MEREDITH BRODSKY
Special Education Department, Western Oregon State College

The process involved in selecting assessment instruments, administering tests, and using assessment results can be difficult, complex, controversial, and time-consuming. Scheduling people for assessment, performing the evaluation and discussing results can be a source of frustration for parents, teachers, and support services staff. However, assessment is critical in providing services to children and youth. Only through careful and accurate assessment can we determine eligibility for services, design effective instruction plans, and track progress made as a result of the school program.

THE PURPOSES OF ASSESSMENT

Browder (1987) discusses the many purposes of assessment, which can be summarized as follows:

Screening

Screening is used to determine whether a child should be further tested to diagnose a disabling condition or to establish eligibility for services. Screening instruments are usually broad in scope and take a minimum amount of time to administer. In a screening, for instance, the American Association on Mental Retardation (AAMR) adaptive behavior scale indicates that a child is engaging in many maladaptive behaviors. The child's functioning level is considerably below his peers. However, no diagnosis has been determined. The child needs to be tested to determine a diagnosis.

Diagnosis

Diagnosis confirms a specific disabling condition and is usually determined by medical and/or psychological professionals. Some infants considered for early intervention services may not yet have a specific diagnosis that can be used to assist in eligibility determination. For some children, diagnosis is quite elusive. For instance, the diagnosis of fetal alcohol syndrome in a child may only be determined by the physician's noting impulsivity and noncompliance and exploring family history. However, most students with severe disabilities will have diagnostic records upon entering elementary school.

Eligibility

Testing for eligibility under P.L. 94-142 requires the use of norm-referenced tests to determine accurately the specific delays related to mental retardation and other severe disabilities. A complete listing of norm-referenced tests for use in special education can be found in Gearhart and Gearhart (1990, pp. 63–230). Assessment measures used with children with severe disabilities can be found in Fewell and Cone (1983, pp. 60–68). School district policy will dictate which of these are acceptable for determining eligibility.

Individualized Education Plans

Results of eligibility testing may be used to begin assessment for developing Individualized Education Plans (IEPs). In addition, teams may use criterion-referenced assessments and curriculum materials such as the Teaching Research Curriculum or the Project Quest functional assessment of student needs, which are described later, as well as systematic observations, to write IEP goals, objectives, and strategies.

Monitoring Progress

Assessment is an ongoing process as the student progresses through the school year. Gains made toward IEP goals and objectives should be continuously monitored, and the documentation of such monitoring should be used to make adjustments in instruction strategies and to develop new goals and objectives for the next IEP. Such assessment techniques have been described by numerous authors, including Haring, Liberty, and White (1980), the Staff of the Teaching Research Infant and Child Center (1982), Snell (1983), Browder (1987), and Lehr (1989).

Program Evaluation

By compiling results of the progress of all children in a program, the overall quality of the program can be assessed. Progress summaries, in addition to other information, can assist with decisions about curriculum, materials, schedules, staff development, administration, and other potential areas for program improvement. For instance, summaries that indicate poor progress in communication skills by a large number of students in a program may

indicate to administrators the need for curriculum revision or further staff training.

Chapter Focus

This chapter will focus on only one of the previously described types of assessment: assessment for the development of an IEP, and will emphasize a kind of assessment procedure known as functional assessment.

WHAT IS FUNCTIONAL ASSESSMENT?

Before effective teaching can occur, the teacher needs to know certain essential elements. The first of these is the overall purpose of the educational process. This purpose is usually expressed in the form of goals and objectives and is supported by a curriculum that allows fulfillment of the goals and accomplishment of the objectives.

The well-qualified teacher also recognizes that all children are different and so attempts to individualize instruction for each student, based on the student's current competencies and deficits. In other words, the teacher assesses the knowledge and skills the student possesses, thereby determining the parts of the curriculum in which the student needs instruction.

In most traditional education settings, the teacher follows curricula that are developmentally oriented, so that the student acquires knowledge in a building-block type of format, each new block of subject matter building on the preceding ones. These developmental curricula are usually correlated with age or grade level. Browder (1987) provides a history of the development of curricula and assessment approaches for students with severe disabilities (pp. 8–11). Initially, schools congregated students by types and severity of disabling conditions. This approach essentially modeled the age placement of children in regular education; consequently, all children in the congregate setting were taught the same curriculum. The curriculum taught in these settings was frequently geared to mental age rather than developmental age. Thus, one could see adolescents in school situations playing with preschool toys. In the 1960s the diagnostic-prescriptive approach emerged, and with it the development of criterion-referenced testing. This approach allowed greater individualization of instruction, but usually moved a child through an established developmental curriculum that correlated with the criterion-referenced testing instruments.

Brown, Nietupski, and Hamre-Nietupski (1976) were among the first professionals to postulate that such developmental curricula are not suitable for students with severe disabilities. If one were to teach a student with severe disabilities in such a curriculum, one would expect that over the student's school life, she might progress only one or two grade levels, if at all in certain curricular domains. Therefore, professionals have proposed that students with severe disabilities need to be taught within a functional curriculum. They have reached this position by considering primarily the environment in which the student must be prepared to function. Brown and associates (1976) postulated the *criterion of ultimate functioning.* This concept focused on skills that adolescents and adults with severe disabilities would need in order to function as effectively and independently as possible in vocational, residential, and social environments. In other words, they advocated judging all curricula against the criterion of usefulness for future adult life and community functioning.

Obviously, this concept had some difficulty in application for students at the preschool level or in the early elementary grades. Vincent, Salisbury, Walter, Gruenwald, and Powers (1980), therefore, built on the concept of Brown and associates (1976) by suggesting that a functional curriculum should also include those skills a student would need in the next environment. For instance, in the case of a preschool student, the next environment might be a kindergarten class. Vincent and associates (1980) postulated certain survival skills for kindergarten, recognizing that even those needed to be individualized for the student with severe disabilities. Thus, combining the concept of Brown and associates (1976) and that of Vincent

and associates (1980), educators were now to consider in the preparation of a functional curriculum not only the student's ultimate functioning in the adult world, but also the student's functioning in the next educational environment. In 1983, Petersen, Trecker, Egan, Fredericks, and Bunse published an assessment procedure for adolescents and adults. This work was based on the work of Brown and associates (1976) and Vincent and associates (1980) but added one additional concept, the need to consider the functioning of the student in the immediate environment. Thus, with this last work, the scope of the functional curriculum, and therefore the guidelines of what must be considered in assessment for a functional curriculum, were complete. A functional curriculum could be defined as the life skills needed by a student in the current environment in which he or she was functioning, the life skills needed in the student's immediate next educational environment, and the skills the student would need after leaving school to function in vocational, residential, and recreational environments.

THE FUNCTIONAL ASSESSMENT PROCESS

This section discusses certain procedures that need to be considered and implemented in conducting a functional assessment, including team input and the utilization of assessment instruments and observation. Some considerations for the preschool and elementary levels are discussed. Then a detailed explanation of the process as it would be conducted at the secondary level is offered, with the recognition that the example could be extrapolated to the preschool and elementary educational levels.

The following steps constitute the functional assessment process:

1. Conduct an ecological inventory.

2. Assess the current functioning of the student *vis à vis* the ecological inventory, determining those skills currently possessed by the student and those that are needed.

3. From the list of student needs, prioritize with the student's parents or guardians the instructional items to be taught.

4. From this prioritization, prepare with the parents or guardians the instructional items to be taught.

Conduct an Ecological Inventory

An ecological inventory is a compilation of life skills needed by the student in settings in which she or he currently functions or in which she or he will function in the future (Browder & King, 1987). In discussing this part of the functional assessment with teachers, we find that this process is one of the more difficult and time-consuming. Thus, it is important that this process be streamlined to ease the pressure on the teacher's time and yet comprehensive enough to gather the necessary information, for this is the part of the process that determines the curriculum within which the student will be taught.

We have found that the use of checklists by both teachers and parents (or guardians) facilitates the process of inventory. The checklists are based on curricular priorities that might be necessary for most students. Numerous checklists have been published; five sources are cited here as being reasonably comprehensive. At the preschool and elementary level, *The Teaching Research Curriculum for Moderately and Severely Handicapped,* published in three volumes, has been found to be useful (Fredericks et al., 1980a, 1980b [two volumes]; Makohon & Fredericks, 1985). Covering all ages are the curricula developed by Bender and Valletutti (1976a, 1976b), published in two volumes and containing comprehensive checklists that could be useful for parents and teachers. *The Syracuse Community-Referenced Curriculum Guide* (Ford et al., 1989) also contains some checklists across all ages, although they are not as conveniently arranged for teacher use as others cited here. One of the more comprehensive publications is IMPACT (Neel & Billingsly, 1990), which includes environmental inventions for both home and community. The checklists in Petersen, Trecker,

Egan, Fredericks, and Bunse (1983) are primarily designed for students at the secondary level.

In addition to using checklists, an ecological inventory can be conducted by observing the student in various environments and determining what he or she needs in order to function well in those environments. This process, of course, will not provide information as to what will be needed in the next educational environment, or in the adult world.

Finally, but by no means least important, the ecological inventory can be conducted through discussions with the parents or guardians to determine what they perceive to be the needs of the child for the present and for the future.

Assess the Current Functioning of the Student

The second step in the functional assessment process is to assess the student's current level of functioning in comparison with the skills that are necessary in the student's current educational, residential, and community environments, what will be needed in the next educational environment, and what will ultimately be needed by the student when he or she enters the adult world. The process in this assessment utilizes the same tools that were used in the ecological inventory. There are essentially four means by which the student's current functioning level can be assessed: (1) the use of checklists, (2) discussions with parents, guardians, and significant others, (3) observations of the student in the various environments in which he or she must function, and (4) formal testing instruments.

The same checklists used to formulate an ecological inventory can be used to determine the skills that the student possesses and those that he or she needs. We suggest that the parents or guardians take the checklists home with them so that they can be discussed and the student observed in environments not accessible by the teacher. The teacher, of course, can use the checklists to assess the student's competencies in the educational environment. After a period of observation by both parents and teacher, they should meet and compare their findings regarding the competencies and needs of the student. We essentially recommend that the use of checklists be combined with observations of the student in his or her natural environments and, finally, with a detailed discussion between parents and teacher.

Such a process will provide a good picture of the student's current needs across environments. It does not address the student's needs in future educational environments, nor in the ultimate environment of the adult world. The teacher should primarily address needs that the student may have in the next educational environment and should share those with the family so that they can be considered when the teacher and parents prioritize the skills to be taught.

The long-range needs of the student are more difficult to determine. The parents need to project what they envision for their child in the future and what will be needed to allow him or her to function in the adult world as independently as possible. Some parents may need assistance in such projections especially if they are not familiar with the types of adult programs or their requirements. A recent survey conducted by Fredericks (1990) indicated that parents wanted the following for their children in the future:

1. To be able to interact effectively with those who are not disabled, as well as with those who are disabled; to have bona fide friends from both groups.

2. To be able to work in the same environments as those who are not disabled.

3. To be able to access with comfort and confidence facilities and events available to those who are not disabled.

4. To live in housing of their choice that is within their economic means.

5. To be happy.

Although this list does not assist parents in determining what specific skills should be taught, it does indicate the need for continued communication training and assistance in community-based skills.

Although we mention the possibility of utilizing formal tests to assist in the process of assessing the student's current functional levels, we have found such tests to be of little use. Checklists based on actual needs in educational, community, and residential environments have been of greatest use. However, for those who wish to explore the use of formal tests in this type of functional assessment, Gearhart & Gearhart (1990) provide the most comprehensive and current listing of instruments that may be of assistance.

Prioritize What Needs to Be Taught

Up to this point, a great deal of information has been gathered about the skills that the student may need, those the student currently has, and those in which he or she may need training. The task that the parent and teacher now face is to prioritize those skills so that they can be formulated into an IEP. There are no prescribed rules or guidelines for this prioritization. We do know that all the skills identified cannot possibly be included in the IEP. Therefore, those that are immediately essential are probably included. The point at which the next educational transition occurs will probably dictate when those skills will be taught. It is likely that age-appropriate community-based activities can help to prepare the student for adult life. The parent and the teacher are faced with difficult decisions during this part of the functional assessment process, but they must make the choices that best meet the present and future needs of the student. This process becomes even more difficult as the student grows older and the end of the school years becomes imminent. The parent then recognizes that it may not be possible for some essential skills to be taught. Alternative adaptations and supports will have to be considered to compensate for skills that will not be taught or could not be learned.

Develop the IEP

This entire assessment process has been designed to develop an IEP that has as its basis a functional curriculum and has been carefully designed to meet the individual needs of the student.

FUNCTIONAL ASSESSMENT AT THE PRESCHOOL/ELEMENTARY LEVEL

Fredericks (1990) postulates that the curriculum for the preschool and elementary-age child should have the following priorities:

1. Communication/socialization
2. Self-help skills
3. Motor skills/recreation
4. Academics/functional academics

These were based on the rationale that throughout a person's life, especially in integrated settings, communication and socialization are the most important skills needed by any individual, including those who are disabled. Self-help skills, the second priority, are necessary to facilitate the student's acceptance in integrated environments. Toilet training and hygiene are paramount among these skills. For each of these areas, Fredericks (1990) offers a checklist that can be used by the teacher and the parent to determine what skills are most needed by the child in the current environments of school, home, and community, what skills will be needed by the student in the next educational environment, and what skills will be needed ultimately. One such checklist for personal hygiene at the preschool and early elementary level is shown in Figure 2.1.

Although the rationale offered by Fredericks (1990) may be acceptable for curriculum choices for many students with severe disabilities, the determination of what constitutes a functional curriculum and, in turn, what constitutes a functional assessment can be more difficult at the elementary level than in the secondary years. When a student reaches high school, both parents and teachers will be more focused toward the future of the youth and will be more concerned about the youth's acquiring a large number of functional skills before

---

CURRICULAR AREA: PERSONAL HYGIENE

Washes hands

Dries hands

Washes face

Dries face

Blow and wipes nose when requested

Wipes self after toileting

Brushes teeth

Washes self in bath or shower with supervision

Combs hair

FIGURE 2.1   Personal hygiene checklist.

---

graduation in order to prepare him or her for maximum independence as an adult.

At the elementary level, the choices are not quite so clear. Certainly, the student who has the ability to acquire skills in math, reading, and other academic areas should be taught those skills, and so should be assessed in those areas, via assessment instruments commonly used for academic curricula. The difficult choice is in determining how long a student with disabilities should remain in a formal academic program. Fredericks (1990) suggests that a formal academic program should be maintained as long as the student is making a one-third year gain, as measured by standardized tests, for every academic year. When the student falls below that rate of gain, a functional academic curriculum should be considered.

FUNCTIONAL ASSESSMENT AT THE SECONDARY LEVEL

As previously stated, traditionally, education has been provided through curricula based on normal human development. Skills were taught in the order in which they normally develop in an individual who is not disabled. We have indicated that such a curricular strategy is probably not relevant for those students who are severely disabled. That concept is especially true for adolescents.

> *As severely handicapped students become adolescents and young adults, the outcome of such curricular strategies often results in the delivery of instruction which is nonfunctional, artificial and inappropriate for their chronological age. Though they may in fact evidence progress through bottom-up curriculum sequences, the obvious performance discrepancies between them and their non-handicapped chronological age-mates actually increase over time. (Brown et al., 1979)*

If one accepts the hypothesis that traditional curricular models are, by and large, inappropriate for the adolescent or adult with severe disabilities, it becomes the responsibility of the teacher to determine curricular content that emphasizes the teaching of functional and chronological-age-appropriate skills in the natural environment.

The following section presents a strategy for identifying the skills that each individual student needs to function as independently as possible in the current and postschool environments. Through this approach, teachers and parents should be able to develop IEPs and supporting instructional programs that will ensure performance of functional skills in the natural environment.

A critical element in the assessment and instructional planning process for adolescent students with disabilities is the identification of probable future environments. This is a task most appropriately handled by the parent-teacher partnership. It requires the best efforts of those who know the student well to determine accurately where the student is most likely to find him- or herself at the termination of a secondary school educational program. Siperstein, Reed, Wolraish, and O'Keefe (1990) highlight needs in residential settings and attempt to scale skills as essential, helpful, or not relevant.

As the result of careful analysis of postschool environment requirements for a large number of individuals with severe disabilities, four major curricular domains have been found to be most critical to those settings. The wide array of needed skills have been grouped into these four domains, which are listed in order of priority:

1. *Social skills,* including communication, are considered to constitute the single most important curricular area, because these skills are generic in their applicability to all other areas: vocational, recreational, and functional living. Included in this broad domain is sexual awareness. There is sufficient evidence to support the notion that it is the lack of acceptable social skills development in individuals with severe disabilities that leads to their termination in residential and vocational placements, more than their inability to learn specific tasks. Included within the social domain are the curricular areas of communication, socialization, and sexual awareness. Petersen and associates (1983) have developed checklists, not only of social skills, but of all curricular domains that can be used by parents and teachers to determine those functional skills to be taught to the adolescent. Examples of the communication and social checklists are shown in Figures 2.2 and 2.3.

2. *Independent living skills* are ranked second in importance for the postschool success of young adults with severe disabilities. The independent living domain comprises the following curricular areas: personal hygiene, dressing, clothing care and selection, self-feeding, meal planning, shopping and storing, food preparation, home and yard maintenance, health and safety, community mobility, personal information, money management, and time management. The large number of skills within this domain affect the individual's ability to function in the vocational, residential, and recreational environments. It is clear that an individual reporting late for work, poorly groomed and carelessly dressed, has diminished the opportunities for success without ever having demon-

---

CURRICULAR AREA: COMMUNICATION

Responds to requests, commands, conversation of others

Expresses wants and needs in verbal or nonverbal manner

Communicates so that others understand basic idea being expressed

Maintains appropriate social distance during conversation

Touches listener only appropriately

Maintains appropriate eye contact during conversation

Obtains listener's attention before speaking

Gives truthful information

Gives relevant information

Uses social courtesies (e.g., please) appropriately (does not overuse)

Listens to speaker without frequent interruption

Responds appropriately to speaker questions

Maintains topic of conversation

Asks for assistance when appropriate

Requests only needed information

Indicates when a message is not understood

Typically laughs only at comments or situations intended to be humorous

Uses appropriate volume according to situation

Uses acceptable language (not obscenities)

FIGURE 2.2   Example of communication checklist.

strated his or her actual work skills. Examples of checklists for two of the skill areas, personal hygiene and food preparation, are shown in Figures 2.4 and 2.5.

3. *Leisure skills* are viewed as important support skills in the individual's integration into the community. The ability to participate in meaningful and enjoyable activities during one's free time either at home or in the community becomes a vital part of developing independence. It is imperative that adolescents who are severely disabled become equipped with appropriate leisure time skills before they are placed in community settings

where large blocks of unstructured time are often available. The current national unemployment situation must be viewed as having a potential impact on the employment continuity of the worker who is disabled, which may therefore increase nonvocational time. The far-thinking educator will be prompted to prepare young adult students to deal with extended periods of free time in appropriate ways. The assessment procedures of Petersen and associates (1983) have categorized leisure skills as either home based or community based. Their lists are not considered exhaustive and certainly should be expanded to reflect the leisure time opportunities of the local

CURRICULAR AREA: SOCIAL SKILLS

Engages only in socially acceptable self-stimulatory behaviors

Manages anger in an appropriate way that is not harmful to self or others

Gains attention only in appropriate manner

Complies to legitimate requests in a timely fashion

Shows and accepts affection appropriately at home, school, work and community

Responds to and initiates appropriate greetings and farewells

Makes appropriate introduction of self and others

Responds appropriately to change in routine

Ignores inappropriate behaviors/comments of others

Maintains self-control when faced with failure, problems, disappointments

Accepts most criticism with no unreasonable outbursts

Typically deals with others in courteous and respectful manner

Discriminates when to comply to requests from peers

Recognizes when it is prudent to leave a provoking situation

Responds appropriately to emotions of others

Talks about personal problems at appropriate times

Discusses differences reasonably with others and negotiates resolutions (with third party)

Laughs, jokes and teases at appropriate times

Shares own property within reason

Borrows property of others appropriately

Respects privacy and property of others

Voluntarily accepts legitimate blame

Responds appropriately to compliments

Engages in appropriate dating behaviors

Takes part in peer group activities

Initiates social activities

Responds appropriately to social invitations

Uses phone to make local calls (unless not viable means of communication)

Uses phone to make direct long distance or collect calls

Uses pay phone to make local calls

FIGURE 2.3   Example of social skills checklist.

CURRICULAR AREA: PERSONAL HYGIENE

Uses appropriate toileting skills

Bathes or showers regularly

Uses deodorant as needed

Practices proper skin care as needed

Combs/brushes hair as needed

Washes hair regularly

Practices proper oral hygiene

Cares for menstrual needs

Shaves underarms and legs

Shaves face as needed

Cares for nails

Blows and wipes nose

Cares for hearing aid

Cares for eyeglasses

Purchases or arranges purchase of personal care items as needed

Uses cosmetics or other grooming items appropriately

FIGURE 2.4   Example of personal hygiene checklist.

CURRICULAR AREA: FOOD PREPARATION

Prepares work area and self for cooking

Cleans food when necessary

Peels and grates food

Dices food with knife

Cleans up spills

Opens and closes various types of containers

Prepares food from recipe

Prepares food from can/box

Sets and cleans table

Scrapes and rinses dishes

Washes dishes by hand so they are clean and sanitary

Dries dishes or stacks in drying rack

Cleans kitchen after use

Operates dishwasher

Stores food left over from meal

Prepares five different nutritionally balanced breakfasts

Prepares five different nutritionally balanced lunches

Prepares sack lunch

Prepares dinner using prepackaged foods

Prepares five main dishes suitable for evening meal

Prepares frozen vegetables

Prepares two different salads

Prepares two side dishes of pasta, potatoes or rice

FIGURE 2.5   Example of food preparation checklist.

CURRICULAR AREA: LEISURE SKILLS—COMMUNITY BASED

Roller skates	Uses a buffet/cafeteria style restaurant
Takes a bicycle ride	Uses food/pop machines
Takes a walk or hike	Uses a restaurant where one is seated and served
Utilizes a park for private space and relaxation	Fast dances without physical contact with partner
Utilizes swimming facilities	Slow dances with physical contact with partner
Uses a tavern	Prepares for and attends a potluck
Attends church services	
Flies a kite	Plays Frisbee™
Uses YMCA, spa	Plays tennis
Ice skates	Plays bingo
Golfs	Plays mini-golf
Bowls	Attends movie
Plays pool	Attends concert, theater, play
Plays racquetball	Visits museum or art center
Uses a fast-food restaurant	Attends sports events

FIGURE 2.6   Example of community based leisure skills checklist.

environment. The checklist by Petersen and associates (1983) for community based leisure skills is shown in Figure 2.6.

4. *Vocational and associated work skills* are included in the fourth curricular domain. Vocational skills are those specific to a given task, such as wiring a circuit board, and are related mostly to an individual's motor and perception abilities. Associated work skills are not vocationally relevant per se, but are those behaviors that influence an individual's production and employment options. These are skills that can generalize to any number of other work settings, for example, a worker's ability to use a time clock or to request more work from a supervisor. Examples of other associated

work skills are found in the other curricular areas, such as appropriate grooming and hygiene and appropriate social and communication skills. A sample part of the associated work skills checklist is shown in Figure 2.7.

The Assessment Process—An Example

To determine within the major curricular domains where a student needs training, Petersen and associates (1983) recommend the following procedures.

A determination is made of the long-range placement of the student, both residentially and vocationally. In addition, consideration is made of deficits that exist in the repertoire of skills needed by the student to function in his or her current

---

CURRICULAR AREA: ASSOCIATED WORK SKILLS—VOCATIONAL

Checks own work

Corrects mistakes

Works alone without disruptions for specified periods with no contact from supervisor/teacher

Works continuously at a job station for specified amount of time

Safety:

    - Uses appropriate safety gear

    - Responds appropriately during fire drill

    - Follows safety procedures specific to classroom/shop

    - Wears safe work clothing

    - Cleans work area

    - Identifies and avoids dangerous areas

    - Responds appropriately to emergency situation (sickness, injury, etc.)

Participates in work environment for specified periods of time

Works in group situation without being distracted

Works faster when asked to do so

Completes work by specified time when told to do so

Time management:

    - Comes to class/work for designated number of times per week

    - Arrives at class/work on time

    - Recognizes appropriate time to change task

    - Returns promptly from:

        -break

        -restroom

        -lunch

    - Uses time clock/clock appropriately

Observes classroom/shop rules

Does not leave work station without permission

FIGURE 2.7   A segment of the Associated Work Skills Checklist.

---

placement and in the immediate next placement. Based on these pieces of information, a determination is then made of the student's current needs, the skills that must be taught to meet those needs, and the environment where those skills are going to be taught, whether in school or elsewhere.

The steps in this process are detailed in the following paragraphs and summarized in Table 2.1.

Step 1. Determine the requirements of the postschool environment. To design an instructional program that will prepare students who are

TABLE 2.1   Steps for Functional Assessment Process at the Secondary Level

Step 1.   Determine the requirements of the postschool environment.

Step 2.   Complete top portion of Student Needs and Priorities Form.

Step 3.   Complete student assessment form for each student.

Step 4.   Complete lower portion of Student Needs and Priorities Form.

Step 5.   Develop the IEP.

severely disabled to be as independent as possible in current and postschool environments, the teacher must gather specific information about the requirements of those environments. Petersen and associates (1983) have developed an extensive system of surveying the postschool vocational and residential environments. The system they describe provides a complete environmental assessment of the requirements of the postschool service providers. However, the information from the providers may be gathered in a much easier manner. A letter sent to individual providers, asking them to indicate what essential skills are required for an individual to access their facilities, will give the teacher the baseline information needed to ensure that at least those basic skills are taught to the student.

We emphasize that the purpose of this survey is to ensure that the student has at least the necessary skills to qualify for placement in the service facilities extant in the community. The teacher's goal, however, must always be to teach as many skills as possible, so that the student can be optimally independent upon graduation from high school. The teacher must also be concerned about teaching those skills that the student needs immediately in his or her current environment. The following procedure assists in determining those skills to be taught to achieve both long-range independence and to satisfy immediate environmental needs.

Step 2. Complete top portion of the Student Needs and Priorities Form. The second step in the assessment process is the determination of the most probable residential and vocational long-range placement of the student. This information is entered in the top portion of the Student Needs and Priorities Form (Figure 2.8). The long-range placement is the "best guess" on the part of the teacher and parents relative to the student's placement(s) following termination of the school program. The parent has at his or her disposal a great deal of information about the student's independent living skills, social abilities in various situations, and inclination toward certain vocational tasks. The teacher has additional information to supplement that of the parents and occasionally has accumulated more objective data about the student than has the parent. If there is doubt as to what particular environment a student will be in, the decision must always reflect the less restrictive environment. In other words, if the parents and teacher cannot determine whether the student will live in a group home or a supported community living situation, the program should be designed to prepare him or her to live in the supported community setting, because it is less restrictive than the group home.

"Immediate Placement Needs," the next section on the form, refers to skills the student needs to survive in his or her current placement—usually the school. These are situation-specific to the student's school and may include skills such as purchasing lunch tickets, dressing for a physical education activity, or unlocking a combination lock. The next item on the form is "Immediate Future," referring to skills required for survival in transition situations between current placement (school) and long-range placement (supported employment). An immediate future need might be of shorter range. For example, if a student currently placed in a junior high program does not know how to work a combination lock, and that skill is required in his immediate future placement—high school, it would be considered a priority skill. If the student is trained in this skill during the current year, the transition to the high school environment might be made more smoothly.

STUDENT NEEDS AND PRIORITIES FORM

NAME: ___Sam Student___

DATE OF BIRTH: ___9/20/69___

LONG-RANGE PLACEMENT: RESIDENTIAL: ___Group Home___

IMMEDIATE PLACEMENT NEEDS: VOCATIONAL: ___Supported employment___

Current:	1.	Uses cafeteria line
ABC Junior	2.	Locates own bus
High	3.	
	4.	
	5.	
Immediate	1.	Uses combination lock
Future:	2.	
DEF High	3.	
School	4.	
	5.	

PRIORITIES (Based on Immediate Needs and attached Student Assessment information):

1. _____
2. _____
3. _____
4. _____
5. _____
6. _____
7. _____
8. _____
9. _____
10. _____
11. _____
12. _____
13. _____
14. _____
15. _____
16. _____
17. _____
18. _____

FIGURE 2.8   Student Needs and Priorities Form.

Step 3. Complete the Student Assessment Form for each student. Once future placement decisions and immediate priorities have been established, information must be gathered relative to the student's current repertoire of skills. The Student Assessment Form developed by Petersen and associates (1983) contains checklists for all four domains previously described. In addition, it has a column where the teacher and/or parent can check those skills determined to be necessary for either long-range vocational or residential placement. (A sample page of the Student Assessment Form is shown in Figure 2.9.)

In the column headed "Has Skill" in Figure 2.9 the teacher records those skills the student already has. It should be noted that unless the student performs the skill independently, consistently, and accurately under appropriate circumstances, he should not be given credit for having that skill. Parental input is very useful at this stage of the assessment process. The teacher may send the form home and ask parents to check those skills they know their child has, or the teacher can "interview" the parents.

Deficit skills are marked in the next column, headed "Needs Training." After determining that a certain skill needs training, the teacher and parent, or caregiver, must negotiate as to where training would best occur—in the school, at home, or at some other location. During this process it should be kept in mind that the school is not equipped to provide optimum training in all areas. Some students are more efficiently trained in the home setting, and still others are best trained in the community. Likewise, many parents are unsure of their ability to teach certain skills (money handling, for example) to their children and would prefer they be trained at school (see the example in Figure 2.10).

Step 4. Complete the lower portion of the Student Needs and Priorities Form. After the Student Assessment is completed, the teacher meets with the parents to discuss the child's assessed needs, to receive further information from the parents, and to prioritize instructional programs. The professional must allow the parents the opportunity to respond to the information gathered on the Student Assessment Form. Most important, the teacher must also listen very carefully to any information the parent may share about any of the curricular areas or about opportunities for the student to engage in activities that could teach certain skills at home. Information about social and work habits of the student may be especially valuable. The parent has known the youth much longer than the teacher and possesses much information that may enhance the entire assessment process. The teacher should make every effort to elicit from the parent as much of that information as possible.

In the determination of priorities, it must be recognized that the array of skills needed by the student may be so extensive that it would not be possible to teach all of them in the school setting, given time and staff limitations. Teachers should, therefore, encourage parents to teach those skills that can best be taught at home. Certainly, many practical living and leisure time skills can better be taught in the home than in school. The home should also be used as a place to generalize skills taught in the school.

A balance of priorities between all four major curricular domains is ideal. However, such a balance will not be in the best interests of some students. If a student's social-sexual skills are significantly deficient, her entire program may justifiably focus on the skills in that curricular domain. Another student may be performing quite adequately in the social-sexual domain, but be in desperate need of training in practical living skills to make him more independent in a targeted semi-independent living environment. His program would certainly emphasize that curricular domain. Priorities are recorded on the lower portion of the Student Needs and Priorities Form (Figure 2.8).

Step 5. Develop the Individualized Education Plan. From the list of priority skills agreed upon by the parents and teacher, the completion of the IEP should be a relatively simple process. Most local

STUDENT ASSESSMENT FORM

Name:

Date of Assessment:

Evaluation Team:

Curricular Area: CLOTHING CARE AND SELECTION	Required Home/Voc	Has Skill	Needs Training	Location		
				School	Home	Other
Selects clothing appropriate to weather and occasion						
Determines daily clothing independent of adult supervision						
Distinguishes between clothing to be worn in public/private						
Wears clothing that fits						
Determines when clothing needs to be laundered						
Sorts clothing for laundry						
Washes and dries clothing on a regular basis						
Uses community laundry facilities						
Uses commercial dry cleaners						
Stores clothing in a neat manner						
Irons clothes as needed						
Makes simple clothing repairs						
Selects and buys appropriate clothing						

FIGURE 2.9   One page from the Student Assessment Form.

STUDENT ASSESSMENT FORM

Name: Sam Student

Date of Assessment:

Evaluation Team:

Curricular Area: PERSONAL HYGIENE	Required Home/Voc	Has Skill	Needs Training	Location		
				School	Home	Other
Uses appropriate toileting skills	X	X				
Bathes or showers regularly	X		X		X	
Uses deodorant as needed	X		X		X	
Practices proper skin care as needed						
Combs/brushes hair as needed	X	X				
Washes hair regularly	X		X		X	
Practices proper oral hygiene	X	X				
Cares for menstrual needs*						
Shaves underarms and legs*						
Shaves face as needed*						
Cares for nails	X		X	X		
Blows and wipes nose	X		X	X		
Cares for hearing aid*						
Cares for eyeglasses*						
Purchases or arranges purchase of personal care items as needed						
Uses cosmetics or other grooming items appropriately						

*Dependent on individual client needs

FIGURE 2.10   One page from the Student Assessment Form.

education agencies have developed IEP formats and procedures to be used throughout the district. The assessment process described in this chapter is designed to pull together needed IEP information and can interface with any IEP format.

SUMMARY

The process of functional assessment can be summarized as follows: A determination is made of the potential future placement of the student both residentially and vocationally. An analysis of basic skill requirements for maintenance in those placements is completed. In addition, the student's current placement and immediate future placement are examined to determine skills requirements. The student's current repertoire of skills is assessed against the required skills of future placements, and from this information is developed a set of needed skills. The pool of "need to teach" skills are prioritized by the parents and teacher, and individual instructional goals for the student are developed.

REFERENCES

Bender, M., & Valletutti, P. J. (1976a). *Teaching the moderately and severely handicapped: Behavior, self-care and motor skills.* Baltimore: University Park Press.

Bender, M., & Valletutti, P. J. (1976b). *Teaching the moderately and severely handicapped: Communication, socialization, safety, leisure time and functional academics.* Baltimore: University Park Press.

Browder, D. M. (1987). *Assessment of individuals with severe handicaps.* Baltimore: Paul H. Brookes Publishing Co.

Browder, D. M., & King, D. (1987). Comprehensive assessment for longitudinal curriculum development. In D. M. Browder (Ed.), *Assessment of individuals with severe handicaps* (p. 14). Baltimore: Paul H. Brookes Publishing Co.

Brown, L., Nietupski, J., & Hamre-Nietupski, S. (1976). The criterion of ultimate functioning and public school services for severely handicapped students. In M. Thomas (Ed.), *Hey, don't forget about me: New directions for serving the severely handicapped* (pp. 2–15). Reston, VA: Council for Exceptional Children.

Fewell, R., & Cone, J. (1983). Identification and placement of severely handicapped children. In M. E. Snell (Ed.), *Systematic instruction of the moderately and severely handicapped* (2nd ed.). Columbus: Charles E. Merrill.

Ford, A., Schnorr, R., Meyer, L., Davern, L., Black, J., & Dempsey, P. (1989). *The Syracuse community referenced curriculum guide for students with moderate and severe disabilities.* Baltimore: Paul H. Brookes Publishing Co.

Fredericks, B. (1990). Education for the child with Down syndrome. In S. Pueschel (Ed.), *Parent's guide to Down syndrome* (pp. 179–212). Baltimore: Paul H. Brookes Publishing Co.

Fredericks, H. D., & the Staff of the Teaching Research Infant and Child Center. (1980a). *The Teaching Research curriculum for moderately and severely handicapped: Self-help and cognitive.* Springfield: Charles C. Thomas.

Fredericks, H. D., & the Staff of the Teaching Research Infant and Child Center. (1980b). *The Teaching Research curriculum for moderately and severely handicapped: Gross and fine motor.* Springfield: Charles C. Thomas.

Gearhart, C., & Gearhart, B. (1990). *Introduction to special education assessment: Principles and practices.* Denver: Love Publishing Co.

Haring, N. G., Liberty, K. A., & White, O. R. Rules for data based strategy decisions in instructional programs: Current research and instructional implications. In W. Sailor, B. Wilcox, & L. Brown (Eds.), *Methods of instruction for severely handicapped students* (pp. 159–192). Baltimore: Paul H. Brookes Publishing Co.

Lehr, D. H. (1989). Educational programming for young children with the most severe disabilities. In F. Brown & D. H. Lehr (Eds.), *Persons with profound disabilities: Issues and Practices* (pp. 213–238). Baltimore: Paul H. Brookes Publishing Co.

Makohon, L., & Fredericks, H. D. (1985). *Teaching expressive and receptive language to students with moderate and severe handicaps.* Austin: PRO-ED.

Neel, R., & Billingsley, F. (1990). IMPACT: A functional curriculum handbook for students with moderate to severe disabilities. Baltimore: Paul H. Brookes Publishing Co.

Petersen, J., Trecker, N., Egan, I., Fredericks, H. D., & Bunse, C. (1983). *The Teaching Research curriculum for handicapped adolescents and adults: Assessment procedures.* Monmouth, OR: Teaching Research Publications.

Salvia, J., & Ysseldyke, J. E. (1988). *Assessment in special and remedial education.* Boston: Houghton Mifflin.

Siperstein, G. N., Reed, D., Wolraish, M., & O'Keefe, P. (1990). Capabilities essential for adults who are mentally retarded to function in different residential settings. *Education and Training in Mental Retardation, 13,* 45–51.

Snell, M. E. (1983). Developing the IEP: Selecting and assessing skills. In M. E. Snell (Ed.), *Systematic instruction of the moderately and severely handicapped* (2nd ed.) (pp. 54–77). Columbus: Charles E. Merrill.

The Staff of the Teaching Research Infant and Child Center (1982). *A data based classroom for the moderately and severely handicapped.* Monmouth, OR: Teaching Research Publications.

Vincent, L. J., Salisbury, C., Walter, G., Gruenwald, L. J., & Powers, M. (1980). Program evaluation and curriculum development in early childhood/special education: Criteria of the next environment. In W. Sailor, B. Wilcox, & L. Brown (Eds.), *Methods of instruction for severely handicapped students* (pp. 303–328). Baltimore: Paul H. Brookes Publishing Co.

CHAPTER 3

PROGRAM DEVELOPMENT, EVALUATION, AND DATA-BASED DECISION MAKING

K. RICHARD YOUNG
RICHARD P. WEST
Utah State University

CHRISTINE A. MACFARLANE
University of Northern Iowa

The purpose of education is to help each individual reach his or her potential for successful, independent functioning in the community. Educating persons with severe and profound disabilities is a challenge, but they deserve an opportunity to live with dignity, respect, and purpose in life just as individuals do who have no disabilities. Persons with severe disabilities are entitled to the same rights enjoyed by those without disabilities: to make choices, to participate in a wide range of activities, to associate with persons without disabilities as well as those with disabilities, to work, and to enjoy leisure activities. The enjoyment of these rights is greatly enhanced by educational programs that use proven instructional procedures to build crucial skills. The most effective teachers will collect pertinent information (data) to evaluate the progress of each learner toward his or her goals and, thereby, the teaching procedures that were used.

DEVELOPING INSTRUCTIONAL PROGRAMS

Program Planning

Using information gathered during the assessment process, a transdisciplinary team can create an In-

dividualized Education Program (IEP) for the learner. The process of developing an IEP and then carrying it out prompts the team to target appropriate instructional goals, implement instruction using best practices, and evaluate the success of instruction. Without this instructional road map, the teacher and learner would waste precious time and resources. Good planning does not ensure success, but poor planning guarantees failure.

Program planning takes place on three distinct levels and results in the development of a comprehensive, individualized instructional program. Initially, long-term goals are selected, based on the learner's need for skill acquisition in general curriculum domains with respect to his or her immediate and subsequent environments. Then, several short-term objectives are chosen for each long-term goal. Finally, an instructional plan is developed through which the learner will complete each objective.

Long-Term Goals. To develop timely long-term goals, the teacher should start with the most significant deficit of each student in each general curriculum domain (i.e., domestic and community, vocational, recreational and leisure, communication, and academics; see Part II of this book) that, if corrected, would improve the learner's quality of life. For example, Annie (an 8-year-old student with a severe disability) has significant deficits in the domestic domain. She does not know how to make a bed, wash dishes, or get herself a drink from the refrigerator. Eventually, she will need to learn all of these skills, but her present quality of life would greatly improve if she could learn to get a drink when she is thirsty. A long-term goal for Annie might read, "Annie will learn to independently get a drink." David, age 18, on the other hand, will be moving into a group home in the near future. He is self-sufficient in his parents' home, but needs to acquire house-cleaning skills so that he can do his share of chores in the group home. A long-term goal for David might read, "David will learn to independently perform routine house-cleaning chores." As a rule of thumb, long-term goals should reflect skills that might require a year to learn.

Short-Term Objectives.   Once long-term goals have been selected for each major curriculum area, the next step is to develop short-term objectives for each goal. Generally speaking, a teacher devises a sequence of three or more objectives per goal. For instance, in Annie's case, the objectives might target getting a drink from a pitcher, a carton, a jug, and an individual serving container. Objectives might also reflect gross motor skills (e.g., walking to the refrigerator), fine motor skills (e.g., opening a milk carton, pouring from a pitcher), cognitive skills (e.g., identifying milk, orange juice, and apple juice), social skills (e.g., getting a friend a soft drink), or communication skills (e.g., using the correct preposition: in [the refrigerator], on [the table]). For David, the objectives might cover separate, but related, skills: (1) vacuuming, (2) dusting, and (3) sweeping.

A short-term or behavioral objective consists of three specific parts: (1) condition, (2) behavior, and (3) criterion. Table 3.1 contains examples of several short-term objectives. The condition delineates the cue, circumstances, and/or materials that should evoke the behavior. Through a series of objectives, David might advance from initially learning the mechanics of sweeping to finally completing this chore as part of a schedule. For David, the ultimate cue may be his name on a chart with a picture of the broom and the verbal reminder that it is time to do chores, or a personal calendar with chores written on specific days. At first, however, the condition would relate to the presence of cleaning supplies. Whenever possible,

TABLE 3.1   Examples of Short-term Objectives

CONDITION	BEHAVIOR	CRITERION
When thirsty,	Annie will get a drink of milk from a gallon plastic jug	in less than 2 minutes with 100% accuracy for 1 week.
Given a broom, dustpan, wastebasket, and dirty floor,	David will sweep a 9' × 12' floor, push the debris into the dustpan, and empty the dustpan into the wastebasket	in less than 5 minutes with 100% accuracy for eight consecutive trials.
Given the verbal cue, "Annie, please get the pitcher of Kool-Aid from the refrigerator,"	Annie will go to the refrigerator and get the pitcher of Kool-Aid	within 10 seconds of the verbal cue for 4 out of 5 consecutive days.

the condition, or final condition in a series of objectives, should specify the learner's performance in the natural environment.

The behavior is a description of the learner's verbal or motoric response. A precise description of the required response is a necessary prerequisite to data collection. An in-depth discussion on how to define behaviors follows in a later section of this chapter.

Establishing Performance Criteria.   A criterion establishes a standard by which to judge when the learner has completed the objective. Each criterion should include both a measure of accuracy and fluency. The level of accuracy should reflect realistic standards in order to demonstrate competence. Some behaviors naturally lend themselves to less stringent standards. For instance, very few people correctly pronounce every word used in conversation. Even with a few mispronunciations, conversation can still take place. However, a high frequency of mispronounced words will affect the quality of conversation. A criterion of 80 to 90 percent correct would probably suffice. In contrast, certain tasks, such as reciting a telephone number, must be performed perfectly or the desired outcome is never achieved. In this case, a criterion of 100 percent is essential.

The ability to respond fluently also denotes competence. Assessing the fluency of performance requires measures of time to be added to measures of accuracy. Such time-based measures are then included in the criterion portion of each objective. (Time-based measures are explained later in this chapter.) There are several ways to establish appropriate criteria (aims) for fluency (see Koorland, Keel, & Ueberhost, 1990). One method involves observing nondisabled peers perform the target behavior. The average time required to complete the task can serve as a guide, although sometimes the teacher must consider the motoric limitations of learners. Frequently, the demands of the setting dictate time limits. For example, if there are only 15 minutes between the time lunch ends and when students arrive for P.E.,

then Bobbie must clear, wipe, and store the tables in 15 minutes or less. A specific rate that demonstrates a high level of automatic responding can also serve as a standard for fluency. Research supports the premise that learners who are able to respond quickly will retain the skill, generalize it to other settings and persons, and maintain it over time (Young, West, & Crawford, 1985; Young, West, Howard, & Whitney, 1986).

Instructional Plans

The teacher next writes an instructional plan that serves as a blueprint for delivering and evaluating systematic instruction. The process of developing an instructional plan begins with a thorough analysis of the instructional steps needed to perform the target skill.

Task Analysis.   A task analysis is a step-by-step breakdown of the specific responses required to complete a target behavior (i.e., objective). The size or scope of each step depends on the person's learning history and the complexity of the task. For example, Table 3.2 is a task analysis for "sweeping." The task analysis could include just the four main steps or the main steps and all the substeps.

The critical factor in determining the amount of detail is the learner's progress. For instance, if the teacher elects to teach only the four main steps and the learner consistently scores an error on a step, it would be difficult to pinpoint the exact problem. If the teacher utilizes a more complex task analysis, he or she would have additional information and might discover the source of the error. At that point, a branch to a more complex task analysis (the substeps) might improve instruction. Discovering the right balance between steps that are too small or too large takes practice. Skills already in the learner's repertoire can be consolidated into large steps. Steps covering new responses will need to be more discrete. For learners with more severe disabilities, the teacher typically develops more detailed task analyses with more, but smaller, steps. During the development of a task

TABLE 3.2   An Example of a Task Analysis for Sweeping a Floor

1. Obtain a broom and dustpan.
   a. Locate broom closet.
   b. Open broom closet door.
   c. Grasp broom with right hand.
   d. Grasp dustpan with left hand.
   e. Transfer dustpan to right hand.
   f. Close broom closet door.
2. Sweep up dirt.
   a. Walk to floor that needs sweeping.
   b. Set dustpan down (out of the way).
   c. Sweep dirt on floor into pile.
   d. Pick up dustpan.
   e. Place dustpan on floor with edge next to pile of dirt.
   f. Sweep dirt into dustpan.
3. Discard contents of dustpan into wastebasket.
4. Return broom and dustpan.
   a. Walk to broom closet.
   b. Open broom closet door.
   c. Return broom.
   d. Return dustpan.
   e. Close broom closet door.

analysis, the teacher should test and fine tune the task analysis to ensure that all of the necessary steps are included and that the task analysis works. A common mistake that many teachers make is to assume that the same task analysis will work for all learners. The unique characteristics of each learner and each setting necessitates the development or adaptation of individualized task analyses. For example, a broom could be kept in a broom closet, hanging on a hook in a utility room, or stored between the wall and refrigerator. Annie may prefer ice in a drink of juice, but not with milk. A generic task analysis for getting a drink could provide a starting point, but individual modifications would be vital.

Task analyses that focus strictly on the basic motoric responses necessary to complete the skill are incomplete. Brown, Evans, Weed, and Owen (1987) presented a component model for delineating functional competencies. They add additional components that enhance the quality of the instructional plan and promote integration of related skills. Based on the model program of Brown and associates (1987), planning should include (a) task initiation, (b) task preparation, and (c) task termination. In addition, they suggest that the learner ought to monitor quality and tempo and learn to solve problems when necessary. The task analysis for sweeping included obtaining the necessary materials (preparation) and putting the materials away (termination). Additional steps could include (1) checking a chart or calendar for chore assignment (initiation), (2) checking the floor after sweeping to make sure all dirt is swept up (monitoring quality), (3) finishing before a timer goes off (monitoring tempo), and (4) searching or asking for the dustpan if it is missing from the broom closet (problem solving). The inclusion of these steps in a task analysis leads to independent functioning.

Further enrichment can occur if the teacher incorporates opportunities for communication, choice, and social skills within the framework of the task analysis (Brown, Evans, Weed, & Owen, 1987). As Annie is learning to get herself a drink, she can also learn to ask siblings, parents, or peers whether they would like a drink. If milk, juice, and soft drinks are all in the refrigerator, then Annie can choose what she wants. The added benefits for the learner make the extra effort involved in creating an extended task analysis very worthwhile.

Partial Participation. The concept of partial participation (Baumgart et al., 1982) has challenged many educators to rethink their ideas about which activities learners with severe disabilities should or should not be involved in. Rather than exclude someone because of an inability to complete the entire task, the use of this technique promotes a sense of accomplishment and provides a measure of dignity and self-respect.

Consider Annie's goal to get a drink independently. If Annie lacks mobility and fine motor skills, the goal is still appropriate, but the steps involved in getting a drink must be restructured. Realistically, Annie may never be able to open the refrigerator independently. A more practical approach would be simply to have a helper open the door. At that point, Annie could indicate which beverage she wanted. The helper would remove it from the refrigerator. Next, she could select a glass and specify how much she wanted. In order to get a drink, Annie definitely needs assistance. Yet in this scenario, she is firmly in control of the situation and, therefore, independent.

Instructional Strategies

A task analysis outlines "what to teach." In the next phase of program planning, the teacher defines all of the parameters associated with the actual delivery of instruction. The instructional planning process presented in this chapter results in a systematic plan of "how to teach," as well as decisions on what to teach. At this point, the teacher considers such things as (1) whether to teach the skill with other learners present, (2) the number of opportunities that must be provided to practice the skill, (3) whether this is a new skill or a continuation of previous instruction, (4) the setting where teaching will occur, (5) the persons who will do the teaching, and (6) which instructional materials to use. The teacher also identifies reinforcers and a correction procedure. Ultimately, the instructional plan reflects a synthesis of "best practices" across all considerations.

Because persons with severe and profound disabilities characteristically have a difficult time transferring to another environment the use of skills learned in a first environment, a teacher must consider where to first teach the skill and in what context to teach the skill. In the past, instruction always occurred in the classroom and involved multiple, repetitive presentations of trials (i.e., massed trials) during structured time blocks. Instruction may still occur in the classroom, but attempts to simulate within the classroom the fea-

tures of future environments have proven successful. Moreover, instruction can and should take place in community environments. Learners need frequent opportunities to respond, but the relevance of the response is also important. Learning the vocabulary associated with cooking makes more sense in the kitchen while preparing a meal than in an isolated training session. Nevertheless, if the learner is going to make satisfactory progress, cooking should occur every day rather than just once a week.

Group or Individual Instruction.   Instruction can take place in a group of learners or in a one-on-one situation. There are several advantages to teaching in a group. For instance, group instruction can occur naturally in a conversation or during the playing of a board game and may therefore be more efficient. Working within a group may approximate future work environments. Learners may work on diverse tasks within a group (e.g., one learner sorts paper for recycling, another learner stuffs envelopes, and a third learner collates hand-outs), but still benefit from individualized instruction. In a group, there are opportunities for learners to observe one another's behavior and learn from others' successes and/or mistakes. A more advanced learner who needs practice can serve as a model for a less-skilled learner. However, if a learner is easily distracted by a peer, then one-on-one instruction may be more appropriate. When utilizing group instruction, the primary concern is to keep all learners actively engaged in the learning process by providing frequent opportunities to respond.

Teaching Format

Teaching may occur in any of several formats (e.g., discrete trial training, incidental teaching, milieu training). Jenson and Young (1985) describe the discrete trial training approach.

The use of discrete trials is a standard approach to the treatment of autistic persons and has been the basis of most behavioral interven-

tions (Donnellan, Gossage, LaVigna, Schuler, & Traphagen, 1977; Koegel, Schreibman, Britten, Burke, & O'Neill, 1982). Essentially, a discrete trial consists of (1) a clear beginning (signaled by a discriminative stimulus) and ending of a trial, (2) a behaviorally defined standard (observable and measurable) to judge a behavior, (3) a consequence for the behavior, and (4) an intertrial interval of very short duration (3 to 5 seconds) in which no teaching occurs and data are recorded. A series of prompts can be used with discrete trials to initially shape a behavior, although these prompts are generally faded out. (p. 182)

Incidental Teaching/Milieu Training.   The basis for incidental teaching (Hart & Risley, 1975, 1982)/milieu training (Cipani, 1988) is that opportunities for instruction occur naturally. For instance, if Heather drops her spoon during a meal, the teacher could use the opportunity to ask, "What did you drop?" and also prompt a response to ask for a clean utensil. Unfortunately, teaching opportunities may slip by unnoticed. Some teachers structure the classroom environment so that teaching opportunities will arise. Instead of automatically giving a person a spoon with a bowl of pudding, the learner gets only the pudding. The learner must then ask for the missing spoon. A good guideline for developing a contrived situation is whether that situation might actually occur in the real world. An instance of "missing silverware" may happen infrequently. Generally, the reasons for learning to identify silverware relate to setting the table, sorting, and eating with the appropriate utensil. In most situations, unless the learner could not physically obtain a spoon, there would be no need to ask. The incidental teaching approach has also been used successfully in teaching social skills (Oswald, Lignugaris-Kraft, & West, 1990).

Learning trials may be massed, distributed, or spaced. Massed trials provide the learner with multiple opportunities to respond during an instructional session. Instruction focuses on one skill or on a series of related behaviors that the learner can practice repeatedly. Criticism of massed trial training has occurred primarily because of its association with nonfunctional skills and a lack of planning for generalization to nonschool environments. These legitimate concerns should not result in the abolition of massed trials, because the number of opportunities to respond is a critical variable in learning (Greenwood, Delquadri, & Hall, 1984). Rather, teachers must always remember to focus on functional skills and plan for transition.

When using distributed trials, a predetermined number of trials are interspersed with other instructional targets across a day or session. Rather than focusing strictly on one skill during an instructional time block, instruction occurs repeatedly in small segments. If the target behavior is the identification of silverware, then the teacher might schedule five mini-sessions of three trials during the school day.

Spaced trials can occur within the context of group instruction. The teacher presents each learner with one or two trials at a time and then moves on to the next learner. After each learner in the group has received an instructional set, the teacher repeats the sequence. The greatest disadvantage in using spaced trials is the "downtime" that occurs while the teacher works with other learners. The impact of downtime can be lessened by keeping the group small, presenting trials rapidly, and having learners work on similar tasks. If three learners needed to know their phone numbers and addresses, the teacher could work with them together, rotating instruction on the various skills.

Daily Routines.   Providing instruction within daily routines expands the concept of teaching in the natural environment. Instead of waiting for a teaching opportunity or manipulating the environment, the teacher develops a schedule of activities that closely approximates naturally occurring routines. Then he or she targets specific behaviors within those routines for instruction. Each component in the routine leads to the next. Given that Annie needs to sort silverware, instruction could occur during the course of unloading a dishwasher, washing and drying silverware, or setting the table. Additional instruction could take place on related skills. One advantage of implementing instruction during daily routines is the immediate access to natural cues (e.g., the sound of the dishwasher clicking off) and consequences (e.g., a clean floor).

Stage of Learning.   In addition to considering the context or instructional format, teachers must also consider the stage of learning when developing instructional plans. Depending on the learner's stage of learning for a particular skill, the method of instruction, the setting for instruction, and the number of opportunities to respond may be different. In the acquisition stage of learning, the learner is learning how to perform the skill. The priority at that time is to provide intense instruction. In the next stage of learning, fluency building, the learner can perform the skill accurately but needs the opportunity to practice the skill and develop fluency. Finally, during the generalization and maintenance stage of learning, the teacher increases the likelihood that the learner will perform the skill correctly and fluently in subsequent environments by providing practice in the actual environments or simulations of those environments. Stages of learning are explored further in a discussion of data-based decisions later in this chapter.

Instructors.   Teachers, paraprofessionals, occupational and physical therapists, and speech and language pathologists can all deliver instruction. Additional instructional resources are peer tutors, volunteers, job coaches, and, of course, parents, siblings, and extended family members. Although teaching specialists should be responsible for designing and evaluating instruction, nearly anyone can teach a skill if he or she has been trained properly to do it. A speech and language pathologist should not be the only person delivering language

instruction. Rather, all persons working with a learner should incorporate language into instruction. However, the speech and language pathologist may be the person best qualified to deliver training on a complex skill during the acquisition stage of learning. As a rule of thumb, the most difficult and important skills should be taught by the most qualified teacher.

The Delivery of Instruction.   Once the conceptual aspects of developing an instructional plan have been decided, the teacher must specify exactly how instruction will be delivered. This process involves identifying the cue, prompt(s), correction procedure, reinforcer(s), and instructional material(s), as well as related schedules and/or levels of implementation. It is important to approximate naturally occurring cues and consequences. If the natural cue for giving an order to the counter person at McDonald's is, "May I take your order, please?" the instructor should use the same cue when instruction has to occur elsewhere. Similarly, if Annie is learning to choose from a variety of beverages, the materials (examples) should be the actual containers rather than line drawings of the items.

Selecting Reinforcers.   Selecting potential reinforcers and determining an appropriate schedule of delivery is another crucial step in developing an instructional plan. Again, the best reinforcers occur as a natural consequence of completing a skill. Saying, "Hello," to a peer and receiving a greeting in return, satisfying one's thirst, or seeing a clean floor may eventually function as reinforcers for learning a greeting, getting a drink, or sweeping a floor. However, in the initial stages of learning or when the natural reinforcer is not strong enough, other reinforcers may be necessary. The teacher should select the most powerful, effective reinforcers that have previously demonstrated an ability to increase the occurrence of a desired behavior. If the teacher has not identified potential reinforcers, then he or she should conduct a reinforcer survey and establish preferences (see Blair, Young, & Macfarlane, 1991; Dyer, 1987). Other factors to consider in selecting reinforcers are (1) cost, (2) dietary restrictions (e.g., allergies), (3) likelihood of satiation, (4) potential for injury (e.g., has sharp edges, breakable, swallowable), (5) potential for spoilage or contamination, (6) ease of presentation, and (7) ease of destruction. Once the teacher has developed objectives and strategies for delivering instruction, the process of measurement and evaluation must be designed.

MEASUREMENT AND EVALUATION

Formal and Informal Evaluations

Evaluations may take many forms, ranging from informal to formal. The most informal evaluations are largely intuitive and lack a systematic, reproducible form. These evaluations are also typically quite subjective and often rely heavily on second-hand evidence that may be neither valid (accurate) nor reliable. These informal evaluations are characterized by teachers who state, "I think Billy is finally getting it," "She really seems to be paying attention more," or "He is cooperating more now than he was before." Each of these statements reflects the change over time that must be present for learning to be inferred, but none of them is based on evidence that can support the conclusion. Informal evaluations are fine for forming preliminary hypotheses requiring further and more formal analyses. Formal evaluations are generally more objective and more likely to be valid and reliable. They are conducted in a systematic and reproducible fashion. These evaluations include sound and operational response definitions, with accurate and reliable measurement of student performance.

The purpose of *measurement* in education is to provide teachers with the information necessary to *evaluate* progress and make decisions concerning it. An important distinction to draw at this juncture is the difference between measurement and evaluation. Both measurement and evaluation should be used in determining the instructional progress in all domains.

Measurement versus Evaluation.   Measurement has been defined by Tawney and Gast (1984)

as the systematic and objective quantification of objects, events, or behaviors according to a set of rules. Basic steps or rules to be followed in the measurement process include (a) identifying what is to be measured, (b) defining the behavior or event in observable terms, and (c) selecting an appropriate data-recording system for observing, quantifying, and summarizing behavior. (p. 79)

They define evaluation "as the analysis or comparison of data collected during the measurement process, upon which instructional decisions can be based" (p. 80). Evaluation is based on measurement(s). Without the systematic quantification of events (measurement) there can be no evaluation. Evaluation characteristically has been broken down into two different types. The first type is summative evaluation. Summative evaluation is a static process that measures student progress at two points in time, usually via a pretest-posttest evaluation paradigm (i.e., at the beginning and at the end). The second type is formative evaluation. Formative evaluation is a dynamic, ongoing process that emphasizes frequent and repeated measures taken over time. Formative evaluation allows teachers to measure the day-to-day changes in target behaviors.

Measurement should be accurate and reliable and collected on a regular basis, preferably daily. Without accurate information, appropriate program evaluation and instructional decisions are not likely to occur. To be effective, educators must regularly and systematically evaluate instructional programs. Teachers should collect data on a regular basis and systematically use the data to make adjustments in each learner's instructional program. With this type of data-based evaluation, persons with severe disabilities can make progress and achieve their instructional goals.

Behavioral Definitions

When formulating instructional goals and objectives, it is necessary to define a behavior in specific, observable terms. For a teacher to observe behavior, the learner must make detectable movements. The behavioral definition should also be valid; in other words, the definition should reflect the needs identified during the functional assessment (see Chapter 2). The definition should also help produce reliable data; that is, if two independent observers watched the learner, using the behavioral definition, they would generally agree that the behavior had occurred or that it had not.

There are two general approaches to defining target behaviors: defining a behavioral response by its topography or by its function (see White & Haring, 1980). To define a behavior topographically, one describes the learner's bodily movement or the physical features of a response product. In defining the behavior "points to," a topographical definition would describe the learner moving his or her arm, hand, and finger toward an object and then holding that position for some prescribed period of time, perhaps as brief as 1 second. A topographical definition of "finger sucking" might be "one or more fingers or the thumb touching the lips or inserted in the mouth."

Describing a behavior functionally focuses on the effects of the response on the person's environment. Functionally defining the behavior "property destruction" would describe the impact of the learner's action. For example, a child's throwing a toy would not be "property destruction" unless the toy was damaged or the toy damaged another object. The definition of "putting on shirt" could describe the movement involved in performing the behavior (topographical definition) or the results of the actions (functional definition). If we are concerned about teaching a person to dress him- or herself, we could functionally define dressing by describing how the learner should look with each item of clothing on. When teaching learners with severe disabilities, functional definitions are often more helpful than topo-

graphical definitions, inasmuch as it is the function of the behavior that we are ultimately concerned with and the behavioral movements necessary to accomplish that function may vary from learner to learner.

Each individual instance of the behavior is referred to as a response. A collection of many responses, similar in topography and/or function, can be grouped together into a response class. For example, a learner might yell, cry, fall on the floor, and/or stamp his or her feet to gain attention or to obtain something from another person. A teacher concerned with these problem behaviors could define each individual behavior and collect data on the occurrence of each. The behaviors might also be grouped into a response class, because they serve the same function. The response class could be called "tantruming" and a definition could include an example of each of the behaviors. Behaviors may be similar in both topography and function. Teaching "drinking from a container" might be a response class that would include several behaviors, such as drinking from a glass, drinking from a cup, and drinking from a soft drink bottle. Each behavior is topographically similar, but they all serve the same function, consuming liquid. Therefore, the use of response class definitions can make teaching efficient as well as effective by capitalizing on the use of one intervention to bring about change in several related behaviors.

Methods for Data Collection

Following the selection and defining of target behaviors, a method for measuring behavior must be selected and a data collection system designed. In order to select appropriate data collection procedures, teachers must understand the advantages and limitations of each method. Two general approaches to data collection are measuring response products and observing behavior as it occurs. Some responses produce permanent products, such as a written response to a math problem or the writing of one's name. Other responses (e.g., stating the time, throwing a softball) do not produce a tangible product; therefore, data must be collected by observing the behavior as it occurs.

With a permanent product, one can observe and record the effect of the behavior by evaluating its final product. For example, defining "getting dressed" topographically would require an observer to watch the learner get dressed and score each step in a task analysis. By focusing on the function of the behavior or the end product, having "clothes on," allows us to check and record whether the learner is dressed correctly (e.g., socks, shoes, pants, shirt, and other accessories put on correctly).

Some products are more permanent than others. For example, a written response to a question or a problem could easily be retained and scored hours later. A worker on an assembly line might produce many assembled products. At the end of the shift, these products could be counted, inspected, and scored for accuracy. Audiotapes and videotapes can be used to produce permanent products of behaviors that typically leave no visible product (e.g., conversation). The teacher can replay the tapes to score the occurrence and accuracy of target behaviors. For behaviors that do not produce products or have not been tape-recorded, the teacher can record data on a form while observing the learner perform the behavior. Six methods for recording data—event recording; discrete categorization; duration, latency, interval, and momentary time sampling—are discussed in the following section.

Methods for Recording Data

Event Recording. Event or frequency recording is achieved by counting the number of times a response occurs within a specified period of time. Event recording is generally an easy way for a teacher to collect data, and this information provides a good basis for instructional decision making. The frequency with which a behavior has occurred in the past is one of the best predictors of how likely the behavior is to occur under the same

conditions in the future. For example, if during a vocational training activity David has completed five tasks each day for the past 4 days, and nothing has changed in his environment, the best prediction of how many tasks he will complete on the fifth day would be five. Obviously, many uncontrolled variables (e.g., sickness, fire drill) could increase or decrease the number of tasks completed. Event recording can be accomplished by observing a learner while he or she performs a behavior and tallying the number of occurrences of the target behavior, or by examining the products of the learner's responding and counting the items. Liberty and Paeth (1990) have described devices that learners with severe disabilities can use as they observe their own behavior and record its frequency. This method of self-assessment forms a valuable part of a self-management program.

We recommend the event recording method of collecting data as the first choice for a teacher, provided the target behavior meets the following requirements: the beginning and end of the behavior can be easily detected, the length of each instance of the behavior is approximately the same, and the behavior occurs at a rate low enough for the teacher to count each occurrence (the behavior should not be occurring so rapidly that observers cannot reliably observe and record each instance of the behavior).

Discrete Categorization Recording. When opportunities to respond are limited or controlled, teachers are primarily interested in whether the learner performed the behavior correctly. Kazdin (1982) describes the use of discrete categorization recording:

> *Often it is very useful to classify responses into discrete categories, such as correct-incorrect, performed-not performed, or appropriate-inappropriate. In many ways, discrete categorization resembles a frequency measure because it is used for behaviors that have a clear beginning and end and a constant duration. Yet there are at least two important differences. With a*

frequency measure, performances of a particular behavior are tallied. The focus is on a single response. Also, the number of times the behavior may occur is theoretically unlimited. For example, how often one child hits another may be measured by frequency counts. How many times the behavior (hitting) may occur has no theoretical limit. Discrete categorization is used to measure whether several different behaviors may have occurred or not. (pp. 27–28)

The teacher should (1) watch for response opportunities, (2) observe learner performance, (3) classify learner responses into the discrete categories of "performed-not performed" or "correct-incorrect," and (4) score the behavior on a checklist. Two examples of this type of recording are presented in Figure 3.1. One is an example of recording the occurrence or nonoccurrence of a social behavior, and the second is an example of scoring the steps as correct, incorrect, or omitted from the task-analyzed skill of purchasing a soft drink from a vending machine. The discrete categorization method of recording data is often used with discrete trial training activities.

Duration and Latency Recording.   Sometimes the most critical feature of a behavior is the length of time that it occurs or the amount of time that elapses prior to the behavior's first occurrence. When behaviors persist for long periods of time, or when they occur at very high rates with little time between each occurrence (which makes it difficult to identify and count each individual response), or when the performance criterion states that a behavior is to continue for a specific time period, the duration method of collecting data is most appropriate. Duration data are collected by starting a stopwatch (or other timing device) when the behavior begins and stopping it when the behavior ceases. Each occurrence of a behavior may be timed and recorded separately. Summarizing both the number of occurrences and either the individual or average durations yields a record of both the frequency and the duration of each re-

sponse. A second method is to total the amount of time across all the responses within the observation period. This provides a measure of the total time the student engaged in the behavior during the observation period. For either method, the total length of the observation period should also be recorded. This enables the teacher to compare the amount of behavior with the total time during which the behavior could occur. The duration data collection method is appropriate for behaviors such as time on-task, time engaged in continuous physical exercise, time spent engaged in appropriate conversation, time engaged in self-stimulatory behavior (e.g., rocking or repetitive hand movements), and the length of time required to complete specific tasks, such as sorting silverware.

Latency is the length of time between the end of an antecedent stimulus (the stimulus intended to prompt the response to occur) and the beginning of the response. Latency data are collected when the speed with which the learner initiates the response is of primary interest. For example, when someone greets another person or asks a question such as "What's your phone number?" a response is expected within a few seconds. If a response is slow in coming, the person may be viewed as unfriendly or incapable of answering. Therefore, teaching would not be successful until the learner can respond correctly within an appropriate latency (e.g., 3 seconds).

Interval Recording Methods.   Interval recording procedures are used to estimate the occurrence or nonoccurrence of a behavior. Data from interval recording are not as precise as measures collected by the event recording or duration methods, because all of the instances of the behavior may not be recorded. However, interval procedures are helpful when the behavior does not have a discrete beginning or ending. To use the interval method of recording, the teacher first specifies the length of an observation time period. Then the observation period is broken into small, equal intervals. The size of each interval typically ranges from 5 seconds to 1 minute. The observer records whether

Target Behavior: Greeting Others

Student: _____

Observer: _____

Date: _____

	1	2	3	4	5	6
1. Was there an opportunity to greet someone?	Y	Y	Y	Y	Y	Y
2. Did the student respond?	Y	Y	N	Y	Y	N
3. Did the student:						
A. Look at the person?	Y	Y		Y	Y	
B. Smile?	Y	N		Y	Y	
C. Use a pleasant voice?	Y	Y		Y	Y	
D. Say "hi" (or other appropriate greeting)?	Y	Y		Y	Y	
4. Context--Did the response occur at an appropriate time and situation?	Y	Y		N	Y	

Target Behavior: Operating a Soft Drink Vending Machine

Student: _____

Observer: _____

		Date				
Steps	10/08	10/08	10/09	10/10	10/10	10/11
1. Insert one quarter in coin slot.	+	+	+			
2. Insert another quarter in coin slot	+	+	+			
3. Press selection button	-	+	+			
4. Pick up canned drink	o	o	+			
5. Reach in coin return and get change	o	o	o			

Key:
    + = Correct
    - = Incorrect
    o = Omitted

FIGURE 3.1   (a) A sample form for a discrete categorization recording of social behavior; (b) a sample recording form for discrete categorization recording of a task-analyzed skill.

the behavior was observed at least once during each interval. Interval data are typically collected by using one of two procedures: whole-interval or partial-interval recording.

Whole-interval recording works best for behaviors with an unclear beginning and end that continue for longer periods of time (e.g., 30 seconds or more), such as talking, playing, or on-task behaviors. A response is recorded only when the behavior lasts throughout the entire interval. If the behavior continues across several intervals without stopping, each interval is scored. Partial-interval recording is best suited for behaviors of shorter duration (e.g., an off-task behavior). An interval is scored if a response occurs at any time during the interval. Additional responses during the same interval are not scored. A disadvantage of interval recording is that this procedure generally requires an observer who can devote total attention to observing and recording and who has no teaching duties during the observation time period. If the teacher has limited time and personnel resources, the interval recording method may not be a viable method for collecting data.

Momentary time sampling is also an interval recording procedure. Again, the observation period is divided into small intervals but, unlike the whole-interval and partial-interval recording procedures, momentary time sampling does not require constant attention to data collection. A teacher can use momentary time sampling while carrying on some other instructional activities. For example, an audible sound from an audiocassette tape might be used to signal that an interval has ended. At that moment, the teacher observes whether or not the target behavior is occurring. Behaviors occurring before or after the timed interval are not recorded. Although momentary time sampling places a relatively low demand on the teacher, the major disadvantage is the potential for inaccuracy in the data, because the occurrence of behaviors may be over- or underestimated. Accuracy can be improved with the use of many short intervals (e.g., 5 to 10 seconds), but shorter intervals also increase demands on the teacher.

In summary, we recommend that if at all possible, a teacher collect data from permanent products and, when collecting observational data, use the event or discrete categorization recording methods of data collection. If that is not suitable, then we recommend the duration method. A summary of data collection procedures and guidelines for applying them are presented in Table 3.3.

Training Versus Probe Data

Some teachers distinguish between training data and probe (or test) data. Training data are collected during instruction and reflect the characteristics of instruction (e.g., prompts, cues, and corrective strategies). Teachers must exercise caution when interpreting training data and not infer improvements in performance when improvement is more a function of the teacher's assistance than the learner's ability.

Training data are useful in representing the degree of teacher assistance required to perform the skill. In the case of recording the amount of assistance required, the teacher might record an "f" for a full physical prompt, a "p" for a partial physical prompt, a "g" for a gestural prompt, and a "v" for a verbal prompt. By comparing changes in assistance over time, the teacher can study the effects of teaching even though the numbers of correct and incorrect responses remain the same. For example, in a self-feeding program, the number of spoonfuls of food inserted in the learner's mouth may remain the same over several sessions, but then, four days later, nearly all of the responses are unprompted.

Unlike training data, probe data represent the use of a skill under natural conditions. These data reflect the ability of the learner to perform the skill independently without prompts or assistance. If the teacher records only those learner responses that occur unaided, most of the scores will be zero in the initial part of the training program. The teacher may not see the improvements in performance that may have occurred when unaided performance has not changed; i.e., the level of

TABLE 3.3   Data Collection Methods and Guidelines for Application

METHOD AND DEFINITION	APPLICATION	STANDARD UNITS OF MEASUREMENT
Permanent Products		
Measurement of behavior taken from products (e.g., assembled parts, written responses, audio- or videotaped behaviors, photographs) collected within a specific time period.	1. When behavior produces a lasting product. 2. When behavior is difficult to observe and a video- or audiotape can be produced and data collected from the tape.	1. Convert to rate of correct and incorrect behavior. 2. Convert to percentage correct. 3. Count total responses (if time or opportunities to respond are constant).
Event Frequency Recording		
The observer counts each occurrence of the behavior during a predefined time period.	1. When behavior is discrete (clear beginning and ending). 2. When each occurrence is similar in length. 3. When behavior is occurring at a moderate or low rate. 4. May be used to observe more than one behavior or person at a time when behavior is easy to observe. 5. Interested in the numerical dimension of behavior.	1. Rate of correct (appropriate) and incorrect (inappropriate) behaviors. 2. Total count (if time and opportunities are constant). 3. Percentage of correct and incorrect responses.
Discrete Categorization Recording		
Scoring the occurrence of correct responses on a checklist or task analysis.	1. For task-analytic data. 2. For checklists. 3. Correct and incorrect responding. 4. Occurrence vs. nonoccurrence of a behavior.	1. Percentage of correct responses. 2. Total number of responses (if number of response opportunities is constant).

(continued)

TABLE 3.3 Continued

METHOD AND DEFINITION	APPLICATION	STANDARD UNITS OF MEASUREMENT
Duration Recording		
Length of a behavior; observer measures time from the beginning of the behavior to the conclusion of the behavior.	1. When behavior is discrete (clear beginning and ending). 2. Usually used with one person and one behavior. 3. When each occurrence of the behavior varies in length. 4. When behaviors occur for long periods of time (e.g., tantrums, talking, crying). 5. When frequency of behavior is high (and pauses between behaviors are very short, less than 1 second) (e.g., head banging 100 times per minute). 6. When temporal dimension of behavior is of interest.	1. Convert raw data to percentage of total time that target behavior occurred. 2. Total time (if length of observation period is constant).
Latency		
Length of time between the end of the antecedent stimulus and the beginning of the response.	1. Behavior is discrete (clear beginning and ending). 2. When primary interest is the speed with which the behavior is initiated.	Time recording in seconds or minutes.
Interval Recording		
Observation period divided into equal number of intervals (e.g., 30 minutes divided into 180 10-second intervals). Observer records occurrence or nonoccurrence of target behavior within interval. Whole interval—behavior scored only if it lasts for the entire interval. Partial interval—behavior scored if behavior occurs in any part of the interval. Multiple responses scored only once per interval.	1. Behavior need not have easily determined beginning or ending. 2. For high-frequency behaviors. 3. When frequency or duration do not work. 4. When independent observer (without other teaching responsibilities) is available. 5. When observing multiple persons or behaviors at once. 6. When both the numerical and temporal dimensions of behavior are of interest.	1. Percentage of scored or unscored intervals. 2. Total number of scored or unscored intervals (if length of observation period is constant).

TABLE 3.3   Continued

METHOD AND DEFINITION	APPLICATION	STANDARD UNITS OF MEASUREMENT
Momentary Time Sampling		
Observations are made at specific times throughout observation period.	When interval data method is called for but no independent observer is available.	1. Percentage of scored intervals. 2. Total number of scored intervals (if length of observation periods is constant.

assistance required can be reduced considerably. Rather than relying on one or the other, we recommend a combination of the two systems that permits a glimpse of the learner's ability to perform at the ultimate criterion level, but also allows the teacher to see initial improvement as independent functioning emerges.

Summarizing and Graphing Data

The only reason for collecting data is to enable the teacher to make decisions regarding a learner's progress and the effectiveness of an instructional program. To make the data useful and easy to manage, and to facilitate decision making, raw data need to be summarized and visually displayed on charts or graphs. In converting raw data to standard units of measurement, there are two key variables: (1) time and (2) the number of response opportunities. Table 3.3 summarizes the most commonly used units of measurement for the data collection methods discussed in this chapter. For permanent product data collection, responses may be reported as rate, total occurrences, or percentage correct.

When the amount of time allowed for a particular instructional activity is constant from day to day, the teacher may total correct and incorrect responses and chart the results each day. However, if the amount of time available for respond-

ing varies (and this is often the case because of the many disruptions that occur naturally within the classroom and community, or because of interfering behaviors), then it is not fair to compare behavior across days without data conversion. The teacher should convert the count to rate or percentage data. The formula for rate is behavior divided by time. If a learner in a food-preparation vocational training program made six chef salads in 1 hour, the supervisor would determine the rate of salad preparation by dividing 6 salads by 60 minutes, which equals .10 salads per minute. If the learner worked only 30 minutes the next day and completed three salads, the rate would still be .10 salads per minute and the supervisor would have a fair comparison.

Data collected from permanent products may also be presented as percentage of occurrences. The formula for percentage is the number of correct responses divided by the total number of correct and incorrect responses. Most teachers are quite familiar with percentages as a way to summarize data. However, percentages allow us to monitor only improved accuracy, not improved rate of performance or fluency.

Data collected during the fluency-building stage of learning are typically converted to rate and graphed as rate per minute. Frequency data may also be tallied and graphed simply as total count, provided the length of the observation periods remains constant. Discrete categorization data are usually converted to the percentage of correct or incorrect responses. Duration data are often converted to percentage by dividing the total duration (the sum of the length of time that each instance of the behavior lasted) by the total observation time. When the length of the observation periods is constant, duration may be reported as length of time the behavior occurred. Latency data are reported in units of time (e.g., seconds or minutes) and often as the average latency (the average number of seconds or minutes) per session. Interval and momentary time-sampling data are typically converted to percentage of total intervals (total number of scored intervals divided by the total number of intervals in the observation period); however, these data may also be presented as the total number of scored intervals (if time is constant).

Graphing Data.   A graphic display helps to analyze student progress. A "key" is placed on the graph to label different types of data points (see upper right-hand corner of Figure 3.2). Line graphs are constructed by drawing a vertical line and a horizontal line, called axes. The horizontal axis is the X axis and is used to display units of time such as days, weeks, months, or sessions. The vertical line is the Y axis and is used to display the occurrences of behavior, using a standard unit of measurement (e.g., frequency, rate, percentage). Educators have traditionally used equal-interval line graphs (i.e., all lines an equal distance apart). For example, the Y axis is labeled as the percentage of correct matches and the scale is marked off in 10 equal intervals. Consecutive school days are plotted on the X axis. Condition change lines are drawn to separate different teaching interventions. Each condition, or phase, is labeled. A key briefly describes the data points. The figure number and legend are placed at the bottom of the graph to provide a brief description of the purpose of the graph, the behaviors, and the interventions implemented.

Another type of graph is the standard celeration chart, which is also referred to as a semilogarith-

mic chart because the vertical or day lines are an equal distance apart but the horizontal spaces (between number lines) are unequal and based on a logarithmic scale. Figure 3.3 is an illustration of the standard behavior chart. One hundred forty successive calendar days are plotted along the X axis, and frequencies are plotted on the Y axis. The top three cycles of the chart represent whole numbers ranging from 1 through 1000; the three cycles include 1–10, 10–100, and 100–1000. The bottom three cycles of the chart represent behaviors that occur less than once per minute and range from .000695 (one behavior in 24 hours) to .09. To a person unfamiliar with the standard celeration chart, it may seem difficult or confusing to use; however, there are a number of advantages to the standard celeration chart (Lindsley, 1990; West & Young, 1992; West, Young, & Spooner, 1990). The standard celeration chart permits a wide range of frequencies to be recorded on the same chart, from 1 behavior in 24 hours to 1000 behaviors per minute. Therefore, the chart standardizes the display and accommodates a wide variety of behaviors such as vocational skills, self-help skills, communication behavior, academic responses, and challenging problem behaviors, as well as high-frequency and low-frequency behaviors. Standard charting conventions are used to make the chart easy to interpret (charting conventions are illustrated in White, 1986). The standard celeration chart covers 140 calendar days on one sheet of paper; two charts would cover an entire school year and three charts would cover an entire year.

Because the chart is standardized (i.e., does not change across learners, teachers, or behaviors), data are always plotted on the same scale; thus, trend lines are always comparable. One of the most important features of the standard celeration chart is that trend lines drawn on a semilogarithmic scale make it possible to accurately predict behavior for several days or weeks into the future. Teachers can see how fast the learner is progressing and predict how many days, weeks, or other periods of time it might take for the learner to master a specific target

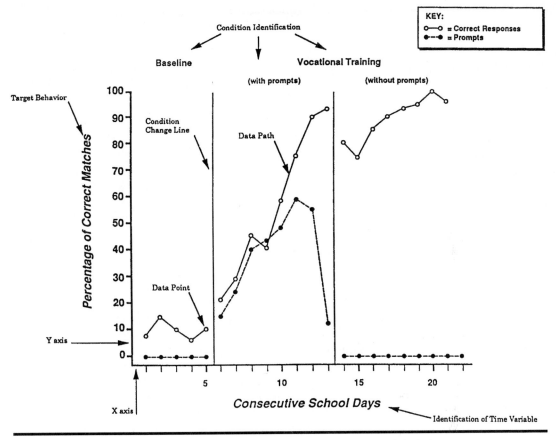

FIGURE 3.2   Sample equal-interval line graph with components labeled.

behavior. If learning occurs too slowly, then the instructional procedures can be modified. After all, the reason for analyzing data is to make informed data-based decisions. For additional information on the standard celeration chart, see Lindsley, 1990; West & Young, 1992; West, Young, & Spooner, 1990; White, 1986; and Young & West, 1985.

Data-Based Decision Making

The data collected in and out of the classroom provide evidence of the effects of teaching on learning. When those data are transformed into pictures on graphs or charts, teachers can use the pictures to make a wide range of judgments concerning the effect of instruction. Researchers have developed rules for making these judgments based on learning or performance data (Browder, 1987; Haring, Liberty, & White, 1980; Macfarlane, Young, & Weeks, 1989; Sailor & Guess, 1983; West, Young, Johnson, & Freston, 1985; Young, Macfarlane, & Kemblowski, 1990; Young & West, 1985). Using data and decision rules, teachers can determine (1) whether learning or performance is satisfactory and (2) if learning is not satisfactory, what changes in instruction might produce satisfactory learning.

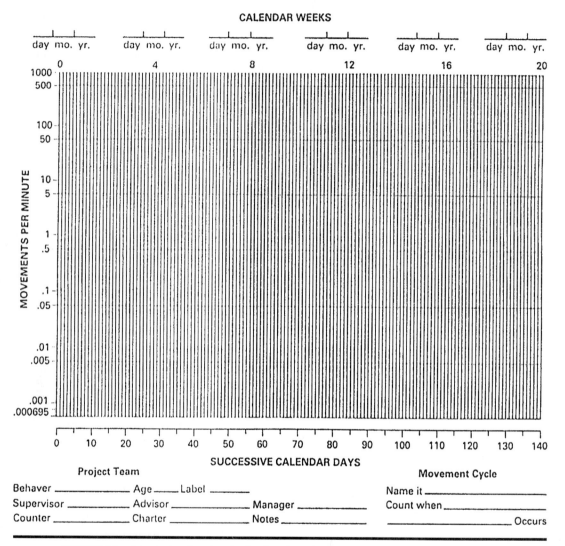

FIGURE 3.3   A sample of a standard celeration chart.

The best rules help teachers decide when a change in instruction is warranted and give them some ideas about what the changes ought to be.

Data Analysis

Analyzing data presented in a visual format consists of studying the pattern of the data and making comparisons of patterns across the various phases

of instruction. Data-based decision making requires a careful inspection of three dimensions of effect or changes in (1) trend or slope, (2) variability, and (3) level of performance. Figure 3.4 shows how improvement might look in each of these three areas. A given instructional strategy has had an effect on learning if we can easily detect changes in one or more of the dimensions when we compare preinstruction data (sometimes called

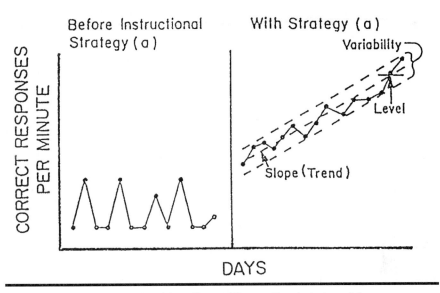

FIGURE 3.4   Visual analysis of the effects of instructional strategy (a).

"baseline") to data collected during instruction. The process of data analysis and decision making is depicted in the flow diagram in Figure 3.5. Each of the decisions that must be made in this process is explained in the following sections.

Changes in Trend. Changes in trend or the slope of data displayed on a graph may indicate an instructional or treatment effect. These changes may be either in magnitude (i.e., amount of change) or in direction (i.e., up, down, or flat), or both. Reversing the direction of the trend (e.g., going from an accelerating or positive direction to a decelerating or negative direction) is generally regarded as a convincing demonstration of the impact of instruction. Consider an automobile traveling along the highway. The automobile represents a learner in the classroom. The current location of the automobile represents the learner's present performance level. The speed with which the automobile travels from a previous location to the present location is represented by the trend line on the graph. Actually, the trend line represents learning rate, or how quickly the learner has ac-

quired the skill. A driver can influence the automobile's rate by pressing down the accelerator pedal, applying the brakes, or changing the direction completely by shifting gears from forward to reverse. Likewise, a teacher can accelerate the learner's performance by increasing opportunities to respond or by other tactics. To enable a learner to accomplish a particular curricular objective, the teacher should look for ways to accelerate learning rate and reach that objective as quickly as possible. The results of these efforts will be a trend line. The power or effectiveness of the intervention will be reflected in the amount of change in the slope or trend. The most powerful interventions can change the amount of slope, as well as the direction of the slope (assuming that a change in direction was intended). The trend of the data describes the speed with which responses are "accelerating" or "decelerating" over time; therefore, we sometimes refer to the trend line (and the trend it represents) by the root word, *celeration*. Trends moving upward are often called *acceleration* or *times celeration* (because the responses are "multiplying"), whereas downward trends may be

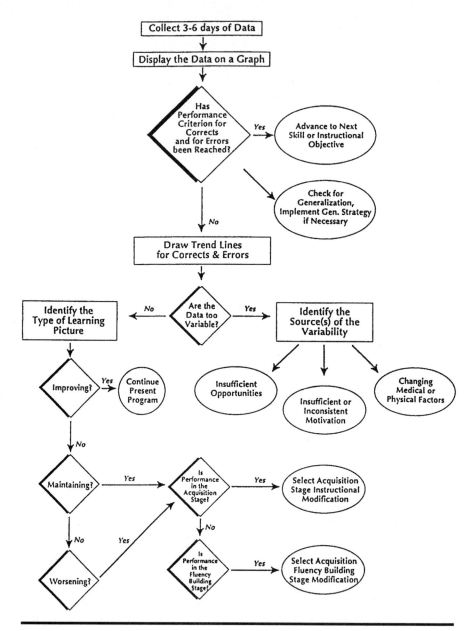

FIGURE 3.5   Flow diagram depicting the process of data analysis and decision making.

called *deceleration* or *divide-by celeration* (because the responses are "dividing").

Drawing Trend Lines. Trend lines can be drawn for any set of data consisting of two or more data points. Six data points are recommended, especially for school data, so as to prevent faulty decisions based on weekly trends that could mask treatment effects. It is not uncommon for Friday's performance to be considerably higher than the following Monday's performance, thus reflecting the possible effects of a lack of response opportunities over the weekend. Therefore, a trend line based only on the five daily data points in a given week might appear to have an upward slope, even though inspection of the data over several weeks might reveal no overall improvement.

Data Patterns and Learning Pictures. Teachers who attempt to make good data-based decisions will find it useful to study the picture of learning represented by trend lines. The teacher should always collect information on the number of responses that were performed correctly and incorrectly. We refer to these two types of data as a "fair pair." Both correct and incorrect responses are calculated and charted. When a trend line for correct performance is viewed along with a trend line for incorrect performance, a special type of data pattern emerges, which we refer to as a "learning picture." Learning pictures are grouped into three categories: (1) improving, (2) maintaining, and (3) worsening. Examples of the three types of learning pictures are presented in Figure 3.6.

The most important question in evaluating instruction is whether the criterion in the behavioral objective has been reached. Once it has been met, the teacher advances to the next skill in the instructional hierarchy. If not, the teacher determines what effect the instruction has had so far on learning. Improving pictures do not suggest that the learner has learned everything, but they do mean that the learner is making satisfactory progress and no changes in instruction are needed at present. Maintaining pictures suggest that the

learner has reached a plateau and is failing to make progress. The instructional program should then be modified. Worsening pictures indicate serious problems, in that previous gains in performance are now in jeopardy. The learner whose performance is represented by a worsening picture requires immediate and substantial modifications in instruction.

Variability. The effects of instruction or motivation may also be reflected by variability of performance data. Variability is the degree to which one score varies from the other scores. Generally, powerful instructional methods will reduce the amount of variability in performance scores. Of course, this statement presumes that variability is the result of factors related to instruction and not to changes in the learner's opportunity to engage in the behavior or other influences (e.g., medical or physical factors). A learner's compliance to teacher-issued commands that varies greatly from session to session may simply reflect variation in the number of commands issued by the teacher. Therefore, teachers must exercise caution in judging an instructional program as ineffective because of variability in scores when, in fact, the variability only reflects opportunities to respond, rather than inconsistencies in the quality of responding.

Nevertheless, variability in performance scores may furnish the teacher with valuable information. At the very least, it should prompt the teacher to look carefully for sources of variability. The learner may not have a complete understanding of the expected response or the conditions under which to display the response. The motivation to perform the response may be delivered inconsistently, or the reinforcement may be insufficient to evoke the response consistently. Many factors can account for variability in performance; however, as long as data remain variable, the teacher will never know what the learner's true ability is.

To determine when data are too variable, two parallel lines can be drawn: one above the original trend line and one below (see Figure 3.4). The dis-

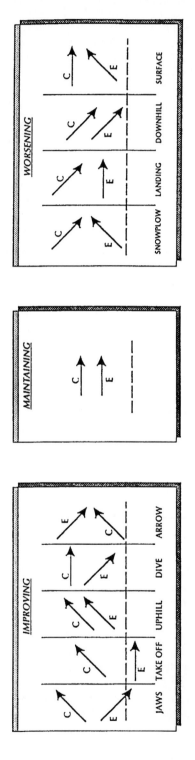

C = Corrects
E = Errors

FIGURE 3.6   Learning pictures.

tance between these two parallel lines can be used to establish the limits of acceptable variability. If several data points fall outside the envelope created by the parallel lines, the data are too variable. Of course, the teacher must decide how far apart the lines should be, thus determining how much variability in performance will be allowed. Another, perhaps simpler, method is to look at the trend line that has been drawn and visually compare its slope with the overall appearance of the data. If there is no discernible trend in the data or if any apparent trend seems to be different from the trend line that has just been drawn, the data are too variable.

Performance Level. Evaluating performance level consists of two considerations: (1) is the change in performance large enough to be important, and (2) what stage of learning is represented by the current performance level? Determining the importance of changes in performance levels requires a careful consideration of two issues. First, is the average level of recent performance different in a practically significant way than the level of prior performance? This question can be answered by using the process of social validation (Wolf, 1978). By comparing the learner's improvement in performance with the expectations for improvement held by teachers and parents, the practical significance of the improvement can be determined.

A teacher also needs to determine the stage of learning represented by the learner's current performance. Establishing the boundaries of the stages of learning for any skill is based on the learner's rate of performance in comparison with the criterion. The teacher examines the three most recent data points and determines whether they represent performance in the acquisition, fluency-building, or generalization and maintenance stage of learning.

The two-step process requires (1) the establishment of an aim, or criterion of successful performance, and (2) an estimation of the value representing roughly one-third of the aim. The

lowest third represents the acquisition stage of learning. The range of performance from the upper boundary of the acquisition stage to the aim value represents the fluency-building stage. The performance range at and beyond the level of the aim constitutes the generalization and maintenance stage.

Determining the stage of learning is associated with different instructional strategies. An instructional strategy selected for use when learning is in the acquisition stage may not be useful when learning is in the fluency-building stage. Figure 3.7 illustrates the stages of learning and some instructional strategies associated with each stage.

Performance in the acquisition stage of learning is characterized by an emphasis on the accuracy or quality of each response. Responding often requires a great deal of effort and usually occurs at a low rate. As performance becomes more accurate and fluent (higher rate, possibly approaching "habitual" or "automatic" performance), the learner moves into the fluency-building stage of learning. Once the learner's performance becomes proficient (accurate and fluent) and performance of the skill emerges in new settings and conditions, the generalization and maintenance stage has been reached (Young et al., 1986). The generalization and maintenance stage may also be characterized by performance that continues even though training and encouragement for the performance are not provided.

If learning seems to stall while performance is in the acquisition stage, modifications in the instructional plan should focus on the antecedents of behavior (events and conditions that precede the target behavior), as well as the topography of the behavior itself. The antecedents that are of greatest importance are those that control the response, such as commands, instructions, and other conditions associated with increased probability of reinforcement. When the relationship between the stimuli and the response is well established, the response occurs consistently. In the acquisition stage of learning, this relationship is being developed. To evoke the response, the teacher can use

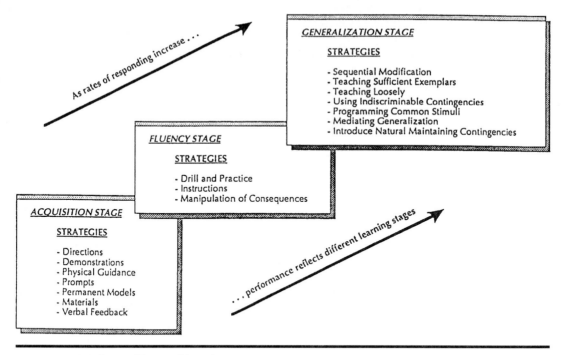

FIGURE 3.7   Stages of learning.

prompts, cues, and other forms of assistance, which will then become stronger as opportunities to respond become more numerous. Table 3.4 presents sample questions. The answers to these questions will help the teacher to identify the sources of learning problems in the acquisition stage of learning and to modify instruction.

Strategies selected for use when learning falters in the fluency-building stage are those associated with the consequences of behavior more than with the antecedents. Because the emphasis in this stage of learning is more on building fluency than on building accuracy (which was developed in the acquisition stage), the most successful strategies will "accelerate" performance. Two types of interventions have been shown to be very successful: increasing the reinforcement for performing correctly and providing more response opportunities (practice). Actually, both of these strategies accomplish

the same thing: they produce many instances of the behavior. By definition, reinforcement increases the probability that behavior will reoccur. Increasing opportunities to respond, especially when reinforcement is available, will increase the number of responses as well. It is the number of responses that results in fluent performance, which, in turn, increases the probability that responses will make contact with naturally occurring "communities of reinforcement" (reinforcers that naturally exist within the context of the learner's behavior) or natural consequences. Answering the questions in Table 3.5 will help the teacher to analyze the appropriateness of reinforcers used in the learner's program.

Stokes and Baer (1977) suggested strategies that can be used to increase the probability of generalized responding. However, research has indicated that when responding reaches the proficiency aim,

TABLE 3.4   Considerations for Problems in the Acquisition Stage of Learning

Sample Questions for Analyzing Problems with Instruction

1. Is the learner attending?
2. Are there interfering behaviors?
3. Do you have an effective reinforcer?
4. Is the cue appropriate? Specific? Functional? Consistent?
5. Is the error correction procedure appropriate? Does it provide feedback? Does it interrupt or prevent errors?
6. Has the learner mastered the necessary prerequisite skills?
7. Is the skill too complex?
8. Are you using functional materials? Are materials age-appropriate?
9. Is the task too difficult?
10. Does instruction occur during a daily routine?

Sample Questions for Evaluating the Effectiveness of Prompts

1. Does the prompt occur before the learner attempts the task?
2. Does the prompt occur when the learner makes an error?
3. Do or could you use a system of least prompts?
4. Do or could you use the most-to-least prompt structure?
5. Do or could you use graduated guidance?
6. Do or could you use time delay?
7. Do or could you use a visual prompt?
8. Do or could you use a model?
9. Is the learner prompt-dependent?
10. Are you trying to fade the prompt?

Sample Questions for Analyzing Errors

1. Is the learner making more errors than correct responses?
2. Is a correct answer really several responses?
3. Do errors occur only at the beginning of the session?
4. Do errors occur only at the end of the session?
5. Do errors occur randomly throughout the session?
6. Do errors and correct responses occur evenly (50-50)?
7. Does the learner receive feedback after an error?
8. Does the learner try to prevent errors or interrupt?
9. Does the learner always make the same error?

(continued)

TABLE 3.4   Continued

*Sample Questions for Analyzing the Antecedent Stimuli
and Learner's Response Mode*

1. Does the learner have a hearing problem? Is the antecedent stimulus auditory?
2. Does the learner have vision problems? Is the antecedent stimulus visual?
3. Does the learner have motoric problems? Is the antecedent stimulus tactile?
4. Is the cue multisensory?
5. How complicated is the required response?
6. How closely does the present required response approximate the final required response?
7. Can the learner perform a similar task that has a different antecedent stimulus?
8. Does the learner use a different response when performing a similar task?
9. Is the antecedent stimulus appropriate for the learner's ability?
10. Does the learner have the motoric skills to complete the response?
11. Does the topography of the response match the learner's capability?
12. Can the critical effect be achieved through a different response mode?
13. Can you shape the response?
14. Could you accept an approximation of the required response?

Sample Questions for Evaluating Learner Characteristics

1. Is the learner hungry?
2. Is the learner thirsty?
3. Does the learner take medication? Are there side effects? Is medicine given on time and correctly?
4. Is the learner sick?
5. Is there a problem with hearing?
6. Is there a problem with seeing?
7. Is the learner tired?
8. Is there a problem at home?
9. Is there a problem at school?
10. Is the learner dressed comfortably?
11. Does the learner get to choose when to work?
12. Does the learner have similar contingencies and expectations in all environments?
13. Is the learner bored? Has the learner worked on this task for a long time? Is the skill functional?
14. Does the learner need adaptive equipment?
15. Is the learner positioned properly?

TABLE 3.4   Continued

Sample Questions for Analyzing the Learning Environment

1. Is the instructional environment too noisy?
2. Is the learner distracted by noise?
3. Is the lighting adequate?
4. Is the temperature adequate?
5. Is the learner distracted by peers?
6. Is instruction delivered in a group or one-on-one?
7. Do different instructors work with the learner? Are they qualified? Consistent?
8. Is the instructional environment appropriately decorated? Not too distracting? Not too barren?
9. Is the learner distracted by visual stimuli?
10. Does the learner have an appropriate chair and/or work space?

generalized responding emerges with no additional programming (Young et al., 1986). Perhaps we have serendipitously noted the benefits of the technique referred to by Stokes and Baer (1977) as "introduce to natural maintaining contingencies." Nevertheless, these authors have described strategies that have been used with varying degrees of effectiveness to produce generalization. Among these are sequential modification, training sufficient exemplars, training loosely, using indiscriminable contingencies, programming common stimuli, mediating generalization, and training to generalize. If teachers encounter problems with learning in this stage, then they must consider issues related to the functional transfer of the skill from the instructional environment to the ultimate environment.

Data analysis never stops. As previously stated, the purpose of data collection is to provide the teacher with information for decision making. Effective teachers must continually plan, collect data, analyze data, make data-based decisions, and change instruction as necessary. This entire process can overwhelm teachers, regardless of their experience levels. One answer to this dilemma

TABLE 3.5   Considerations for Problems in the Fluency-Building Stage of Learning

Sample Questions for Analyzing Reinforcement

1. Do you have evidence that you are using the most effective (powerful) reinforcer?
2. Do you vary reinforcers to avoid satiation?
3. Do you use the least amount of reinforcement possible?
4. Do or can you use a natural reinforcer?
5. Do you deliver the reinforcer immediately after a correct response?
6. Do you deliver the reinforcer only after a correct response?
7. Can the learner see the reinforcer or a facsimile?
8. Can the learner choose different reinforcers?
9. What type of schedule of reinforcement do you use? Fixed? Variable?
10. Do you use a denser rate of reinforcement initially?
11. Do you need to thin the rate of reinforcement?
12. Do you need to use a primary reinforcer?
13. Do you need to use a secondary reinforcer?
14. Do you avoid the use of negative reinforcement?

may be the use of computer software to assist teachers in managing their classrooms.

Word processors and IEP generators can help teachers in the program planning stage. Other commercially available programs can help them to collect, store, and graph data. However, the most promising help for teachers appears to lie in computer programs developed through the use of artificial intelligence techniques. Classroom Advisor (Macfarlane et al., 1989) is an expert system that helps teachers to monitor and make data-based decisions about functional communication programs for learners with severe disabilities. Decel (Young et al., 1990) is the first expert system to employ decision rules for decelerating problem behavior. These two computer programs should help novice teachers acquire decision-making skills and systematically enhance those of more experienced teachers.

CONCLUSION

In this chapter, we have presented a great deal of information about planning effective instructional programs, collecting learner performance data, and using those data to make data-based decisions to improve the quality of instruction. Effective teaching is a challenging task that requires dedication and effort, but anything less is not likely to result in effective outcomes. It is only through this kind of intense effort on the part of teachers that we can ensure that learners with severe disabilities will learn to function as independently as possible in natural communities. In spite of the best efforts of teachers, sometimes learners will still have difficulty in making progress. Table 3.6 lists a series of questions that teachers can review to ensure that their approach to program planning and evaluation has been complete. Answers to these questions should guide teachers either to step back and carry out missing tasks or to realize that their programming and evaluation has been thorough. In some cases, teachers may need to think of new and more creative ways to teach a skill or reinforce a student. It is our experience that when a teacher plans thoroughly and evaluates progress systematically, most students make the desired progress.

TABLE 3.6   Considerations for Effective Programs: Planning, Evaluation, and Data-Based Decision Making

1. Have you completed the instructional planning work sheet?
2. Have you considered the learner's wants, needs, preferences, and culture?
3. Do you have data on student performance? Are you collecting data on a "fair pair"?
4. Do the data reflect both the accuracy and the fluency of performance?
5. Has the student had many opportunities to respond?
6. Is there a discrepancy between the student's performance level and the criteria (aim) for successful completion of the objective?
7. Has the level of performance changed?
8. Is the trend in the desirable or undesirable direction?
9. Is the rate of progress acceptable? For correct responses? For errors? (celeration statement).
10. Are errors (inappropriate behaviors) excessive?
11. Are errors consistent or random? (error analysis).
12. What is the stage of learning? (acquisition vs. fluency building).
13. What type of learning picture do you have? (pictures reflecting changes in both appropriate [correct] and inappropriate [errors] behavior) (improving; maintaining; worsening).
14. Does the student have the necessary motor skills?
15. Has the student mastered the prerequisite behaviors at both the accuracy and fluency criteria?
16. How long has the problem existed?
17. What have you already tried?

REFERENCES

Baumgart, D., Brown, L., Pumpian, I., Nisbet, J., Ford, A., Sweet, M., Messina, R., & Schroeder, J. (1982). Principle of partial participation and individualized adaptations in educational programs for severely handicapped students. *The Journal of The Association for the Severely Handicapped, 7*(2), 17–27.

Blair, M., Young, K. R., & Macfarlane, C. A. (1991). Reinforcer evaluation. Unpublished manuscript. Logan: Utah State University, Department of Special Education.

Browder, D. M. (1987). *Assessment of individuals with severe handicaps: An applied behavior approach to life skills assessment.* Baltimore: Paul H. Brookes Publishing Co.

Brown, F., Evans, I. M., Weed, K. A., & Owen, V. (1987). Delineating functional competencies: A component model. *Journal of the Association for Persons with Severe Handicaps, 12*(2), 224–227.

Cipani, E. (1988). The missing item format. *Teaching Exceptional Children, 21,* 25–27.

Dyer, K. (1987). The competition of autistic stereotyped behavior with usual and specially accessed reinforcers. *Journal in Research and Developmental Disabilities, 8*(4), 607–626.

Greenwood, C. R., Delquadri, J., & Hall, R. V. (1984). Opportunity to respond and student academic performance. In W. L. Heward, T. E. Heron, J. Trap-Porter, & D. S. Hill (Eds.), *Focus on behavior analysis in education* (pp. 58–88). Columbus, OH: Charles E. Merrill.

Haring, N. G., Liberty, K. A., & White, O. R. (1980). Rules for data-based decisions in instructional programs: Current research and instructional implications. In W. Sailor, B. Wilcox, & L. Brown (Eds.), *Methods of instruction for severely handicapped students* (pp. 159–192). Baltimore: Paul H. Brookes Publishing Co.

Hart, B. M., & Risley, T. R. (1975). Incidental teaching of language in the preschool. *Journal of Applied Behavior Analysis, 8,* 411–420.

Hart, B. M., & Risley, T. R. (1982). *How to use incidental teaching for elaborating language.* Lawrence, KS: H & H Enterprises.

Jenson, W. R., & Young, K. R. (1985). Childhood autism: Developmental considerations and behavioral interventions by professionals, families, and peers. In R. J. McMahon & R. DeV. Peters (Eds.), *Childhood disorders: Behavioral-developmental approaches* (pp. 169–194). New York: Brunner/Mazel.

Kazdin, A. E. (1982). *Single-case research designs: Methods for clinical and applied settings.* New York: Oxford University Press.

Koorland, M. A., Keel, M. C., & Ueberhost, P. (1990). Setting aims for precision learning. *Teaching Exceptional Children, 22*(3), 64–66.

Liberty, K. A., & Paeth, M. A. (1990). Self-recording for students with severe and multiple handicaps. *Teaching Exceptional Children, 22*(3), 73–75.

Lindsley, O. R. (1990). Precision teaching: By teachers for children. *Teaching Exceptional Children, 22*(3), 10–15.

Macfarlane, C. A., Young, K. R., & Weeks, R. A. (1989). Classroom advisor (computer program). Logan: Utah State University, Department of Special Education.

Oswald, L. K., Lignugaris-Kraft, B., & West, R. P. (1990). The effects of incidental teaching on the generalized use of social amenities at school by a mildly handicapped adolescent. *Education and Treatment of Children, 13*(2), 142–152.

Sailor, W., & Guess, D. (1983). *Severely handicapped students: An instructional design.* Boston: Houghton Mifflin.

Stokes, T. F., & Baer, D. M. (1977). An implicit technology of generalization. *Journal of Applied Behavior Analysis, 10,* 349–367.

Tawney, J. W., & Gast, D. L. (1984). *Single subject research in special education.* Columbus, OH: Charles E. Merrill.

West, R. P., Young, K. R., & Spooner, F. (1990). Precision teaching: An introduction. *Teaching Exceptional Children, 22*(3), 4–9.

West, R. P., Young, K. R., West, W. J., Johnson, J. I., & Freston, C. W. (1985). Monitoring instructional decision making (computer program). Logan: Utah State University, Developmental Center for Handicapped Persons.

West, R. P., & Young, K. R. (1992). Precision teaching. In R. P. West & L. A. Hamerlynck (Eds.), *Designs for excellence in education: The legacy of B. F. Skinner* (pp. 133–146). Longmont, CO: Sopris West.

White, O. R., & Haring, N. G. (1980). *Exceptional teaching* (2nd ed.). Columbus, OH: Charles E. Merrill.

White O. R. (1986). Precision teaching-precision learning. *Exceptional Children, 52,* 522–534.

Wolf, M. M. (1978). Social validity: The case for subjective measurement or how applied behavior analysis is finding its heart. *Journal of Applied Behavior Analysis, 11,* 203–214.

Young, K. R., Macfarlane, C. A., & Kemblowski, E. J. (1990). Decel (computer program). Logan: Utah State University, Department of Special Education.

Young, K. R., & West, R. P. (1985). *Precision teaching: Strategies for instructional decision making.* Logan, UT: Behavioral and Educational Training Associates.

Young, K. R., West, R. P., & Crawford, A. (1985). The acquisition and maintenance of reading skills by intellectually handicapped deaf students. *Journal of Precision Teaching, 5,* 73–86.

Young, K. R., West, R. P., Howard, V. F., & Whitney, R. (1986). The acquisition, fluency development, generalization, and maintenance of dressing skills. *Education and Treatment of Children, 9*(1), 16–29.

THE TECHNOLOGY OF INSTRUCTION

FELIX F. BILLINGSLEY
University of Washington

KATHLEEN A. LIBERTY
University of Canterbury

OWEN R. WHITE
University of Washington

tech·nol·o·gy.
1.a. The application of science [to achieve stated] objectives. b. The entire body of methods and materials used to achieve such objectives.
—The American Heritage Dictionary (1979)

Educational practice has always been swayed by fads and fancies, with various approaches to curriculum and instruction swinging in popularity (Slavin, 1989). Most often, decisions about the tools of instruction and curriculum are made by popular consensus, with little consideration of their merits as indicated by scientific investigation (Carnine, 1992; Lindsley, 1992a). However, a science of learning and instruction does exist, based on the empirical study of learning and ways in which learning can be influenced, and provides the principles and practices of an effective educational technology (Carnine, 1992; Lindsley, 1992a, 1992b). Application of those principles and practices results in effective instruction for any learner, because they are derived from the scientific study of the learning and teaching process,

not on the presumably immutable internal characteristics of the learner. In this chapter is presented the application of those principles and practices to learners with severe disabilities.

A technology of instruction is not based on guesses of what method *should* help students learn, but is derived from the careful and replicated experimental study of what *does* help students learn. Principles and practices are supported by reference to investigations that compared learning under varying instructions conditions with learners displaying severe disabilities.

Instructional Best Practices. The goal of integrating students with severe disabilities into the mainstream of school and community life guides the selection and definition of appropriate curriculum. The goal of helping a student learn a skill that

The authors shared equally in the development of this chapter. Preparation of the chapter was supported in part by the U.S. Department of Education, Grant Number HO86C80019. However, the opinions expressed herein do not necessarily reflect the position or policy of the U.S. Department of Education, and no official endorsement by the Department should be inferred.

extends performance in school and society is defined as effective application of instructional technology. *Best practices* are those curricular and instructional strategies that are best for the student—those that have been experimentally shown to facilitate the development of skills that provide the student with the greatest possible independence in mainstream family, school, and community life settings.

One criterion for a best practice is that it is technologically sound; that is, that it works. In the case of an instructional practice, effectiveness is determined by the extent to which learning is accelerated as compared with learning under a different instructional method.

Effectiveness is not the only factor governing the selection of instructional procedures. The technology of instruction is designed to accelerate skilled behavior, not decelerate inappropriate behavior. The use of aversive stimuli, such as reprimands, and punishment procedures, such as "time-out" or exclusion, are not effective in facilitating skill acquisition and are not included in this chapter.

Identifying the Best Practices for Individual Pupils. Although it would be simple if the same instructional procedures were effective with all pupils, this is not the case. Because the technology of instruction is only a few decades old, and because each learner is a unique individual, it is understandable that what might prove to be an effective procedure for one student could fail utterly to help another student, or even the same student at a different time or in another instructional program.

Current research in the technology of instruction is aimed at helping to make successful matches between practices and the particular learning needs of each student during the development of each skill. Guidelines for when to change from one method to another, and for selecting another instructional strategy on the basis of individual pupil performance, are provided where possible. It is crucial that each instructional program be continuously monitored to evaluate student progress. Regardless of what the research

literature says should work, if acceptable progress is not observed, the approach does not represent a best practice for that student, and alternative approaches should be explored.

BEFORE INSTRUCTION BEGINS

The Aims of Instruction

Teaching a learner how to perform a skill accurately should be only the first step of instruction. Instruction should continue until the skill is fluent, can be generalized to new situations, and is maintained over time. Instruction can be designed to facilitate these important stages of learning by application of instructional technology, whereas naive instructional practices can produce skills that are performed slowly, do not transfer to new environments, and are forgotten.

Development of an overall curriculum plan for an individual is accomplished by a multidisciplinary team. The plan for each individual will comprise a number of objectives, which include descriptions of the skills to be taught, the quality and fluency of performance of each, and the nature of target settings in which skill should be performed. In addition, each objective might include descriptions of the natural stimuli that are to signal the onset of the skill, the amount of assistance, if any, to be provided by others in the setting, and any materials or items that the learner is to manipulate during the performance of the skill. The overall curriculum plan should also identify how skills fit into the natural school, family, community, and work routines, if this is not apparent.

Task Analysis

Most skills are composed of chains of behavior (e.g., items are grasped, manipulated, and released) and occur in a consistent sequence. Instruction is facilitated if the behavior chains are carefully analyzed and understood prior to instruction. *Task analysis* refers to the process and product of identifying component behaviors in their chains (cf. Wolery, Bailey, & Sugai, 1988). Figure 4.1 provides examples of two completed task analyses, one of which (top panel) includes both learner and teacher behaviors for each step.

Brown, Evans, Weed, and Owen (1987) have observed that the beginning and ending points of behavior chains identified in task analyses "are often determined in an arbitrary and inconsistent manner" (p. 118). This may result in a first step with a cue that does not exist in natural environments and a final step that does not evoke natural reinforcers, thereby inhibiting generalization (cf. Falvey, Brown, Lyon, Baumgart, & Shroeder, 1980). It could be more productive to develop task analyses as "routines" that begin with a description of the natural cue for the skill and finish with the behavior that evokes the natural reinforcer necessary for maintenance (Donnellan & Neel, 1985; Neel & Billingsley, 1989).

Brown and associates (1987) suggested that task analyses should also extend and enrich core skills (see Figure 4.2). Extended analyses promote performance of routines under the demands of natural environments, for example, by including skills to initiate and prepare for tasks, to ensure adequate quality of performance, to resolve problems, to perform fluently, and to complete tasks necessary to end routines. Enrichment components are not required for independent functioning of the core skill, but enhance its performance and often involve communicating, interacting, and choosing.

No firm rules currently exist for determining the number of component behaviors that should be included in task analyses. In one of the few empirical studies of the number of steps in a task analysis, Crist, Walls, and Haught (1984) indicated that longer task analyses with smaller skill increments were learned with fewer errors by students with severe disabilities, and that training time was not lengthened by having small steps. Neel and Billingsley (1989) and Sailor and Guess (1983) have suggested that long chains of behaviors are generally undesirable and recommended that task analyses generally consist of no more

than 15 or 20 steps, respectively. Ultimately, it appears that educators must make decisions regarding the optimum number of steps, and the degree of difficulty added with each, on the basis of task difficulty and the skill level of the learner (Bellamy, Horner, & Inman, 1979).

Task analyses may be purchased, copied from published articles, or constructed by the teacher, but each must be validated by first making sure that the final skill that results from the task analysis is a good match with the instructional objective. Next, task analyses should be checked by comparing the step-by-step description of the component behaviors with an actual performance of the skill by the learner, by the instructor, and by an expert in the skill, inasmuch as "one's own practices may not lead to identifying the safest, most hygienic, or nutritious practice" (Browder, 1987, p. 59).

Initial Assessments

The purpose of the initial assessment is to determine the discrepancy between the learner's current performance level on each component of the task and the ultimate performance quality and level in the instructional objective. Observation of the learner's attempts to perform the skill can help identify existing responses on which to build (Browder, 1991), determine whether adequate attention has been given to the motoric and sensory capabilities of the learner, and discover whether the learner has alternate (and perhaps unique) ways of performing parts of the skill, which may be both acceptable and efficient. If possible, repeated opportunities should be provided during assessment to provide the most complete picture.

Initial assessments should occur in the context in which the skill is to be ultimately performed, and occur in a positive atmosphere. The student should be provided demonstrations, assistance, and lots of positive feedback, regardless of how poorly initial performance is judged. Providing no assistance, little or no feedback, or negative corrective feedback during an initial assessment may set up an inauspicious beginning for instruction and establish

Task Analysis - Reaching

Objective:

From a variety of <u>positions</u>, S moves his hand/arm/upper torso to contact objects placed 1-2 inches out of <u>arm's reach</u>.

<u>positions</u> = lying on stomach, back, side, or sitting.

<u>arm's reach</u> = the full extension of S's arm (straight at elbow, or as straight as possible for S's physical condition). Objects should be placed in front of S, to his side, above his head.

1. Position the object within 2 inches of S's hand. Vary the position of the object to require S to use different hand movements (up, down, sideways).	1. S <u>moves his hand</u> to contact an object.
2. Position the object far enough from S's hand that he must move his forearm (at least 5 inches) to contact it. Vary the position of the object to require S to move his arm in different directions (up, sideways, down).	2. S <u>moves his forearm</u> and hand to contact an object.
3. Position the object far enough away from S's hand so that he must move his entire arm to contact it. Vary the position of the object to require S to extend his arm in different directions (up, forward, sideways, down).	3. S <u>moves his whole arm</u> to contact an object.
4. Position the object in front of S, 1-2 inches out of his reach, so that he must extend his arm and shift forward slightly to reach it. Vary the position of the object to require S to reach forward from different positions. Insure that if S is sitting upright, he is positioned so that his shift in weight will not cause him to fall over.	4. S <u>shifts his upper torso</u> slightly forward and <u>extends his arm</u> to contact an object positioned just out of his reach (forward only).
*5. Position the object 1-2 inches out of S's reach so that he must move his hand/arm/upper torso to contact it. Vary the position of the object to require S to reach in different directions (up, down, forward, sideways).	*5. Target—from a variety of positions, S moves his hand/arm/upper torso to contact objects positioned 1-2 inches out of arm's reach.

FIGURE 4.1 *This page:* Task analysis for reaching. (Reprinted from Tawney, J., Knapp, D. S., O'Reilly, C. D., & Pratt, S. S. [1979]. *Programmed environments curriculum.* Columbus, OH: Charles E. Merrill). *Next page:* Task analysis of social interaction sequence at break time. (Reprinted with permission from Breen, C., Haring, T., Pitts-Conway, V., & Gaylord-Ross, R. [1985]. The training and generalization of social interaction during breaktime at two job sites in the natural environment. *The Journal of The Association for Persons with Severe Handicaps, 10,* 41–50.)

TASK ANALYSIS—BREAKTIME SOCIAL SEQUENCE

1. S. leaves work area.

2. S. pours a cup of coffee.

3. S. adds 1 spoon/packet of sugar.

4. S. adds 1 ounce of milk.

5. S. takes coffee to any table and sits down.

*6. S. asks familiar NH coworker/peer "Hi, how are you?"

*7. S. asks NH "Would you like coffee?"

8. S. pours a cup of coffee for NH.

*9. S. hands coffee to NH.

*10. S. asks NH "What's new?"

*11. S. responds appropriately to NH question "What have you been doing at work?" (i.e., "doing dishes," "raking," "weeding.")

*12. S. responds to NH statement "Take it easy" with "Take it easy."

13. S. returns to work.

NOTE: Steps with asterisks are social behaviors. Steps without asterisks are motor behaviors.

FIGURE 4.1   Continued

the instructor as a neutral, aversive, or punishing person. A neutral "baseline" may be appropriate for research, but generally neither appropriate nor adequate for initial instructional assessments.

Teach Task Steps Forward, Backward, or All at Once?

Although task analyses of extended and enriched routines specify skill performance that moves from the first to the last step in a temporal sequence, instruction may not necessarily proceed in that order (Liberty, 1985). Three general methods for sequencing instruction have commonly been employed to teach skills with multiple task steps to learners with severe disabilities: forward chaining, backward chaining, and total task instruction. The intent of each method is to produce a seamless

chain, in which each behavior is both a discriminative stimulus that evokes the next response in the chain and is a conditioned reinforcer for the previous response (Spooner & Spooner, 1984).

In forward and backward chaining (often referred to as *serial* or *part* methods), steps are introduced in a cumulative fashion over successive instructional trials (McDonnell & McFarland, 1988). In *forward chaining,* instruction begins with the behavior that a person would normally perform first to accomplish the skill (or, the first one failed during initial assessment), and in *backward chaining,* steps are instructed in the reverse order. In a *total task* approach (also called *whole task* or *concurrent* methods), the student practices all the task steps during each instructional trial. For example, in forward chaining, the first step of instruction for eating with a spoon would be

Routine:	Grooms Nails
Domain:	Self-Management
Interval/Form:	Episodic/Fixed
Component	Behavior
Initiate	Grooms or indicates to another the need to groom nails at times such as when nails are dirty, jagged, or long
Prepare	Finds and selects needed materials such as clippers, scissors, or file
Core	Cleans and trims nails
Monitor quality	Checks nails for cleanliness and neatness
Monitor tempo	Grooms nails within acceptable amount of time
Problem solve	If a problem arises, such as cannot find materials or has hangnail, will take action to address the problem
Terminate	Puts trimming supplies away, throws nail clippings in trash
Communicate	Communicates about any aspect of nail grooming such as nail care, length, materials used
Choice	Makes choices concerning nail grooming such as length of nails, color of nail polish
Social	Does routine at appropriate time and place

FIGURE 4.2 Component analysis for a "Grooms Nails" routine. (Reprinted with permission from Brown, F., Evans, I. M., Weed, K. A., & Owen, V. [1987]. Delineating functional competencies: A component model. *The Journal of The Association for Persons with Severe Handicaps, 12,* 117–124.)

grasping the spoon; then the student would be assisted through the steps of scooping, bringing the spoon to the mouth, and so on. Once grasping was acquired, instruction would focus on the next step in the chain, scooping food with the spoon. In backward chaining, the learner would be assisted through all the steps, and then given an instructional trial to bring the spoon the final few inches to the mouth. In a total task approach, the learner would be instructed on each step for each spoonful of food.

Instruction using part procedures typically requires students to complete the step trained for, as well as those that were previously learned (direct repetitive part method). In variations, each part of the task may be learned individually before the parts are combined (pure part method), or a part may be taught in isolation before performance of that part is required in conjunction with previously acquired parts (progressive part method). In addition, the student may or may not be guided through untrained steps. If the instructor completes untrained steps (a common procedure in backward chaining), completion may or may not occur within the student's view. As suggested by the work of Martin, Koop, Turner, and Hanel

(1981) and Spooner, Spooner, and Ulicny (1986), backward chaining may be improved by reducing excessive step repetitions.

Both total task and part methods have been successfully used to teach learners with severe disabilities a variety of vocational, personal management, leisure, self-help, and motor skills (McDonnell & McFarland, 1988), but backward chaining has often been recommended as the method of choice, based largely on the idea of "always having a readily available conditioned reinforcer to strengthen each new response that is added to the sequence in a backward order" (Martin et al., 1981, p. 134). Recently, it has been argued that total task methods are to be preferred (e.g., Neel & Billingsley, 1989) because they provide instruction on the response topography and response sequence simultaneously (Bellamy et al., 1979), and because they are also highly compatible with training demands in the community and other performance settings (McDonnell & McFarland, 1988).

In fact, a number of comparative studies have demonstrated faster acquisition by learners with severe disabilities when instruction involved total task procedures (e.g., Kayser, Billingsley, & Neel, 1986; Martin et al., 1981; McDonnell & McFarland, 1988; Spooner, Weber, & Spooner, 1983). However, some studies with other skills have indicated no substantial differences (e.g., McDonnell & Laughlin, 1989). In addition, Weld and Evans (1990) found that a pure part method generally produced more desirable outcomes than a whole task method when learners with moderate to severe mental retardation were taught to make greeting cards and prepare a bag lunch. Of particular interest was that more excess behaviors or inappropriate behaviors were observed under the whole task condition. Comparison of backward and forward chaining has generally produced findings of no differential effects (e.g., Banks & Baer, 1966; Walls, Zane, & Ellis, 1981).

Although it is possible that some skills might be taught more effectively with one method of in- . structional sequencing than another, research has identified neither the skill categories nor the influ-

ence of accompanying instructional practices (e.g., various prompting and prompt-fading techniques) that would allow prediction. Liberty (1985) has pointed out that the total task approach can be tried initially and that data on student learning will "quickly identify if a total task approach is too demanding" (p. 41). It would then be appropriate to try either forward or backward chaining.

THE INSTRUCTIONAL CONTEXT

The context of instruction includes the physical, temporal, and human dimensions of instruction. Decisions regarding whether instruction will occur in the classroom, in some other setting, or in multiple settings, whether instruction will occur at a preset time, whether the instructor will be teacher, peer, or the student him- or herself, whether instruction will be individual or in a group, and the general approach to presenting or arranging instructional examples all involve the instructional context. Decisions about the context of instruction are often dictated by tradition (e.g., the school day is divided into periods, and one objective or "subject" is assigned to each period). However, the context in which instruction occurs will influence not only how quickly skills are acquired, but also their mastery, generalization, and maintenance. Care and consideration must begin with decisions about the instructional context.

Instructional Settings

The first step in determining an appropriate instructional setting is to identify where the skill is to be used by the student in current school, home, and community environments, and where it is likely to be needed in future environments. However, except when the possible universe of settings is limited (e.g., there are only two grocery stores in town), it is usually not practical to teach in all possible current and future environments. Instruction, therefore, should occur in multiple settings that reflect the general characteristics of, and include the range of relevant cues (Horner, McDonnell, &

Bellamy, 1986) in, the environments in which the skill is ultimately to be used, in order to avoid problems with generalization and maintenance (Stokes & Baer, 1977).

Some skills (e.g., grasping objects, communicating, moving around) are performed in virtually all types of settings (e.g., at home, at school, at the store), and learning will be facilitated if the setting of instruction is systematically varied to include exemplars of all types of situations. Other skills are performed in a range of environments that share certain characteristics (e.g., playing ball in gyms, parks, playgrounds, yards, ball courts), and learning is facilitated by instructing in representative settings that share key stimuli.

Finally, some skills are performed only in specific classes of environments (e.g., toileting in bathrooms; shopping in stores), and learning is likely to be facilitated if instruction occurs directly in those settings. For example, to ensure that the student will be capable of using bathrooms available in a variety of locations, toileting instruction might occur in each bathroom available at school, at the student's home, in public rest rooms in the community, at friends' homes, and so on. If the skill is one in which there are no school settings representative of the current or future environments, then (1) the skill must be taught off school grounds (a proposal requiring that arrangements be made regarding time, transportation, and staff), and/or (2) the skill will need to be acquired in the classroom under simulated conditions, and its usefulness tested by assessments in nonschool settings (discussed later in this chapter, in "Making Skills Useful").

Decisions about settings should be made on the basis of the best match between current and future environments and the practicality of achieving acquisition within a reasonable length of time. For example, it may be extremely desirable to teach grocery shopping in the store near the learner's home. If the grocery store can be accessed only once a week for instruction, however, acquisition might be lengthy or fail to result in generalization (cf. White et al., 1988; Neef, Iwata, & Page, 1978).

In such cases, instructional trials might be increased by including simulated settings (at the school store, in the cafeteria purchase line, in the school office, etc.) and then evaluating instruction by conducting community probes.

Selecting and Sequencing Exemplar Stimuli

Instruction should systematically introduce the student to the natural variations that will be encountered when the skill is performed in its natural contexts (Day & Horner, 1989; Falvey, 1989; Liberty & Billingsley, 1988; Stokes & Baer, 1977). The natural features of target settings should be identified during the initial assessment (Liberty, 1985). Such stimuli include any verbal cues in the environment (e.g., the bank teller saying, "Next"), other people in the environment (e.g., the person in the front of the line), furniture or other objects (e.g., the counter at which the bank teller stands), items to which the learner is to respond (e.g., deposit slips), and so on. Key stimuli that are to function to evoke the steps in the behavior chain are very likely to be slightly different in each setting. During instruction, representative stimuli that exemplify the range of stimuli used in performance of the skill should be systematically introduced and taught (Ford & Mirenda, 1984; Horner et al., 1986).

Exemplars may be used in instruction serially or concurrently. In *serial* presentation, the student first masters the skill under one set of exemplars, and then is presented with the second set (e.g., walking on a carpeted surface is acquired before walking on wooden floors, linoleum, uneven surfaces, lawns, slopes, or stairs). In *concurrent* presentations, the student is exposed to the range of exemplars from the first (e.g., any trial might occur on carpets, rugs, ramps, floors, grass, and so on).

Which method produces quicker acquisition? Investigations have produced mixed results. For example, Schroeder and Baer (1972) found that neither procedure was more efficient than the other in teaching word imitation, but Waldo, Guess, and Flanagan (1982) observed that receptive labels were acquired more rapidly when a serial training format was employed. Serial training may cause problems if an easy-to-hard sequence results in response distortions on more difficult tasks (Horner, McDonnell, & Bellamy, 1986; Horner, Sprague, & Wilcox, 1982). According to Horner and associates (1982), overall mastery of all exemplars required for generalization is actually quicker for most skills with concurrent presentation.

Instructional Ratio

A one-to-one teacher-pupil ratio for students with severe disabilities has been regarded as optimal for skill development; however, many students with severe disabilities can learn skills in groups just as quickly as in one-to-one instruction (Reid & Favell, 1984). Group instruction increases the amount of instructional time and the number of instructional opportunities. It can also provide for natural variance in the people with whom the skill is practiced and less opportunity for the learner to become overdependent on a single teacher or person—thus increasing the potential for successful generalization.

Instruction in a group can begin by arranging the learners in proximity to one another and to the teacher. Depending on the makeup of the group, instructional procedures might involve the teacher's providing appropriate cues to one learner at a time and allowing that learner to respond before moving to the next learner. The learners who are not responding at a particular point in time would be intermittently reinforced for appropriate waiting or self-practice, or provided an interactive skill to practice with each other. Instruction may be directed at (1) different skills for each learner, (2) identical skills, but with different levels of prompting and independence for each learner, or (3) similar skills for all learners. Groups can be structured so that individuals must interact with each other (cf., Kamps et al., 1992) or cannot interact with each other (Brown, Holvoet, Guess, & Mulligan 1980; Collins, Gast,

Ault, & Wolery, 1990). In addition, group instruction can be implemented within carefully developed cooperative team structures (cf. Cosden & Haring, 1992; Johnson & Johnson, 1989).

For some skills, one-to-one instruction is best. Private skills such as dressing, toileting, grooming, sexual behaviors, and so on should not be taught in groups, and such teaching may be unsuccessful (e.g., Alberto, Jobes, Sizemore, & Doran, 1980; Reid & Favell, 1984). Skills that are not practiced in groups, such as grocery shopping, should not be instructed in groups. Additional teachers for one-to-one instruction can be enlisted from peers with disabilities, peers without disabilities (Haring & Breen, 1992), volunteers, parents, and members of a teaching team.

Frequency and Scheduling of Instruction

An instructional trial is a unit of instruction consisting of antecedent events, an opportunity for the student to respond (a practice opportunity), and a consequence. The speed with which a skill is acquired will be directly related to the number of instructional trials: the more trials, the quicker the learning. Scheduling trials just for sheer quantity, however, might interfere with generalization. For example, a student who is instructed in hand washing at 10:00 A.M., regardless of what he or she was doing, is not being taught the exemplar stimuli for handwashing (e.g., before meals, after toileting).

Further, if the child must wash hands 10 times in a row, he or she is not only being taught an excess behavior, but is also not experiencing the natural reinforcers for hand washing (e.g., clean, dry hands and access to a new activity, such as a meal). A balance between the number of practice opportunities and a natural context should be considered.

When instructional trials are not formally scheduled, trials may occur as the skill would normally be performed in a natural school or home routine. For example, instructional cues for a trial in grasping would occur any time an object (e.g., a coat cuff, a hat, a game box, a computer disc, a coin, a toy, or a sandwich) was in reach. Such *natural opportunities* (also called *naturally distributed trials*) for instruction can improve acquisition and, potentially, generalization, because they provide a contextual sequence that duplicates the occasions in which the skill should naturally occur after instruction ceases (cf. Bambara, Warren, & Komisar, 1988; Mulligan, Guess, Holvoet, & Brown, 1980; Neel & Billingsley, 1980).

An alternative for repetitively performed skills (e.g., taking steps, sorting utensils for storage, washing dishes, and putting Lego pieces together) is the use of *massed* trials (Mulligan et al., 1980), in which several trials are presented sequentially. Massed trials are not appropriate for nonrepetitive skills such as greeting, toileting, dressing, asking questions, and so on, because the salient cues are missing or distorted (cf. Falvey et al., 1980; Sailor & Guess, 1983; Snell & Zirpoli, 1987).

Natural trials may also be *spaced*, so that a pause or a rest period falls between trials. For example, taking bites during a meal is normally a spaced response; using a massed format may well result in teaching gobbling behavior or in digestive problems. Arranging for *distributed trials* is an alternative when there are only a few natural opportunities and when massed trials are inappropriate (Mulligan et al., 1980). For example, opportunities to teach greeting can be planned and programmed to occur throughout the day with the help of peers and teachers "dropping in" or by sending the student on errands. Students not only learn skills with distributed trial formats, but may also like the instruction better and engage in fewer excess behaviors (Dunlap, 1984; Dunlap & Koegel, 1980; Horner, Day, Sprague, O'Brien, & Heathfield, 1991; Winterling, Dunlap, & O'Neill, 1987).

ACQUIRING SKILLS

Two effective methods for teaching the learner how to perform a new skill are shaping and prompting.

Shaping

Reinforcing successive small improvements toward a new behavior (Panyan, 1980) can shape performance of new skills. Instruction begins by reinforcing a motor movement that the student can perform independently. For example, a slight movement in the hand or fingers might be initially reinforced in teaching grasping. Once the slight extension is reliably established, a further movement would be required before reinforcement. The movements required to obtain reinforcement would be continually increased until grasping the object is required for reinforcement. Shaping may also be used to change frequency, duration, or intensity of behavior. Horner (1971) successfully reinforced a child with intellectual disabilities and spina bifida for successive increases in the number of forward crutch movements.

In order to employ shaping effectively, it is necessary to ensure that reinforcement be provided *only* for responses that meet the performance criteria for each step and that the student not continue to be reinforced for completion of any step for an extended period of time. The steps should not be so large that it would be virtually impossible for the student to gain reinforcement. The shaping process can be slow (Rusch, Rose, & Greenwood, 1988), and prompts of various types are often used to increase the efficiency of the process (e.g., Horner, 1971).

Prompting

Prompts are added to natural cues and consequences to increase the likelihood that the correct behavior will occur, thus increasing opportunities for reinforcement (Billingsley & Romer, 1983; Shoen, 1986; Wolery & Gast, 1984).

Stimulus manipulations involve altering the configuration or appearance of elements of the stimulus complex (e.g., varying size, color, position, texture, or other dimension) (Etzel, LeBlanc, Schilmoeller, & Stella, 1981; Schoen, 1986). For example, Mosk and Bucher (1984) taught children with moderate to severe intellectual disabilities to hang their toothbrushes on a specific peg by first reinforcing hanging when only one peg was available, and then gradually introducing increasing numbers of distracter pegs so the children could discriminate "their" pegs from others. Distracter pegs were too short to hang the toothbrushes on, thus preventing errors, but were gradually lengthened until they matched in appearance the designated peg and the learner was still making the correct discrimination.

Best results are likely when the prompt emphasizes critical features of the target stimuli (Cipani, 1987; Dowler, Walls, Haught, & Zawlocki, 1984; Etzel & LeBlanc, 1979). Therefore, if a discrimination is based on shape, it is desirable that stimulus variations enhance shape rather than, say, a color cue. These procedures may not be appropriate for complex functional skills because of the time that may be required for the preparation of materials and the possibility that stimulus manipulations may be insufficient to evoke responses from many learners with severe disabilities (cf. Schoen, 1986; Ault, Wolery, Doyle, & Gast, 1989). In some instances, however, stimulus manipulations may be combined with other types of prompts to produce desired outcomes (e.g., Mosk & Bucher, 1984).

Auditory prompts are typically verbal cues or directions that provide more information about responding than are provided by natural stimuli (Hourcade, 1988). *Visual prompts* include gestures and modeling (or demonstration). Gestures should direct the learner's attention to critical task requirements through the trainer's touching, tapping, or pointing to correct choices (Hourcade, 1988; Snell & Zirpoli, 1987) or motioning in such a way as to suggest the correct movement (Billingsley & Romer, 1983). Demonstration, which can be a highly effective and efficient technique, should be used only if the learner is able to imitate (Wolery, Ault, & Doyle, 1992). (Techniques for training imitative behaviors may be found in many sources including Charlop and Walsh [1986], Cooper, Heron,

and Heward [1987], Schoen [1989], and Sternberg, McNerney, and Pegnatore [1985].)

Picture prompts (Wolery, Gast, Kirt, & Schuster, 1988) may be used to prompt behavior chains (e.g., pictures illustrating the sequence of steps in a vocational task or simplified, adapted maps to popular destinations) or to provide models of the desired behavior (e.g., a snapshot of a properly set table), as long as the learner has been taught to follow the prompts.

Tactile or kinesthetic prompts include touching and partially assisting the learner physically to direct the correct movement of the student in order that he or she might be reinforced. Physically guiding the student completely through the skill gives the learner the feel of the response and molds the appropriate physical movements (see Alberto & Troutman 1986; Falvey et al., 1980; Rusch et al., 1988). A student who resists physical guidance is unlikely to benefit from such prompts. In some cases, the teacher may need to desensitize the individual to physical contact and establish contact as a conditioned reinforcer before tactile prompts can be used in an effective manner (Wolery et al., 1988).

It is important that the type of assistance selected for use be one that will reliably and efficiently evoke the desired response, so that reinforcement occurs for the correct response (Bijou, 1981; Neel & Billingsley, 1989). However, when more help is given than is required, particularly in the form of extensive physical guidance, there is a danger that students will respond by attempting to exert countercontrol (Schoen, 1986; Schoen, Lentz, & Suppa, 1988) or will become dependent on teacher assistance (Wolery & Gast, 1984). A careful assessment procedure should, therefore, be employed to select appropriate prompts.

Under some conditions, stimulus manipulations have been found to yield more desirable results than prompts provided by the teacher (e.g., Schreibman, 1975; Wolfe & Cuvo, 1978). Such an outcome, however, is by no means invariable (e.g., Schreibman, Charlop, & Koegel, 1982; Wolery, Gast, Kirk, & Schuster, 1988).

Prompt Systems

Graduated guidance is a system that involves the use of physical prompts. Initially, the learner is provided with the amount of physical guidance he or she requires to perform the response. Assistance is then reduced on a moment-by-moment basis, depending on the student's responsiveness. Prompts are reduced by moving the location of the prompt away from the initial site of control (e.g., hand to wrist, wrist to forearm, forearm to shoulder) or by reducing the intensity of the prompt (Schoen, 1986) and then simply shadowing the student's movements. If errors occur, assistance is immediately increased to the extent necessary to produce correct movements. Verbal praise for improved independence accompanies the changes in prompts (cf. Foxx & Azrin, 1973; Foxx, 1982).

In the *increasing assistance*[1] system, prompts are ordered in a presumed sequence of lesser to greater assistance and applied sequentially, subsequent to errors or hesitations in responding. Typically, this system involves auditory prompts (e.g., verbal directions), visual prompts (e.g., pointing), and tactile prompts (e.g., partial physical assistance), and the same prompt sequence is followed in each trial (for an interesting and effective exception, see Steege, Wacker, & McMahon [1987]). An investigation in which students with severe disabilities were taught to use liquid soap dispensers (Pancsofar & Bates, 1985) illustrated use of the increasing assistance method. First, students were given the opportunity to respond independently after their hands were wet (natural cue for obtaining soap). If students did not use the dispenser correctly within 5 seconds, the instructor provided a verbal direction ("Get the soap"). A second incorrect response or a failure to respond within 5 seconds was followed by a repetition of

the verbal instruction with a gesture toward the soap dispenser. Finally, a third error was followed by repetition of the direction and physical guidance to operate the dispenser. This system has the potential for relatively high initial error rates. Falvey et al. (1980) and Schoen (1986) have expressed concern that students will learn to delay responding to gain teacher guidance, that the prompts are inconsistent with events in natural environments, and that prompts are not consistent with training requirements for potentially dangerous tasks.

The *decreasing assistance system*[2] also involves a presumed hierarchy of prompts. Instruction begins with the most assistance needed to evoke the response. The initial prompt is often full physical assistance (e.g., Csapo, 1981; Luyben, Funk, Morgan, Clark, & Delulio, 1986); however, it is preferable to select the prompt based on assessment data (e.g., McDonnell & Ferguson, 1989; see also Neel & Billingsley, 1989; Wuerch & Voeltz, 1982) in order to ensure that reinforcers are accessed without the provision of more assistance than necessary. After the student is able to perform with the "most" prompt, successively lesser prompts are used, contingent on correct responding. If the student makes an error, the sequence is usually "backed up" to provide more assistance (see Neel & Billingsley, 1989). It is preferable to provide the prompt prior to the response in order to maximize correct responding. For example, as soon as the student has finished wetting his or her hands, the teacher prompts the student with the assessed level of prompt, for instance, tapping the elbow toward the soap dispenser. If, say, three trials are completed successfully, the tapping is replaced by pointing or by a less intense tap.

Errors During Acquisition

Acquisition occurs only through reinforcement. Each error reduces reinforcement and interferes with learning. Moreover, undesirable behaviors

---

[1]Also known as the *system of least prompts, least-to-most prompting* and *least intrusive prompts.*

[2]Also known as *most-to-least prompting.*

may accompany frequent errors and corrections (Weeks & Gaylord-Ross, 1981; Carr & Durand, 1985; Bellamy et al., 1979; Horner, 1988), excessive errors may reduce motivation to perform (Koegel & Egel, 1979), and error responses may persist (Terrace, 1963; Bereiter & Engelmann, 1966).

Shaping and prompting increase correct responding and decrease the possibility of error. Shaping reduces errors by successively and gradually increasing the quality of behavior required for reinforcement. Sensitive shaping can result in each trial's producing reinforcement.

Prompts can be provided antecedent to student responses, subsequent to responses as error-correction procedures (e.g., Haught, Walls, & Crist, 1984; Miller & Test, 1989), or both. In teaching the use of a paper towel dispenser, for example, a gesture could be provided immediately following the last step in hand washing (antecedent prompt) and/or assistance could be used following errors, such as the learner's attempting to pull down the towels without using the handle (subsequent prompt or corrective feedback).

Antecedent prompts prevent errors; subsequent prompts are corrective. If assistance is insufficient, undesirable levels of error responding may occur. Given the potential problems associated with error responding, it is prudent to employ techniques that, at least initially, involve the antecedent presentation of prompts (Day, 1987; Zane, Walls, & Thvedt, 1981). Skills in recognizing and correcting one's own errors are necessary for successful adaptation to natural settings. Programs should, therefore, be implemented to instruct learners in adapting and in handling problems (cf. Demchak, 1990), but correcting errors during instruction may not have a beneficial impact on acquisition and will not teach the student to self-monitor or to deal with problems.

It should be noted, however, that antecedent prompts may hide student progress. Because the controlling prompts are provided before the student has a chance to respond to the natural cue without assistance (or with less assistance), the teacher may not see how the student would do without any assistance and the student may be capable of performing with greater independence than can be observed. Acquisition might, therefore, be delayed because of overprompting.

Assessments are needed to determine when assistance may be reduced (Neel & Billingsley, 1989). In the *antecedent prompt and test strategy* (Ault et al., 1989; Wolery et al., 1988; Zane et al., 1981), the prompt is presented simultaneously with the natural cue before the learner responds. Then trials without the prompt (but with reinforcement for corrects) are programmed. A correct response to the "test" trial results in elimination of the prompt. This method "may not provide sufficient assistance to some students with severe handicaps" (Wolery et al., 1988, p. 255), but this danger should be present for only a few trials, because if correct responses do not occur, the level of prompting should be increased.

Eliminating Cues and Prompts

Manipulated stimuli and other prompts can come to control the response. Then, when these stimuli are not available in natural environments, the learner may not respond, but may wait for help or cues. To prevent this, control of the behavior must be gradually transferred to the natural stimulus: this process is often referred to as *fading*. The effective transfer of stimulus control will ensure, for example, that traffic signals, rather than a tap on the elbow, control street-crossing behavior; the sight of a desired compact disc evokes behaviors for operating a disc player; and the sight and smell of a plate of food evoke eating skills in a hungry student.

Where stimulus materials have been modified to serve as prompts, transfer of control occurs by gradually changing the manipulated property or properties of stimuli, in successive trials, to match the natural stimuli (cf. Deitz & Malone, 1985; Irvin & Bellamy, 1977), as illustrated in Figure 4.3. Verbal cues can be faded by the teacher's using successively fewer words and a quieter voice

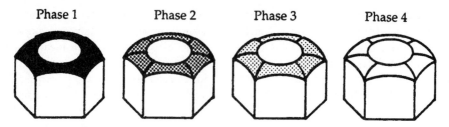

Condition I - Adding and Fading Redundant Dimensions (AFRD)

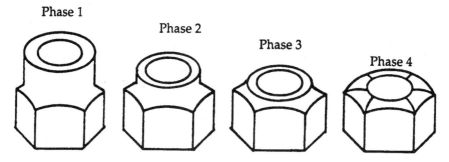

Condition II - Adding and Reducing Large Cue Differences (ARLCD)

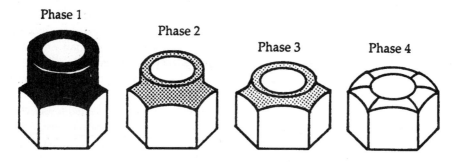

Condition III - Combined ARLCD/AFRD

FIGURE 4.3   The instructional objective is to assemble a bicycle brake. At one step in the task analysis, the learner must pick up a nut and put the flat side of it over the brake axle. A natural cue for placement would be that the nut fits in only one position. However, in this task, the learner must be taught placement by discriminating the flat side of the nut, inasmuch as the nut fits with either face down. Color (AFRD), shape (ARLCD), and color plus shape (ARLCD/AFRD) prompts were manipulated. (Reprinted with permission from Bellamy, T., Horner, R., & Inman, D. P. (1979). *Vocational habilitation of severely retarded adults: A direct service technology* (p. 130). Baltimore: University Park Press.)

volume; a model can be faded by placing it farther and farther away from the learner; and a demonstration can be faded by using it on alternate trials and then increasing the number of trials without a demonstration.

Fading methods for the different prompt systems have been developed to transfer control of a skill from the prompt to the natural stimulus. Transfer is usually achieved in decreasing and increasing assistance systems by the teacher's moving through a hierarchy of prompt types that are presumed to provide different amounts of information. As the student's errors drop out, the prompt is first replaced with a lesser one and then eliminated altogether. Fading may also be accomplished *within* a given type of prompt, for example, by systematically reducing the amount of physical assistance provided, or moving from more to less directive verbal prompts (Billingsley & Romer, 1983; Wilcox & Bellamy, 1982). Verbal directions that do not control the response and that will not be present in nontraining settings can be avoided entirely, thus reducing the fading process (cf. Neel & Billingsley, 1989).

In the antecedent prompt and fade strategy (Ault et al., 1989), fading reduces the magnitude of the prompt or decreases the frequency of delivery. Billingsley (1987), for example, faded physical prompts for gestural requests for food by reducing the number of prompted trials and increasing the number of unprompted trials across instructional sessions.

Time delay procedures employ systematic temporal variation in a negative reinforcement paradigm. In *progressive time delay* (e.g., Godby, Gast, & Wolery, 1987; Snell, 1982), prompting occurs simultaneously with the natural stimuli for a number of trials. Next, the prompt is delayed for a short period of time (for instance, 1 second), during which the student has an opportunity to respond independently to the natural stimuli. If he or she does so respond, reinforcers are provided and the next trial or the next step in the skill sequence is presented. If no response occurs during the interval, the prompt is delivered. If a correct re-

sponse does occur, it is reinforced. Delay in the following trials is gradually extended to a maximum interval in preselected increments contingent upon some number of correct independent or prompted responses. Walls, Haught, and Dowler (1982) suggested that 1-second increments may produce quicker transfer to the natural stimuli than 3- or 5-second increments. The effect of the increasing interval is to gradually delay reinforcement; if the reinforcer is powerful enough and the student can perform the behavior, the learner should respond before the prompt in order to avoid the delay. Gast, Wolery, Ault, Doyle, and Alig (1988) have recommended that if transfer does not occur, only unprompted correct responses should be reinforced. In *constant time delay* (e.g., Kleinert & Gast, 1982; McDonnell, 1987), the trial-by-trial method of increasing the delay is replaced by repeated sets of trials in which the length of delay between the natural cue and the prompt remains constant.

Time delay systems may be relatively complicated to apply (McDonnell & Ferguson, 1989; Snell, 1982) and, in such cases, may be less preferable to teachers than other prompt-fading methods (i.e., decreasing assistance) (McDonnell & Ferguson, 1989). However, a careful consideration of available practices and variations (see Handen & Zane, 1987) should allow educators to tailor systems that will be manageable within many instructional contexts (see also Gast et al., 1988; Wolery et al., 1992; Schuster & Griffen, 1990).

Instructor assistance is often used to establish skills because it requires less effort and expense than stimulus manipulation procedures. It is possible, however, that the individual who provides assistance may become a controlling stimulus for student behavior. In such a case, the student will be unlikely to demonstrate skill performance unless the instructor is nearby (cf. Chandler, Fowler, & Lubeck, 1992). Should that outcome be observed, it will be necessary to treat instructor proximity as a prompt and implement a plan to gradually fade the instructor's presence (e.g., by the instructor's moving farther and farther away until out of sight).

Recommendations based on research regarding the comparative utility of methods for fading prompts must be considered tentative rather than definitive. Studies reviewed in such sources as Ault et al. (1989), Demchak (1990), Schoen (1986), and Wolery et al. (1992), however, suggest that transfer of control from prompts to natural stimuli will be quicker with the use of systems that minimize the number of errors the learner makes in the presence of the natural stimuli. In choosing among those systems, educators should apply the principle of parsimony and "seek the least complex but still effective procedure for changing behavior" (Etzel & LeBlanc, 1979, p. 362).

Reinforcement Guidelines

Skills are acquired when they are followed by reinforcing events. Reinforcement increases the probability that the skill will occur in the presence of those antecedent stimuli that precede it. For skill utility, skills must be taught so that they are evoked and reinforced in the presence of the natural antecedents (Billingsley & Romer, 1983; Wolery & Gast, 1984; Ford & Mirenda, 1984). The selection and presentation of positive reinforcers will determine whether skills will be acquired and maintained. It is therefore necessary to plan carefully for the effective use of reinforcers throughout the instructional process.

The initial step is to identify the event that should "naturally" serve as a positive reinforcer for the behavior (e.g., getting food into one's mouth is the natural positive reinforcer for using a spoon and a fork). Many frequently occurring behaviors are reinforced by events whose reinforcing properties are not learned. Those *unconditioned reinforcers* include sensory stimulation, especially novel stimulation, which reinforces television watching, keeping one's head up, picking up objects, and so on. There are other events that are unconditioned positive reinforcers in some situations: food, when a person is hungry; liquid, when thirsty; warmth,

when cold; coolness, when warm; kinesthetic stimulation resulting from body movement, especially after periods of enforced stillness, and from being touched.

When events in the social environment occur simultaneously with unconditioned positive reinforcers, those events may become learned, or conditioned, positive reinforcers. Praise is a conditioned reinforcer; it *must be learned*. Children from an environment in which they were abused or neglected, or children with sensory impairments, may not have learned that praise, or attention from an adult, or physical touching, is reinforcing. Playing with toys, games, friends— all of these social and interactive events can become conditioned reinforcers, but only if they are presented simultaneously and contingently with unconditioned reinforcers for many instructional trials. A child with physical disabilities that have interfered with his or her interactions with the physical environment, a child with uncaring or neglectful caretakers or parents, or a child with sensory disabilities may not respond to events that are commonly considered to be "reinforcing."

The way to select a reinforcer is to present a likely event contingently during instruction. If learning occurs, the event is a positive reinforcer; if learning does not occur, a different event must be programmed. Although formal systems designed to assist in identifying potential reinforcers are available (cf. Fisher et al., 1992), they should not be considered foolproof for several reasons: (1) an event that is a positive reinforcer for one skill may not reinforce a different skill; (2) the learner may become satiated with a particular event, thus reducing the available events; and (3) an event that is not a positive reinforcer may later become one.

What are likely events? The best choice is the natural reinforcer. If a natural reinforcer cannot be identified and controlled, "a behavior that a student performs frequently can be used to reinforce a behavior the student seldom performs" (Popovich, 1981, p. 71) *if* the learner will be in a state of deprivation for the contingent response until he or she performs the instrumental response (Konarski, 1987; Konarski, Johnson, Crowell, & Whitman, 1980). For example, access to a snack-vending machine at coffee break could potentially be used to reinforce quality work, as long as the learner has not been permitted to obtain snacks prior to the break.

Time to engage in leisure activities is used widely as a reinforcer in schools and is a common consequence for task completion in natural environments (e.g., after helping to wash the dishes, a youngster may get "free time" to watch television). Liberty (1985) has cautioned that students with disabilities may not have the skills necessary to engage in many common free-time activities (e.g., playing with various toys or games, engaging in social conversations) and, therefore, that free time may not function as a reinforcer. It is critical that students be taught to participate in available leisure and play activities if free time is to be effective as a reinforcing consequence. Remember, however, that free time or any other event (e.g., sensory stimulation, touching, praise, opportunity to engage in another behavior) will not reinforce a skill if the learner is able to obtain as much of the reinforcer as he or she wants without improving skill performance. To the maximum reasonable extent, the teacher should attempt to confine the delivery of reinforcers to those instances in which they follow target behaviors (Liberty, 1985). In addition, the teacher should attempt to reduce the student's opportunity to receive reinforcement for the performance of high-probability behaviors other than the target behavior(s) during the instructional process (Aeschleman & Williams, 1989).

Where appropriate and possible, it is important to vary the reinforcers or let the learner select from a number of available events so as to avoid satiation and subsequent decreases in responsivity (Egel, 1981; Liberty, 1985). For example, in teaching a learner to request snacks or recreational activities, it would be sound practice to avoid using only a single food item or game for an extended period of time.

Instructional reinforcers are events that are used to increase response strength, but that do not occur naturally. Praise or a carrot stick that is provided as a reinforcer for putting on a jacket is an instructional reinforcer, because praise and food are not the natural reinforcers. The natural reinforcer for putting on a jacket is either warmth (if cold), or the opportunity to go outdoors (potential unconditioned positive reinforcer of novel sensory and kinesthetic stimuli, and possible access to preferred activities or conditioned reinforcers, such as social interaction). Instructional reinforcers must be faded if the student is to respond under natural conditions. When such reinforcers are used, they should be paired with the presentation of events in the natural environments that should ultimately function as reinforcers, be as similar as possible to those that are frequently employed in natural environments, and be systematically faded as the target skill is acquired (cf. Liberty, 1985; Wolery et al., 1988).

Frequent reinforcement in the presence of the natural stimuli for a behavior will promote the development of desirable stimulus control, and skill acquisition will occur most efficiently, if *every correct or improved response is reinforced.* However, when performance of a particular behavior in natural environments is to be reinforced on a noncontinuous (intermittent) schedule, it will be necessary to reduce gradually the frequency with which reinforcers are delivered as instruction progresses. This issue is discussed further in the section "Making Skills Useful" later in this chapter.

The teacher should deliver reinforcers immediately following the correct response (Cooper, Herron, & Heward, 1987), inasmuch as a delay of even a few seconds can have undesirable effects. If the learner does not receive immediate reinforcement, he or she may emit other behaviors before reinforcement. Learning may be delayed because the student is unable to discriminate which response was reinforced and an undesired behavior (e.g., excess behavior) may be strengthened (Streifel & Cadez, 1983).

Reinforcing events must be presented *contin-*

gently. During instruction, the teacher must control reinforcers so that they occur if, and only if, the desired response occurs. Moreover, reinforcement should be made contingent on quick starts. The teacher should determine an appropriate period of time between the stimulus for the target behavior and the student's initiation of the response and reinforce only those correct responses that occur within that time period (this is known as a *latency limit* or *wait-time*). The longer the teacher waits for a response, the greater the probability that the behavior will be associated with irrelevant stimuli in the instructional environment or with waiting itself (Liberty, 1985). It is also possible that the student will engage in behaviors that may interfere with learning. In research conducted with students with severe disabilities, White (cited in Liberty, 1985) found that latency limits of 3 seconds or less accelerated learning more effectively than longer limits (e.g., 5 seconds). Such an effect, however, may not be found if tasks are of questionable functionality and if consequences for appropriate performance are either withheld or consist only of verbal feedback (Lee, O'Shea, & Dykes, 1987; Valconte, Roberson, Reid, & Wolking, 1989).

There is, in addition, a reinforcement procedure that can be initiated during acquisition that is designed to shape adaptable responses. In this procedure, teacher-controlled reinforcement is delivered for only the first instance of a response to a particular set of stimuli, or for the first instances of a response with a particular topography. For example, in teaching a youngster to share, the teacher might arrange several different stimulus conditions, involving different times of day, play supervisors, peers, toys, and so forth. The teacher might then give praise only the first time the youngster offers a particular toy, but not again when that same toy is shared. Similarly, praise would follow the first sharing interaction with a particular child, but sharing with that child again would not be praised. The purpose of this procedure is to prevent the restricted stimulus control that might be exerted by a particular toy or a par-

ticular child-peer. Repeated reinforcement of a single type of situation-toy-peer combination could result in the learner's playing almost exclusively with one child or offering to share only a particular toy. This procedure is also sensitive to individual preferences, because if the youngster wants to play only with a special friend, those interactions will be sustained by natural reinforcers and not by the intrusive reinforcers of the teacher.

After accurate performance has been achieved, the teacher should fade instructional reinforcers. Fading can be achieved by presenting the natural reinforcer first and delaying the instructional reinforcer for longer and longer periods of time. One-to-one schedules of reinforcement can be faded by gradually increasing the number of responses, or the amount of time spent responding, before reinforcement is delivered. The reduction of reinforcers must be done gradually to prevent performance deterioration or extinction.

Aims During Acquisition

An aim such as "100 percent correct for 3 consecutive days" strengthens teacher reinforcement contingencies for accuracy, but it is far more important to guarantee that the skill is fluent, maintains, and generalizes. It is best to use aims that include fluency standards from the outset, such as "will still be meeting employer standards for speed and accuracy after 3 months" or "will be correctly dressed *in time to make the bus* for 5 days in a row" or "will correctly pay the clerk in three different consumer situations *without causing a delay for others.*"

It is especially important that repeated demonstrations of accurate performance not be required at intermediate stages, or skill steps, in acquisition. Such repetitions serve no purpose in terms of the ultimate mastery of the skill (inasmuch as the skill at one step is incorporated or required at subsequent steps) and may act to establish a reinforcement history of "careful but slow" that is difficult to break. For example, if backward chaining were employed to teach sock removal, a learner might be reinforced for drawing the sock off her toes. If she were required to repeat this act for 10 of 10 trials for 4 of 5 days, she would be likely to have had a minimum of 40 reinforcers for only the tiniest step in sock removal, and it is more likely that she would have received 100 or 200 reinforcers. She would also have been able to evoke the natural reinforcer (a bare foot) for performing only part of the target skill in conjunction with allowing the instructor to remove all of the sock except for the toe. At the next step, when she must draw the sock off from her ankle, there may be a long latency period as she waits for the instructor to do his or her bit before she does hers, in accordance with the way she was trained during the first step. Then, when she finally completes the last two steps independently, the reinforcer may act to reinforce her doing the steps slowly.

A reinforcement history for slowness, and for dependency on the instructor to do part of the skill, may be cumulative over time and tasks and may help to explain why it is so difficult to teach generalization, maintenance, and independence to older learners with a long history of such reinforcement practices. An alternative is to accept that one accurate performance is sufficient until the entire skill is acquired, and that proficiency should not be assumed until fluency, generalization, and maintenance, as well as accuracy, have been measured. For example, once the learner has pulled the sock off her toe in one trial, she would be required to pull it off from her ankle on the very next trial.

Assessment During Acquisition

Measures of learning during acquisition are usually counts of the number of times a response is performed accurately and inaccurately (usually summarized by teachers as "percent correct") and, perhaps, records of the degree of independence or prompting needed to achieve accuracy (e.g., Browder, 1991). The teacher can use these performance data to make decisions about employing a

particular instructional procedure during acquisition, as discussed in the section that follows.

Selection of Instructional Procedures

Unfortunately, many acquisition strategies, as typically implemented, result in fluency and generalization problems. Those problems can frequently be reduced by: (1) avoiding the use of verbal directions, cues, feedback, schedules of reinforcement, and reinforcers that are not present in settings in which the skill is ultimately to be performed, (2) avoiding reinforcing only accuracy during initial acquisition (improvements in fluency should be reinforced too), and (3) avoiding performance aims that require more than one session at 85 percent accuracy or better before moving to the next curricular step.

There are several methods for teaching new behaviors, many different prompts and cues that can be used, and numerous types of events that might be reinforcing. The use of decision rules, which help to match instructional procedures to student performances, can be applied to data collected on acquisition performance and can dramatically improve the chances of selecting effective interventions. The following decision rules are adapted from 5 years of research involving 1264 decisions in 234 programs for 109 students with severe disabilities, by 46 teachers in three different states (Haring, Liberty, & White, 1981).

1. *When to leave well enough alone.* When acquisition is occurring at a satisfactory rate of improvement, there is no point in changing the instructional procedure.

2. *When to change.* If the introduction of a procedure does not produce improvement in performance within three instructional sessions, the procedure should be changed (further instructional sessions have less than a 12 percent chance of improving learning).

3. *When to make the skill easier to perform.* Cut back to an easier version of the skill, or a smaller piece of the skill, or a prerequisite movement if 0 correct performances have been recorded. In one study, teachers moved to an easier skill 30 percent of the time they made performance changes, but this helped only 5 percent of the time and only when the learner's performance was at 0 (Haring, White, & Liberty, 1976). If the instructional procedure is wrong for the learner, the use of the same instructional procedures at a different level of difficulty is unlikely to be effective.

4. *When to make the skill more difficult to perform.* Move ahead to the next step in the task analysis, reduce the level of prompting, or teach a more difficult skill entirely if performance bounces from near criterion to very low levels from day to day. High variability is a sign that the stimuli are no longer adequately controlling the behavior and that reinforcement is no longer sufficient to maintain improved levels. Switching reinforcers may be effective for a short time, but this is not desirable if natural reinforcers should be or are controlling the skill. Advancing to a more difficult skill permits access to new sets of stimuli, reinforcing simply in their newness, plus access to additional covert self-reinforcement resulting from performing the more difficult skill.

5. *When to provide more help and information.* Additional prompts, cues, and feedback on how to perform the skill accurately should be provided if the number of correct performances is decreasing and accuracy has never reached 83 percent, or if errors are made more frequently than correct responses.

MAKING SKILLS USEFUL

Instructional programs initially focus on skill acquisition, during which the student learns the stimulus discriminations and response requirements for reinforcement. Acquisition is the first step in a learning hierarchy, and a skill is acquired when it can be accurately performed without instructional prompts. Unfortunately, accuracy in performance does not guarantee proficiency in natural environments (Bailey & Wolery, 1984; Haring, Liberty, & White, 1980; White & Haring, 1980; Horner, Bellamy, & Colvin, 1984). Concluding instruction after acquisition will not ensure that skills are adaptable to present and future environments, can be performed as components of functional skill routines, and are integrated into the learner's behavioral repertoire. Instruction must continue until three additional stages of learning competency are achieved: fluency, generalization, and maintenance (Becker, 1986; Haring, 1988; Haring, Liberty, & White, 1980; Stokes & Baer, 1977; White & Haring, 1980).

Fluency is evident when the learner can perform a skill at the speed or with the quality of performance that is necessary to access natural reinforcers, and when prompts and special training procedures are not required for accurate and independent performance. *Generalization* is evident when the learner is able to apply the skill to new conditions and in new situations. *Maintenance* is evident when the skill continues to be performed at fluent levels in natural settings after instruction has ended.

Building Fluency

In natural environments, fluency deficits often evoke naturally punishing consequences—the person with the slow gait arrives after all the seats are taken; the person who takes a long time to answer a question or remark is later avoided; the child who dresses slowly ends up being reprimanded and dressed by his father; a worker misses the bus; a janitor is fired for taking too long to finish cleaning; the person who takes too long to pay the cashier evokes the complaints of other customers.

Most descriptions of individuals with severe disabilities include "slowness" as a characteristic, even though they can learn to perform as fast and as accurately as learners without disabilities (Barrett, 1979; Gold, 1972; Lindsley, 1964). Slowness is caused by a failure to teach to necessary levels of fluency. Some consequences of an instructor's failing to teach fluency to children with severe disabilities are frightening. For example, children with multiple disabilities who are not taught to be fluent walkers are often confined to wheelchairs for the convenience of staff who do not have the time to "wait" while a student walks independently. Then, once in a wheelchair, the student may not be taught to use the wheelchair independently and fluently, thereby completely reducing personal freedom. Similarly, children who are not taught to chew and swallow fluently, and with a wide variety of foods, are often fed, placed on restricted diets of food that caregivers can easily handle, and may even be fed through gastronomy feeding systems because they are not receiving appropriate nutrition through self- or caregiver-feeding, or because self- or caregiver-feeding takes too long.

Skills that are not fluent are generally not maintained because they cannot be reinforced within natural schedules. Further, lack of fluency means that learners will be slow to respond to the stimulus conditions that should evoke generalization.

Measurement of Fluency

During fluency building, measures of the temporal dimensions of a behavior are critical (Haring et al., 1981; White & Haring, 1980). The functional temporal dimensions include: *duration* (i.e., the length of time it takes to perform the skill or routine); *latency* (i.e., the hesitation before initiating a skill, such as the time before beginning to follow a direction or to answer a question); *endurance* (e.g., the length of time one is able to work on a task); and *frequency* (the speed with which one is able to perform a skill). A clock, watch, or stopwatch is used to record the temporal dimension. Accuracy may be assessed as during acquisition.

A fluency criterion can often be appropriately established through actually timing the performance of a competent peer or by identifying the schedule or wage constraints of the target setting (Liberty, 1985; White, 1984). Often, however, it is more important to evaluate the fluency of less de-

sirable competing behavior(s) and set standards for the new target skill sufficiently high to "break old habits" (cf. Horner & Billingsley, 1988). For example, the fluency standard for walking might be set at a level one and a half times faster than the student is able to crawl (White, 1984, 1985a, 1985b, 1985c).

Identifying Fluency Problems

A teacher can identify fluency problems by naturalistic observations or by asking someone not connected with the instruction of the skill to provide a "layperson's" evaluation of the skill. Methods similar to those discussed later in this chapter for assessing generalization problems can be used. Research into the stages of learning has also shown that fluency problems can be identified early in the instructional process by the frequent measuring of performance. A skill that is once measured at or above 83 percent accuracy without subsequent improvement is likely to reflect a fluency problem, although sometimes a flat performance pattern is excused as a *plateau* in a "blame the victim" approach to learning (Haring et al., 1980). Slow but accurate performance without improvements in speed indicates the need for instructional change.

Fluency Interventions

One of the first approaches is to shift contingencies for reinforcement from accurate performance to fluent performance, until fluency aims match requirements for performing fluently in the target environments (e.g., O'Brien, Azrin, & Bugle, 1972). A *changing criterion for reinforcement* can be applied on a trial-to-trial basis to shift contingencies gradually (Alberto & Troutman, 1986). The aim standard may be communicated to the student before the session.

Cues, prompts, timers, and speed contests can be used to establish fluency, but they will have to be faded once their usefulness is completed. For example, a kitchen timer may be set and placed next to the student. If he has finished (met the criterion level of fluency) before the timer bell rings, the reinforcer is provided; if he is not finished, he is told that he did not "beat the clock" and that the reinforcer will not be made available. For children with dual sensory impairments, a special tactile watch (such as those used by pilots, which give a mild prick to the wrist or a vibration as an alarm) might be employed, or other touch cues used to tell the child what is expected. Or cues might be provided while the child is responding, such as "Hurry up, or you'll miss P.E." or "That was a fast one." Of course, such cues must be faded; otherwise the student may learn to respond only in the presence of nagging. Nonverbal cues, such as seeing a door slowly close, can also be effective. A teacher or peer demonstration of fluent performance, perhaps accompanied by a description of it, can be a useful technique. Often the best demonstration is provided by having a peer work alongside the learner (but not for private behaviors, except in certain circumstances; e.g., when both the peer and student get dressed in the locker room following a swim session).

Additional reinforcers or richer schedules of reinforcement may be implemented for a short period of time to build fluency, although use must be carefully monitored to avoid generalization and maintenance problems, and then the reinforcers must be faded.

It is sometimes necessary to teach a fluent response topography. For example, table setting might be more fluent if, instead of counting out all of the spoons and then taking them to the table, the learner takes all the spoons to the table, sets them at the places, and then returns the unneeded ones, thus "saving" the time spent in counting. Often a physical therapist can describe ways in which a young child can strengthen muscles or use alternative muscles or positions to increase fluency and ease of physical movement.

If one is not successful in building fluency, alternative ways of achieving the critical effect of the behavior must be considered. For example, if a teacher is not able to improve latency of question answering, he or she might teach a student to use fillers, such as "uh" (which normalizes communication patterns) or to make a restraining motion with a hand, communicating to listeners that an answer will be forthcoming. Or if fluency in shoe tying is not achieved, the teacher might consider eliminating tie-shoes from the wardrobe. In either case, it is of no educational value for an individual to acquire skill accuracy without achieving fluency; such skills are simply not maintained.

Ensuring Generalization and Maintenance

Generalization and maintenance are requirements for the function of skills in new environments and over time, regardless of learner disability. Unless instruction continues until the ability to solve problems and respond appropriately in new situations is established, the skills themselves are disabled in new environments and thus will eventually be extinguished from skill repertoires (Liberty, 1985; Stokes & Baer, 1977; Streifel & Cadez, 1983).

The disastrous effects of failing to program generalization and maintenance can be seen in analyses of Individualized Education Plans for children and in the curricula: identical requests from parents for teaching particular skills year after year because instructional gains achieved at school failed to transfer to the home or to the next teacher, identical target objectives year after year because the skill was "lost" over summer vacation, and a cumulative failure to teach students skills that can lead to meaningful lives in community, home, and vocational settings. Fortunately, there is currently a considerable technology of instruction to prevent and remediate generalization and maintenance problems (Haring, 1988; Horner, Dunlap, & Koegel, 1988; Stokes & Baer, 1977).

Measuring Generalization and Maintenance

Generalization may occur at any time; however, it is conventionally evaluated once the skill is acquired and fluent, because generalization appears more likely to occur once the initial hurdles have been cleared (Liberty, White, Billingsley, & Haring, 1988). Naturalistic observations or reports of how a learner behaved when he or she encountered a new situation are the most direct methods of identifying problems in generalization or maintenance (White, 1988). The basic principles include the following: (1) Evaluate generalization under more than one set of conditions; (2) evaluate generalization when all important stimulus dimensions of instruction are changed; (3) evaluate whether the skill generalizes to inappropriate situations as well; (4) evaluate only the first opportunity to perform under a set of new conditions to assess generalized performance; and (5) evaluate periodically over time to assess maintenance (White, 1988).

Any measure of generalization must involve an opportunity for the student to respond to cues, directions, settings, individuals, and events that were not included in instruction. The universe of possible situations in which many skills might be needed in current and future environments is very broad, and a sample of only one or two of these will not provide an adequate measure of generalization. It is much more crucial to obtain measures in multiple settings than it is to insist on repeated demonstrations of accuracy without fluency, generalization, or maintenance. In addition, it is important to evaluate generalization when all important stimulus dimensions are changed from those present during instruction.

The teacher should also evaluate whether the skill generalizes to inappropriate situations (Horner et al., 1984). Problems, in which the student responds to a new situation with the wrong skill, are relatively common. For example, a student was very carefully and fluently trained to wash and wax linoleum floors. When he was hired to clean an office building, however, he washed and waxed the carpeted offices. The same type of problem can be observed in the student who greets all other people with a handshake, every day and throughout the day, no matter how many times they are encountered.

It is also important to remember that only the very first chance to perform a skill in a new setting can provide a true measure of generalization. Once the stimulus conditions in the new setting have occurred, that situation becomes a learning environment, and once the skill is performed, or a mistake is made or the skill is not performed, the events that naturally follow complete the natural instructional trial. If the response occurs, it may be reinforced, punished, or ignored by natural events in the setting; if the response is not performed, whatever else the learner does may also be reinforced, punished, or ignored by natural events in the setting. Whatever it is that follows the initial introduction to the generalization situation (untrained stimuli) produces learning (stimulus discrimination) in regard to that particular situation. Thus, "true" generalization can be measured only once in each situation.

Maintenance can be measured anytime after instruction ceases, but instruction will generally continue until generalization is achieved. Maintenance, then, will be measured after generalization is achieved and instruction ends. When assessing maintenance, it is usually sufficient to see whether performance continues over time at satisfactory levels.

Identifying Generalization and Maintenance Problems

Problems exist if an acquired and fluent skill does not occur in the proper circumstances (e.g., a plate of spaghetti is set in front of the learner at the restaurant, but he does not eat it) or is performed at the wrong time, or in the wrong circumstances (e.g., a waiter eats from a plate he is serving); an inappropriate skill is performed instead (e.g., the individual eats with her fingers) or is performed incorrectly or incompletely (e.g., a child might begin to eat the food with the utensils, but slop the food on her clothes or the table, or chew with her mouth open); or the skill is performed in only a few generalization situations (e.g., generalization is to restaurants with family members but not to restaurants with peers).

Generalization can fail to occur because of some problem with the stimulus conditions in the uninstructed situation. If stimulus conditions are properly instructed, the skill should generalize at least once. However, if the skill does occur once, but is not reinforced, it is less likely to occur a second time in the particular setting. The failure of appropriate reinforcement has turned the situation into an "instructional" one, although one that is poor and unplanned. Subsequent problems in that particular environment, however, are not ones of generalization, but of maintenance. Maintenance problems occur because of some problem with the reinforcement conditions in the situation in which the behavior should naturally occur.

Selection of Instructional Strategies

When the learner does not generalize, the type of performance problem has implications for the type of intervention that might be needed (Horner & Billingsley, 1988; Liberty, 1985; Liberty & Billingsley, 1988; Liberty, Haring, White, & Billingsley, 1988; Haring & Liberty, 1990; Stokes & Baer, 1977).

1. *If there is no response* when a skill should be performed, the stimulus conditions in the new setting are not evoking the skill. Such problems may be linked to oversuccessful instruction to respond precisely one way to precisely one set of stimuli under one set of conditions. As a result of such instruction, when the student encounters an untrained situation, he or she is unlikely to recognize novel, but relevant, stimuli. The approach to preventing this problem is to introduce variability into stimulus conditions from the first instances of instruction, so that stimulus control is established for a range of stimuli representative of the range the student will encounter in generalization situations (Albin & Horner, 1988; Horner et al., 1986, 1988; Liberty, 1985; Stokes & Baer, 1977).

Intervention for this problem may be effected through continued instruction with a wider variety of stimuli (e.g., Sprague & Horner, 1984). If there

are only a limited number of stimuli, the simplest solution might be to repeat or initiate instruction in the environment in which the skill is required (e.g., Tucker & Berry, 1980). This solution satisfies an immediate need, but it is not a solution to generalization of the skill in other, new situations. It should be noted that teaching in the natural environment may be the least effective single strategy to achieve generalization to other environments (White et al., 1988), perhaps because teachers are less likely to program, or unable to manipulate, a wide variety of representative stimuli and reinforcers in natural settings.

It may also be possible to provide cues and prompts in the natural environment, such as using color cues, tactile cues, and so forth, to signal when a skill should occur or to help an individual link components of a skill chain. In fact, individuals with severe disabilities can be taught to deliver the instructions or other stimuli that control their own skills or performance of routines (e.g., Wacker & Greenbaum, 1984).

If it is not possible to make changes in all of the target environments, or if greater independence and autonomy are desired, then teaching self-delivery of antecedent stimuli is an excellent approach, even though it involves instructing the learner in both the behaviors involved in self-control and in how the self-control is to be applied to the target skill (e.g., Wacker & Greenbaum, 1984). For example, the learner could use a wallet-size booklet of photos as cues to the skill steps. If carefully instructed, the self-control skill itself can generalize to be used with other skills in other situations. A related approach to this skill is to teach peers, friends, parents, or an interpreter to deliver the special additional stimuli unobtrusively (e.g., Laski, Charlop, & Schreibman, 1988).

2. *If the problem is that the skill is performed when it should not be,* it is important to review carefully the instructional history to make sure that the appropriate "not-conditions" have been taught. Instruction that focuses on where, when, and how a skill is to be used, but fails to include teaching examples of where, when, and how the skill is *not* appropriate (Becker, 1986), may result in generalization problems in which the student responds inappropriately in new situations. For example, a child may be expected to wait until all of the family is served before beginning a meal, but may begin eating immediately when his plate is put in front of him. In that case, it is important to ensure that the child has been successfully taught (a) to "wait until all are served before eating" and (b) for the length of time required by the family situation (the fluency aim might vary between 90 seconds and 10 minutes).

3. *If the skill is performed incorrectly or if an inappropriate behavior occurs,* it is important to determine whether the "error response" is followed by the reinforcer that should be available only for competent demonstration of the target skill, or by a different, but preferred, reinforcer. In those cases, the inappropriate behavior competes with the target behavior for the reinforcer, or the reinforcer for the inappropriate behavior competes with the reinforcer available for the target behavior, respectively (Billingsley & Neel, 1985; Carr, 1988). If the reinforcer for the inappropriate behavior is preferred, then the inappropriate behavior will "ace out" the instructed one. For example, the learner might not begin to walk when told, "It's time for the bus." If the learner is then led or carried to the bus, he receives the natural reinforcer of riding the bus for a "no response." He might also be receiving an unconditioned reinforcer (the physical contact used to lead or carry him) for dawdling. In future situations, it is probable that he will wait to be led or carried rather than walk, because waiting behaviors have been reinforced.

To avoid the delivery of reinforcers following generalization failures, it is of critical importance to try to establish what the likely consequences will be before setting up initial probes of generalization. In the preceding example, the problem could have been avoided by using a bus that was acceptable for the student to miss for the first

probe, so that the bus driver was not forced into a situation in which the student *had* to get on the bus. Instead, if the student was allowed to miss the bus, the "no response" could be followed by natural consequences (e.g., not getting on the bus is followed by not getting to go on the field trip), which transforms the situation into an excellent instructional situation. In other instances in which an inappropriate behavior was performed in response to a new situation, an appropriate intervention might focus on instruction designed to make the desired behavior more efficient and/or reliable in its ability to produce a reinforcing effect (e.g., Horner & Day, 1991).

4. *If the skill generalizes once, but not again,* the skill actually generalized, but *did not maintain*. In that case, there is a failure in accessing the natural reinforcers that should exist for the skill. It may be that the skill is so successfully controlled by the reinforcers and contingencies programmed during instruction that the reinforcement available in natural situations is unable to adequately maintain skill responding. If natural events have been properly introduced and paired with conditioned or unconditioned reinforcers and have acquired reinforcing properties, and if the schedule of reinforcer delivery approximates the schedule in natural settings and there is still a problem, then there are two basic approaches: to determine whether reinforcement that should be available is actually available, and to determine whether there are responses that compete for the reinforcers that exist. If the boss never praises or if the daddy never hugs, then the probability of maintenance is reduced. Some form of training or prompting to teach persons in the environment to provide the reinforcers that should be available is a good alternative when reinforcement is inadequate or improperly delivered.

If it is not possible to rearrange the reinforcement contingencies in the natural environment, if the natural contingencies occur too infrequently for reliable control, or if personal independence is the goal, the learner can be taught to deliver his or her own reinforcers, supplementing or supplanting the natural reinforcers (cf. Liberty & Michael, 1985; Wolery et al., 1988). Self-delivered reinforcers can be as unobtrusive as a whispered "good" or a small tally on a pad of paper. Teaching self-reinforcement has the additional advantages of promoting independence from control by others and individual responsibility. It is also a process that can generalize to other skills.

Another alternative is to teach the learner to solicit reinforcement from individuals within the environment (e.g., Mank & Horner, 1987). This can be done by teaching such strategies as asking questions designed to evoke feedback (e.g., "Is this right?"), showing a finished product, demonstrating facial and body movements of expectancy under certain conditions, or even asking directly for the event ("I want a hug.").

TECHNOLOGICALLY SOUND "SYSTEMS"

The instructional approaches discussed earlier in this chapter offer a wide range of possibilities for developing effective programs. Often, because of the unique abilities and needs presented by each new student, having the ability to pick and choose from among such a cornucopia of possibilities will be a blessing to the teacher. It can also be helpful, however, to begin with a previously tested "system" for program design and instruction. In closing this chapter, we briefly describe a few of the more thoroughly tested systems available.

Precision Teaching

Precision Teaching (Lindsley, 1964, 1971, 1990) is a highly standardized approach for the evaluation of daily student progress in virtually any program. The basic steps in Precision Teaching include: (1) pinpoint—describe the behavior of interest, the instructional objective, and the instructional plan; (2) count—record the average number of correct behaviors and errors emitted during each minute of assessment; (3) chart—display the student's progress record on a standard

"celeration" chart; and (4) evaluate—decide whether, when, and how a program might be improved to facilitate student progress (White & Haring, 1980). Objective data-based decision rules have also been developed to facilitate evaluation (e.g., Albrecht, 1982; Liberty, 1972; White, 1985e).

The impact of Precision Teaching on student progress has been evaluated through a number of studies, and Precision Teaching projects have been validated as effective by the U.S. Department of Education's Joint Dissemination and Review Panel (White, 1986; Binder & Watkins, 1989; Binder, 1988).

Direct Instruction

Direct Instruction (Bereiter & Engelmann, 1966) entails a logical analysis of concepts and operations involved in a given task, followed by an empirical testing and refinement of instructional strategies designed to teach those concepts and operations. The application of Direct Instruction principles most fully explored in the development of programs for students with severe disabilities is *General Case Programming* (cf. Day & Horner, 1989; Sprague & Horner, 1984). To facilitate proper generalization of a skill, three types of stimuli are considered: positive stimuli (S^+), which should evoke the skill (e.g., a vending machine); negative stimuli (S^-), which should suppress the use of a skill (e.g., an "out of order" sign); and irrelevant stimuli (S^i), stimuli that might accidentally come to control performances, but that should not (e.g., a particular color for a vending machine). The task of the instructional program designer is to select the fewest number of positive, negative, and irrelevant stimuli possible that will adequately represent the "universe" of situations to which generalization is desired, and then to arrange the presentation of those stimuli in a manner that will facilitate learning (Binder and Watkins, 1990).

The effectiveness of Direct Instruction has been evaluated through many studies. Perhaps the most dramatic evidence of effectiveness was obtained via Project Follow Through, a federally funded study that has been called the largest and most expensive social experiment ever undertaken (Watkins, 1988). Applications of the principles of Direct Instruction, and especially the use of General Case Programming, have been most thoroughly investigated by Horner and his colleagues (cf. Day & Horner, 1989; Sprague & Horner, 1984).

The Individualized Curriculum Sequencing Model

The Individualized Curriculum Sequencing Model (ICS) (Guess et al., 1978) is a strategy for integrating several of a student's IEP objectives into a cohesive training sequence. ICS focuses on skill clusters—skills that can be learned independently of one another, but that often occur together or in various sequences during daily living, and so might be taught together. For example, shoe tying can be taught alone, but most often occurs naturally in the context of an entire dressing sequence, and dressing is often part of the more extended routine of getting up, washing, brushing teeth, dressing, and going down for breakfast. Arranging instruction for all those skills within the context of an extended routine improves the student's opportunity to encounter natural stimuli and consequences (Sailor & Guess, 1983).

Because the ICS model represents the combination of several strategies that have been studied separately (see earlier sections of this chapter), its effectiveness is often assumed. Studies of the complete model, although somewhat rare, tend to confirm that assumption (cf. Bambara et al., 1988).

IMPACT

IMPACT (Neel & Billingsley, 1989) is a functional curriculum for students with moderate to severe disabilities. It has many features in common with the ICS model, but provides more specific suggestions for evaluating skill development needs, establishing instructional priorities, and arranging instruction.

IMPACT has several characteristics, including: (1) an analysis of the functional intents of the student—determining what the *student* wants to accomplish, instead of simply looking at what *we* think is important, (2) integrating traditional related services into a comprehensive instructional program, (3) teaching skills that are critical for maintaining the student in the least restrictive environment, (4) developing skills to a level of fluency and proficiency that ensures their maintenance after instruction has been terminated, (5) teaching skills that allow students to access and function successfully within an ever-increasing number of natural environments, and (6) evaluating the ultimate success of instruction in terms of the application of skills in appropriate environments outside the instructional situation.

Critical features of the IMPACT curriculum are drawn from the best-practices literature reviewed earlier in this chapter, and so are relatively well researched. In addition, data related specifically to the IMPACT model have been provided by Donnellan and Neel (1985), Neel, Billingsley, & Lambert (1983), and Kayser et al. (1986). A complete overview of the IMPACT curriculum, its logic, and the procedures for its implementation may be found in Neel and Billingsley (1989).

The Teaching Research Curriculum

Unlike the ICS model and IMPACT, the Teaching Research Curriculum (TRC) represents a detailed, step-by-step curriculum for the development of individual skills in four major domains: gross motor, fine motor, self-help (self-feeding, dressing, personal hygiene, table skills), and cognitive skills (personal information, prereading and reading, writing, number concepts). Each curricular target is broken down into subordinate behaviors, the terminal objective, prerequisite skills, phases of skill development, and instructional steps. A list of suggested materials, materials for placement assessments, guidelines for assessing progress, and a set of teaching notes are also provided. Unlike the ICS model and IMPACT, the TRC system provides no guidelines for teaching skills in clusters or naturally occurring routines, but it could be adapted to employ those instructional approaches.

The TRC is one of the most thoroughly tested curricula ever developed (cf. Fredericks et al., 1979), and the Teaching Research Model as a whole was validated by the U.S. Department of Education's Joint Dissemination and Review Panel. The complete curriculum is available in several volumes (e.g., Fredericks et al., 1980a, 1980b).

SUMMARY

The systems described briefly in the preceding section range from the completely "contentless" evaluation strategies of Precision Teaching to the Teaching Research Curriculum that specifies precisely what, when, and how skills should be taught. Between those extremes Direct Instruction represents a set of principles for developing effective instructional programs and selecting instructional "exemplars"; the Individualized Curriculum Sequencing Model provides general strategies for identifying and teaching functional skill clusters; and IMPACT extends the concept of clusters and routines by providing specific procedures for identifying and prioritizing routines, integrating other services, forming partnerships with teachers, parents, and others, and evaluating the impact of instruction on behavior in nonschool settings.

Each of these standard systems is based largely on validated "best practices," and each has been found to be effective in meeting the needs of students with severe disabilities. However, it is not enough to pick a system that has proven to be effective in the past. Student progress must be continually evaluated, and if the student is not progressing satisfactorily, the program should be changed. Ultimately, an instructional program can be considered "technologically sound" only to the degree that it meets the needs of the individual pupil *now,* not just in the past.

REFERENCES

Aeschleman, S. R., & Williams, M. L. (1989). A test of the response deprivation hypothesis in a multiple-response context. *American Journal on Mental Retardation, 93,* 345–353.

Alberto, P. A., & Troutman, A. C. (1986). *Applied behavior analysis for teachers* (2nd ed.). Columbus, OH: Charles E. Merrill.

Alberto, P., Jobes, N., Sizemore, A., & Doran, D. (1980). A comparison of individual and group instruction across response tasks. *The Journal of the Association for the Severely Handicapped, 5,* 285–293.

Albin, R. W., & Horner, R. H. (1988). Generalization with precision. In R. H. Horner, G. Dunlap, & R. L. Koegel (Eds.), *Generalization and maintenance: Life-style changes in applied settings* (pp. 99–120). Baltimore: Paul H. Brookes Publishing Co.

Albrecht, P. (1982). *Data decision rules.* Paper presented at the Second Annual Precision Teaching Conference. Orlando, Florida.

Anderson, S., & Spradlin, J. (1980). The generalized effects of productive labeling training involving common object classes. *The Journal of the Association for the Severely Handicapped, 5,* 143–157.

Ault, M. J., Wolery, M., Doyle, P. M., & Gast, D. L. (1989). Review of comparative studies in the instruction of students with moderate and severe handicaps. *Exceptional Children, 55,* 346–356.

Bailey, D., & Wolery, M. (1984). *Teaching infants and preschoolers with handicaps.* Columbus, OH: Charles E. Merrill.

Bambara, L. M., Warren, S. F., & Komisar, S. (1988). The individualized curriculum sequencing model: Effects on skill acquisition and generalization. *The*

Journal of The Association for Persons with Severe Handicaps, 13, 8–19.

Banks, M. E., & Baer, D. M. (1966). Chaining in human learning. Working Paper 138. Unpublished manuscript. Parsons, KS: Parsons Research Center.

Barrett, B. (1979). Communitization and the measured message of normal behavior. In R. York & E. Edgar (Eds.), *Teaching the severely handicapped*, vol. 4 (pp. 301–318). Seattle: American Association for the Education of the Severely/Profoundly Handicapped.

Becker, W. (1986). *Applied psychology for teachers: A behavioral cognitive approach.* Chicago: Science Research Associates, Inc.

Bellamy, G. T., Horner, R. H., & Inman, D. P. (1979). *Vocational habilitation of severely retarded adults: A direct service technology.* Baltimore: University Park Press, 1979.

Bereiter, C., & Engelmann, S. (1966). *Teaching disadvantaged children in the preschool.* Englewood Cliffs, NJ: Prentice Hall.

Bijou, S. W. (1981). Behavioral teaching of young handicapped children: Problems of application and implementation. In S. W. Bijou & R. Ruiz (Eds.), *Behavior modification: Contributions to education* (pp. 97–110). Hillsdale, NJ: Lawrence Erlbaum.

Billingsley, F. F. (1987). A probe intermix procedure for fading response prompts. *Behavioral Disorders, 12*, 111–116.

Billingsley, F.F., & Neel, R.S. (1985). Competing behaviors and their effects on skill generalization and maintenance. *Analysis and Interventions in Developmental Disabilities, 5*, 357–372.

Billingsley, F. F., & Romer, L. T. (1983). Response prompting and the transfer of stimulus control: Methods, research, and a conceptual framework. *The Journal of the Association for the Severely Handicapped, 8*, 3–12.

Binder, C. (1988). Precision teaching: Measuring and attaining exemplary academic achievement. *Youth Policy* (July) 12–14.

Binder, C., & Watkins, C. L. (1989). Promoting effective instructional methods: Solutions to America's educational crisis. *Future Choices, Youth Policy Institute, 1*(3), 33–39.

Binder, C., & Watkins, C. L. (1990). Precision teaching and direct instruction: Measurably superior instructional technology in schools. Draft of a paper submitted for publication and distributed at the Ninth Annual Precision Teaching Conference, Boston, Massachusetts, October 31–November 3.

Browder, D. M. (1987). *Assessment of individuals with severe handicaps: An applied behavior approach to life skills assessment.* Baltimore: Paul H. Brookes Publishing Co.

Browder, D. M. (1991). *Assessment of individuals with severe disabilities: An applied behavior approach to life skills assessment* (2nd ed.). Baltimore: Paul H. Brookes Publishing Co.

Brown, F., Evans, I. M., Weed, K. A., & Owen, V. (1987). Delineating functional competencies: A component model. *The Journal of The Association for Persons with Severe Handicaps, 12*, 117–124.

Brown, F., Holvoet, J., Guess, D., & Mulligan, M. (1980). The individualized curriculum sequencing model (111): Small group instruction. *The Journal of the Association for the Severely Handicapped, 5*, 352–367.

Carnine, D. (1992). Expanding the notion of teachers' rights: Access to tools that work. *Journal of Applied Behavior Analysis, 25*, 13–19.

Carr, E. A. (1988). Functional equivalence as a mechanism of response generalization. In R. H. Horner, G. Dunlap, & R. L. Koegel (Eds.), *Generalization and maintenance: Life-style changes in applied settings* (pp. 221–241). Baltimore: Paul H. Brookes Publishing Co.

Carr, E. G., & Durand, V. M. (1985). Reducing behavior problems through functional communication training. *Journal of Applied Behavior Analysis, 18*, 111–126.

Chandler, L., Fowler, S., & Lubeck, R. (1992). An analysis of the effects of multiple setting events on the social behavior of preschool children with special needs. *Journal of Applied Behavior Analysis, 25*, 249–263.

Charlop, M. H., & Walsh, M. E. (1986). Increasing autistic children's spontaneous verbalizations of affection: An assessment of time delay and peer modeling procedures. *Journal of Applied Behavior Analysis, 19*, 307–314.

Cipani, E. (1987). Errorless learning technology: Theory, research, and practice. *Advances in Developmental Disorders, 1*, 237–275.

Collins, B. C., Gast, D. L., Ault, M. J., & Wolery, M. (1990). *Small group instruction: Guidelines for teachers of students with moderate to severe handi-caps.* Lexington, KY: Group Errorless Teaching Strategies Research Project, University of Kentucky.

Cooper, J. O., Heron, T. E., & Heward, W. L. (1987). Applied behavior analysis. Columbus, OH: Charles E. Merrill.

Cosden, M. A., & Haring, T. G. (1992). Cooperative learning in the classroom: Contingencies, group interactions, and students with special needs. *Journal of Behavioral Education, 2,* 53–71.

Crist, K., Walls, R. T., & Haught, P. A. (1984). Degrees of specificity in task analysis. *American Journal of Mental Deficiency, 89,* 67–74.

Csapo, M. (1981). Comparison of two prompting procedures to increase response fluency among severely handicapped learners. *The Journal of the Association for the Severely Handicapped, 6*(1), 39–47.

Day, H. M. (1987). Comparison of two prompting procedures to facilitate skill acquisition among severely mentally retarded adolescents. *American Journal of Mental Deficiency, 4,* 366–372.

Day, H. M., & Horner, R. H. (1989). Building response classes: A comparison of two procedures for teaching generalized pouring to learners with severe disabilities. *Journal of Applied Behavior Analysis, 22,* 223–229.

Deitz, S. M., & Malone, L.W. (1985). Stimulus control terminology. *The Behavior Analyst, 8,* 259–264.

Demchak, M. A. (1990). Response prompting and fading methods: A review. *American Journal on Mental Retardation, 94,* 603–615.

Donnellan, A. M., & Neel, R. S. (1985). New directions in educating students with autism. In R. H. Horner, L. H. Meyer, & H. D. B. Fredericks (Eds.), *Education of learners with severe handicaps: Exemplary service strategies* (pp. 99–126). Baltimore: Paul H. Brookes Publishing Co.

Dowler, D. L., Walls, R. T., Haught, P. A., & Zawlocki, R. J. (1984). Effects of preference, prompt, and task agreement on the discrimination learning of mentally retarded adults. *American Journal of Mental Deficiency, 88,* 428–434.

Dunlap, G. (1984). The influence of task variation and maintenance tasks on the learning and affect of autistic children. *Journal of Experimental Child Psychology, 37,* 41–64.

Dunlap, G., & Koegel, R. L. (1980). Motivating autistic children through stimulus variation. *Journal of Applied Behavior Analysis, 13,* 619–627.

Egel, A. L. (1981). Reinforcer variation: Implications for motivating developmentally disabled children. *Journal of Applied Behavior Analysis, 14,* 345–350.

Etzel, B. C., & LeBlanc, J. M. (1979). *Journal of Autism and Developmental Disorders, 9,* 361–382.

Etzel, B. C., LeBlanc, J. M., Schilmoeller, K. J., & Stella, M. E. (1981). Stimulus control procedures in the education of young children. In S. W. Bijou and R. Ruiz (Eds.), *Behavior modification: Contributions to education* (pp. 3–37). Hillsdale, NJ: Lawrence Erlbaum.

Falvey, M. A. (1989). *Community-based curriculum: Instructional strategies for students with severe handicaps* (2nd ed.). Baltimore: Paul H. Brookes Publishing Co.

Falvey, M., Brown, L., Lyon, S., Baumgart, D., & Schroeder, J. (1980). Strategies for using cues and correction procedures. In W. Sailor, B. Wilcox, & L. Brown (Eds.), *Methods of instruction for severely handicapped students* (pp. 109–133). Baltimore: Paul H. Brookes Publishing Co.

Fisher, W., Piazza, C. C., Bowman, L. G., Hagopian, L. P., Owen, J. C., & Slevin, I. A comparison of two approaches for identifying reinforcers for persons with severe and profound disabilities. *Journal of Applied Behavioral Analysis, 25,* 491–498.

Ford, A., & Mirenda, P. (1984). Community instruction: A natural cues and corrections decision model. *The Journal of The Association for Persons with Severe Handicaps, 9,* 79–88.

Foxx, R. M. (1982). *Increasing behaviors of severely retarded and autistic persons.* Champaign, IL: Research Press.

Foxx, R. M., & Azrin, N. H. (1973). *Toilet training the retarded: A rapid program for day and nighttime independent toileting.* Champaign, IL: Research Press.

Fredericks, H. D., Hanks, S., Makohon, L., Fruin, C., Moore, W., Piazza-Templeman, T., Blair, L., Dalke, B., Hawkins, P., Coen, M., Renfroe-Burton, S., Bunse, C., Farnes, T., Moses, C., Toews, J., McGuckin, A. M., Moore, B., Riggs, C., Baldwin, V., Anderson, R., Ashbacher, V., Carter, V., Gage, M. A., Rogers, G., & Samples, B. (1980a). *The teaching research curriculum for moderately and* severely handicapped: Gross and fine motor. Springfield, IL: Charles C. Thomas.

Fredericks, H. D., Makohon, L., Fruin, C., Moore, W., Piazza-Templeman, T., Blair, L., Dalke, B., Hawkins, P., Coen, M., Renfroe-Burton, S., Bunse, C., Farnes, T., Moses, C., Toews, J., McGuckin, A. M., Moore, B., Riggs, C., Baldwin, V., Anderson, R., Ashbacher, V., Carter, V., Gage, M. A., Rogers, G., & Samples, B. (1980b). *The teaching research curriculum for moderately and severely handicapped: Self-help and cognitive.* Springfield, IL: Charles C. Thomas.

Gast, D. L., Wolery, M., Ault, M. J., Doyle, P. M., & Alig (1988). *How to use time delay.* Lexington, KY: University of Kentucky, Department of Special Education.

Godby, S., Gast, D. L., & Wolery, M. (1987). A comparison of time delay and system of least prompts in teaching object identification. *Research in Developmental Disabilities, 8,* 283–306.

Gold, M. W. (1972). Stimulus factors in skill training of retarded adolescents on a complex assembly task: Acquisition, transfer, and retention. *American Journal of Mental Deficiency, 76,* 517–526.

Guess, D., Horner, D., Utley, B., Holvoet, J., Maxon, D, Tucker, D., & Warren, S. (1978) A functional curriculum sequencing model for teaching the severely handicapped. *AAESPH Review, 3,* 202–215.

Handen, B. L., & Zane, T. (1987). Delayed prompting: A review of procedural variations and results. *Research in Developmental Disabilities, 8,* 307–330.

Haring, N. G., (Ed.). (1988). *Generalization for students with severe handicaps: Strategies and solutions.* Seattle: University of Washington Press.

Haring, N. G., & Liberty, K. A. (1990). Matching strategies with performance in facilitating generalization. *Focus on Exceptional Children, 22*(8), 1–16.

Haring, N., Liberty, K., & White, O. (1980). Rules for data-based strategy decisions in instructional programs: Current research and instructional implications. In W. Sailor, B. Wilcox, & L. Brown (Eds.), *Methods of instruction for severely handicapped students* (pp. 159–192). Baltimore: Paul H. Brookes Publishing Co.

Haring, N. G., Liberty, K. A., & White, O. R. (1981). *An investigation of phases of learning and facilitating instructional events for the severely/profoundly handicapped* (Final project report). (U.S. Department of Education, Contract No. G007500593). Seattle: University of Washington, College of Education.

Haring, N. G., White, O. R., & Liberty, K. A. (1976). *An investigation of phases of learning and facilitating instructional events for the severely/profoundly handicapped* (Second annual report). (U.S. Department of Education, Contract No. G007500593). Seattle: University of Washington, College of Education.

Haring, T., & Breen, C. (1992). A peer-mediated social network intervention to enhance the social integration of persons with moderate and severe disabilities. *Journal of Applied Behavior Analysis, 25,* 319–333.

Haught, P., Walls, R. T., & Crist, K. (1984). Placement of prompts, length of task, and level of retardation in learning complex assembly tasks. *American Journal of Mental Deficiency, 89,* 60–66.

Horner, R. D. (1971). Establishing use of crutches by a mentally retarded spina bifida child. *Journal of Applied Behavior Analysis, 4,* 183–189.

Horner, R. H. (1988, May). Functional analysis in applied settings. In A. J. Cuvo (Chair), *Behavior analysis of community referenced skills: Issues in promoting and transferring stimulus control.* Symposium conducted at the 14th annual convention of the Association for Behavior Analysis, Philadelphia.

Horner, R., Bellamy, T., & Colvin, G. (1984). Responding in the presence of non-trained stimuli: Implications of generalization error patterns. *The Journal of The Association for Persons with Severe Handicaps, 9,* 287–296.

Horner, R., & Billingsley, F. (1988). The effect of competing behavior on generalization and maintenance of adaptive behaviors in applied settings. In R. Horner, G. Dunlap, & R. Koegel (Eds.), *Generalization and maintenance: Lifestyle changes in applied settings* (pp. 197–220). Baltimore: Paul H. Brookes Publishing Co.

Horner, R. H., & Day, M. (1991). The effect of response efficiency on functionally equivalent competing behaviors. *Journal of Applied Behavior Analysis, 24,* 719–732.

Horner, R. H., Day, M., Sprague, J. R., O'Brien, M., & Heathfield, L. T. (1991). Interspersed requests: A nonaversive procedure for decreasing aggression and self-injury during instruction. *Journal of Applied Behavior Analysis, 24,* 265–278.

Horner, R. H., Dunlap, G., & Koegel, R. L., (Eds.). (1988). *Generalization and maintenance: Life-style changes in applied settings.* Baltimore: Paul H. Brookes Publishing Co.

Horner, R. H., McDonnell, J. J., & Bellamy, G. T. (1986). Teaching generalized skills: General case instruction in simulation and community settings. In R. H. Horner, L. H. Meyer, & H. D. B. Fredericks (Eds.), *Education of learners with severe handicaps: Exemplary service strategies* (pp. 289–314). Baltimore: Paul H. Brookes Publishing Co.

Horner, R. H., Sprague, J., & Wilcox, B. (1982). General case programming for community activities. In B. Wilcox & G. T. Bellamy (Eds.), *Design of high school programs for severely handicapped students* (pp. 61–98). Baltimore: Paul H. Brookes Publishing Co.

Hourcade, J. J. (1988). Effectiveness of gestural and physical guidance prompts as a function of type of task. *Education and Training in Mental Retardation, 23,* 38–42.

Irvin, L. K., & Bellamy, G. T. (1977). Manipulation of stimulus features in vocational-skill training of severely retarded individuals. *American Journal of Mental Deficiency, 81,* 486–491.

Johnson, D. W., & Johnson, R. T. (1989). Cooperative learning and mainstreaming. In R. Gaylord-Ross (Ed.), *Integration strategies for students with handicaps.* Baltimore: Paul H. Brookes Publishing Co.

Kamps, D. M., Leonard, B. R., Vernon, S., Dugan, E. P., Delquadri, J., Gershon, B., Wade, L., & Folk, L. (1992). Teaching social skills to students with autism to increase peer interactions in an integrated first-grade classroom. *Journal of Applied Behavior Analysis, 25,* 281–288.

Kayser, J. E., Billingsley, F. F., & Neel, R. S. (1986). A comparison of in-context and traditional instructional approaches: Total task, single trial versus backward chaining, multiple trials. *The Journal of The Association for Persons with Severe Handicaps, 11,* 28–38.

Kleinert, H. L., & Gast, D. L. (1982). Teaching a multihandicapped adult manual signs using a constant time delay procedure. *The Journal of the Association for the Severely Handicapped, 6*(4), 25–32.

Koegel, R. L., & Egel, A. L. (1979). Motivating autistic children. *Journal of Abnormal Psychology, 88,* 418–426.

Konarski, E. A. (1987). Effects of response deprivation on the instrumental performance of mentally retarded persons. *American Journal of Mental Deficiency, 91,* 537–542.

Konarski, E. A., Johnson, M. R., Crowell, C. R., & Whitman, T. L. (1980). Response deprivation and reinforcement in applied settings: A preliminary analysis. *Journal of Applied Behavior Analysis, 13,* 595–609.

Laski, K. E., Charlop, M. H., & Schreibman, L. (1988). Training parents to use the natural language paradigm to increase their autistic children's speech. *Journal of Applied Behavior Analysis, 21,* 391–400.

Lee, J., O'Shea, & Dykes, M. K. (1987). Teacher wait-time: Performance of developmentally delayed and non-delayed young children. *Education and Training in Mental Retardation, 22,* 176–184.

Liberty, K. (1972). *Decide for progress: Dynamic aims and data decisions* (Working paper). Eugene: University of Oregon, Regional Resource Center for Handicapped Children.

Liberty, K. A. (1985). Enhancing instruction for maintenance, generalization, and adaptation. In K. C. Lakin & R. H. Bruininks (Eds.), *Strategies for achieving community integration of developmentally disabled citizens* (pp. 29–71). Baltimore: Paul H. Brookes Publishing Co.

Liberty, K. A., & Billingsley, F. F. (1988). Strategies to improve generalization. In N. G. Haring (Ed.), *Generalization for students with severe handicaps: Strategies and solutions.* Seattle: University of Washington Press.

Liberty, K., Haring, N., White, O., & Billingsley, F. (1988). A technology for the future: Decision rules for generalization. *Education and Training in Mental Retardation, 23,* 315–326.

Liberty, K. A., & Michael, L. J. (1985). Teaching retarded students to reinforce their own behavior: A review of process and operation in the current literature. In N. Haring (Principal Investigator), *Investigating the problem of skill generalization* (3rd ed.). (U.S. Department of Education, Contract No. 300-82-0364.) Seattle: University of Washington, College of Education.

Liberty, K. A., White, O. R., Billingsley, F. F., & Haring, N. G. (1988). Effectiveness of decision rules for generalization. In N. Haring (Ed.), *Generalization for students with severe handicaps: Strategies and solutions* (pp. 101–120). Seattle: University of Washington Press.

Lindsley, O. R. (1964). Direct measurement and prostheses of retarded behavior. *Journal of Education, 147,* 62–81.

Lindsley, O. R. (1971). From Skinner to Precision Teaching: The child knows best. In J. B. Jordan & L. S. Robins (Eds.), *Let's try doing something else kind of thing: Behavior principles and the exceptional child* (pp. 1–11). Reston, VA: The Council for Exceptional Children.

Lindsley, O. R. (1990). Precision Teaching: By teachers for children. *Teaching Exceptional Children, 22,* 10–15.

Lindsley, O. R. (1992a). Why aren't effective teaching tools widely adopted? *Journal of Applied Behavior Analysis, 25,* 21–26.

Lindsley, O. R. (1992b). Precision Teaching: Discoveries and effects. *Journal of Applied Behavior Analysis, 25,* 51–57.

Luyben, P. D., Funk, D. M., Morgan, J. K., Clark, K. A., & Delulio, D. W. (1986). Team sports for the severely retarded: Training a side-of-the-foot soccer pass using a maximum-to-minimum prompt reduction strategy. *Journal of Applied Behavior Analysis, 19,* 431–436.

Mank, D. M., & Horner, R. H. (1987). Self-recruited feedback: A cost-effective procedure for maintaining behavior. *Research in Developmental Disabilities, 8,* 91–112.

Martin, G., Koop, S., Turner, G., & Hanel, F. (1981). Backward chaining versus total task presentation to teach assembly tasks to severely retarded persons. *Behavior Research of Severe Developmental Disabilities, 2,* 117–136.

McDonnell, J. (1987). The effects of time delay and increasing prompt hierarchy strategies on the acquisition of purchasing skills to students with moderate handicaps. *The Journal of The Association for Persons with Severe Handicaps, 12,* 227–236.

McDonnell, J., & Ferguson, B. (1989). A comparison of time delay and decreasing prompt hierarchy strategies in teaching banking skills to students with moderate handicaps. *Journal of Applied Behavior Analysis, 22,* 85–91.

McDonnell, J., & Laughlin, B. (1989). A comparison of backward and concurrent chaining strategies in teaching community skills. *Education and Training in Mental Retardation, 24,* 230–238.

McDonnell, J., & McFarland, S. (1988). A comparison of forward and concurrent chaining strategies in teaching laundromat skills to students with severe handicaps. *Research in Developmental Disabilities, 9,* 177–194.

Miller, U. C., & Test, D. W. (1989). A comparison of constant time delay and most-to-least prompting in teaching laundry skills to students with moderate retardation. *Education and Training in Mental Retardation, 24,* 363–370.

Mosk, M. D., & Bucher, B. (1984). Prompting and stimulus shaping procedures for teaching visual-motor skills to retarded children. *Journal of Applied Behavior Analysis, 17,* 23–34.

Mulligan, M., Guess, D., Holvoet, J., & Brown, F. (1980). The individualized curriculum sequencing model (1): Implication from research on massed, distributed, or spaced trial training. *The Journal of the Association for the Severely Handicapped, 5,* 325–336.

Neef, N., Iwata, B., & Page, T. (1978). Public transportation training: In vivo versus classroom instruction. *Journal of Applied Behavior Analysis, 11,* 331–344.

Neel, R. S., & Billingsley, F. F. (1989). *IMPACT: A functional curriculum handbook for students with moderate to severe disabilities.* Baltimore: Paul H. Brookes Publishing Co.

Neel, R. S., Billingsley, F. F., & Lambert, C. (1983). IMPACT: A functional curriculum for educating autistic youth in natural environments. In R. B. Rutherford, Jr. (Ed.), *Monograph in behavioral disorders: Severe behavior disorders of children and youth* (Series No. 6, pp. 40–50). Reston, VA: Council for Children with Behavioral Disorders.

O'Brien, F., Azrin, N., & Bugle, C. (1972). Training profoundly retarded children to stop crawling. *Journal of Applied Behavior Analysts, 5,* 131–137.

Pancsofar, E. L., & Bates, P. (1985). The impact of the acquisition of successive training exemplars on generalization. *The Journal of The Association for Persons with Severe Handicaps, 10,* 95–104.

Panyan, M. (1980). *How to use shaping.* Austin, TX: PRO-ED.

Popovich, D. (1981). *Effective educational and behavioral programming for severely and profoundly handicapped students: A manual for teachers and aides.* Baltimore: Paul H. Brookes Publishing Co.

Reid, D. H., & Favell, J. E. (1984). Group instruction with persons who have severe disabilities: A critical review. *The Journal of The Association for Persons with Severe Handicaps, 9,* 167–177.

Rusch, F. R., Rose, T., & Greenwood, C. R. (1988). *Introduction to behavior analysis in special education.* Englewood Cliffs, NJ: Prentice Hall.

Sailor, W., & Guess, D. (1983). *Severely handicapped students: An instructional design.* Boston: Houghton Mifflin.

Schoen, S. F. (1986). Assistance procedures to facilitate the transfer of stimulus control: Review and analysis. *Education and Training of the Mentally Retarded, 21,* 62–74.

Schoen, S. F. (1989) Teaching students with handicaps to learn through observation. *Teaching Exceptional Children, 22*(1), 18-21.

Schoen, S. F., Lentz, F. E., & Suppa, R. J. (1988). An examination of two prompt fading procedures and opportunities to observe in teaching handicapped preschoolers self-help skills. *Journal of the Division for Early Childhood, 12,* 349–358.

Schreibman, L. (1975). Effects of within-stimulus and extra-stimulus prompting on discrimination learning in autistic children. *Journal of Applied Behavior Analysis, 8,* 92–112.

Schreibman, L., Charlop, M. H., & Koegel, R. L. (1982). Teaching autistic children to use extra-stimulus prompts. *Journal of Experimental Child Psychology, 33,* 475–491.

Schroeder, G., & Baer, D. M. (1972). Effects of concurrent versus serial training on generalized vocal imitations in retarded children. *Developmental Psychology, 6,* 293–301.

Schuster, J. W., & Griffen, A. K. (1990). Using time delay with task analyses. *Teaching Exceptional Children, 22*(4), 49–53.

Slavin, R.E. (1989, June). PET and the pendulum: Faddism in education and how to stop it. *Phi Delta Kappan,* pp. 752–758.

Snell, M. E. (1982). Analysis of time delay procedures in teaching daily living skills to retarded adults. *Analysis and Intervention in Developmental Disabilities, 2,* 139–155.

Snell, M. E., & Zirpoli, T. J. (1987). Intervention strategies. In M. E. Snell (Ed.), *Systematic instruction of persons with severe handicaps* (3rd ed.) (pp. 110–149). Columbus, OH: Charles E. Merrill.

Spooner, F., & Spooner, D. (1984). A review of chaining techniques: Implications for future research and practice. *Education and Training of the Mentally Retarded, 19,* 114–124.

Spooner, F., Spooner, D., & Ulicny, G. (1986). Comparisons of modified backward chaining: Backward chaining with leap-aheads and reverse chaining with leap-aheads. *Education and Treatment of Children, 9,* 122–134.

Spooner, F., Weber, L. H., & Spooner, D. (1983). The effects of backward chaining and total task presentation on the acquisition of complex tasks by severely retarded adolescents and adults. *Education and Treatment of Children, 6,* 401–420.

Sprague, J. R., & Horner, R. H. (1984). The effects of single instance, multiple instance, and general case training on generalized vending machine use by moderately and severely handicapped students. *Journal of Applied Behavior Analysis, 17,* 273–278.

Steege, M. W., Wacker, D. P., & McMahon, C. M. (1987). Evaluation of the effectiveness and efficiency of two stimulus prompt strategies with severely handicapped students. *Journal of Applied Behavior Analysis, 20,* 293–299.

Sternberg, L., McNerney, C., & Pegnatore, L. (1985). Developing co-active imitative behaviors with profoundly mentally handicapped students. *Education and Training of the Mentally Retarded, 20,* 260–267.

Stokes, T., & Baer, D. (1977). An implicit technology of generalization. *Journal of Applied Behavior Analysis, 10,* 349–367.

Striefel, S., & Cadez, M. J. (1983). *Serving children and adolescents with developmental disabilities in the special education classroom: Proven methods.* Baltimore: Paul H. Brookes Publishing Co.

Terrace, H. S. (1963). Errorless transfer of a discrimination across two continua. *Journal of the Experimental Analysis of Behavior, 6,* 223–232.

Tucker, D., & Berry, G. (1980. Teaching severely multihandicapped students to put on their own hearing aids. *Journal of Applied Behavior Analysis, 13,* 65–75.

Valconte, G., Roberson, W., Reid, W. R., & Wolking, W. D. (1989). Effects of wait-time and intertrial interval durations on learning by children with multiple handicaps. *Journal of Applied Behavior Analysis, 22,* 43–55.

Wacker, D. P., & Greenbaum, F. T. (1984). Efficacy of a verbal training sequence on the sorting performance of moderately and severely retarded adolescents. *American Journal of Mental Deficiency, 88,* 653–660.

Walls, R. T., Haught, P., & Dowler, D. L. (1982). Moments of transfer of stimulus control in practical assembly tasks by mentally retarded adults. *American Journal of Mental Deficiency, 87,* 309–315.

Walls, R. T., Zane, T., & Ellis, W. D. (1981). Forward and backward chaining, and whole task methods: Training assembly tasks in vocational rehabilitation. *Behavior Modification, 5,* 61–74.

Watkins, C. L. (1988, July). Project Follow Through: A story of the identification and neglect of effective instruction. *Youth Policy,* pp. 7–11.

Weeks, M., & Gaylord-Ross, R. (1981). Task difficulty and aberrant behavior in severely handicapped students. *Journal of Applied Behavior Analysis, 14,* 449–463.

Weld, E. M., & Evans, I. M. (1990). Effects of part versus whole instructional strategies on skill acquisition and excess behavior. *American Journal on Mental Retardation, 94,* 377–386.

White, O. R. (1984). Aim*star wars (setting aims that compete): Episode I. *Journal of Precision Teaching, 5,* 55–64.

White, O. R. (1985a). Aim*star wars (setting aims that compete): Episodes II and III. *Journal of Precision Teaching, 5,* 86–94.

White, O. R. (1985b). Aim*star wars (setting aims that compete): Episode IV. *Journal of Precision Teaching, 6,* 7–13.

White, O. R. (1985c). Aim*star wars (setting aims that compete): Episode V. *Journal of Precision Teaching, 6,* 30–34.

White, O. R. (1985d). Evaluation of severely mentally retarded populations. In D. Bricker and J. Filler (Eds.), *Severe mental retardation: From theory to practice* (pp. 161–184). Reston, VA: Council for Exceptional Children.

White, O. R. (1985e). Decisions, Decisions . . . . *B.C. Journal of Special Education, 9,* 305–320.

White, O. R. (1986). Precision teaching/precision learning. In B. Algozzine and L. Maheady (Eds.), *Exceptional Children* (Special issue: *In search of excellence: Instruction that works in special education classrooms*), *52,* 522–534. Reston, VA: Council for Exceptional Children.

White, O. (1988). Probing skill use. In N. Haring (Ed.), *Generalization for students with severe handicaps: Strategies and solutions* (pp. 131–141). Seattle: University of Washington Press.

White, O. R., & Haring, N. G. (1980). *Exceptional Teaching* (2nd ed.). Columbus, OH: Charles E. Merrill.

White, O. R., Liberty, K. A., Haring, N. G., Billingsley, F. F., Boer, M., Burrage, A., Connors, R., Farman, R., Fedorchak, G., Leber, B. D., Liberty, S., Miller, S., Opalski, C., Phifer, C., & Sessoms, I. (1988). Review and analysis of strategies for generalization. In N. Haring (Ed.), *Generalization for students with severe handicaps: Strategies and solutions* (pp. 13–52). Seattle: University of Washington Press.

Wilcox, B., & Bellamy, G. T. (1982). *Design of high school programs for severely handicapped students.* Baltimore: Paul H. Brookes Publishing Co.

Winterling, V., Dunlap, G., & O'Neill, R. (1987). The influence of task variation in the aberrant behavior of autistic students. *Education and Treatment of Children, 10,* 105–119.

Wolery, M., Ault, M. J., & Doyle, P. M. (1992). *Teaching students with moderate to severe disabilities: Use of response prompting strategies.* New York: Longman.

Wolery, M., Bailey, D. B., Jr., & Sugai, G. M. (1988). *Effective teaching: Principles and procedures of applied behavior analysis with exceptional students.* Boston: Allyn & Bacon.

Wolery, M., & Gast, D. L. (1984). Effective and efficient procedures for the transfer of stimulus control. *Topics in Early Childhood Special Education, 4,* 52–77.

Wolery, M., Gast, D. L., Kirk, K., & Schuster, J. (1988). Fading extra-stimulus prompts with autistic children using time delay. *Education and Treatment of Children, 11,* 29–44.

Wolfe, V. F., & Cuvo, A. J. (1978). Effects of within-stimulus and extra-stimulus prompting on letter discrimination by mentally retarded persons. *American Journal of Mental Deficiency, 83,* 297–303.

Wuerch, B. B., & Voeltz, L. M. (1982). *Longitudinal leisure skills for severely handicapped learners: The Ho'onanea curriculum component.* Baltimore: Paul H. Brookes Publishing Co.

Zane, T., Walls, R. T., & Thvedt, J. E. (1981). Prompting and fading guidance procedures: Their effect on chaining and whole task teaching strategies. *Education and Training in Mental Retardation, 16,* 125–135.

CHAPTER 5

NONAVERSIVE BEHAVIORAL INTERVENTION IN THE COMMUNITY

GLEN DUNLAP
JOLENEA FERRO
MARIA DEPERCZEL
Florida Mental Health Institute, University of South Florida

The goal of education for people with severe disabilities is to prepare them for a satisfying and useful life in the community. As reflected in the chapters of this book, such preparation is multifaceted. It includes systematic instruction in a variety of curricular domains, and it encompasses individualized programming and support for students who exhibit a diversity of strengths, needs, and challenges. Some of these students display behavior problems, including responses that are undesirable because they are dangerous or stigmatizing, or because they interfere with instructional efforts. Approaches for managing these undesirable behaviors have been the topic of substantial research efforts and considerable advocacy during the past few decades. As knowledge and experience have accumulated, and as people with disabilities have gained increasing entrance into our general society, the clear trend in behavior management has been toward interventions that are not only effective, but are also nonaversive. This chapter is intended to provide a framework for describing and understanding the character of nonaversive interventions, and to present an overview of some strategies that make up the nonaversive approach.

Nonaversive behavior management refers to a broad set of strategies that are designed to reduce behavior problems while preserving a student's rights to dignity and to interactions that are free from pain and humiliation. Nonaversive interventions minimize the use of punishment and aversive stimulation. They seek instead to reduce behavior problems in a proactive way by increasing desirable behaviors and enhancing the positive features of a student's environment and life-style. Nonaversive interventions are compatible with community-based programs because they seek to manage problem behaviors with methods that are acceptable in typical, integrated settings. In this chapter, we refer to the community as the range of environments that are inhabited by people who have disabilities and by people who are nondisabled. Such environments include schools, homes, workplaces, restaurants, stores, recreation settings, and other locales that are occupied by members of the general community (Falvey, 1989). Nonaversive interventions are part of the behavioral supports that foster community participation by people with severe disabilities.

This chapter, which offers a summary of nonaversive intervention in the community, consists of two main sections. The first provides descriptive and background information that is relevant to

Preparation of this manuscript was supported by Cooperative Agreement No. GOO87CO434 from the National Institute on Disability and Rehabilitation Research. However, the opinions are those of the authors, and no official endorsement should be inferred.

117

the current status of nonaversive interventions. Included in this section are descriptions of behavior problems, a brief overview of behavioral interventions and discussions of the controversy regarding aversive procedures, the development of nonaversive alternatives, some of the premises that underlie nonaversive approaches to behavior management, and a review of behavioral explanations for the presence of behavior problems in persons with severe disabilities. The second main section of the chapter is reserved for a presentation of components that make up the nonaversive armamentarium, including comprehensive and functional assessment, positive reinforcement, and antecedent and ecological manipulations. The final section of the chapter indicates that nonaversive intervention is a comprehensive approach that is represented best when it includes multiple components and strives for significant life-style improvements.

BEHAVIOR PROBLEMS EXHIBITED BY PERSONS WITH SEVERE DISABILITIES

Students with severe disabilities may engage in a variety of maladaptive behaviors that interfere with optimal community functioning. Behavior problems that require some form of intervention can include a range of potentially injurious and disruptive actions. Such behaviors can often result in injury to self or others, property destruction, and interference with skill acquisition and community involvement (Reichle, 1990). Specifically, self-injurious, aggressive, stereotypic and self-stimulatory, disruptive, and noncompliant responses that interfere with community participation are those behaviors that are discussed in this chapter as problematic, undesirable, and challenging.

Behaviors that may result in physical injury include self-inflicted head banging, slapping, pinching, scratching, and biting; eye-gouging; trichotillomania (i.e., hair pulling); rumination; vomiting; withholding oxygen; and pica (i.e., ingestion of inedible objects). Self-injurious behaviors (SIB) among students with autism and

retardation occur with greater frequency and severity than among individuals who are nondisabled and those with mild disabilities (Favell et al., 1982; Gast & Wolery, 1987). Rates of SIB among institutionalized individuals with mental retardation have been reported to be approximately 8 percent to 14 percent (Baumeister & Rollins, 1976; Maurice & Trudel, 1982). Although affecting only a small number of persons overall, self-injurious behaviors receive considerable attention because of the serious risks they pose for those who engage in such behavior.

Self-injurious behavior is especially serious, as it often results in physical injuries, including bleeding, bruising, permanent tissue damage, hearing or vision loss, and poisoning (from ingestion of harmful substances). Whereas self-injurious behaviors put the student in danger, aggressive behaviors may result in physical harm to others, including support personnel, family members, and friends. Aggressive behaviors take both physical and verbal forms and are directed toward others or property. Aggressive behaviors include hitting, kicking, pinching, punching, spitting, screaming, cursing, and throwing objects. Gast and Wolery (1987) reported that aggressive behaviors are included among the behavior problems most often identified by teachers of students with moderate or severe disabilities.

Although usually not dangerous, other behaviors are targets of intervention because they disrupt instructional activities and may limit opportunities for community involvement. Students with severe disabilities may engage in behaviors described as stereotypic. These actions occur with repetition (Baumeister, 1978), appear nonfunctional, and range widely—from rocking and arm flapping to mouthing objects or body parts. Sterotypic behaviors are frequently referred to as "self-stimulation"; however, this term implies a specific sensory purpose for the behavior, and that purpose may not be present in all cases (e.g., Durand & Carr, 1987).

Many maladaptive behaviors disrupt ongoing activities and interfere with other persons. These include tantrums, throwing objects, crying, yelling, and arguing. In addition, socially inappropriate activities such as perseveration, public masturbation, inappropriate toileting, feces smearing, and excessive messiness are considered problematic and are often targeted for intervention. Failure to respond appropriately to teacher requests and instructions (i.e., noncompliance) is similarly likely to result in behavioral treatment. Withdrawal, including social avoidance and elective mutism, may also be considered as a pattern of behavior that interferes with community involvement.

All of the behaviors described here increase the likelihood that the social environments of persons exhibiting them will be limited. Unusual behaviors often result in more restrictive placements (Danforth & Drabman, 1989), as well as avoidance by others, because they identify a person as being different. Furthermore, there is evidence that problem behaviors, including stereotypic responding, can interfere substantially with a student's acquisition and performance of skills (e.g., Koegel & Covert, 1982). In addition, some of the intervention procedures that have been used to manage serious problem behaviors may be restrictive and stigmatizing in and of themselves.

OVERVIEW OF BEHAVIOR
MANAGEMENT INTERVENTIONS

Systematic, replicable interventions for the behavior problems of individuals with severe disabilities emerged from operant psychology about 25 years ago. Initially, the research was conducted in highly controlled settings such as state hospitals and clinical laboratories, but investigations were also conducted in natural home environments. The early studies served to demonstrate that contingency management procedures can be effective in reducing behavior problems and increasing desirable behaviors. These studies typically used combinations of procedures to demonstrate the effectiveness of behavior modification interventions (e.g., Corte, Wolf, & Locke, 1971; Risley, 1968). For example, Bostow and Bailey (1969) addressed the aggressive responding of an institutionalized 7-year-old boy with a treatment package that included time-out and differential reinforcement. Each time the boy displayed aggressive behavior, he was placed in a time-out booth for a short period of time. For reinforcement, he was given small amounts of cookies, soda, or milk every time 2 minutes elapsed without aggression. This treatment produced dramatic reductions in the boy's disruptive responding.

The orderly manipulation of consequences for desirable and undesirable behaviors formed the basis and the essence of behavior management strategies in the 1960s and 1970s. The fundamental approach was to use the principles of positive reinforcement and punishment to modify behavior patterns. Frequent and powerful rewards were used to increase responses other than the targeted behavior problem, and, if necessary, punishers were used directly to suppress the undesirable behavior. Applied research in the area of behavior management tended to replicate these operations with assorted behavior problems (e.g., stereotypy, self-injury, aggression, tantrums) and with various stimuli used as the reinforcers and punishers. The stimuli that were used as positive reinforcers included favored foods, drinks, attention, tokens, and sensory stimulation. The stimulus events that were used as punishers ranged from time-out to a diversity of contingent aversives, such as slaps, electric shock, water mist, facial screening, forced exercise, noxious odors, noxious tastes, and overcorrection (see Axelrod & Apsche, 1983). In general, these strategies have been reported as successful in producing rapid decreases in the behavior problems of people with severe disabilities.

Although consequence manipulations have dominated the behavior management literature, other reports have shown that behavior problems can be influenced through additional kinds of procedures. These additional strategies have broadened the array of practical behavior management alternatives and have gained increasing recognition and popularity over the past decade. They can be divided roughly into two categories: (1) instructional strategies, which seek to reduce behavior problems by teaching specific skills, and (2)

stimulus-based interventions, which seek to reduce behavior problems by removing or ameliorating those antecedent stimuli that have been
shown to evoke the problem. Instructional strategies are designed to establish skills, such as communication or instruction following, that are
assumed to covary with the problem behavior. The
logic is that the establishment of these new functional competencies will replace the existing behavior problem. A number of studies have shown
recently that this approach can produce powerful
and durable effects (e.g., Carr & Durand, 1985b;
Durand & Carr, 1991; Gardner, Cole, Berry, &
Nowinski, 1983; Slifer, Ivancic, Parrish, Page, &
Burgio, 1986).

Stimulus-based interventions are designed to
prevent behavior problems by altering features of
the person's immediate environment and context.
This approach is based on the identification and
manipulation of stimulus events that control behavior problems. Such stimulus events may be almost anything, but are frequently such things as a
demanding instruction, an unpleasant task, or the
proximity of a disagreeable person. The associated intervention is to eliminate or modify the
stimulus and replace it with another stimulus that
controls more desirable behavior. As we discuss
later in this chapter, studies have demonstrated a
variety of strategies for accomplishing this objective (e.g., Carr, Newsom, & Binkoff, 1980;
Touchette, MacDonald, & Langer, 1985; Weeks
& Gaylord-Ross, 1981; Winterling, Dunlap, &
O'Neill, 1987).

Although behavior management operations
continue to center on the use of consequences, recent years have contributed knowledge and perspectives that have expanded the field of behavior
management in important ways. This expansion
has coincided with the growing strength of advocacy and civil rights movements and the transition
of people with severe disabilities from institutions
to community-based environments. The development of additional and alternative strategies has
also accompanied the dissatisfactions with, and
the increasing repudiation of, aversive conse-

quences. The controversy and debate surrounding
the use of aversive contingencies to suppress behavior problems have occupied a prominent position in the area of severe disabilities. This
controversy has also spurred articulations of
nonaversive alternatives to aversive interventions.

Controversy over Aversive Interventions

The question of whether aversive consequences
should be used to punish severe behavior problems
has aroused more heated discussion of scientific
and ethical viewpoints than any other issue in the
field of severe disabilities. The debate has been
aired at special federally sponsored conferences
(e.g., Horner & Dunlap, 1988; National Institutes of
Health, 1990), on national network news programs
(e.g., ABC's *Nightline*), within professional organizations, within courts of law, and in the pages of
numerous books on the topic of severe behavior
problems (e.g., Cipani, 1989; Evans & Meyer,
1985; LaVigna & Donnellan, 1986; McGee,
Menolascino, Hobbs, & Menousek, 1987; Meyer &
Evans, 1989; Repp & Singh, 1990). Opponents of
aversive procedures call for an immediate cessation
and legal prohibitions, while others insist that some
use of powerful aversive techniques is necessary
for the effective resolution of the most destructive
and intransigent of behavior problems. Arguments
are marshalled from many perspectives, including
ethics, legal and civil rights, and science. It is not
likely that the controversy will be fully resolved for
many years. However, it is possible to define some
of the issues so as to narrow the debate to a manageable breadth and to offer an impetus for constructive action.

One issue has to do with definition. Horner and
his colleagues (1990) note that the term *aversive*
has created confusion because its technical meaning differs from its typical use in the behavior
management controversy. The technical definition of *aversive* refers to a class of stimuli that
produce escape or avoidance responses (Azrin &
Holz, 1966; Van Houten, 1983). When they follow a behavior, aversive stimuli can produce re-

ductions in the future probability of the behavior. That is, they can serve as punishers. As in other technical definitions (e.g., reinforcement, punishment), *aversive* is defined on the basis of its effects on behavior, and not as a finite set of stimuli. The technical definition does not apply adequately to the debate. It fails to distinguish between mildly aversive events (such as a frown, a correction, or a gentle reprimand) and severely aversive events (such as electric shock). If the technical definitions are invoked, there are very few advocates who would argue that all aversive or punishing events could be, or should be, eliminated (Evans & Meyer, 1990).

The controversy focuses not on the use of punishment per se, but rather on the use of extremely aversive events that have been reported and used with some regularity with people who have severe disabilities. According to Horner and associates (1990), the procedures that are subject to such scrutiny and restriction include those that cause pain (such as electric shock, slaps, and the administration of other noxious stimuli), involve the withholding of basic human needs, and produce social humiliation. These authors advocate that a social validation standard (Wolery & Gast, 1990; Wolf, 1978) be applied to *all* behavioral interventions. The point of this standard is that any intervention should support and maintain a person's dignity, and that any procedure that may exceed the community's norms for dignified interactions should be subjected to scrutiny, monitoring, regulation, and possible prohibition.

When the debate is narrowed to those interventions that are unambiguously aversive, the arguments focus on issues having to do with ethics and the efficacy of treatment. Those who defend the use of aversive interventions acknowledge a preference for nonaversive approaches, but argue that some extremely challenging cases exceed the current capacities of strictly positive procedures (Iwata, 1988). This position holds that there are individuals whose destructive behaviors are so severe that denying access to aversive contingencies is unethical because it is tantamount to withhold-

ing effective treatment (cf. Favell et al., 1982; Van Houten et al., 1988). Because the literature clearly indicates that aversive contingencies can suppress behavior problems, at least in the short term, there are those who believe that such a technology should not be dismissed.

Arguments against the use of aversives are diverse. One common contention is that it is morally wrong to inflict pain and humiliation on a vulnerable person, especially when it is clear that the same procedures are not used with nondisabled individuals (Guess, Helmstetter, Turnbull, & Knowlton, 1987). There is great concern that aversives have been and are being used routinely by inadequately trained (or untrained) providers in blatantly inappropriate, and thus abusive, circumstances (Neisworth & Smith, 1973). Despite efforts to the contrary (cf. Lovaas & Favell, 1987), it can be argued that there are no substantive mechanisms other than prohibition for limiting this negative dissemination (Durand, 1990). It is also argued that effective, nonaversive options *do* exist (LaVigna & Donnellan, 1986) and that they can serve not only to reduce the behavior problem, but also to produce desirable outcomes that are meaningful from an ecological and life-style perspective (Meyer & Evans, 1989). The debate regarding aversives is far more complex than can be suggested by this brief overview. Readers who are interested in further information are encouraged to pursue the references in this chapter, including those that explicitly explore the issues surrounding the aversives-nonaversives controversy (e.g., Repp & Singh, 1990). It is also recommended that readers refer to the position statements that have been issued by many professional and advocacy organizations concerned with people who experience severe disability. These organizations include The Association for Persons with Severe Handicaps (TASH), the Association for Retarded Citizens (ARC), the American Association on Mental Retardation (AAMR), the Autism Society of America (ASA), Division 33 (Mental Retardation and Developmental Disabilities) of the American Psychological Association (APA), and the Association for Behavior Analysis (ABA). Their statements range from unambiguous calls for the elimination of all aversive treatments (e.g., TASH), to declarations of a person's rights to effective treatment, which might include restrictive and aversive procedures under some circumstances (e.g., ABA). None of the resolutions support the routine use of aversive or highly restrictive procedures, and none suggest that aversives should ever be used by individuals who are not expertly trained and monitored.

Rationale for Nonaversive Intervention

Although there will be lingering scientific and ethical contentions regarding the role of aversives in restricted circumstances, there is nevertheless a strong rationale for the adoption of nonaversive approaches. In addition to the pervasive moral and human rights issues, there are ample reasons to be derived from (1) the practical exigencies of community integration, (2) the growing data base of effective, nonaversive procedures, and (3) the logic of functional analysis and functional intervention. First, the fact that education and support for people with severe disabilities are occurring in community settings (e.g., supported employment, supported living) can be considered tantamount to a mandate for nonaversive, respectful interventions. Aversive interactions between people with severe disabilities and their supervisors will not be tolerated in public settings. Therefore, the procedures that are well suited for community participation are those that prevent behavior problems and those that seek durable solutions through alternative skill development. Prevention and skill training are characteristics of the nonaversive approach.

A second reason for nonaversive approaches is found in their increasing empirical support. As discussed in subsequent sections of this chapter, recent years have produced extensive data that demonstrate the efficacy of reinforcement-based strategies, skill development approaches, and a variety of stimulus-based interventions (Carr, Robinson, Taylor, & Carlson, 1990). These behavioral support

programs are being implemented in schools, homes, workplaces, and a variety of other community settings. Although the literature is far from presenting a conclusive case that all problem behaviors can be solved completely with nonaversive methods, the growing accumulation of case studies and experimental reports offers increasingly persuasive testimony.

An additional reason to support nonaversive interventions is that they are based on attempts to understand the reasons that the problem behaviors occur and that they seek to relate those reasons directly to their design. Procedures that attempt to suppress undesirable responses through aversive contingencies are not based on such understanding. In a related discussion, Carr, Robinson, and Palumbo (1990) distinguish between functional and nonfunctional treatment by noting that functional interventions are: (1) based on functional analyses with a focus on an understanding of the behavior problem, (2) proactive, in the sense that they occur when behavior problems are not present, (3) designed primarily to increase desirable behaviors, and (4) long term, because the essential goal is to maintain desirable behaviors. Attractive aspects of this orientation are that its interventions are logical, its emphases are instructional, and its management of behavior problems is a side effect of increased competence in skills that are important for community living.

UNDERSTANDING BEHAVIOR PROBLEMS

The variables potentially related to the acquisition and maintenance of severe behavior problems are diverse and have generated a great deal of theoretical and empirical analysis. For example, possible biological factors related to self-injurious behavior were identified by Cataldo & Harris (1982). They noted that some medically diagnosed syndromes, such as Lesch-Nyhan syndrome, have been associated with high rates of severe self-injury. They describe possible biochemical and developmental factors that may be implicated in the etiology of behavior problems.

However, the evidence relating self-injury and biological factors is correlational at best; a causal relationship has not been clearly demonstrated. More persuasive is research literature that clearly identifies challenging behavior as a learned response. When challenging behaviors are related to environmental factors, three possible hypotheses have been consistently offered: positive reinforcement, negative reinforcement, and sensory stimulation (Carr, 1977; Iwata, Vollmer, & Zarcone, 1990; Repp & Karsh, 1990).

Positive Reinforcement Hypothesis

Positive reinforcement describes a condition in which the probability of the occurrence of a behavior is increased when an event is delivered contingent upon performance of that behavior. Challenging behaviors have been shown to be maintained by positive reinforcement that includes social attention and the presentation of tangibles, such as toys or snacks (Carr & Durand, 1985b; Day, Rea, Schussler, Larsen, & Johnson, 1988; Iwata, Dorsey, Slifer, Bauman, & Richman, 1982; Lovaas & Simmons, 1969).

Iwata et al. (1982) provided a demonstration of SIB maintained by positive social reinforcement. They described a condition of social attention in which expressions of concern, touching, and experimenter proximity, when provided contingent on the occurrence of self-injury, resulted in increased rates of self-injury. This condition was designed to approximate events that may occur in the natural environment, especially in institutional settings.

The positive reinforcement hypothesis receives further support from evidence demonstrating that challenging behavior is reduced when the positive reinforcement contingency is eliminated through extinction. For example, Day and associates (1988) demonstrated that SIB was maintained by positive reinforcement when they took preferred toys away from children after the toys had been played with for a short period of time. When access to toys was denied contingent on SIB, these authors found that responses decreased. Other

studies have documented reductions when a time-out procedure (removing access to all forms of reinforcement for a specified period of time) was implemented contingent on the occurrence of the challenging behavior (Bostow & Bailey, 1969; Lovaas & Simmons, 1969).

Research indicating that challenging behaviors can come under stimulus control not only supports the positive reinforcement hypothesis but also provides additional information about variables related to the acquisition and maintenance of such behavior. When the behavior comes under stimulus control, the behaver learns that the presence of certain stimuli signals an opportunity to receive a desired event. For example, higher levels of a target behavior may occur in the presence of other people, as opposed to when the person is alone (Iwata et al., 1982; Lovaas, Freitag, Gold, & Kassorla, 1965), or in the presence of certain items (Day et al., 1988). These observations suggest that the target behavior is probably exhibited in order to obtain the stimuli that are present.

Negative Reinforcement Hypothesis

Negative reinforcement describes a condition in which the probability of a behavior is increased when an event is removed or delayed contingent upon performance of that behavior. A number of studies have demonstrated conditions under which challenging behavior was maintained as a function of negative reinforcement (Carr, Newsom, & Binkoff, 1976; Durand & Carr, 1987; Iwata et al., 1982; Weeks & Gaylord-Ross, 1981). For example, Durand and Carr (1987) provided for presentation of stimuli selected because they were identified as difficult tasks during preassessment data collection. The authors found that the rate of stereotyped behaviors increased in all subjects when difficult tasks were presented. A negative reinforcement function was further verified in the second assessment phase. During this phase, time-out was made contingent on occurrences of stereotyped behavior. This resulted in an increase in the target response. The time-out procedure removes the event and provides an opportunity for the subject to escape task demands, thus providing negative reinforcement (Solnick, Rincover, & Peterson, 1977).

Antecedent stimuli may also exert stimulus control over negatively reinforced behaviors. That is, in the presence of certain stimuli, the challenging behavior serves to remove or delay an event. Stimuli that may assume aversive properties include type of task (Carr & Durand, 1985a; Weeks & Gaylord-Ross, 1981), form of instruction (Iwata, 1987; Winterling, Dunlap, & O'Neill, 1987), and setting events such as density of other people in the same area (McAfee, 1987) or prolonged sitting (Bailey & Pyles, 1989).

Sensory Stimulation/Automatic Reinforcement Hypothesis

In a comprehensive review of the literature, Carr (1977) examined the hypothesis that some challenging behaviors provide sensory stimulation to an organism experiencing a less than optimal level of kinesthetic, tactile, or vestibular stimulation. Maladaptive behaviors are exhibited as a person attempts to manipulate the environment in such a way as to increase stimulation when he or she is in a deprivation state or to attenuate stimulation when too much is being provided.

Identification of challenging behaviors maintained by self-stimulation presents a problem, in that the events hypothesized as maintaining the behavior can only be inferred and not directly observed. In addition, either positive reinforcement (increasing stimulation) or negative reinforcement (attenuating stimulation) processes can apply. In spite of these difficulties, the self-stimulation hypothesis is supported by studies that have demonstrated decreases in stereotypic behaviors (Rincover, Cook, Peoples, & Packard, 1979) and SIB (Rincover & Devany, 1982) when sensory extinction procedures were introduced. For example, Rincover and Devany (1982) successfully treated face scratching by covering the subject's hands with thin rubber gloves, and head banging by providing a padded helmet.

In addition, exhibition of higher rates of chal-

lenging behavior in environments that are not stimulating when compared with those that provide opportunities for activities, may provide evidence supporting the self-stimulation hypothesis. Iwata et al. (1982) devised a condition approximating a barren environment that might allow for the identification of challenging behavior maintained by self-stimulation when a person is in a deprivation state. That is, in this condition, behavior is positively reinforced by increasing stimulation. The authors placed a child alone in a room that contained no toys or other stimulation. Four subjects exhibited higher levels of self-injury while in this condition, suggesting self-stimulation as a maintaining factor.

Although single functions tend to be reported in the research literature, severe behavior problems may also serve multiple functions. The following example provides an illustration. Paul bites himself. Episodes of self-injury seem to occur randomly throughout the day, are sometimes associated with tasks, but just as often occur without apparent provocation. Paul's teachers are baffled, but in fact his behavior serves very specific functions in his environment. For example, Paul's favorite activity is watching television. His teachers have learned that his biting decreases when they "distract" him by turning on the television. Although the immediate result is a decrease in biting, Paul's teachers have inadvertently provided positive reinforcement for the very behavior they are trying to eliminate. Paul also bites himself during tasks in which he has a very low rate of correct responding. These tasks vary across the curriculum, making it difficult to identify the function of biting under different tasks. When he bites himself, Paul's teacher removes the task materials for a short period of time. If the biting becomes severe, he is restrained. Implementation of this intervention sometimes takes as long as 30 minutes. Often the schedule prohibits a return to the original task, providing Paul with negative reinforcement through escape. Finally, Paul is sometimes expected to sit quietly in a chair while his teacher works with another student. Usually no materials are provided, because Paul destroys them unless closely supervised. In this instance, Paul's biting may provide positive reinforcement in the form of stimulation. The possibility that one behavior serves multiple functions will have significant impact on the design of an intervention, requiring different treatments depending on the situation in which the behavior is observed.

Communicative Intent

Some authors have suggested that a thorough understanding of the factors affecting challenging behavior should include an analysis of the communicative intent (Carr & Durand, 1985a; Donnellan, Mirenda, Mesaros, & Fassbender, 1984; Doss & Reichle, 1989). This position considers behavior from the standpoint of pragmatics, the study of language within the social context, which suggests that all behaviors have some type of communicative value and carry a message. A number of authors have delineated possible intentions and have suggested how behavior problems may communicate these meanings (Donnellan et al., 1984; Doss & Reichle, 1989).

This hypothesis complements, rather than replaces, the learned functions of behavior as discussed previously. For example, when self-injurious behavior is found to be maintained by positive reinforcement, as described by Day and associates (1988), the communicative hypothesis might interpret the behavior as a request for access to preferred toys. The treatment implemented in this study supported this hypothesis. Teaching an alternative communicative behavior for toy requests resulted in reductions in SIB. Alternatively, when stereotypic behavior is found to be maintained by negative reinforcement, as described by Durand and Carr (1987), the communicative function hypothesis might identify the behavior as a request for escape from, or help with, a difficult task. Teaching the children in this study to request assistance with the task also resulted in reductions of the target behavior.

The results of a number of studies have been consistent with a communicative intent hypothesis; that is, challenging behavior was reduced when a communicative behavior was provided (Carr et al., 1980; Carr & Durand, 1985b; Day et al., 1988; Durand & Carr, 1987; Horner & Budd, 1985). This suggests that viewing many behavior problems as communication can be a productive and positive perspective. However, it is not yet possible to interpret all behavior problems as intentional. The process through which communicative functions are developed and identified requires much more extensive study.

Components of Nonaversive Intervention.   Nonaversive behavioral intervention is a broad approach that is difficult to describe simply as a set of procedures or techniques. Although there are specific manipulations that can be prescribed, best practices in nonaversive intervention are individualized on the basis of comprehensive assessment and typically include more than one intervention component. In the rest of this chapter, a sampling of intervention strategies are categorized according to key components of nonaversive behavioral intervention. It is important to acknowledge that the full array of interventions can only be suggested by this categorization.

Comprehensive and Functional Assessment

As previously discussed, severe behavior disorders can develop and be maintained by a number of factors, both biological and environmental. Functional assessment is a method for identifying these factors. First, interviews, record review, and naturalistic observation may be used to develop hypotheses about the antecedents and consequences relevant to the maintenance of a target behavior. Then specific conditions are designed to test the hypotheses within controlled manipulations. Systematic changes (increases and decreases) in the behavior as a result of functional analysis manipulations establish the validity of a hypothesis and demonstrate control of the behavior by specific antecedent or consequent events.

A completed functional assessment should provide three outcomes. The challenging behavior should be operationally described and measured, the time and situations when the behavior will and will not occur should be predictable, and the function or maintaining reinforcers that the behavior produces should be described (O'Neill, Horner, Albin, Storey, & Sprague, 1990). This information allows for hypothesis-driven treatment; that is, intervention procedures are designed consistent with observed relationships between the behavior and the surrounding environment (Iwata et al., 1982; Repp, Felce, & Barton, 1988).

Three methods for obtaining information about the variables maintaining a behavior may be identified in the literature. These methods differ in their ease of implementation and in the precision of the data collected. Although each of these methods may be a primary source of assessment information, they are more likely to be effective when used in combination, each providing for refinement and greater specificity of hypotheses (Durand, 1990; O'Neill et al., 1990; Lennox & Miltenberger, 1989).

Informant-Based Methods. Interviews, rating scales, questionnaires, and record review rely on the reporting of an informant (e.g., Durand & Crimmins, 1988; Iwata, Wong, Reardon, Dorsey, & Lau, 1982; O'Neill et al., 1990). They provide a simple, efficient strategy for beginning a functional assessment, usually requiring much less time and fewer staff persons' effort to complete than either direct observation or experimental manipulation. However, the data obtained provide only indirect information about the relationship between the behavior and the environment. That is, the data are composed of staff recollections about behavior rather than the direct observation of the behavior at the point in time it occurs. Because they are a product of memory, the data may be influenced by factors unrelated to the behavior or events in question and, therefore, may be unreliable. The informant-based assessment is most effective when used to enumerate potential functional relationships that can be subjected to more rigorous assessment.

A number of formal informant-based assess-

ment instruments have been developed. For example, the Motivational Assessment Scale (MAS) (Durand & Crimmins, 1988) is a 16-item rating scale designed to identify the consequences that are maintaining a target behavior along the dimensions of sensory stimulation, escape or avoidance, social attention, and tangible rewards. The scale requires only a few minutes to complete and is easily scored and interpreted. The ratings for the questions in each dimension are summed, and the dimension with the highest score is assumed to be maintaining the behavior in question.

Durand (1990) suggests that the MAS is most effective when the target behavior and the setting are specified and a separate MAS is completed in each setting and for each target behavior. A definition that is too broad, of either the behavior (e.g., tantrum) or the setting (e.g., school), can mask different behavioral functions, making interpretation more difficult. The MAS is one of the few instruments for which an attempt has been made to establish reliability and validity.

The Functional Assessment Interview Form (O'Neill et al., 1990) has nine sections of questions designed to assess variables that are potentially relevant to both occurrence and nonoccurrence of the behavior(s) of interest. Questions provide for a topographical definition of each target behavior, identification of factors that are predictive of the target behavior (i.e., antecedent stimuli, physiological factors, and setting events), and possible maintaining consequences. This form requires more time to complete than the MAS, but addresses a wider range of possible variables and relationships. It includes a summary page and an assessment guide that provides directions and examples of completed forms.

Two additional informant-based assessments may be helpful in determining possible relationships between variables. Gardner, Cole, Davidson, and Karan (1986) developed a checklist specifically to assess the influence of setting events on behavior. Bailey and Pyles (1989) proposed a list of questions that address variables across four categories that include setting events, physiological variables, operant variables (consequences), and other possible influencing factors. Interested readers are referred to the references cited above for more complete information about each instrument.

Descriptive Analysis.   A descriptive analysis involves direct observation of the occurrence of the target behavior and events in the environment that may be related (Bijou, Peterson, & Ault, 1968; O'Neill et al., 1990; Touchette et al., 1985). An assumption is made that over time a pattern will emerge from this recording that will identify a relationship between the behavior in question and either specific or general classes of antecedents and consequences.

Possibly the most often used method of descriptive analysis is the antecedent-behavior-consequence (A-B-C) assessment. An A-B-C assessment is composed of a narrative account of ongoing behavior that provides for recording of any environmental events that occur contiguous in time with the behavior in question (Bijou, Peterson, & Ault, 1968; Kazdin, 1980). To provide for the most accurate observation, guidelines are usually suggested for data recording that include length of observation, objectivity of data gathered (i.e., report only what is actually seen and heard without making inferences), and identification of response definitions and categories.

As part of their comprehensive assessment package, O'Neill et al. (1990) developed an A-B-C observation form that is structured to provide for the recording of events identified through the Functional Assessment Interview Form. This simplifies and focuses the observation on variables and settings already thought to be related to the occurrence of the target behavior. The form is designed so that data can be easily summarized in a way that makes patterns of events clear. Their assessment guide presents a description of procedures and provides examples of completed forms.

Touchette et al. (1985) also described a method of direct observation, called a "scatter plot" assessment (see Figure 5.1). It provides for identification of correlations between the time of day and differential rates of the target behavior. This method is relatively simple to use and may require less effort than other methods of direct observation. However, the data provide only a categorization of the number of incidents rather than an absolute count and do not identify other environmental correlates. The results of this assessment may be used to provide a temporal focus for a more extensive A-B-C assessment.

Direct observation offers a more objective and systematic assessment method, as compared with informant-based methods. However, it is limited in that it provides only correlational information that may or may not identify functional relations. That is, a causal relationship may not exist. For example, when a number of events occur before and after a target behavior, the event actually maintaining the behavior may be difficult to identify. In addition, the behavior may be maintained by highly intermittent reinforcement or by events that do not occur in temporal contiguity with the behavior. Setting events, which may be temporally distal, exemplify events that may affect behavior but may not be apparent in a descriptive observation. Nonetheless, when the results of a descriptive analysis provide clear and consistent data patterns, interventions that are based on these data are likely to be effective.

Experimental Analysis.   Experimental, or "functional," analysis provides for the manipulation of the environment so that systematic differences in the challenging behavior will be produced (Carr & Durand, 1985b; Iwata et al., 1982). The important dimension of this procedure is that it is experimental; that is, the relationship is verified through the direct manipulation of variables and replication of effect (Axelrod, 1987; Carr, Robinson, & Palumbo, 1990; Iwata et al., 1990). Conducting a functional analysis can be time-consuming and labor intensive, but it is the only method that provides a demonstration of a causal relation (Bailey & Pyles, 1989; Carr, Robinson, & Palumbo, 1990; O'Neill et al., 1990).

The procedure involves direct observation of

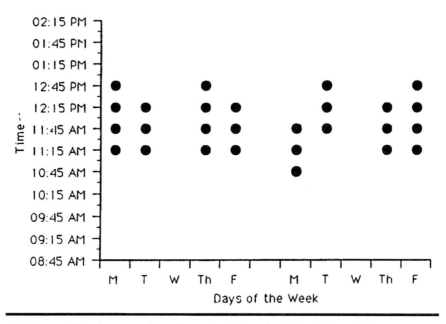

FIGURE 5.1   Tony's aggressions throughout the school day. Data points represent 30-minute intervals during which at least three aggressions occurred. Response pattern reveals consistent aggressions following a minimally structured free-play activity that ends each day (except Wednesday, when activity is not conducted), at 11:30 A.M.

behavior under preselected and controlled conditions. For this reason, functional analyses have generally been conducted in an analogue environment, one that is contrived but similar to the natural environment. At least two conditions must be constructed, one in which the variable of interest is present and one in which the variable is absent. More conditions are constructed as the number of variables to be manipulated are increased. Decisions about what conditions are to be used in the analysis are more efficient when they are based on the results of previously conducted assessment methods, as described earlier.

Steege, Wacker, Berg, Cigrand, and Cooper (1989) provide a good example of the manner in which conditions are constructed. They designed four experimental conditions to assess the influence of different antecedent and consequent stimuli on

self-injurious behavior: (1) a solitary condition, in which the participant was left alone in a classroom without ready access to toys or play materials, (2) a demand condition, in which the participant was prompted to complete academic tasks, (3) a control condition consisting of unstructured play, in which the participant was given access to toys, no demands were made, and social attention was provided contingent upon no occurrence of self-injury, and (4) a response cost condition, in which toys or objects were taken away from the participant and given to other children. The response cost condition approximated events in the home environment that had been reported to elicit self-injury. Differential rates of self-injurious behavior across conditions provide the experimenter with a hypothesis of the variables maintaining the self-injurious behavior. For example, finding higher rates of responding in the solitary condition can indicate that the behavior may function to provide sensory stimulation, whereas finding higher rates of responding in the demand condition can indicate that the self-injurious behavior may function as escape under this condition for the individual student. Table 5.1 summarizes the components of the functional assessment process.

Although they are extremely helpful for developing appropriate interventions, conducting functional analyses prior to intervention is still the exception rather than the rule (Carr, Robinson, Taylor, & Carlson, 1990; Lundervold & Bourland, 1988). A few research studies document the functional relationship between behavior and its consequences (Bird, Dores, Moniz, & Robinson, 1989; Day, Rea, Schussler, Larsen, & Johnson, 1988; Durand & Carr, 1987; Iwata et al., 1982;

Steege et al., 1989). Other efforts have emphasized the role of a wide range of antecedents that compared curricular content (Dunlap, Dunlap, Koegel, & Koegel, 1991), hard versus easy tasks (Carr & Durand, 1985b), varied versus repetitive tasks (Winterling et al., 1987), or easy tasks versus nonpreferred requests (Horner, Day, Sprague, O'Brien, & Heathfield, 1991).

Experimental manipulations can be complex and costly in that they require highly trained staff and an extensive amount of time to implement. These concerns have led to efforts to simplify and shorten the time required for implementation (Wacker et al., 1990) or to adapt the experimental procedures for use in the natural environment (Durand, 1990; O'Neill et al., 1990). O'Neill and his associates (1990) suggest examples of a functional analysis that allow for scheduling manipula-

---

TABLE 5.1 Components of the Functional Assessment Process

Functional Assessment Methods for Generating Hypotheses

INFORMANT-BASED	DESCRIPTIVE ANALYSIS
Record Review	Narrative Account
Collateral Report	Antecedent-Behavior-Consequence
Interview	Scatter Plot (Touchette, MacDonald,
Rating Scales	& Langer, 1985)
Motivational Assessment	
Scale	
Questionnaires	
Functional Assessment	
Interview Form	
Checklist	
Standardized Test	
Vineland Adaptive Behavior	
Scales	

Functional Analysis (Hypothesis Testing Within Analog or Natural Environments)

  Consequence Manipulation

  Antecedent Manipulation

tions during regular instructional periods. For example, if interviews and initial observations indicate that the behavior occurs during the presentation of difficult tasks, teaching sessions might be conducted in which only easy tasks are presented. These could then be followed by sessions in which only difficult tasks are presented. The authors caution, however, that control of the events or situations is imperative even in the natural environment.

Another strategy may be to shorten the time spent in doing the functional analysis. In general, conditions must be repeated until behaviors are clearly differentiated, requiring many sessions distributed over a number of days. However, extensive and thorough interviews and naturalistic observations may enable one to identify clear hypotheses that may then be confirmed in only a few sessions. Using this method, Dunlap, Dunlap, Koegel, and Koegel (1991) and Horner et al. (1991) completed experimental manipulations in natural settings within only a few days.

Wacker and associates (1990) described an outclinic assessment model. The authors combined a behavioral interview with a functional analysis procedure that required only 90 minutes to implement. First, a tentative hypothesis was developed from a review of client history. Analogue conditions were then designed to test the hypothesis. Presentation of analogue conditions was followed by a "replication analysis" in which the conditions with the highest and lowest occurrence of the target behavior were repeated. Finally, within a "contingency reversal" condition, the event previously reinforcing the challenging behavior was provided for occurrences of an appropriate behavior.

Linking Assessment to Intervention.   The main purpose of the functional assessment process is to identify functional relationships in such a way that the information can then be linked to intervention (Lennox & Miltenberger, 1989). When a functional assessment is completed, the results are in the form of hypotheses (Repp et al., 1988) or state-

ments that relate environmental consequences and antecedent conditions to occurrences of the problem behavior. These statements must then be translated into specific programmatic operations that relate logically to the assessment data. Although this can be a complex process (Carr, Robinson, & Palumbo, 1990; Iwata et al., 1982; Lennox & Miltenberger, 1989; Lovaas & Favell, 1987), linking assessments to interventions can enhance the effectiveness of treatment and help to ensure that intervention programs are responsive to the idiosyncratic needs of individual students. Table 5.2 lists hypotheses about the function of a given behavior and examples of treatment procedures that can be used to alter the relationship between occurrences of the problem behavior and environmental events.

If interventions are not linked to functional assessment information, the treatment can be nonfunctional (Carr, Robinson, & Palumbo, 1990), ineffective, and related more to the behavior's appearance than to its purpose. Consider, for example, a situation in which a student's disruptive tantrums are motivated by the desire to escape from demanding instructional activities. This student has learned that when the environment becomes unpleasant because of too much work, escape is achieved by screaming and destroying the instructional materials. Without a functional assessment, the student's teacher may very well use some intervention(s) that might have been effective with other behaviors or other students, or that might be prescribed as "cookbook" standard treatment for tantrums. For instance, if a teacher uses differential attention (or even time-out) to solve the problem, there is little chance that the treatment will be successful. Attention is not functionally related to the problem, and as long as the tantrums are the student's effective means of terminating the activity, they will continue.

Functional assessment data are linked to intervention programs in several ways. In the preceding example, in which escape was identified as controlling the student's tantrums, the intervention would focus on the escape function. Prior to a

TABLE 5.2   Linking Assessment Information to Functionally Based Intervention

HYPOTHESIS	FUNCTION	EXAMPLES OF INTERVENTION COMPONENTS
Positive Reinforcement	Obtain tangible Obtain social Obtain activity	**Teach an Alternative Behavior** 1. Teach the student to ask for the item verbally, to use a picture or sign. 2. Teach general social interaction skills that will include appropriate ways to obtain social reinforcers. **Change the Reinforcement Schedule** 1. Make sure that the problem behavior no longer results in access to the reinforcer. 2. Provide the reinforcer only when the student exhibits appropriate behavior. 3. Provide an enriched environment in which the student is given unlimited access to the reinforcer.
Negative Reinforcement	Escape event Avoid event	**Teach an Alternative Behavior** 1. Teach the student to use pictures or signs, or to verbally request a break. Then gradually increase the length of work time before a break can be requested. 2. Teach the student to request help. **Change the Characteristics of the Task or Instruction** 1. Intersperse easy and hard tasks. 2. Gradually fade in or fade out stimuli so that there are a limited number of errors. 3. Add choices. For example, allow the student to choose the order in which tasks will be completed. 4. Provide exercise or a break before an instructional session. Change the type of break provided.
Sensory Stimulation/ Automatic Reinforcement	Increase Stimulation Attenuate Stimulation	1. Check for possible health problems, such as an ear infection. 2. Provide an enriched environment. Be especially careful to provide stimuli that match that provided by the behavior. For example, provide textured items to replace behavior that seems to provide tactile stimulation. 3. Pad the area stimulated and the environment if necessary to prevent tactile stimulation. For example, cover a small area of the floor and wall with foam-filled mats. 4. Teach appropriate toy play.

future occurrence of the tantrum, at least two logical interventions could be implemented: (1) the task could be eliminated or characteristics of the instruction could be modified, so that the student would no longer seek to escape, and (2) the student could be taught a more desirable way to request a break from the activity. The same logic can be applied to any results that may be produced by a functional assessment process.

The links between assessment and intervention usually result in intervention programs that involve teaching adaptive skills, changing schedules of positive reinforcement, and/or changing the immediate or contextual stimuli that are antecedent events. Strategies that represent these components are discussed in the following section.

Teaching Adaptive Behaviors

Functional analysis, as it matures, and the growing body of literature on skill development increasingly suggest that behavior problems are not only purposeful, but can be viewed profitably as manifestations of skill *deficiencies,* rather than simply as excess behaviors. This means that the behavior problem occurs because it serves a purpose *and* because the person does not have a more effective and efficient way to achieve that purpose. Although it is not yet possible to identify the functions of all behavior problems, research has shown that many undesirable behaviors are governed (or motivated) by clear environmental operations. As discussed previously, research has shown, for example, that many behavior problems are exhibited because they function to obtain something (e.g., attention) from the environment, or to produce escape from something that is aversive (e.g., an instructional demand). One way to regard these phenomena is to say that the person has "excessive" attention-seeking behavior, or exhibits "too much" escape responding. Operating from such a perspective, one might choose to ignore the problem behavior or even punish it. However, if the problem is regarded as a deficiency, rather than an excess, the behavior would be interpreted as a sign

that the person requires instruction in a more adaptive attention-seeking or escape response. The process would be the same as that used when a mother observes that her young son has not learned the rules for crossing the street, or when a teacher notes that his class does not know the name of the president. A skill deficiency is detected, and instruction is provided.

Given such an orientation, a constructive approach would be to identify an alternative to the behavior problem and to initiate an instructional program with the objective of teaching a more desirable topography. As long as the replacement behavior is more efficient and effective in producing the objective (e.g., attention or escape), it is likely that the instructional program will serve not only to teach a new behavior (thus remediating the deficiency), but also to reduce the undesirable behavior. This general strategy is incorporated in nonaversive recommendations for positive programming (LaVigna, Willis, & Donnellan, 1989) and has been described as an educational orientation (Evans & Meyer, 1985) to the management of problem behavior.

The constructive approach is most clearly exemplified when communication is targeted for instruction. *Functional communication training* (Carr & Durand, 1985b; Durand, 1990) is based on a functional analysis of the communicative properties of a behavior problem. For example, some behavior problems that are motivated by escape may be equivalent to the message, "I want a break from this unpleasant activity." Other undesirable behaviors may convey a strong desire for attention, food, or some other tangible or sensory stimulation. Other communicative functions may also be identified (Donnellan, Mirenda, Mesaros, & Fassbender, 1984). When the purpose is identified, an appropriate and more desirable communicative alternative is scheduled to replace the problem behavior. For some individuals, the communicative alternative may involve speech or other language topography, but for many people who have severe disabilities, communication may be in a more rudimentary form. For example, people with severe disabilities have been taught to raise a hand, to use a gesture, to hold a sign, to activate a microswitch, or to use other simple signals as functionally equivalent substitutes for disruptive responding. The issue is not the level of sophistication, but rather the effectiveness of the communication. For functional communication training to be effective in reducing the behavior problem, several conditions must be present: (1) the function of the behavior problem needs to be clearly identified; (2) a replacement behavior needs to be established that is as efficient as or more so than the behavior problem; (3) the replacement behavior needs to be taught under the conditions that otherwise would produce the behavior problem; and (4) the replacement behavior needs to be functional, in the sense that it must produce the same result that was intended by the behavior problem, and it must do so with at least as high a level of consistency and predictability. Functional communication training has been shown in many recent investigations to be very effective in reducing a variety of severe behavior problems (e.g., Bird, Dores, Moniz, & Robinson, 1989; Carr & Durand, 1985b; Durand & Carr, 1987), and it has been demonstrated to produce a level of maintenance not often seen with other types of intervention (Durand & Carr, 1991).

Although functional communication training is a highly focused tactic for reducing specific behavior problems, there is also evidence that more general instruction in communication and social interaction skills can produce similar reductions. Hunt, Alwell, and Goetz (1988) taught high school students with severe disabilities to initiate and maintain conversations with their nondisabled peers. As the students learned to extend these social interactions, their inappropriate behaviors declined. In another study of indirect behavior management, Mace, Kratochwill, and Fiello (1983) reduced behavior problems by establishing increased rates of compliance (Russo, Cataldo, & Cushing, 1981). In the study by Mace and colleagues (1983), the aggression and tantrums of a young man with severe disabilities were de-

creased in a variety of settings, with a number of people, and over an extended time period when direct efforts were undertaken to reinforce and prompt compliance to instructions. Another demonstration was provided by Santarcangelo, Dyer, and Luce (1987). These authors focused on the disruptive behavior of children with autism in unstructured play settings. After the children received instruction on how to play with specific toys, their disruptions decreased significantly.

Another tactic that reflects the constructive approach to behavior management involves training in self-management techniques. Although most of the work in this area has been with people who have moderate, rather than severe, disabilities, there is growing evidence that some self-management approaches can be implemented effectively with individuals who have autism, severe learning challenges, and severe problem behaviors (Dunlap, Johnson, Winterling, & Morelli, 1988). Studies that relate to this area include work on relaxation training, self-monitoring, self-recording, and self-reinforcement (Browder & Shapiro, 1985; Gardner & Cole, 1984; Reese, Sherman, & Sheldon, 1984; Shapiro & Klein, 1980). Koegel and Koegel (1990) tested the efficacy of a self-management program to reduce the stereotypic behaviors of four children (aged 9 to 14) with severe autistic disabilities. First, the children were taught to make immediate discriminations regarding the presence and absence of their own stereotypies. Then, the children learned to self-record (e.g., make a check mark) following gradually increasing durations of time without stereotypy. With reinforcement and prompting, the children learned to be accurate in their self-recordings. The schedules of prompts and reinforcement were thinned until the children were monitoring their behavior for periods of more than an hour. The results of the study showed substantial reductions in stereotypy for each of the children in their treatment settings, and, for two of the children, the program was applied successfully in community settings that had not been associated with previous interventions. Although the explanations for the success of the self-monitoring package are not fully articulated, the authors of this research suggest that the procedures have important potential for helping people with disabilities to gain greater success and independence in community settings (Dunlap, Dunlap, Koegel, & Koegel, 1991).

Teaching adaptive behavior is an extremely important focus of nonaversive behavior management. It is probably most effective when it follows a functional assessment process and when the adaptive behavior produces the same reinforcer that had maintained the problem behavior (Carr, Robinson, Taylor, & Carlson, 1990), as in functional communication training (Durand, 1990). However, research also suggests that the occurrence of behavior problems is, in general, related to adaptive responding in an inverse manner. Therefore, a number of authors have suggested that strong instructional programs, which develop relevant skills and which increase access to rewarding events in the environment, are among the most critical short- and long-term measures that can be taken to reduce and prevent the occurrence of behavior problems among people with severe disabilities (Dunlap, Johnson, & Robbins, 1990; Evans & Meyer, 1985).

Strategies Using Positive Reinforcement

Reinforcement-based strategies are designed to increase the probability of the occurrence of desirable responses by arranging for reinforcement to be made contingent on those responses. In this section, we discuss those reinforcement procedures that are not designed to teach new adaptive behaviors, but are designed to reduce problem behaviors indirectly by increasing other behaviors. These positive reinforcement strategies include noncontingent reinforcement and procedures involving the use of differential reinforcement.

An important element of any reinforcement strategy is the selection of stimuli that are powerful enough to compete with the reinforcer provided by the undesirable behavior. Results of recent investigations suggest at least two procedures that may increase the likelihood of choosing

an effective reinforcer: functional analysis and assessment of reinforcer preference.

A functional analysis provides general information about the consequences maintaining a problem behavior that could be used to select a reinforcer for desirable behavior (Durand, Crimmins, Caulfield, & Taylor, 1989; Iwata et al., 1990). For example, behavior maintained by sensory stimulation may be more effectively treated when similar stimulation is provided for a desirable response. However, sensory stimulation may be ineffective as a reinforcer when the behavior problem is maintained by social or tangible consequences.

Assessment of reinforcer preferences allows for the empirical identification of reinforcers that should be both effective and powerful (Datillo, 1986; Green et al., 1988; Pace, Ivancic, Edwards, Iwata, & Page, 1985; Steege, Wacker, Berg, Cigrand, & Cooper, 1989; Wacker, Berg, Wiggins, Muldoon, & Cavanaugh, 1985). The procedure, as described by Pace and his colleagues (1985), is relatively simple. First, potential reinforcers are identified by getting suggestions from the student or from others who are familiar with the student's likes and dislikes. Next, the frequency of occurrence, or percentage of time, the student approaches, requests, or engages specific stimuli is recorded. Data that measure student approaches to stimuli can be accumulated in a very few short sessions. For example, Pace and colleagues (1989) conducted only eight sessions consisting of 20 stimulus presentations. Steege and colleagues (1989) measured approaches to stimuli in the classroom during five 10-minute sessions.

Stimuli identified as preferred (as described in the preceding step) are then delivered contingently on the occurrence of an arbitrarily selected target response. Those stimuli that increase the occurrence of the target response are identified as reinforcers. Examples of possible target responses have included motor responses to commands such as "reach" (Pace et al., 1985), presses on a microswitch (Datillo, 1986; Steege et al., 1989), or correct responses in a skill training program (Green et al., 1988).

This last step may take a little longer because it requires at least a baseline condition in which the request is made without providing consequences for the target response, and a second condition in which the preferred stimuli are provided contingent on the occurrence of the target response. In addition, each condition must continue long enough so that differences in levels of responding will be apparent.

Combining the two assessment procedures may provide for an even more effective treatment. Using this strategy, Steege and colleagues (1989) demonstrated rapid decreases in the self-injurious behavior of two children with severe disabilities. A functional analysis enabled the investigators to identify one child's self-injurious behavior as occurring during solitary conditions, indicating that the behavior served a self-stimulatory function. The reinforcer assessment identified stimuli that could be activated by the child independently, were appropriate for use during solitary conditions, and would provide an alternative source of sensory stimulation.

In contrast, the second child's self-injurious behavior occurred during task demand conditions, suggesting that the behavior was maintained by negative reinforcement (i.e., escape from task demands). The treatment prescription for this child included reinforcement of appropriate on-task behavior using the preferred stimuli identified during the reinforcer assessment and extinction of self-injurious behavior by preventing escape from the task.

Noncontingent Reinforcement. Persons in a state of deprivation may exhibit challenging problem behavior in order to access the reinforcing stimuli of which they have been deprived. Therefore, if the stimuli are made available freely, or at least very frequently, and noncontingently, that is, without regard to the behavior being exhibited, the state of deprivation may be eliminated and the basis for reinforcement removed (Iwata et al., 1990; LaVigna et al., 1989). Thus, if an undesirable behavior is maintained by attention, and attention is then provided often and freely, it is

probable that the undesirable behavior will decline owing to satiation.

Although the logic has appeal, there has been little research on noncontingent reinforcement. When used by itself, there is reason to suspect that the procedure may be insufficient to reduce many challenging behaviors. Horner (1980) assessed the effect on challenging behavior when a large number of toys and objects were provided noncontingently, a condition that he referred to as an enriched environment. He then compared the enriched environment condition with two others. In one, noncontingent social reinforcement was added to the enriched environment, and in the second, differential reinforcement for adaptive behavior was added. He found that simply providing noncontingent access to toys and social interaction was not sufficient to reduce the challenging behaviors. To this end, including differential reinforcement for desirable behavior was most successful.

Differential Reinforcement. Differential reinforcement provides for a combination of extinction of the target behavior and a differential schedule of reinforcement for some other behavior. Two broad categories of differential reinforcement may be identified: differential reinforcement of other behavior (DRO) and differential reinforcement of incompatible behavior (DRI). Other differential reinforcement operations have been noted in the literature, including differential reinforcement of alternative behaviors (DRA) and differential reinforcement of communicative behavior (DRC); however, procedures that are functionally the same as these have been discussed previously under "Teaching Adaptive Behaviors" and functional communication training.

DRO describes a procedure in which reinforcement is delivered whenever a specified period of time has elapsed and any behavior other than the target behavior occurs. Although DRO procedures have been in use for a number of years, research findings are mixed. Studies have shown reductions of challenging behavior (Repp & Dietz, 1974), no effect, and in a few cases, increased occurrence of the challenging behavior (Carr, Robinson, Taylor, & Carlson, 1990). It is likely that the effectiveness of the DRO procedure could be increased if it were based on a functional analysis. However, no studies to date have attempted to do this. In addition, the DRO procedure does not provide explicitly for the acquisition of any functional or life-style-enhancing behaviors.

DRI describes a procedure in which reinforcement is delivered for a response that is physically incompatible with the challenging behavior. As with the DRO procedure, previously noted, research results have been mixed, providing examples of both successful and unsuccessful interventions. If the incompatible behavior is selected without careful planning, it is possible that the replacement behavior could be nonfunctional or even interfere with more functional behaviors. For example, Young and Wincze (1974) reinforced an incompatible response that consisted of a student's sitting erect with hands lowered. In this position, the student was unable to hit her head with her fists, but she was also unable to perform any tasks of relevance to her curriculum.

Although the research findings offer inconsistent results, differential reinforcement procedures are important. Several authors have provided guidelines for using the techniques most effectively (e.g., LaVigna & Donnellan, 1986). DRO and DRI may also be most effective when they are combined with other strategies and when they are based on functional analyses of reinforcers.

Strategies Involving
Antecedent Manipulations

Although consequences are instrumental in modifying the future probability of undesirable and desirable behaviors, antecedent stimuli also exert great influence on the occurrence of target responses. Stimulus control is a pervasive phenomenon that is evident any time that antecedent stimuli affect the rate of a behavior. The basic idea in using antecedent manipulations is to identify those stimulus events that are associated with high rates of problem behavior and then eliminate or ameliorate those stimuli. To produce more positive responding, those stimuli that control the occurrence of desirable behaviors can be presented. In one example of an antecedent manipulation, Touchette, MacDonald, and Langer (1985) identified the presence of a particular staff member as being related to the occurrence of high rates of self-injurious behavior in an adult with autism. The behavior was reduced by rescheduling the subject's time so that he was no longer in the presence of that staff member. As another example, problem behaviors may be displayed during the presentation of tasks in which the student makes a great number of errors, but not during the presentation of tasks that the student has mastered or in which he or she makes only a few errors. Alternatively, a student may exhibit problem behavior when a stimulus is presented in repeated trials; for instance, the student is presented with 20 trials in which he or she is asked to receptively and/or expressively identify a fork in the presence of a fork.

When task characteristics are implicated in the occurrence of behavior problems, it is possible to change the manner with which instructions are delivered. Effective interventions have included errorless learning procedures (Weeks & Gaylord-Ross, 1981) and a collection of strategies that may be described as "task variation" or "task interspersal" (Winterling et al., 1987).

Task variation is a process of presenting both mastered and unmastered tasks intermittently during a teaching session. The strategy has been used successfully in situations where repeated presentations of a single instruction have been associated with high or increasing rates of behavior problems or inattentiveness (Dunlap, 1984; Dunlap & Dunlap, 1987; Dunlap & Koegel, 1980). For example, Winterling et al. (1987) identified repetitious (constant) task presentations as producing higher levels of disruptive and self-stimulatory behaviors in three students with autism. When the authors interspersed a variety of maintenance tasks among the teaching trials, the students exhibited lower levels of challenging behavior and improved acquisition of the unmastered task.

Singer, Singer, and Horner (1987) used a related strategy with students who experienced difficulties when they were asked to make a transition from a play period to a period of group instruction. In this study the authors identified a set of brief instructions (e.g., "give me five") that were associated with high levels of compliance. These "pre-task requests" were presented in rapid succession immediately before the instruction to make a transition, and the approach was associated with greatly improved performance. Mace and his colleagues (1988) have reported similar procedures, which they describe in terms of establishing a "behavioral momentum."

In a recent study, Horner and colleagues (1991) demonstrated that interspersing requests was effective both in reducing levels of aggression and self-injury and in increasing the completion of an instructional task. Prior to intervention, these authors implemented a functional analysis assessment that identified the challenging behavior as being motivated by escape. Because the behavior served to avoid the instructional task, the authors could expect that a sufficient change in the manner with which the task was presented would probably be effective. On the other hand, if the behavior had been motivated by social or sensory reinforcement, it is unlikely that the interspersal procedure would have been effective.

Another antecedent strategy that has been shown to be effective in reducing challenging behavior related to task presentation is to add a choice-making component to the instruction (Dyer, Dunlap, & Winterling, 1990; Shevin & Klein, 1984). In this approach, students are given the opportunity to make choices among instructional tasks, reinforcers, or both. Dyer et al. (1990) studied the effects of choice-making opportunities on the serious problem behaviors of three students with severe disabilities. They found that the opportunity to select tasks and rewards from a limited set of curricular options was related to substantial decreases in behavior problems. The results also indicated that these students' productivity was not diminished and that the students tended to vary their choices across sessions.

Strategies for manipulating antecedent conditions represent an important component of nonaversive intervention. A variety of manipulations in this category have reduced problem behavior by altering the antecedent stimuli so as to prevent, rather than suppress, the undesirable responding. However, in order to effect widespread changes with behaviors that occur under multiple circumstances, it is likely that antecedent manipulations may need to be implemented in package programs and in coordination with instructional strategies and positive reinforcement.

Strategies Involving Manipulations of Context and Setting Events

There is a growing acknowledgment that behavior occurs in an environmental context that may include more than a simple stimulus-response-consequence relationship (Bailey & Pyles, 1989; LaVigna et al., 1989; Wahler & Fox, 1981). These contextual and setting factors can involve complex and temporally distant phenomena and include influences that may accrue from events such as fitness training (Jansma & Combs, 1987) or social exchanges that occurred earlier in the day (Wahler, 1980). They may also include circumstances, such as noise, crowding, or predictability of schedule, that occur in temporal contiguity with a response, but that do not have a direct stimulus-response relationship.

These factors are often referred to as *setting events*. Setting events, in this sense, are occurrences in the environment that do not produce a problem behavior directly, but that may serve to increase the probability that a problem behavior will occur under future (or additional) circumstances. The setting events for a student with severe disabilities may include the number of students (crowding) in the classroom, the content or scheduling of the curriculum, the temperature, the quality of peer interactions, the onset of a headache, skipping breakfast, or any number of other factors.

Consider skipping breakfast as an example of the way in which a setting event can influence behavior. Each morning at 7:30 A.M., Mary is given breakfast. On some mornings she refuses to eat what is offered and is not allowed to substitute any other foods. She goes to school or work without having eaten. By 10:00 A.M. Mary begins to feel the effects of skipping breakfast. Her stomach contracts and she gets a headache. She is hungry. When Mary is presented with a task under these conditions, she throws a tantrum. The differences in Mary's condition that are related to eating or skipping breakfast are correlated with a change in control exerted by the eliciting stimulus, task presentation. Although this kind of task presentation would not produce a tantrum when she is feeling well, the task instructions in combination with the effects of skipping breakfast may be sufficient to occasion the problem.

Most family members and support personnel are familiar, in a general sense, with the effects that various setting factors may have on problem behavior. This is evident when supervisors recognize that a student has not slept well, or is suffering an ear infection, and is thus more likely to be irritable and, possibly, disruptive. However, the specification of setting events' influences is often difficult to determine. The relationship between a setting event and a particular behavior problem may appear inconsistent and may be very difficult to observe on a regular basis. The case of Mary's breakfast provides a good example. Because she does not get hungry at the same time every day, Mary's tantrums occur during different activities. On some days she may get a snack before she gets hungry, or she may encounter a particularly pleasing interaction that might represent a distraction or a setting event that might compete with the hunger. On other days she may eat breakfast, but the food might irritate her digestion, thus creating an apparent contradiction between the fact that she both ate breakfast and displayed a subsequent tantrum. As these illustrations suggest, such setting factors can be influential, but their influence may be variable and difficult to document.

There are only a few investigations in which setting events have been manipulated in an effort to control challenging behaviors. Examples include manipulating diet (Rast & Johnston, 1986; Rast, Johnston, Ellinger-Allen, & Drum, 1985), controlling noise (Adams, Tallon, & Stangl, 1980) or crowding (McAfee, 1987), and providing for gross motor activities or exercise (Baumeister & McLean, 1984; Jansma & Combs, 1987; Kern, Koegel, & Dunlap, 1984; Lancioni, Smeets, Ceccarani, Capodaglio, & Campanari, 1984). Nevertheless, there are many more setting event manipulations that have occurred in practice than have been documented in the literature. These interventions are evident whenever teachers or family members use preventive strategies when a student is ill or agitated or when a student encounters a context that is disorienting or historically associated with challenging circumstances. In addition, authors are describing with increasing frequency the behavior management implications that are relevant to a person's physiological well-being and to the overall stability and satisfactions present within a person's life-style (Bailey & Pyles, 1989; Brown, 1990).

The manipulation of context and setting events can contribute importantly to a package of nonaversive intervention. Functional assessment procedures, including interviews and direct observations, can be helpful in narrowing the range of possible factors and focusing on those variables that may warrant attention (Bailey & Pyles, 1989; O'Neill et al., 1990). Although research is needed to improve the technologies of assessment and intervention, investigation of setting events is a high priority in nonaversive behavior management because of their broad influences on behavior problems and all other areas of functioning.

Comprehensive Nonaversive Intervention (Programming for Generalized, Life-style Change)

Although an assortment of procedures have been described in the preceding sections, nonaversive intervention is considered to be a broad approach that is not defined adequately on the basis of particular behavioral interventions. Rather, nonaversive intervention addresses a person's life-style in a comprehensive effort to develop increased competencies and adaptive interactions in integrated community settings (Horner et al., 1990; Turnbull & Turnbull, 1990). Included in nonaversive programs of behavioral support are efforts to establish functional skills, increased ratios of reinforcement, alterations of the antecedent stimuli that evoke undesirable responding, and modifications of the context in which a person lives and which may precipitate undesirable patterns of behavior.

A distinguishing factor of comprehensive nonaversive intervention is that it incorporates multiple components. Instead of depending on a single procedure (e.g., DRO), programs might include several concurrent manipulations. For example, it is possible that an individualized program for one student could simultaneously change the schedule of reinforcement, deliver training for staff, offer increased opportunities for choice making, change the curriculum to target functional skills, develop new options for augmentative communication, and increase the number of social contacts. The positive effects that might accrue from such widespread changes are difficult to replicate experimentally because they are so highly individualized. However, a growing number of case descriptions are contributing information relevant to the design and implementation of comprehensive interventions.

In one detailed presentation concerning a 3-year-old boy with autism, Dunlap, Robbins, Morelli, and Dollman (1988) described a multi-component intervention strategy that served to reduce the boy's aggression and tantrums. The authors began with a period of functional assessments in community and instructional contexts. These assessments led to a program of intervention that included training in functional communication, extinction of the disruptive behaviors, generalized training in functional life skills, information and training for the boy's parents, and placement in a socially integrated preschool program. This multicomponent approach was demon-strated to be helpful in reducing aggression and in promoting appropriate speech and other adaptive skills. In addition, standardized assessments and anecdotal reports indicated that the boy's social behavior and community participation were improved substantially.

Turnbull and Turnbull (1990) published an example of comprehensive behavioral support that they described as an illustration of the dramatic changes that can accrue from significant adjustments in a person's life-style. Their case report is of their son, Jay, whose disabilities were identified as "low moderate mental retardation, mild autism, and intermittent bipolar emotional states." In their article the authors first described Jay's behavior, as well as his daily life experiences, when he was in relatively segregated residential and work settings. They compared these circumstances with substantial changes that had been incorporated over a 4-year period and that amounted to a major alteration in Jay's life-style. The changes included a new residence (from a group home to a home of his own with college-age roommates), a change of employment (from a sheltered workshop to supported employment with a job coach), incorporation of choice making across a great range of typical choice-making opportunities, and the development of a social support network that included a chance to establish genuine friendships. Although this example is not accompanied by quantified data, the report indicates significant qualitative gains, with great improvements in Jay's adaptive behavior and reductions in aggression and bipolar mood swings. Jay's experiences represent the substantial impact that can be produced by multicomponent interventions that focus on life-style adjustments.

Another illustration of multicomponent intervention, described by Dunlap, Kern-Dunlap, Clarke, and Robbins (1991), involved "Jill," an adolescent who was described as having multiple intellectual and emotional disabilities. Jill had displayed extremely aggressive and disruptive behavior throughout her school years and had spent significant portions of her school days confined in

TABLE 5.3 "Jill": From Assessment to Intervention

PHASE I: DATA REVIEW AND HYPOTHESIS DEVELOPMENT	PHASE II: HYPOTHESIS TESTING	INTERVENTION
Tested via Reversals of Conditions Alternated Across School Day		
File Review (school records)	Jill is better behaved when:	
Collateral Interviews		
Structured Interviews (school, medical, family)	H1: She is engaged in gross motor activities.	H1: Fine vs. Gross Motor Activities	Curriculum Revision
	H2: Difficult task requirements are brief.	H2: Short vs. Long Tasks	
Standardized Assessment	H3: Activities interest her and they result in outcomes that are meaningful.	H3: Meaningful vs. Analogue Tasks	
Direct Observation			
Rating Scale	H4: She has some choice regarding her activities.	H4: Choice vs. No Choice	

140

a time-out room. The authors' efforts began with an extensive functional assessment that was designed to yield hypotheses (Repp, Felce, & Barton, 1988) regarding the environmental conditions associated with Jill's desirable and undesirable behaviors. Four hypotheses were developed; these were then tested (and confirmed) within the school setting with use of the direct manipulations of functional analysis. The four hypotheses were related to Jill's curriculum. They stated that Jill behaved more positively when she: (1) participated in gross, as opposed to fine, motor activities; (2) worked on difficult tasks in short, as opposed to long, sessions; (3) worked on functional, as opposed to analogue (e.g., workbook), tasks; and (4) had opportunities to make choices among instructional activities. Intervention consisted of revising Jill's curriculum to incorporate guidelines that were derived directly from these four hypotheses. Data collected over a 6-month period showed that Jill's disruptions were eliminated immediately and that her on-task responding increased to very high and stable levels. Improvements were also

noted in her appropriate speech, social behavior, and performance of adaptive life skills. These improvements occurred without explicit changes in the consequences that were scheduled for her behavior; however, the elimination of the disruptions meant that she no longer was placed in the time-out chamber. Table 5.3 depicts the assessment to intervention process used with Jill.

These two examples illustrate the design and implementation of comprehensive packages of nonaversive intervention. In each case, an individualized program was built on the basis of functional assessment information, and each took advantage of multiple intervention strategies. The intervention program for both Jay and Jill involved substantial changes in activity patterns and in the personal control that the two exerted in the form of choice making. In addition, the two cases reflect essential aspects of nonaversive intervention in community settings; that is, they minimized the use of aversive stimuli, and they focused on the establishment of positive repertoires of functional behavior.

REFERENCES

Adams, G. L., Tallon, R. J., & Stangl, J. M. (1980). Environmental influences on self-stimulatory behavior. *American Journal of Mental Deficiency, 85,* 171–175.

Axelrod, S. (1987). Functional and structural analyses of behavior: Approaches leading to reduced use of punishment procedures? *Research in Developmental Disabilities, 8,* 165–178.

Axelrod, S., & Apsche, J., (Eds.). (1983). *The effects of punishment on human behavior.* New York: Academic Press.

Azrin, N. H., & Holz, W. C. (1966). Punishment. In W.K. Honig (Ed.), *Operant behavior: Areas of research and application* (pp. 380–447). New York: Appleton-Century-Crofts.

Bailey, J. S., & Pyles, D. A. M. (1989). Behavioral diagnostics. In E. Cipani (Ed.), *The treatment of severe behavior problems* (pp. 85–106). Washington, DC: American Association on Mental Retardation.

Baumeister, A. A., Sr. (1978). Origins and control of

stereotyped movements. In C. E. Meyers (Ed.), *Quality of life in severely and profoundly mentally retarded people: Research foundations for improvement* (pp. 353–384). Washington, DC: American Association on Mental Deficiency.

Baumeister, A. A., & McLean, W. E. (1984). Deceleration of self-injurious and stereotypic responding by exercise. *Applied Research in Mental Retardation, 5,* 385–393.

Baumeister, A. A., Sr., & Rollins, J. P. (1976). Self-injurious behavior. In N. R. Ellis (Ed.), *International review of research in mental retardation,* vol. 8 (pp. 1–30). New York: Academic.

Bijou, S. W., Peterson, R. F., & Ault, M. H. (1968). A method to integrate descriptive and experimental field studies at the level of data and empirical concepts. *Journal of Applied Behavior Analysis, 1,* 175–191.

Bird, F., Dores, P. A., Moniz, D., & Robinson, J. (1989). Reducing severe aggressive and self-injurious behaviors with functional communication training. *American Journal on Mental Retardation, 94,* 37–48.

Bostow, D. E., & Bailey, J. (1969). Modification of severe disruptive and aggressive behavior using brief timeout and reinforcement procedures. *Journal of Applied Behavior Analysis, 2,* 31–37.

Browder, D. M., & Shapiro, E. S. (1985). Applications of self-management to individuals with severe handicaps: A review. *The Journal of The Association for Persons with Severe Handicaps, 10,* 200–208.

Carr, E. G. (1977). The motivation of self-injurious behavior: A review of some hypotheses. *Psychological Bulletin, 84,* 800–816.

Carr, E. G., & Durand, V. M. (1985a). The social-communicative basis of severe behavior problems in children. In S. Reiss and R. Bootzin (Eds.), *Theoretical issues in behavior therapy* (pp. 219–254). New York: Academic Press.

Carr, E. G., & Durand, V. M. (1985b). Reducing behavior problems through functional communication training. *Journal of Applied Behavior Analysis, 18,* 111–126.

Carr, E. G., Newsom, C. D., & Binkoff, J. (1976). Stimulus control of self-destructive behavior in a psychotic child. *Journal of Abnormal Child Psychology, 4,* 139–153.

Carr, E. G., Newsom, C. D., & Binkoff, J. (1980). Escape as a factor in the aggressive behavior of two retarded children. *Journal of Applied Behavior Analysis, 13,* 101–117.

Carr, E. G., Robinson, S., & Palumbo, L. W. (1990). The wrong issue: Aversive versus nonaversive treatment. The right issue: Functional versus nonfunctional treatment. In A. C. Repp & N. N. Singh (Eds.), *Perspectives on the use of nonaversive and aversive interventions for persons with developmental disabilities* (pp. 362–379). DeKalb, IL: Sycamore Press.

Carr, E. G., Robinson, S., Taylor, J. C., & Carlson, J. I. (1990). Positive approaches to the treatment of severe behavior problems in persons with developmental disabilities: A review and analysis of reinforcement and stimulus-based procedures. *Monograph of the Association for Persons with Severe Handicaps, Number 4.* Seattle, WA: TASH.

Cataldo, M. F., & Harris, J. (1982). The biological basis for self-injury in the mentally retarded. *Analysis and Intervention in Developmental Disabilities, 6,* 265–282.

Cipani, E., (Ed.). (1989). *The treatment of severe behavior problems.* Washington, DC: American Association on Mental Retardation.

Corte, H. E., Wolf, M. M., & Locke, B. L. (1971). A comparison of procedures for eliminating self-injurious behavior of retarded adolescents. *Journal of Applied Behavior Analysis, 4,* 201–213.

Danforth, J. S., & Drabman, R. S. (1989). Aggressive and disruptive behavior. In E. Cipani (Ed.), The treatment of severe behavior disorders: Behavior analysis approaches. *Monographs of the American Association on Mental Retardation, 12,* 111–127.

Dattilo, J. (1986). Computerized assessment of preference for severely handicapped individuals. *Journal of Applied Behavior Analysis, 19,* 445–448.

Day, R. M., Rea, J. A., Schussler, N. G., Larsen, S. E., & Johnson, W. L. (1988). A functionally based approach to the treatment of self-injurious behavior. *Behavior Modification, 12,* 565–589.

Donnellan, A. M., Mirenda, P. L., Mesaros, R. A., & Fassbender, L. L. (1984). Analyzing the communicative functions of aberrant behavior. *The Journal of The Association for Persons with Severe Handicaps, 9,* 201–212.

Doss, S., & Reichle, J. (1989). Establishing communicative alternatives to the emission of socially motivated excess behavior: A review. *The Journal of The Association for Persons with Severe Handicaps, 14,* 101–112.

Dunlap, G. (1984). The influence of task variation and maintenance tasks on the learning and affect of autistic children. *Journal of Experimental Child Psychology, 37,* 41–64.

Dunlap, L. K., & Dunlap, G. (1987) Task Variation: A method for motivating handicapped students. *TEACHING Exceptional Children, 19*(3), 16–19.

Dunlap, G., Kern-Dunlap, L. K., Clarke, S., & Robbins, F. R. (1991). Functional assessment, curriculum revision, and severe behavior problems. *Journal of Applied Behavior Analysis, 24,* 387–397.

Dunlap, L. K., Dunlap, G., Koegel, L. K., & Koegel, R. L. (1991). Using self-monitoring to increase students' success and independence. *TEACHING Exceptional Children, 23*(3), 17–22.

Dunlap, G., Johnson, L. F., & Robbins, F. R. (1990). Preventing serious behavior problems through skill development and early intervention. In A. C. Repp

& N. N. Singh (Eds.), *Perspectives on the use of nonaversive and aversive interventions for persons with developmental disabilities* (pp. 273–286). DeKalb, IL: Sycamore Press.

Dunlap, G., Johnson, J., Winterling, V., & Morelli, M. A. (1988). The management of disruptive behavior in unsupervised settings: Issues and directions for a behavioral technology. *Education and Treatment of Children, 10,* 367–382.

Dunlap, G., & Koegel, R. L. (1980). Motivating autistic children through stimulus variation. *Journal of Applied Behavior Analysis, 13,* 619–627.

Dunlap, G., Robbins, F. R., Morelli, M. A., & Dollman, C. (1988). Team training for young children with autism: A regional model for service delivery. *Journal of the Division for Early Childhood, 12,* 147–160.

Durand, V. M. (1990). *Functional communication training: An intervention program for severe behavior problems.* New York: Guilford Press.

Durand, V. M., & Carr, E. G. (1987). Social influences on "self-stimulatory" behavior: Analysis and treatment application. *Journal of Applied Behavior Analysis, 20,* 119–132.

Durand, V. M., & Carr, E. G. (1991). Functional communication training to reduce challenging behavior: Maintenance and application in new settings. *Journal of Applied Behavior Analysis, 24,* 251–264.

Durand, V. M., & Crimmons, D. B. (1988). Identifying the variables maintaining self-injurious behavior. *Journal of Autism and Developmental Disorders, 18,* 99–117.

Durand, V. M., Crimmins, D., Caulfield, M., & Taylor, J. (1989). Reinforcer assessment: I. Using problem behavior to select reinforcers. *The Journal of The Association for Persons with Severe Handicaps, 14,* 113–126.

Dyer, K., Dunlap, G., & Winterling, V. (1990). The effects of choice-making on the serious problem behaviors of students with developmental disabilities. *Journal of Applied Behavior Analysis, 23,* 515–524.

Evans, I. M., & Meyer, L. H. (1985). *An educative approach to behavior problems.* Baltimore: Paul H. Brookes Publishing Co.

Evans, I. M., & Meyer, L. H. (1990). Toward a science in support of meaningful outcomes: A response to Horner et al. *The Journal of The Association for Persons with Severe Handicaps, 15,* 133–135.

Falvey, M. A. (1989). *Community-based curriculum*

(2nd ed.). Baltimore: Paul H. Brookes Publishing Company.

Favell, J. E., Azrin, N. H., Baumeister, A. A., Carr, E. G., Dorsey, M. F., Forehand, R., Foxx, R. M., Lovaas, O. I., Rincover, A., Risley, T. R., Romanczyk, R. G., Russo, D. C., Schroeder, S. R., & Solnick, J. V. (1982). The treatment of self-injurious behavior. *Behavior Therapy, 13,* 529–554.

Gardner, W. I., & Cole, C. L. (1984). Aggression and related conduct difficulties in the mentally retarded: A multicomponent behavior model. In S. E. Breuning, J. L. Matson, & R. P. Barrett (Eds.), *Advances in mental retardation and developmental disabilities,* vol. 2 (pp. 41–84). Greenwich, CT: JAI Press.

Gardner, W. I., Cole, C. L., Berry, D. L., & Nowinski, J. M. (1983). Reduction of disruptive behaviors in mentally retarded adults. *Behavior Modification, 7,* 76–96.

Gardner, W. I., Cole, C. L., Davidson, D. P., & Karan, O. C. (1986). Reducing aggression in individuals with developmental disabilities: An expanded stimulus control, assessment, and intervention model. *Education and Training of the Mentally Retarded, 21,* 3–12.

Gast, D. L., & Wolery, M. (1987). Severe maladaptive behaviors. In M. E. Snell (Ed.), *Systematic instruction of persons with severe handicaps* (pp. 300–332). Columbus, OH: Charles E. Merrill.

Green, C. W., Reid, D. H., White, L. K., Halford, R. C., Brittain, D. P., & Gardner, S. M. (1988). Identifying reinforcers for persons with profound handicaps: Staff opinion versus systematic assessment of preferences. *Journal of Applied Behavior Analysis, 21,* 31–43.

Guess, D., Helmstetter, E., Turnbull, H.R., & Knowlton, S. (1987). *Use of aversive procedures with persons who are disabled: An historical review and critical analysis.* Seattle, WA: The Association for Persons with Severe Handicaps.

Horner, R. D. (1980). The effects of an environmental "enrichment" program on the behavior of institutionalized profoundly retarded children. *Journal of Applied Behavior Analysis, 13,* 473–491.

Horner, R. H., & Budd, C. M. (1985). Teaching manual sign language to a nonverbal student: Generalization of sign use and collateral reduction of maladaptive behavior. *Education and Training of the Mentally Retarded, 20,* 39–47.

Horner, R. H., Day, M., Sprague, J., O'Brien, M., &

Heathfield, L. T. (1991). Interspersed requests: A nonaversive procedure for decreasing aggression and self-injury during instruction. *Journal of Applied Behavior Analysis, 24,* 265–278.

Horner, R. H., & Dunlap, G., (Eds.). (1988). Behavior management and community integration for individuals with developmental disabilities and severe behavior problems. *Monograph of the Research and Training Center on Community-Referenced Behavior Management.* Eugene: University of Oregon.

Horner, R. H., Dunlap, G., Koegel, R. L., Carr, E. G., Sailor, W., Anderson, J., Albin, R. W., O'Neill, R. E. (1990). Toward a technology of "nonaversive" behavioral support. *The Journal of The Association for Persons with Severe Handicaps, 15,* 125–132.

Hunt, P., Alwell, M., & Goetz, L. (1988). Acquisition of conversation skills and the reduction of inappropriate social behaviors. *The Journal of The Association for Persons with Severe Handicaps, 13,* 20–27.

Iwata, B. A. (1987). Negative reinforcement in applied behavior analysis: An emerging technology. *Journal of Applied Behavior Analysis, 20,* 361–378.

Iwata, B. A. (1988). The development and adoption of controversial default technologies. *The Behavior Analyst, 11,* 149–157.

Iwata, B. A., Dorsey, M. F., Slifer, K. J., Bauman, K. E., & Richman, G. S. (1982). Toward a functional analysis of self-injury. *Analysis and Intervention in Developmental Disabilities, 2,* 1–20.

Iwata, B. A., Vollmer, T. R., & Zarcone, J. H. (1990). The experimental (functional) analysis of behavior disorders: Methodology, applications, and limitations. In A. C. Repp & N. N. Singh (Eds.), *Perspectives on the use of nonaversive and aversive interventions for persons with developmental disabilities* (pp. 301–330). Sycamore, IL: Sycamore Publishing Co.

Jansma, P., & Combs, C. S. (1987). The effects of fitness training and reinforcement on maladaptive behaviors of institutionalized adults, classified as mentally retarded/emotionally disturbed. *Education and Training in Mental Retardation, 22,* 268–279.

Kazdin, A. E. (1980). *Behavior modification in applied settings* (rev. ed.). Homewood, IL: The Dorsey Press.

Kern, L., Koegel, R. L., & Dunlap, G. (1984). The influence of vigorous versus mild exercise on autistic self-stimulation. *Journal of Autism and Developmental Disorders, 14,* 57–67.

Koegel, R. L., & Koegel, L. K., (1990). Extended reduc-

tions in stereotypic behavior of students with autism through a self-management treatment package. *Journal of Applied Behavior Analysis, 23,* 119–127.

Lancioni, G. E., Smeets, P. M., Ceccarani, P. S., Capodaglio, L., & Campanari, G. (1984). Effects of gross motor activities on the severe self-injurious tantrums of multihandicapped individuals. *Applied Research in Mental Retardation, 5,* 471–482.

LaVigna, G. W., & Donnellan, A. M. (1986). *Alternatives to punishment: Solving behavior problems with non-aversive strategies.* New York: Irvington Publishers.

LaVigna, G. W., Willis, T. J., & Donnellan, A. M. (1989). The role of positive programming in behavioral treatment. In E. Cipani (Ed.), *The treatment of severe behavior disorders: Behavior analysis approaches* (pp. 61–83). Washington, DC: American Association on Mental Retardation.

Lennox, D. B., & Miltenberger, R. G. (1989). Conducting a functional assessment of problem behavior in applied settings. *The Journal of The Association for Persons with Severe Handicaps, 14,* 304–311.

Lovaas, O. I., & Favell, J. E. (1987). Protection for clients undergoing aversive/restrictive interventions. *Education and Treatment of Children, 10,* 311–325.

Lovaas, O. I., Freitag, G., Gold, V. J., & Kassorla, I. C. (1965). Experimental studies in childhood schizophrenia: Analysis of self-destructive behavior. *Journal of Experimental Child Psychology, 2,* 67–84.

Lovaas, O. I., & Simmons, J. Q. (1969). Manipulation of self-destruction in three retarded children. *Journal of Applied Behavior Analysis, 2,* 143–157.

Lundervold, D., & Bourland, G. (1988). Quantitative analysis of treatment of aggression, self-injury, and property destruction. *Behavior Modification, 12,* 590–617.

Mace, F. C., Hock, M. L., Lalli, J. S., West, B. J., Belfiore, P., Pinter, E., & Brown, D. K. (1988). Behavioral momentum in the treatment of noncompliance. *Journal of Applied Behavior Analysis, 21,* 123–141.

Mace, F. C., Kratochwill, T. R., & Fiello, R. A. (1983). Positive treatment of aggressive behavior in a mentally retarded adult: A case study. *Behavior Therapy, 14,* 689–696.

Maurice, P., & Trudel, G. (1982). Self-injurious behavior prevalence and relationships to environmental events. In J. H. Hollis & C. E. Meyers (Eds.), *Life-threatening behavior: Analysis and intervention* (pp. 81–103). Washington, DC: American Association on Mental Deficiency.

McAfee, J. K. (1987). Classroom density and the aggressive behavior of handicapped children. *Education and Treatment of Children, 10,* 134–145.

Meyer, L. H., & Evans, I. M. (1989). *Nonaversive intervention for behavior problems: A manual for home and community.* Baltimore: Paul H. Brookes Publishing Co.

National Institutes of Health (1990). *Treatment of destructive behaviors in persons with developmental disabilities* (Consensus Development Statement). *Journal of Autism and Developmental Disorders, 20,* 403–429.

Neisworth, J. T., & Smith, R. M. (1973). *Modifying retarded behavior.* Boston: Houghton Mifflin Co.

O'Neill, R. E., Horner, R. H., Albin, R. W., Storey, K., & Sprague, J. R. (1990). *Functional analysis: A practical assessment guide.* Chicago: Sycamore Press.

Pace, G., Ivancic, M., Edwards, G., Iwata, B., & Page, T. (1985). Assessment of stimulus preferences and reinforcer values with profoundly retarded individuals. *Journal of Applied Behavior Analysis, 18,* 249–255.

Rast J., & Johnston, J. M. (1986). Social versus dietary control of ruminating by mentally retarded persons. *American Journal of Mental Deficiency, 90,* 464–469.

Rast, J., Johnston, J. M., Ellinger-Allen, J. A., & Drum, C. (1985). Effects of nutritional and mechanical properties of food on ruminative behavior. *Journal of the Experimental Analysis of Behavior, 44,* 195–206.

Reese, R. M., Sherman, J. A., & Sheldon, J. (1984). Reducing agitated disruptive behavior of mentally retarded residents of community group homes: The role of self-recording and peer prompted self-recording. *Analysis and Intervention in Developmental Disabilities, 4,* 91–107.

Reichle, J., (Ed.). (1990). *National working conference on positive approaches to the management of excess behavior: Final report and recommendations.* Minneapolis: Center on Community Integration, University of Minnesota.

Repp, A. C., & Dietz, S. M. (1974). Reducing aggressive and self-injurious behavior of institutionalized retarded children through reinforcement of other behaviors. *Journal of Applied Behavior Analysis, 7,* 313–325.

Repp, A. C., Felce, D., & Barton, L. E. (1988). Basing the treatment of stereotypic and self-injurious behaviors on hypotheses of their causes. *Journal of Applied Behavior Analysis, 21,* 281–289.

Repp, A. C., & Karsh, K. G. (1990). A taxonomic approach to the nonaversive treatment of maladaptive behavior of persons with developmental disabilities. In A. C. Repp & N. N. Singh (Eds.), *Perspectives on the use of nonaversive and aversive interventions for persons with developmental disabilities* (pp. 331–347). DeKalb, IL: Sycamore Press.

Repp, A. C., & Singh, N. N., (Eds.). (1990). *Perspectives on the use of nonaversive and aversive interventions for persons with developmental disabilities.* DeKalb, IL: Sycamore Press.

Ricover, A., Cook, A., Peoples, A., & Packard, D. (1979). Using sensory extinction and sensory reinforcement principles to program multiple treatment gains. *Journal of Applied Behavior Analysis, 12,* 221–233.

Rincover, A., & Devany, J. (1982). The application of sensory extinction procedures to self-injury. *Analysis and Intervention in Developmental Disabilities, 3,* 67–81.

Risley, T. R. (1968). The effects and side effects of punishing the autistic behaviors of a deviant child. *Journal of Applied Behavior Analysis, 1,* 21–35.

Russo, D. C., Cataldo, M. F., & Cushing, P. J. (1981). Compliance training and behavioral covariation in the treatment of multiple behavior problems. *Journal of Applied Behavior Analysis, 1,* 21–35.

Shapiro, E. S., & Klein, R. D. (1980). Self-management of classroom behavior with retarded/disturbed children. *Behavior Modification, 4,* 83–97.

Shevin, M., & Klein, N. K. (1984). The importance of choice-making skills for students with severe disabilities. *The Journal of The Association for Persons with Severe Handicaps, 9,* 159–166.

Singer, G. H. S., Singer, J., & Horner, R. H. (1987). Using pretask requests to increase the probability of compliance for students with severe disabilities. *The Journal of The Association for Persons with Severe Handicaps, 12*(4), 287–291.

Slifer, K. J., Ivancic, M. T., Parrish, J. M., Page, T. J., & Burgio, L. D. (1986). Assessment and treatment of multiple behavior problems exhibited by a profoundly retarded adolescent. *Journal of Behavior Therapy and Experimental Psychiatry, 17,* 203–213.

Solnick, J., Rincover, A., & Peterson, C. (1977). Some

determinants of the reinforcing and punishing effects of timeout. *Journal of Applied Behavior Analysis, 10,* 415–424.

Steege, M. W., Wacker, D. P., Berg, W. K., Cigrand, K. K. & Cooper, L. J. (1989). The use of behavioral assessment to prescribe and evaluate treatments for severely handicapped children. *Journal of Applied Behavior Analysis, 22,* 23–33.

Touchette, P. E., MacDonald, R. F., & Langer, S. N. (1985). A scatter plot for identifying stimulus control of problem behavior. *Journal of Applied Behavior Analysis, 18,* 343–351.

Turnbull, A. P., & Turnbull, H. R. (1990). A tale about lifestyle changes: Comments on "Toward a technology of 'nonaversive' behavioral support." *The Journal of The Association for Persons with Severe Handicaps, 15,* 142–144.

Van Houten, R. (1983). Punishment: From the animal laboratory to the applied setting. In S. Axelrod & J. Apsche (Eds.), *The effects of punishment on human behavior* (pp. 13–44). New York: Academic Press.

Van Houten, R., Axelrod, S., Bailey, J. S., Favell, J. E., Foxx, R. M., Iwata, B. A., & Lovaas, O. I. (1988). The right to effective treatment. *The Behavior Analyst, 11,* 111–114.

Wacker, D. P., Berg, W. K., Wiggins, B., Muldoon, M., & Cavanaugh, J. (1985). Evaluation of reinforcer preferences for profoundly handicapped students. *Journal of Applied Behavior Analysis, 18,* 173–178.

Wacker, D., Steege, M., Northup, J. Reimers, T., Berg, W., & Sasso, G. (1990). Use of functional analysis and acceptability measures to assess and treat severe behavior problems: An outpatient clinic model. In A. C. Repp & N. N. Singh (Eds.), *Perspectives on*

the use of nonaversive and aversive interventions for persons with developmental disabilities (pp. 331–348). Sycamore, IL: Sycamore Publishing Co.

Wahler, R. G. (1980). The insular mother: Her problems in parent-child treatment. *Journal of Applied Behavior Analysis, 13,* 207–219.

Wahler, R. G., & Fox, J. J. (1981). Setting events in applied behavior analysis: Toward a conceptual and methodological expansion. *Journal of Applied Behavior Analysis, 14,* 327–338.

Weeks, M., & Gaylord-Ross, R. (1981). Task difficulty and aberrant behavior in severely handicapped students. *Journal of Applied Behavior Analysis, 14,* 449–463.

Winterling, V., Dunlap, G., & O'Neill, R. (1987). The influence of task variation on the aberrant behavior of autistic students. *Education and Treatment of Children, 10,* 105–119.

Wolery, M. & Gast, D. L. (1990). Re-framing the debate: Finding middle ground and defining the role of social validity. In A. C. Repp & N. N. Singh (Eds.), *Perspectives on the use of nonaversive and aversive interventions for persons with developmental disabilities* (pp. 129–143). Sycamore, IL: Sycamore Publishing Company.

Wolf, M. M. (1978). Social validity: The case for subjective measurement or how applied behavior analysis is finding its heart. *Journal of Applied Behavior Analysis, 11,* 203–214.

Young, J. A., & Wincze, J. P. (1974). The effects of the reinforcement of compatible and incompatible alternative behaviors on the self-injurious and related behaviors of a profoundly retarded female adult. *Behavior Therapy, 5,* 614–623.

PART TWO

CURRICULUM DOMAIN AND CONTENT AREAS

The chapters in Part II of this book deal with specific assessment and teaching strategies for general domains and specific content areas. Each chapter also includes a curriculum section and a critical issues section, relevant to the domain or curriculum content area under consideration. The first chapter in Part II (Chapter 6) provides an overview of the importance of training domestic and community skills. The assessment strategies in this chapter (as well as in other chapters) rely heavily on the principles espoused in Chapter 2, on functional assessment. Similarly, the chapter on instructional technology (Chapter 3) provides the foundation for the training programs and procedures described in each chapter of Part II.

Persons with severe disabilities need to acquire relevant work skills for meaningful work, and engaging in such work results in a more fruitful, productive life. With an emphasis on supported employment, Chapter 7, on vocational training, presents assessment and instructional approaches for teachers to utilize in working with persons with severe disabilities. Both trainer-directed and self-managed instructional programs are detailed.

Chapter 8 presents techniques in teaching recreational and leisure skills. In the first three chapters in this section, the reader will notice an emphasis on developing learner competence in specific environments. Therefore, an infusion of other curriculum content areas (e.g., language,

self-care, motor skills) in these domains is inherent in this model. For example, language skills needed in a specific leisure environment would be taught within a specific social context involving a leisure activity. Therefore, the type of language skill to be developed will vary as the function of the context. These three chapters also provide a methodology for identifying the relevant needed skills for each specific context.

The following two chapters focus on language development and communication. One of the most glaring deficiencies in persons with severe disabilities is their inability to use language in a functional, socially successful manner (Gaylord-Ross & Holvoet, 1985). Chapter 9 provides a number of techniques to build language both in the natural context as well as in structured training programs. Chapter 10 is an important chapter, in that many persons with severe disabilities are nonvocal. Thus, it is incumbent upon the teacher to identify and design an alternative method of communication, one that can allow the individual to express his or her wants and needs and interact with other members of society in an everyday context. Chapter 11, on social skills, is an extension of the previous two chapters dealing with communication skills. Social skills comprise many component behaviors, many of which are language oriented. This chapter also takes a functional approach in designing a program to teach appropriate acceptable social skills, which can often compete with undesirable aberrant behaviors.

The next chapter (Chapter 12) provides the reader with a wealth of information on teaching academics. Again, the format is the same as in other chapters, in that a discussion on selecting and assessing relevant skills is followed by a consideration of critical issues and curriculum areas. The types of academic skills to be taught derive from the natural contexts of home and community environments.

Chapter 13, the last in Part II, involves techniques for using adaptive equipment. The severe disabilities of some people often include physical disabilities. Therefore, the teacher needs to be competent in the identification and use of specialized adaptive equipment to allow such individuals to function as independently as possible in everyday environments.

_____ CHAPTER 6 _____

DOMESTIC AND COMMUNITY LIVING SKILLS

FRED SPOONER
DAVID W. TEST
University of North Carolina at Charlotte

If asked to describe what they do in a "typical" day, most people would probably include many of the following activities: getting dressed, brushing teeth, making coffee and breakfast, fixing a lunch or perhaps eating at a fast-food restaurant, using public transportation, stopping at a convenience store, and cooking dinner. On a weekly basis, most people do laundry, shop for groceries, and go out to eat. Because these activities are part of our everyday life, we often take them for granted. However, persons with severe disabilities often do not develop such skills readily (Brimer, 1990; Meyer, Peck, & Brown, 1991; Sailor & Haring, 1977; Sontag, Burke, & York, 1973). Their ability to live in a home of their own choosing, independently, and to access the community to engage in preferred activities and events is often limited because of their extreme skill deficits in everyday tasks. The following example illustrates how lack of these skills can restrict a person's freedom.

George is 18 years old, has a tested IQ of 25, has been in school for 12 years, but has never been served in any setting other than an elementary school. George can do several things that he could not do 10 years ago. He can put 100 pegs in a board in less than 10 minutes with 95 percent accuracy, but he cannot put coins in a vending machine. He can, when given the command to touch his nose, ear, and other body parts, touch those selected parts, but he cannot blow his nose when needed. He can sort blocks by 10 different colors, but cannot sort clothes—whites from colors—for doing the laundry. He can string beads in alternating colors and match the sequence to a pattern on a Developmental Learning Materials (DLM) card, but cannot lace or tie his shoes. He can sing his ABCs and tell the names of all letters of the alphabet, when they are presented on a card in upper case, with 85 percent accuracy, but he cannot tell the men's room from the ladies' room when he goes to McDonald's. He can identify with 100 percent accuracy 100 different Peabody Picture Cards by pointing, but cannot order a hamburger by pointing to a picture or gesturing. He can count to 100 by rote, but does not know how many dollars to pay the waitress for a $1.95 McDonald's coupon special. He can sit in a circle with appropriate behavior and sing songs and play "Duck, Duck, Goose," but nobody else his age in his neighborhood seems to want to do that.[1]

It is obvious that George has some skills, but do

[1]Adapted from the O'Berry Center's (Goldsboro, NC) *Family Focus Newsletter*.

The preparation of this manuscript was supported in part by U.S. Department of Education, Office of Special Education and Rehabilitative Services Grant, #H02900047. However, the opinions expressed do not necessarily reflect the policy position of the U.S. Department of Education, and no official endorsement of the U.S. Department should be inferred.

they allow him to participate with others his own age who are not disabled? Do the skills that George has learned allow him to functionally and independently participate in the community? No! It is the functional, age-appropriate skills (the skills George did not have), which allow a person to reside in his or her own preferred style and access community activities, that are the focus of this chapter.

DEFINITION

Domestic and community living skills can be defined as those skills used on a regular (daily, weekly, monthly) basis that are necessary for a person to function within domestic (home) and community environments and that allow an individual to become a contributing member of his or her household and community. At the simplest level, *domestic skills* occur at home and include such self-help activities as dressing, grooming, toileting, self-feeding, and household chores (e.g., cooking, cleaning, doing laundry). On the other hand, *community living skills* occur outside the home and include activities such as traveling in the community, going shopping, eating out, and using other services (e.g., laundromat, post office).

Importance of Domestic and Community Living Skills

Domestic and community living skills are important for a number of reasons. First, they allow an individual to become independent. Because most domestic and community living skills are essential to an individual's everyday existence, if individuals cannot perform all or part of a skill, someone else will do it for them. For example, if Sally, a 13-year-old girl, cannot dress herself, then Sally's mother or caregiver must do it. If Sally cannot independently select her own clothes for the day, and then put them on by herself, she must wear what her mother chooses for her. Second, domestic and community living skills allow individuals greater personal choice. By being able to cook, shop, or order in a restaurant, a person is able to

choose his or her own favorite food. Finally, as an individual's domestic and community living skills increase, the responsibilities of that person's parents or family are reduced. This is reflected in a recent survey of 202 parents of students with severe and profound disabilities (Epps & Myers, 1989). The results of this study indicated that parents rated domestic skills as the most important curricular domain, followed by vocational, community, and leisure and recreation skills.

Historical Review of Domestic and Community Living Skills

The importance of domestic and community living skills is also supported by the large amount of research that has been conducted in this area. Figure 6.1, a time line of domestic and community living skills, is a sampling of articles that have been published in this area between 1965 and 1990. As can be seen, individuals with mental retardation have been taught a variety of domestic and community living skills, ranging from brushing teeth and washing hands and face to cooking their own meals.

It is interesting to note from the time line that in the early years (1965–1975) research was largely focused on self-help skills, such as dressing, toilet training, and toothbrushing. Except for the one citation to travel training (Cortazzo & Sansone, 1969), the focus was not on training skills in the community, but rather in these persons' residences in the 1960s and early 1970s—in institutions. The advent of Public Law 94-142 and the application of the principles of normalization (Wolfensberger, 1972) have had a significant impact not only on the skills that were the new focal point of training, but on the environment in which those skills were trained—the community.

SELECTING, ASSESSING, AND TEACHING RELEVANT DOMESTIC AND COMMUNITY LIVING SKILLS

Clearly, domestic and community living skills are important for individuals with severe disabilities

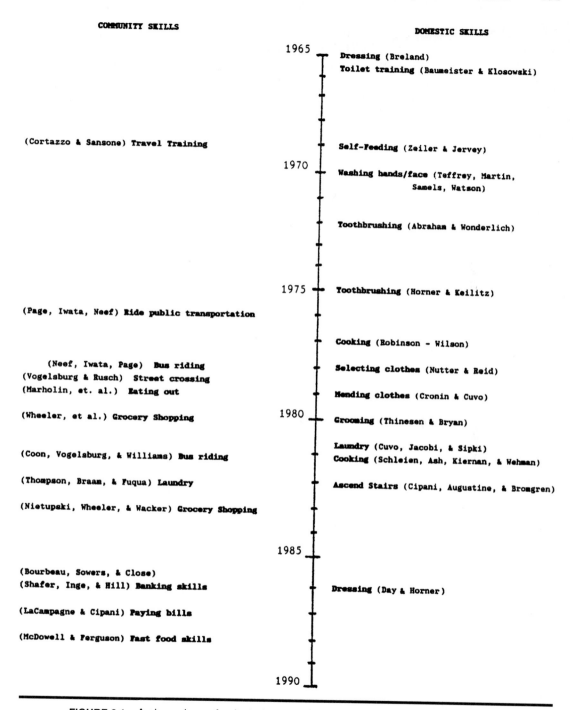

FIGURE 6.1   A chronology of selected community and domestic living skills from 1965–1990.

if they are to function effectively in their home and community living situations. Aveno (1987), in a national survey of 298 group homes and 138 foster homes, gives an exhaustive list of community skill competencies ranging from general skills, such as using a home telephone and frequenting a video arcade, to consumer services such as using a bank or a laundromat.

Although an extensive number of domestic and community living skills can be important, one needs to keep in mind that persons who reside in different places may need different skills. For example, it would not be necessary to teach a student to ride the bus if there was no bus service where the individual lived. Therefore, it is important for teachers to be able to (1) select appropriate skills and (2) assess and teach domestic and community living skills that allow individuals with severe disabilities to become contributing members of their households and communities. The following sections focus on procedures for selecting, assessing, and teaching domestic and community living skills—addressing the question, how do teachers make decisions as to what skills to select for the specific students in their classrooms, and then how do they assess and teach those skills?

Selecting Skills

Simply stated, community and domestic skills should be chosen because they are skills that each individual student will need in present and future settings (see Chapter 2). Although it may be "the bottom line," this response is too general. To plan effectively for future placements teachers need to know (1) several detailed pieces of information about the current skill levels of the student, as well as (2) the skills that will be needed to function effectively in the student's next placement.

When selecting functional and chronologically age-appropriate skills, teachers will need to survey peers of the same approximate age group who are not disabled so that the skills selected will be socially valid for that particular age group, in that particular community or that part of the country

(Haring, 1991). Surveying peers can be accomplished in at least three ways. First, peers can be interviewed to determine the activities in which they engage during breaks and lunch at school, as well as during nonschool hours. Haring, Roger, Lee, Breen, and Gaylord-Ross (1986) used this strategy to identify topics of conversation to use in training social skills to students with severe disabilities attending regular public schools. Second, peers can be asked to respond to a checklist of items. For example, Haring, Breen, and Laitinen (1989) ask nondisabled teenagers to rate catalog clothing items to determine age and situational appropriateness. Third, teachers can observe peers in the natural environment to determine sequences of activities in both domestic and community settings by conducting an inventory of activities (e.g., Ford et al., 1984).

Surveying peers in selecting socially valid, chronologically age-appropriate skills is viewed as an overarching strategy that can be applied to each of the following six considerations for selecting appropriate domestic and community living skills. These include the three influences of functional assessment identified in Chapter 2 of this book, the criterion of ultimate functioning, the criterion of the next environment, and the criterion of the immediate environment, as well as the three criteria identified by Falvey (1986), functionality, chronological age-appropriateness, and reflection of transitions.

Six considerations. The first consideration is the *criterion of ultimate functioning* (Brown, Nietupski, & Hamre-Nietupski, 1976). Brown and colleagues define the criterion of ultimate functioning as "an ever changing, expanding, localized, and personalized cluster of factors that each person must possess in order to function as productively and independently as possible in socially, vocationally, and domestically integrated adult community environments" (p. 8). The criterion of ultimate functioning was introduced in 1976 by Brown and his colleagues as a guideline for the field to follow. Although our thinking in some areas of care and treatment for persons with severe disabilities has shifted, such as in the movement away from widespread use of aversive interventions, Brown's statement still holds true today, some 14 years later. The criterion of ultimate functioning suggests that in order for individuals with severe disabilities to function independently in integrated adult environments, the educational services they receive should be longitudinal and continuous, as opposed to short term; that they should be trained with "real" materials, as opposed to artificial materials; and that they should be placed in regular, integrated community schools that facilitate the development of skills, values, and attitudes necessary to perform and interact effectively in a heterogeneous society, as opposed to segregated (self-contained) schools.

To illustrate the criterion of ultimate functioning, consider two examples: first, an example that illustrates the principle; and second, one that does not. If the criterion of ultimate functioning is followed, Richard, an 18-year-old who is being trained in a community-based training program to clean hotel rooms, would actually receive that training at the Holiday Inn or a similar "real" hotel in the community, with real beds, sheets, mirrors, and furniture. On the other hand, if the criterion of ultimate functioning is not followed, Richard might be receiving that training, to work as an attendant to clean hotel rooms, in his classroom, with his teacher and fellow students playing the roles of guests in a "simulated" hotel. The bed might be real, but it would need to be made twice to simulate a double room (i.e., Richard would make the bed, the teacher would unmake it, and Richard would make it again).

The focal point should be on integration, the student's attending regular community schools, which increases the probability of their interaction with their chronological-aged peers, working and living in the community, longitudinal applications, and functional materials. The applications of the criterion of ultimate functioning should be in the community, not in assimilate classroom settings with make-believe people and unrealistic setups.

The second consideration is the *criterion of the next environment* (Vincent, Salisbury, Walter, Gruenwald, & Powers, 1980), which specifically addresses the skills and competencies that the student will need in his or her next educational placement. For example, Vincent and colleagues (1980) considered the skills necessary for a young child to function effectively in the next educational placement. In the case of preschool-aged children with disabilities, the next logical classroom environment would be the public school kindergarten. The logic is that if teachers know what skills their students will need for the next educational placement, then they can better prepare students to successfully make the transition to those educational settings. For example, children entering kindergarten usually recognize primary colors (i.e., red, blue, green, yellow, etc.), recognize the four basic shapes (i.e., triangle, square, circle, and rectangle), recognize numbers 1 through 10, recognize their own name in a written format, recognize letters of the alphabet, and demonstrate appropriate social skills such as sharing, getting along with others, and not aggressing toward other children. In addition, children who enter kindergarten are typically toilet trained and can put on and take off their own coats. Although these are some of the skills expected of a child entering a kindergarten classroom, they are also taught during the kindergarten year because children come to this experience with such varied backgrounds. If the skills needed in the next environment are known, then teachers can work on them prior to placement, but not necessarily as prerequisites. When such a wide variance of skill level is accepted as entry-level behavior, the probability is increased for young children with disabilities to participate with their chronological-aged peers in the kindergarten experience.

Another consideration is the *criterion of the immediate environment* (Petersen, Trecker, Egan, Fredericks, & Bunse, 1983). The criterion of the immediate environment, as one might expect, focuses directly on identifying and teaching skills that the student needs at present to function effectively in all of his or her different environments (e.g., school, home, YMCA, community). Does John, who is 8 years old and attends Newell Elementary, need to be able to use public transportation? Or does he just need to be able to ride the school bus with the other children? Is it necessary for students who attend elementary school, like John, to pack a lunch box each day? Should a particular junior high school student be proficient at making a bed, cleaning his or her room, ordering at a fast-food restaurant, or going shopping?

A fourth consideration is *functionality,* another integral component to selecting skills. Recent publications have stressed a functional approach to teaching practically all skills to learners with severe disabilities (Brown et al., 1980; Falvey, 1986; Sailor & Guess, 1983; Snell, 1987; Wilcox & Bellamy, 1982). Functionality is a practical perspective and is similar to the criterion of ultimate functioning in that it concentrates on identifying curriculum areas or domains (e.g., domestic, community, vocational, leisure and recreation) in which each student will be involved in both the present and future environment.

Brown and colleagues (1979) suggest that in order to determine whether a skill is functional, the teacher should ask the following question: If the student does not learn to perform this skill, will someone else have to do it for him or her? If the answer is yes, it is highly probable that the skill is functional. For example, for Bill, who is 12 years old, brushing teeth is a critical domestic skill, because if teeth are not brushed well two or three times a day, food caught in teeth will cause one's breath to smell bad, affecting potential social interaction; food caught in teeth will, over time, cause teeth to decay, which may cause them to be pulled. If enough teeth are pulled and not replaced, physical appearance can be affected.

A fifth consideration is *chronological age-appropriateness.* When skills and materials are chronologically age-appropriate, they reflect activities and equipment that are performed and used by nondisabled peers of the same age (Bates, Renzaglia, & Wehman, 1981; Meyer, 1989, Fore-

word to Neel & Billingsley, 1989; Neel & Billingsley, 1989; Sailor & Guess, 1983). The consideration of age-appropriate skills taught with age-appropriate materials is an integral component of current state-of-the-art thinking for selecting, assessing, and teaching appropriate skills to people with severe disabilities. Travis, who is 14 years old, should not spend leisure time listening to nursery rhymes, but to music that is more oriented toward his chronological-aged peers, such as some of the latest releases from Madonna, Aerosmith, or Bon Jovi. Moreover, it would be inappropriate to allow Travis, an adolescent with a disability, to spend time playing Ring-Around-the-Rosie, when daily or weekly access to Nintendo's Super Mario Brothers would be a much more age-appropriate activity for him. It is important that we keep in mind that a person's peers, classmates, and friends are usually about the same chronological age. Yet when mental age has been used for grouping students with severe disabilities, this is often not the case. Older students with disabilities are often placed in classes where their classmates are younger children without disabilities or with younger children who have less severe disabilities. An example of such a grouping by mental age might be the placement of a 10-year-old child with a severe disability in a regular kindergarten classroom because test results show that he or she functions, mentally, at about that level. Although the child's mental functioning might be within the range of a normal 5-year-old, there would be other drastic differences, size for one, that would be clear indicators that this child does not fit in a kindergarten classroom. In situations based on grouping by mental age, older students are not exposed to the same materials that children of their own chronological age would encounter. Clearly, this violates the age-appropriate criterion.

A sixth and final consideration is the *reflection of transitions.* When planning and placement reflect transition, they prepare the student for the next or subsequent environment and the next set of expectations. For example, it is appropriate for high school-aged children to become involved in community activities, because these are the activities they will need to access when their school program is finished. Although one might ride a school bus to and from school, school buses are free transportation and often include assistance, such as in making sure a student gets on the right bus. Because free bus rides and assistance will not be available after the school program has been completed, training should focus on accessing public transportation. In addition to transportation issues, school training should also take into account living and employment in the community. High school-aged students should be taught to cook meals and to do laundry, as well as numerous household tasks that will allow them to live independently in the community. Another focus should be employment preparation skills (see Chapter 7).

These six considerations force teachers to make both philosophical and practical decisions. In fact, a teacher's philosophy, which might be thought of as the first ingredient, to a very significant extent helps to dictate practical application. For example, if a person's philosophical view is that the most appropriate residential option for adults with severe disabilities is a state-operated residential facility, and the most appropriate vocational placement is a sheltered workshop, then behaviors selected for assessing and teaching would likely coincide with compliance training for outbursts of aberrant or aggressive behavior. On the other hand, if a teacher believes, as we do, that the community is the most appropriate residential and vocational placement, then assessment and training in accessing public transportation, eating in a fast-food restaurant, and crossing busy intersections would be selected.

Assessing Skills

In assessing the environment of a student's placement, it is important to consider both *immediate skills* (i.e., skills that the learner will need to function effectively in his or her current setting) and *long-term skills*. Assessing the skills necessary to

successfully negotiate present and future environmental situations, and then using the list of skills to form an assessment tool, is an excellent way to determine what skills a student currently has in his or her repertoire and the skills that are not present that can enhance the probability of success in these environments. Brown and colleagues (1979) and Falvey (1986) have referred to the process of assessing the environment as an *ecological inventory*. In doing an ecological inventory, it is important to identify skills that are performed by nondisabled age peers in a variety of domestic and community environments. Falvey (1986) indicates that there are five basic steps to conducting an ecological inventory: (1) dividing the curriculum into curriculum domains (in this case, domestic and community), (2) delineating the environments within each domain that are available to nondisabled age peers, (3) delineating the subenvironments within each environment, (4) delineating the activities that occur within each subenvironment, and (5) delineating the specific skills required or expected of a student in order to participate in each activity. See Figure 6.2 for an example of the steps in conducting an ecological inventory.

In most situations where teachers are working with young children with severe disabilities who have very few skills, common sense, in conjunction with some foresight, can be a good guide to decision making. For example, suppose the following information is known about a 10-year-old child: (1) the child is not toilet trained, but has the ability to sit independently on the toilet; (2) he or she can pull pants and underpants up and down successfully; and (3) the child can feed him- or herself independently with a spoon, but cannot use a fork or knife. Based on the current assessment information just described, two targets immediately come to mind: first, toilet training, as it would not be advantageous to be 10 years old and not toilet trained; second, learning to eat certain foods that require the use of a fork; and next, perhaps, discrimination training with spoon and fork, as to which foods are appropriately eaten with each utensil. Keep in mind that there can be mul-

Domain: Community
Environment: Torrance Hospital
Subenvironment: Coffee Shop

Activity: Locating a seat
Skills: Enter doorway
Scan area for empty table/chair
Go to empty table/chair
Sit down in empty chair

Activity: Looking at menu
Skills: Scan selections
Determine desired food and beverage
Replace menu in menu holder

Activity: Ordering desired food and beverage
Skills: State or point to choice
Answer waitress/waiter's questions
Wait for order

FIGURE 6.2   Sample abbreviated ecological inventory. Reprinted with permission from: Falvey, M. (1989). *Community-based curriculum: Instructional strategies for students with severe handicaps*, second edition (p. 47). Baltimore: Paul H. Brookes Publishing Co.

tiple training targets, with additional assessments being done on other functional skills (e.g., dressing, grooming).

The outcomes of the assessment process need to be practically based and directly related to functional skills that will help students in immediate and next environments. When domestic skills are considered, can the learner dress him- or herself? Can the individual eat with a spoon? Is selecting clothes for the day a possibility? Additional generic, yet very critical, skills in the domestic area also include grooming, toileting, feeding, cooking, and cleaning, to name but a few. When community skills are considered, can the learner use the local public transportation system? In communities where a public transportation system is not available, can the individual in question effectively call a cab and pay the appropriate amount when the destination is reached? Other critical community skills include using a public tele-

phone, grocery shopping, eating at a fast-food restaurant, and attending local community recreation facilities, such as a swimming pool or a park. Finally, it is important always to return to considering the skills that nondisabled peers of the same chronological age will be performing in domestic and community environments.

Teaching Skills

Once skill assessment has taken place, the next step is to teach the skill. Teaching skills includes selection of both curriculum and instructional methods. *Curriculum* refers to the skills that need to be acquired (e.g., feeding, toileting, riding public transportation), whereas *methods* represent the instructional procedures such as chaining, prompting, and fading that are used to teach the items of the curriculum. Curriculum selection will flow directly from the environmental demand and functional assessments. Any curriculum for students with severe disabilities should be individualized and based on individual strengths and weaknesses as suggested by the functional assessment process. An important component to curriculum selection in teaching in the domestic and community domains is sequencing the curriculum. Gaylord-Ross and Holvoet (1985) refer to curriculum sequencing as the when and why of instruction. This means that skills should be taught at natural times during the day, and in a sequence that is functional (i.e., useful and timely). For example, because brushing teeth typically occurs in the morning after breakfast, perhaps after lunch and dinner, and in the evening before bedtime, there are a total of four functional times each day in which this domestic skill could be practiced. In most school situations where children receive breakfast at school, the teacher could focus on at least two of those training times (after breakfast and after lunch). The other two toothbrushing opportunities could be handled where the child lives. It is neither appropriate nor functional to have a toothbrushing session at 10:00 A.M. on Monday, Wednesday, and Friday. After all, what is functional about brushing teeth at ten o'clock? Nothing, unless that is the time you get up on Saturday after a late night on Friday. Other domestic skills in the curriculum should be sequenced in the same way. For example, there are several naturally occurring times during the day when dressing, making a snack, riding the bus, and going to a fast-food restaurant could be practiced.

Once the necessary domestic and community skills are selected and the "when and why" issues decided, the teacher (or trainer) will need to choose instructional methods (techniques) to help the learner acquire the identified skills. From a general perspective, Sontag, Burke, and York's (1973) statement about an inverse relationship between the skills of the learner and those skills required by the trainer still rings true in the 1990s. The lower the skill performance of the learner, the more skills the trainer needs to possess. In addition, it is essential that a full spectrum of learning include acquisition, fluency building, generalization, and maintenance (Haring, 1988; Haring et al., 1985; Haring, Liberty, & White, 1980; Horner, Dunlap, & Koegel, 1988; see also Chapter 3). Although some authors (e.g., Haring et al., 1980) discuss the stages of learning in four distinct categories, we combine generalization and maintenance into a single category, thus making only three distinctions (see Chapter 3).

Stages of Learning. *Acquisition,* the initial stage of learning, involves learning to perform a skill accurately. During the acquisition phase, if a student's performance falters, a good remediation strategy is to provide the student with information about how to perform the task or the target step (Haring, Liberty, & White, 1980). Such strategies as giving directions and demonstrations, using physical guidance, and providing prompts (e.g., physical or verbal) are listed among the ways to provide information to the student. For example, if the student is learning to cook French toast using a recipe (not the prepackaged type) that involves a 25-step task analysis, and he fails to turn the appropriate knob to control the temperature on the burner he is using, or to select the correct temperature, then giving a verbal prompt such as, "What's the correct temperature, Fred?" or physically guiding Fred's hand to the correct knob and turning it to the appropriate reading would be a possible acquisition-enhancing strategy.

The next stage of learning, according to Haring et al. (1980), is *fluency building.* Fluency involves going beyond accuracy by increasing efficiency. The fluency stage requires changes in instructional strategy that motivate and improve efficient performance of the student. Strategies that have been effective in promoting fluency have been drill and practice, instructions such as, "Go fast," and manipulating consequences (e.g., consequences for correct, fluent performance, as well as consequences for disfluent performance). This could involve increasing the rate of the behavior, increasing or decreasing the duration of the behavior, or decreasing the latency of response time. Let us continue with our example of Fred, cooking French toast according to a recipe. The typical amount of time needed to cook one serving of French toast is approximately 15 minutes. Yet current data indicate that 30 minutes have elapsed from the time Fred starts the process (e.g., getting the appropriate cooking utensils) until he is ready to sit down to eat his breakfast. Because Fred now performs each step accurately, the present overall strategy should focus on decreasing the time that Fred spends cooking the French toast. Specifically, instructions might be given to Fred during the time he is stirring batter to "stir it faster" rather than at the slow pace he is currently using.

The third stage of learning, *generalization,* is an essential component of overall learning. Generalization occurs when a learned response is seen to occur in the presence of "untaught" stimuli (Haring et al., 1980; Horner et al., 1988; Stokes & Baer, 1977; Stokes & Osnes, 1988). Stokes and Baer (1977) initially identified seven strategies to influence generalization that include sequential modification and training sufficient exemplars. Several generalization strategies are exemplified in the section "Generalization: A Critical Issue." We return now to Fred, who is currently able to make French toast accurately (acquisition) and quickly (fluency building) in approximately 15 minutes. However, if all he can make is French toast, there is a generalization problem. One possible strategy for teaching Fred to cook other breakfast dishes is to use the technique known as *providing sufficient exemplars.* Every morning Fred is instructed to make a different breakfast, which involves following a recipe, mixing ingredients, and using the stove or oven. In addition, the techniques *loose training* (sometimes the batter is mixed right next to the stove, and sometimes it is mixed on the counter across from the stove) and *indiscriminable contingencies* (sometimes Fred is reinforced for not getting parts of the eggshell in the batter, and sometimes he does just fine, with no pieces of shell in the batter, and is left alone) are used.

Maintenance involves performing the newly acquired behavior or skill over time (e.g., generalization over time). Maintenance is said to have occurred if 6 days later, 6 weeks later, 6 months later, and 6 years later, the student can still successfully perform the skill. Generally, one of the strategies for maintaining skills is to have the student practice the targeted skills frequently and to provide feedback on the appropriate completion of the requisite steps (Horner, Williams, & Knobbe, 1985). Even if Fred is not attempting to be the gourmet chief of the 1990s, in order to successfully care for himself properly and as independently as possible, he will need to practice making various breakfast dishes that he likes, as well as preparing food for other meals.

Community and domestic skills, like all other skills, are not learned until they are performed in the environment where they are expected to be performed naturally. Teachers cannot simply teach skills in the classroom (unless that is the place where the behavior is to ultimately be performed) and expect the student to perform those skills in another environment. Real-life settings must be identified, analyzed, and used to significantly enhance future placement and success in the real world. Chaining and response prompting

procedures are discussed next, as methods for teaching domestic and community living skills.

Chaining Procedures.   Although there are many training strategies that can be used to teach domestic and community living skills, the application of *chaining* procedures has been used in teaching domestic skills (i.e., dressing) since at least 1965, when Breland discussed the use of backward chaining. Even though a complete description of the application of chaining procedures to teaching a wide variety of skills to students with severe disabilities can be found in Chapter 4, we briefly reiterate here their application to domestic and community living skills.

Table 6.1 presents a task analysis of a first-aid skill, communicating an emergency. This task analysis will be used to demonstrate the relationship of task analysis to types of chaining procedures.

TABLE 6.1   Task Analysis of First-Aid Skill Trained

Communicating an Emergency

1. Locate phone.
2. Pick up receiver.
3. Dial 9.
4. Dial 1.
5. Dial 1.
6. Put receiver to ear.
7. Listen for operator.
8. Give full name.
9. Give full address.
10. Give phone number.
11. Explain emergency.
12. Hang up after operator does.

Adapted from Spooner, F., Stem, B., & Test, D. W. (1989). Teaching first-aid skills to adolescents who are moderately mentally handicapped. *Education and Training in Mental Retardation, 24,* 341–351.

To review briefly, there are three types of chaining procedures. The first type is *backward chaining* (BC), teaching the last step of the task first, reaching a predetermined criterion at that step before moving to the next step, and progressing one step at a time. If we consider the task analysis for communicating an emergency (Table 6.1), and we wanted to use BC, we would start at step 12, "Hang up after operator does." In this case, the trainer would have to perform the preceding 11 steps, let the learner do the last one, and then reinforce the learner for hanging up the phone. After step 12 was performed to criterion (for instance, three times in a row without error or assistance), the trainer would train step 11, "Explain emergency," and the learner would complete step 12 after step 11. The training sequence would, as the criterion is reached for each individual step, move back up the chain.

A second type is *forward chaining* (FC), teaching the first step of the task first, reaching a predetermined criterion on that step before moving to the next step, and progressing one step at a time. Using the example of communicating an emergency, FC would start with the first step of the task, "Locate phone." This step would be trained to criterion, then step 2 would be trained, and so on, progressing in a forward fashion.

A third type of chaining procedure is *total task* (TT), starting with the first step of the task and training every step in every trial until the student performs the whole task at a predetermined criterion (Spooner & Spooner, 1984). Again using the example of communicating an emergency, if TT were being employed, one training trial would consist of taking the learner through all 12 steps, starting at step 1, "Locate phone," and ending with step 12, "Hang up after operator does."

The first two chaining procedures (BC and FC) are usually described as serial training methods because learning progresses one step at a time, usually in a multiple-trial format (Kayser, Billingsley, & Neel, 1986; Sailor & Guess, 1983). Backward chaining has been employed to teach a wide variety of domestic skills, but dressing has

typically been one of the key skill areas where researchers have focused their attention (Ball, Seric, & Payne, 1971; Bensberg, Colwell, & Cassell, 1965; Bensberg & Slominski, 1965; Watson, 1972). On the other hand, TT is described as a concurrent method, because all steps are trained at once or concurrently, usually in a single-trial format (Kayser et al., 1986; Sailor & Guess, 1983). The TT procedure has also been used to teach a wide variety of domestic and community living skills, including dressing (Azrin, Schaeffer, & Wesolowski, 1976), use of public transportation (Coon, Vogelsberg, & Williams, 1981; Neef, Iwata, & Page, 1978), brushing teeth (Horner & Keilitz, 1975), and cooking (Schleien, Ash, Kiernan, & Wehman, 1981).

Response Prompting Procedures. The use of *response prompting procedures* is another instructional method to consider when teaching relevant domestic and community living skills to students with severe disabilities. Response prompts can be defined as stimuli in the form of instructions, modeling, or physical guidance, which are added (and subsequently faded) to the naturally occurring cues either before or after a response, and which increase the likelihood that the target behavior will be performed and consequently reinforced (Billingsley & Romer, 1983; Demchak, 1990; Schoen, 1986; Snell & Smith, 1978). According to Demchak (1990), there are four methods for systematically fading response prompts: (1) *increasing assistance,* (2) *decreasing assistance,* (3) *graduated guidance,* and (4) *time delay.* Like the previous discussion on chaining procedures, a complete and thorough critique can be found in Chapter 4. To illustrate the types of response prompting procedures, Table 6.2 presents an example of using a washing machine in the teaching of laundry skills.

Increasing assistance is sometimes called the system of least prompts (e.g., verbal, model, physical). Consider the washing machine example. If Debbie, an 18-year-old, failed to put in the detergent, she would first be given a verbal cue, "Debbie,

TABLE 6.2 Task Analysis for Using a
Washing Machine

1. Open lid.
2. Pick up pile of clothes.
3. Put pile of clothes in washing machine.
4. Pick up premeasured detergent.
5. Put in premeasured detergent.
6. Close lid.
7. Turn wash/rinse knob to warm/warm setting.
8. Turn load size knob to middle setting.
9. Push cycle knob in.
10. Turn cycle knob to the right.
11. Pull cycle knob out.

Adapted from Miller, U. C., & Test, D. W. (1989). A
comparison of constant time delay and most-to-least
prompting in teaching laundry skills to students with
moderate retardation. *Education and Training in Mental
Retardation, 24,* 363–370.

put in the detergent." If the verbal cue produced the appropriate response, Debbie would be reinforced, verbally, and would move on to the next step. If, on the other hand, the verbal cue did not elicit Debbie's putting the detergent into the washing machine, the next level prompt would be used, a verbal cue with a model. Debbie's teacher would say, "Debbie, the detergent goes in the machine like this," at the same time putting the packet of One Shot Fab into the washing machine. If the verbal cue plus the model did not produce the desired response (putting the detergent into the washing machine), then the verbal cue would be paired with a full physical prompt. The teacher would take Debbie's hand, get the packet of One Shot Fab, and assist Debbie in putting the detergent into the washing machine. Increasing assistance has been used successfully to teach a variety of community skills, such as grocery shopping (Gaule, Nietupski, & Certo, 1985; Nietupski, Welch, & Wacker, 1983), pinball machine use (Hill, Wehman, & Horst, 1982), cooking (Schleien, Ash, Kierman, & Wehman, 1981), and

break-time skills (Breen, Haring, Pitts-Conway, & Gaylord-Ross, 1985), as well as domestic skills, such as toothbrushing (Horner & Keilitz, 1975).

Decreasing assistance is sometimes called the system of most-to-least prompts (e.g., physical, model, verbal). If we were to use decreasing assistance to teach Debbie to use the washing machine, the following might occur. If Debbie did not put the detergent into the washing machine independently, the first-level prompt to be used would be the full physical prompt. The teacher would take Debbie's hand, get the packet of One Shot Fab, and assist Debbie in putting the detergent into the washing machine. Debbie would be praised for her assistance in getting the detergent into the washing machine. Perhaps on the next trial, Debbie's teacher would model how the detergent is put into the washing machine. If that teacher prompt produced the correct response, then in the next trial or so the teacher would just verbally tell Debbie, "Put the detergent into the washing machine." Decreasing assistance has also been used successfully for domestic skills such as dressing and undressing (Ball, Seric, & Payne, 1971; Minge & Ball, 1967), and community-oriented skills such as making a snack (Kayser et al., 1986) and mobility skill training (Colozzi & Pollow, 1984).

Graduated guidance involves providing the assistance necessary for the individual to complete a step, but varies from decreasing assistance in that the assistance provided from trial to trial can vary. Once again, using the example of Debbie and the washing machine, if graduated guidance is used and Debbie did not independently put the detergent into the washing machine, Debbie's teacher would start with full physical assistance. However, on the next trial, if it appeared that Debbie was in the process of reaching for the detergent, Debbie's teacher would, probably, let her see what she could do by herself and supply a prompt only if necessary. According to Demchack (1990), graduated guidance has been documented in the literature primarily with domestic skill training such as for self-feeding (Azrin & Armstrong, 1973) and dressing skills

(Azrin, Schaeffer, & Wesolowski, 1976; Diorio & Konarski, 1984).

Similarly, *time delay* involves systematically inserting increasing amounts of time between the task direction and the controlling prompt. If time delay were applied to help Debbie put detergent into the washing machine, it would work like this, with a 0 (zero)-second delay: If Debbie failed to put the detergent into the washing machine, Debbie's teacher would simultaneously provide a prompt with the presentation of each step. After Debbie was performing all of the steps in washing clothes with a zero-second delay, Debbie's teacher could then move to a 2-second delay. With a 2-second delay, if Debbie did not put the detergent in the washing machine independently, her teacher would wait 2 seconds between the steps of the task analysis and the prompt. Time delay has been employed to teach domestic skills such as making a bed (Snell, 1982), using a washer and dryer (Miller & Test, 1989), and requesting a lunch (Halle, Marshall, & Spradlin, 1979), as well as skills that can be used in both community and domestic situations, such as manual signing (Browder, Morris, & Snell, 1981) and use of language (Halle, Baer, & Spradlin, 1981).

Evaluating Instructional Effects

Evaluating the effects of instruction has been, and continues to be, a major focus within the field of special education. Teachers who are working with students who have severe disabilities have been no less interested than those who work with students who have milder learning problems in evaluating the effects of their instructional efforts on their learners. Chapter 3 presents a comprehensive program for evaluation of instructional effects in students with severe disabilities. It highlights the differences between measurement and evaluation and provides a detailed explanation of types of recording systems. Our task in this chapter is to show how measurement and evaluation and data-recording systems specifically apply to the training of domestic and community living skills.

As stated in Chapter 3, when student outcome data are collected on a frequent basis, typically daily, it is necessary for the teacher to define the target behavior in observable and objective terms. Once the target behavior is identified and operationalized, the next step is to decide the salient features of the target behavior. Is it the number of times in which the student engages in the behavior that is important? Or is it the amount of time the student spends engaging in the behavior that is of most importance? The answers to these questions determine the type of recording system used to quantify the target behavior. Table 6.3 presents a set of guidelines to determine what, where, and how to collect data.

Applications of Types of Recording Systems for Domestic and Community Living Skills. There are five types of observational recording systems: (1) event recording, (2) interval recording, (3) momentary time sampling, (4) duration recording, and (5) latency recording. The following are examples of how these data-recording systems can be used in the training of domestic and community living skills.

Event recording would be used in the following two situations. Tom is working in a community-based janitorial program at a nearby hotel, and his task is to make beds. The task analysis for bed making consists of 43 steps, and Tom's job coach counts the number of correct and incorrect steps as a bed is made. After Tom has made one bed, the job coach tallies up the number of steps that Tom got correct (these are steps performed independently without error or assistance from the trainer). He got 20 steps correct and made 23 errors. The 20 steps correct and the 23 steps incorrect represent the counts, or events. If rate is a desired outcome, then the job coach would have to keep track of the amount of time that it took Tom to make one bed. Assume that it took Tom 15 minutes to make one bed. If 15 minutes is the amount of time it took to make a bed, then 20/15 (1.33 correct per minute) would be the *correct* rate and 23/15 (1.53 incorrect per minute) would be the *incorrect* rate.

TABLE 6.3   Decision Rules for Collecting Data

STEPS

1. Identify Skill:
2. Identify Skill

Dimension:	Frequency	Rate	Duration	Latency	Topography
	(# or count; %)	(# time unit)	(length of time)	(S^D—R time)	(form of response)
3. Identify Recording System:	Event	Event	Duration Internal MTS	Latency	Event

4. Identify Stage
   of Learning:

	What type data?	How often collected?	Where collected?
Acquisition	From Step #2	Each time taught	In training environment
Fluency	Step #2 + time-based measure (rate, duration, latency)	At least weekly	In training environment
Generalization	Same as above	Weekly or monthly	In training environment Outside training environment
Maintenance	Same as above	At least monthly	Same as above

EXAMPLE

STEPS

1. Setting table for lunch
2. Frequency   Student must accurately put all utensils at each place and all condiments on table. Use % because number of items will vary from day to day.
3. Event Recording

	What type data?	How often?	Where?
4. *Acquisition*	Frequency	Daily	In lunchroom
Fluency	Frequency & Duration (add duration because only have 5 minutes to set table before lunch is served)	Daily	In lunchroom
Generalization	Frequency & Duration	Weekly	At home
Maintenance	Same as above	Monthly	In lunchroom At home

Interval recording would be the recording system of choice in the following example. Michele is an 18-year-old who has a long history of finger flapping, which significantly interferes with other functional uses of her hands. Michele engages in this finger flapping at such a high rate that it is virtually impossible to identify discrete events (difficult to tell the end of one behavior and the beginning of another). Because it is very difficult to determine the cycle of the behavior, interval recording would be a likely way to proceed to quantify Michele's finger flapping behavior. Typically, in interval recording, an observation period in which the target behavior will be observed is identified. The observation period is then divided into equal intervals, not usually longer than 30 seconds in length. If the target behavior occurs at any time during the interval, a mark is made on the data collection sheet, which could resemble a series of boxes that divide a 1-minute observation period into six 10-second intervals. See Figure 6.3.

In this example, using interval recording requires Michele's teacher to observe at all times. An alternative for the teacher would be to use *momentary time sampling*. With momentary time sampling, the target behavior is recorded *only* if it was occurring at the end of the sample or time interval. Once again, Michele's stereotypic hand flapping occurs at such a high rate that it is difficult to discern one event from another, except this time, the observer looks at and records the occurrence of the target behavior *only* at the end of the interval.

Duration recording is the system of choice if the amount of time in which the student engages in the target behavior is the salient feature of the behavior. If Joe, a 5-year-old, is spending too much time in the bathroom during his regular bathroom break, then it is important to clearly define how long is "too long." One way to find out is to "put Joe on the clock." Joe's teacher would start the clock when the students were released for their bathroom break. Then the teacher would stop the clock when Joe returned to his seat or to the activity in which he should be engaging at that time. An effective recording strategy would document the amount of time that Joe was out of his seat and involved in the presumed activity of going to the bathroom. Similarly, an effective treatment should shorten the amount of time that Joe spends taking bathroom breaks.

Finally, *latency recording* is the system used if the target behavior is one for which the focus is on how quickly a student responds to a request or stimulus situation. Again, we look at Joe from our previous example, but this time we focus on latency. Joe's teacher issues the command (antecedent stimulus), "All right class, everyone in their seats." All of Joe's classmates head in the direction of their respective seats, except for Joe, who is still playing with water in the sink. In this situation, Joe has a latency problem. Joe does not move toward his seat when the teacher says he should and when the rest of the class responds. As in the duration example, an effective strategy for this situation would be to decrease, shorten, the amount of time it takes Joe to respond.

Decision Making.   Although there are systems designed to assist teachers in deciding when and how to change their instructional procedures (e.g., Haring, Liberty, & White, 1980), these rules for decision making are complex and not usually employed by teachers without specific and extensive

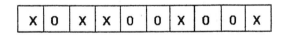

Behavior: On-task

X	O	X	X	O	O	X	O	O	X

x = Behavior occurred

o = Behavior did not occur

FIGURE 6.3   An example of an Interval or Momentary Time Sampling recording sheet.

training. The simplest form of decision making about the effects of an intervention strategy is to carefully watch the data and change (or not change) things accordingly. The data (on the target behavior) should be collected (by one of the methods of recording identified previously) on a regular basis (we recommend daily, or whenever the skill is taught) and transformed into a visual display (graph) that influences the teacher's decision making. This process of collecting, charting, and visually analyzing data, which has a long and substantiated history in behavior analysis, is covered in detail in most beginning textbooks on behavior analysis (e.g., Rusch, Rose, & Greenwood, 1988).

When trying to make instructional decisions based on charted data, teachers should look for two things: (1) stability versus variability and (2) trends (either ascending or descending) in the data. The following example will illustrate. Sam is a 12-year-old who is learning to make an unmade bed from scratch (putting linens and blankets on a bare mattress). The task analysis has been identified, and there are 40 steps that need to be mastered (see Table 6.4). Sam's teacher has chosen to use the total task procedure (train every step in every trial and begin in a forward fashion) to teach Sam to make a bed. Data on the 40 steps, prior to training (baseline), indicate that Sam, at best, can perform only 20 of the 40 steps correctly without assistance. It is evident in reviewing the baseline data that for the last 4 days Sam's performance has fluctuated between 15 and 20 steps correct. It is also obvious that Sam is not going to learn to make his bed without training. Now is the time for Sam's teacher to make a decision about what to do. Does he need more baseline data? Or is there enough data and the variability (bounce) in the data is small enough that it will be potentially evident when the intervention (total task training) is employed, so that the effects of the intervention will be seen immediately? Our decision at this juncture would be that, yes, there probably is enough data, and that the bounce in the data is

small enough that when the total task procedure is implemented we should be able to see the effect. Moreover, the baseline data are not ascending, although initially, days 1, 2, 3, and 4 show progress, and correct responses dropped and stayed at 15 for two days in a row (days 5 and 6). The decision then is to implement the total task procedure. When the total task procedure is implemented Sam responds immediately, and correct responses "jump" to 30. For some reason, however, correct responding plateaus at 30. Sam cannot seem to get more than 30 steps correct. How many days does Sam's teacher stay at 30 correct with no progress? Good question! It is time for another decision. Sam's teacher clearly sees what Sam's problem is. Step 30 of the task analysis calls for Sam to "fold top of spread back about twice the width of pillow," which Sam cannot seem to visualize. Sam's teacher has been giving feedback, but Sam just gets frustrated and quits, thus leaving the rest of the steps unfinished. The teacher makes a change in the task analysis by adding a few steps that require Sam to lay the pillow on the bed to judge the approximate distance he is to fold the spread back. The change works, and Sam goes on to complete all of the steps in the task analysis correctly (see Figure 6.4).

In real-life training situations, things may not always work as smoothly as they did in the bed-making example with Sam. The first alteration is not always the change that proves to be the one that makes the difference. If the first modification does not produce the desirable change, then try again. The point is that because data are charted, they can be used to make a decision about when to change (e.g., when to try something different). If no changes were made in the bed-making task analysis for Sam, based on his performance, he might not be able to make a bed. The program would be reported as no progress and Sam would be viewed as not able to make a bed, just like many students who fail to learn the task at hand. The only problem is that this time it really was not Sam's fault.

TABLE 6.4   Making a Bed

Instructional Objective: Given a bed, pillow, 2 sheets, pillowcase, blanket, bedspread, and chair or table to put linens on, S will make the bed in 20 minutes, with 100% accuracy for 3 consecutive training days.

Prerequisite Skills: Pincer or palmar grasp and full extension of one upper extremity.

Task Analysis:

1. S puts linen on chair or chest near bed.
2. S differentiates between bottom and top sheets.
3. S takes bottom sheet from stack on chair.
4. S unfolds sheet on bed.
5. S grasps bottom of sheet (narrow hem) with both hands.
6. S pulls bottom of sheet to bottom of mattress.
7. S grasps top of sheet (wide hem) with both hands.
8. S pulls top of sheet to top of mattress.
9. S centers and straightens sheet.
10. S smooths wrinkles in sheet.
11. S tucks right side of sheet under mattress.
12. S tucks left side of sheet under mattress.
13. S takes top sheet from chair.
14. S unfolds sheet on bed.
15. S grasps bottom of sheet (narrow hem) and pulls to bottom of mattress.
16. S grasps top of sheet (wide hem) and pulls to top of bed.
17. S centers, straightens, and smooths sheet.
18. S takes blanket from chair.
19. S unfolds blanket on bed.
20. S grasps bottom of blanket with both hands and pulls to bottom of bed.
21. S grasps top of blanket and pulls to top of bed.
22. S centers and straightens blanket over top sheet.
23. S smooths all wrinkles.
24. S tucks both top sheet and blanket under mattress at bottom of bed.
25. S folds top of sheet back to cover top of blanket.
26. S takes spread from chair.
27. S pulls bottom of spread to bottom of bed.
28. S centers and smooths out spread.
29. S pulls top of spread to top of bed and smooths.
30. S folds top of spread back about twice the width of pillow.
31. S takes pillow from chair.
32. S places pillow on bed lengthwise in front of self.
33. S holds one edge of open end of pillowcase in each hand.
34. S pulls pillowcase over bottom of pillow about 4 inches.
35. S pulls pillow up against his or her chest, holding it with his or her chin.
36. S shakes pillow down halfway into pillowcase.
37. S shakes pillow rest of the way into pillowcase.
38. S lays pillow at top of bed.
39. S folds spread up over pillow.
40. S smooths out all wrinkles of spread, including top of pillow.

Teaching Suggestions: If S has difficulty centering the sheets, blanket, or spread on the bed, use two pieces of tape, one on the bed and one on the sheet, blanket, or spread. Have S match the pieces of tape to center the sheet, blanket, or spread. Gradually fade the tape by shortening it until S can center them without cues.

Use a large pillowcase while S is learning to put the case on the pillow so it will slide more easily. If you normally use a smaller case, fade back to this after S has learned to put on the larger case.

Reprinted from Wehman, P., & McLaughlin, P. J. (1980). *Vocational curriculum for developmentally disabled persons.* Austin, TX: PRO-ED.

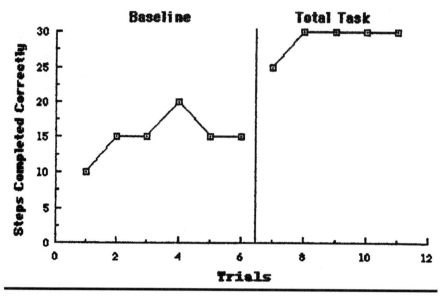

FIGURE 6.4   Bed making data decision making example.

GENERALIZATION: A CRITICAL ISSUE

Angela spent months in her school's home eco-
nomics classroom learning to cook a balanced dinner for herself consisting of macaroni and cheese,
hot dogs, a frozen green vegetable, a beverage,
and a microwave cake. Angela's teacher also
spent many hours designing and implementing her
instructional program. Angela's training included
picture recipe cards, color-coded symbols on both
the stove and microwave, and specially marked
measuring spoons and cups. Although at times it
seemed as if Angela was doomed to a life of TV
dinners, she finally managed to prepare the entire
meal on her own. Everyone in her class was excited, and Angela was so happy that she decided to
cook dinner for her family.

The following day Angela came to school very
upset. Dinner had been a disaster. Nothing had
worked out right. While she had tried to use her
recipe cards neither the stove, microwave, nor
measuring utensils were the same as she had
learned to use at school.

Angela's situation is typical of a particular type
of teaching failure. For Angela's new cooking
skills to be truly useful, she must be taught in such
a manner that her new skill can be used over time
and in different situations. Unfortunately, this
does not happen automatically. Students must be
taught in ways that will promote the generalization of newly learned skills. The following discussion describes some of the techniques that can be
used by teachers in designing instruction to promote generalized behavior changes.

Generalization refers to expanding a student's
capability of performance beyond those conditions
set for initial acquisition (Alberto & Troutman,
1990). The three types of generalization are stimulus generalization, response generalization, and
maintenance. *Stimulus generalization* refers to performing a response under conditions other than
those present when the response was learned. If
Angela had successfully cooked the same meal at
home, it would have been an example of stimulus
generalization. *Response generalization* refers to
changes in behaviors not specifically targeted or

developed by the intervention program. In Angela's case, response generalization would occur if she cooked a microwave dessert that was different from the one she was taught to make. Finally, *maintenance* refers to the continued performance of a behavior once instruction has ended. If Angela can still make her meal at a later time (e.g., next week, next month), her cooking behavior would be said to have maintained.

Strategies for Promoting Generalization

As mentioned earlier in this chapter, Stokes and Baer (1977) have suggested a number of techniques that can be included in a lesson to help promote generalization of new behaviors. (See Table 6.5 for a brief definition of each technique.) In this section we briefly discuss and give examples of the following techniques: *Introduce to Natural Contingencies, Teach Enough Examples,* and *Use Common Stimuli.*

Introduce to Natural Contingencies.   This strategy involves teaching students behaviors that will be reinforced in their natural environment. It can be facilitated in two ways. First, observe the student's natural (home) environment and choose a behavior that will be reinforced. For example, before teaching Angela to use a microwave, it would be prudent to see whether she has a microwave at home. Before teaching Ted to wash his clothes, it is important to know whether his family have a washer and dryer *and* if they will let Ted use them. Second, teach students to recruit their own reinforcers. For example, Katie has learned to flush the toilet at appropriate times at school. However, at home her parents notice only when she does not do so. To help Katie, her teacher might teach her how to "recruit" reinforcers from her family by telling a family member each time she flushes the toilet appropriately.

Teach Enough Examples.   For a newly learned behavior to generalize, it must (1) be performed in appropriate, nontrained stimulus situations that

TABLE 6.5   Stokes and Baer's (1977) Strategies for Promoting Generalization

1. Train and Hope—involves teaching the desired response and then hoping that generalization will occur.

2. Sequential Modification—involves applying the *full* intervention in all settings in which the behavior must occur.

3. Introduce to Natural Contingencies—involves teaching behaviors that will be reinforced in the student's natural environment.

4. Teach Enough Examples—involves training the behavior in a number of settings or situations and/or with several different trainers.

5. Train Loosely—involves training the behavior in such a manner that the controlling stimuli are constantly changing (varying the antecedents).

6. Use Indiscriminate Contingencies—involves the use of intermittent schedules of reinforcement (varying the consequences).

7. Use Common Stimuli—involves making the training setting similar to the real or natural environment.

8. Use Self-Management—involves teaching students strategies to monitor and record their own behavior.

9. Reinforce Generalization—involves reinforcing the occurrence of new behaviors in settings outside the training setting.

include new materials, individuals, and settings and (2) not occur in inappropriate, nontrained situations (Horner, Bellamy, & Colvin, 1984). To ensure these conditions, teaching examples and nonexamples must be chosen carefully. Examples must sample the range of possible situations, and nonexamples should be selected that include minimal and maximal differences. For example, Horner, Albin, and Ralph (1986) taught six young adults with mental retardation to select or reject grocery items, using picture cards as cues. To teach selecting Heinz ketchup, their training included the appropriate picture card cue, as well as a nonexample with minimal differences (i.e., Heinz 57 Barbecue Sauce) and a nonexample with maximal differences (Durkee's Louisiana Red Hot Sauce). Following instruction, students were able to both select the correct grocery items and reject the wrong items.

Use Common Stimuli. Using common stimuli involves making the training setting similar to the real, or natural, environment. One way to do this is to use real (rather than simulated) materials and situations. For example, Trask, Grossi, and Heward (1989) taught three young adults who were blind and developmentally disabled to prepare two different microwave food items (french fries, cheesecake) and make automatic drip coffee, using tape-recorded instructions. A remote-controlled tape recorder allowed students to move more freely around the kitchen while being able to start and stop the recorded instructions as needed. Common stimuli were programmed by using food items and cooking utensils to which the students had access in their home environment. In addition to using common stimuli, instruction included the previously discussed strategies of introducing to natural contingencies and teaching enough examples. First, the natural contingency of reinforcement for eating and sharing food was used. During the training, Lisa and Carl shared their completed food products with other students and staff, and Steve invited his girlfriend to sample his cooking. Second, teaching enough examples was included by incorporating the strategy called general case instruction.

General Case Instruction. General case instruction involves using teaching examples that sample the full range of appropriate responses the learner will need to perform if generalization is to occur. In the present example, french fries and cheesecake were chosen as teaching examples for the microwave because they sampled the full

range of microwave food preparation behaviors (i.e., cooking french fries included opening a box, putting an item into the microwave correctly, and pushing the appropriate buttons; making cheesecake involved mixing eggs, water, and cheesecake mix before placing in the microwave). Following instruction, all three students were able to cook untrained microwave items that required following directions similar to those for cooking french fries (i.e., pizza, popcorn, pudding) as well as directions similar to those for cheesecake (i.e., brownies and cake). In addition, each student was able to make tea using the automatic drip coffee maker. Thus, through carefully chosen teaching examples that sampled the range of possible microwave preparation techniques, students learned skills that they could use in different situations and with different foods. These are just a few examples of how instruction can be designed to program for generalization. More information can be found in Alberto and Troutman (1990), Cooper, Heron, and Heward (1987), and Horner, Dunlap, and Koegel (1988).

Decision Rules for Generalization

Even after a teacher is familiar with the various techniques for promoting generalization, it is often difficult to decide which one(s) to use. To help teachers make this difficult decision, Liberty, Haring, White, and Billingsley (1988) developed a set of decision rules for generalization (see Table 6.6). The purpose of these "rules" is to help teachers select the most effective technique(s) from among the variety of strategies. The information used to answer questions in the decision table can assist teachers in identifying when a specific strategy should be applied for it to be most effective.

To demonstrate the decision rule strategy, let us return to Angela and use the decision rules to select a strategy for promoting generalization. The answer to Question A (Has the skill generalized?) is "No, it is not occurring at home." The answer to Question B (Has skill been acquired?) is "Yes, she can do it at school." The answer to Question C (Is

TABLE 6.6   Decision Rules for Generalization

QUESTION	PROCEDURES	ANSWER	NEXT STEP/DECISION
A. Has skill generalized at the desired level in all target situations?	Probe for generalization in all desired situations, then compare performance with criteria (IEP objective).	yes	1. SUCCESSFUL INSTRUCTION Step ahead to a more difficult level of skill. Choose a new skill to teach. EXIT sequence
		no	CONTINUE with question B.
B. Has skill been acquired?	Compare performance in instructional situation with criteria for acquisition or performance levels specified in IEP objective. Answer yes if student has met performance levels in training situation but not in generalization.	yes	CONTINUE with question C.
		no	2. SKILL MASTERY PROBLEM Continue instruction. EXIT sequence
C. Is generalization desired to only a few situations?	Analyze function of skill in current and future environments available to student.	yes	CONTINUE with question D.
		no	CONTINUE with question E.
D. Is it possible to train directly in those situations?	Are all situations frequently accessible for training so that training time is likely to be adequate to meet aim date in IEP objective?	yes	3. LIMITED GENERALIZATION SITUATIONS Train in desired situation. Train sequentially in all situations (sequential modification). EXIT sequence
		no	CONTINUE with question E.
E. Does student perform inappropriate or other behaviors instead of the target skill *and* is the student reinforced? OR Does the student fail to respond *and* is reinforced (accesses reinforcers)?	Observe student behavior during probes and note events that follow appropriate, inappropriate, target, and nontarget skills. Determine whether those events are those that should follow the target skill, or have been shown to reinforce other skills.	yes	To either question, CONTINUE with question F.
		no	To both questions, CONTINUE with question G.

(continued)

TABLE 6.6   Continued

QUESTION	PROCEDURES	ANSWER	NEXT STEP/DECISION
F. Are reinforcers contingent on others?	Observe how student is reinforced. If other people deliver the reinforcement, answer yes. If student accesses reinforcer directly, answer no.	yes	4. COMPETING REINFORCER PROBLEM Alter generalization contingencies. Amplify instructed behavior. EXIT sequence
		no	5. COMPETING BEHAVIOR PROBLEM Increase proficiency. Amplar instructed behavior. Alter generalization contingencies. EXIT sequence
G. Did the student generalize once at close to criterion performance levels and then not as well on other opportunities? (Consider performance in current and past probes.)	Compare student performance for each response opportunity with performance level specified in objective. If near criterion performance occurred on the first response opportunity, and performance was poor or nonexistent after that, answer yes.	yes	6. REINFORCING FUNCTION PROBLEM Program natural reinforcers. Eliminate training reinforcers. Use natural schedules. Use natural consequences. Teach self-reinforcement. Teach to solicit reinforcement. Reinforce generalized behavior. Alter generalization contingencies. EXIT sequence
		no	CONTINUE with question H.
H. Did the student respond partially corrrectly during at least one response opportunity?	Analyze anecdotal data and observational notes from probes.	yes	7. DISCRIMINATION FUNCTION PROBLEM Vary stimuli. Use all stimuli. Use frequent stimuli. Use multiple exemplars. Use general case exemplars. EXIT sequence
		no	CONTINUE with question I.
I. Did the student fail to perform any part of the target skill?	Analyze student performance during probe situation.	yes	8. GENERALIZATION TRAINING FORMAT Increase proficiency. Program natural reinforcers. Use natural schedules. Use appropriate natural stimuli. Eliminate training stimuli. EXIT sequence
		no	STOP. You have made an error in the sequence. Begin again at Question A.

Reprinted from Liberty, K. A., Haring, N. G., White, O. R., & Billingsley, F. F. (1988). A technology for the future: Decision rules for generalization. *Education and Training in Mental Retardation,* 23, 318–319.

generalization desired to only a few settings?) is "Yes, only to her home." The answer to Question D (Is direct training possible?) is "No, both of Angela's parents work and do not want people in the house when they are not home." Next, because the answer to both parts of Question E is "No, Angela is trying to do it right," we go on to Questions G and H where once again the answer is "No, Angela's first attempt at cooking at home was a complete disaster." This response leads to Question I, to which we answer, "Yes, she used her picture recipe cards in the correct order, but the kitchen appliances at home are not marked as they are at school." At this point the decision rules suggest a variety of strategies from which we choose "Use appropriate (common) stimuli" and "Eliminate training stimuli." This can be done by replacing the picture cards she uses at school with pictures of her home appliances and gradually eliminating the color coding from her picture cues. Of course, if Angela's teacher had designed her instruction with skill generalization as the goal, this might not have been necessary.

In conclusion, to avoid the frustration that occurs in situations similar to Angela's, instruction must be designed with generalization as the goal. By building strategies for building generalization into instruction and using the decision rules, teachers will be better able to guarantee that the domestic and community living skills they teach will be truly functional.

CURRICULUM MODELS

This section reviews a number of commercially available curricula for use by teachers of students with severe disabilities. For our purposes, we have categorized curricula as domain-based, activities-based, or non-domain-based. Typically, *domain-based* curricula divide content into a number of areas or domains. For example, Falvey (1989) divides curricula into seven domains, which include community, domestic, recreation, employment, motor, communication, and functional academic skills, whereas the Syracuse Community-Refer-

enced Curriculum Guide (Ford et al., 1989) includes the three domains of community living, functional academics, and embedded social, communication, and motor skills. These curricula typically include tables containing the scope and sequence of skills to be taught in each domain or area.

An *activities-based* curriculum is similar to a domain-based curriculum. However, instead of including scope and sequence skill lists, sets of "activities" are provided. An activity, as defined by Wilcox and Bellamy (1987), is a "chain of behavior which, if performed under appropriate natural conditions, produces an outcome that is functional to the individual" (p. 12). For example, one activity listed under "Food" is learning to use vending machines.

Finally, curriculum can be *non-domain-based*. Basically, a non-domain-based curriculum is just that—one that does not include domains. Instead, the curriculum includes procedures that are designed to identify functional skills and instructional practices that will work best with individual students (Neel & Billingsley, 1989). Therefore, instead of scope and sequence lists, a non-domain-based curriculum presents information on how to determine which skills a person must learn to function in his or her own environment and the most appropriate instructional techniques for teaching each skill.

Domain-Based Curriculum

In this section we look at three different curricular approaches to domestic and community living skills, which are: (1) Community-Based Curriculum (Falvey, 1989), (2) the Syracuse Community-Referenced Curriculum Guide (Ford et al., 1989), and (3) Community Living Skills: A Taxonomy (Dever, 1988).

Community-Based Curriculum. The Community-Based Curriculum (Falvey, 1989) is designed for use by individuals who work and/or live with individuals who are severely disabled. The curriculum includes strategies for developing and implementing training in seven skill areas or domains, including community, domestic, recreation, employment, motor, communication, and functional academics. For our purposes, we focus on the two domains of domestic and community skills.

The domestic domain includes self-help and social-sexual skills. Table 6.7 includes a list of the sample scope and sequence for domestic skills.

The community skills domain does not include sample scope and sequence lists. Instead of listing potential skills, this section focuses on how to (1) identify specific community skills for each student and (2) teach the skills once they are identified. This is to ensure that skills are taught that are functional (useful) to each individual student's situation.

Syracuse Community-Referenced Curriculum Guide. The Syracuse Community-Referenced Curriculum Guide (Ford et al., 1989) was designed for people who teach (parents, teachers, therapists) students with moderate and severe disabilities (ages 5 to 21). The scope and sequence

charts are designed as "guides," providing teachers with a framework for deciding what each student needs on an individual basis. Each scope and sequence chart is accompanied by a set of decision-making rules that focus teachers on the most important goals for each student. The curriculum guide includes the community living domain, functional academic skills, and embedded social, communication, and motor skills. Included in the community living domain are self-management and home living, vocational skills, recreation and leisure, and general community functioning.

In terms of our definition of domestic and community living skills, the relevant areas are self-management, home living, and general community functioning. The scope and sequence charts for each area are arranged by skill with example activities given for age and grade levels (Kindergarten to Transition). Goal areas within self-management and home living include eating and food preparation, grooming and dressing, hygiene and toileting, safety and health, assisting and taking care of others, budgeting, planning and scheduling. See Table 6.8 for an example of the eating and food prepara-

TABLE 6.7 A Summary of the Community-Based Curriculum Scope and Sequence for Domestic Skills

PERSONNEL HEALTH CARE	HOME CARE	HOME MANAGEMENT	SOCIAL INTERACTION	SOCIAL-SEXUAL
Physical Appearance	Laundry	Schedules/Routines	Family	Self-Awareness/Esteem
Hygiene	Clothing	Time	Neighbors	Health and Hygiene
Safety	House Cleaning	Money	Friends	Self-Protection
Wellness	Eating Skills	Materials		Relationships
Nutrition	Home Maintenance	Use of Space		
Emotional/ Mental Health	Yard Maintenance	Organization		
	Appliances	Choices		

Adapted from Eshilian, L., Haney, M., & Falvey, M. A. (1989). Domestic Skills. In M. A. Falvey (Ed.), *Community-based curriculum: Instructional strategies for students with severe handicaps* (pp. 115–140). Baltimore: Paul H. Brookes Publishing Co.

TABLE 6.8 Scope and Sequence for Self-Management/Home Living

Age and Grade Levels

| GOAL AREAS | Elementary School | | | | | |
	KINDERGARTEN (AGE 5)	PRIMARY GRADES (AGES 6–8)	INTERMEDIATE GRADES (AGES 9–11)	MIDDLE SCHOOL (AGES 12–14)	HIGH SCHOOL (AGES 15–18)	TRANSITION (AGES 19–21)
Eating and food preparation	Eat meals and snacks.	Eat balanced meals.	Eat balanced meals with appropriate manners.	Eat balanced meals with appropriate manners.	Eat balanced meals with appropriate manners.	Eat balanced meals with appropriate manners.
	Prepare simple snack for self; pour own drink.	Prepare simple snacks for self; pour own drink.	Plan and prepare simple snacks for self.	Plan and prepare snacks for self.	Plan and prepare snacks for self and others.	Plan menu for self/family/roommates.
	Serve snack to peers.	Serve snack to peers.	Serve food items to others.	Serve food items to others.	Serve food items to others.	Serve food items to others.
	Clean own place after snack/meal.	Clean up table after snack.	Clean up preparation area and table after snack.	Clear table and do dishes after food preparation.	Clear table and do dishes after food preparation.	Clean up after meals.
		Choose nutritious foods: snack.	Choose nutritious foods: snack.	Choose nutritious foods: breakfast, lunch, snacks.	Choose nutritious foods: breakfast, lunch, snacks.	Choose nutritious foods (including when eating out).
				Prepare simple meals: breakfast, lunch (some cooking).	Prepare various types of meals.	Prepare meal for self/others.
				Store food and leftovers.	Store food and leftovers.	Store food and leftovers.
						Make weekly grocery list.

Reprinted from Ford, A., Schnorr, R., Meyer, L., Davern, L., Black, J., & Dempsey, P. (1989). Self-Management/Home Living. In A. Ford, R. Schnorr, L. Meyer, L. Davern, J. Black, & P. Dempsey (Eds.), *The Syracuse community-referenced curriculum guide for students with moderate and severe disabilities* (p. 30). Baltimore: Paul H. Brookes Publishing Co.

tion goal area. Goal areas within general community functioning include travel, community safety, grocery shopping, general shopping, eating out, and using services.

Community Living Skills: A Taxonomy.   The Community Living Skills Taxonomy (Dever, 1988) is different from the previous two domain-based curricula in that it is not a curriculum. Instead it is a taxonomy; that is, it classifies skills required for daily life in the community. Therefore what is provided are "statements of endpoints of instruction in community living" (Dever, 1988, p. 7). Whereas the taxonomy was developed for persons with moderate, severe, and profound mental retardation, it would be useful for anyone (e.g., administrators, teachers) who wishes to develop a community-living skills curriculum.

The taxonomy is organized into the five do-mains of personal maintenance and development, homemaking and community life, vocational, leisure, and travel. An interesting part of each domain is the inclusion of goals that focus on dealing with "glitches." The reason for including "glitches" is that daily life is full of minor problems with which we must all learn to deal. According to Dever (1988), "glitches" fall into three categories: (1) tool and equipment breakdowns, (2) running out of materials, and (3) scheduling problems. Therefore, all three types of problems are included in each domain. See Table 6.9 for an example in one domain.

Activities-Based Curriculum

We turn now to an example of an activities approach to curriculum development for students with severe disabilities. As noted earlier, the ac-

---

TABLE 6.9   Taxonomy of Community Living Skills (List of Major Goals)

DOMAIN H: Homemaking and Community Life

I.   *The learner will obtain living quarters.*
   A.   Find appropriate living quarters.
   B.   Rent/buy living quarters.
   C.   Set up living quarters.

II.   *The learner will follow community routines.*
   A.   Keep living quarters neat and clean.
   B.   Keep fabrics neat and clean.
   C.   Maintain interior of living quarters.
   D.   Maintain exterior of living quarters.
   E.   Respond to seasonal changes.
   F.   Follow home safety procedures.
   G.   Follow accident/emergency procedures.
   H.   Maintain foodstock.
   I.   Prepare and serve meals.
   J.   Budget money appropriately.
   K.   Pay bills.

III.   *The learner will coexist in a neighborhood and community.*
   A.   Interact appropriately with community members.
   B.   Cope with inappropriate conduct of others.
   C.   Observe requirements of the law.
   D.   Carry out civic duties.

IV.   *The learner will handle glitches in the home.*
   A.   Cope with equipment breakdowns.
   B.   Cope with depletions of household supplies.
   C.   Cope with unexpected depletions of funds.
   D.   Cope with disruptions in routine.
   E.   Cope with sudden changes in the weather.

Reprinted from Dever, R. B. (1988). *Community living skills: A taxonomy.* Washington, DC: American Association on Mental Retardation.

tivities approach is similar to a domain-based approach, but rather than a scope and sequence of skills list, sets of "activities" are provided.

The Activities Catalog.   The Activities Catalog (the alternative curriculum) (Wilcox & Bellamy, 1987) is designed to assist parents, teachers, service providers, and individuals with severe disabilities to make thoughtful decisions about how to invest training time. The catalog is a new curriculum for adolescents and adults with moderate and severe disabilities. It provides a way to implement recent curriculum innovations and integrate procedural developments for a total effect of comprehensive system change. It provides a way to translate what professionals say should happen in training into "how to" instruction for families, school personnel, and residential training staff.

The catalog is a two-volume set in which the text discussion and rationale are outlined in Volume 1 (a comprehensive guide) and how to order from the catalog is graphically described in Volume 2. Volume 1 contains 11 chapters that provide (1) discussion on the question, Why a new curriculum? (2) an overview of the total curriculum system, (3) alternative performance strategies, (4) discussion on using the catalog in program evaluation, and sections on using the catalog in planning for high school, residential placement, employment programs, and life-style.

An underlying premise to Volume 2, the actual catalog, is explained in the introduction. "Basic to the catalog is the assumption that since we simply can't learn everything, decisions about what to teach an individual with severe disabilities are more dependent on values—of family, friends, advocates, and of course, the individual him or herself—than upon any logical sequence" (Wilcox & Bellamy, 1987, p. 4). Major sections in the catalog include leisure (exercise; games, crafts, and hobbies; events; media; and other topics), personal management (self, food, space and belongings, personal business), and work (introduction and categories of activities). An example of the types of activities that best relate to the training of domestic

and community living skills are found in the personal management section. Table 6.10 presents the activity of planning meals.

Non-Domain-Based Curriculum

Finally, we look at one example of a non-domain-based curricular approach—the IMPACT curriculum (Neel & Billingsley, 1989). The non-domain-based approach to curriculum includes areas such as self-help or cooking and identifies procedures that illustrate functional skills and instructional practices.

IMPACT Curriculum.   The IMPACT curriculum (Neel & Billingsley, 1989) is designed for teachers, parents, and other professionals who are involved in the development and implementation of quality programs for students with moderate to severe disabilities. The curriculum guide includes three major sections: (1) an introduction, (2) getting started (how to put IMPACT to work), and (3) learning with IMPACT. The first section contains five chapters that discuss what IMPACT is, introduce functional curricula, discuss assumptions about IMPACT, and present a primer on language and communication programming. The second section contains three chapters that help the consumer (i.e., teacher, parent, or other professional) use the curriculum guide. These three chapters discuss how to use the included inventories, setting priorities for educational programming, and writing an individualized education program. The third major section presents the learning process with the curriculum guide. The five chapters in this section include information on the instructional process, teaching communication in context, behavior problems, building alternative responses to behavior problems, and scheduling the day. In addition to the three sections, the guide includes four appendices that (1) display blank forms for record keeping and data collection, (2) provide an environmental inventory for home and community, (3) provide an environmental inventory for school and community, and

TABLE 6.10   What's for dinner? Or lunch? Or breakfast?

Meal planning occurs as part of a larger system of food management designed for an individual or for a household.

Meal planning can take many forms, depending on that system. It can be so elaborate that it requires the skills of a licensed dietitian or it can be as simple as pulling a picture menu and recipe cards from a file of "balanced meals." Meal planning can be done each day or for an entire week or month. As items are used up, there must be a strategy to add them to the shopping list.

Systems should be devised with the collaboration of parents, teachers, or advocates. The development of picture menu and recipe cards, picture grocery shopping cards, coded systems for monitoring the availability of ingredients, and so on, all will require some external support.

To maximize choice and independence, we suggest a system that relies on a limited set of menus developed by a parent, teacher, or advocate.

Relying on prepared foods rather than "cooking from scratch" may be somewhat more expensive but controls portions and promotes greater independence.

Care, of course, should be taken to ensure that the standard menus developed are indeed nutritionally balanced and responsive to the preferences of the individual(s).

ITEM 2-2-10 Planning Meals

Note: This activity should be coordinated with ITEM 2-2-7: Buying Groceries.

Once a meal is planned, there is still work to be done!

Activity includes:

- Selecting menu/recipe
- Gathering necessary equipment and ingredients
- Following recipe or instructions
- Serving
- Eating
- Cleaning up
- Continuing to next activity

The activity lends itself to partial participation or collaboration since some components—especially serving and cleaning up—are substantial tasks in their own right.

The major decisions should address the range of items/menus to be prepared, and the format for presenting the target recipes or instructions. Picture recipes can be specific to each dish or designed to accommodate a range of items that require similar preparation.

ITEM 2-2-11 Preparing Meals

a. Breakfast	c. Dinner
b. Lunch	d. Snacks

Note: This activity can be coordinated with ITEM 2-2-10: Planning Meals, and ITEM 2-2-7: Buying Groceries. See Williams, J., & Horner, R. H. (1986). General case cooking. Unpublished manuscript, Specialized Training Program, University of Oregon, for a set of picture recipe cards designed to teach four general food preparation routines, each of which can be used with a large number of items.

Reprinted from Wilcox, B., & Bellamy, G. T. (1987). *The activities catalog: An alternative curriculum for youth and adults with severe disabilities.* Baltimore: Paul H. Brookes Publishing Co.

(4) provide a parent guide to understanding the curriculum.

Table 6.11 presents an excerpt from the environmental inventory for home and community.

This example is particularly germane to the training of domestic and community living skills and is representative of the other inventories presented in the IMPACT curriculum guide.

TABLE 6.11   What Can Your Child Do Independently?

One of the main objectives of the IMPACT program is to help children with autism and other handicaps, moderate to severe, to learn to function as independently as possible. The training required to reach this goal must start earlier than it does for other children. This section will tell us which skills your child currently has, and which skills you would like us to work on next.

For each of the following self-help skills, please check "Independently" if your child does not require any assistance or supervision to complete the tasks in the routine, "Yes" if your child can complete the routine with assistance, "No" if the child does not do the routine (e.g., child tantrums, you do it for him or her).

There may be several tasks that you want your child to learn that are not included on this list. If you identify one or more tasks that your child can do, or that you would like your child to learn how to do, add them to the list in the spaces provided at the end of this section.

Can your child prepare a snack or simple meal (e.g., get some fruit, get a sandwich or a drink)?

_____Independently

_____Yes, but needs help (describe) _____

_____

_____No (explain) _____

_____

Can your child complete mealtime tasks (i.e., serve food/drink, use utensils)?

_____Independently

_____Yes, but needs help (describe) _____

_____

_____No (explain) _____

_____

Can your child clean up after meals (i.e., clear table, wash/dry dishes)?

_____Independently

_____Yes, but needs help (describe) _____

_____

_____No (explain) _____

_____

Can your child handle toileting by himself or herself (i.e., get to and from bathroom, wash and dry hands)?

_____Independently

(continued)

TABLE 6.11   Continued

_____Yes, but needs help (describe) _____

_____

_____No (explain) _____

_____

Can your child complete hygiene tasks (i.e., wash and dry hair, brush teeth)?

_____Independently

_____Yes, but needs help (describe) _____

_____

_____No (explain) _____

_____

SUMMARY AND CONCLUSIONS

The following two paragraphs present two different groups of students and how their lives are affected by the training of functional skills. Which of these two scenarios best represents the students in your classroom?

There are no bells in the school, but that's all right, because nobody is going anywhere. Jimmy, Billy, and Susie stay with Mrs. Jones all day long in their room at the end of the hall. Pictures of snowmen and red woolen mittens hang on the bulletin board. In the back of the room, Bobby rocks back and forth, occasionally banging his head on the wall. No one tries to stop him. Susie and Jimmy get out their work sheets and point to the blue or red or green squares as Mrs. Jones instructs. Billy is carefully putting pegs into his pegboard. When he is finished, Mrs. Jones dumps them out for him so he can start again. Jimmy comes back from the bathroom with his shirttail out and his fly unzipped. No one reminds him. Susie, Jimmy, and Billy like Mrs. Jones. They have been in her class for 3 years now, and next year they will go to the workshop. They wonder who will put on their boots and gloves and who will hug them at the end of each day.

The bell rings and Lisa, Zak, and Brian leave homeroom to go to their first-bell class. Zak makes a stop at his locker to get his coat, because he is going to his job site at a fast-food restaurant and he has to be there by nine. The beeper on his watch has told him that it is eight o'clock now, so he needs to hurry to catch the bus on time. Lisa wheels her chair into the computer lab, and, while the other kids learn programming, she practices her keyboarding skills. The teacher comes by periodically to check her accuracy and gives her a smile that says she is doing fine. Brain walks to Mr. Green's class, where he is working on counting money and making change. Tomorrow they will go to the mall to check on how well he can really do. After school he will go with the other seniors to the music room where he will practice for graduation. His parents have already arranged some meetings with his rehab counselor, and they have been talking about what kind of work he wants to do after school.[2]

We would like to think that we are training more Zaks. In the 1990s the technology is in place to deliver appropriate service in the appropriate setting.

[2]Adapted from the *ECAC News Line* (Exceptional Children's Assistance Center, P.O. Box 16, Davidson, NC 28036, 704-892-1321).

REFERENCES

Abramson, A. E., & Wunderlich, R. A. (1972). Dental hygiene training for retardates: An application of behavioral techniques. *Mental Retardation, 10*(3), 6–8.

Alberto, P. A., & Troutman, A. C. (1990). *Applied behavior analysis for teachers* (3rd ed.). Columbus, OH: Charles E. Merrill.

Ault, M. J., Gast, D. L., & Wolery, M. (1988). Comparison of progressive and constant time-delay procedures in teaching community-sign word reading. *American Journal on Mental Retardation, 93*, 44–56.

Aveno, A. (1987). A survey of activities engaged in and skills most needed by adults in community residences, *The Journal of The Association for Persons with Severe Handicaps, 12*, 125–130.

Azrin, N. H., & Armstrong, P. M. (1973). The "mini-meal"—A method for teaching eating skills to the profoundly retarded. *Mental Retardation, 11*(1), 9–13.

Azrin, N. H., Schaeffer, R. M., & Wesolowski, M. D. (1976). A rapid method of teaching profoundly retarded persons to dress by a reinforcement-guidance method. *Mental Retardation, 14*(6), 26–33.

Ball, T. S., Seric, K., & Payne, L. E. (1971). Long-term retention of self-help skill training in the profoundly retarded. *American Journal of Mental Deficiency, 76*, 378–382.

Bates, P., Renzaglia, A., & Wehman, P. (1981). Characteristics of an appropriate education for severely and profoundly handicapped students. *Education and Training of the Mentally Retarded, 16*, 142–149.

Baumeister, A., & Klosowski, R. (1965). An attempt to group toilet train severely retarded patients. *Mental Retardation, 3*(6), 24–26.

Bensberg, G. J., Colwell, C. N., & Cassel, R. H. (1965). Teaching the profoundly retarded self-help activities by behavior shaping techniques. *American Journal of Mental Deficiency, 69*, 674–679.

Bensberg, G. J., & Slominski, A. (1965). Helping the retarded learn self-care. In G. J. Bensberg (Ed.), *Teaching the mentally retarded: A handbook for ward personnel*. Atlanta: Southern Regional Education Board.

Billingsley, F. F., & Romer, L. T. (1983). Response prompting and the transfer of stimulus control: Methods, research, and a conceptual framework. *The Journal of The Association for the Severely Handicapped, 8*(2), 3–12.

Bourbeau, P. E., Sowers, J., & Close, D. W. (1986). An experimental analysis of generalization of banking skills from classroom to bank settings in the community. *Education and Training of the Mentally Retarded, 21*, 98–107.

Breen, C., Haring, T., Pitts-Conway, B., & Gaylord-Ross, R. (1985). The training and generalization of social interaction during break-time at two job sites in the natural environment. *The Journal of The Association for Persons with Severe Handicaps, 10*, 41–50.

Breland, M. (1965). Application of method. In G. J. Bensberg (Ed.), *Teaching the mentally retarded: A handbook for ward personnel*. Atlanta: Southern Regional Education Board.

Brimer, R. W. (1990). *Students with severe disabilities: Current perspectives and practices*. Mountain View, CA: Mayfield.

Brown, L., Branston, M. B., Hamre-Nietupski, S., Pumpian, I., Certo, N., & Gruenwald, L. (1979). A strategy for developing chronological age appropriate and functional curricular content for severely handicapped adolescents and young adults. *Journal of Special Education, 13*(1), 81–90.

Brown, L., Falvey, M., Pumpian, I., Baumgart, D., Nesbit, J., Ford, A., Schroeder, J., & Loomis, R., (Eds.). (1980). *Curricular strategies for teaching severely handicapped students functional skills in school and nonschool environments*. Madison, WI: Madison Metropolitan School District.

Brown, L., Nietupski, J., & Hamre-Nietupski, S. (1976). Criterion of ultimate functioning. In M. A. Thomas (Ed.), *Hey, don't forget about me!* Reston, VA: The Council for Exceptional Children.

Browder, D. M., Morris, W. M., & Snell, M. E. (1981). Using time delay to teach manual signs to a severely retarded student. *Education and Training of the Mentally Retarded, 16*, 252–258.

Cipani, E., Augustine, A., & Blomgren, E. (1982). Teaching profoundly retarded adults to ascend stairs safely. *Education and Training of the Mentally Retarded, 17*, 51–54.

Colozzi, G. A., & Pollow, R. S. (1984). Teaching independent walking to mentally retarded children in a public school. *Education and Training of the Mentally Retarded, 19*, 97–101.

Coon, M. E., Vogelsburg, R. T., & Williams, W. (1981). Effects of classroom public transportation instruction on generalization to the natural environment.

The Journal of the Association for the Severely Handicapped, 6(2), 46–53.

Cooper, J. O., Heron, T. E., & Heward, W. L. (1987). *Applied behavior analysis.* Columbus, OH: Charles E. Merrill.

Cortazzo, A., & Sansone, R. (1969). Travel Training. *TEACHING Exceptional Children, 1*(3), 67–82.

Cronin, K. A., & Cuvo, A. J. (1979). Teaching mending skills to mentally retarded adolescents. *Journal of Applied Behavior Analysis, 12,* 401–406.

Cuvo, A. J., Jacob, L., & Sipko, R. (1981). Teaching laundry skills to mentally retarded students. *Education and Training of the Mentally Retarded, 16,* 54–64.

Day, H. M., & Horner, R. H. (1986). Response variation and the generalization of a dressing skill: Comparison of single instance and general case instruction. *Applied Research in Mental Retardation, 7*(2), 189–202.

Demchack, M. (1990). Response prompting and fading methods: A review. *American Journal on Mental Retardation, 94,* 603–615.

Dever, R. B. (1988). Community Living Skills: A taxonomy. In M. J. Begab, (Ed.), *Monographs of the American Association on Mental Retardation, 10.* Washington, DC: American Association on Mental Retardation.

Diorio, M. S., & Konarski, E. A. (1984). Evaluation of a method for teaching dressing skills to profoundly mentally retarded persons. *American Journal of Mental Deficiency, 89,* 307–309.

Epps, S., & Myers, C. L. (1989). Priority domains for instruction, satisfaction with school teaching, and postschool living and employment: An analysis of perceptions of parents of students with severe and profound disabilities. *Education and Training of the Mentally Retarded, 24*(2), 157–167.

Eshilian, L., Haney, M., & Falvey, M. A. (1989). Domestic skills. In M. A. Falvey (Ed.), *Community-based curriculums: Instructional strategies for students with severe handicaps* (2nd ed.) (pp. 115–140). Baltimore: Paul H. Brookes Publishing Co.

Falvey, M. A. (1986). *Community-based curriculum: Instructional strategies for students with severe handicaps.* Baltimore: Paul H. Brookes Publishing Co.

Falvey, M. A. (1989). *Community-based curriculum: Instructional strategies for students with severe handicaps* (2nd ed.). Baltimore: Paul H. Brookes Publishing Co.

Ford, A., Brown, L., Pumpian, I., Baumgart, D., Nisbet, J., Schroeder, J., & Loomis, R. (1984). Strategies for developing individualized recreation and leisure programs for severely handicapped students. In N. Certo, N. Haring, & R. York (Eds.), *Public school integration of severely handicapped students: Rational issues and progressive alternatives* (pp. 245–275). Baltimore: Paul H. Brookes Publishing Co.

Ford, A., Davern, L., Meyer, L., Schnorr, R., Black, J., & Dempsey, P. (1989a). General community functioning. In A. Ford, L. Davern, L. Meyer, R. Schnorr, J. Black, & P. Dempsey (Eds.), *The Syracuse community-referenced curriculum guide for students with moderate and severe disabilities* (pp. 77–92). Baltimore: Paul H. Brookes Publishing Co.

Ford, A., Davern, L., Meyer, L., Schnorr, R., Black, J., & Dempsey, P. (1989b). Overview. In A. Ford, L. Davern, L. Meyer, R. Schnorr, J. Black, & P. Dempsey (Eds.), *The Syracuse community-referenced curriculum guide for students with moderate and severe disabilities* (pp. 3–16). Baltimore: Paul H. Brookes Publishing Co.

Ford, A., Schnorr, R., Meyer, L., Davern, L., Black, J., & Dempsey, P. (1989c). Community living domains. In A. Ford, L. Davern, L. Meyer, R. Schnorr, J. Black, & P. Dempsey (Eds.), *The Syracuse community-referenced curriculum guide for students with moderate and severe disabilities* (pp. 29–44). Baltimore: Paul H. Brookes Publishing Co.

Gaule, K., Nietupski, J., & Certo, N. (1985). Teaching supermarket shopping skills using an adaptive shopping list. *Education and Training of the Mentally Retarded, 20,* 53–59.

Gaylord-Ross, R., & Holvoet, J. (1985). *Strategies for educating students with severe handicaps.* Boston: Little, Brown & Company.

Halle, J. W., Baer, D. M., & Spradlin, J. E. (1981). Teachers' generalized use of delay as a stimulus control procedure to increase language use in handicapped children. *Journal of Applied Behavior Analysis, 14,* 389–410.

Halle, J. W., Marshall, A. M., & Spradlin, J. E. (1979). Time delay: A technique to increase language use and facilitate generalization in retarded children. *Journal of Applied Behavior Analysis, 12,* 431–440.

Haring, N. G. (1988). *Generalization for students with severe handicaps: Strategies and solutions.* Seattle: University of Washington Press.

Haring, N. G., Liberty, K., Billingsley, F., White, O.,

Lynch, V., Kayser, J., & McCarty, F., (Eds.). (1985). *Investigating the problem of skill generalization* (3rd ed.). Seattle: Washington Research Organization.

Haring, N. G., Liberty, K. A., & White, O. R. (1980). Rules for data-based strategy decision in instructional programs: Current research and instructional implications. In W. Sailor, B. Wilcox, & L. Brown (Eds.), *Methods of instruction for severely handicapped students* (pp. 159–192). Baltimore: Paul H. Brookes Publishing Co.

Haring, T. G. (1991). Social relationships. In L. H. Meyer, C. A. Peck, & L. Brown (Eds)., *Critical issues in the lives of people with severe disabilities* (pp. 195–217). Baltimore: Paul H. Brookes Publishing Co.

Haring, T. G., Breen, C. G., & Laitinen, R. (1989). Stimulus class formation and concept learning: Establishment of within- and between-set generalization and transitive relationships via conditional discrimination procedures. *Journal of the Experimental Analysis of Behavior, 52,* 13–25.

Haring, T. G., Roger, B., Lee, M., Breen, C., & Gaylord-Ross, R. J. (1986). Teaching social language to moderately handicapped students. *Journal of Applied Behavior Analysis, 19,* 159–171.

Hill, J. W., Wehman, P., & Horst, G. (1982). Toward generalization of appropriate leisure and social behavior in severely handicapped youth: Pinball machine use. *The Journal of the Association for the Severely Handicapped, 6*(4), 38–44.

Horner, R. D., & Keilitz, I. (1975). Training retarded adolescents to brush their teeth. *Journal of Applied Behavior Analysis, 8,* 301–309.

Horner, R. H., Albin, R. W., & Ralph, G. (1986). Generalization with precision: The role of negative teaching examples in the instruction of generalized grocery item selection. *The Journal of The Association for Persons with Severe Handicaps, 11,* 300–308.

Horner, R. H., Bellamy, G. T., & Colvin, G. T. (1984). Responding in the presence of nontrained stimuli: Implications of generalization error patterns. *The Journal of The Association for Persons with Severe Handicaps, 9,* 287–296.

Horner, R. H., Dunlap, G., & Koegel, R. L. (1988). *Generalization and maintenance.* Baltimore: Paul H. Brookes Publishing Co.

Horner, R. H., Williams, J. A., & Knobble, C. A. (1985), The effect of "opportunity to perform" on the maintenance of skills learned by high school students with severe handicaps. *The Journal of The Association for Persons with Severe Handicaps, 10,* 172–175.

Kayser, J. E., Billingsley, F. F., & Neel, R. S. (1986). A comparison of in-context and traditional instructional approaches: Total task, single trial versus backward chaining, multiple trials. *The Journal of The Association for Persons with Severe Handicaps, 11,* 28–38.

LaCampagne, J., & Cipani, E. (1987). Training adults with mental retardation to pay bills. *Mental Retardation, 25,* 293–303.

Liberty, K. A., Haring, N. G., White, O. R., & Billingsley, F. F. (1988). A technology for the future: Decision rules for generalization. *Education and Training in Mental Retardation, 23,* 315–326.

Marholin, D., II, O'Toole, K. M., Touchette, P. E., Berger, P. L., & Doyle, D. A. (1979). "I'll have a Big Mac, large fries, large Coke™, and apple pie," . . . or Teaching adaptive community skills. *Behavior Therapy, 10,* 236–248.

McDonnell, J. J., & Ferguson, B. (1988). A comparison of general case in vivo and general case simulation plus in vivo training. *The Journal of The Association for Persons with Severe Handicaps, 13,* 116–124.

Meyer, L. H. (1989). Foreword. In R. S. Neel & F. F. Billingsley (Eds.), *Impact: A functional curriculum handbook for students with moderate to severe disabilities* (pp. vii–xii). Baltimore: Paul H. Brookes Publishing Co.

Meyer, L. H., Peck, C. A., & Brown, L. (Eds.). (1991). *Critical issues in the lives of people with severe disabilities.* Baltimore: Paul H. Brookes Publishing Co.

Miller, U. C., & Test, D. W. (1989). A comparison of constant time delay and most-to-least prompting in teaching laundry skills to students with moderate retardation. *Education and Training in Mental Retardation, 24,* 363–370.

Minge, M. R., & Ball, T. S. (1967). Teaching of self-help skills to profoundly retarded patients. *American Journal of Mental Deficiency, 71,* 864–868.

Neef, N. A., Iwata, B. A., & Page, T. J. (1978). Public transportation training: In vivo versus classroom instruction. *Journal of Applied Behavior Analysis, 11,* 331–344.

Neel, R. S., & Billingsley, F. F. (1989). *IMPACT: A functional curriculum handbook for students with moderate to severe disabilities.* Baltimore: Paul H. Brookes Publishing Co.

Nietupski, J., Welch, J., & Wacker, D. (1983). Acquisition, maintenance, and transfer of grocery item purchasing skills by moderately and severely handicapped students. *Education and Training of the Mentally Retarded, 18,* 279–286.

Nutter, D., & Reid, D. H. (1978). Teaching retarded women a clothing selection skill using community norms. *Journal of Applied Behavior Analysis, 11,* 475–487.

Petersen, J., Trecker, N., Egan, I., Fredericks, H. D. B., & Bunse, C. (1983). *The Teaching Research curriculum for handicapped adolescents and adults: Assessment procedures.* Monmouth, OR: Teaching Research.

Robinson-Wilson, M. A. (1977). Picture recipe cards as an approach to teaching severely and profoundly retarded adults to cook. *Education and Training of the Mentally Retarded, 12,* 69–73.

Rusch, F. R., Rose, T., & Greenwood, C. R. (1988). *Behavior analysis in special education.* Englewood Cliffs, NJ: Prentice Hall.

Sailor, W., & Guess, D. (1983). *Severely handicapped students: An instructional design.* Boston: Houghton Mifflin Co.

Sailor, W., & Haring, N. G. (1977). Some current dimensions in the education of the severely/multiply handicapped. *AAESPH Review, 2,* 3–23.

Schleien, S. J., Ash, T., Kiernan, J., & Wehman, P. (1981). Developing independent cooking skills in a profoundly retarded woman. *The Journal of the Association for the Severely Retarded, 6*(2), 23–29.

Schoen, S. F. (1986). Assistance procedures to facilitate the transfer of stimulus control: Review and analysis. *Education and Training of the Mentally Retarded, 21,* 62–74.

Shafer, M. S., Inge, K. J., & Hill, J. (1986). Acquisition, generalization, and maintenance of automated banking skills. *Education and Training of the Mentally Retarded, 21,* 265–272.

Snell, M. E. (1982). Analysis of time delay procedures in teaching daily living skills to retarded adults. *Analysis and Intervention in Developmental Disabilities, 2,* 139–155.

Snell, M. E. (1987). *Systematic instruction of persons with severe handicaps* (3rd ed.). Columbus, OH: Charles E. Merrill.

Snell, M. E., & Smith, D. D. (1978). Intervention Strategies. In M. E. Snell (Ed.), *Systematic instruction of the moderately and severely handicapped* (pp. 74–100). Columbus, OH: Charles E. Merrill.

Sontag, E., Burke, P. J., & York, R. (1973). Considerations for serving the severely handicapped in the public schools. *Education and Training of the Mentally Retarded, 8,* 20–26.

Spooner, F. (1984). Comparisons of backward chaining and total task presentation in training severely handicapped persons. *Education and Training in Mental Retardation, 19,* 15–22.

Spooner, F., & Spooner, D. (1984). A review of chaining techniques: Implication for future research and practice. *Education and Training of the Mentally Retarded, 19,* 114–124.

Stokes, T. F., & Baer, D. (1977). An implicit technology of generalization. *Journal of Applied Behavior Analysis, 10,* 349–367.

Stokes, T. F., & Osnes, P. G. (1988). The developing applied technology of generalization and maintenance. In R. H. Horner, G. Dunlap, & R. L. Koegel (Eds.), *Generalization and maintenance: Life-style changes in applied settings* (pp. 5–19). Baltimore: Paul H. Brookes Publishing Co.

Thinesen, P. J., & Bryan, A. J. (1981). The use of sequential pictorial cues in the initiation and maintenance of grooming behavior with mentally retarded adults. *Mental Retardation, 19,* 246–250.

Thompson, T. J., Braam, S. J., & Fuqua, R. W. (1982). Training and generalization of laundry skills: A multiple probe evaluation with handicapped persons. *Journal of Applied Behavior Analysis, 15,* 177–182.

Trask, S. A., Grossi, T. A., & Heward, W. L. (1989, May). *Teaching young adults who are blind and developmentally handicapped to use tape-recorded recipes: Acquisition, generalization, and maintenance of cooking skills.* Paper presented at the Association for Behavior Analysis Conference. Nashville, Tennessee.

Treffry, D., Martin, G., Samels, J., & Watson, C. (1970). Operant conditioning of grooming behavior of severely retarded girls. *Mental Retardation, 8,* 29–33.

Vincent, L. J., Salisbury, C., Walter, G., Gruenwald, L. J., & Powers, M. (1980). Program evaluation and curriculum development in early childhood special education: Criteria of the next environment. In W. Sailor, B. Wilcox, & L. Brown (Eds.), *Methods of instruction for severely handicapped students* (pp. 303–328). Baltimore: Paul H. Brookes Publishing Co.

Vogelsburg, R. T., & Rusch, F. R. (1979). Training severely handicapped students to cross partially controlled intersections. *AAESPH Review, 4,* 264–273.

Watson, L. S. (1972). *How to use behavior modification with mentally retarded and autistic children: Programs for administrators, teachers, parents, and nurses.* Libertyville, IL: Behavior Modification Technology.

Wheeler, J., Ford, A., Nietupski, J., Loomis, R., & Brown, L. (1980). Teaching moderately and severely handicapped adolescents to shop in super-markets using pocket calculators. *Education and Training of the Mentally Retarded, 15,* 105–112.

Wilcox, B., & Bellamy, G. T. (1982). *Design of high school programs for severely handicapped students.* Baltimore: Paul H. Brookes Publishing Co.

Wilcox, B., & Bellamy, G. T. (1987). *A comprehensive guide to* The Activities Catalog: *An alternative curriculum for youth and adults with severe disabilities.* Baltimore: Paul H. Brookes Publishing Co.

Wolfensberger, W. (1972). *The principle of normalization in human services.* Toronto: National Institute on Mental Retardation.

Zeiler, M. D., & Jervey, S. S. (1968). Development of behavior: Self-feeding. *Journal of Consulting Psychology, 32,* 164–168.

CHAPTER 7

EMPLOYMENT PREPARATION OF STUDENTS WITH SEVERE DISABILITIES

MARTIN AGRAN
Department of Special Education, Utah State University

DAVID TEST
Special Education Program, University of North Carolina at Charlotte

JAMES E. MARTIN
School of Education, University of Colorado–Colorado Springs

Although Public Law 94-142 has had a significant impact in the last decade and a half in ensuring that students with severe disabilities receive quality education in a least restrictive environment, there is, nevertheless, a continued concern among educators that these students are being served in less than optimal educational settings. Often such settings are segregated and, thus, provide few, if any, opportunities for students with severe disabilities to interact with peers without disabilities in instructional, social, or recreational experiences. In addition, the instructional focus in such programs may be nonfunctional. Rather than providing skills that will enhance these students' independence and quality of life, instruction may instead be based on teaching skills that correspond to the developmental level of a student but have no functional outcomes (e.g., teaching an 18-year-old student with profound mental retardation to sort plastic geometric shapes). Given these discrepancies, there is now a strong commitment to guarantee that students with severe disabilities are provided education in integrated settings in which they have ample opportunity to learn, socialize, and recreate with students without disabilities, and where the focus is on providing community-referenced, functional instruction.

Similar to this shift in educational focus and service delivery has been a shift in the focus and nature of vocational education or employment preparation services for students with severe disabilities. Rather than a continued practice of placing individuals in segregated (i.e., sheltered) sites in which they will have few opportunities to interact with co-workers without disabilities and where they may be engaged in unvalued or busywork (e.g., making unmarketable trinkets), efforts are being directed to providing appropriate work experiences in natural, community settings. Although educators may differ in what they think are appropriate work experiences for persons with severe disabilities, there appears to be a general consensus that the need to provide employment

The National Institute for Disability Rehabilitation Research, Colorado Division of Vocational Rehabilitation, and the Mid-Colorado Regional Commission for the Developmentally Disabled provided partial support for the preparation of this chapter. For further information, contact Martin Agran, Department of Special Education, Utah State University, Logan, UT 84322-2865. For additional information about the Consumer Directed Supported Employment Partnership at the University of Colorado, contact James E. Martin, University of Colorado, Special Education Program, Colorado Springs, CO 80933-7150.

preparation services to students with severe disabilities is indeed critical.

OVERVIEW OF CHAPTER

This chapter describes current efforts to provide transition services to persons with severe disabilities. Specifically, four functions are addressed. First, it provides information on the factors responsible for the current professional interest in providing appropriate transition and supported employment services for persons with severe disabilities. Second, the chapter describes recommended instructional technologies, as well as a comparison of teacher-directed and student-directed strategies. Third, a description of the adaptability instructional model, which seeks to provide students with a range of problem-solving and adaptability skills needed for successful transition, is discussed. Last, this chapter describes the supported employment initiative. Employment preparation for students with severe disabilities is a complex, multifaceted process, and this chapter seeks to provide current, state-of-the-art information on how these issues are being addressed.

Postschool Transition Outcomes

The current interest in providing appropriate vocational or transition programs for students with severe disabilities has been engendered by several factors. Foremost has been the realization that to ensure successful community work outcomes, effective employment preparation programs need to be implemented as early as possible. Historically, persons with severe disabilities were totally denied programs to develop marketable work skills or were placed in sheltered facilities where they performed work activities that were low paying, seasonal, and often meaningless (e.g., producing worthless crafts). Little or no effort was committed to moving the consumer to a progressively less restrictive, community-based work setting. In particular, the need for appropriate transition programs has been underscored by reports on the postschool outcomes of students with severe dis-

abilities. In general, the data revealed the lack of effectiveness of traditional vocational programs on (1) status and wages, (2) movement through the service delivery continuum, (3) specificity in training, and (4) training in problem solving. The following section describes these findings.

Status and Wages

Wehman, Kregel, and Seyfarth (1985) examined the employment status of 117 individuals with moderate to profound disabilities who had received educational services in Virginia. Of this sample, 78.6 percent were unemployed, 9.4 percent were employed in a sheltered facility, and 12 percent were competitively employed. In respect to earnings, 71 percent earned $100 or less per month, 21 percent earned $101 to $500 a month, and 8 percent earned between $501 and $700 a month. Mithaug, Horiuchi, & McNulty (1987) examined the postschool status of 234 students with disabilities who had received special education services in Colorado. Only 32 percent were employed full-time, and 57 percent earned less than $4.00 an hour. Hasazi, Gordon, and Roe (1985) reported data on the status of more than 400 students who had received special education services in Vermont. Of the 55 percent who were employed, only 33 percent were working full-time.

Mithaug, Martin, Agran, and Rusch (1988) noted that students with disabilities have only a 35 percent to 45 percent chance of working full-time. Inasmuch as the majority of participants in the studies of both Mithaug, Horiuchi, and McNulty (1987) and Hasazi et al. (1985) had mild disabilities and tended to be the members of the group who earned the most money and worked the greatest number of hours, the employment status of persons with severe disabilities is that much more despairing.

Lack of Movement

Traditionally, work placement options for persons with severe disabilities has been based on a flow-through service-delivery continuum. Accordingly, individuals were to be placed into increasingly less restrictive work settings as they acquired the skills needed for their new placements. Investigations of the movement of consumers from low-level programs (e.g., work- or day-activity programs) to high-level programs (e.g., competitive employment) have, however, revealed rates of movement from 1 percent to 3 percent (Bellamy, Rhodes, Mank, & Albin, 1988). Thus, once placed into the service delivery system, the odds of moving through it (and eventually to competitive employment) were minuscule. With such findings it became clear that the service delivery system was not transitional or dynamic, but resulted in extended placements in low-level programs. As a result of these placements, low wages and limited skill development were, regrettably, virtually guaranteed.

Lack of Specificity

Unsuccessful employment outcomes and low movement rates have been attributed in part to a lack of specificity in both focus and training. Rather than teach specific work skills to meet the requirements of specified jobs, employment preparation programs for persons with severe disabilities have instead relied on a readiness model, which sought instead either to change consumers' attitudes about work (Rusch & Menchetti, 1981) or to provide them with a repertoire of generic skills assumed to be necessary. Not surprisingly, changing the attitudes of persons with severe disabilities or teaching them skills that have not been validated as essential did not produce successful outcomes (Rusch, Mithaug, & Flexer, 1986). Further, training difficulties were often compounded by the staff's use of vague and unsystematic instruction and supervision (Gifford, Rusch, Martin, & White, 1984) and a failure to incorporate maintenance and generalization programs into training strategies (Rusch & Mithaug, 1980; Wacker & Berg, 1986).

Lack of Problem Solving

Mithaug, Martin, and Agran (1987) suggested that the postschool employment success of students

with disabilities will depend on their abilities to acquire new skills and adapt to changing situations. Because of the many changes that occur in work environments (e.g., changes in routine, supervisors), individuals need to know how to identify potential problems in their work environments, then come up with an appropriate course of action. For example, if an employee cannot find the appropriate tool to use, he or she needs to be able to ask a coworker where the tool is. Inability to make these adjustments has been cited as a major reason for job termination (Mithaug, Martin, Husch, Agran, & Rusch, 1988). Mithaug, Martin, Agran, and Rusch (1988) suggested that many employment-preparation programs represent teacher-controlled procedures that reinforce dependence and discourage individuals from making choices for themselves and managing their own behavior. To ensure success, training in acquiring problem-solving skills must be incorporated into instructional procedures; at present, they are not.

HISTORICAL REVIEW OF THE TRANSITION INITIATIVE

Although reports on the vocational competence of students with severe disabilities began to appear in the late 1960s and early 1970s (see Crosson, 1969; Gold, 1972; Bellamy, Horner, & Inman, 1979), there was limited interest in this area at this time and transition-related research and demonstration projects remained few. In the late 1970s and early 1980s, however, interest in providing transition programs for students with severe disabilities accelerated. Several factors were responsible for this. Although Public Law 94-142 did not mandate that vocational goals must be included in IEPs, it is clear that an IEP without such goals, especially for older students with disabilities, would not be considered appropriate (Phelps & Frasier, 1988). Because Public Law 94-142 stipulated that instruction needs to take place in the least restrictive setting, students with severe disabilities began to be provided work experiences at real job sites in their communities.

Concurrent with the provision of these services,

transition outcome data and unemployment figures for persons with severe disabilities began to appear. As discussed earlier, the employment prospects for these individuals were dismal. Aware of these problems, Congress hoped to ameliorate the situation by passing two pieces of legislation: Public Law 98-199 and the Developmental Disabilities Act of 1984 (Public Law 98-527) (see "Federal Definition and Characteristics" later in this chapter).

Public Law 98-199 amended Public Law 94-142 and put a priority on transition services. The law encouraged school districts to base their programs on the students' progress to their adulthood (i.e., their likely work placements when they leave school). Accordingly, districts were encouraged to do careful planning through an Individual Transition Plan. This plan included the transition goals for the student and was appended to the Individualized Education Plan (IEP). Moreover, districts were encouraged to establish links with other relevant service agencies (e.g., Division of Vocational Rehabilitation) so that the student would be able to receive needed services when he or she left the school system.

The Developmental Disabilities Act of 1984 stipulated that employment for persons with disabilities should be considered a priority and that efforts must be made to ensure that persons with disabilities are provided sufficient assistance to achieve successful outcomes. Specifically, the Developmental Disabilities Act offered guidelines on providing supported employment services for persons with severe disabilities. *Supported employment* refers to paid employment in competitive or integrated environments, with ongoing support services (for fuller discussion, see "Federal Definition and Characteristics" in this chapter). As a result, persons with severe disabilities began to be more fully involved in programs that provided them with opportunities to work in community jobs and receive all the assistance they may need.

TRANSITION MODELS

The following section describes several key transition models.

Will's Transition Model

In 1984, Madeline Will, former assistant secretary for the Office of Special Education and Rehabilitative Services (OSERS), the agency responsible for the monitoring of educational and transition services for persons with disabilities, presented a transition model that has received wide acceptance (Will, 1984). Transition in this model was defined as the extent to which support services are provided to students with disabilities to facilitate their movement from school to work. Three tiers were presented. The first referred to transition services that involved little or no special services other than generic services available to anyone in the community. The second level of support involved short-term or "time-limited" services (e.g., vocational rehabilitation counseling). The third level referred to ongoing services in which a person receives support as long as needed (e.g., supported employment). Given the varied and complex needs of persons with disabilities, the OSERS model seeks to provide each student with the level of support he or she needs to achieve successful outcomes.

From Will's original concept, several other approaches evolved, sharing Will's components or branching off in new directions. Brief descriptions of several models follow.

Community Living Transition Model

Halpern (1985) questioned Will's belief that employment is the primary outcome of an effective school transition program. Instead, this author believes, the purpose of transition is to prepare exiting students to live successfully in their community. In addition to employment, this includes establishing a quality home environment and a satisfying social network. The levels of support specified in the Will model (generic services, time-limited services, and ongoing services) are included in the Halpern model. However, unlike those in the Will model, these services are not restricted to work programs, but also include home and social skills programs. Successful community adjustment is achieved only if success in all of these domains is achieved. Although Halpern considers the social and interpersonal network to be the most important of the three domains, teaching is suggested for all domains, inasmuch as success in one domain will not necessarily generalize to another.

Wehman's Transition Model

Like Will, Wehman and associates believe that employment is the primary outcome of a transition program (Wehman, Kregel, & Barcus, 1985). These authors consider any one of three vocational placements as a suitable outcome: competitive employment, placement in a work crew or enclave, or employment at a specialized sheltered work arrangement. Early development of an individualized transition plan, with input from parents, students, school, staff, and adult agency personnel, helps ensure an orderly transition from school to work.

Four aspects of this model are noteworthy. First, it calls for the establishment of a detailed "transition plan" to coordinate postschool services. Second, it describes specific school services that may lead to a successful outcome. Third, the need to use a functional curriculum and to provide training in integrated community job sites is strongly emphasized. Fourth, it introduces an array of vocational outcomes, supported by long-term follow-up.

Severe-Needs Model

Brown and associates believe that meaningful work for students with severe disabilities in community environments should be a major school goal (Brown, 1986). According to Brown et al., meaningful work represents "a series of actions that, if not performed by a severely handicapped person, must be performed by a nonhandicapped person for money" (Brown et al., 1986, p. 133). Such work *must* be in a community environment, where the number of people with severe disabilities does not exceed 1 percent of the total work force and where interactions with co-workers without disabilities are encouraged. It is recommended that such community-based training needs to begin early (i.e., by age 11). The amount of time students spend at work increases as they get older, so that by the last year of school, students work full-time at their jobs.

The Council for Exceptional Children's Division on Career Development Transition Statement

The Council for Exceptional Children's (CEC) Division on Career Development (DCD) transition statement also considers work the major goal of transition (Razeghi, Kokaska, Gruenhagen, & Fair, 1987). Work occurs when individuals are "contributing to their own benefit" (Razeghi et al., 1987, p. 4). Work can be paid or unpaid. A parent who raises a child and does not work outside the home is engaged in an important career role—one as important as the person who works at a child care center for pay.

Career development is "an on-going, sequential process of assisting disabled children, youth, and adults in achieving meaningful work roles such as that of student, consumer, citizen, family member, and employee" (Razeghi et al., 1987, p. 4). Passing through the career education phases helps prepare students for their worker roles. Implementation starts during the early years and continues throughout the school years and beyond. Noteworthy in this model is the belief that transition programming starts at preschool and that all personnel in the school community are responsible for career development, under the leadership of the special educator.

Student-Directed Transition Model

Should students provide input about their own futures? Can we teach them to make choices? Should they not have an active role in their transition programs? Unlike the previously described models that ignore *active* student involvement, the student-directed approach seeks to empower students (Agran & Moore, 1987; Martin, Mithaug, Agran, & Husch, 1990; Mithaug, Martin, Agran, & Rusch, 1988). Such student empowerment provides them with "the opportunity to choose, to set goals, and to make decisions" (Martin et al., 1990, p. 360). In this model, systematic instruction is provided to enable students to plan and make their own decisions. Rather than telling students what types of jobs they should be interested in, what to do at every step, and how to correct their work performance, this model seeks to shift responsibility from the teacher to the student. The shift is accomplished by teaching students to use a variety of self-management strategies. This model seeks to put participants into a decision-making role, regardless of the severity of their disabilities.

Summary

These are several transition models (see Berkell & Brown, 1989; Wehman, Moon, Everson, Wood, & Barcus, 1988, for a more detailed review). Each possesses positive attributes, no one model fully meeting the transition needs of all students. We suggest combining approaches into a unique model to meet the unique needs of all students.

SELECTING, ASSESSING, AND TEACHING RELEVANT WORK SKILLS

Trainer-Directed Instruction

Based on experiences with persons without disabilities or persons with mild disabilities, it was once believed that vocational competency represented a developmental process that could be shaped by maturational or attitudinal changes. These changes, it was further believed, could be produced by increasing students' exposure to new situations and by providing them with more counseling. Needless to say, we have realized that to produce desired changes for persons with severe disabilities, we need to provide systematic, behavior-analytic programs. Such programs involve the use of task analyses, which allow trainers to break down a work task into discrete, sequential steps; then, with the use of behavioral procedures (i.e., the manipulation of cues and consequences), desired responses can be shaped. Although components differ among transition programs, many programs include the components listed in Table 7.1.

This section describes the instructional procedures commonly used in transition programs. (For detailed information on training strategies, see McLoughlin, Garner, and Callahan, 1987, and Rusch and Mithaug, 1980.)

Selecting Appropriate Instructional Procedures. As Mithaug, Martin, Agran, and Rusch (1988) noted, the use of prompt hierarchies has been recommended for transition and supported employment programs. These procedures are comparable to the direct instruction approaches teachers use in classrooms and involve a determination by the trainer as to the type and amount of assistance a student needs. Based on this system, independence for the student is gauged by the level of assistance he or she needs to complete a task appropriately. At the highest level, the student will need only a verbal cue from the trainer on what needs to be done; at the lowest level, full or partial physical assistance is provided. When trainer cues are no longer needed, independence is said to be achieved. (For further specifics on data collection methods and instructional techniques appropriate for teaching work skills, see Chapters 3 and 4.)

TABLE 7.1 Components in Teacher-Directed Transitional Programs

1. Use of prompt hierarchies
2. Use of fading procedure
3. Development and use of a meaningful data collection system
4. Use of peer-instruction strategies
5. Use of co-worker strategies

Peer Instruction.   One cost-efficient approach to employment training for students with severe disabilities is the use of peer trainers (Wacker & Berg, 1984). Such training reduces personnel costs, may be highly motivating for students with disabilities, may save teacher training time, and may prove to be as effective as teacher-delivered instruction. Further, several researchers (Agran, Fodor-Davis, Moore, & Martella, 1992; Knapczyk, Johnson, & McDermott, 1983; Wacker & Berg, 1984) have suggested that peers with disabilities can be trained to serve effectively as trainers. For example, Knapczyk and colleagues (1983) reported that there were no differences in the production rates or accuracy of work performed by six students with severe mental retardation whether they were supervised by a teacher or by a peer with severe disabilities.

The roles that peer trainers can serve are many. Peers can be trained to provide systematic, work-related instruction to students, collect data, provide necessary feedback, and serve as advocates. Peers may also be used to teach appropriate social responses, teach relevant academic or functional living skills (e.g., time management, pedestrian skills), or manage the challenging behaviors of their tutees. Needless to say, before a peer trainer is asked to serve in an instructional capacity, it is assumed that he or she will be able to perform the task in question fluently, be able to deliver reinforcement and correction to an established expectation level, and be knowledgeable as to what he or she can say or do when delivering the intervention.

Co-worker Strategies.   Work environments are often busy places with competing stimuli. Such an environment may cause an employee to attend to irrelevant stimuli and to be unable to complete a work task. To minimize such occurrences, Hughes, Rusch, and Curl (1990) suggest that co-worker involvement represents a natural means to assist supported employees in maintaining their independent performance. Generally, co-workers are employees who perform the same duties as supported employees and work in the same area. In roles similar to those peer trainers have assumed, co-workers have been trained to implement interventions, collect data, provide subjective evaluations about the quality of work of a supported employee, and serve as advocates and social acquaintances at and outside the workplace. Although co-workers may serve a helpful role to employees with disabilities by demonstrating a job task or providing the new employees with general information, formal instruction is needed if they are to be effective training agents (Hughes et al., 1990). For example, Hughes and colleagues (1990) indicate that without such instruction, co-workers tend to not ask supported employees to perform a task after they have demonstrated it, or to allow supported employees to continue a task even though they may be doing the job incorrectly. As with peer trainers, co-workers need to meet established expectations regarding their instructional delivery prior to their formal instructional interactions with supported employees.

Student-Directed Instruction

Parents of students who have been out of school for several years complain that their special education graduates lack initiative, self-confidence, and problem-solving skills (Mithaug et al., 1987). These parents reported that their children do not know what to do, what they can do, or what they need to do in order to become more independent and successful. In a sense, this is not surprising, inasmuch as the dominant instructional approach of special education programs is one in which teachers make the decisions and students respond passively. Students learn to *react to* and *depend on* teacher cues and consequences. They complete tasks, answer questions, go where teachers want them to go, receive feedback, meet teacher or supervisor expectations (not their own), comply with class rules and teacher instructions, follow teacher schedules, and pay attention to teacher directions. The situation in teacher-controlled work environments is no different. There are few, if any, opportunities for students to make choices and to act upon them (Guess, Benson, & Siegel-Causey, 1985).

Guess and Siegel-Causey (1985) argue that current practice determines what students in special education should learn, how they will be taught, where instruction will take place, and why it is important for them to learn assigned skills. Rather than being viewed as "self-directing and purposeful human beings," persons with learning or behavior problems are perceived as "mere objects of external manipulation." Opportunities to express preferences, make choices, and behave spontaneously and autonomously are not provided. Perhaps the failure of many students to adapt to community life after school is not due to their inability to learn, but rather to the approach we use to teach. If learning is to be enhanced, students must have strategies for controlling their environment by deciding for themselves. Perhaps our perceptions of students with severe disabilities, based on the controlling technology we use for their education, have diminished our ability to see students with severe disabilities as individuals capable of ever making choices, let alone the right choices (Guess et al., 1985).

Central to the concept of student-directed instruction is instruction of students in the use of self-management strategies, which include those listed in Table 7.2. Such strategies permit students to manage and direct their classroom or work behavior, independent of external manipulation. Descriptions of these self-management strategies, commonly used in transition programs, follow (see Agran & Martin, 1987, for a complete review).

Self-Monitoring. Self-monitoring refers to a strategy in which a student records whether a target behavior has occurred, compares his or her recording to a standard given, and then determines whether the performance was satisfactory. Interestingly, researchers have suggested that as students become more aware of the desired behavior, a change in a positive direction will occur, even if their recordings are inaccurate (Agran & Moore, 1987). Mithaug, Martin, Agran, and Rusch (1988) suggest that self-monitoring allows students to draw conclusions about meeting goals when they are able to compare their evaluations with a standard.

Self-Reinforcement. Self-reinforcement involves the determination and/or self-delivery of reinforcement. That is, students are provided opportunities to select preferred reinforcers and to reinforce themselves when they believe they have responded appropriately. In this respect, self-reinforcement involves some degree of self-monitoring. In a number of studies conducted in work settings, researchers have reported that participants may perform as well, if not better, under self-reinforcing conditions than under conditions of externally administered reinforcement. An obvious advantage of this strategy is that it provides students with an opportunity to be immediately reinforced for performing appropriately rather than having to wait for a teacher or trainer who is not present.

Permanent Cues. Permanent cues involve the use of picture cues to facilitate performance. Rather than depend on teachers to tell them what to do, students are trained to refer to pictures. In particular, this strategy allows students who have difficulty remembering what to do to refer to a picture and to perform the response illustrated. As Mithaug, Martin, Agran, and Rusch (1988) note, by reading a picture sequence indicating tasks to do, a student can complete a day's work independent of external supervision. The use of such cues may allow a student to perform at a higher level of independence than previously experienced.

TABLE 7.2 Self-Management Strategies

Self-monitoring
Self-reinforcement
Permanent cues
Self-instructions
Goal setting

Self-Instructions. Self-instructions are verbalizations that students emit to cue, direct, or maintain their behavior. Such self-instructions may acquire discriminative stimulus control over succeeding responses. Thus, students can direct themselves to a task, independent of external manipulation. Agran and associates have trained students with moderate and severe disabilities to use self-instructions to facilitate job-task sequencing (Agran, Fodor-Davis, & Moore, 1986), promote instruction following (Agran, Fodor-Davis, Moore, & Deer, 1989), increase production rates (Moore, Agran, & Fodor-Davis, 1989), and complete complex food preparation tasks (Agran, Fodor-Davis, Moore, & Martella, 1992). In addition, self-instructional training has been recommended as a strategy to facilitate problem solving. When trained to define a problem verbally, consider a solution, and evaluate the action taken, students may be able to resolve existing problems independently at their jobs.

Goal Setting. Goal setting involves the student's determination of a desired goal. For example, students can be trained to establish their own production goals (e.g., number of units to be assembled). Several researchers have suggested that self-determined contingencies may be as effective as externally determined contingencies. Mithaug, Martin, Agran, and Rusch (1988) suggest that the advantages of teaching students to set their own goals are many. First, students are better able to see a relationship between what they indicate they will do and what they actually do. Second, by setting goals, they can better plan their work schedule and determine appropriate reinforcers. Most important, goal setting provides the student an opportunity to be a very active member of the educational process.

In summary, each of these strategies has been effectively used by students with severe disabilities. Further, their use in combination has been found to be even more powerful (Mithaug, Martin, Agran, & Rusch, 1988). Such combinations provide a level of independence difficult to achieve in an environment that is externally managed.

ADAPTABILITY INSTRUCTIONAL MODEL

This section describes a student-directed transition model developed by Mithaug, Martin, and Agran (1987). If independence is to serve as an indicator of a successful transition program, strong efforts must be made to promote it. The adaptability instructional model seeks to do this.

The adaptability model identifies 43 skills that students need to succeed at their jobs (Mithaug, Martin, & Burger, 1987). The instructional units comprised by the model are (1) decision making, (2) independent performance, (3) self-evaluation, and (4) adjustment. These skills are listed in Table 7.3.

Decision Making

In decision making, students identify their needs, interests, and abilities, consider alternatives, and then select their work goals. In other words, they complete their own job match (Martin, Mithaug, & Husch, 1988), determining which jobs are most suitable for them. Student-centered situational assessments allow individuals with severe disabilities *to evaluate their own needs.*

The job-match assessment is a two-part process. First, students determine what they like. Second, they match their strengths and weaknesses to the demands of available jobs.

Students complete three different preference forms, which consist of several line drawings representing locally available entry-level work conditions, tasks, and jobs. Figures 7.1 through 7.3 present samples: "Work conditions I like," "Tasks I like," and "Jobs I like." During a job club session, students circle the drawings representing what they like. Afterward, they visit a job site to learn if what they selected is what they actually like. This process is repeated until the student's choice is consistent.

Prior to completing a self-directed job-match assessment, many students with severe disabilities do not know what they like, have an unrealistic view of their strengths and weaknesses, or lack knowledge about present vocational opportunities. Therefore, the student-centered job-match process teaches while assessing vocational interest and ability.

The forms must be adapted to meet the needs of individual learners. For instance, if a multipictured

TABLE 7.3   Adaptability Skills

Decision Making

GOALS

Does the student indicate goals

1. To work at preferred tasks?
2. To work at easy tasks?
3. To work at difficult (challenging) tasks?
4. To work at tasks that earn money or rewards?

OPTIONS

Given several tasks or assignments, can the student predict

5. How many problems or units could be completed for each task or assignment?
6. The accuracy of work on each task or assignment?
7. How much money or reward could be earned for each assignment?

DECISIONS

Given several tasks or assignments to choose from, does the student choose and then perform tasks for which he or she has

8. Expressed preferences in the past?
9. Demonstrated the ability to perform quickly and accurately?
10. Previously completed difficult work tasks?
11. Earned money or rewards in the past?

Given tasks or assignments the student has selected to work on, does the student

12. Determine the times to begin and end work on each task?
13. Specify the number to be completed, the accuracy level, and the rewards to be earned for work during that period?

Independence

PERFORMANCE

Does the student

1. Learn how to complete new tasks without teacher assistance?
2. Perform a required number of tasks quickly and accurately?

SEQUENCE

Does the student complete a sequence of tasks by

3. Getting the needed materials?
4. Setting up the materials?
5. Starting the task on time?
6. Ending work on time?

(continued)

TABLE 7.3 Continued

7. Delivering the finished product and remaining materials to a specified location?

8. Getting materials needed for the next task?

MONITORING

Does the student record the

1. Time he or she started work on a task?

2. Time he or she ended work on a task?

3. Number of tasks (steps or problems) completed?

4. Number of tasks (steps or problems) completed correctly?

5. Amount of reward or money received from completing a task or assignment correctly?

Self-Evaluation

COMPARING

Does the student compare self-recorded results with a standard and then determine if he or she

1. Started a task early, late, or on time?

2. Completed a task early, late, or on time?

3. Completed fewer, the same number, or more tasks (steps or problems) than expected?

4. Accurately completed fewer, the same number, or more tasks than expected?

5. Earned less, the same amount, or more rewards or money than expected?

Adjustment

ADJUSTMENT OF OWN BEHAVIOR

Does the student use a standard to determine that next time he or she should

1. Start a task earlier, later, or at the same time?

2. Complete a task earlier, later, or at the same time?

3. Complete fewer, the same, or more tasks?

4. Accurately complete fewer, the same, or more tasks?

5. Earn less, the same, or more rewards or money?

6. Change the number of tasks he or she plans to complete?

7. Change the number of tasks he or she plans to complete correctly?

8. Change the number of rewards he or she plans to earn?

9. Change task selections?

10. Change goal selections?

11. Change task options?

12. Change goal options?

FIGURE 7.1   Work conditions I like.

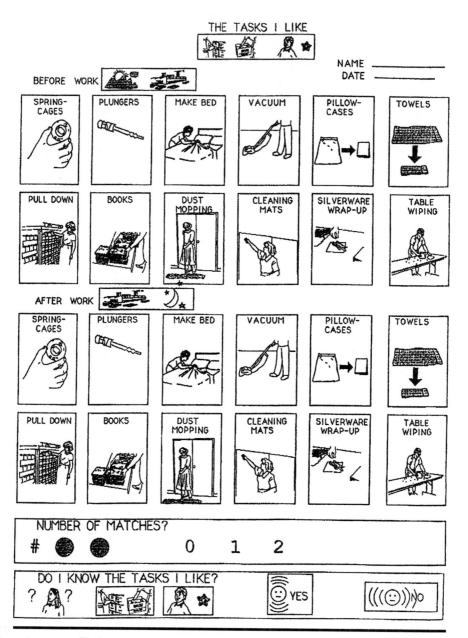

FIGURE 7.2   Tasks I like.

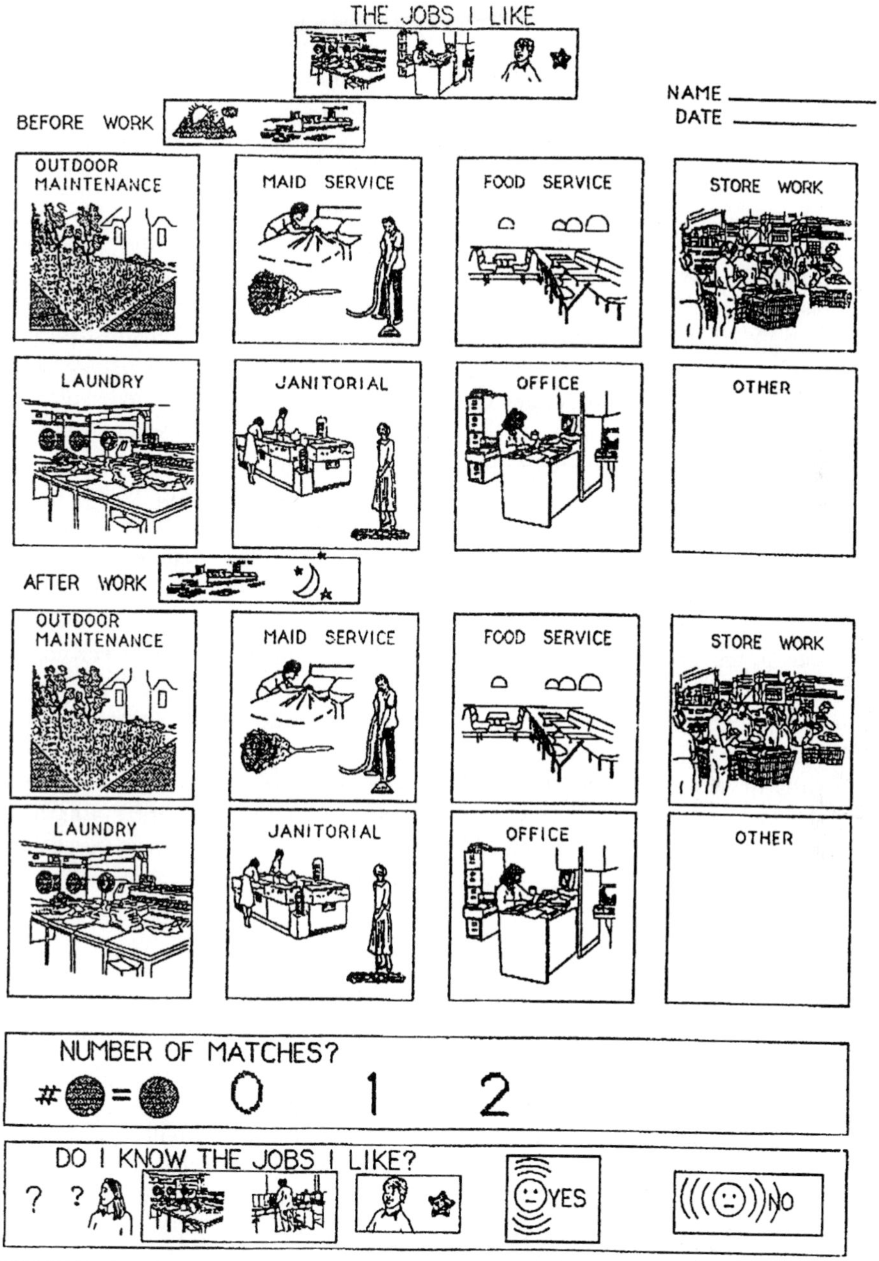

FIGURE 7.3 Jobs I like.

form is too difficult, then a form with only one drawing per page is appropriate. Used systematically, this process can provide reliable information regarding vocational choice for most students with special vocational needs.

Independent Performance

Following the decision-making phase, students demonstrate independent performance by following through on their action plan. They perform tasks independently at a job site they like by using learning-to-learn or self-management strategies, including self-instructions or permanent cues. Students are instructed to use these cues to aid them in completing tasks.

Self-Evaluation

While working, students self-evaluate their performance by monitoring and recording performance outcomes, then comparing their results with supervisor expectations (i.e., job coach or teacher's observations). In job settings, self-evaluations usually focus on being on time, task completion, productivity, accuracy, and earnings. These self-evaluations provide students with opportunities to evaluate the quality of their own performance.

Adjustment

Students use their self-evaluations to decide what to do next to meet the desired standard. For example, they may change their goals regarding the number of products they need to complete or the time they need to start.

Adjustments are essential to success. They connect future action to past performance. Before beginning another assignment, students review previous adjustment decisions and select goals, plans, and performance objectives accordingly. To allow them to make these changes, *adaptability contracts* are used. Adaptability contracts are self-management forms that students use to (1) set goals and performance objectives, (2) develop

work schedules, (3) monitor their own progress, (4) evaluate their results, and (5) decide what adjustment to make next time.

The adaptability contract reflects day-to-day changes on the job. It is a means for workers to monitor their performance, make short-term decisions, and make on-the-job performance adjustments. The contract includes sections for Plan, Work, Evaluate, and Adjust. The plan details the day's responsibilities, and the work section allows students to self-monitor their performance. In the evaluation section they compare actual performance with expectations. The plan can be expanded to include unique issues. Figure 7.4 presents a sample contract.

Performance feedback is crucial to long-term job success (Mithaug, Martin, Husch, Agran, & Rusch, 1988). The contract provides a means to shape the feedback process. For this reason, the teacher or job coach evaluates the student's performance daily. The student then compares his or her evaluation to the trainer's. Discrepancies require new decisions, which are expressed by marking directly on the contract. Over time, we have found that many workers with severe disabilities can master on-the-job problem solving. The forms, of course, must be adapted to meet unique student needs.

Summary

Although the adaptability model seeks to facilitate a student's transition from school to work, the adaptability skills that constitute the model can be taught to students as they move through their school grades. These skills can be included in the student's individualized transition plan. Figure 7.5 is a sample of a transition policy statement from a school district that has adopted the model.

CURRICULUM MATERIALS

Because the focus of transition programming is to provide training in community-based job sites where it is most probable that students will ultimately be placed, it will be necessary to develop

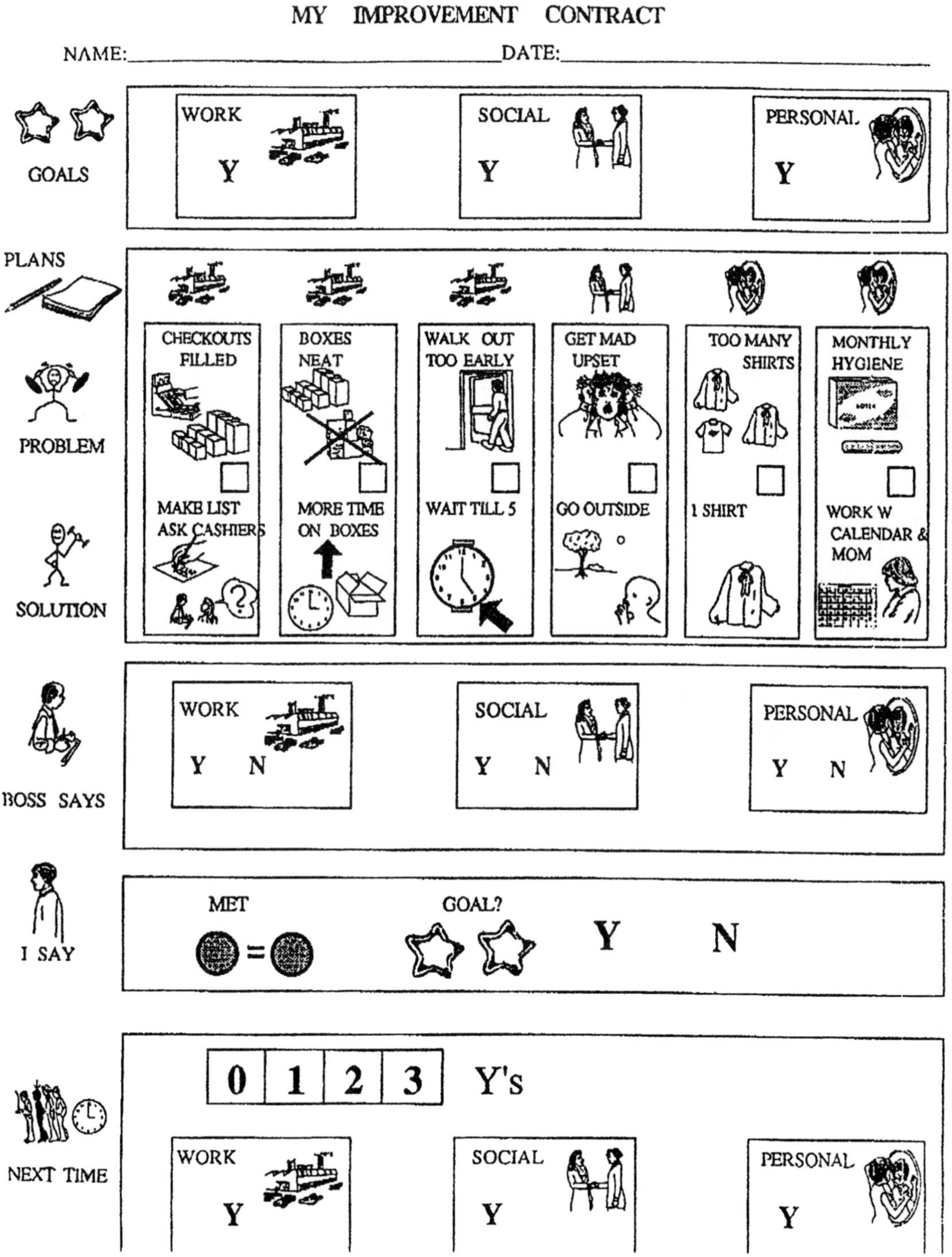

MY IMPROVEMENT CONTRACT

NAME:_____ DATE:_____

FIGURE 7.4 Improvement contract.

Components Of A Comprehensive School To Work Transition Policy*

Outcomes	Implementation Stages			
	Elementary	Middle School	High School	Post-School

Adaptability Skills

Goal Setting

Independent Performance

Self-Evaluation

Adjustment

Educational and Transition Planning

Observation & Limited Participation

Participation

Management

Career

Awareness

Exploration

Preparation

Placement

Follow-up

Linkage To Post -School Service

Referral

Transfer

FIGURE 7.5 Transition plan used by Academy School District, Colorado Springs, Colorado. Modified from Air Academy's School District Special Education's Transition Policy Statement, Colorado Springs, CO. Developed by a joint school-district, community, and university committee.

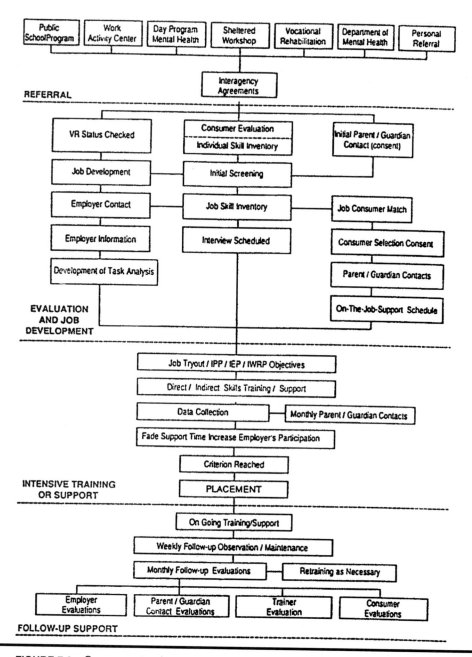

FIGURE 7.6   Components of comprehensive supported employment.

curricula relating to the specific requirements of specified jobs. This will necessitate at least four activities by the teacher: developing job analyses, writing task analyses for the jobs, assessing the student's work skills, and conducting evaluations of the student's performance. A brief description of each follows.

Job Analysis

The function of a job analysis is to identify the requirements of a specific job (i.e., the responses that will need to be performed to complete the task), as well as the characteristics of the environment that may influence responding (e.g., noise level, structural characteristics) (see "Supported Employment Components" later in this chapter). This will involve at least one visit to the job site to provide the teacher an opportunity to observe the site (*Note:* McLoughlin, Garner, and Callahan [1987] recommend that a week be spent). It is also recommended that the teacher meet with the job supervisor and one or more potential co-workers to find out more about job requirements. Finally, it is recommended that the teacher perform the job so that he or she can do a precise task analysis.

Task Analysis

A detailed task analysis for each of the required work tasks must be developed. Such analyses should be broken down to the level the teacher thinks appropriate for the student. In addition, when developing task analyses, teachers should identify the naturally occurring cues and consequences in the environment to facilitate instruction.

Student Assessment

Several transition-related assessment instruments are available (see Agran & Morgan, 1991; Menchetti & Flynn, 1990). Generally, these instruments provide teachers with an overall profile of their students' work skills and deficits. Behav-

iors required for specific jobs may not be included, and the teacher will need to develop an assessment form that includes these behaviors. This may take the form of a simple checklist, or the teacher may elect to obtain observational data on the specified behaviors.

Work Evaluation

To ensure that students are making progress and maintaining desired performance levels, teachers will need to obtain evaluation data. Collection of these data will require the development of one or more forms. These forms will include the specific jobs skills, as well as other work behaviors the teacher thinks important to evaluate (e.g., interactive skills during breaks). As an adjunct to the teacher's observations, input from co-workers, supervisors, and the consumer should be actively sought.

CRITICAL ISSUES IN SUPPORTED EMPLOYMENT INITIATIVE

Every day for the past 2 years, Dale has gotten up at 6:30 A.M. in order to catch the bus so that he will be on time for his job. Dale works in the dish room at a local hospital and has received salary increases each year he has worked. This description may sound as though Dale is "just another employee," but he is not. Not long ago, Dale would have been spending his adult life in a sheltered workshop; however, because of the current interest in providing supported employment, Dale is now working in a real job for real pay. Although he may not know it, Dale is part of what has been called "a national rights movement on the part of people with severe disabilities who have been excluded, devalued, and disenfranchised on the basis of their perceived lack of vocational competence" (Wehman, Kregel, & Shafer, 1989, p. 2). This section discusses the supported employment initiative—what it is, what its benefits are, and, most important, what its impact has been.

Federal Definition and Characteristics

Supported employment has emerged from a combination of factors, including (1) growing evidence from research and service demonstration projects showing that people with severe disabilities can and want to work, (2) a renewed focus on integration based, in part, on the fact that, although deinstitutionalization and mainstreaming have enabled people with severe disabilities to live and to be educated in the community, individuals continue to work in segregated workshops, and (3) the need for ongoing (often lifelong), rather than time-limited, services (e.g., traditional vocational rehabilitation services) to allow persons with severe disabilities to maintain employment (Bellamy, Rhodes, Mank, & Albin, 1988). In effect, the function of transition programs is to provide students with adequate preparation for supported employment.

As a result of these factors, supported employment has emerged as the most desirable work placement option for persons with severe disabilities. The Developmental Disabilities Act of 1984 defined supported employment as:

> *Paid employment which (i) is for persons with developmental disabilities for whom competitive employment at or above the minimum wage is unlikely and who, because of their disabilities, need ongoing support to perform in a work setting; (ii) is conducted in a variety of settings, particularly work sites in which persons without disabilities are employed; and (iii) is supported by any activity needed to sustain paid work by persons with disabilities, including supervision, training, and transportation. (Federal Register, 1984)*

Although the 1984 Developmental Disabilities Act provided the initial definition, it was not until the Vocational Rehabilitation Act Amendments of 1986 (P.L. 99-506) that supported employment were included in the national rehabilitation system. The 1986 amendments set forth regulations guiding the standards for providing supported employment services, as well as defining persons with severe disabilities as the target population for supported employment.

> *The supported employment program is intended to provide services to individuals who, because of the severity of their handicaps, would not traditionally be eligible for vocational rehabilitation services. Individuals who are eligible for services under the program must not be able to function independently in employment without intensive ongoing support services for the duration of their employment. Such term includes transitional employment for individuals with chronic mental illness. (P.L. 99-506, Title I, Sec. 103, i)*

These acts are important because they defined the three primary characteristics of supported employment as (1) paid employment, (2) integrated work settings, and (3) the provision of ongoing support for persons with severe disabilities.

Paid Employment

Supported employment requires a minimum of 20 hours of paid work per week, but does not specify production or wage levels. Although "real wages for real pay" is not a particularly radical idea in general, when applied to persons with severe disabilities, it is. Until recently, most persons with severe disabilities were shunted away to day centers where they received little or no work activity and little or no remuneration. For individuals who were placed in work activity centers or sheltered workshops, the work provided was often of a temporary or seasonal basis, with substandard wages. Providing persons with severe disabilities opportunities to perform meaningful work and receive appropriate wages for their efforts does indeed represent a change of major significance.

Integrated Work Settings

Given that community integration is an important outcome of supported employment, it is not surprising that one of the characteristics of supported employment is that work must be conducted in integrated settings. Federal guidelines state that a work site can be considered integrated only if eight or fewer persons with disabilities work together with persons without disabilities in a location not adjacent to another disability program. Although this does not guarantee integration, if persons are to become contributing members of their communities, they must have an opportunity to interact with others during lunch and breaks on a regular basis.

Ongoing Support

Prior to the advent of supported employment, the lack of appropriate work skills and behaviors exhibited by many people with disabilities were often viewed as a lack of "readiness." That is, it was felt that their inability to perform appropriately and achieve successful employment outcomes was due to their lack of prerequisite skills. As a result, it was felt that placement into integrated work settings was not appropriate until such skills were acquired. With the establishment of supported employment, these skill deficits are now viewed as indicating the need for ongoing support. Based on individuals' needs, such support may involve intensive daily assistance or infrequent follow-up checks. In fact, the 1986 Rehabilitation Act Amendments require follow-up at the job site at least two times each month. In either case, there must be an effort to provide consumers with the appropriate level of support that they need.

SUPPORTED EMPLOYMENT COMPONENTS

The three previously discussed characteristics have been combined into a delivery package for providing supported employment services that includes five components: (1) community survey and job analysis, (2) job match and placement, (3) job training, (4) follow-up services, and (5) interagency coordination (Rusch & Hughes, 1989).

Community Survey and Job Analysis

In the component comprising the community survey and job analysis, the job coach attempts to identify potential work sites through telephone calls, letters, or personal contact. Such canvassing allows the job coach to identify potential jobs in a cost-efficient manner. Once possible work sites are identified (i.e., the employer indicates that he or she would be interested in hiring persons with disabilities or would allow his or her business to be used as a training site), the job coach visits each site to view and work at potential jobs. This process of identifying job tasks and requirements is called *job analysis*. A job analysis involves scrutinizing all of the characteristics of a work environment that may influence work performance. Such factors as noise and light levels, the expected work pace, and the frequency and nature of social interactions with co-workers and customers are considered. In addition, the work tasks are analyzed and other skill requirements are identified (e.g., time management, mobility). Rusch (1986) recommends that certain items be included in job analyses (see Table 7.4).

Job Match and Placement

At the same time a job coach is conducting the community job analysis, he or she is also gathering information about the potential worker. For example, this could include information on the student's specific work skills, as well as social skills, vocational interests, and previous employment history. By carefully matching the information gathered through job analysis with student assessment data, the best job for each person can be identified.

Job Training

Once a worker has been placed, the job coach is responsible for teaching the person how to do the job. The job coach needs to provide all the neces-

TABLE 7.4   Items in Job Analysis

1. OVERVIEW	4. EMPLOYMENT CONDITIONS
Name, address, and telephone of firm	Work hours per day, per week
Type of industry	Shift
Name and title of person interviewed	Pay scale
Title of position	Bonuses and overtime pay
Total number of people employed	Union (if applicable)
Number of employees in position	Name and address of union representative
Stability of job	Travel requirements
Reasons for previous firings or abandonments	Training
	Criteria for promotion
2. WORK ENVIRONMENT	
Type of firm	**5. EMPLOYEE REQUIREMENTS**
Importance of speed	Education requirements
Number of co-workers consumer will work with	Previous experience
Degree and type of supervision available	Licenses and certificates
Cooperation of other employees	Special social and functional, academic and vocational skills
General social environment	
Physical appearance	Tests
Physical conditions	Insurance and other benefits
3. TASK ANALYSIS	
Tasks performed	
Approximate times tasks performed	

Modified from Rusch, F. R. (1986). *Competitive employment issues and strategies.* Baltimore: Paul H. Brookes Publishing Co.

sary training and still ensure that the job will be done to company standards. In addition to teaching the new job, the job coach often must train appropriate social skills and other job-related tasks, such as using public transportation, grooming, and dealing with money.

Follow-up Services

As the worker learns to do the new job independently, the job coach begins to "fade" from the scene. Such fading involves a systematic reduction in the amount and type of assistance provided to the worker. Needless to say, the amount of assistance to be faded differs from one worker to the next. Ultimately, the job coach's responsibility is to provide the least amount of support the worker needs to maintain the job. Often this includes recruiting co-workers to lend a hand if needed, or teaching the worker self-management skills so that he or she can continue to work at acceptable levels when the job coach is no longer present. Rusch and Mithaug (1980) suggest that follow-up programs include certain components (see Table 7.5).

TABLE 7.5 Components in
Follow-up Programs

1. Identify consumer's competencies and deficits.

2. Obtain objective and subjective assessments of consumer's performance.

3. Provide feedback to consumer and significant others (e.g., employer, work supervisor).

4. Prioritize skill deficits.

5. Set training objectives.

6. Deliver necessary work performance evaluation data on a systematic basis.

7. Obtain work performance evaluation data on a systematic basis.

8. Report progress to consumer and significant others.

9. Maintain a placement log.

Adapted from Rusch, F. R., & Mithaug, D. E. (1980). *Vocational training for mentally retarded adults: A behavioral analytic approach.* Champaign, IL: Research Press.

Interagency Coordination

Throughout the delivery of supported employment services, interagency coordination is a must for at least two reasons. First, most services are funded through a combination of vocational rehabilitation and mental retardation/developmental disability dollars. To ensure that available funds are being used expeditiously, coordination of cooperating agencies is essential. Second, making sure that each worker keeps his or her job during follow-up requires coordinating many different areas, including Social Security benefits, residential services, and case management. Without cooperation of all these agencies, supported employment services could not be provided.

SUPPORTED EMPLOYMENT MODELS

In accord with the federal definition and the five components of supported employment, a number of methods for delivering services have emerged, based on available placements. These include the individual placement, enclave or work station, mobile crew, and small business models. A description of each follows.

Individual Placement

In the individual placement model, also known as the job coach or individual supported jobs model, supported employment services are provided on an individual basis by a trained specialist. Depending on the agency, the person providing direct services is known as a job coach, employment specialist, or vocational training specialist (Winking, Trach, Rusch, & Tines, 1989). The individual placement model typically involves a job coach who locates a job for an individual, provides on-the-job training, systematically fades training support, then provides follow-up services at least twice each month.

Enclaves and Work Stations in Industry

In the enclave or work station model, also known as the clustered placement model (Rusch & Hughes, 1989), small groups of not more than eight individuals with disabilities work in a host business. Typically, individuals work in close proximity and perform similar tasks. The host industry provides the work task and the workplace, and often pays the employees directly. In most cases, a supported employment agency provides direct supervision and training; however, in some instances workers are supervised by host industry personnel.

Mobile Crews

The mobile crew is another small-group model that gets its name from the fact that services are often provided from a van. In this model, the job coach, who can also serve as the driver, together with a small group of workers (legally eight or fewer, but in practice usually four or five) drive from work site to work site. Mobile crews typically provide employment in the areas of landscaping/groundskeeping and janitorial/custodial services.

Small Business Models

Also known as the entrepreneurial approach or benchwork model, the small business model provides supported employment services by manufacturing and/or selling specific products or services (e.g., a bakery). This model allows for up to eight persons with severe disabilities to be in

one location, with all other employees being staff or co-workers without disabilities.

Alternative Models of Job Support

Although the four supported employment models described above are the most widely known, Nisbet and Hagner (1988) have suggested a number of alternative support strategies that involve active participation on the part of company supervisors and co-workers. These include the mentor model, training consultant option, job sharing option, and attendant option. Table 7.6 provides a

TABLE 7.6   Summary of Supported Employment Models

OPTION	Support Person/Role		RESPONSIBLE TO	AGENCY ROLE
	INITIAL	ONGOING		
Individual jobs, enclave, work crew, small business	Job coach trains.	Coach fades; worker is presumed independent.	Agency	Direct: Training and follow-up
Mentor	Job coach trains; supervision is transferred to mentor.	Mentor remains on site, providing support and supervision.	Company	Indirect: Matching and support for mentor
Training consultant	Job coach trains with the co-workers and/or supervisor.	Co-workers and/or supervisor provides support, supervision, and additional training.	Company	Indirect: Consultation and stipend
Job sharing	Job coach identifies job sharer, then trains and assists.	Job sharer remains on site.	Agency and company	Indirect: Matching support for job sharer; stipend
Attendant	Attendant trains and assists (may need some assistance from job coach).	Attendant remains on site at worker's discretion.	Worker	Possibly initial training; afterward little or no intervention

Adapted from Nisbet, J., & Hagner, D. (1988). Natural supports in the workplace: A reexamination of supported employment. *The Journal of The Association for Persons with Severe Handicaps, 13,* 265.

summary of the various supported employment service delivery options.

In conclusion, it is clear that the supported employment definition does allow flexibility in terms of how services are provided. As we learn more about taking advantage of natural supports in the workplace, it is probable that new and better models will emerge.

SUPPORTED EMPLOYMENT SERVICES INDICATORS

Probably the single most distinguishing characteristic of the supported employment movement has been its focus on producing measurable outcomes. Much of the data evaluating the impact of supported employment on workers have been collected by Paul Wehman and his colleagues at the Rehabilitation Research and Training Center at Virginia Commonwealth University (Hill & Wehman, 1983; Hill, Wehman, Kregel, Banks, & Metzler, 1987; Wehman et al., 1982; Wehman, Hill, & Koehler, 1979a, 1979b; Wehman, Hill, Wood, & Parent, 1987; Wehman, Kregel, & Shafer, 1989). Their research has demonstrated positive outcomes in terms of numbers of individuals placed, job retention, absentee rates, increased wages, and taxes paid. In this section, we present some of the most recent findings from a study of the 27 states that received systems change model demonstration funds from the Rehabilitation Services Administration in 1986 and 1987 (Wehman et al., 1989). These grants were given to states for the purpose of modifying or changing existing adult day services for persons with severe disabilities and providing supported employment.

Who Is Being Served?

In the 27 states reviewed, the number of individuals engaged in supported employment has risen from 9633 in fiscal year (FY) 1986 to 24,187 in FY 1988. By far the largest percentage of these consumers are persons labeled mentally retarded (71.6 percent), and persons labeled long-term

mentally ill constitute the second largest group (14.6 percent). Within the nearly 72 percent of persons with mental retardation who are receiving supported employment services, 57.7 percent are labeled borderline or mildly retarded, 31.3 percent moderately mentally retarded, and 11 percent severely and profoundly mentally retarded.

How Are Consumers Served?

Data indicate that in FY 1988 approximately 65 percent of all consumers were served in the individual placement model. The second most prevalent model was the enclave or work station (20 percent). Finally, about 10 percent of consumers were served with a work crew or small business model.

How Much Do Consumers Earn?

Data indicate that in the 15 states that kept data on earnings in FY 1988, supported employees earned more than $12 million. In terms of individual wages, data indicate that consumers who were placed in individual jobs received $3.93 per hour, which compared favorably with earnings of individuals in mobile crews ($2.29 per hour) and enclaves ($2.08 per hour). In terms of hours worked per week, two out of five individuals worked 20 to 30 hours per week, and about one out of four worked 30 to 40 hours per week or less than 20 hours per week. Finally, one out of three consumers was employed in the custodial field, and one out of five was employed in food services.

Summary of Outcome Findings

Although Wehman et al. reviewed the supported employment outcomes of only 27 states, it is clear that supported employment is producing positive outcomes by putting people to work in integrated settings for real wages. However, the data also indicate that more effort is needed to ensure that supported employment services are made available for all individuals with severe disabilities.

Other Success Indicators

Although outcome data are important, they are not the only indicators of the success of supported employment. Data exist that indicate that supported employment programs are more productive in terms of consumers' earnings, as well as being less costly than typical adult day programs, work activity centers, or sheltered workshops (Noble & Conley, 1987; Wehman et al., 1989).

In addition to being more cost-effective, it is often felt that supported employment has a number of social benefits, such as increased social integration and societal acceptance. For example, the social interactions of supported employees are typically similar to those of co-workers without disabilities (Chadsey-Rusch & Gonzalez, 1987; Farebrother, Test, & Spooner, 1988). In terms of social acceptance, Shafer, Rice, Metzler, and Haring (1989) found that co-workers of supported employees were more comfortable and accepting of working with persons labeled as mentally retarded than were individuals who were not co-workers. In addition, co-workers also felt that persons with mental retardation were more socially and vocationally competent than did non-co-workers.

SUMMARY AND CONCLUSIONS

Appropriate transition services for students with severe disabilities represent a compelling need. Without extensive instruction in integrated community work environments and detailed, coordinated planning, the individuals who achieve successful work outcomes will remain few in number.

Typically, transition programs have been delivered by teachers or job coaches, who have relied upon prompt hierarchies to produce desired outcomes. A limitation of this instructional approach is that it may promote student dependence on the trainer. Consequently, a consumer-directed transition program has been suggested in which students are responsible for monitoring their own performance, evaluate the quality of their work, and make whatever adjustments are necessary. There is no question that transition and supported employment programs have helped persons with severe disabilities to earn higher wages than previously received in sheltered programs, and have provided them with increased opportunities to interact with persons without disabilities. However, efforts to enhance independence have essentially remained unrealized.

Regardless of the type of placement or the severity of the disability of the consumer, maximal efforts must be made so that consumers can have greater control over their own lives—at work and in the community. A frequently cited reason for the job termination of persons with severe disabilities is their dependence on trainers and difficulty in adjusting to changes that occur in their work settings. Persons involved in supported employment programs need all possible support to help them achieve desired outcomes. Likewise, they need all possible independence training to be independent of trainer manipulation. At best, this is a delicate balance, but one that we can ill afford to ignore.

REFERENCES

Agran, M., Fodor-Davis, J., & Moore, S. (1986). The effects of self-instructional training on job-task sequencing: Suggesting a problem-solving strategy. *Education and Training of the Mentally Retarded, 21,* 273–281.

Agran, M., Fodor-Davis, J., Moore, S., & Deer, M. (1989). The application of a self-management program on instruction-following skills. *The Journal of The Association for Persons with Severe Handicaps, 14,* 147–154.

Agran, M., Fodor-Davis, J., Moore, S., & Martella, R. (1992). Effects of peer-delivered self-instructional training on a lunch-making work task for students with severe handicaps. *Education and Training in Mental Retardation, 27,* 230–240.

Agran, M., & Martin, J. E. (1987). Applying a technology of self-control in community environments for individuals who are mentally retarded. In M. Hersen, R. M. Eisler, & P. M. Miller (Eds.), *Progress in behavior modification* (pp. 108–149). Beverly Hills, CA: Sage.

Agran, M., & Moore, S. (1987). Transitional programming: Suggesting an adaptability model. In S. E. Breuning, J. L. Matson, & R. P. Barrett (Eds.), *Advances in mental retardation and developmental disabilities* (pp. 170–208). Greenwich, CT: JAI Press.

Agran, M., & Morgan, R. (1991). Current transition assessment practices. *Research in Developmental Disabilities, 12,* 113–126.

Bellamy, G. T., Horner, R. H., & Inman, D. P. (1979). *Vocational habilitation of severely retarded adults: A direct service technology.* Baltimore: University Park Press.

Bellamy, G. T., Rhodes, L. E., Mank, D. M., & Albin, J. M. (1988). *Supported employment: A community implementation guide.* Baltimore: Paul H. Brookes Publishing Co.

Berkell, D. E., & Brown, J. M. (1989). *Transition from school to work for persons with disabilities.* White Plains, NY: Longman.

Brown, L. (1986). Teaching severely handicapped students to perform meaningful work in nonsheltered vocational environments. In R. J. M. Blatt (Ed.), *Special education research and trends* (pp. 131–189). New York: Pergamon Press.

Chadsey-Rusch, J., & Gonzalez, P. (1987). *Social ecology of the workplace: Employer's perception versus direct observation.* Champaign, IL: University of Illinois, Secondary Transition Intervention Effectiveness Institute.

Crosson, J. (1969). A technique for programming sheltered workshop environments for training severely retarded workers. *American Journal of Mental Deficiency, 73,* 814–818.

Farebrother, C., Test, D. W., & Spooner, F. (1988). A comparison of the social interactions of workers with and without disabilities. *Journal of Employment Counseling, 25,* 122–131.

Federal Register (1984). *Developmental Disabilities Act of 1984.* Report 98-1074, Section 102(11)(F). Washington, DC: U.S. Government Printing Office.

Gifford, J. L., Rusch, F. R., Martin, D. E., & White, D. M. (1984). Autonomy and adaptability in work behavior of retarded clients. In N. W. Ellis & N. R. Bray (Eds.), *International review of research on mental retardation,* vol. 12 (pp. 285–318). New York: Academic Press.

Gold, M. W. (1972). Stimulus factors in skill training of retarded adolescents on a complex assembly task: Acquisition, transfer, and retention. *American Journal of Mental Deficiency, 76,* 517–526.

Guess, D., Benson, H. A., & Siegel-Causey, E. (1985). Concepts and issues related to choice-making and autonomy among persons with severe disabilities. *The Journal of The Association for Persons with Severe Handicaps, 10,* 79–86.

Guess, D., & Siegel-Causey, E. (1985). Behavioral control and education of severely handicapped students: Who's doing what to whom? And why? In J. Filler & D. Bricker (Eds.), *Severe mental retardation: From theory to practice* (pp. 230–244). Reston, VA: The Council for Exceptional Children.

Halpern, A. S. (1985). Transition: A look at the foundations. *Exceptional Children, 51,* 479–486.

Hasazi, S., Gordon, L., & Roe, C. (1985). Factors associated with the employment status of handicapped youth exiting high school from 1979 to 1983. *Exceptional Children, 51,* 455–469.

Hill, M., & Wehman, P. (1983). Cost benefit analysis of placing moderately and severely handicapped individuals into competitive employment. *The Journal of the Association for the Severely Handicapped, 8*(1), 30–38.

Hill, M., Wehman, P., Kregel, J., Banks, P., & Metzler, H. (1987). Employment outcomes for people with moderate and severe disabilities: An eight-year longitudinal analysis of supported competitive employment. *The Journal of The Association for Persons with Severe Handicaps, 12,* 182–189.

Hughes, C., Rusch, F. R., & Curl, R. (1990). Extending individual competence, developing natural support, and promoting social acceptance. In F. R. Rusch (Ed.), *Supported employment: Model, methods, and issues* (pp. 181–197). Sycamore, IL: Sycamore.

Martin, J. E., Mithaug, D. E., Agran, M., & Husch, J. V. (1990). Consumer-centered transition and supported employment. In J. L. Matson (Ed.), *Handbook of behavior modification with the mentally retarded* (2nd ed., pp. 357–389). New York: Plenum Press.

Martin, J. E., Mithaug, D. E., & Husch, J. V. (1988). *How to teach adaptability in community training and supported employment.* Colorado Springs, CO: Ascent Publications.

McLoughlin, C. S., Garner, J. B., & Callahan, M.

(1987). *Getting employed, staying employed.* Baltimore: Paul H. Brookes Publishing Co.

Menchetti, B. M., & Flynn, C. C. (1990). In F. R. Rusch (Ed.), *Supported employment: Models, methods, and issues* (pp. 111–130). Sycamore, IL: Sycamore.

Mithaug, D. E., Horiuchi, C. N., & McNulty, B. A. (1987). *Parent reports on the transitions of students graduating from Colorado special education programs in 1978 and 1979.* Denver: Colorado Department of Education, Special Education Programs.

Mithaug, D. E., Martin, J. E., & Agran, M. (1987). Adaptability instruction: The goal of transitional programming. *Exceptional Children, 53*(6), 500–505.

Mithaug, D. E., Martin, J. E., Agran, M., & Rusch, F. R. (1988). *Why special education graduates fail: How to teach them to succeed.* Colorado Springs, CO: Ascent Publications.

Mithaug, D. E., Martin, J. E., & Burger, D. L. (1987). *VITAL checklist and curriculum guide.* Colorado Springs, CO: Ascent Publications.

Mithaug, D. E., Martin, J. E., Husch, J. V., Agran, M., & Rusch, F. R. (1988). *When will persons in supported employment need less support?* Colorado Springs, CO: Ascent Publications.

Moore, S. C., Agran, M., & Fodor-Davis, J. (1989). Using self-management strategies to increase the production rates of workers with severe handicaps. *Education and Training in Mental Retardation, 24,* 324–332.

Nisbet, J., & Hagner, D. (1988). Natural supports in the workplace: A reexamination of supported employment. *The Journal of The Association for Persons with Severe Handicaps, 13,* 260–267.

Noble, J. H., & Conley, R. W. (1987). Accumulating evidence on the benefits and costs of supported and transitional employment for persons with severe disabilities. *The Journal of The Association for Persons with Severe Handicaps, 12,* 163–174.

Phelps, L. A., & Frasier, J. R. (1988). In R. Gaylord-Ross (Ed.), *Vocational education for persons with handicaps* (pp. 3–29). Mountain View, CA: Mayfield.

Razeghi, J., Kokaska, C., Gruenhagen, K., & Fair, G. (1987). *The transition of youth with disabilities to adult life: A position statement.* Reston, VA: Council for Exceptional Children.

Rusch, F. R. (1986). *Competitive employment issues and strategies.* Baltimore: Paul H. Brookes Publishing Co.

Rusch, F. R., & Hughes, C. (1989). Overview of supported employment. *Journal of Applied Behavior Analysis, 22,* 315–363.

Rusch, F. R., & Mithaug, D. E. (1980). *Vocational training for mentally retarded adults: A behavioral analytic approach.* Champaign, IL: Research Press.

Rusch, F. R., Mithaug, D. E., & Flexer, R. W. (1986). Obstacles to competitive employment and traditional program options for overcoming them. In F. R. Rusch (Ed.), *Competitive employment issues and strategies* (pp. 7–21). Baltimore: Paul H. Brookes Publishing Co.

Rusch, F. R., & Menchetti, B. M. (1987). Increasing compliant work behaviors in a non-sheltered work setting. *Mental Retardation, 19*(3), 107–111.

Shafer, M. S., Rice, M. L., Metzler, H. M. D., & Haring, M. (1989). A survey of nondisabled employees' attitudes toward supported employees with mental retardation. *The Journal of The Association for Persons with Severe Handicaps, 14,* 137–146.

Wacker, D. P., & Berg, W. K. (1984). Use of a peer instruction to train a complex photocopying task to moderately and severely retarded adolescents. *Analysis and Intervention in Developmental Disabilities, 4,* 219–234.

Wacker, D., & Berg, W. (1986). Generalizing and maintaining work behavior. In F. R. Rusch (Ed.), *Competitive employment issues and strategies* (pp. 129–140). Baltimore: Paul H. Brookes Publishing Co.

Wehman, P., Hill, M., Goodall, P., Cleveland, P., Brooke, V., & Pentecost, J. H. (1982). Job placement and follow-up of moderately and severely handicapped individuals after three years. *Journal of the Association for the Severely Handicapped, 7,* 269–276.

Wehman, P., Hill, J. W., & Koehler, F. (1979a). Placement of developmentally disabled individuals into competitive employment: Three case studies. *Education and Training of the Mentally Retarded, 14,* 269–276.

Wehman, P., Hill, J. W., & Koehler, F. (1979b). Helping severely handicapped persons enter competitive employment. *AAESPH Review, 4,* 274–290.

Wehman, P., Hill, J. W., Wood, W., & Parent, W. (1987). A report on competitive employment histories of persons labeled severely retarded. *The Journal of The Association for Persons with Severe Handicaps, 12,* 11–17.

Wehman, P., Kregel, J., & Seyfarth, J. (1985). Outlook

for young adults with mental retardation. *Rehabilitation Counseling Bulletin, 25*(2), 90–99.

Wehman, P., Kregel, J., & Shafer, M. S. (1989). *Emerging trends in the national supported employment initiative: A preliminary analysis of 27 states.* Richmond: Virginia Commonwealth University, Rehabilitation Research and Training Center on Supported Employment.

Will, M. (1984). *OSERS programming for the transition of youth with disabilities: Bridges from school to working life.* Washington, DC: Office of Special Education and Rehabilitative Services.

Winking, D. L., Trach, J. S., Rusch, F. R., & Tines, J. (1989). Profile of Illinois supported employment specialists: An analysis of educations, background, experience, and related employment variables. *The Journal of The Association for Persons with Severe Handicaps, 14,* 278–282.

CHAPTER 8

LEISURE AND RECREATION PROGRAMMING TO ENHANCE QUALITY OF LIFE

LINDA A. HEYNE
STUART J. SCHLEIEN
University of Minnesota—Minneapolis

To answer the question, "How can one best meet the leisure and recreation needs of individuals with severe disabilities?", one must first seek to understand the role of leisure and recreation in the lives of individuals who are not disabled. Recognition of the commonalities between individuals who do and do not have disabilities sets the stage for personalized leisure and recreation programming that provides meaningful and diverse experiences to enhance the quality of the lives of individuals with disabilities.

Leisure may be defined as an individual's personal "free time." Leisure implies both a freedom *from* work or school obligations and a freedom *to* choose among a wide range of recreational options. Leisure may be viewed from a *quantitative* perspective—the amount of free time available—and, more important, from a *qualitative* perspective—the evaluative, emotive content of leisure and recreation behavior (Goodale & Witt, 1985; Wuerch & Voeltz, 1982).

For the population at large, many benefits— social, emotional, intellectual, and physical—are derived from participation in recreational activities. Active engagement in leisure and recreation activities renews, refreshes, and provides us with opportunities for relaxation, spontaneity, and playfulness. Through recreation, we enjoy the company of others, learn the give and take of social relationships, and build friendships and a sense of community. By developing our leisure repertoires, we learn new skills, strengthen our physical and mental well-being, and build our self-esteem.

For persons with severe disabilities, participation in recreational activities offers these same vital benefits. However, unlike the general population, which typically learns recreation skills through trial and error and by observing others, persons with severe disabilities require systematic instruction in order to develop leisure repertoires (Schleien & Ray, 1988; Wehman & Schleien, 1981). Individual needs, abilities, and preferences must be assessed, environments must be analyzed, adapted, and engineered to promote inclusive recreational participation, instruction must be pro-

The development and dissemination of this report was partially supported by Rehabilitative Services and Cooperative Agreement No. H133B80048 funded by the National Institute on Disability and Rehabilitation Research and Grant Project No. H029F90067 funded by the Office of Special Education and Rehabilitative Services, both of the U.S. Department of Education. The opinions expressed herein do not necessarily reflect the opinion of the U.S. Department of Education, and no official endorsement should be inferred.

vided via state-of-the-art behavioral methodologies, and ongoing evaluation must be provided (Peterson & Gunn, 1984; Schleien & Ray, 1988).

Without a leisure repertoire, most individuals with disabilities experience feelings of isolation and social withdrawal (Schleien & Meyer, 1988; Wuerch & Voeltz, 1982). In many cases, the absence of meaningful leisure life-styles means the development and perpetuation of maladaptive or aggressive behaviors (Gaylord-Ross, 1980; Kissel & Whitman, 1977). Through the development of leisure competencies, however, people with disabilities can build friendships, learn greater self-sufficiency, develop physical fitness, and become active participants in their communities (Heyne, 1987; Schleien & Ray, 1988).

Consider, for example, Susan, a 14-year-old girl with a severe intellectual disability and cerebral palsy. She lives in a care facility with other youngsters with multiple disabilities, has little contact with nondisabled peers, and is highly dependent on adult supervision and assistance for nearly all activities of daily living. Without instruction in recreational activities, Susan's life could become increasingly insular and disparate from the lives of nondisabled teens her age. To help promote Susan's self-sufficiency, develop her leisure repertoire, and widen her social circle, Susan's recreational program would include the provision of opportunities and instruction in how to participate in preferred recreational activities with nondisabled peers at home, school, and in the commmunity. Through systematic instruction in leisure skills, individuals with disabilities like Susan can avoid the isolation and exclusion that has typically characterized the lives of persons with disabilities, and can lead meaningful and fulfilling lives.

Purpose of Therapeutic Recreation

People with disabilities characteristically have an abundance of unstructured free time (Schleien & Wehman, 1986; Voeltz, Wuerch, & Wilcox, 1982). Activities in which they typically engage are either sedentary activities, such as watching television or listening to music (Powers & Ball, 1983), or stereotypic activities, such as bowling, swimming, arts and crafts, or field trips (Schleien & Werder, 1985). Many people with disabilities lack the means, skills, and opportunities to participate in a greater variety of more active leisure pursuits.

To address these and the aforementioned problems of social isolation and the potential for maladaptive behaviors, certified therapeutic recreation specialists seek to teach persons with disabilities appropriate, functional, and normalizing leisure skills that will expand their leisure repertoires, friendships, and level of independence. Therapeutic recreation specialists consider individual needs and preferences while implementing systematic instruction that promotes acquisition, maintenance, and generalization of lifelong leisure skills. Principal goals of therapeutic recreation specialists, outlined in Table 8.1, are as follows:

Increase Range of Lifelong Leisure Skills. The ability to choose from a variety of leisure pursuits can enhance the quality and fullness of a person's life. Expanding one's leisure repertoire to include activities in which one may engage throughout a lifetime can reinforce skill development, participation, and enjoyment over extended periods of time.

Increase Socialization and Cooperation Skills. Opportunities to participate in community and mainstream recreation programs can enhance a

---

TABLE 8.1 Principal Goals of Therapeutic Recreation

- Increase lifelong leisure skills.
- Increase socialization and cooperation.
- Increase self-concept and self-esteem.
- Increase independence and interdependence.
- Increase opportunities to perform acquired recreation skills.
- Increase collateral or support skills.

person's ability to learn appropriate social behaviors and make friends. Cooperatively structured, integrated experiences can help people with and without disabilities to learn about, accept, and interact with each other.

Increase Self-Concept and Self-Esteem. Through repeated failures or lack of choice, many people with disabilities experience low self-esteem. Therapeutic recreation specialists seek to teach leisure skills in such a way that the participant experiences success often. Successful participation in meaningful leisure activities can enhance a person's self-image and build self-confidence.

Increase Independent and Interdependent Leisure Behavior. The concepts of *independence* and *interdependence* are equally normalizing principles. Adaptations of equipment, environments, or rules can contribute to a person's access to self-directed leisure behavior. Learning to select and self-initiate appropriate activities can also promote independent functioning. Partial participation, in which assistance in performing targeted skills is provided by another person, promotes interdependency.

Increase Opportunities to Perform Acquired Skills. It is not sufficient for people with disabilities to learn new skills; they must be given opportunities to practice skills frequently. Horner, Williams, and Knobbe (1985) found that individuals with severe disabilities needed at least two opportunities per month to maintain performance of newly acquired skills. Increased opportunities to practice new skills in different settings can also enhance generalization to nontrained environments and help individuals adjust to involvement in the community (Goetz, 1987; Voeltz, Wuerch, & Wilcox, 1982).

Increase Collateral or Support Skills. Few leisure skills are performed in isolation without support from leisure-related collateral skills. Collateral skills include self-care, communication, motor and physical fitness, money management, and cognition and attention span competencies. The development of collateral skills is essential for maintaining almost any leisure skill.

Historical Perspective

A historical view of recreational programming for persons with disabilities reveals a gradual shift from segregated, specialized services to the provision of integrated options that include individuals with disabilities in mainstream recreational activities and environments.

Prior to the 1900s, little interest was shown in the role of recreation in the lives of individuals with disabilities. In 1906, the Playground Association of America (later renamed the Playground and Recreation Association, and still later known as the National Recreation Association) was formed. This service organization declared that their programs were open to all people, including those individuals who had previously experienced discrimination because they had a physical disability. For more than half a century, local recreation and park associations promoted the cause of community recreation.

In the 1920s and 1930s, public schools began to offer after-school programs exclusively for students with disabilities. During World War II, the National American Red Cross was active in providing recreational opportunities for military personnel. In the late 1940s, recreation programs began to appear in public hospitals. The Veterans Administration, which provided therapeutic recreation services to patients with emotional disorders in hospitals and state institutions, was a pioneer in this effort.

The use of outdoor and wilderness areas as therapeutic environments also first became popular in the 1940s. Outdoor therapeutic programs, which continue to operate actively across the country, include such activities as backpacking, mountaineering, rock climbing, canoeing, camping, and cross-country skiing. The interest in outdoor therapeutic programs also gave rise to summer camping programs for children, adolescents, and adults with disabilities. In the camping programs of the 1940s, efforts were made to assess the needs of individual campers, and new ways of meeting those needs were explored.

Beginning in the 1950s centers were developed in some cities, which provided "special" recreational services for people with disabilities. In particular, the National Association for Retarded Children (NARC) took the initiative to provide recreational services for individuals with intellectual disabilities.

Special, segregated recreational programs for persons with disabilities continued to flourish as the primary service delivery model in the 1960s and 1970s. After-school programs were designed especially for children with developmental disabilities. In 1968, Special Olympics began. During this period there emerged numerous state and national organizations that attempted to respond to the recreational needs of people with disabilities. These organizations included the American Foundation for the Blind, the Association for Retarded Citizens of the United States (ARC-US), Goodwill Industries, The Joseph P. Kennedy, Jr., Foundation, the Muscular Dystrophy Association, the National Easter Seal Society for Crippled Children and Adults, the National Multiple Sclerosis Society, the New York Service for Orthopedically Handicapped Persons, and the United Cerebral Palsy Associations, Inc.

Owing to several factors, however, in therapeutic recreation preference has shifted from providing specialized services to including persons with disabilities in regular recreational programs. This shift in philosophy has resulted from a series of national trends propelled by the advent of the concept of *normalization* or *social role valorization* (Wolfensberger, 1972, 1983) and the movement toward deinstitutionalization. Normalization was introduced by Wolfensberger in 1972 and defined as:

the utilization of means which are as culturally normative as possible, in order to establish or

maintain personal behaviors or characteristics which are as culturally normative as possible. (Wolfensberger, 1972, p. 28)

As applied to recreation, normalization implies both a *goal* and a *process* (Reynolds, 1981). As a normalization *goal,* recreational programming offers people with disabilities opportunities for physical access to settings with nondisabled peers as a means to learning social, as well as leisure and recreation, skills. As a normalization *process,* integrated programming promotes the total leisure life-styles of people with developmental disabilities. That is, recreation providers look beyond individual techniques and programs to the broader scope of leisure delivery systems and how they influence the inclusion of people with disabilities in regular recreational settings.

Since the principle of normalization was first coined, it has evolved into a new concept, *social role valorization.* In Wolfensberger's words:

the most explicit and highest goal of normalization must be the creation, support, and defense of valued social roles for people who are at risk of social devaluation. (Wolfensberger, 1983, p. 234)

The concept of social role valorization acknowledges the necessity to bring to the lives of typically devalued people socially valued roles and life conditions. This can be accomplished in two ways: (1) by developing the competencies of the culturally devalued individual and (2) by enhancing the individual's social image or value as perceived by others in the society.

As the concept of normalized and socially valued leisure and recreation services gained momentum throughout the 1970s and 1980s, community-based inclusive leisure programming began to emerge. This period also saw the beginning of empirical research to develop instructional strategies for people with developmental disabilities in integrated leisure settings. With the development of new instructional technologies, research began to demonstrate that persons with severe disabilities could acquire leisure skills in integrated environments. Moreover, research documented that leisure skill instruction in integrated settings could promote social interactions between participants with and without disabilities, and the development of positive attitudes toward persons with disabilities by nondisabled participants (Kennedy, Austin, & Smith, 1987; Schleien & Ray, 1988).

Impact of Federal Legislation on Recreational Programming. The philosophical shift from segregated to inclusive recreational programs has been fueled primarily by landmark federal legislation regarding services for persons with disabilities. Acts of pertinent legislation are listed in Table 8.2, and a thumbnail sketch of each and how it has influenced recreational services follows:

The *Architectural Barriers Act* of 1968 (P.L. 90-480) required that all buildings and facilities designed, constructed, altered, or leased with federal funds be made accessible and usable by individuals with physical disabilities. This legislation included recreational facilities built with federal contributions.

The *Rehabilitation Act* of 1973 (P.L. 93-112) was the first law to address rehabilitative services for persons with severe disabilities, authorizing more than one billion dollars for training and placing people with intellectual and physical disabilities in employment. *Section 504* of this act, entitled "Nondiscrimination Under Federal Grants" or the "Civil Rights Act for Persons with Handicaps," prohibited discrimination solely on the basis of disability. This act has served as the legal basis for many civil rights lawsuits involving discrimination against people with disabilities.

In 1975, the *Education for All Handicapped Children Act* (P.L. 94-142) mandated "free and appropriate public education and related services" for all children with disabilities in the "least restrictive environment." Individualized Education Plans (IEPs) were required by local school dis-

TABLE 8.2   Federal Legislation and Its Impact on Recreational Services

1968	The Architectural Barriers Act (P.L. 90-480)	Required recreation facilities to be made accessible.
1973	The Rehabilitation Act (P.L. 93-112)	Prohibited discrimination in recreation programs on the basis of disability.
1975	The Education for All Handicapped Children Act (P.L. 94-142)	Identified recreation as a "related service" in public education.
1986	Education of the Handicapped Act Amendments (P.L. 99-457)	Mandated early intervention programs, including recreational services.
1990	Americans with Disabilities Act (P.L. 101-336)	Expanded civil rights in the areas of employment, public accommodations, public services, transportation, and telecommunications.

tricts based on the unique needs of each child. Under this law, recreation was identified as a "related service." This implied that any parent who chose to have a child receive instruction in recreational activities could insist that recreation goals be included in his or her IEP.

In 1986, the *Education of the Handicapped Act Amendments* (P.L. 99-457) strengthened the Education for All Handicapped Children Act by mandating preschool programs for 3- to 5-year-olds with disabilities. Early intervention program plans for infants and toddlers (i.e., 0 to 2 years) with disabilities and their families were also required.

In 1990, the *Americans with Disabilities Act* (P.L. 101-336) comprehensively eliminated discrimination against persons with disabilities in the areas of employment, transportation, public accommodations, public services, and telecommunications. Potential employers could no longer discriminate against qualified individuals with disabilities, and reasonable accommodations for a disability had to be provided at work sites. All new public transportation and demand-response service vehicles were required to be made accessible. All areas of public accommodation, including recreational areas, were to be made accessible, and nondiscriminatory practices were to be implemented. In addition, telephone companies were to provide relay services to individuals with hearing and speech impairments.

Because of these landmark federal policy changes and their subsequent impact on services for people with disabilities, therapeutic recreation specialists and "generic" recreation providers (those professionals who have not received traditional training in services for people with disabilities) have actively sought ways to provide equal access for persons with disabilities in mainstream recreational environments. Although many totally segregated programs continue to be offered today, the trend is toward new, inclusive alternatives that provide options for those individuals with disabilities who want to take part in normalized, mainstream leisure life-styles.

Looking ahead to the end of the century, it is anticipated that practitioners and researchers will continue to examine, even more closely, effective means to promote inclusive programming in leisure and recreation environments. Topics of particular interest might include the development of friendship between people who do and do not have disabilities, the impact of integration on neighborhoods and communities, overcoming architectural and attitudinal barriers to integration, and how systems must change to provide more inclusive services.

Chapter Overview

The rest of this chapter sets forth guidelines for assessing individual needs and preferences, and strategies for including persons with disabilities in natural community leisure environments. Obstacles that typically inhibit integrated leisure participation and solutions for overcoming those obstacles are presented. "Best professional practices" in providing recreational programming for people with disabilities in the community are defined, and four curriculum models that employ exemplary practices are described. Finally, a model integration program and its impact on the community are presented as an illustrative example of integration in motion.

Underlying the instructional strategies presented herein is a values base that supports the inalienable right of people with severe disabilities to enjoy a full range of leisure options and to participate in school and community leisure environments alongside their nondisabled peers. In addition, the authors believe that by including people with disabilities in regular recreational programs, the entire community benefits. Through exposure to and interaction with people with disabilities, individuals without disabilities gain knowledge about disabilities, become more sensitive to individual differences, develop more accepting attitudes toward people with disabilities, and broaden their own opportunities for friendship.

SELECTING, ASSESSING, AND TEACHING RELEVANT LEISURE AND RECREATION SKILLS

Individualized Assessment

To develop programs to meet lifelong leisure needs, individualized assessments of peoples' needs and abilities are essential. Assessments should highlight abilities, potentialities, personal preferences, and accessibility issues, rather than focus on skill deficits and functional limitations.

In conducting assessments, it is necessary to respect a family's right to privacy. Families with children with disabilities typically are bombarded with questions of a personal nature regarding their children and life-styles. Although it is essential to understand how to address competently a child's specific medical emergency or physical limitation (e.g., seizures, special physical handling, safety concerns), any information requested should pertain solely to programming. That is, in most cases, it would be inappropriate to inquire into family issues such as life-style, marital relations, substance abuse, values, or religious beliefs. Although family situations definitely have an impact on a child's well-being, trust and mutual inclination would have to be established before such issues could be discussed. Moreover, in the assessment process, it is extremely important to reassure families that any information they disclose will be held confidential. In all respects, confidentiality must be honored.

To understand the total leisure and recreational needs of an individual, it is useful to gather information from a variety of sources. Family members, care providers, peers, teachers, related service personnel, and other support staff can contribute a wealth of pertinent information about the individual's needs and abilities. Important information to gather would include: (1) leisure preferences, (2) current leisure competencies, (3) social and communication needs regarding peer relationships, methods of communication, types of effective reinforcers, means of selecting activities, and behavioral concerns, (4) physical and medical needs, as they pertain to physical handling, physical fitness, seizure disorders, sensory disorders, or any physical or motor limitations, (5) preferred leisure activities of the family, and (6) personal resources, such as any activities or materials that might be available to the individual on a regular basis, or community agencies and activities that are frequently used by the family. Recommended needs assessment inventories include the "Client Home Environment Checklist" (Wehman & Schleien, 1981), the "Home Leisure Activities Survey" (Wuerch & Voeltz, 1982), and the "Student Interest Survey" (Wuerch & Voeltz, 1982).

Preferences and Choice Making. Inherent in the definition of leisure is the freedom to choose to participate in preferred recreational activities. Dattilo and Barnett (1985) suggest that the omission of choice in the participation process actually prevents individuals from genuine leisure experiences. Too often, recreational activities are selected on behalf of persons with severe disabilities. Common practice is to identify the chronological age, physical characteristics, and current functioning level of the individual and subsequently select an activity for instruction based on this information only (Wehman & Schleien, 1981; Wuerch & Voeltz, 1982).

As previously noted, people with disabilities are often relegated to participation in only stereotypic activities (e.g., bowling, swimming, arts and crafts). Research in preferences and choice making, however, supports the view that stereotypic leisure activities are not necessarily those most preferred by persons with severe disabilities. These activities may have been selected for instruction because they were convenient for staff or because the system had always offered such a program. In fact, Matthews (1980) has found many similarities in recreational preferences of children with and without mental retardation, suggesting that chronologically age-appropriate, integrated activities are possible. Others have discovered that persons with developmental disabilities have interests in the same general outdoor activities as nondisabled persons. West (1981) found hiking, camping, and other outdoor educational pursuits to be preferred over typical indoor offerings. Indeed, many activities that have typically been associated with persons with severe multiple disabilities have been stereotyped, inaccurate ideas of what these individuals are capable of doing and enjoying.

Neglecting to include persons with severe disabilities in their own leisure choice making is probably not so much intentional as it is indicative of the real difficulties in determining the preferences of persons with significant functional limitations. For instance, individuals with severe disabilities generally have limited communication skills. Many are unable or have not yet learned to speak. Determining the leisure preferences of these individuals tends to become much more subjective and suspect than when one is able to ask persons who are verbal to indicate their choices. In addition, individuals with severe multiple disabilities often demonstrate very few functional preferences (Dattilo & Mirenda, 1987). Selecting leisure skills for instruction based on their current repertoires could result in the strengthening of nonfunctional behavior, such as increased rates of stereotypic behavior or participation in age-inappropriate activities. Another difficulty in assessing preferences results from the fact that people with severe disabilities generally have not been exposed to a wide range of leisure options from which to choose. Lack of exposure begets lack of participation and self-initiation or participation only in stereotypic activities.

To overcome these problems and assess true leisure preferences, the use of direct behavioral observation techniques can be extremely helpful. That is, one may present an individual with opportunities to participate in a variety of recreational activities, such as toys, games, hobbies, and sports (Wehman & Schleien, 1981). The observer may note any appropriate or inappropriate interactions with the materials during a preference assessment and record the participant's responses. Quality indicators to observe and evaluate may include the following:

1. Affect of the participant (e.g., evidence of smiling, concentration, interest, displeasure, etc.)
2. Attraction of participant to particular objects over others (i.e., as evidenced by approaching, reaching for, touching, or manipulating an object)
3. Duration of eye contact (i.e., visual acuity) with play materials
4. Duration of active engagement in activity or manipulation of materials

Those activities in which the participant expresses or demonstrates most interest and engages in longest can be prospective activities to target for instruction.

Needs Assessment Based on Environmental Analysis Inventory.   At times it may be desirable to assess an individual's level of proficiency in a particular activity. An *Environmental Analysis Inventory,* or *ecological assessment* (Belmore & Brown, 1976; Certo, Schleien, & Hunter, 1983; Schleien & Ray, 1988; Voeltz & Wuerch, 1981) can be conducted to determine the specific components of the activity that the individual has already mastered and those that require additional training. Certo, Schleien, and Hunter (1983) defined this inventory as "a systematic method of conducting an observation of an event as it occurs in a natural setting under typical conditions" (p. 33).

Through the environmental analysis inventory, component tasks of an activity are identified and instructional sequences developed. An individual is then given opportunities to perform the component tasks in order to determine current levels of proficiency and highlight further instructional needs. This inventory is also instrumental in identifying appropriate teaching strategies, as well as modifications to enhance participation. (A fuller description of the uses of the Environmental Analysis Inventory as a tool for instruction may be found later in this chapter in "Leisure and Recreation Instructional Strategies.")

Skill and Activity Selection

Following an initial needs assessment, skills and activities must be identified for instruction as part of a comprehensive leisure and recreation program. Key considerations in selecting skills and activities for instruction include functionality and chronological age-appropriateness.

Functional skills are those that are frequently used throughout an individual's daily routine as they naturally occur in home, school, work, or community environments. A nonfunctional skill is one that has a "low probability of being required by daily activities" (Brown et al., 1979).

Functional skills help an individual perform as independently as possible in normalized settings. When developing a leisure skills curriculum for an individual, one may assess the validity of the activities by their adherence to the principle of functionality. For example, a nonfunctional approach to curriculum design and skill selection would be the development of an elementary-age student's palmar grasp and voluntary release skills by teaching the child to push a medicine ball, an activity not commonly performed by nondisabled youngsters. A functional alternative would be to teach the student to grasp and release the edge of an inflated parachute within the context of a cooperative game, a popular skill frequently performed by same-age peers. Another example of a nonfunctional activity, which is often incorporated into recreational curricula, is placing pegs into a pegboard to increase a child's pincer grasp and release skills. A functional option would be to teach the child to play with a Lite-Brite (Hasbro) game. Both activities have identical topography, but Lite-Brite offers additional sensory stimulation and reinforcement (through the illumination of pegs), and is an age-appropriate activity for school-age children that can also be practiced and enjoyed at home.

Functionality by itself, however, is an insufficient criterion for curriculum development. Activities must also be *chronologically age-appropriate* (Brown et al., 1979). The age-appropriateness of a leisure activity may be determined by asking whether a nondisabled individual of the same chronological age would typically engage in the activity during his or her free time (Wehman & Schleien, 1980).

Chronological age-appropriateness is of particular concern when developing curricula for secondary-age students and young adults. In state institutions, group homes, and other living environments, unfortunately, one may still find adults with severe disabilities inappropriately playing with dolls, busy boxes, and preschool puzzles. To solve the problem of identifying age-appropriate activities for the older student, a teacher may select preferred activities and target them for instruction by breaking down component skills into small, teachable behaviors. Recreational activities that a person may enjoy throughout a lifetime (e.g., plant care, playing a musical instrument, walking, jogging, biking, cooking, woodworking, painting, dancing, photography, working out at a YM or YWCA or neighborhood community center, etc.) are optimal activities to choose for leisure instruction for the secondary-age student or young adult in preparation for adult life experiences.

As a guide to selecting activities for leisure skill instruction, Voeltz and Wuerch (1981) have developed the Leisure Activity Selection Checklist. Three elements make up this checklist: normalization, individualization, and environmental aspects. *Normalization* addresses concerns for socially appropriate and socially valid activities. Questions in this area focus on whether nondisabled peers would be interested in and engage in the activity, how many people could use the activity, and whether the activity is potentially lifelong in nature. *Individualization* addresses the adaptability of the activity in relation to a participant's unique needs and preferences. *Environmental aspects* of recreational materials refer to such factors as availability, durability, safety, noxiousness (i.e., noisy, space consuming, distracting), and expense.

In addition, Wehman and Schleien (1980) suggested a systematic review of criteria for skill selection. These criteria must be carefully assessed before beginning a program. They include the participant's leisure skill preference, functioning level, and physical characteristics; age-appropriateness of the skill; access to materials; and the quality of support available in the home and leisure environment.

Collateral Skill Development. One of the most significant outcomes of leisure skill instruction for persons with severe disabilities may be its contribution to collateral skill development. As individuals practice newly acquired leisure skills in positive and naturally occurring environments, social, communication, problem-solving, motor and physical fitness, money-management, self-monitoring, and other collateral skills are repeatedly practiced and reinforced.

There are few empirical investigations that conclusively substantiate the development of skills in other curriculum areas through play. However, the results of research that has been conducted are compelling and suggest the need for further study of leisure-related collateral skill development. Vandercook (1987) reported that as persons with severe disabilities became more proficient in two recreational activities (i.e., pinball and bowling), their social repertoires became more sophisticated. A likely hypothesis for this phenomenon is that increased competency in a recreational skill allows individuals more freedom to devote their efforts to monitoring their social behavior.

Favell (1973) found a significant decrease in inappropriate behaviors following an individual's acquisition of appropriate object manipulation skills. Similarly, Alajajian (1981) discovered that as students with severe sensory impairments and cognitive deficits improved their physical fitness through a jogging program, their self-abusive and self-stimulatory behaviors were noticeably reduced.

Verhoven, Schleien, and Bender (1982) reported that successful play experiences encouraged positive perceptions of body image and self-image by children with severe disabilities. As self-image is cultivated, social and personal security can also increase.

If collateral skill competencies can be improved "incidentally" within the context of age-appropriate recreational activities, valuable intervention time can be saved. In addition, people with disabilities can receive practice in basic life skills within multiple environments where it is appropriate for them to be performed. Other collateral skills that can be acquired within the context of a leisure program include communication and language skills (Bates & Renzaglia, 1982; Rogow, 1981), social skills, such as cooperation, relationship building, taking turns, and sharing materials (Kibler, 1986; Schleien & Wehman, 1986), object manipulation and motor skills (Orelove & Sobsey, 1987; Sherrill, 1986), and those needed for activities of daily living.

Leisure and Recreation Instructional Strategies

Task/Environmental/Discrepancy Analyses. In the earlier discussion of Individualized Assessment, the Environmental Analysis Inventory is described as a method for identifying components of an activity that an individual has already mastered and those that require additional instruction. Here the Environmental Analysis Inventory is presented as it relates specifically to leisure skill instruction.

The Environmental Analysis Inventory provides a systematic, comprehensive approach to teaching leisure skills and facilitating the involvement of persons with disabilities in school and community settings (Certo et al., 1983; Schleien & Ray, 1988). This inventory enables the professional to look closely at the component skills required to perform a particular activity, from start to finish. It also allows the professional to incorporate individualized adaptations, partial participation strategies, and/or special teaching techniques into instructional procedures. There are four main advantages to using the Environmental Analysis Inventory:

1. It provides a *step-by-step, task-analyzed* instructional procedure that can be easily implemented by any number of service providers consistently.

2. It offers an *individualized approach* to leisure skill instruction.
3. It identifies basic and vital skills as *compared with the performance of nondisabled peers*.
4. It provides critical *information* to school personnel, caregivers, and community recreation professionals regarding how to plan and prepare for current and future leisure programming.

The flexibility and utility of the Environmental Analysis Inventory can be attributed to the task-analytic nature of the instrument. A *task analysis* breaks down skills into smaller components that may be more easily learned by the participant. It provides a precise, consecutive, step-by-step description of the individual behaviors that are expected in a given recreational situation.

In the sample Environmental Analysis Inventory: Activity/Discrepancy Analysis shown in Figure 8.1, steps required to participate in an exercise class at a neighborhood recreation center have been delineated. Following the development of the task analysis, a *discrepancy analysis* is conducted. That is, as noted in the directions on the form, a plus (+) is given if the participant is able to perform the step, and a minus (-) is given if the participant is not able to perform the step independently. For those steps marked with a minus (-), specific teaching procedures, adaptations or modifications, or strategies for partial participation are then suggested.

Behavioral Teaching Methods. When developing the Environmental Analysis Inventory and planning instructional procedures, useful behavioral teaching methods to consider include: (1) an instructional cue hierarchy and prompting system, (2) shaping and chaining, and (3) positive reinforcement.

A basic instructional model includes a *cue hierarchy* of *prompts* to elicit specific behaviors on the task analysis. Prompts are presented to the participant in a "hierarchy" of least-to-most intrusive instructional interventions. That is, prompts may range from verbal instruction (least intrusive), to

modeling appropriate behaviors, to physical guidance in performing the behavior (most intrusive). To encourage independent performance and avoid dependency on the instructor, prompts should be gradually faded, or withdrawn, as the student gains competency in acquiring skills. The overall goal is to allow the actual leisure environment and materials to become the natural reinforcers that elicit appropriate and independent leisure behavior.

Task-analyzed skills are usually taught through sequential procedures called shaping and chaining. *Shaping* refers to the reinforcement of small steps, or "approximations," toward a final response, rather than the response itself. That is, in developing a new leisure behavior, it may be necessary to provide reinforcement for approximations of the desired behavior. As the learner's response gains accuracy, approximations should no longer be reinforced; reinforcement should only be delivered for the correct (final) response.

For example, an individual may initially learn to purchase a snack from a vending machine by using push buttons with built-up extensions on them. Successful manipulation of the push buttons with extensions would be reinforced as approximations of the final response. As the individual's responses increase in accuracy, the size of the extensions would be reduced until the person is able to manipulate standard-size push buttons.

Chaining involves the sequencing of responses within a task; that is, the order in which steps of the task analysis are presented. Skills may be taught using a *forward* or *backward* chain. To use the vending machine of the preceding example, in a forward chain, the instructor teaches the first step of the task analysis (i.e., locate the vending machine) and then guides the individual consecutively through the subsequent steps. In a backward chain, however, instruction is initially provided for the final step of the task analysis (i.e., consume the snack item) until that step is mastered. The remaining steps of the task analysis are then taught in reverse order, one by one, always including previously instructed step in the teaching sequence. Backward chaining allows the learner to

ENVIRONMENTAL ANALYSIS INVENTORY
ACTIVITY/DISCREPANCY ANALYSIS

Leisure Skill Inventory

Activity/Skill: _____*Exercise Class*_____

Leisure Setting: _____*Hiawatha Recreation Center*_____

Directions: Below, give a step-by-step breakdown
of those *basic* and *vital* skills a nondisabled
person would need in order to participate in the
activity. Include all components (i.e., breaks,
using restrooms, drinking fountain, telephone, etc.)

Inventory for Participant with Disability

Name: _____*Sue Winters*_____

Directions: Read the step(s) in left column. If participants
can perform the step independently, mark a plus (+) in the
center column. If the participant cannot perform the step
independently, make a minus (-) in the center column. If the
participant's performance is marked (-), identify a teaching
procedure or adaptation/modification for that step in the
right column.

STEPS (Activity Analysis)	- / +	Teaching Procedure, Adaptation/Modification, Strategy for Partial Participation
1. *Enter the recreation center.*	+	1.
2. *Acknowledge recreation staff and others, if appropriate.*	-	2. *Initially, group home staff will appropriately model interactions with rec. staff and others. (Staff may not be available.)*
3. *Locate and proceed to the multipurpose center.*	-	3. *Group home staff will teach Sue to ask for assistance in locating the room. After a few classes, Sue will know where the room is.*
4. *Locate coat rack along the wall and proceed in that direction.*	-	4. *Initially, group home staff will model and assist Sue in this step.*
5. *Take coat off, hang on coat rack or place it with other belongings (i.e., sport bag, purse) along the wall.*	+	5.

FIGURE 8.1   Environmental Analysis Inventory: Activity/Discrepancy Analysis.
Reprinted with permission from Schleien, S., & Ray, M.T. (1988). *Community
recreation and persons with disabilities: Strategies for integration.* Baltimore: Paul
H. Brookes Publishing Co.

STEPS (Activity Analysis)	− / +	Teaching Procedure, Adaptation/Modification, Strategy for Partial Participation
6. *Find a space on the excercise mat and proceed in that direction.*	−	6. *Initially, group home staff will model and assist Sue in this step.*
7. *Wait for class to begin.*	+	7.
8. *Optional: appropriately speak with others and stretch out.*	−	8. *Appropriate role modeling needed.*
9. *When class starts, listen to and follow instructor's instructions.*	+	9.
10. *Do warm-up exercises.*	+	10.
11. *Do strength training exercises.*	−	11. *Sue may have difficulty with some of these exercises. The instructor will provide modified exercises or assistance as needed.*
12. *When instructor offers a break, use drinking fountain if necessary.*	+	12.
13. *Do aerobic exercises.*	−	13. *Assistance/modification, as needed.*

FIGURE 8.1   Continued

STEPS (Activity Analysis)	− / +	Teaching Procedure, Adaptation/Modification, Strategy for Partial Participation
14. *Check heart rate (3x).*	−	14. *Assistance/modification, as needed.*
15. *Do cool-down exercises.*	+	15.
16. *Upon completion of class, help put mats away.*	−	16. *Appropriate role modeling/teaching may be needed.*
17. *Optional: talk to other participants.*	−	17. *Group home staff will appropriately model interactions with others.*
18. *Optional: use drinking fountain/restroom, if necessary.*	+	18.
19. *Collect personal belongings.*	+	19.
20. *Put on coat.*	+	20.
21. *Exit recreation center.*	+	21.

FIGURE 8.1   Continued

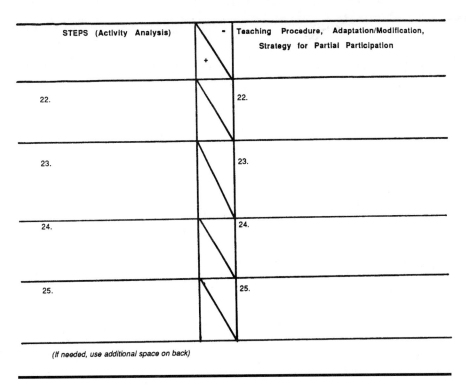

STEPS (Activity Analysis)	− / +	Teaching Procedure, Adaptation/Modification, Strategy for Partial Participation
22.		22.
23.		23.
24.		24.
25.		25.

(If needed, use additional space on back)

FIGURE 8.1   Continued

enjoy the naturally reinforcing consequences of an activity early in the instructional process, thereby enhancing the individual's motivation to acquire the skill.

Positive reinforcement can provide powerful motivation to learn new skills as taught through task analyses. Reinforcers are situational events that follow a behavior and increase the likelihood that the behavior will recur. Reinforcement should be learner-specific and contingent upon desired skill performance. Ideally, the activity itself should be a strong reinforcer to encourage participation, skill acquisition, and a feeling of personal reward (Amado, 1988). Reactive recreational materials such as the game Simon (Milton Bradley), video games, cameras, remote control vehicles,

and vending machines that provide sensory feedback (i.e., flashing lights, electronic sounds, visual stimulation, tastes) offer participants *natural* reinforcers (Schleien & Ray, 1988). Other powerful natural reinforcers are those that come from other people—special educators, community recreation staff, or peers—who provide positive attention through social interaction. Reinforcing social interactions may include conversation, praise, smiles, appropriate touch (e.g., pats on the back, handshakes, or hugs), and cooperative assistance in performing particular skills within the context of the activity (Amado, 1988).

Secondary reinforcers, those not necessarily associated with a particular activity, can also serve as strong motivators in a leisure and recreation program. Examples of secondary reinforcers include stickers, food items, switch-activated buzzers, and access to more preferred recreational activities (Schleien & Ray, 1988). In developing programs, it is important to observe students to determine what is naturally motivating to them, and then select activities in which those reinforcers naturally occur (Amado, 1988).

Adaptations. To facilitate active involvement in leisure activities, it may be necessary to provide programmatic adaptations. In planning for adaptations, three main guidelines should be considered:

1. *Provide adaptations on an individual basis to meet individual needs.* Adaptations that work for one person may not necessarily be suitable for another. For example, just because one person with mental retardation may need continual one-on-one assistance to participate in a basketball program, it does not follow that all people with mental retardation will automatically require such intensified instruction. Depending on individual needs, a participant may require adult assistance only at particular times during an activity, assistance from a peer may be adequate, or the person may be able to perform the activity independently.

2. *Provide adaptations only when necessary.* Based on the discrepancy analysis of the Environmental Analysis Inventory, identify the individual's need for adaptation and provide ample modifications to promote participation, success, and enjoyment.

3. *View any changes or adaptations as temporary. Adapt to ultimately facilitate independent engagement in the original, nonmodified activity.* Unless the adaptation is inherently necessary (e.g., a prosthetic adaptation such as a built-up tennis shoe for a person with one leg shorter than the other, or a sighted guide for a cross-country skier who is blind), program modifications should be designed as temporary changes. A primary goal of adaptations is to support a person in learning the necessary skills to eventually perform the activity as a nondisabled peer would perform it. For ex-

ample, a person may initially need one-on-one assistance to participate in an aerobics program. As the participant gains familiarity with the protocol of the environment and learns the exercise routines, support should be gradually faded until the person is able to participate independently.

Programmatic adaptations may include modifications to one or more of the following items: materials or equipment, rules of the game, the skill sequence, or the environment. Lead-up activities may also be provided in preparation for teaching complex leisure skills. Materials or equipment may be adapted to facilitate the participant's physical manipulation of objects during an activity. The original rules of a game may be changed to simplify the activity. Component steps of skill sequences may be rearranged to enhance safety and efficiency. Barriers in the environment may be modified to promote architectural accessibility of facilities and outdoor recreation areas. Finally, lead-up activities may be provided to allow practice in basic component skills of an activity prior to full participation in a more difficult activity. Table 8.3 presents specific examples of programmatic modifications within the context of a variety of recreational activities.

Program Evaluation

The evaluation of leisure and recreation programs is necessary for several reasons. It helps determine whether program goals and participant learning objectives are being met. It provides valuable information to instructors for making objective programmatic decisions and revisions. It enhances accountability to administrators (e.g., provides data regarding participant outcome, records feedback regarding participant satisfaction). It helps gain support for additional programming from administrators, parents, caregivers, participants, and professional colleagues. It provides concrete information that can be used to secure funding for future programs. Finally, evaluation offers a measure for understanding how the program is im-

TABLE 8.3   Examples of Programmatic Adaptations to Facilitate Leisure and Recreation Participation

ADAPTATIONS	EXAMPLES OF ADAPTATIONS
Material and Equipment	Adaptive switches and head wands to activate video games
	Extended shutter release buttons on cameras
	Color-coding on electronic keyboards
	Adjustable basketball backboards
	Handle-grip bowling balls
	Tubular steel bowling ramps
	Sport and power versus standard wheelchairs
	Braille reading materials
	Closed-captioned videotapes
	Sort versus hard rubber balls
	Built-up handles on paint brushes
	Picture cards of recreation center activities to facilitate activity selection
Rules	Allow two-handed basketball dribble
	Stand closer to pallina to ensure greater accuracy in bocce ball
	Allow table tennis ball to bounce on same side before going over net
	Use personal item as collateral instead of driver's license for material checkout at community recreation center
	Allow one-handed instead of two-handed play on fooseball table
Skill Sequence	Perform one-half of the normally required exercise routine
	Place food item in cold oven before turning oven on
	Wear swimming suit under street clothes in advance of aquatics program at recreation center
	Enter leisure setting earlier than other participants
	Place index finger on camera shutter release button before raising camera to eye level
Environment	Cut-away curbs
	Ramp steps
	Handrails from building to ice skating rink
	Accessible sinks, toilets, water fountains
	Asphalt instead of sand or dirt walking paths
	Tree branches trimmed to prevent injury to people with visual impairments

(continued)

TABLE 8.3 Continued

ADAPTATIONS	EXAMPLES OF ADAPTATIONS
Lead-Up Activity	Kickball leads to baseball
	Tricycle leads to bicycle
	Boot hockey or broomball leads to skate hockey
	Game of "catch" over a net (i.e., newcomb) leads to volleyball
	Adult assistance leads to participation with friend or independent access
	Use of low numbers leads to use of high numbers to score on cricket dart board

proving the participant's quality of life (Schleien & Ray, 1988).

Evaluation provides the professional with a systematic, ongoing procedure, or process, from which to gain important insights, feedback, and information concerning the impact of the program on the participant. The process of program evaluation is a dynamic one as the program evaluator must continually seek ways to improve the program to benefit the participant. The evaluation process contains the following component steps:

1. Determine the need for the leisure and recreation program.
2. Determine program goals and objectives.
3. Determine instructional procedures.
4. Select instructional tool(s) to determine attainment of program goals.
5. Implement the leisure and recreation program.
6. Gather data on the performance of participants.
7. Analyze the data.
8. Incorporate necessary revisions into the program.
9. Conclude the program.
10. Summarize the data.
11. Develop program revisions and recommendations, and submit these to administrators, participants, and other interested persons.
12. Commence a new program, implementing revised goals and instructional procedures.

Two primary forms of evaluation influence the effectiveness of an individual's program. The first is *baseline assessment,* an initial observation of the participant's ability level prior to actual implementation of the program. Baseline assessment makes it possible to identify which skills are already present in the participant's repertoire and which skills need to be taught. The discrepancy analysis presented earlier is an example of baseline assessment.

The second form of evaluation is *ongoing* or *formative* evaluation. This form enables the professional to track and verify the participant's progress throughout the program. Three elements must be considered in ongoing evaluation of participant progress: frequency, reliability, and validity of the evaluation methodology.

Frequency of evaluation refers to how often short-term instructional objectives are evaluated. Objectives may be evaluated at the end of each day, weekly, biweekly, or once a month. As a general rule, the following guidelines should be followed to determine the frequency with which evaluation is to be conducted:

1. Evaluate often enough to receive feedback on the progress of the participant. The more fre-

quently evaluation is conducted, the easier it is to detect problems.

2. Evaluate often enough to ascertain whether the instructional sequence is effective. If it is not effective, make the necessary modifications in methods and materials to increase effectiveness.

3. Evaluate often enough to verify that the participant has acquired the skill. Once the skill has been acquired, instruction can begin on the next skill in the instructional sequence, with the newly acquired skill being reviewed periodically.

Reliability refers to the accuracy of the data that are collected. Reliability may be influenced by a number of factors: participant or instructor illness, inconsistency in who collects the data, or confusion regarding the method of evaluation. To increase reliability, a second observer may be trained to collect data independent of the primary observer. Both observers would collect data simultaneously, from which an index of consistency of agreement can be established. Reliable recording of participant behavior is the foundation for credible and substantive evaluation.

Validity refers to the accuracy of the evaluation instrument in portraying a true picture of an individual's performance level. Validity addresses the question, "Does the evaluation instrument measure what it purports to measure?" One way to ensure the validity of evaluation instruments is to employ different types of evaluation techniques and cross-check results. For example, to measure a participant's basketball shooting accuracy, an observational assessment of percentage of successful field goals made by the participant can be completed and recorded daily. This is an example of *criterion-referenced* evaluation. Another way to measure the participant's basketball shooting accuracy is to compare the participant's score with scores of other individuals of the same chronological age. This is an example of *norm-referenced* evaluation; that is, performance level is computed on the basis of how well a large number of other respondents have performed the same task. The use of both methods of evaluation allows

for two independent techniques for tracking an individual's progress.

An example of an ongoing, criterion-referenced evaluation tool is the Skill Acquisition Evaluation Form, shown in Figure 8.2. This tool is based on the task-analytic Environmental Analysis Inventory discussed earlier. The primary advantages of this instrument are that it enables instructors to identify (1) skills in which the participant is already proficient, (2) the specific step of the task analysis where further instruction is to begin, and (3) the rate at which the participant is acquiring the skill.

As in the Environmental Analysis Inventory, each step of the task is listed sequentially on the Skill Acquisition Evaluation Form. During each session, following the completion of instruction on a selected skill, the instructor provides a verbal cue to the participant to perform the skill. Without offering any kind of reinforcement, such as positive feedback regarding appropriate behavior, the instructor observes the participant attempting to complete the task. The instructor records a plus (+) beside each step of the task analysis the participant can perform independently, and a minus (-) beside those steps not performed independently. The plus signs indicate which steps of the skill the participant has mastered. The minus signs indicate where instruction should be provided during the following session. By totaling the number of pluses, the instructor can identify the participant's rate of skill acquisition.

In addition to measuring leisure skill acquisition by program participants, it is important to have a means to measure social interaction skills. For many individuals with developmental disabilities, a necessary instructional goal is to initiate and sustain interactions with peers more frequently. One way to assess social interactions is to obtain a simple count of the number of times an individual initiates, receives, sustains, or terminates an interaction (see Figure 8.3). The duration of these interactions may also be recorded. Analyzing the direction of interactions (i.e., *to* whom or *from* whom the interaction is directed) can be helpful in assessing which individuals in the envi-

SKILL ACQUISITION EVALUATION FORM

Directions for Lines A - J:

A. Write the participant's name.
B. Write the participant's goal statement.
C. Write phrase (verbal cue) which you will consistantly use.
D. Write the name of the program, and the day and time it meets.
E.. Step-by-step, write a task-analysis of the skill to be taught.
F. Record a plus (+) by those skills the participant performs independently;
     record a minus (-) by those skills the participant cannot perform independently.
G. Write the total # of pluses for the session.

H. Write your initials.
I. Write the date.
J. Write the name of the skill.

Date: ___4-22-87___

A. Name: _Sue Winters_   D. Program: ___Exercise Class___   M + W : 5 - 6 p.m.
B. Goal Statement: _To independently participate in an exercise class._
C. Verbal Cue: _"Sue, we're here for your exercise class."_

Task Analysis Steps   F.

Step		a	b	1	2	3	4	5	6	7	8	9	10	11	12	13	14	15	16
25																			
24																			
23																			
22																			
21	Exit the recreation center.	−	−	+	+	+	+	+	+	+	+	+	+	+	+	+	+	+
20	Put coat on.	−	−	+	+	+	+	+	+	+	+	+	+	+	+	+	+	+
19	Collect personal belongings.	−	−	−	−	−	+	+	−	+	+	+	+	+	+	+	+	+
18	Optional: use drinking fountain/restroom.	−	−	−	−	+	+	+	+	+	+	+	+	+	+	+	+	+
17	Optional: talk to other participants.	−	−	−	+	+	+	+	+	+	+	+	+	+	+	+	+	+
16	At the end of class, help put mats away.	−	−	+	−	−	−	−	−	−	+	+	+	+	−	+	+	
15	Do cool-down exercises.	−	−	−	−	−	−	−	−	+	+	+	+	+	−	−	−	
14	Check heart rate (3x).	−	−	−	−	−	−	−	−	−	−	−	−	−	−	−		
13	Do aerobic exercises.	−	−	−	−	−	−	−	−	−	−	−	−	−	−	+		
12	When instr. offers break, use drinking fountain.	−	−	−	−	−	−	−	−	−	−	−	−	−	+	+		
11	Do strength training exercises.	−	−	−	−	−	−	−	−	−	−	−	−	−	+	+		
10	Do warm-up exercises.	−	−	−	−	−	−	−	−	−	−	+	+	+	+	+		
9	When class starts, listen to and follow instructor.	−	−	−	−	−	−	+	+	+	+	−	+	+	+	+		
8	Optional: approp. speak w/ others + stretch out.	−	−	−	−	−	+	−	−	+	+	+	+	+	+			
7	Wait for class to begin.	−	−	−	−	−	+	−	−	+	+	+	+	+				
6	Find a space on the mats + go in that direction.	−	−	+	+	+	+	+	+	+	+	+	+	+	+	+		
5	Take off coat, hang it on coat rack.	−	−	−	−	+	+	−	+	+	+	+	+	+				
4	Locate coat rack along wall + walk in that direction	−	−	−	−	−	+	−	+	+	+	+	+	+	+			
3	Locate + procede to the multipurpose room.	−	−	+	+	+	+	+	+	+	+	+	+	+	+	+		
2	Acknowledge rec. staff + others, if approp.	−	−	−	+	+	+	+	+	+	+	+	+	+	+			
E. 1	Enter the recreation center.	−	−	+	+	+	+	+	+	+	+	+	+	+	+	+		

a b 1 2 3 4 5 6 7 8 9 10 11 12 13 14 15 16 17 18 19 20 21
Sessions

	a	b	1	2	3	4	5	6	7	8	9	10	11	12	13	14	15
G. Total # of +'s	0	0	5	7	8	8	11	12	11	12	14	16	16	17	15	17	19
H. Your initials	sf	sf	sf	sf	sf	sf	sf	sf	sf	sf	sf	sf	sf	sf	sf	sf	
I. Date																	

J. Skill: _Partic. in comm. rec. program_

FIGURE 8.2   Skill Acquisition Evaluation Form. Reprinted with permission from Schleien, S., & Ray, M.T. (1988). *Community recreation and persons with disabilities: Strategies for integration.* Baltimore: Paul H. Brookes Publishing Co.

SOCIAL INTERACTION EVALUATION FOR ONE PARTICIPANT

A. Program Title: _Talking Art;_
B. Program Goal: _Increasing social interaction between part._
D. Date: _6-9-87_

C. Name: _Sue Winters_
Evaluator: _E. Fullen_

E. Level of Interaction

Time (preset)	None	Staff	Dis. Part.	Nondis. Part.	Other	Activity	Comments
3:05	A					Taking coat off	
3:10				A		Sitting at table	
3:15				I		Throwing clay	Sue was being ignored by staff and peers
3:25		A				Asking for help	
3:40	A					Working on project	
3:45				I		Pushing mess to neighbor's space	Possibly seeking attention from peer in close proximity
3:55				A		Putting coat on	

H.

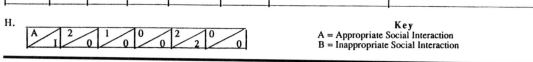

Key
A = Appropriate Social Interaction
B = Inappropriate Social Interaction

FIGURE 8.3   Social Interaction Evaluation Form. Reprinted with permission from Schleien, S., & Ray, M.T. (1988). *Community recreation and persons with disabilities: Strategies for integration.* Baltimore: Paul H. Brookes Publishing Co.

ronment are reinforcing to the participant (e.g., peers, instructors, or family members). For a more complete discussion and examples of social interaction evaluation tools, please refer to Schleien and Ray (1988), *Community Recreation and Persons with Disabilities: Strategies for Integration.*

CRITICAL ISSUES IN TEACHING LEISURE AND RECREATION SKILLS: OVERCOMING OBSTACLES TO INTEGRATED LEISURE PARTICIPATION

Commonly reported obstacles to including individuals with disabilities in community leisure and recreation environments fall within four main categories: *attitudinal, administrative, architectural,* and *programmatic* barriers (Smith, 1985; Vaughan & Winslow, 1979; West, 1984). Although a general understanding of the existence of barriers is neces-

sary and important, one must approach recreational programming as if *everyone* in the community is capable of participating. Through the identification and systematic appraisal of barriers, one can minimize their impact on community recreation participation by individuals with disabilities. Environmental and individualized approaches can be particularly effective in achieving integrated leisure environments (Schleien, Heyne, Rynders, & McAvoy, 1990). In this section, the four most commonly reported obstacles to integration are discussed, and solutions for overcoming those obstacles are presented.

Attitudinal Obstacles

In providing integrated programming, the obstacles that are probably most difficult to overcome are those that arise from stereotyped, negative attitudes toward individuals with disabilities. Lack of information about people with disabilities, lack of opportunities for contact with people with disabilities, and recreational services that strictly adhere to models of segregation and specialization all reinforce the stigmatization of people with disabilities.

To reverse misconceptions and the social exclusion of individuals with disabilities, positive perceptions must be cultivated. One way to promote more positive attitudes is to provide accurate information about disabilities, and people who have them, to agency administrators, staff, and nondisabled consumers. Disability awareness and friendship training can be provided to nondisabled program participants. Programmatic supports can be arranged for participants with disabilities to enable them to demonstrate successful leisure and recreation competencies. Finally, opportunities for persons with and without disabilities to interact together on an ongoing basis are essential for promoting mutual understanding and acceptance.

Administrative Obstacles

In planning for integrated programming, many practical administrative questions may arise: How will staff receive training to work with individuals with disabilities? How will people with disabilities be recruited to participate in integrated programs? How will transportation be provided? How will funding be secured to provide supports for integration?

Many administrative concerns can be allayed by an intentional reassessment of agency priorities. Including in an agency's mission statement support for the involvement of *all* people in leisure and recreation programming establishes a precedent for finding ways of overcoming administrative obstacles to integration. If an agency currently provides segregated programming, some of its programs may be phased out in favor of integrated options. Specialized personnel can be engaged to facilitate integration. An integration coordinator can be designated or hired to oversee the integration process. In-service training can be provided to increase the instructional competencies of staff.

Program participants can be actively recruited through agency brochures, advocacy organizations (e.g., Association for Retarded Citizens, United Cerebral Palsy, etc.), schools, residences, and local newspapers. Once a philosophical foundation for inclusive programming is set by a board of directors, funding and supports should follow to alleviate administrative concerns.

Architectural Obstacles

Physical barriers to integration may include obstacles that prevent access to buildings, recreational facilities, or outdoor environments. Access to buildings may be deterred by inaccessible parking spaces and entrances, or curbs that are not cut away. Recreational facilities, which may include a locker room, pool, gymnasium, running and walking track, or weight room, may be architecturally inaccessible. In addition, pathways, hiking trails, playgrounds, and camping areas may be unusable by participants with physical disabilities.

To solve architectural inaccessibility, one must analyze environments to identify physical barriers, then adapt facilities and structures to reduce or eliminate obstacles. Examples of architectural modifications include cut-away curbs, handicapped-only parking spaces, accessible restrooms and drinking fountains, ramps or elevators instead of stairs or escalators, and paved pathways instead of dirt trails. Planning for barrier-free environments heightens societal awareness of the right of *all* people, including those with physical disabilities, to be included in leisure and recreation environments.

Programmatic Obstacles

Programs themselves may present obstacles to integration if staff are untrained in assessing the needs of people with disabilities and providing appropriate instructional strategies to meet those needs. Staff may lack appropriate curricula or specialized equipment to effectively teach leisure and recreation skills to persons with disabilities. Problems may also arise when programs emphasize competition or individual prowess and achievement, because such programs tend to exclude people with disabilities.

To alleviate programmatic constraints, several strategies may be employed. In-service training in integration techniques can be provided for program staff. Individualized assessments of participant and family needs, abilities, and leisure preferences can be conducted. Regular curricula and equipment can be adapted to meet individual needs. Volunteers can be recruited and trained to provide participants with one-on-one programmatic support. Programs can be structured to promote cooperative learning and active participation by all participants. Integration efforts can be evaluated to refine integration strategies and further reduce programmatic barriers (Schleien et al., 1990).

CURRICULUM MODELS IN LEISURE AND RECREATION

The integration strategies and techniques described in the previous section have come to be known as "best professional practices" in recreation and leisure programming for individuals with disabilities. Best professional practices include those strategies that support the integration of people with developmental disabilities into mainstream community environments. These strategies include the use of needs and preference assessments, guidelines for skill selection, individualized instructional programming, adaptations and modifications, a concern for the maintenance and generalization of acquired skills, and ongoing evaluation (Schleien, Light, McAvoy, & Baldwin, 1989). This section presents four exemplary curriculum models that employ best professional practices.

Leisure Programs for Handicapped Persons: Adaptations, Techniques, and Curriculum

Authors: Paul Wehman and Stuart Schleien
Austin TX: PRO-ED (1981)

This curriculum model presents detailed instructional strategies for teaching leisure and recreation skills to people with developmental disabilities. Chapters include information on lei-

sure skills assessment, instruction, adapting leisure skills, and curriculum design and format. One hundred and twenty-six (126) leisure and recreation skills are presented, which include activities suitable for preschool, elementary, secondary-age, young adult, or adult instruction. Leisure and recreation skills are grouped in four categories: hobbies, sports, games, and object manipulation. For each skill, a complete task analysis, instructional objective, listing of materials, and verbal cues are provided. The authors present five case studies illustrating recreational competence by persons with developmental disabilities.

Longitudinal Leisure Skills for Severely Handicapped Learners: The Ho'onanea Curriculum Component

Authors: Bonnie Biel Wuerch and Luanna M. Voeltz
Baltimore: Paul H. Brookes Publishing Co. (1982)

This curriculum addresses the direct training of leisure activities and skills to enable students with severe disabilities to adapt to and participate in community environments. A philosophy of leisure education is presented. Ten field-tested lifetime leisure skills, which involve the manipulation of reactive materials, are task-analyzed, each according to specific instructional objectives. The curriculum provides guidelines for incorporating leisure skill instruction into existing educational programs. It also includes an in-home training component to facilitate parental involvement in leisure skill instruction. Validated curriculum assessment forms are provided, including the "Home Leisure Activity Survey," "Leisure Activity Selection Checklist," "Student Interest Inventory," and "Leisure Time at Home Needs Assessment."

Mainstreaming: A Total Perspective

Authors: Laura Wetherald and Joy Peters
Silver Spring, MD: Montgomery County Department of Recreation, Therapeutic Section (1986)

Developed as a guide for recreation staff to integrate public recreation services in Montgomery County, Maryland, this manual provides a useful integration resource for other municipal and county park and recreation agencies. It provides a comprehensive rationale for mainstreaming and discusses barriers to integration and methods to promote accepting environments. Implementation of the integration process is covered extensively, including the role and training of volunteer mainstreaming companions. Useful forms include the "Mainstreaming Companion Contract," "Volunteer Evaluation," "Mainstreaming Facilitation Sheet," "Mainstreaming Accommodations Plan," and various evaluation tools. The appendices offer valuable information on eight specific disabilities (e.g., autism, hearing impairments, mental retardation, etc.) and examples of sensitivity training exercises to promote disability awareness.

Therapeutic Recreation and Adapted Physical Activities for Mentally Retarded Individuals

Authors: Michael E. Crawford and Ron Mendel
Englewood Cliffs, NJ: Prentice Hall (1987)

This curriculum model specifically addresses the leisure needs of individuals with mental retardation. Learning theory, motor learning theory, perceptual motor learning, and behavioral modifications are emphasized. An extensive "Behavior Modification Self-Study Module" is presented, which includes detailed recommendations regarding target behaviors, methods of observation and recording, factors affecting reinforcement, guidelines for increasing and decreasing behavior, methods of teaching, and the maintenance and generalization of leisure behaviors. This resource also provides aquatics, bowling, and camping skill programs in a behavioral format. An appendix includes a glossary of related terms, syndromes, and definitions for perceptual-motor development and dysfunction.

MODEL PROGRAM: JEWISH COMMUNITY CENTER OF THE GREATER ST. PAUL AREA

An example of "best professional practices" in action is the Special Needs Program at the Jewish Community Center (JCC) of the Greater St. Paul Area, Minnesota.

The beginnings of the Special Needs Program illustrate the deliberate, systemwide approach to facilitating integration at the JCC. Prior to initiating the program, the JCC had offered segregated aquatics classes and a social club for a small group of elementary-age youngsters with Down syndrome. In the spring of 1984, however, administrators noticed several additional children with developmental disabilities who were coming to the JCC with their families, but who were not actively involved in regularly scheduled, structured programming. To determine the needs of these children and how the JCC might best respond, administrators called an open meeting for the parents of the children.

At that meeting parents agreed that opportunities already existed in the community for their children to participate in segregated recreational activities. What their children needed were integrated options. Parents believed that through integrated recreational activities their children could build friendships with nondisabled peers, learn appropriate social behaviors, develop lifetime leisure skills, gain self-confidence, and become active participants in the larger community.

Administrators took the concerns of these parents to the JCC board of directors, requesting authorization to seek funding to initiate a pilot integration project. Some reservations were expressed by board members: Would integration interfere with programming? Were current staff capable of meeting the needs of children with disabilities? Would the children with disabilities require a disproportionate amount of staff attention at the expense of learning by nondisabled participants? Despite these reservations, the board unanimously supported the philosophy of integration and granted permission to seek funding to explore how integration might be realized at the JCC.

With authorization from the board of directors, funding was sought and secured through the State of Minnesota Developmental Disabilities Council to implement a 1-year demonstration project. A certified therapeutic recreation specialist (CTRS) was hired as integration coordinator, and the process of involving youngsters with disabilities in regular programming commenced. Initial individualized child-family assessments were conducted to determine participant needs, abilities, and preferences. JCC staff were trained in how to include youngsters with disabilities in their programs and classes. To determine where individual children would need supports in order to have a successful experience, programmatic environmental analyses were conducted. One-on-one "trainer advocates" were recruited to assist children in classes, as needed. Nondisabled participants received sensitization orientations regarding disabilities and individual differences and were taught ways to interact with children with disabilities and include them in activities. Individualized instructional strategies, as discussed earlier in this chapter, were designed to support participants in programs. Ongoing evaluation of integration occurred via communication with and feedback from the children with disabilities, parents, administrators, staff, trainer advocates, nondisabled peers, and members of the board of directors.

To oversee the process of integration, a lay committee was formed. This committee was composed of leaders in the community, parents, and professionals. The committee discussed and set policy regarding such issues as eligibility criteria for participation in the program, agency membership for families with children with disabilities, accessibility at camp, and funding resources.

As a result of these integration efforts, children with disabilities began to participate successfully in a variety of mainstream community activities. Integrated programs included gymnastics, aquatics, dance, after-school day care, theater productions, social outings for youth, summer day camp, and woodworking, among many others.

The key to the success of the Special Needs Program has been inclusion on an agencywide scale. The system change, which was necessary to achieve integration, required the active and coordinated involvement of each of the key players in the integration process: children and youth with disabilities and their families, the board of direc-

tors, the lay committee, administrators, program staff, trainer advocates, and nondisabled peers. The coordination of the key players' involvement was made possible through the daily intervention of the CTRS.

With the success of the first-year demonstration project, the initial concerns of the board of directors were relieved; in fact, its members emphatically supported the continuation of integration at the JCC. Staff time was designated to develop and submit grant proposals seeking funds to extend the program. Subsequently, financial backing for the program was secured from the U.S. Department of Special Education, the United Way of Greater St. Paul, private foundations, and several private donors.

The benefits of integration at the JCC were demonstrated in several ways. Leisure skill acquisition by the children and youth with disabilities was documented via task-analytic "Skill Acquisition Evaluation Forms" (described earlier in this chapter). The building of social interaction skills was evidenced by the friendships that developed between the children with disabilities and their nondisabled peers. The benefits of integration for the youngsters with disabilities can probably best be understood, however, through the comments of their parents. At the end of every program quarter, parents were asked to complete "parent satisfaction questionnaires" regarding their thoughts on how integration worked for their children. Parents consistently reported that their children benefited from integration in terms of making friends, enjoying activities, developing self-confidence, becoming more independent, learning appropriate play behaviors, strengthening motor skills, and developing a sense of belonging in the community. The JCC became their children's neighborhood recreation center, *their* place to go to meet friends and feel a part of the larger community.

Nondisabled peers also benefited from integration. Every summer for 6 years, pre- and postprogram attitude surveys were administered to nondisabled children at the JCC day camp for grades K–6. Each summer, the attitudes of the nondisabled children grew more accepting toward the children with disabilities. Moreover, from one summer to the next, positive attitudes were maintained, demonstrating the longitudinal effects of integration on shaping positive attitudes of nondisabled children.

Integration also had an impact on regular program staff at the JCC. On pretest and posttest program attitude assessments, staff indicated that integration taught them not to be afraid of people with disabilities, that children with disabilities are disabled only to the extent that we perceive them to be disabled, and that with careful planning, integration can work to everyone's advantage.

When integration began at the JCC, no one anticipated the positive impact it would have on the total community. Not only did the children with disabilities and their families benefit, but the entire community as well. The JCC Special Needs Program demonstrates that when everyone is actively involved in the integration process, from policy makers and administrators to actual program participants, everyone benefits (Heyne, 1987; Schleien et al., 1990).

SUMMARY AND RECOMMENDATIONS FOR FUTURE RESEARCH

This chapter presents instructional strategies for teaching leisure and recreation skills to individuals with disabilities within the context of regular recreational activities and mainstream school and community environments. In summary, the key points to remember in providing leisure and recreation programming are as follows:

1. All individuals with developmental disabilities have an inalienable right to participate in a full range of leisure and recreation activities with nondisabled peers.
2. Leisure and recreation skills must be systematically taught to individuals with disabilities, through the use of state-of-the-art instructional strategies.

3. Leisure and recreation instruction must be individualized according to the unique needs, abilities, and preferences of participants.
4. Environments must be engineered and adaptations provided in order to support individuals with disabilities in mainstream leisure and recreation settings.
5. Evaluation of leisure and recreation programming must be conducted to determine participant progress and refine instructional strategies.
6. Philosophical support for the inclusion of individuals with disabilities in normalized leisure and recreation environments is essential to overcome attitudinal, administrative, architectural, and programmatic obstacles to integration.
7. Successful integrated programming in the community results from active and coordinated involvement of all key players in the integration process: program participants, their families, integration facilitator, boards of directors, administrators, program staff, trainer advocates, and nondisabled peers.
8. When people with disabilities are included in regular leisure and recreation programming, the entire community benefits.

Although there have been important strides in integrated leisure and recreation programming in recent years, further research is needed to ensure quality services for individuals with disabilities. Potential areas for further study include: (1) how to promote friendships between people with disabilities and nondisabled peers, (2) how to build support in the community to promote the active inclusion of individuals with disabilities in leisure and recreation environments, (3) the correlation between leisure and recreation skill acquisition by individuals with disabilities and friendship development with nondisabled peers, (4) how to systematically remove attitudinal, administrative, architectural, and programmatic barriers to integration, and (5) how to implement system changes for agencies that seek to include individuals with disabilities in their generic delivery of services.

REFERENCES

Alajajian, L. (1981). Jogging program for deaf-blind students improves condition and reduces self-stimulation. *News . . . About Deaf-Blind Students: Programs and Services in New England, 6*(1), 3–4.

Amado, R. (1988). Behavioral principles in community recreation integration. In S. J. Schleien & M. T. Ray (Eds.), *Community recreation and persons with disabilities: Strategies for integration.* Baltimore: Paul H. Brookes Publishing Co.

Bates, P., & Renzaglia, A. (1982). Language instruction with a profoundly retarded adolescent: The use of a table game in the acquisition of verbal labeling skills. *Education and Treatment of Children, 5*(1), 13–22.

Belmore, K., & Brown, L. (1976). A job skill inventory strategy for use in a public school vocational training program for severely handicapped potential workers. In L. Brown, N. Certo, K. Belmore, & T. Crowner (Eds.), *Papers and programs related to public school services for secondary age severely handicapped students,* vol. 6, part 1. Madison, WI: Madison Metro School District. Revised and republished in N. Haring & D. Bricker (Eds.), (1977), *Teaching the severely handicapped,* vol. 3. Columbus, OH: Special Press.

Brown, L., Branston, M., Hamre-Nietupski, S., Pumpian, I., Certo, N., & Gruenewald, L. (1979). A strategy for developing chronological age-appropriate and functional curricular content for severely handicapped adolescents and young adults. *Journal of Special Education, 13*(1), 81–90.

Certo, N., Schleien, S., & Hunter, D. (1983). An ecological assessment inventory to facilitate community recreation participation by severely disabled individuals. *Therapeutic Recreation Journal, 17*(3), 29–38.

Crawford, M., & Mendel, R. (1987). *Therapeutic recreation and adapted physical activities for mentally retarded individuals.* Englewood Cliffs, NJ: Prentice Hall.

Dattilo, J., & Barnett, L. (1985). Therapeutic recreation for individuals with severe handicaps: An analysis of the relationships between choice and pleasure. *Therapeutic Recreation Journal, 19*(3), 79–91.

Dattilo, J., & Mirenda, P. (1987). An application of a leisure preference assessment protocol for persons with severe handicaps. *The Journal of The Association for Persons with Severe Handicaps, 12,* 306–311.

Favell, J. (1973). Reduction of stereotypes by reinforcement of toy play. *Mental Retardation, 11*(4), 21–23.

Gaylord-Ross, R. (1980). A decision model for the treatment of aberrant behavior in applied settings. In W. Sailor, B. Wilcox, & L. Brown (Eds.), *Methods of instruction for severely handicapped students.* Baltimore: Paul H. Brookes Publishing Co.

Goetz, L. (1987). Recreation and leisure: Practices in educational programs which hold promise for adult service models. In A. Covert & H. Fredericks (Eds.), *Transition for persons with deaf-blindness and other profound handicaps: State of the art* (pp. 119–130). Monmouth, OR: Teaching Research.

Goodale, T., & Witt, P. (1985). *Recreation and leisure: Issues in an era of change.* State College, PA: Venture Publishing, Inc.

Heyne, L. (1987). *Integrating children and youth with disabilities into community recreation agencies: One agency's experience and recommendations.* St. Paul: Jewish Community Center of the Greater St. Paul Area.

Horner, R., Williams, J., & Knobbe, C. (1985). The effect of "opportunity to perform" on the maintenance of skills learned by high school students with severe handicaps. *The Journal of The Association for Persons with Severe Handicaps, 10*(3), 172–175.

Kennedy, D., Austin, D., & Smith, R. (1987). *Special recreation: Opportunities for persons with disabilities.* Philadelphia: Saunders College.

Kibler, C. (1986). Board games for multihandicapped players. *Perspectives for Teachers of the Hearing Impaired, 4*(4), 21–23.

Kissel, R., & Whitman, T. (1977). An examination of the direct and generalized effects of a play-training and overcorrection procedure upon the self-stimulatory behavior of a profoundly retarded boy. *AAESPH Review, 2,* 131–146.

Matthews, P. (1980). Why the mentally retarded do not participate in certain types of recreational activities. *Therapeutic Recreation Journal, 14*(1), 44–50.

Orelove, F., & Sobsey, D. (1987). *Educating children with multiple disabilities: A transdisciplinary approach.* Baltimore: Paul H. Brookes Publishing Co.

Peterson, C., & Gunn, S. (1984). *Therapeutic recreation program design: Principles and procedures* (2nd ed.). Englewood Cliffs, NJ: Prentice Hall.

Powers, J., & Ball, T. (1983). Video games to augment

leisure programming in a state hospital residence for developmentally disabled clients. *Journal of Special Education Technology, 6*(1), 48–57.

Reynolds, R. (1981). Normalization: A guide to leisure skills programming for handicapped individuals. In P. Wehman & S. Schleien (Eds.), *Leisure programming for handicapped persons: Adaptations, techniques, and curriculum* (pp. 1–13). Baltimore: University Park Press.

Rogow, S. (1981). Developing play skills and communicative competence in multiply handicapped young people. *Visual Impairment and Blindness, 5,* 197–202.

Schleien, S., Heyne, L., Rynders, J., & McAvoy, L. (1990). Equity and excellence: Serving all children in community recreation. *Journal of Physical Education, Recreation & Dance, 61*(8), 45–48.

Schleien, S., Light, C., McAvoy, L., & Baldwin, C. (1989). Best professional practices: Serving persons with severe multiple disabilities. *Therapeutic Recreation Journal, 23*(3), 27–40.

Schleien, S., & Meyer, L. (1988). Community-based recreation programs for persons with severe developmental disabilities. In M. Powers (Ed.), *Expanding systems of service delivery for persons with developmental disabilities* (pp. 93–112). Baltimore: Paul H. Brookes Publishing Co.

Schleien, S., & Ray, M. T. (1988). *Community recreation and persons with disabilities: Strategies for integration.* Baltimore: Paul H. Brookes Publishing Co.

Schleien, S., & Wehman, P. (1986). Severely handicapped children: Social skills development through leisure skills programming. In G. Cartledge & J. Milburn (Eds.), *Teaching social skills to children: Innovative approaches* (2nd ed.) (pp. 219–245). Elmsford, NY: Pergamon.

Schleien, S., & Werder, J. (1985). Perceived responsibilities of special recreation services in Minnesota. *Therapeutic Recreation Journal, 19*(3), 51–62.

Sherrill, C. (1986). *Adapted physical education and recreation: A multi-disciplinary approach* (3rd ed.). Dubuque, IA: William C. Brown.

Smith, R. (1985). Barriers are more than architectural. *Parks and Recreation, 20*(10), 58–62.

Vandercook, T. (1987). Generalized performance of community leisure skills with peers. Unpublished manuscript. Minneapolis: University of Minnesota.

Vaughan, J., & Winslow, R. (1979). *Guidelines for community based recreation programs for special populations.* Alexandria, VA: National Therapeutic Recreation Society.

Verhoven, P., Schleien, S., & Bender, M. (1982). *Leisure education and the handicapped individual: An ecological perspective.* Washington, DC: Institute for Career and Leisure Development.

Voeltz, L., & Wuerch, B. (1981). Monitoring multiple behavioral effects of leisure activities training upon severely handicapped adolescents. In L. M. Voeltz, J. A. Apffel, & B. B. Wuerch (Eds.), *Leisure activities training for severely handicapped students: Instructional and educational strategies.* Honolulu: University of Hawaii, Department of Special Education.

Voeltz, L., Wuerch, B., & Wilcox, B. (1982). Leisure and recreation: Preparation for independence, integration, and self-fulfillment. In B. Wilcox & G. Bellamy (Eds.), *Design of high school programs for severely handicapped students* (pp. 175–209). Baltimore: Paul H. Brookes Publishing Co.

Wehman, P., & Schleien, S. (1980). Assessment and selection of leisure skills for severely handicapped individuals. *Education and Training of the Mentally Retarded, 15*(1), 50–57.

Wehman, P., & Schleien, S. (1981). *Leisure programs for handicapped persons: Adaptations, techniques, and curriculum.* Baltimore: University Park Press.

West, P. (1981). *Vestiges of a cage: Social barriers to participation in outdoor recreation by the mentally and physically handicapped,* Monograph 1. Ann Arbor: University of Michigan, Natural Resources Sociology Research Lab.

West, P. (1984). Social stigma and community recreation participation by the mentally and physically handicapped. *Therapeutic Recreation Journal, 23*(3), 27–40.

Wetherald, L., & Peters, J. (1986). *Mainstreaming: A total perspective.* Silver Spring, MD: Montgomery County Department of Recreation, Therapeutic Section.

Wolfensberger, W. (1972). *The principle of normalization in human services.* Toronto: National Institute on Mental Retardation.

Wolfensberger, W. (1983). Social role valorization: A proposed new term for the principle of normalization. *Mental Retardation, 21*(6), 234–239.

Wuerch, B., & Voeltz, L. (1982). *Longitudinal leisure skills for severely handicapped learners: The Ho'onanea curriculum component.* Baltimore: Paul H. Brookes Publishing Co.

CHAPTER 9

COMMUNICATION INTERVENTION FOR PERSONS WITH DEVELOPMENTAL DISABILITIES

JOE REICHLE
University of Minnesota

JEFF SIGAFOOS
University of Queensland

IMPORTANCE OF COMMUNICATION SKILLS

The ability to communicate with other individuals is an inherently important component of virtually every activity we undertake. Without the ability to understand or produce communication, it is virtually impossible to function independently. There is a well-established body of literature supporting the fact that individuals with limited communicative repertoires can easily fall victim to the phenomenon of "learned helplessness" (Guess, Benson, & Siegel-Causey, 1985). That is, without the ability to communicate their likes and dislikes, individuals, over time, may more and more come to rely on others to make most of their choices. Eventually they may come to exhibit very little control over their lives. Other individuals who fail to acquire a functional repertoire of communicative behavior may develop classes of socially unacceptable behavior that are used communicatively. A number of investigators (see Durand, 1991) have described individuals who engage in aggression and/or self-injury in order to communicate their desire for attention, goods, or services, or their dislike for certain items or events. Although most people learn how to communicate without any special assistance, some individuals with developmental disabilities may require more systematically organized instruction if they are to learn to produce and understand spoken language.

HISTORICAL REVIEW OF COMMUNICATION INTERVENTION

Early efforts to delineate communication intervention programs focused on teaching learners to understand and produce *syntax* (sentence structure that includes word order, inflections, and relationships between words). However, interventionists soon realized that many individuals (who were either very young or more severely disabled) lacked the ability to understand and produce the simple word meanings that represent the building blocks of syntactic relations. This realization led to the development of a wave of intervention programs aimed at establishing initial understanding and production of individual vocabulary. *Semantics* (the study of meaning and rules for linking meaning to words), to a great extent, guided the intervention programs of the 1970s. The 1980s brought a number of revelations to the discipline of language intervention. Interventionists found themselves working with very young toddlers and with individuals with severe disabilities who could not understand or produce specific meaning, yet could make known a wide variety of wants and needs. Other learners had rather extensive repertoires of spoken words, yet had great difficulty using them to express a variety of different communicative intents (i.e., requesting, commenting, providing

241

information, requesting information, answering, etc.). These learners required intervention to establish *pragmatic* competencies (rules governing how communication is used in social contexts). Today public school professionals are finding themselves responsible for providing communication intervention to infants and preschoolers who, in addition to requiring intervention in the areas of *semantics* and *pragmatics,* may also require the use of an augmentative communication system (gestures or graphic symbols—see Chapter 10) to supplement speech output.

In addition to understanding the classes of communicative behavior described thus far, it is important to realize that communicative behavior can either be *produced* (spoken) or *comprehended* (understood). There is not always a direct correspondence between what an individual communicatively produces and what he or she understands. For this reason, the communication interventionist must be careful not to make any assumptions regarding a learner's ability to produce communicative behavior based on his or her ability to understand communicative behavior, or vice versa.

The purpose of this chapter is to acquaint the reader with the range of considerations that are important in developing communication intervention options for individuals who have moderate to severe developmental disabilities. We believe that the available best practice standards suggest that communication intervention can proceed with the youngest infant. We also believe that there are a wide variety of intervention techniques from which interventionists may choose. Although this variety of techniques represents an equally wide variety of theoretical underpinnings, we believe that any approach for which empirical data demonstrate the establishment of functional communication should not be overlooked.

In the paragraphs that follow, we first describe the range of communicative behaviors that interventionists often choose to teach beginning communicators to produce and understand. With respect to the content of intervention procedures designed to teach communicative production and

comprehension, we focus on both pragmatic and semantic skills. Subsequently, we discuss a continuum of teaching procedures that emphasize the use of naturally occurring interactions as the basis for communication intervention.

SELECTING, ASSESSING, AND TEACHING COMMUNICATION SKILLS

Identifying a Repertoire of Communication Production

McLean and Snyder-McLean (1988) identified a hierarchy of initial communicative forms that reflect an individual's growing ability to engage in communication. They described what they called "primitive," "conventional," and "referential" acts. Primitive acts include an individual's actions that have occurred often enough that they have been conditioned (i.e., pulling away when an undesired item is offered). Conventional acts are those that have been "streamlined from their earlier primitive forms" (i.e., requesting by offering an open palm without an object in one's hand, or pointing at an object). Referential acts include using speech. Although the primary thrust of this chapter is to describe more conventional aspects of communication, it is important to point out that intervention may begin at the level of establishing primitive communicative forms.

Adults who frequently interact with young children, during their first few months of life, tend to assign intent to the action of a learner even though the learner is expressing no intent. For example, when an infant fusses, an adult may conclude that the infant is communicating, "I'm hungry." If the infant likes food, and if the adult regularly offers food as a consequence of the child's crying near mealtime, the infant may come to use crying as an intentional strategy to obtain food. In this instance, the adult would have taught a primitive communicative form.

All intentional communicative behavior has some social motivation. We believe that there are two distinct components to pragmatic aspects of communication. On one level, the interventionist can ask, "Why was an utterance produced?" That is, was it emitted in an effort to request goods or service, request information, provide information, greet, or for some other purpose? On a second level, the interventionist can concern him- or herelf with how these "reasons to communicate" are emitted across communicative turns. That is, how does taking turns among participants in a conversation proceed in an orderly fashion to maintain, add to, and gain closure on conversational topics? Of course, critically related to both of these aspects of pragmatics are the specific word meanings that are selected to teach the learner to use in communicating requests, or rejection or protest, within the context of initiating, maintaining, or terminating an interaction.

Pragmatic Functions. Interventionists have begun to recognize the importance of establishing a variety of communicative functions. There is a plethora of procedures describing the range of communicative functions used by both nondisabled children and individuals with developmental disabilities. Some of the more frequently used taxonomies are those developed by Dore (1975), Cirrin and Rowland (1985), and Wetherby and Prizant (1989). Examples of the latter two systems are displayed in Table 9.1. Reichle (1991) provides a detailed discussion of several of these systems. Most systems that describe pragmatic intents include many similar classes of behavior, such as request, direct attention or comment, protest or reject, answer, and so forth.

In the initial wave of language intervention programs, there was but limited attention given to the variety and sequencing of communicative intents (Guess, Sailor, & Baer, 1974; Kent, 1974; Bricker, Dennison, & Bricker, 1975). For the most part, the intervention strategy of choice seemed to be to teach the learner to "direct attention" or "comment" by labeling targeted objects and events (i.e., The interventionist says, "What's this?" as she holds up an apple. The learner responds "apple," even though he does not desire

one). The assumption of many programs was that the learner, having been taught in this fashion, would be able to use his or her newly acquired vocabulary for other communicative intents, such as requesting. Unfortunately, generalized use may not occur for all learners. Reichle (1990) reported that learners taught to reject offers of items that they strongly disliked, failed to use the same vocabulary to reject items that they normally liked, but for which they had reached a state of satiation. Other investigators have reported similar breakdowns in learners' abilities to generalize their use of specific communicative intents. Lamarre and Holland (1985), for example, investigated the functional independence of mands (requests) and tacts (provisions of information) in normal preschool children. Some preschoolers initially learned to direct the experimenter's placement of objects by producing prepositional phrases, "on the left" and "on the right." At regular intervals during acquisition, probes were implemented to determine whether learners could use the same prepositions to describe the experimenter's action that had already taken place. With the remaining children, the experimental conditions were implemented in the opposite order. Results demonstrated that acquisition of the phrases to direct the actions of the experimenter did not lead to the collateral acquisition of a corresponding repertoire to describe actions that had already been performed, and vice versa, even though the same vocabulary was involved in both repertoires.

A similar lack of generalization across the response classes of requesting and providing information has been observed among disadvantaged preschoolers (Hart & Risley, 1968) and among learners with developmental disabilities (Glennen & Calculator, 1985; Hall & Sundberg, 1987; McCook, Cipani, Madigan, & LaCampagne, 1988; Reichle & Yoder, 1985; Romski, Sevcik, & Pate, 1988). However, among this latter group there appear to be certain training parameters that may facilitate transfer from describing to requesting relationships (Sigafoos, Doss, & Reichle, 1989; Sigafoos, Reichle, Doss, Hall, & Pettitt,

TABLE 9.1 Taxonomies of Pragmatic Functions of Communicative Utterances

CIRRIN & ROWLAND (1985)		WEATHERBY & PRIZANT (1989)	
Request action	Seeks the performance of an action by the listener in which the child awaits a response. The child may specify the action (e.g., "sit"), or the child's immediately preceding behavior gives evidence that he or she realizes that some action is a necessary step to obtaining some object (e.g., signaling "help" to open a jar).	Request action	Acts used to command another to carry out an action.
Request object	Seeks the receipt of a specific object from the listener in which the child awaits a response. The object may be out of reach because of some physical barrier.	Request object	Acts used to demand a desired tangible object.
Request information	Seeks information, approval, or permission from the listener in which the child awaits a response. This includes directing the listener to provide specific information about an object, action, or location.	Request information	Acts used to seek information, explanation, or clarification about an object, event, or previous utterance. Includes wh-questions and other utterances having the intonation contour of an interrogative.
Direct attention to self	Direction of listener's attention to the child as a general attention-getter for some unspecified social purpose.	Show off	Acts used to attract another's attention to oneself.
Direct attention for communication	Direction of listener's attention to self as a preface to another communcative behavior that follows immediately.	Call	Acts used to gain the attention of others, usually to indicate that a communicative act is to follow.
Direct attention to object	Direction of listener's attention to an external, observable referent, or some object identified by the child. This includes the speaker taking notice of an object, or labeling an object in absence of a request.	Comment on object	Acts used to direct another's attention to an entity.

TABLE 9.1   **Continued**

CIRRIN & ROWLAND (1985)		WEATHERBY & PRIZANT (1989)	
Direct attention to action	Direction of listener's attention to an ongoing action or event in the environment. The focus may be the movement or action of an object rather than the object itself. A "comment" on some ongoing activity.	Comment on action	Acts used to direct another's attention to an event.
Answer	A communicative response from a child to a request for information from the adult listener. This typically takes the form of indicating a choice or answering a question.	Protest	Acts used to refuse an undesired object or to command another to cease an undesired action.
		Clarification	Acts used clarify the previous utterance.
		Acknowledg-ment	Acts used to indicate notice of another person's previous statement or utterance.
		Greet	Acts used to gain another's attention to indicate notice of their presence, or to indicate notice of the initiation or termination of an interaction.
		Request permission	Acts used to seek another's consent to carry out an action; involves the child's carrying out or wishing to carry out the action.
		Request social routine	Acts used to command another to commence or continue carrying out a gamelike social interaction

1990). More recent intervention literature has sought to address the individualized selection of communicative functions in the initial decisions that must be made to establish a communication intervention program.

We believe that some learners may be more interested in requesting desired items while other learners may be more interested in maintaining the attention of others. In the former case, requesting objects represents an important initial communicative function. For other learners, the ability to produce greetings may be a more salient initial pragmatic function to develop. Unfortunately, some learners have not yet learned to enjoy the company of others. When approached by other people, they retreat immediately or appear to spend most of their time plotting an escape. For such an individual, a more salient initial pragmatic function to teach may be a communicative strategy that will allow the learner to leave.

Rather than arbitrarily selecting initial pragmatic functions to target for intervention, implementing a careful analysis of those communicative functions that might be of the greatest salience to the learner may result in the quickest route to demonstrate to a fledgling communicator the advantage of learning to communicate with the use of a conventional communicative system. The selection of initial communicative functions to teach should be based on the learner's needs and interests. In addition, there is no reason to assume that only a "single" communicative function should be selected for implementation during the early phases of an intervention program.

Selecting Initial Word Meanings.   On one hand, the interventionist wants to select vocabulary that can be used frequently. On the other hand, it is important that vocabulary be selected that can address important communicative opportunities and obligations imposed by the learner's environments.

A number of investigators have described the use of an ecological inventory to describe an initial vocabulary to teach. The ecological inventory identifies vocabulary that would be used frequently in the learner's current and future environments. Unless ecologically valid strategies for vocabulary selection are utilized, it is quite possible that a fair amount of vocabulary that is taught will focus on some objects or events that the learner may have little need to communicate about.

Once the interventionist identifies relevant communicative functions for specific environments, the degree of specificity of the initial vocabulary must be considered. The specificity with which one represents referents may have a significant impact on the learner's initial acquisition and use of vocabulary. Does one develop communicative behaviors that are general in nature (e.g., to communicate "food") or very specific (e.g., "cheeseburger")? The decision may depend on several factors. For learners having a number of preferred items/events, it may be most practical to teach a request that could be used in the presence of a wide variety of objects and events (i.e., "more," "want"). For example, a learner's initial repertoire of vocabulary used to request attention may consist of "hey," and his or her generalized protesting or rejecting vocabulary might consist of "no." In the case of requesting, more generalized requests (e.g., "want") may also be effective for learners whose preferences shift tremendously, because even if some preferences change there may still be a large enough pool of reinforcers available to maintain generalized requesting. In addition, the varied reinforcement associated with a more generalized request may enable the interventionist to implement a higher density of instructional opportunities without the learner's becoming satiated with the items being requested (Egel, 1980, 1981). This may be especially important for learners who require a large number of instructional opportunities to acquire new skills.

In contrast to more generalized vocabulary, explicit vocabulary has its own advantages. In particular, explicit vocabulary is often required for clear communication in community settings with unfamiliar listeners. One cannot, for example, order dinner at a restaurant by simply asking for "food." More explicit vocabulary would thus seem to place less burden of interpretation on the part of the listener, reducing, in turn, the frequency of requests for clarification. In the case of requesting, for learners with a few specific and relatively stable preferences, or for those who tend to acquire vocabulary relatively quickly, teaching explicit vocabulary may be a practical option.

It is clear that explicit as well as more generic vocabulary can be taught to learners with moderate and severe disabilities. Equally clear is that explicit vocabulary can be taught subsequent to more generic vocabulary, with both strategies then maintained concurrently. What is not clear, however, is whether the difference between explicit and generic vocabulary would significantly impact aspects of interventions, such as speed of acquisition, maintenance, and generalized use resulting in efficient communicative exchanges.

Components of Conversational Exchanges. Conversational, as well as other social, exchanges can usually be divided into three distinct components: initiation, maintenance, and termination. When conversational exchanges are the context of communication intervention, the interventionist must focus on how the vocabulary and communicative intents targeted for intervention interact with these three components of an exchange.

For the most part, the intervention literature seems to have focused on teaching learners with disabilities to maintain interactions that were the result of pleasant overtures initiated by another person. Although such instances are clearly desirable, they may not represent the majority of available communicative opportunities afforded by the range of environments in which most learners operate. For example, it is quite common for many young children to initiate communication contingent on the intrusion of some external event. The learner may drop a desired toy behind the sofa; being unable to retrieve the toy independently creates an opportunity for the child to "complain" or "protest loudly." Two young children may be playing together. One child "steals" the other child's toy. This creates an opportunity for the "wronged" party to initiate an interaction with a parent or to maintain a communicative exchange with the "thief."

The preceding examples suggest that initiating an interaction may occur for a variety of reasons. The same could be said for maintenance and termination functions of a conversation. Too often, interventionists fail to select an instructional format that conforms to the learner's interests. With greater attention paid to whether the focus of earliest opportunities for initiation focus on greetings, supplying

information, requesting, or rejecting, the process of teaching learners to initiate interactions can be more skillfully addressed. Table 9.2 displays the interaction between the communicative intents of requesting and rejecting with the conversational components of initiating, maintaining, and terminating an interaction. Table 9.3 shows a series of commonly encountered environmental scenarios that provide opportunities to initiate (in the first set of examples) and to terminate (in the second set of examples) communicative exchanges. Although little empirical data are available, we believe that focusing on a single "scenario" to establish conversational components is apt to mitigate against generalized use of the conversational component. Consequently, it is important for interventionists to select carefully the context of the intervention opportunities on which they choose to focus. The challenge to the interventionist is to create an intervention procedure that incorporates relevant conversational function, pragmatic function, and correct vocabulary meaning into the same communicative event. Integrating the communicative function of requesting with the conversational function of initiating is a good example.

In working with individuals with moderate and severe developmental disabilities, it is quite common to observe a learner approach an interventionist, provide a request, be consequated, and move away. In such instances, engaging in extended interactional sequences would represent a highly nonpreferred activity for the learner. In this situation, therefore, it may be more promising to focus on establishing communicative functions, such as "requesting," that allow the client to learn that communication is a powerful tool. Doing so puts the focus of early intervention on establishing joint attention between the learner and his or her listener with brief episodes of exchange.

Experience suggests that, over time, the exchanges that we have been describing may become more extended in what, to the observer, appears to be an exchange consisting of numerous instances of taking turns. An example of this phenomenon often occurs during the dinner hour in

TABLE 9.2   Examples of the Interaction between the Communicative Functions of Requesting and Rejecting with the Conversational Components of Initiating, Maintaining, and Terminating Interactions

	INITIATE	MAINTAIN	TERMINATE
REQUEST			
Context	A 6-year-old sees a peer on the playground.	A preschool child is watching his mother blow bubbles.	A learner has lost interest in playing with his younger sibling.
Utterance	He approaches the peer and says, "Wanna play?"	He says, "Do it again."	He says, "Wouldn't you like to watch cartoons now?"
REJECT			
Context	Two children are sitting together. Adult asks one child if he wants to go to a movie.	A preschool child is playing a game with her dad.	A learner and his friend are working on a jigsaw puzzle.
Utterance	The other child says, "I don't want to go to a movie."	The child says, "It's not your turn!"	He says, "I'm tired of doing this."
COMMENT			
Context	A child and an adult are walking at the zoo.	A learner and her friend are talking about a television show.	Two children are waiting to be picked up from school.
Utterance	The child says, "A bear!"	The learner says, "I thought that it was funny."	One child says, "Oh, there's my ride."

From Reichle, J., York, J., & Sigafoos, J. (1991). *Implementing augmentative and alternative communication: Strategies for learners with severe disabilities* (p. 163). Baltimore, MD: Paul H. Brookes Publishing Co. Copyright 1991 by Paul H. Brookes Publishing Co., Inc. Adapted by permission.

most homes. Having just completed her meal, a child asks for and receives a dessert. After consuming it, she requests another instance and is again consequated. These requests for additional helpings may continue until the parent terminates the exchange by saying, "That's it. You've had enough." This example has many of the attributes of a rudimentary communicative exchange. How-

TABLE 9.3   Examples of Commonly Encountered Scenarios Providing Opportunities to Initiate and Terminate Communicative Exchanges

CIRCUMSTANCE	EXAMPLE
Joining activities that are already in progress	Tom Sawyer instilling an interest among his peers in painting a fence
Beginning well-established routines	A learner (taught that you can't eat your snack unless all the children in the group have some), upon receiving several cookies turns to a peer who doesn't have any, offers her a cookie, and says, "Here."
Calling attention to novel events	At snack time when a child spills his milk, a learner gets the teacher's attention to point out what has happened.
Protesting the undesirable actions of another	A waitress, assuming that a customer has finished his meal, attempts to remove a plate that still contains a small amount of food. When this happens, the customer says, "I'm not through."
Ending undesired interactions	A learner participating in a game of cards becomes bored and says, "Let's stop."
Concluding desirable interactions in order to accommodate a schedule	When the bell rings in the school cafeteria, a learner may have to terminate his lunchtime interaction with a peer in order to avoid being late to his next class.
Finishing pleasant interactions to take advantage of a more attractive alternative	A 7-year-old child may be content to play with a 3-year-old child provided no other playmates are available. However, the appearance of another 7-year-old may result in the interaction with the 3-year-old being abruptly terminated.
Discontinuing pleasant interactions owing to environmental disruptions	A learner who sees his little brother fall off his bike may need to terminate a play activity in order to render assistance.

From Reichle, J., York, J., & Sigafoos, J. (1991). *Implementing augmentative and alternative communication: Strategies for learners with severe disabilities* (p. 147). Baltimore, MD: Paul H. Brookes Publishing Co. Copyright 1991 by Paul H. Brookes Publishing Co., Inc. Adapted by permission.

ever, qualitatively, this conversation is very limited. That is, once a topic is introduced, little is done by either participant to expand or elaborate the topic. Over time, learners gradually become more sophisticated in maintaining conversations, adding new information and changing topics with the tact required to keep the interaction interesting to their speaking partner. In succeeding sections of this chapter, we explore more carefully the parameters of establishing interactive exchanges.

Summary.   Selecting the content for communication intervention has changed significantly over the years. It is clear that one cannot assume that a vocabulary item acquired to express one communicative function will necessarily be used to express others. Further, we have learned that identifying initial communicative functions to teach proceeds most smoothly when the interventionist targets communicative outcomes that are already of importance to the learner. We have also learned that a careful consideration of the specificity of early vocabulary can be used to the interventionist's advantage in addressing the discriminability of early vocabulary.

In addition, we have learned that vocabulary and communicative functions must carefully match those communicative opportunities and obligations imposed by the range of environments in which the learner is apt to operate. When the match is good, the interventionist ensures that the natural environment will provide adequate "natural maintaining contingencies." This, in turn, eases the demands for generalization placed on the learner, which is needed if he or she is to derive benefit from communication intervention. Having established a basis for identifying an initial productive communicative repertoire, we can begin to focus attention on identifying the program content important in developing a program to teach the learner to understand the communication of others.

Identifying a Repertoire of Communication Understanding

Learning to understand the communication produced by others can be seen as an amazingly complex task when one considers that to be efficient, a learner must: (1) attend to incoming speech, (2) remember it while it is being processed (inasmuch as there is no permanent product produced), (3) compare the speech to his or her prior knowledge, (4) consider any other verbal or contextual information that preceded the utterance, and (5) formulate a response.

Traditionally, interventionists have sought to isolate verbal utterances from any potential contextual information that may typically accompany such utterances addressed to the learner. This is done so that the learner may more readily attend to the verbal component of the behavior of a communicative partner. This logic has resulted in the observation that by about 12 months of age, most children understand the names of familiar objects or persons around them (Miller, Chapman, Branston, & Reichle, 1980). Within the next several months, they begin to understand the names of common actions that are given to them as instructions (i.e., *stand, run, sing, dance, kiss*). Huttenlocker (1974) has reported that it is at about 12 months of age that the child's use of directed gaze and pointing becomes sufficiently reliable to be used as an indication that a learner has understood the names of objects that are being described by his or her communicative partner.

Although many learners with severe disabilities demonstrate little propensity to reach and point, or to use directed gaze to attend to the spoken words of others, they may act differentially to a host of contextual cues that the environment provides. Consequently, any discussion of communication understanding in very young persons or in persons who have developmental disabilities must address the question of how to scrutinize both the learner's understanding of spoken words and his or her understanding of situational or contextual cues provided by the ecology of the learner's natural environment.

Describing Contexts Used to "Understand" Situations.   Recently, we encountered an adolescent with multiple disabilities. We initiated a "give me five" routine and were fully prepared to prompt a response. Instead, the learner placed his hand independently in the "receiving" position. In this instance, it was clear that extensive effort over time was spent teaching this learner's reaction to the "give me five" social routine. In the context of this game, we were curious as to exactly what portion of our actions served as the cue for him to identify this social game. The next morning, when the learner was approached, the utterance "Hey, give me five" was directed to him without a raised hand and without the speaker's posturing that ordinarily accompanies this game. The learner stared without participating. Over the next few days, when we saw the learner in a variety of settings, our actions and verbal behavior addressed to him were varied. After several days, it become apparent that raising a hand resulted in the learner's response and that any other verbal or gestural antecedents did not occasion the same response.

Most individuals participate in a series of "routines" that occur during the course of a day. Some of these routines occur many times a day (e.g., washing one's hands), whereas others may occur somewhat less often (e.g., doing the laundry). In everyday routines, there are a variety of cues available to assist us in our performance. Some of these cues consist of gestures (e.g., pointing to a door to cue an individual to leave), and others are verbal (e.g., telling a child to get a coat so that he or she can go outside). Still other cues involve the setting in which an event occurs or the time of day when it occurs.

Once a learner is participating actively in a predictable routine, adults appear to perform in a role that supports the child's behavior in that routine by providing opportunities for expansion of the routine. For example, Ninio and Bruner (1978) reported that among children who were familiar with the routine of looking at a book with their mothers, the mother repeated a sequence of four very predictable interactional devices. First, the mother would request the child's attention ("Look!"). Next, she produced an object label. If the child produced any discrete voluntary behavior, it was followed by maternal positive feedback ("Yes"). Children between the ages of 10 months and 19 months became increasingly more participative in this game. At 8 months of age, children produced a response consisting of gesture, vocalization, smile, eye contact, or search for an object in about half of the instances. By a year and a half of age, children responded during 100 percent of

the opportunities by providing the information requested and, in many instances, instigating the book-reading routine.

Very early in their development, children acquire the ability to anticipate what is about to happen in certain familiar situations. For example, adults frequently initiate a variety of games such as "peekaboo" and "gotcha" with infants. In the latter, the adult (1) approaches the child, (2) raises arms over head, (3) wiggles fingers, (4) swoops down over the child, tickling him or her, and (5) says, "Gotcha!" After numerous opportunities to participate in this game, the child comes to anticipate the routine. It is quite common to observe 5-month-olds begin wiggling and laughing upon receiving the first two cues in this game. We know that as early as 3 to 4 months, children begin to understand some situations. Anticipatory responses provide an important basis for making judgments about what portions of environmental routines the learner actually understands. If the adult's motor and verbal components of a given social routine have been paired consistently, it is reasonable to speculate that the learner might continue to participate given only a portion of the motor or verbal components. By rearranging some familiar routines, it should be possible to examine the learner's initial capability to understand spoken language addressed to him or her. A simple sequential set of strategies can be implemented in an effort to differentiate situational understanding from language understanding.

Viewing Comprehension as a Continuum.   If a learner could not comprehend spoken language, that person would find him- or herself overrelying on inconsistently available contextual information to understand others' utterances.

The approach we have advocated involves attempting to establish whether there are any situations in which aspects of a natural event are used by a learner to make decisions about how to act or what to do. If such situations are identified, the interventionist has an opportunity to develop instruction in which relevant verbal utterances are paired with nonverbal cues that may already have value to the learner. As a history of instruction develops, the interventionist can separate the verbal cue from those contextual cues that have been used in the past. Although often the learner will not need to use this skill in the absence of other redundant environmental cues, it will be helpful to know that should it become necessary to rely only on the spoken language of others to receive information, he or she can do so.

Thus far, we have suggested that it is important for learners to understand both the contextual cues that surround communicative events and the verbal behavior marking those events. Communication interventionists often make the assumption that learners can already use contextual information in an effort to "understand situations" at the point they begin participating in programs for learning to understand language. To the contrary, many very young learners and individuals with moderate and severe developmental disabilities fail to benefit from the rich context that often surrounds communicative events. We believe that it is desirable to teach learners to take advantage of contextual cues and subsequently separate them from the speech portion of the communicative event, as previously described.

Corresponding Early Language Comprehension and Production

From the standpoint of the interventionist, an important area of concern is the relationship between early language comprehension and production. If an interventionist teaches a learner to comprehend a given vocabulary item, can he or she assume that the learner will be able to produce it, and vice versa?

Benedict (1979) examined the development of comprehension and production in eight children from the time that they were 9 to 10 months of age until shortly after their second birthday. Data describing the first 50 words comprehended and produced were collected in diary entries made by the children's parents. Comprehension was defined as

a child's "understanding" a word presented in at least two different contexts (e.g., touching a ball when told to "get the ball" and "throw the ball.") Spontaneous production of words constituted the criteria for production. Benedict's (1979) results (as well as those of numerous other investigators) indicate that language comprehension develops earlier and faster than language production. These findings are often interpreted as evidence that comprehension is a necessary prerequisite to productive speech. However, some empirical evidence suggests that there may be a degree of independence between emerging receptive and productive repertoires for some learners (Guess & Baer, 1973; Lee, 1981; Siegel & Vogt, 1984).

Unfortunately, the relationship between the emerging repertoire of comprehension and production skills in learners with developmental disabilities is not completely understood. In the absence of more definitive empirical evidence regarding this topic, the sequencing of language intervention objectives remains somewhat of an arbitrary decision for the language interventionist.

CRITICAL ISSUES

Identifying Instructional Strategies to Teach a Beginning Repertoire of Communication Production

Early systematic attempts at teaching beginning communication skills focused on implementing didactic intervention programs that were conducted in a highly controlled environment. In most instances, the learner interacted with the same interventionist, at the same time each day, and in the same location. Over the course of the 1960s and 1970s, an impressive technology of fine-tuned operant procedures were identified. This work had a tremendous impact on the education community. Suddenly, individuals for whom no hope of establishing a communication repertoire had been held were acquiring communicative behavior. Unfortunately, the enthusiasm generated by the initial successes of the early intervention studies was diminished as empirical work began to identify significant areas of deficiency in the early intervention procedures. Learners with moderate and severe disabilities were reported to have tremendous difficulties maintaining and generalizing their newly established communicative repertoires (Warren & Rogers-Warren, 1983). Stokes and Baer (1977) reported that maintenance and generalization difficulties were not unique to communication intervention, but, in general, proliferated the intervention literature. They identified a number of instructional modifications that could remedy many of the challenges in maintenance and generalization encountered by interventionists serving individuals with severe disabilities.

Meeting the conditions of instruction proposed by Stokes and Baer (1977) is, for the most part, addressed when intervention occurs in the range contexts in which the behaviors being taught are expected to be used. This logic would suggest, then, that in defining intervention targets, care should be taken to sample the entire range of situations in which the interventionist wishes the target behavior to be emitted.

In the realm of establishing generalizable repertoires of initial communicative behavior, Stokes and Baer (1977) suggested that many intervention programs had failed to "teach sufficient exemplars," "train loosely," and "use common training stimuli." Table 9.4 delineates each of these strategies. When taken as an implicit technology, these strategies suggest that a target behavior should be taught under a variety of stimulus conditions (i.e., materials, settings, and people). In addition, materials that are used as part of the cues for a response should be those that would be naturally available. Finally, the conditions to which the learner should *not* constantly attend should be varied. For example, if the goal is for the individual to request independently, verbal prompts such as, "What do you want?" must not be systematically paired with available items/events. If "What do you want?" is used as a verbal prompt, it must be faded if independent requesting is to be established.

TABLE 9.4 Strategies that Promote Generalization

STRATEGY	DESCRIPTION
Train sufficient ememplars	Teach the same behaviors under a variety of conditions (e.g., vary the materials, settings, people).
Use contingencies that are naturally maintained	Teach in conditions that include naturally available cues and consequences so that the behavior comes under control of natural conditions (e.g., teach during naturally occuring daily routines).
Train loosely	Systematically vary the conditions of instruction—specifically the stimuli (e.g., questions, cues, prompts) to prevent the development of narrow stimulus control.
Choose common stimuli	Use stimuli (e.g., materials, people) that are naturally available or present in the array of conditions in which performance is desired.

From Reichle, J., York, J. & Sigafoos, J. (1991). *Implementing augmentative and alternative communication: Strategies for learners with severe disabilities* (p. 164). Baltimore, MD: Paul H. Brookes Publishing Co. Copyright 1991 by Paul H. Brookes Publishing Co., Inc. Adapted by permission.

There seems to be agreement that the general strategies derived by Stokes and Baer (1977) are easiest to address when communication intervention occurs in the milieu of the natural environment. Consequently, in an increasing proportion of intervention programs designed to teach a beginning communicative repertoire, there is a growing shift toward the use of intervention procedures that can be implemented in the context of natural communicative interactions.

In addition to the parameters of maintenance and generalization outlined by Stokes and Baer (1977), there is evidence that active involvement in frequent social interactions is critical to the acquisition of communicative behavior (MacDonald, 1989; McLean & Snyder-McLean, 1978). Tannock and Girolametto (1992) have summarized that styles of interaction that are "congruent and responsive to the child's current focus of attention and interests" are most helpful to the intervention process. There is some evidence demonstrating that persons who have language delays are less apt to engage actively in communicative interactions. When they do interact, it is more often in the role of responder than initiator (Tannock, 1988). Interestingly, adults interacting with persons who have communicative deficits tend to be less responsive than they are to individuals with no communicative disabilities. They also appear to attempt to exert greater control over the conversation (Mahoney & Powell, 1988; Tannock, 1988).

The past 15 years have spawned significant efforts focusing on the development of collections of intervention strategies that can be implemented in the context of natural interactions. These strategies have great intuitive appeal, inasmuch as they are all based on classes of behavior exhibited by individuals who competently engage in desirable communicative interactions. The discussion that follows focuses on several intervention strategies that have been empirically demonstrated to result in the successful establishment of social communicative repertoires.

Incidental Teaching.   Hart and Risley (1978) originally described the critical components of in-cidental teaching techniques. In incidental teaching, the learner actually initiates the teaching opportunity. For example, a learner might initiate a requesting episode by reaching for a snack item that is just out of his or her reach. Seeing this event, the teacher would focus his or her full attention on the child ("creating joint focus of attention on the child's chosen topic"). If the child does not elaborate (in this instance, produce a sign approximation, vocal approximation, or graphic mode approximation), the teacher might ask for elaboration. Requesting elaboration could be accomplished through use of a variety of response prompts. For example, the teacher might say, "What do you want?" Gesturally, the teacher might simply cup her hand to her ear (as if to communicate, "I don't hear anything"). Selection of each of the preceding prompts would occur because the teacher had some evidence that the child had the desired response in his repertoire but on this particular occasion simply failed to produce it. If, on the other hand, the teacher had no evidence that the desired response was already part of the learner's repertoire, she would provide an imitative model of the appropriate elaboration. Finally, the teacher would produce positive feedback to the learner once an approximation occurred.

The logic supporting the use of incidental teaching is compelling. If the learner initiates a teaching episode, there is a far greater possibility that the learner is more highly motivated to attend to the teacher. In fact, there appears to be a base of empirical data describing the emergence of conversational skills to support this point (see Folger & Chapman, 1978). Table 9.5 summarizes an incidental teaching procedure.

Kaiser, Yoder, and Keetz (1991) provided an extensive review of incidental teaching and mand-model intervention procedures. These authors concluded that there is a substantial data base supporting the viability of these procedures in increasing the frequency of infrequently used behavior. There is also support for using these procedures to establish chains of more sophisticated communicative forms (i.e., combinations of individual semantic intents). However, Kaiser and

TABLE 9.5   Examples of Environmentally Nonintrusive Communication Intervention Strategies

OPTION	CHARACTERISTICS	CONSIDERATIONS FOR USE
Incidental teaching	Uses learner-initiated teaching opportunities.	Learners must currently initiate approximations of target behavior. Effective reinforcers must be available in the natural environment.
Mand-model	Uses interventionist initiated teaching opportunities.	Learners need not initiate. Most effective when learners have shown propensity to act on verbal prompts. Mands for communicative behavior may reduce spontaneity.
Time-delay	Interventionist delays the delivery of the controlling mand-mode prompt. Interventionist makes use of naturally arising opportunities.	Learner must be consistently responding to an instructional prompt (e.g., to a mand or model). Learner has shown little or no propensity to initiate approximations of target behavior.

From Reichle, J., York, J. & Sigafoos, J. (1991). *Implementing augmentative and alternative communication: Strategies for learners with severe disabilities* (p. 166). Baltimore, MD: Paul H. Brookes Publishing Co. Copyright 1991 by Paul H. Brookes Publishing Co., Inc. Adapted by permission.

colleagues (1991) also suggest that the empirical support for the generalizability of skills taught is limited (see Kaiser et al., 1991, for a detailed discussion).

A significant portion of the initial incidental teaching literature has focused on learners with mild to moderate developmental disabilities. Unfortunately, many individuals with more severe deficits produce relatively few initiated communicative attempts. Inasmuch as a model of incidental teaching requires learner initiations, it is most easily implemented with learners who have more frequent vocal output. For these learners, the exclusive use of an incidental teaching procedure may fail to result in the generation of a sufficient number of intervention opportunities to establish new communicative behavior. If this is the case, slightly more intrusive intervention alternatives may be warranted.

Mand-Modeling.   A mand-model instructional strategy differs from incidental teaching procedures in that the teacher initiates a teaching opportunity. For example, the teacher may observe a learner to look longingly at a bowl of candy. The teacher may then approach the learner and say, "Tell me what you'd like." If the learner approximates the spoken word "candy," the interventionist must decide whether the utterance was qualitatively sufficient. If so, the candy can be delivered. If, on the other hand, the learner failed to respond to the interventionist's query, a model "candy" would be produced by the interventionist. Contingent on an approximation, candy would be delivered. As is often the case in an incidental teaching procedure, the interventionist presumes that the learner is capable of imitating a communicative partner's spoken utterance.

Once mand-model procedures are efficient in establishing a beginning communicative repertoire, the interventionist must take care to ensure that the learner does not become overdependent on the interventionist's spoken utterances. Consequently, the interventionist must take care to fade the extensive use of verbal prompts in a mand-model instructional strategy. To systematically move the learner from participation in a mand-model instructional procedure to successful participation in an incidental teaching procedure, a prompt fading strategy termed "time-delay" (Halle, 1982; Hart, 1985) has been used.

In a time-delay prompt fading strategy, the interventionist determines a controlling instructional prompt. For example, in a successful mand-model intervention procedure, a verbal direction should predictably result in the emission of an approximation of the target behavior. In implementing a time-delay procedure, initially, the interventionist would pair the delivery of the mand with the contextual features present in the environment where the behavior is to be emitted. Once a substantial number of pairing opportunities had been implemented, the interventionist would delay the delivery of the mand, providing an opportunity for the natural conditions present in the environment to begin to exert instructional control over the learner's response.

The procedures originally delineated by Hart and Risley (1968, 1975) and Hart (1985) were focused primarily on establishing speech. More recently, Tannock and Girolametto (1992) differentiated between several functions that environmentally based communication intervention procedures might address. They described one potential goal of environmentally based language instruction as being designed "to assist the child in inducing the relations between language content, form, and use" (p. 15). Other applications of environmentally based teaching procedures may have as their prime objective the

establishment of balanced turn taking between the learner and interventionist and may be less focused on establishing specific vocabulary or combinations of vocabulary. In such instances the interventionist may attend less to the form of the target behavior and more to the contingency and communicative intent of the learner's production. Simple turn-taking exchanges have been the focus of a number of environmentally based intervention efforts within recent years (Girolametto, 1988; MacDonald, 1989; Mahoney & Powell, 1988).

Identifying Strategies to Teach Simple Understanding in Social Routines

Traditionally, interventionists have attempted to teach learners to understand communication in the absence of the contextual cues that often accompany spoken language. This is an important consideration, particularly for those contextual cues that may not always be present to help the learner decipher a partner's spoken utterances.

Rather than developing intervention procedures that cannot be implemented in the natural environment because contextual cues cannot be controlled adequately, we believe that the natural environment should serve as the context for initial intervention. As the learner becomes increasingly competent in discriminating between utterances offered in natural contexts, the interventionist may gradually and systematically tighten stimulus control so that the learner eventually responds to a spoken message in isolation. In the paragraphs that follow, we offer an example of this naturalistic strategy that can be used to teach communication understanding. We have found this strategy to be particularly efficient with very young children who have not yet acquired sufficient motor competency to engage in the usual behaviors, such as pointing at or manipulating objects, often used to determine whether a learner has understood a spoken utterance.

1. *Identify social routines.* Most young children can be somewhat easily interested in a variety of social routines such as "peekaboo," "so big," "I'm gonna get you," "eensy-weensy spider," and so forth. All of these games have both vocal and motor components. Initially, a learner's participation in these games may be rather passive. However, a discerning interventionist is usually able to identify some beginning discrete, observable behavior. For example, when the interventionist approaches the child saying, "I'm gonna get you," and wiggles his fingers as he reaches for the child, the child may wiggle her body vigorously and laugh. In the initial phases of social interaction, it is important to identify each of several different games that elicit a uniquely different response from the learner.

2. *Anticipate components of social routine.* Once social routines have been selected that the learner appears to enjoy, the interventionist establishes a history of frequent implementation in a variety of settings. Over time, the interventionist hopes to observe that the learner begins to anticipate a portion of the routine. The interventionist may be able to facilitate this anticipation by systematically delaying the presentation of critical components of the routine. For example, if during "peekaboo" the interventionist leans forward and smiles, but refrains from putting his hand over his eye for several seconds, the learner will have an opportunity to anticipate the rest of the routine. If the learner does not anticipate, the entire routine is re-presented in its original form. In this phase of intervention, the teacher's role is to frequently present the routine and occasionally delay the presentation of critical cues to see whether the learner is beginning to anticipate components of the routine.

3. *Systematically separate the vocal from gestural components of the routine.* Because the interventionist's objective is to determine whether the spoken language of another person exerts instructional control over the learner's behavior, it is necessary to separate the spoken component from the rest of the social routine. For example, in the "I'm gonna get you" routine, the adult might approach the child at a time and location in which the

routine is not characteristically implemented. After ensuring that the learner is attending, the interventionist can produce the spoken component of the routine. Subsequently, the interventionist observes to see whether the learner produces the discrete behavior that has been defined as indicative of the learner's understanding the situation. If not, the interventionist can systematically implement a time-delay procedure. In this application, the interventionist presents the spoken stimulus just slightly before delivery of the gestural cues associated with the social routine. Throughout successful opportunities, the delay between the spoken word and the delivery of the gestural cues is increased. Eventually the gestural cues become unnecessary in occasioning the learner's participation in the social routine. Once the spoken utterance associated with a routine controls a learner response, steps can be taken to ascertain exactly which components of the spoken message act as salient cues.

4. *Systematically eliminate intonational cue characteristics from the actual words produced in the verbal component of the routine.* Language may be parsed into a number of different components. For example, language may be thought of as being composed of sounds and sound combinations (segmentals), as well as the pitch, loudness, and duration of voice used to carry those sounds (suprasegmentals). If speech were a song, we might think of segmentals as the lyrics and suprasegmentals as the melody to which the lyrics are applied. Meaning can be altered by changes in suprasegmentals (variations in pitch, stress, and duration of the sound components) or by changes in segmentals (sounds or sound combinations). For example, we know that before young children use words, they emit questions by producing a rising pitch inflection at the end of a spoken word. It appears that early on, suprasegmental features represent very salient stimuli to young learners.

Even though many of the gestural cues may have been eliminated from a social routine, it remains a distinct possibility that a learner relies on suprasegmental cues to respond appropriately when a verbal utterance is addressed to him or her. Of course, this is not necessarily undesirable, because it is quite possible that in the majority of situations in which a learner encounters a particular phrase, it is apt to be marked somewhat similarly in terms of suprasegmental characteristics. On the other hand, we also know that some changes in pitch, duration, and loudness alter or change the communicative intent of the speaker. It may be important to verify that the learner can actually understand certain words or phrases in the absence of a particular suprasegmental marking. To make this determination involves conducting the same type of probe opportunity that we have just described, taking great care to change the suprasegmental characteristics from those typically used. Reducing the learner's dependency on suprasegmental features can be accomplished by remembering to lessen, gradually, yet systematically, the exaggerated intonation of utterances that may typically be associated with common routines.

5. *Ensure that the learner refrains from responding to extraneous vocal or verbal cues.* Assuming that the learner has continued to respond in social routines even though gestures and suprasegmental cues have been diminished, it is important to ensure that the learner responds in the presence of the relevant remaining cues and refrains from responding in the presence of different spoken cues. On some occasions the interventionist may approach the learner and deliver a spoken word(s) other than those associated with the routine of interest. If the learner refrains from emitting the response that is uniquely attributable to the spoken word(s) that has been the focus of the targeted social routine, the interventionist has generated evidence that the learner may be beginning to discriminate spoken words. For example, every evening a learner removes the dishes from the dishwasher when told to "check the dishwasher." To assess the learner's understanding of language, we could ask the learner, some evening at about the same time, to "get the newspaper." If the learner truly understands the cue "check the dishwasher," he or she will refrain from checking the dishwasher and instead retrieve the newspaper. Once the learner is participating in a routine as a function of spoken cues delivered by others, the interventionist can attempt to establish that the learner can act discriminatively on each of two different vocal utterances (each of which is associated with a different action response emitted by the learner). Suppose, for example, that a preschooler had learned to respond consistently to the vocal utterance "I'm gonna get you" by beginning to squirm, laugh, and run away. Next, a second game such as "pattycake" could be identified. In this routine, the learner's response might be to raise his hands to make contact with the adult's in a "patting" motion. As in the establishment of the first routine with the learner, the interventionist would systematically pair a characteristic vocal utterance with the physical prompt that involved reaching for the learner's hand. Once this history was established, the interventionist would engage in a response prompt fading strategy. During the implementation of this strategy, the teacher's spoken word would always signal the beginning of the routine. Eventually, as a result of response prompt fading, the learner would come to participate in the "pattycake" game as a result of the interventionist's spoken word (this, of course, assumes that setting and other contextual variables are not controlling the learner's response).

Originally, the second routine might be established in contexts very different from those in which the initial routine was implemented. Over time, however, one would expect the learner to participate in either of the two game routines as a function of the unique spoken cues associated with each.

When contextual cues exert an influence on a learner's actions, it should be possible to develop intervention procedures to transfer cue value from nonvocal contextual features to vocal utterances associated with the activity (provided that the learner's auditory system is intact). The primary importance for doing so rests in the importance of teaching the learner to discriminate among incoming stimuli regardless of the context in which they occur.

Understanding Spoken Language

Learning to understand spoken language requires that the learner match language spoken by another to referent objects or events. The majority of early language intervention programs emphasize teaching learners to understand individual words in the presence of the objects and activities with which the words are associated. Unfortunately, many of the occasions that require learners to understand language involve situations where objects and events are not present. For example, assume that a learner is seated in the living room of his home. The learner's mother says, "Hey, go get yourself a cookie." Consider what skills are called into play in this situation. First, assuming that the learner has a limited repertoire of comprehended vocabulary, he must separate the critical part of the message, "get" and "cookie," from the rest of the message. In addition, the learner must be able to remember the instruction long enough to get to the referent object (cookie). The learner must also be able to match the targeted item (in this instance) with its storage location. These three skills are not trivial and go significantly beyond simply understanding the word "cookie" or the word "get." In the paragraphs that follow, each of the competencies addressed in the context of the example presented here are explored.

Locating the Important Part of an Utterance. We know that when adults interact with small children, they alter their speech and language in some very predictable ways. For example, they use shorter and more redundant utterances, allow greater pauses between sentences, and place increased stress on important words in the utterance, to name just a few. We also know that when nondisabled developing children tackle the problem of deciphering adult speech, they are most apt

to attend to words that occur near the end of an utterance or words that receive primary stress (Blaisdell & Jensen, 1968).

Few intervention programs have been structured to examine the value of teaching the learner to act on major carriers of meaning that may be embedded in a longer utterance. Keogh and Reichle (1985) suggested that some learners might benefit from a program designed initially to emphasize the critical word in a longer utterance. Throughout instructional opportunities, the loudness level of key words is reduced systematically until the learner can identify critical message-carrying words contained in a longer utterance, based on only natural stress and emphasis produced by the speaker. In a second application, the critical word of an instruction is placed at the end of a more lengthy utterance (e.g., "Please go get a *cookie*"). Throughout instructional opportunities, the critical portions of the instruction are placed in less prominent locations (e.g., "Could you *get* a *cookie* right now?"). Teaching learners strategies to identify critical components in the range of utterances they are apt to encounter in community environments is a significant area of scrutiny that continues to be addressed in a very limited fashion in communication intervention programs designed for individuals with severe disabilities.

Remembering an Utterance. Many learners, like most people, may hear a message directed at them but fail to remember it long enough to use the information it contains. This becomes a particularly important skill for persons with severe disabilities because often they do not have sufficient control over the pragmatic function of requesting a repeated message or a clarification. There are a variety of natural cues that can assist the learner in remembering verbal utterances produced by others. Doss and Reichle (1991) have discussed the use of picture reminder lists to supplement verbal directions delivered to a learner. In addition, we have made use of a delayed matching-to-sample procedure in teaching learners to remember spoken utterances produced by others. If the interventionist chooses not to rely on a graphic prompt, it may be helpful to teach learners to retain verbal information over increasingly longer intervals. Reichle (1990) reported use of the following procedure. During the early phase of intervention, an individual with severe developmental disabilities was taught to follow simple instructions that required him to retrieve supplies needed for work. Initially, the interventionist provided the instruction at a time when the learner was only a short distance from the item to be retrieved. In consecutive opportunities, the distance between the learner and the materials at the point of instruction increased systematically. Over time, the learner was taught to retain verbal instructions for increasingly greater distances. For example, a learner might first be asked to get a Coke when he is within a few feet of the refrigerator (although in a room other than the kitchen). Contingent on successful opportunities, the interventionist would increase the distance between the learner and the location of the target item or event that is the focus of the interventionist's verbal behavior.

CONCLUSION

Communication intervention has become increasingly more sophisticated over the past 20 years. Most intervention strategies aimed at establishing beginning repertoires of communicative behavior emphasize pragmatic aspects of communication. Interventionists of the 1990s are no longer content with teaching clients to produce requests and provide information. Instead, many interventionists are beginning to tackle the task of identifying instructional strategies that focus on teaching learners to initiate, maintain, and terminate conversational exchanges.

Perhaps the greatest advance that has permitted a more conversational approach to early communication intervention rests with a growing evidentiary base demonstrating that in many instances, milieu instructional procedures can be even more advantageous than the exclusive use of the structured didactic intervention strategies that were prevalent in the 1970s. Although there is increasing empirical support for more relaxed instructional strategies, there continues to be a critical need to demonstrate that these intervention strategies result in highly generalized emissions of newly established communicative behavior.

The area of communication comprehension, to a significant extent, continues to be driven by the study of semantics. That is, for the most part, early comprehension intervention targets continue to include names of objects, actions, and so on. Interestingly, there is a small but growing empirical base beginning to examine aspects of communication comprehension from a more pragmatic perspective. One example of this is the increasing emphasis on aspects of situational comprehension as described in this chapter. In addition, there is an increasingly greater body of literature beginning to address the role of a learner's ability to identify communicative breakdowns and repair them in his or her developing communicative competence.

In summary, communication intervention strategies of the 1990s are far more diverse than earlier strategies. The influence of pragmatics has dramatically altered not only the content of communication intervention programs but also the instructional strategies and contexts in which communicative behavior can be taught. As a result, current intervention strategies reflect an increasingly greater sensitivity to the issue of generalization.

REFERENCES

Benedict, H. (1979). Early lexical development: Comprehension and production. *Journal of Child Language, 6,* 183–200.

Blasdell, R., & Jensen, P. (1970). Stress and word position as determinants of imitation in first language learners. *Journal of Speech and Hearing Research, 13,* 193–202.

Bloom, L., & Lahey, M. (1978). *Language development*

and language disorders. New York: John Wiley & Sons.

Bricker, D., Dennison, L., & Bricker, W. (1975). *A language intervention program for developmentally young children.* I. MCCD Monograph series. Miami: Mailman Center for Child Development, University of Miami.

Cirrin, F., & Rowland, C. (1985). Communicative assessment of nonverbal youths with severe/profound mental retardation. *Mental Retardation, 23,* 52–62.

Dore, J. (1975). Holophrases, speech acts, and language universals. *Journal of Child Language, 2,* 21–40.

Doss, L. S., & Reichle, J. (1991). Using graphic aids to promote independent functioning. In J. Reichle, J. York, & J. Sigafoos (Eds.), *Implementing augmentative and alternative communication: Strategies for learners with severe disabilities* (pp. 275–288). Baltimore: Paul H. Brookes Publishing Co.

Durand, V. M. (1991). *Severe behavior problems.* New York: Guilford Press.

Egel, A. L. (1980). The effects of constant versus varied reinforcer presentation responding by autistic children. *Journal of Experimental Child Psychology, 30,* 455–463.

Egel, A. L. (1981). Reinforcer variation: Implications for motivating developmentally disabled children. *Journal of Applied Behavior Analysis, 14,* 345–350.

Folger, J., & Chapman, R. (1978). A pragmatic analysis of spontaneous imitations. *Journal of Child Language, 5,* 25–38.

Girolametto, L. (1988). Improving the social-conversational skills of developmentally delayed children: An intervention study. *Journal of Speech and Hearing Disorders, 53,* 156–167.

Glennen, S. L., & Calculator, S. N. (1985). Training functional communication board use: A pragmatic approach. *Augmentative and Alternative Communication, 1,* 134–142.

Guess, D., & Baer, D. (1973). An analysis of individual differences in generalization between receptive and productive language in retarded children. *Journal of Applied Behavior Analysis, 6,* 311–329.

Guess, D., Benson, H., & Siegel-Causey, E. (1985). Concepts and issues related to choice making and autonomy among persons with severe disabilities. *The Journal of The Association for Persons with Severe Handicaps, 10*(2), 79–86.

Guess, D., Sailor, W., & Baer, D. (1974). To teach language to retarded children. In R. L. Schiefelbusch &

L. Lloyd (Eds.), *Language perspectives: Acquisition, retardation and intervention.* Baltimore: University Park Press.

Hall, G., & Sundberg, M. L. (1987). Teaching mands by manipulating conditioned establishing operations. *Analysis of Verbal Behavior, 5,* 41–53.

Halle, J. (1982). Teaching functional language to the handicapped: An integrative model of natural environment teaching techniques. *The Journal of The Association for Persons with Severe Handicaps, 7,* 29–37.

Hart, B. (1985). Naturalistic language training techniques. In S. F. Warren & A. K. Rogers-Warren (Eds.), *Teaching functional language* (pp. 63–88). Austin, TX: PRO-ED.

Hart, B., & Risley, T. R. (1968). Establishing use of descriptive adjectives in the spontaneous speech of disadvantaged preschool children. *Journal of Applied Behavior Analysis, 1,* 109–120.

Hart, B., & Risley, T. R. (1975). Incidental teaching of language in the preschool. *Journal of Applied Behavior Analysis, 8,* 411–420.

Huttenlocher, J. (1974). The origins of language comprehension. In R. L. Solso (Ed.), *Theories in Cognitive Psychology: The Loyola Symposium.* Hillsdale, NJ: Lawrence Erlbaum Associates.

Kaiser, A., Yoder, P., & Keetz, A. (1991). The efficacy of milieu teaching. Unpublished manuscript. Vanderbilt University, Nashville, TN.

Kent, L. (1974). *Language acquisition program for the retarded or multiply impaired.* Champaign, IL: Research Press.

Lamarre, J., & Holland, J. G. (1985). The functional independence of mands and tacts. *Journal of the Experimental Analysis of Behavior, 43,* 5–19.

Lee, V. L. (1981). Prepositional phrases spoken and heard. *Journal of the Experimental Analysis of Behavior, 35,* 227–242.

MacDonald, J. (1989). *Becoming partners with children.* San Antonio, TX: Special Press, Inc.

Mahoney, G., & Powell, A. (1988). Modifying parent-child interactions enhancing the development of handicapped children. *Journal of Special Education, 22*(1), 82–96.

McCook, B., Cipani, E., Madigan, K., & LaCampagne, J. (1988). Developing requesting behavior: Acquisition, fluency, and generality. *Mental Retardation, 26,* 137–143.

McLean, J., & Snyder-McLean, L. (1978). *Transac-

tional approach to early language training. Columbus, OH: Charles E. Merrill.

McLean, J., & Snyder-McLean, L. (1988). Application of pragmatics to severely mentally retarded children and youth. In R. Schiefelbusch & L. L. Lloyd (Eds.), *Language perspectives: Acquisition, retardation and intervention* (pp. 255–288). Austin, TX: PRO-ED.

Miller, J., Chapman, R., Branston, M., & Reichle, J. (1980). Communicative assessment in twelve (12) to twenty-four (24) months: A reliable method. *Journal of Speech and Hearing Research, 32,* 284–311.

Reichle, J. (1990). Examining subtle generalization patterns within a pragmatic intent. Unpublished manuscript, University of Minnesota, Minneapolis.

Reichle, J. (1991). Developing communicative exchanges. In J. Reichle, J. York, & J. Sigafoos (Eds.), *Implementing augmentative and alternative communication: Strategies for learners with severe disabilities* (pp. 133–156). Baltimore: Paul H. Brookes Publishing Co.

Reichle, J., & Yoder, D. E. (1985). Communication board use in severely handicapped learners. *Language, Speech and Hearing Services in Schools, 16,* 146–157.

Romski, M. A., Sevcik, R. A., & Pate, J. L. (1988). Establishment of symbolic communication in persons with severe mental retardation. *Journal of Speech and Hearing Disorders, 53,* 94–107.

Siegel, G., & Vogt, M. (1984). Pluralization instruction in comprehension and production. *Journal of Speech and Hearing Disorders, 49,* 128–135.

Sigafoos, J., Doss, S., & Reichle, J. (1989). Developing mand and tact repertoires in persons with severe developmental disabilities using graphic symbols. *Research in Developmental Disabilities, 10,* 183–200.

Sigafoos, J., Reichle, J., Doss, S., Hall, K., & Pettitt, L. (1990). "Spontaneous" transfer of stimulus control from tact to mand contingencies. *Research in Developmental Disabilities, 11,* 165–176.

Stokes, T., & Baer, D. (1977). An implicit technology of generalization. *Journal of Applied Behavior Analysis, 10,* 349–367.

Tannock, R. (1988). Mothers' directiveness in their interactions with their children with and without Down syndrome. *American Journal of Mental Retardation, 93,* 154–165.

Tannock, R., Girolametto, L., & Siegel, L. (1990a). Are the social-communicative and linguistic skills of developmentally delayed children enhanced by a conversational model of language intervention? *Proceedings of the Conference on Treatment Efficacy.* Rockville, MD: American Speech-Language-Hearing Foundation.

Tannock, R., Girolametto, L., & Siegel, L. (1990b). The interactive model of language intervention with developmentally delayed children: An evaluation study. Manuscript submitted for publication.

Warren S., & Rogers-Warren, A. (1983). A longitudinal analysis of language generalization among adolescents with severely handicapping conditions. *Journal of The Association for Persons with Severe Handicaps, 8,* 18–31.

Wetherby, A. M., & Prizant, B. M. (1989). The expression of communicative intent: Assessment guidelines. *Seminars in Speech and Language, 10,* 77–90.

CHAPTER 10

AUGMENTATIVE AND ALTERNATIVE COMMUNICATION

LORI GOETZ
PAM HUNT
San Francisco State University and The California Research Institute

Augmentative and alternative communication (AAC) systems play a crucial role in enabling and facilitating effective communication in students with severe disabilities. AAC systems provide an alternative for individuals who have no speech or, through augmentation, support and expand the communicative efficiency of persons who have some speech. The development of an effective AAC system is an essential element of every student's participation throughout all curriculum domains. Changes in fundamental assumptions about the language-learning process and the rapid development of nonspeech communication aids (Mirenda & Iacono, 1990; Musselwhite & St. Louis, 1988) have led to three premises that underlie the selection, development, and use of an AAC system for any individual student.

THREE PREMISES

All persons communicate. Although the means to communicate and convey messages may be highly idiosyncratic, ranging from inappropriate and self-abusive behaviors, to communicative signals such as facial expression, to a breath-activated computerized scanning system, all human beings express preferences and make choices (Donnellan, Mirenda,

Mesaros, & Fassbender, 1984; Siegel-Causey & Guess, 1989).

All communication is multimodal. Everyone uses multiple means to communicate effectively and get a message across—body language, gestures, facial expressions, and proximity between speaker and listener are examples of communicative means used by nearly all speakers. A single AAC aid or technique will rarely be sufficient to meet all of the communication needs of an individual student (Vanderheiden & Lloyd, 1986).

All communication requires partners. Effective communication requires a listener. Although communication curricula for students with severe disabilities have traditionally focused on increasing the communication skill levels of these students, recent evidence suggests that a partner's role may be equally critical in accomplishing effective communication (Hunt, Atwell, & Goetz, 1991). The purpose of communication is to affect others; if this purpose is not met, communication has failed.

GOALS

These premises imply that every student in the classroom should have an effective communica-

Preparation of this chapter was supported in part by the U.S. Department of Education, OSERS, Grant #G008730083 and Grant #H029B80095.
Pat Mirenda's inspiration and leadership in AAC development is gratefully acknowledged.

tion method, whether through conventional speech and language or through an augmentative or alternative communication system. An effective communication system enables each student to experience control, express preferences, interact socially, and make choices. Indeed, the crucial role of communicative competence in both present and future environments, and the learning time that may be needed for a student to become fluent in the use of an augmentative or alternative system, really means that each student in the classroom should have a "today" system, which recognizes and is responsive to the way or ways in which the student currently communicates a message, and should be *preparing* for a "tomorrow" system, which will enable even greater communicative efficiency and effectiveness in the future.

CHAPTER OVERVIEW

Accomplishing these goals for each student requires both knowledge of state-of-the-art resources in AAC and the use of comprehensive assessment and teaching strategies. This chapter includes a discussion of assessment strategies for selection of an AAC system and a review of major AAC systems and resources. Considerations in matching AAC systems to individual users are discussed as well as the role of partners in facilitating effective communication. The chapter then presents two different case examples of the development and use of AAC systems. Finally, discussion about the role of the transdisciplinary team, and the emergence of a new role, that of AAC Specialist, concludes the chapter.

ASSESSMENT PROCESS

All students, even the most physically and cognitively disabled, can learn to communicate when they are provided with a reason to express themselves, a communication system that matches their physical, sensory, and cognitive abilities, and daily routines that promote and support communicative interactions.

There are no prerequisite behaviors that the student must master before he or she can be taught beginning communication skills (Falvey, 1986; Mirenda & Iacono, 1990). Cognitive processes, such as attending to things and people and awareness of contingent relationships between actions and outcomes, are elements of any communicative exchange; however, the student can learn these skills in association with the acquisition of beginning communicative behaviors. For example, a student who is taught to point to objects she wants and then gaze at the communication partner to make a request has learned, at the same time, the contingent relationship between the communicative gesture and gaze and receipt of the item requested; that is, she has developed an awareness that her behavior can produce a specific effect on a communication partner. Cognitive, sensory, and motor skills that are elements of communicative interactions will be learned as the student is taught the communicative behaviors in which they are imbedded. Instruction of component skills (such as pointing or orienting oneself to face a speaker), therefore, happens within, rather than before, instruction of functional communicative responses.

Goals

Assessment of the student's current communicative behaviors, as well as associated cognitive, sensory, motor, and social skills, provides the basis upon which the communication training program is designed. Assessment information guides not only the selection of an appropriate AAC system, but also the identification of communicative behaviors that produce highly motivating outcomes for the student and activities that promote and support attempts by the student to relay a message. Assessments are conducted throughout the activities of the school day in a variety of school and community settings in order to identify situational events that promote communication and to evaluate the extent to which communicative behaviors generalize to settings, people, and events outside classroom settings. A student's communication program is built on the following assessment goals (Mirenda & Icono, 1990; Yorkston & Karlan, 1986).

- Determining whether a student is a candidate for an augmentative or alternative communication system
- Determining how the student will access the system (i.e., what response will "run" the system)
- Identifying the type of nonsymbolic or symbolic communication system that will initially meet the needs and abilities of the student
- Selecting the messages that will initially be taught and, if a symbolic system is being designed, determining how those messages will be organized on the display (i.e., the communication board or book, or the electronic communication system)
- Identifying the daily routines that provide motivating contexts for instruction

Areas and Techniques

The information required to accomplish the program development goals is obtained through assessments of the student's capabilities in a variety of communication-related areas, including the student's current level of communicative competence, cognitive abilities, and sensory and motor functioning. Capability assessments require an assessment team approach with participants representing several disciplines (Yorkston & Karlan, 1986; Musselwhite & St. Louis, 1988). Team members may include the special education teacher, parents, a communication specialist, and physical and occupational therapists. Each member shares information from his or her area of expertise to provide an integrated assessment and intervention plan.

Key assessment questions in each of the major communication-related areas, as well as assessment strategies to obtain answers to those questions, are described in the following paragraphs.

Communicative Competence

Assessment of communicative competence involves an examination not only of the student's communicative behaviors and skills, but also the degree to which his or her abilities match the communicative requirements for full social participation in daily routines. Assessment focuses on the student's use of verbal and nonverbal behaviors to accomplish communicative goals within those activities (Schuler & Goetz, 1981). The orientation is a pragmatic one (see Dore, 1974, for a discussion of communication pragmatics); that is, emphasis is placed on what a child can *do* with language and/or facial expression, gestures, vocalizations, and so on, rather than on the correctness, length, or sophistication of language output. For this purpose, more traditional measures of language structure (i.e., mean length, articulatory proficiency, and grammatical complexity of utterances) need to be supplemented with information on how the student manages to request, protest, comment, and converse (Schuler & Goetz, 1981).

Assessing Nonverbal Behaviors.   Nonverbal behaviors can be analyzed to determine the primary communicative functions (i.e., requests, protests, social comments, and turn taking) expressed through those behaviors, as well as the specific messages relayed (e.g., "I want to go outside," expressed through gesture toward the door and eye gaze at the teacher). Examples of nonverbal communicative behaviors, communicative functions, and specific messages expressed by those behaviors are presented in Table 10.1.

Identification of the message content of nonverbal behaviors provides a picture of the communication needs of the student and, therefore, leads directly to the first messages that the student will be taught to express with a communication system that provides the "next step" in greater communicative effectiveness and efficiency.

Nonverbal behaviors can be assessed through *observation* of the student throughout the activities of the school day (Donnellan et al., 1984; Schuler & Goetz, 1981; Mills & Higgins, 1983). The questions are asked, "What behaviors function to get the child something? What behaviors does the child use to request things and attention, to protest activities or events, and to comment about things, people, or feelings? What are the specific messages expressed?"

TABLE 10.1   Examples of Nonverbal Communicative Behaviors, Communicative Functions, and Specific Messages Expressed

NONVERBAL COMMUNICATIVE BEHAVIORS	COMMUNICATIVE FUNCTIONS	SPECIFIC MESSAGES
Gestures	Requests for:	"I want a hug" (through
Gaze	Attention	gestures, vocalizations,
Vocalizations	Objects	and facial expression).
Facial expression	Events	"I don't like this"
Body movement	Interaction	(through facial expression,
Physical manipulation	Assistance	crying, and physical
Touching	Information	manipulation [throwing]).
Crying	Refusal/protest	"I want a cookie"
Tantrums	Declarations/comments	(through gaze and
Aggression		gesture).

Observations may be supplemented by *experimental manipulation* of outcomes and setting events to "provoke" nonverbal communication (Schuler & Goetz, 1981; Mills & Higgins, 1983). For example, anticipated outcomes can be withheld, routines can be interrupted, or problem-solving situations can be set up. The child may be motivated to use nonverbal behaviors to communicate a request for items or assistance that will remove barriers to desired items or events.

Finally, valuable information may be gained from *interviews* (Schuler, Peck, Willard, Theimer, 1989; Schuler & Goetz, 1981; Grabowski & Shane, 1986) with parents, teachers, caregivers, and others through specific questions such as, "How does your child manage to get your attention? How does he request food or help?" and so on.

The choice of a beginning AAC system for a child who is nonverbal will be guided by the analysis of his or her nonverbal communicative behaviors. For the child who seldom demonstrates the use of behaviors for the purpose of communicating a particular message to another person, initial instruction will be directed toward increasing his or her nonverbal communicative repertoire (see

Siegel-Causey & Guess, 1989, for a description of strategies to enhance the use of nonsymbolic communicative behaviors). For the child who demonstrates a diverse behavioral repertoire, expressing a variety of communicative functions and messages through a number of "conventional" gestures (e.g., pointing, waving, taking a partner by the hand to the object desired), program goals would likely include the introduction of a *symbol system* (e.g., objects, pictures, or iconic signs) to expand the effectiveness of the existing system (Rowland & Stremel-Campbell, 1987).

The nonsymbolic behaviors that students use to communicate will continue to play an important role as a communication means even after symbols (e.g., words, signs, and pictures) are introduced into the AAC system. It is likely that they will continue to develop in amount and complexity and will serve as an adjunct to symbolic communication (Wilcox, 1989).

Assessing Verbal Behaviors.   An approach to the assessment of verbal behaviors that provides a pragmatic extension of more conventional language assessments (see Orelove & Sobsey, 1987, for a discussion of the limited usefulness of standardized assessments for children with severe disabilities) examines the ways in which the child uses speech in a social context. Language samples taken within daily routines can provide valuable information on the level of speech and language that the child uses to achieve communicative goals.

One assessment approach, developed by Stremel-Campbell, Johnson-Dorn, and Guide (1984), uses 10-minute samples of communicative interactions that occur within everyday routines at school. For each communicative act (nonverbal as well as verbal) by the targeted student, recordings are made of the communicative function (e.g., request, comment, or question) of the exchange as well as the specific messages expressed. If a symbolic system was used (i.e., pictorial, sign, or speech), the content of the utterance is recorded. Finally, the role of the student, as initiator or responder within the exchange, is recorded. Language samples analyzed in this way provide a wealth of information that can be directly related to the development of the student's communication program. The following are examples of program objectives that may be developed from such assessment information.

- Instructional procedure objectives: for example, increasing the opportunities to communicate within the routine, the reasons to communicate, and the peers with whom to communicate
- Augmentative communication objectives: for example, increasing the use of natural gestures to convey a variety of messages
- Speech objectives: for example, increasing vocabulary and syntactic complexity of speech responses
- Role objectives: for example, increasing initiation of both speech and nonverbal communicative behaviors

Cognitive Abilities

Assessments of the student's cognitive capabilities are used as aids in determining the design of the AAC system, including the semantic content of the messages taught (i.e., how complex or abstract), the symbol system selected, and the number of symbols presented at one time on the display. *Cognitive assessments are not performed to determine readiness* (Falvey, 1986; Miranda & Iacono, 1990).

Examples of the assessment of communication-related cognitive abilities are presented in the paragraphs. Each ability area can be evaluated with the observation and experimental manipulation assessment methods discussed earlier.

Object Permanence.   Perception of object permanence (Piaget, 1953), or the awareness that an object still exists when it is not in sight, is a skill that has implications for the design of an AAC system (Musselwhite & St. Louis, 1988): for example, can the system include a multipage display that would keep hidden all symbols except those on the opened page? Can a communication book be carried in the student's pocket and, therefore, out of sight? Can the student request items, people, or events not in view?

Robinson and Robinson (1983) described a series of three object-permanence assessment tasks, each one increasing in complexity:

1. Can the student visually follow an object to a place where it is partially hidden, and retrieve it (if physically able to do so)?
2. Can the student observe an object being completely hidden from view and then retrieve it?
3. Can the student search for and recover an object when its location is unknown?

Like other communication-related cognitive skills, object permanence can be taught in association with the communicative responses in which they are imbedded.

Contingency Awareness.   Awareness of the contingent relationship between actions and outcomes (Watson, 1966) is an integral aspect of all intentional communicative responses. Contingency awareness can be assessed by observing whether the student uses behaviors as a tool to achieve specific outcomes: for example, does he or she flip the light switch or depress the "on" button on a radio to turn them on, turn on the faucet for water, or turn the lever on a jack-in-the-box to make the clown appear? Each of these actions would demonstrate an awareness of contingent relationships. For students who are physically disabled, who may not have the motor capabilities to manipulate items, contingency awareness may be assessed through an analysis of their nonverbal behaviors for demonstration of communicative intent.

For the student who does not demonstrate through communicative and other behaviors an awareness of the relationship between his or her actions and their effect on the environment, a simple, nonsymbolic communicative response (e.g., a gesture, a generic request card, or a signal for attention) will be selected for initial training. The environment is arranged to include highly desirable objects and events, responsive communication partners, and communicative opportunities (e.g., objects available but out of reach or the interruption of highly predictable routines) (cf. Halle, 1982; Hunt, Goetz, Alwell, & Sailor, 1986). As the student is systematically taught to use the targeted communicative response to request the desired items or continuation of the routine, contingency awareness is established at the same time.

Conceptual Understanding.   For students with severe disabilities who do not have speech, assessments strategies must rely on the analysis of observable behaviors to determine conceptual understanding (cf. Schuler, 1979). Examples of assessment areas that, together, provide a picture of the child's level of conceptual sophistication include the following: (1) the extent of functional object use and symbolic play (Musselwhite & St. Louis, 1988; Chappell & Johnson, 1976; Miller, Chapman, Branston, & Reichle, 1980), (2) the ability to associate objects by various properties of those objects (Schuler, 1979; Schuler & Goetz, 1981), and (3) receptive understanding of critical terms (e.g., names of favorite objects and people and simple directions) (Falvey, 1986). Schuler (1979) presents a detailed nonverbal assessment

strategy that may be used to clarify a student's understanding of conceptual relationships, the speed of learning, and generalization skills. The assessment of conceptual sophistication aids in determining the level of complexity and abstractness of the first messages the student is taught to express with the AAC system.

Matching Skills for Symbol Assessment.   If the decision is made to include pictorial symbols as one component of the student's AAC system, an assessment must be done prior to the selection of the specific symbol system to ensure a match between ease of interpretation of symbols and the student's discriminative abilities. The results of an investigation by Mirenda and Locke (1989) suggest that there is a hierarchy of symbol systems in terms of cognitive complexity or level of abstractness. Object symbols that were the same as or similar to the objects they represented were the most easily interpreted by participants in the study who experienced severe intellectual disabilities. Colored and black-and-white photographs were next, followed by (in order of increased difficulty) miniatures, line drawings, and abstract symbols such as the Rhebus and Bliss, which are commercially available symbol systems. The symbols used for "today's system" (e.g., colored photographs) should match the student's current ability to interpret. "Tomorrow's system" can introduce symbols that require increasing discriminative ability but allow greater communicative effectiveness (e.g., line drawings).

Sensory and Motor Abilities

An assessment of motor abilities is performed to identify the optimum means of accessing an augmentative communication aid or to determine the possible constraints in using a gestural communication system (Yorkston & Karlan, 1986). Skills are assessed in the general areas of mobility and positioning and manipulation skills. The following are examples of assessment questions in each of these areas (Mirenda & Iacono, 1989):

Mobility and positioning

• What is the optimal positioning to facilitate controlled motor movements when the student is sitting, lying, or standing?

• If the student is ambulatory, what restrictions (if any) exist that might limit the type of communication system recommended? For example, can the student use one or both hands to carry a device when ambulating? Is there a limit to the weight of the device? Can the student carry the device on his or her belt, in a pocket, or in a pouch?

• If the student is not ambulatory, does the method of mobility provide adequate head, trunk, arm, pelvic, and foot support for controlled motor movements? Does the other equipment the student uses (e.g., prone stander, side-lier) provide adequate support?

Manipulation skills

• How well can the student use his or her hands to gesture? to use a conventional keyboard? an adapted keyboard? to point to a symbol that represents what he or she wants to communicate? If a pictorial symbol is used, how large must the symbols be, and how far apart, for accurate pointing?

• If the student does not have efficient use of hands and arms for one of the above techniques, can he or she use a head stick or mouth stick for pointing? or a light pointer mounted on the head?

• If one of the preceding options is not viable, how well can the student use eye gaze to access the system?

• If the student cannot directly select symbols by pointing, can he or she activate a switch accurately and efficiently with any body part in order to select symbols through a scanning process?

Assessment of motor abilities in areas such as those described requires the combined efforts of assessment team members, including the occupational and physical therapist and the teacher.

Sensory and Perceptual Functioning. A student's use of a particular AAC system depends on his or her ability to process incoming information (Mirenda & Iacono, 1990); therefore, assessments

of vision, hearing, and tactile skills are essential. If a vision loss is suspected, vision assessments must be undertaken to evaluate the student's ability to interpret gestures and signs or to see the symbols on an AAC system display. Cress and colleagues (1981) provide a review of formal vision assessments for persons with severe disabilities and offer a nonverbal programmatic assessment program for determining visual acuity. Informal assessments such as those developed by Sailor, Utley, Goetz, Gee, and Baldwin (1982) can be implemented by the classroom teacher and provide relevant information for symbol selection.

A comprehensive audiological evaluation is an essential element of capability assessments. Goetz, Gee, and Sailor (1983) provide a series of instructional programs to prepare students for formal audiological assessment who have previously been considered difficult to test.

Assessment to Program Development. As discussed earlier, assessment of the student's communicative competence and cognitive capabilities yields information that can be used as the basis for the selection of the initial *messages* that the student will learn to convey through a variety of communicative means that, together, constitute the student's AAC system, as well as the identification of *contexts* for instruction that provide highly motivating opportunities for communicative attempts. Information gathered from assessments of the student's sensory and motor functioning aids in the selection of a primary AAC output system through a process of comparisons of student capabilities with the requirements of various communications options. The following section discusses the basic considerations in matching an AAC system to the user.

CRITICAL ISSUES

Matching an AAC System to the User

Figure 10.1 presents a flowchart that provides guidelines for decision making concerning the se-

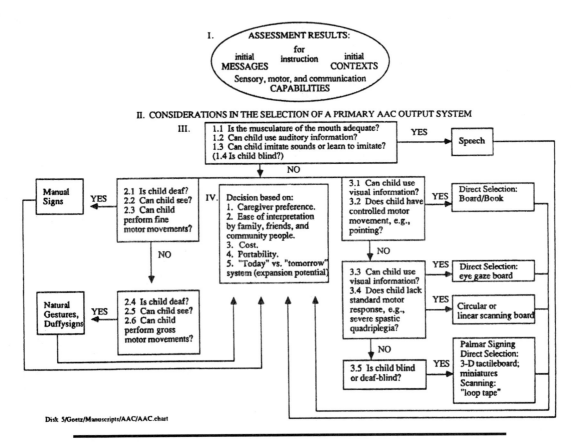

FIGURE 10.1   A set of decision rules for consideration in selecting an AAC system.

lection of an AAC output system. The decision-making process begins with the results of the previously described assessment process. The content and complexity of *initial messages* has been determined by the student's current communicative competence, cognitive functioning, and the contexts in which the student appears to be most highly motivated to communicate. *Initial contexts* for instruction, based on interviews, observations, and ecological inventories, have also been established. Finally, outcomes of sensory, motor, and communication *capability assessments* provide necessary information concerning response modes available to the student to "drive" the AAC system.

With this information in hand, the teacher may ask a series of questions that lead to selection of a particular system. Questions 1.1 to 1.4, if answered positively, may result in a tentative decision to develop speech as the primary output mode. If any or all of these questions are answered negatively, additional sets of questions are asked. Positive answers to questions 2.1 to 2.3 may lead to a tentative decision to teach a formal signing system as the AAC mode of choice, whereas positive responses to questions 3.3 and 3.4 suggest a direct selection or scanning AAC system.

The first selection of a system following application of these guidelines is, however, *tentative*. Each time selection of a tentative system occurs, the system must be evaluated in terms of the questions asked in box IV. Unlike the other assessment processes and questions, box IV questions address the concerns and preferences of significant others and care providers; logistical factors of cost and portability, and the practical factors concerning the expansion potential of the system are also of concern.

To be effective and to achieve its intended purpose, an AAC system must be accessible to *both* the user and his or her communication partners in family, school, and community environments. Caregiver preference and ease of interpretation, for example, are critical factors in deciding between ASL and SEE 2 signs if the AAC system of choice is manual signing. Deaf parents might select ASL, but SEE 2 signs may be more readily learned than ASL by potential partners who speak English. Portability, or the ease with which an AAC system can accompany the student *anywhere,* is another dimension influencing final selection of a system, as is the expansion potential of the system. A student who is deaf and blind, for example, may have a "today" system that uses 3-dimensional objects in a calendar plan (Writer, 1987) while developing palmar signing, which has greater potential for growth in vocabulary and complexity of messages conveyed, as a "tomorrow" system.

Figure 10.1 is intended as an aid to decision making by the transdisciplinary team, not as a series of firm rules. When a tentative AAC system is selected, in addition to the considerations addressed in box IV, the team must also consider the effectiveness of the match between the selected system and the initial messages and contexts for instruction determined in the assessment process. Natural gestures (Nietupski & Hamre-Nietupski, 1979) may be an appropriate "today" system for a student who expresses both limited communicative intents (i.e., expresses only a rejection function) and communicative means (i.e., tantrums and runs to escape) even if the student's hearing is intact. Alternatively, an echolalic student with autism who displays all of the capabilities requested

in questions 1.1 to 1.4 may nevertheless be a candidate for a visual or pictorial system, as indicated by information gained from assessments of cognition and information-processing styles. The seeming complexity of the decision-making process should not overwhelm the teacher and prevent the ultimate selection and development of an AAC system. If the chosen system is not effective, an alternative one can be developed.

The Role of Partners

Much recent research suggests that attempts by students with severe disabilities to communicate may often be ignored or overlooked by others in the classroom, including teachers (Houghton, Bronicki, & Guess, 1987; Peck & Semmel, 1987). Teachers themselves may need to learn to "read" the subtle and nonsymbolic means that students may use to communicate (see Siegel-Causey & Guess, 1989); in addition, teachers may need to teach other classroom staff and the student's nondisabled peers and friends to look for, recognize, and respond to communicative messages that may be expressed through changes in facial expression, body tone, or activity levels.

For students who use augmentative or alternative systems, training peers in use of these systems may be crucial if the system is to be used on a generalized basis (Hunt, Alwell, & Goetz, 1988, 1990b, 1991). Hunt and colleagues, for example, trained a student with severe disabilities and a peer to have conversational exchanges using an AAC adaptation (a book), but use of the adaptation did not generalize to other peers until these other peers received brief instruction in how to use the book during conversational exchanges. Similarly, use of the book taught at school did not generalize to the student's home (despite the parents' involvement in determination and selection of the system) until the parents received brief training in how to use the book to converse with the student.

Table 10.2 presents the script used as part of a brief training session (less than 5 minutes) given to peers who served as partners during instruc-

TABLE 10.2 Partner Training Script

"We are going to be teaching some of our students to have conversations with their friends. They will be using a book with pictures and words in it, because sometimes it's hard to figure out what they are trying to say.

"Your part is to sit with (Joe) for 5 minutes or so and take part in the conversation.

"(Joe) will take a turn by answering your questions and making a new comment (or asking a question). (Joe) will answer your question by pointing to a picture and perhaps saying some words; (he) will ask you a question or make a comment by pointing to a different picture and perhaps saying something.

"If you do not understand what (he) is trying to tell you, you can ask (him) to repeat it. If you still do not understand, try to guess from the picture that (he) points to.

"After (Joe) answers your question, wait until (he) has a chance to point to a new picture. Then it is your turn to talk about that picture.

"You can talk about anything else you want to during your turn, but be sure to end it by asking (Joe) a question.

"So, you always do two things: talk about what (Joe) just pointed to and then ask a new question."

From Hunt P., Alwell, M., & Goetz, L. (1991). Interacting with peers through conversation turntaking with a communication book adaptation. *Augmentative and Alternative Communication, 7*(2), 117–126.

tional sessions. The objectives for the training session were to teach student peers the following: (1) to make comments by referring to pictures in the student's communication book, (2) to cue the student with disabilities to take another "turn" by asking him or her a question related to a picture in the book, and (3) to wait after the student answered the question to give him or her an opportunity to make additional comments or introduce a new topic. Oral instructions were accompanied by demonstration and followed by a brief role-playing activity with the teacher. Training was gener-

ally conducted individually or, occasionally, with pairs of students.

This brief training format was all that was required for peers (and family members) to feel comfortable and successful in communicating with a student using the student's AAC system. The teacher's role in promoting AAC use thus extends beyond training only the student with severe disabilities. Training others in how the AAC system works, however, does not necessarily require an extensive amount of time and may be accomplished as part of general "ability" awareness activities at the school.

CURRICULUM: AAC SYSTEMS AND RESOURCES

History of Development

Successful instruction in nonspeech modes—including gestural language, graphic symbols, and simultaneous communication—for students with severe disabilities was reported as early as the 1970s (e.g., Topper, 1975; Stremel-Campbell, Cantrell, & Halle, 1977). Until recently, however, the AAC field was dominated by the development of "candidacy" models (i.e., Chapman & Miller, 1980) of intervention. Students were considered good "candidates" for AAC use in relation to performance on a fixed set of a criteria, including, for example, a set of complex cognitive prerequisites. Those persons who did not display the presumed cognitive prerequisites to language, such as specific Piagetian sensorimotor stages, were not considered appropriate candidates for communication instruction or AAC use (see Sailor et al., 1980, for comprehensive review).

Today, AAC "candidacy" models are being replaced by models that provide a process for communication assessment and intervention applicable to all students, regardless of ability range (Mirenda & Iacono, 1990; Rosenberg & Beukelman, 1987). An explosion of studies documenting the development and use of a vast array of augmentative and alternative communication strategies and aids for students with severe disabilities, ranging from gesture language (Nietupski & Hamre-Nietupski, 1979), to microswitches (Wacker, Wiggins, Fowler, & Berg, 1988), to tangible symbol systems (Rowland & Schweigert, 1988) has strengthened the basic inclusionary principles that *all* persons can participate in and improve their communicative exchanges (see Kangas & Lloyd, 1988).

Communication *mode* refers to the form in which the content of a message is expressed. There are two broad categories of AAC modes: unaided modes and aided modes. Within these categories are a variety of systems and options. The following discussion includes a brief general description of each category and reviews selected examples and prototypes. The examples are not comprehensive, however, and the reader is referred to Musselwhite and St. Louis (1988) for an excellent and comprehensive review.

Unaided Modes

Unaided modes are those that do not require any aids or devices external to the user. Natural gestures, gesture languages, manual signing systems, and idiosyncratic behaviors such as facial expression are all examples of unaided communication modes.

Nonsymbolic Intent. One category of unaided modes includes nonsymbolic communicative behaviors. Siegel-Causey and Guess (1989) present an approach in which nonsymbolic communication is developed within the context of naturally occurring routines. Working with students who demonstrated severe and profound multiple disabilities, Siegel-Causey and Guess present a model in which all behaviors (vocal, gestural, facial expression, etc.) are viewed as being potentially communicative in nature. Adults consistently respond to these behaviors, which are considered meaningful within predictable activity routines, in order to expand the student's communicative repertoire so that a more

formal system can later be built. For example, a child may consistently reach toward items within many different contexts. The adult interprets the gesture as a request and responds accordingly by giving the child the item. With repeated experience, the child begins to use the reaching behavior intentionally in order to achieve specific environmental outcomes. The expression of nonsymbolic communication behaviors may be idiosyncratic and difficult for the communication partner to read (Campbell, 1989); however, for some students the nonsymbolic expression of communicative intent within consistent routines, such as going out to recess or preparing a snack, may provide an opportunity to introduce successfully more conventionally understood communication modes (Gee et al., 1991).

A related type of unaided communication mode that merits discussion is a person's use of inappropriate or aberrant behaviors (for example, hitting another person or giggling expressively when asked to do a task). A functional analysis of the conditions associated with their occurrence (Carr et al., 1990) may reveal that these behaviors are in fact communicative in nature. The communicative intent may be to maintain social interaction or, alternatively, to avoid doing a task. A growing body of evidence supports the efficacy of replacing these inappropriate behaviors with functionally equivalent communication system responses (Carr & Durand, 1985; Horner & Budd, 1985; Hunt, Alwell, & Goetz, 1988). Although aberrant behaviors are obviously not a desired outcome mode for AAC, recognition of their communicative function is an essential part of the assessment process, as described earlier.

Symbolic Systems. Symbolic systems such as manual signing, gestural language systems, and finger-spelling constitute the most formally developed unaided communication system. Musselwhite and St. Louis (1988) review in detail the range of options for manual signing systems, discussing the pros and cons of each for use by persons with severe disabilities. Two sign systems are of particular importance: American Sign Language (ASL), and Signing Exact English (SEE 2). ASL is the language used by the majority of deaf adults in the United States and Canada. ASL differs in structure from spoken English; it is in fact a unique language and not merely a coded representation of spoken English. SEE 2 was initially developed by concerned parents, educators, and deaf adults as an attempt to represent spoken English manually. There are nearly 4000 SEE 2 signs and nine basic principles used in developing new content. Thus, although ASL is the language most used by the adult deaf community, SEE 2 signs may be more widely used in the younger deaf community.

If the assessment process leads to a decision to develop manual signing as either an alternative or augmentative mode, consideration of which of the many available systems to use will be influenced by these factors: (1) the student's motor proficiency and the complexity of physical production of the system, (2) the linguistic environment in which the student functions, (3) student and family preference, and (4) the student's current communicative functioning abilities, as described in detail in the earlier discussion of the assessment process and shown in Figure 10.1. Although manual signs are the most often reported form of augmentative communication used with persons labeled "severely or profoundly retarded" (Matas et al., 1985), evidence suggests that persons with severe disabilities may never learn a comprehensive sign vocabulary and that spontaneous use may seldom occur (Bryen et al., 1988).

Aided Systems: Nonelectronic

Nonelectronic aided systems offer tremendous variety in terms of the symbol system used to represent messages (e.g., objects, pictures, or line drawings), the motor response that "runs" the system by accessing the message (e.g., pointing to or gazing at the symbol), and the format in which the symbols are displayed (e.g., a communication book or board). The design of a student's communication aid is based on assessments of his or her communicative competence, cognitive abilities, and sensory and motor functioning (see the earlier discussion of assessment goals and strategies, as well as implications of assessment outcomes for design of an AAC system and a communication training program).

Symbols

The message options provided by aided communication systems are represented to the user through a set of static symbols. A symbol is an object or a pictorial representation that stands for a real object, event, person, action, or relationship. Symbol systems can be described by their level of abstractness (i.e., the degree to which they resemble their physical referent). Selection of a symbol system for an individual includes an assessment of his or her ability to interpret symbol sets that represent varying levels of abstraction (Mirenda & Smith-Louis, 1989; Mirenda & Locke, 1989). The following symbol options, most commonly used with students with severe disabilities, are described in order of difficulty of interpretation (cf. Mirenda & Locke, 1989).

Objects. For students who do not yet demonstrate the ability to match pictures to the items, events, or people they represent, the initial symbols introduced in "today's system" may be objects (Vanderheiden & Lloyd, 1986; Goossens' & Crain, 1987; Musselwhite & St. Louis, 1988). Object symbols can be *duplicates* of the objects they stand for, or they can be objects that are different from but *represent* other objects or events (e.g., a spoon may represent food, or a piece of chain from a swing may represent the activity of swinging). Miniature objects can also be used to represent real objects and events; however, some students may find them to be significantly more abstract than real objects (Mirenda & Locke, 1989). Transition from real objects to miniatures or two-dimensional symbol systems for "tomorrow's system" requires the systematic introduction of the more abstract symbols with gradual fading of the original object symbol (see Goossens' & Crain, 1987, for descriptions of various fading strategies).

Photographs. Photographs (including magazine pictures), particularly if they are colored and are actual pictures of the object, person, or event they represent, require minimal symbolic ability (Chapman & Miller, 1980). The results of a study by Mirenda and Locke (1989) suggest that photos may be easier to interpret for individuals with severe intellectual disabilities than black-and-white line drawings; however, caution must be taken in assuming that this is true for all students (cf. Schuler & Baldwin, 1981). The selection of a pictorial or any other symbol system should be done only after considering a number of interrelated factors, including the student's cognitive abilities, visual processing abilities, and prior knowledge and experience (Mirenda & Smith-Louis, 1989).

Line Drawings. Black-and-white line drawings require more symbolic ability for their interpretation (Mirenda, 1985); however, their use presents a number of distinct advantages, including the following:

• The symbol set can be easily developed through hand drawings or selection from commercially available systems.
• Simple line drawings can be interpreted less "literally" than photographs and, therefore, can stand for classes of things, events, and even people (e.g., a ball can stand for any leisure activity; a girl's face can represent friends at school).
• Line drawings can represent abstract concepts such as feelings (e.g., happy, sad), physical states (e.g., tired, sick), and attributes (e.g., color, size).
• Some students have an easier time interpreting symbols that are less complex in configuration (Mirenda & Smith-Louis, 1989; Schuler & Baldwin, 1981) and, therefore, have less difficulty

with line drawings, because of their simplicity, than with photographs that present variation in both shapes and colors.

However, even for those students who are successfully using line drawings to communicate requests, to express protests, and to make simple social comments about things and people of interest, there is still an important place in their AAC system for colored photographs. The work of Hunt, Alwell, and Goetz (1988, 1990a, 1991) has demonstrated that conversation between students with severe disabilities and their nondisabled peers may be greatly facilitated through the use of a communication book filled with colored photographs of the students' favorite activities, things, and people. Each photograph provides a rich source of topics and suggestions for specific comments or questions for both partners in the conversation. Moreover, the photographs in the book promote a more "personal" exchange as they generate topics and comments related to the student's school and family life.

System Display Formats. The basic requirements of an aided communication system are that it be portable, durable, and flexible (Mirenda & Smith-Louis, 1989); that is, as the student moves through his or her day at school and at home, the system must move with the student and messages relevant to each activity of the day must be readily accessible. Symbols for nonelectronic communication aids can be displayed in a variety of formats, including communication books for physically able-bodied students (cf. Mirenda & Smith-Louis, 1989), communication boards for physically disabled individuals (cf. Goossens' & Crain, 1987), and object boxes and boards for object communication systems (cf. Rowland, 1989; Goossens' & Crain, 1985). Figures 10.2 and 10.3 present examples of these types of symbol display formats. The systems in Figure 10.3 all provide voice output.

Response Modes (Symbol Selection Techniques). Symbol selection for nonelectronic aided systems

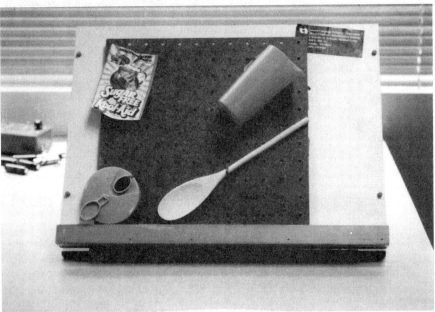

FIGURE 10.2 Shown are a communication vest, an object board, an eye gaze board, and a circular scanner.

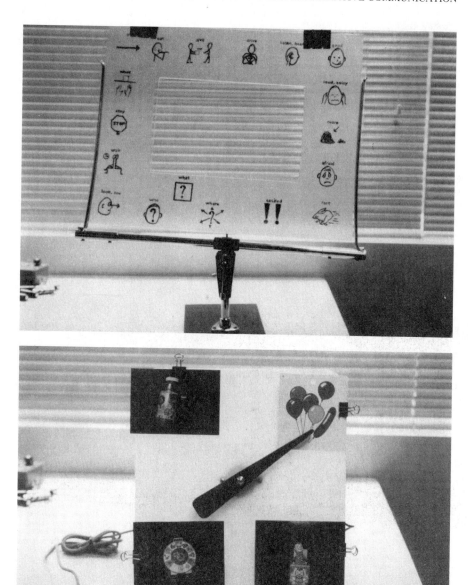

FIGURE 10.2   Continued

is accomplished through "direct selection"; that is, the user chooses directly from available options, using a motor response that points to the symbol by any of the following means:

- An arm, hand, or finger
- A lower extremity or any other body part
- An eye gaze
- A head stick or mouth stick
- A headlight pointer

The selection of a reliable response mode to indicate desired messages is an essential component of the AAC system. The symbol selection technique must clearly identify the message to the communication partner, or communication breakdown will occur. In selecting the optimum response mode for a student, at least the following factors should be considered (Musselwhite, 1987): (1) accuracy of the pointing response, (2) speed, (3) effort, (4) cognitive demands, and (5) listener demands. For the student who lacks sufficient motor control to directly select symbols on a board or book, a scanning system is an alternative. With scanning selection, choices are presented to the individual one at a time, either visually or audibly, and the individual selects the desired symbol by making a specific response—for example, touching a switch—at the proper time. As with the other two major components of an AAC system, the symbol system and the display format, identification of the selection technique is based on assessments of the student's communicative competence, cognitive abilities, and sensory and motor functioning (see the earlier discussion in "Assessment Process").

Aided Systems: Electronic

In recent years there have been rapid and exciting technological advances in the area of electronic communication systems for individuals with severe intellectual disabilities (Romski & Sevcik, 1988; Beukelman & Mirenda, personal communi-

cation, July 1990). Computerized communication systems have been reduced in size and cost, and battery-operated systems allow portability and flexibility. In addition, portable electronic systems are available today that can be designed to match the cognitive capabilities of the most severely intellectually disabled individual (e.g., Zygo's Macaw, Prentke and Romich's Intro-Talker, Touch Talker, and Light Talker, and Adaptive Communication Systems' Alltalk) by allowing a full range of options of symbol systems (e.g., objects, photographs, or line drawings), symbol display formats (including the number, size, and arrangement of the symbols), and selection techniques, including both direct selection and switch-activated "scanning" techniques for individuals who do not have sufficient control of any motor response to directly indicate a symbol choice (cf. Musselwhite & St. Louis, 1988; Vanderheiden & Lloyd, 1986).

Furthermore, the availability of digitized speech output (which is a feature of the products just mentioned) allows for natural voice output; this means that family members and friends of individuals who are nonverbal or severely speech impaired can hear messages relayed by that person in a voice that is matched by sex and age. One can only speculate, as research has not yet caught up with technological advances in this area, as to the profound effect that normalized speech output will have, for individuals with severe intellectual disabilities, on independent participation in integrated school and community activities, perceived levels of competence by nondisabled schoolmates and co-workers, and the establishment of social contacts and friendships.

Finally, recent technological advances have produced electronic communication systems, including those already mentioned, that can be simply and quickly programmed, thereby allowing care providers and teachers to easily modify displayed messages to keep them relevant to the student's communication needs as they change during the activities of the day.

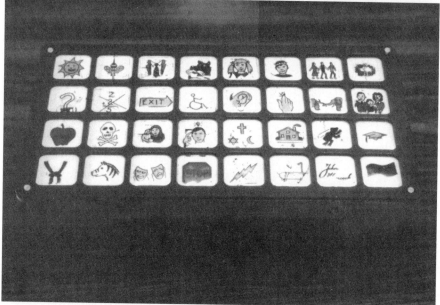

FIGURE 10.3   Shown are Zygo's McCaw; Prentke and Romich's Intro Talker, Touch Talker, and Light Talker; and Adaptive Communication System's Alltalk.
Manufacturers' addresses are as follows:
Zygo's Industries, Inc., P.O. Box 1008, Portland, OR 97207-1008
Prentke & Romich Co., 1022 Hegl Road, Wooster, OH 44691
Adaptive Communication Systems, Inc., P.O. Box 12440, Pittsburgh, PA 15231

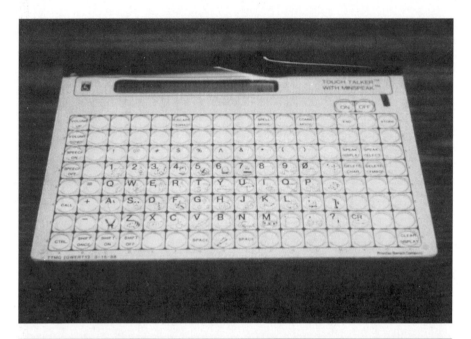

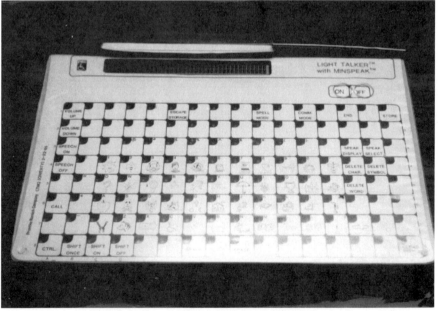

FIGURE 10.3   Continued

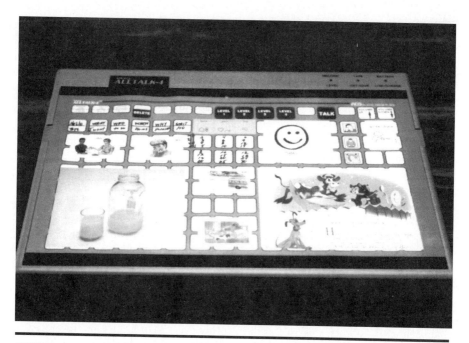

FIGURE 10.3   Continued

CASE EXAMPLES

Mike: Teaching Activation of a Call Buzzer Within Motivating Activity Routines

Mike attends school in a special day class that is integrated into a regular elementary school campus. He has attended the same school for 2 years, and both peer tutoring and special friends programs (Murray & Beckstead, 1983) have been an active part of school life. He is known and liked by many of his same-age peers.

Mike's educational program focuses on participation in the third grade, leisure skills, participation in household and personal care activities, social skills, eating and drinking skills, and building friendships. Mike is 8 years old. His vision is extremely myopic, and he can see large objects only when they are brought extremely close to him. He is nonambulatory and has partial control primarily over one physical movement, which is a head turn to the right. Mike has learned to control this movement to activate contingent switch-operated toys and other items. He is able to bring his arms into extension at times, but has not yet learned to use his arms or hands functionally.

Mike has no formal communication, but uses a number of nonsymbolic means to communicate. He often rolls his eyes upward in response to familiar voices and events. He laughs or smiles when certain physical bouncing or hand shaking movements are done to him, especially by his mother or teacher. He often demonstrates positive affect changes when in the company of nondisabled peers. Mike demonstrates dislikes through crying and frowns.

The introduction of a more easily interpreted response form was prioritized as a goal, so as to create a more effective "tomorrow" system that would facilitate increases in communicative content and provide a perception of increased competence among his peers, family, and staff. An AAC system was developed for Mike with his family, friends, and classroom staff, in order to provide a system that would be desirable and most likely to be used by those close to him.

Mike's head turn was sufficiently consistent to allow him to activate a switch mounted within a half inch of his cheek. This switch was attached to a call device that sounded like a doorbell. Mike's response was to activate the switch long enough to hear the entire bell sound. He was taught to use this call device as an initial "want" (request) function.

The instructional objective and program developed to teach Mike to use his call buzzer is shown in Table 10.3. Four different motivating activity routines were selected for instruction, following procedures described in detail in Goetz et al. (1985) and Gee et al. (1991). Chain interruption (Hunt et al., 1986), in which an ongoing, predictable sequence of events is suddenly interrupted and a communication trial occurs, was used as the basic event for instruction. Mike was instructed in the four activity routines chosen as instructional contexts; regular and systematic assistance from classroom staff enabled him to participate partially (Baumgart et al., 1982). Once Mike's ways of participating in each routine were well established, interruptions occurred at predetermined points, and an instructional trial to teach switch activation as a means of requesting for the routine to continue also occurred (see Gee et al., 1990, for a full discussion of similar procedures). The specific instructional strategy used was a time-delay (Snell & Gast, 1981) procedure, in which the prompt of full physical assistance occurs after longer and longer intervals (see Chapter 4 for full discussion of time-delay).

Selection of this particular AAC system, and the written instructional program for its use, will enable Mike to begin to exercise control and to make choices within highly motivating and age-appropriate contexts through more conventionally understood means. Once Mike learns to activate the switch to request assistance or attention in order to continue his participation, additional functions (such as rejection or negation) might be

taught, using a different auditory cue than the call buzzer. Activation of a scanning device or loop tape might be the long-term goal for Mike's "tomorrow" system. At the same time, continued recognition of Mike's nonsymbolic means of communicating pleasure and distress will remain part of his "today" system.

Matt: Teaching Conversation Turn Taking with a Communication Book Adaptation

Matt, who experiences Down syndrome and severe intellectual disabilities, attends a special education classroom located on a regular high school campus. His school day includes numerous opportunities for social interaction with nondisabled peers—co-workers at his community job site, classmates in some regular education programs, and peer tutors providing instructional assistance. However, Matt's attempts to engage peers in a social exchange have been greatly hampered by his limited speech and language abilities. Moreover, because he desires social contact, he has often resorted to the use of a variety of inappropriate behaviors, including shouting, hitting, kicking, and name calling to capture the attention of peers. His speech, while serving him well for communicative functions related to simple requests, protests, or comments, has not been adequate to sustain the extended exchange of messages required for conversation turn taking.

A conversation training program, which included an augmentative communication system, was implemented for Matt (cf. Hunt, Alwell, & Goetz, 1988, 1990a, 1991; Hunt, Alwell, Goetz, & Sailor, 1990). It provided the support he needed to interact socially through conversation.

A "conversation book" was developed for Matt, which included colored photographs of things, people, places, and activities that he liked best. He carried the book throughout the school day in a "trendy" sports pouch attached to the waistband of his pants. The book was organized conceptually by the major environments in his

TABLE 10.3   Instructional Program Plan

STUDENT: Mike	**DATE:** 3/90	**BASIC SKILL PROGRAM:** Call buzzer activation	

GOAL/OBJECTIVE: When interrupted at predetermined spots during motivating activity routines, Mike will turn his head to the right to activate a call device in three out of four consecutive occasions for each activity.

PEERS INVOLVED?/HOW?   Nondisabled peers bring Mike to the door on their way out to recess.

Implement within the following activity contexts (indicate paired skills)	Natural and/or designated cues	Instructor does this prior to response (antecedent procedures)	Performance criteria (response)	This naturally occurs, or the instructor implements/ensures occurrence following response
1. Going out to recess (10:00 A.M. and 2:00 P.M.) 2. Preparing lunch using microwave 3. Preparing snack using blender 4. Using Casio as a leisure activity	1. ND students exit and door slams, leaving Mike behind. 2. When bell goes off, the usual assistance to get food is not provided. 3. While Mike is actively blending juice, circuit is suddenly broken. 4. While activating Casio using extended arms, switch is turned off and further movement will not reactivate it.	1. Assist Mike as usual to participate in routines until the point of interruption. 2. *Prompt:* Physical assistance at chin to turn head. *Time delay increments:* 0 seconds 1 seconds (1') 3 seconds (3') 5 seconds (5') Independence Increase delay each time criterion is met.	1. Mike turns head to R. to activate switch	Immediate resumption of activity routine and social praise and enthusiasm, i.e., "Oh, they almost forgot to take you with them to recess!"

DATA SUMMARY: LIST TIMES OR SESSIONS IN WHICH DATA WILL BE COLLECTED ON THIS SKILL.

Session↓ Date→	3/12 1'	3/13								
Recess	+ +	+ +	(Criterion met. Increase delay interval.)							
Lunch/Microwave	+ −	+ +	"	"	"	"	"			
Snack/blender	− +	− +								
Casio	+ +	+ −	"	"	"	"	"			

Adapted from Gee, K., Graham, N., Goetz, L., Oshima, G., & Yoshioka, K. (1991). Teaching students to request the continuation of routine activities by using time delay and decreasing physical assistance in the context of chain interruption. *The Journal of The Association for Persons with Severe Handicaps, 16,* 154–167.

world, including his home, school, and favorite community activities. Some pictures were grouped by special events such as parties and trips. Figure 10.4 shows a sample conversation book.

The communication book served as a conversation medium; that is, Matt was taught to pair spoken words and phrases with a point to the relevant picture in the book, through a prompt-fading procedure by which gesture and verbal prompts were gradually eliminated (cf. Hunt, Alwell, & Goetz, 1990b, for a detailed description of the conversation training program). This strategy ensured that his questions, comments, and answers would be understood by a communication partner. The pictures in his book also provided cues for comments and answers to his partner's questions.

Both Matt and his potential communication partners were taught a specific "turn-taking" structure that supported a balanced, sustained interaction. Each conversation "turn" included both *responding* to the partner's message and then *cueing* that person to respond again.

Instruction was delivered in a variety of campus and community settings, with schoolmates or co-workers serving as communication partners (e.g., during lunch or break periods at community job sites, en route to a local store, laundromat, or bank, on the bleachers during lunch period, or in P.E. class).

In one semester's time, Matt has demonstrated that he can carry on lengthy conversations with peers, not only in instructional contexts but also during a variety of naturally occurring opportunities for conversation with peers at school and at work. Finally, not only is Matt initiating and participating in conversations with peers throughout the school day, but he is no longer resorting to those inappropriate behaviors he had been using prior to the implementation of the training program to sustain social contact.

SUMMARY ISSUES

Achieving an effective "today" and "tomorrow" AAC system for each student requires input from many disciplines. The occupational and physical therapists may provide particularly valuable infor-

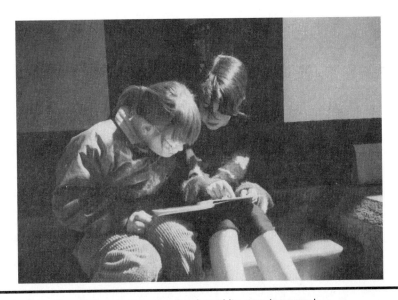

FIGURE 10.4 A sample conversation book and its carrying pouch.

mation concerning a student's motor function, or positioning and handling needs, and the speech and language therapist may provide useful information concerning current communication competence or specific alternative communication symbol systems. Assessments of hearing and vision capability may be performed by an audiologist or vision specialist. Information about particularly motivating contexts or expression of current communicative intents may be offered by the classroom teacher, a parent, a significant other, or a peer. The composition of the team—who its members are and how and when it meets—will vary according to the ability and needs of individual students. A number of different team approaches have been discussed in the literature (Fewell & Cone, 1983). Regardless of the type of team model that is used, all team members should share a common vision of the quality of life they want for a particular student, which will be reflected in the ultimate AAC system that is utilized.

Continuing rapid growth in the field of AAC, and particularly in the development of high-tech devices and systems, suggests that a new role may be emerging: that of an AAC facilitator. Within a school district, an AAC facilitator may participate in assessment, coordinate team planning, and provide the latest information concerning state-of-the-art system and device options to the team as they complete the assessment process and match system to user. In the absence of this role, however, the special education teacher may well fill the role of coordinator of team input, while turning to outside resources such as university-affiliated assessment clinics or training programs; local, regional, or national AAC conferences; or published materials, including books and articles (a brief list of resources is included in "References" at the end of this chapter). Input from a strong and supportive team will greatly expand the knowledge base used in decision making.

The recognition that all persons do communicate, using a variety of modes to express themselves, and that all communication requires a partner, makes the development of an effective AAC system essential for every student who can benefit. Once established, AAC systems will become an integral part of the student's full participation at home, at school, and in the community at large.

REFERENCES

Baumgart, D., Brown, L., Pumpian, I., Nisbet, J., Ford, A., Sweet, M., Messina, R., & Schroeder, J. (1982). Principle of partial participation and individualized adaptations in educational programs for severely handicapped students. *Journal of the Association for the Severely Handicapped, 7*(2), 17–28.

Bryen, D., Goldman, A., & Quinlisk-Gill, S. (1988). Sign language with students with severe/profound mental retardation: How effective is it? *Education and Training in Mental Retardation, 23,* 129–137.

Campbell, P. (1989). Dysfunction in posture and movement in individuals with profound disabilities. In F. Brown & D. Lehr (Eds.), *Persons with profound disabilities: Issues and practices* (pp. 163–189). Baltimore: Paul H. Brookes Publishing Co.

Carr, E. G., & Durand, V. M. (1985). Reducing behavior problems through functional communication training. *Journal of Applied Behavior Analysis, 18*(2), 111–126.

Carr, T., Robinson, S., Taylor, J., & Carlson, J. (1990). *Positive approaches to the treatment of severe behavior problems in persons with developmental disabilities: A review and analysis of reinforcement and stimulus based procedures.* Seattle, WA: The Association for Persons with Severe Handicaps.

Chapman, R., & Miller, J. (1980). Analyzing language and communication in the child. In R. Schiefelbusch (Ed.), *Nonspeech language and communication: Analysis and intervention* (pp. 160–195). Baltimore: University Park Press.

Chappell, G., & Johnson, G. (1976). Evaluation of cognitive behavior in the young child. *Language, Speech, and Hearing Services in Schools, 7,* 17–27.

Donnellan, A. M., Mirenda, P. L., Mesaros, R. A., & Fassbender, L. L. (1984). Analyzing the communicative function of aberrant behavior. *The Journal of The Association for Persons with Severe Handicaps, 9*(3), 201–212.

Dore, J. (1974). A pragmatic description of early language development. *Journal of Psycholinguistic Research, 3,* 343–350.

Falvey, M. A. (1986). *Community-based curriculum: Instructional strategies for students with severe handicaps.* Baltimore: Paul H. Brookes Publishing Co.

Fewell, R., & Cone, J. (1983). Identification and placement of severely handicapped children. In M. Snell (Ed.), *Systematic instruction of the moderately and severely handicapped* (2nd ed., pp. 46–73). Columbus, OH: Charles E. Merrill.

Gee, K., Graham, N., Goetz, L., Oshima, G., & Yoshioka, K. (1991). Teaching students to request the continuation of routine activities by using time delay and decreasing physical assistance in the context of chain interruption. *The Journal of The Association for Persons with Severe Handicaps, 16,* 154–167.

Goetz, L., Gee, K., & Sailor, W. (1985). Using a behavior chain interrupted strategy to teach communication skills to students with severe disabilities. *The Journal of The Association for Persons with Severe Handicaps, 10*(1), 21–30.

Goetz, L., Gee, K., & Sailor, W. (1983). Using crossmodal transfer of stimulus control: Preparing students with severe multiple disabilities for audiological assessment. *Journal of the Association for the Severely Handicapped, 8*(4), 3–13

Goossens', C. A., & Crain, S. S. (1987). Overview of nonelectronic eye-gaze communication techniques. *Augmentative and Alternative Communication, 3*(2), 77–89.

Goossens', C., & Crain, S. (1986). *Augmentative communication: Intervention resource.* Birmingham: Sparks Center for Developmental and Learning Disorders, University of Alabama at Birmingham.

Grabowski, K., & Shane, H. (1986). Communication profile for severe expressive impairment. Unpublished manuscript. Communication Enhancement Clinic, Children's Hospital, Boston.

Halle, J. (1982). Teaching functional language to the handicapped: An integrative model of natural environment teaching techniques. *The Journal of The Association for Persons with Severe Handicaps, 7,* 29–37.

Horner, R. H., & Budd, C. M. (1985). Acquisition of manual sign use: Collateral reduction of maladaptive behavior, and factors limiting generalization. *Education and Training of the Mentally Retarded, 20,* 39–47.

Houghton, J., Bronicki, G. J. B., & Guess, D. (1987). Opportunities to express preferences and make choices among students with severe disabilities in classroom settings. *The Journal of The Association for Persons with Severe Handicaps. 12*(1), 18–27.

Hunt, P., Alwell, M., & Goetz, L. (1991). Interacting with peers through conversation turntaking with a communication book adaptation. *Augmentative and Alternative Communication, 7*(2), 117–126.

Hunt, P., Alwell, M., & Goetz, L. (1990a). Using a communication book adaptation at home: Informed family members as conversation partners. Manuscript in submission.

Hunt, P., Alwell, M., & Goetz, L. (1990b). *Teaching conversation skills to individuals with severe disabilities with a communication book adaptation: Instructional handbook.* San Francisco: Department of Special Education, San Francisco State University.

Hunt, P., Alwell, M., & Goetz, L. (1988). Acquisition of conversation skills and the reduction of inappropriate social interaction behaviors. *The Journal of The Association for Persons with Severe Handicaps, 13,* 20–27.

Hunt, P., Alwell, M., Goetz, L., & Sailor, W. (1990). Generalized effects of conversation skill training. *The Journal of The Association for Persons with Severe Handicaps, 15*(4), 250–260.

Hunt, P., Goetz, L., Alwell, M., & Sailor, W. (1986). Using an interrupted behavior chain strategy to teach generalized communication responses to students with severe disabilities. *The Journal of The Association for Persons with Severe Handicaps, 11*(3), 196–204.

Kangas, K., & Lloyd, L. (1988). Early cognitive skills as prerequisites to augmentative and alternative communication use: What are we waiting for? *Augmentative and Alternative Communication, 4,* 211–221.

Matas, J., Mathy-Laikko, P., Beukelman, D., & Legresley, K. (1985). Identifying the nonspeaking population: A demographic study. *Augmentative and Alternative Communication, 1,* 17–31.

Miller, J., Chapman, R., Branston, M., & Reichle, J. (1980). Language comprehension in sensorimotor stages V and VI. *Journal of Speech and Hearing Research, 23,* 284–311.

Mills, J., & Higgins, J. (1983). *Non-oral communication assessment and training guide.* Encinitas, CA: Authors.

Mirenda, P., & Smith-Louis, M. (1989). Teaching communication skills. In A. Ford, R. Schnorr, L. Meyer,

L. Davern, J. Black, & P. Dempsey (Eds.), *The Syracuse community-referenced curriculum guide* (pp. 189–209). Baltimore: Paul H. Brookes Publishing Co.

Mirenda, P., & Iacono, T. (1990). Communication options for persons with severe and profound disabilities: State of the art and future directions. *The Journal of The Association for Persons with Severe Handicaps, 15,* 3–21.

Mirenda, P., & Locke, P. (1989). A comparison of symbol transparency in nonspeaking persons with intellectual disabilities. *Journal of Speech and Language Disorders, 54,* 131–140.

Musselwhite, C. (1987). Augmentative communication. In E. McDonald (Ed.), *Treating cerebral palsy: For clinicians by clinicians* (pp. 209–238). Austin, TX: PRO-ED.

Musselwhite, C., & St. Louis, K. (1988). *Communication programming for persons with severe handicaps: Vocal and augmentative strategies* (2nd ed.). Boston: College-Hill.

Nietupski, J., & Hamre-Nietupski, S. (1979). Teaching auxiliary communication skills to severely handicapped learners. *AAESPH Review, 4,* 107–124.

Peck, C. A., & Semel, M. I. (1982). Identifying the least restrictive environment (L.R.E.) for children with severe handicaps: Toward an empirical analysis. *The Journal of The Association for the Severely Handicapped, 7*(1), 56–63.

Piaget, J. (1953) *The origins of intelligence in children.* London: Routledge and Kegan Paul.

Robinson, C., & Robinson, J. (1983). Sensorimotor functions and cognitive development. In M. Snell (Ed.), *Systematic instruction of the moderately and severely handicapped.* Columbus, OH: Charles E. Merrill.

Romski, M. A., & Sevcik, R. A. (1988). Augmentative and alternative communication systems: Considerations for individuals with severe intellectual disabilities. *Augmentative and Alternative Communication,* 83–93.

Rosenberg, S., & Beukelman, D. (1987). The participation model. In C. A. Coston (Ed.), *Proceedings of the National Planners Conference on Assistive Device Service Delivery* (pp. 159, 161). Washington, DC: RESNA, The Association for the Advancement of Rehabilitation Technology.

Rowland, C., & Schweigert, P. (1988). *Tangible symbol systems.* Eugene, OR: Oregon Research Institute.

Rowland, C., & Stremel-Campbell, K. (1987). Share and share alike: Conventional gestures to emergent language for learners with sensory impairments. In L. Goetz, D. Guess, & K. Stremel-Campbell (Eds.), *Innovative program design for individuals with dual sensory impairments.* Baltimore: Paul H. Brookes Publishing Co.

Sailor, W., Guess, D., Goetz, L., Schuler, A., Utley, B., & Baldwin, M. (1980). Language and severely handicapped persons: Deciding what to teach to whom. In W. Sailor, B. Wilcox, & L. Brown (Eds.), *Methods of instruction for severely handicapped students.* Baltimore: Paul H. Brookes Publishing Co.

Schuler, A. (1979). *An experimental analysis of conceptual and representational abilities in a mute autistic adolescent: A serial vs. a simultaneous mode of processing.* Ph.D. diss., University of California, Santa Barbara.

Schuler, A. L., & Baldwin, M. (1981). Nonspeech communication and childhood autism. *Language, Speech, and Hearing Services in Schools, 12,* 246–257.

Schuler, A., & Goetz, L. (1981). The assessment of severe language disabilities: Communicative and cognitive considerations. *Analysis and Intervention in Developmental Disabilities, 1,* 333–346.

Schuler, A. L., Peck, C. A., Willard, C., & Theimer, K. (1989). Assessment of communicative means and functions through interview: Assessing the communicative capabilities of individuals with limited language. *Seminars in Speech and Language, 10*(1), 51–62.

Siegel-Causey, E., & Guess, D. (1989). *Enhancing nonsymbolic communication interactions among students with severe disabilities.* Baltimore: Paul H. Brookes Publishing Co.

Snell, M., & Gast, D. (1981). Applying time delay procedure to the instruction of the severely handicapped. *The Journal of The Association for Persons with Severe Handicaps, 6,* 3–14.

Stremel-Campbell, K., Cantrell, D., & Halle, J. (1977). Manual signing as a speech initiator for the nonverbal severely handicapped student. In E. Sontag, J. Smith, & N. Certo (Eds.), *Educational programming for the severely and profoundly handicapped.* Reston, VA: CEC Division on Mental Retardation.

Stremel-Campbell, K., Johnson-Dorn, N., & Guide, J. C. (1984). *Prelanguage/language communication sample.* Monmouth, OR: Teaching Research Integration Project.

Topper, S. (1975). Gesture language for a nonverbal severely retarded male. *Mental Retardation, 13,* 30–31.

Vanderheiden, G., & Lloyd, L. (1986). Communication systems and their components. In S. Blackstone (Ed.), *Augmentative communication: An introduction* (pp. 49–161). Rockville, MD: American Speech-Language-Hearing Association.

Wacker, D., Wiggins, B., Fowler, M., & Berg, W. (1988). Training students with profound or multiple handicaps to make requests via microswitches. *Journal of Applied Behavior Analysis, 18,* 331–343.

Watson, J. S. (1966). The development and generalization of "contingency awareness" in early infancy:

Some hypotheses. *Merrill-Palmer Quarterly, 12,* 123–135.

Wilcox, M. J. (1989). *Children with dual sensory impairments series: Guidelines for obtaining ecologically-based communication assessments.* Akron, OH: Children's Hospital Medical Center of Akron, Family Child Learning Center.

Yorkston, K. M., & Karlan, G. (1986) Assessment procedures. In S. Blackstone (Ed.), *Augmentative communication: An introduction.* Rockville, MD: American Speech-Language-Hearing Association.

CHAPTER 11

STRATEGIES AND INSTRUCTIONAL PROCEDURES TO PROMOTE SOCIAL INTERACTIONS AND RELATIONSHIPS

THOMAS G. HARING
University of California–Santa Barbara

DIANE RYNDAK
State University College at Buffalo

IN MEMORY OF THOMAS G. HARING
1953–1993

The following chapter is dedicated to the memory of Tom Haring, friend, colleague, behavioral scientist, and person extraordinaire, who lost his bout with brain cancer January 17, 1993. Tom's passing is both a professional and a personal loss to many of us in the field of severe developmental disabilities. His primary research focus has been to assist in the understanding of social contexts and social relationships that would facilitate inclusion for full and meaningful participation in community life for persons with severe disabilities. This chapter, co-authored with Diane Ryndak, is a reflection of his program of research and the practical applications of that research in the instruction of master's level as well as undergraduate students interested in the teaching of social skills to persons with severe disabilities.

There are many measures of the success Tom Haring enjoyed. One is his professional accomplishments: he published more than 50 articles since completing his doctoral training at the University of California, Berkeley, and San Francisco State University in 1983; he was a full professor in the Department of Special Education, University of California at Santa Barbara, associate editor of several major journals (including *The Journal of The Association*

for Persons with Severe Handicaps [JASH]), and principal investigator on several federally funded research projects. Another measure of his success is the friendships he developed with his students (Florene Bednersh, Jan Weiner, Craig Kenedy, and Richard Laitinen) and his colleagues across the continent (Cap Peck, Mark Wolery, Rob Horner, Glen Dunlap, Sam Odom, and Jim Halle) who knew not only Professor Thomas Haring, but the person, Tom Haring. Some of us had an opportunity to help Tom celebrate one of his recent accomplishments, the 1992 TASH Distinguished Professional Award, in San Francisco. It was always a pleasure to accompany Tom on a dining adventure, and that evening in San Francisco was no different. A third measure of Tom's success is the relationship he enjoyed with his family—his wife, Catherine Breen Haring, and their three children, Lauren Elizabeth, Anna Elise, and Catherine Taylor Haring, and his parents, Norris and Dorothy Haring. Tom and Catherine frequently co-authored papers such as the study on peer-mediated social network interventions that appeared in the *Journal of Applied Behavior Analysis, 25,* 1992, in addition to many cooperative presentations at professional meetings. Yet their collective focal point was their children. A fourth measure, one that rounds out the balance of an individual, is the development of an extracurricular activity. For Tom, it was a true appreciation for the automobile, particularly in regard to the restoration of "classic cars," a hobby he and his father, Norris, both enjoyed.

Tom, thank you for your contribution and your friendship. You have done some significant work in a short period of time. It will not go unnoticed, nor will it be forgotten.

DEFINITION, IMPORTANCE, AND HISTORICAL REVIEW

The goal of special education for students with severe disabilities is to impart the critical skills needed and provide the necessary service supports to create maximally integrated life-styles. Social relationships and social interaction skills are key ingredients in achieving this goal. Within this chapter, we discuss strategies and interventions that teachers and other support personnel can use to teach social interaction skills and to facilitate the development of friendships and other social relationships between students with disabilities and nondisabled peers within integrated settings.

Social Skills Defined

Social interaction is a behavioral event in which the responses of one person affect or control the responses of others. Defined in this way, a social interaction includes diverse events, such as two people throwing a ball back and forth, instructional interactions between a teacher and a student, a conversation among a group of friends, or an individual asking for a glass of water. A social skill, defined most broadly, is a potential repertoire of behavior that an individual can use in a given situation to affect (that is, influence or in some way constrain) the behavior of others. In this definition, the term "to affect the behavior of others" requires some elaboration. The effect must be a *reciprocal* effect. That is, if a person initiates a conversation with a statement such as "How's it

going?" the social behavior of the respondent is at least partially constrained or influenced to the extent that some responses, such as "Fine," become more highly probable. The instruction of social skills is, therefore, the teaching of responses that are used reciprocally to affect the behavior of others. Social skills include initiating interactions, taking turns, responding to others, and maintaining and elaborating on an interaction. Clearly, as the focus of special education moves in the direction of teaching skills in the natural context and promoting integration, the role of social skills instruction forms an important foundation. Social interaction is the basis for integration and the raw material from which friendships are built.

The Importance of Social Skills Instruction

Integration, social interaction, and friendship are critical educational goals for students with disabilities. Increasingly, policy makers, teachers, parents of students in special education, and students themselves are advocating for more than increases in physical proximity to nondisabled students as the defining feature of integration (Haring & Breen, 1990). At present, the outcome variables most actively sought are:

1. Changes in the social networks of students so that increased numbers of nondisabled students are within the network of a student with disabilities. Although students with disabilities are members of social networks, these networks are composed disproportionately of family members, service providers, and other people with disabilities (Romer & Heller, 1983; Kennedy, Horner, & Newton, 1989). The most critical need for students with disabilities is the provision of services that allow and support friendships and social interactions with nondisabled peers of their own age.

2. Increases in opportunities for social interaction with members of a stable network of acquaintances and friends within typical school, home, and community contexts. This includes increasing contacts between students with disabilities and their peers within mainstreamed classes, as well as in other natural contexts in which friends spend time with each other.

3. Increased support in problem solving, learning, and emotional well-being derived from interactions with friends rather than service providers (e.g., Forest, 1991). Many educational support functions currently performed by teachers and other paid adults can be effectively provided by peers in a more naturalistic fashion. Indeed, there have been numerous observations that describe how adult service providers who assist a student in a mainstreamed classroom, or in the community, can isolate the student from the natural social interactions that are available.

Policy Basis of Social Skills and Integration Intervention: The Least Restrictive Environment

The "least restrictive environment" (LRE) mandate is by now a well-known component of Public Law 94-142. Yet in spite of this mandate, there has been continuing controversy over its definition and how it should be implemented (e.g., Gartner & Lipsky, 1987; Sailor et al., 1986; Stainback & Stainback, 1984). Typically, the translation of the LRE mandate into practice has been the physical placement of students with disabilities onto regular school campuses. When physical integration is achieved, a goal that many educational systems are now meeting, there is little administrative motivation to promote social interactions or social

relationships. It is entirely possible to live a physically integrated life-style and yet be socially segregated. A physically integrated but socially segregated life-style does not achieve the intention of the current policy emphasis on school integration and community-based services (Will, 1986). That intention includes the development and maintenance of a network of friends and acquaintances and the creation of opportunities for social interactions.

Current policy at both federal and state levels defines the concepts of LRE and integration with two components: (1) an administrative and organization component that defines the placement of students in physical proximity to students without disabilities and (2) a curricular and programmatic component to support the social integration of students. For example, the state of California's policy on LRE defines an integrated educational program as including principles to guide the physical placement of students with disabilities in proximity to students without disabilities, as well as principles that entail participation in school activities, acceptance by peers, development of sustained interactions between students with and without disabilities, and use of friendship-based programs (Sailor et al., 1990). The purpose of this chapter is to describe the curricular and programmatic components that have been validated to achieve the social integration mandates in current policy.

Program Quality Indicators

A major indicator of integrated programming is an active effort to promote and facilitate the development of social interaction skills so that people with disabilities have the necessary skills to participate in social networks, as well as active efforts to allow opportunities for social interaction and the formation of relationships. An emphasis on social skill training and promoting opportunities for social relationships is consistent with current best practice models (e.g., Horner, Meyer, & Fredericks, 1986). Meyer, Eichinger, and Park-Lee (1987) conducted a comprehensive study to determine the degree of agreement on program quality indicators to be used in judging classroom programs. The following items were found to be indicators of best practices in the area of social integration and social skills instruction:

- The program philosophy emphasizes the goal of maximum participation in integrated community environments.
- The program philosophy emphasizes the goal of social acceptance and adjustment.
- Each Individualized Education Plan (IEP) contains objectives to develop social skills.
- Each IEP includes objectives to teach the learner to interact with and help others.
- Each IEP includes at least one measurable behavioral objective involving interactions with a peer who is not disabled.
- Nondisabled peers spontaneously interact with students when passing them in the hall or meeting them in central areas, such as the lunchroom.
- Students eat lunch in the cafeteria with peers.
- Students participate in extracurricular activities typical for their age range with nondisabled students.
- Students participate in daily social and leisure activities with same-aged peers, such as recess or sports.
- The classroom program includes planned daily interactions with same-aged nondisabled peers.
- Students participate in heterogeneously grouped instruction with nondisabled peers at least three times a week.

As the list of program quality indicators demonstrates, the instruction of social skills and creation of opportunities to socially interact should not be viewed as an adjunctive part of the curriculum: they are centrally important.

Social Skills Training and Integration

Social skills training and social integration form an interactive process of habilitation for students with severe disabilities. Social integration facilitates so-cial skill development by providing peers as models for appropriate social behavior, increasing the opportunities to practice social skills within multiple contexts, and providing environments that are more responsive to the social initiations of students with severe disabilities (cf. Sailor et al. 1986; Falvey, 1989; Haring & Breen, 1990; Gaylord-Ross, 1989). Conversely, increased social interaction skills allow for more meaningful (and more competent) interaction with nondisabled people within integrated settings. Thus, increased social development facilitates integration and, simultaneously, increased integration provides for greater opportunities for social development.

Given the importance of social skill development to the integration of persons with severe disabilities (as well as to their long-term habilitation), it is not surprising that considerable research has focused on this topic. Strategies such as *Peer Initiation Training* (e.g., Goldstein & Wickstrom, 1986; Odom & Strain, 1986) directly increase the frequency of social interactions by prompting and reinforcing peers to initiate contacts with students with disabilities. Strategies that use *Student Initiation Training* (e.g., Haring, Roger, Lee, Breen, & Gaylord-Ross, 1986; Hunt, Alwell, & Goetz, 1988) further increase the social interactions of students with disabilities by prompting and reinforcing students to initiate interactions with their nondisabled peers. Systematic instruction of social skills within the context of *activity-based participation* creates stronger generalization and more interaction with persons without disabilities (e.g., Gaylord-Ross, Haring, Breen, & Pitts-Conway, 1984; Haring & Lovinger, 1989). These and related strategies have a consistent record of increasing the frequency of social exchanges between peers with and without disabilities in integrated settings (e.g., Brady & McEvoy, 1989; Brady, Shores, McEvoy, Ellis, & Fox, 1987; Fox, Shores, Lindeman, & Strain, 1986; James & Egel, 1986; Lancioni, 1982; McEvoy et al., 1988; Sasso, Hughes, Swanson, & Novak, 1987; Sasso & Rude, 1987; Sisson, Babeo, & Van Hasselt, 1988).

Social skills research with students who have

disabilities has been concerned with the training of social exchange responses within dyads. The primary focus of much of the current research has been to teach social interaction skills, such as greetings and play responses, between a target student and one peer, with little reference to the application of these skills to participation in group contexts or the impact that group interactive variables could exert on modifying appropriate social repertoires. However, it should be recognized that there are powerful determinants of social responding (hence, potential foci of interventions) located beyond the level of the dyad. For example, a group's willingness to include a new member can operate as a strong determinant of a person's being provided with opportunities to interact. Thus, interventions designed solely to teach social responding within a dyad (i.e., traditional social skills training strategies) potentially ignore the impact of other variables on reciprocal social behavior and have typically not targeted integration into wider social networks.

SELECTING, ASSESSING, AND TEACHING SOCIAL INTERACTION SKILLS

Assessment

There are three facets of assessment of social skills and the support of relationships that require consideration in curricular planning. First, it is important to assess the existing social skills repertoire of a student and, using this repertoire as a basis, to develop objectives for the direct instruction of social interaction skills. Second, it is also important to assess the social environments in which a student will be interacting, so as to choose contexts that best support social interaction, or to change contexts in which the student must necessarily be, but which do not sufficiently support social interaction. Third, it is important to assess periodically the social relationships in which a student is participating in order to document that relationships exist and to provide an analysis to support further efforts to create and support social interactions and relationships.

Assessing Social Interaction Skills. The determination of which social responses are most pivotal or central to increasing interactions and creating social relationships underlies the assessment of social interaction skills. Social behavior under natural conditions includes an infinite array of possible targets for measurement. The complexity of the assessment problem can be fully appreciated when (1) variations of behavior, (2) differences in contexts, and (3) differences in the functional effects of social behavior require simultaneous discrimination by the observer. This problem entails determining which behavior, contexts, and functional effects to define, observe, and count within this infinite set. Fortunately, both conceptual and empirical analyses exist to guide the selection of responses that are most critical to assess. From a conceptual analysis, the developing literature in language pragmatics (Bates, 1976; Prutting, 1982; Warren, Baer, & Rogers-Warren, 1979) and social interaction research (e.g., Cairns, 1980) identifies classes of variables, such as initiation strategies, sharing, and conversational repair strategies, which describe the success of social and communicative events under natural conditions. In addition, there has been more than a decade of research that has identified and validated social interaction variables directly with students with severe disabilities within school settings, including: instruction of social initiations (Gaylord-Ross, Haring, Breen, & Pitts-Conway, 1984), conversational expansion strategies (e.g., Haring, Roger, Lee, Breen, & Gaylord-Ross, 1986; Hunt, Alwell, & Goetz, 1988), play organization (Odom & Strain, 1986), selection of peers (Sasso & Rude, 1987), and responsiveness to others (Koegel & Koegel, 1988). Thus, the process of defining which responses to assess can be guided by empirical findings that have demonstrated the sufficiency of skills for entering and maintaining social interactions.

There are four basic social interaction measures that are indicators of the development of social competence: frequency of social initiation, measurement of responsiveness to others, number of social turns within interactions, and duration of interactions. As previously mentioned, the selection of social interaction skills for assessment can be guided by both conceptual analysis and empirical analysis of pivotal social interaction skills. A *pivotal social skill* (Koegel & Koegel, 1988) is defined as a response that enables a person to participate in a broad series of opportunities that would otherwise be unavailable. For example, teaching a student a simple social initiation response, such as approaching a familiar peer and handing him or her an interactive hand-held video game, can set the occasion for extended durations of mutually engaged social interaction. The pivotal social interaction measures are defined as follows:

• *Social initiation* is any behavior that serves to begin an interaction or changes the focus of the interaction to a new topic or event. For example, Hunt, Alwell, and Goetz (1988) developed an initiation strategy wherein students with severe disabilities were given photo albums that displayed pictures of favorite activities, pets, and family members. The students were taught to approach and show this book to peers. Thus, the book served as both an object with which to initiate an interaction, as well as a topic for ongoing social interaction. For many students with severe disabilities, social initiations are nonverbal and consist of responses such as showing objects or pictures, waving hello, or pointing to an interesting occurrence in the present context. The initiation can be coded as to its direction (person A to person B), as linguistic (e.g., a spoken or signed utterance) or nonlinguistic (e.g., smile, eye contact, physical contact), as social or instructional, and as prompted or independent. Each of these descriptions provides information about the role of the targeted individual, his or her success, and the extent to which that individual is supported within a social group.

• *Social responsiveness to others* is defined as any behavior that serves to acknowledge and respond to the initiation of another person. When a peer initiates an interaction with a student with severe dis-

abilities, the ability to acknowledge the social bid of the peer is an important skill for that student. Peers learn relatively rapidly what types of social initiation strategies work successfully to start interactions. Responding to the social initiations of others is therefore critical to social interaction because, eventually, if the student fails to respond at least minimally to social initiations, people within the student's social world will gradually stop initiating. For some students with severe disabilities, social responding to others includes responses such as making eye contact and smiling, whereas for others (such as students with autism), social responsiveness entails giving elaborated answers to questions. As with initiations, a response can be coded within multiple dimensions: linguistic or nonlinguistic, and prompted or spontaneous.

• *Turn taking* is generally assessed by counting the number of social turns that occur within an interaction. This gives information as to the complexity or sophistication of an interaction. A *turn* is defined as an expansion or elaboration of an initiation, or a response that is followed by a response. Therefore, in a dyad, a turn requires participation by both individuals to define one social turn. After an initiation, each "give and take" interaction between people is defined as a turn:

Person A		Person B	
Initiation	–>	Response	(Turn 1)
	/		
Response	–>	Response	(Turn 2)
	/		
Termination			

• *The duration of the social interaction* is measured to assess the endurance of the interaction to provide a measure of the overall degree of social involvement in a given context. Duration is recorded by starting a stopwatch whenever an interaction is initiated. The stopwatch is turned off when the activity is terminated or when joint attention is broken off. Thus, the assessment of the duration of interaction is a different measure than the number of turns, because it simply assesses whether students are maintaining joint attention to an ongoing activity or event. For example, if two students are playing a game of UNO®, the entire duration of the game is recorded. This provides a relatively efficient measure of time spent in mutual contact.

The assessment of these pivotal social interaction measures provides a way to determine those responses that promote successful dyadic and group interactions and those that are missing from an individual's repertoire, the lack of which creating fewer opportunities for future interactions. Figure 11.1 gives an example of an assessment form used to measure the existing social interaction skills employed by students. Assessment is based on a 10-minute observation of a student with severe disabilities in a natural social interaction context (e.g., during a break between classes, eating lunch in the cafeteria, an interactive instructional event within a mainstreamed classroom). From left to right on the scoring sheet, the observer records the time of the event (e.g., 9:00 A.M.), the context (e.g., walking to class), the peer (e.g., Joe), the interaction as dyadic (i.e., a one-to-one interaction) or a group interaction, the initiator of the interaction (i.e., the student with disabilities or a nondisabled peer), the social nature of the interaction (i.e., S is checked if the interaction was primarily social in nature [versus tutorial]), the presence of an acknowledgment by another interaction (*AC* is checked), the number of turns in the interaction, and the duration of mutually engaged contact. From these data it is possible to assess the four pivotal social interaction functions. To get an accurate summary of a student's social interaction repertoire, it is important to conduct such assessments within each integrated social interaction context.

Assessing Environmental Support and Structure.

There are two classes of support and structure variables that have been shown to affect the quality and quantity of social interactions. One major class of such support variables includes the orga-

nizational strategies that define roles and create contexts for interactions. In addition, teachers can promote interaction through direct prompting.

- *Direct behavioral support and structure.* Teachers frequently structure interactions and social roles that affect the degree and types of social interaction behaviors. *Nonstructured contexts* are situations, such as free time during a break between classes, wherein there is no organized activity and no teacher or peer involvement in structuring or prompting interactions. An unstructured context is exemplified by a student with a severe disability taking a break between classes, with no prompts to interact, activities with which to interact, or designated peers with whom to interact. *Context organized* refers to situations wherein an organized activity is taking place, but in which there is no teacher or peer prompting of social behavior. A context organized activity is exemplified by a student with a severe disability taking a break between classes, carrying a hand-held video game with which he or she has been taught to initiate social interactions. Context organized situations can also exist when a nondisabled peer is participating in interactions with some degree of prior definition and assignment to a definite role. For example, if a peer is taught to behave as a peer tutor and coached to interact in a specific manner, the social context is organized. A defining characteristic of this level of structure is that social interaction is not prompted directly or reinforced. *Directed contexts* refers to structured activities that also include direct teacher or peer prompting of social behaviors. An example of this is seen when a student with a disability is taking a break with a nondisabled peer who prompted participation within a larger group of students by directly including that student in a conversation or interactive episode. Context notes as to the degree of structure and support for interactions can be entered on an assessment form, such as Figure 11.1, within the description of the context.

- *Types of settings.* Levels of social interaction are also affected by the location of the interaction.

Social Interaction Assessment Form

Social Context Research Project

University of California, Santa Barbara

Name: __Mike__   Date: __November 7__

Time	Context	Peer	Relationship	SH<-->NH	S	AC	Turns	Duration
9 25	1st-2nd period Locker A	Joe	peer tutor	←	+	+	TTTT	3 min
9:32	Hallway	Karen	pe friend	→	+	+		2 s
10.15	2nd-3rd period outside office	Matt	office aide buddy	←	+	+	① I	2 min
10:17	In office	Kyle	office aide worker	→	+	+		2 s
10.20	3rd period office aide	Matt		←	T	+	TTTT TTTT HHt	10 min
11.20	3rd-4th period leaving office	Matt		→	+	+		2 s
11.22	Locker A	blonde male	acquaint.	→	+	+		2 s
11.23	hallway	John	Lunch Club Friend	←	+	+	++++	2 min
12:15	lunch (field)	Scott John Glen	lunch friends	←	+	+	Continuous	40 min

FIGURE 11.1   Data collection sheet for assessing social interactions. The columns record the following information: (1) the time of the interaction, (2) the context of the interaction, (3) the name of the peer or peers, (4) whether the interaction was dyadic or group; (5) each initiation is recorded with an arrow showing who initiated the interaction (SH indicates student with severe disabilities, NH indicates nondisabled student). (6) Mark a + if the interaction was social; (7) indicate AC if the initiation was acknowledged by the other person(s); (8) count the number of subsequent interaction turns; and (9) record the duration of the interaction.

Some physical settings offer greater opportunities for social interaction. For example, supported education in highly academic classes that use lecture formats may offer fewer opportunities for interaction than supported education in elective or nonacademic classes, or during other school or community events. Within this model, it is critical not only to assess the frequency of interactions in all settings, but also to assess and document the frequency with which a student is exposed to all relevant settings necessary for habilitation. Data indicating the simple frequency of interaction or mean frequency across settings would help clarify the social interaction opportunities available within a setting.

Placing a student within a given environment without assessing the opportunities that naturally exist within that environment could inadvertently result in the identification of situations with an unusually reduced number of opportunities. Within this model, an opportunity for an interaction is defined as any social situation that would conventionally create a context for a social exchange. For example, in completing a purchase at a grocery store, approaching the cashier constitutes an opportunity to interact. Similarly, if two students are eating lunch together and a third student approaches the dyad and says, "Hi," another opportunity for interaction is available. As defined in this system, an opportunity exists whether or not that opportunity is actually used by the people in that context. This variable is conceptualized as an assessment of the social richness of environments, rathter than the abilities of the interactants.

Regardless of degree of disability, students should be exposed to interactions in vocational and regular campus settings, regular classrooms, and community settings. Because environments vary as to the number of opportunities for interaction, these data should be evaluated to determine which environments of the many possible choices available are optimal for interactions. Note that although the opportunities for social interaction are a critical consideration in selecting environments, other equally critical factors must be considered, such as needed life skills, parent and student prioritization of the activity, and availability of the environment and activity for repeated participation.

To assess those environments and contexts that will provide the greatest number of socially rich opportunities for interaction, a profile, which can be referred to as a Setting Utilization Matrix, can be produced (see Figure 11.2). This matrix identifies a student's current use of the range of potential settings within the school and community. The matrix is produced by first designating the range of settings within the school and the community to which a student should be exposed. For most high school-aged students, the range of settings should include a vocational setting, community settings (such as stores or restaurants), campus settings, and classroom settings (including regular education classes). Substantial gaps in the profile can then become potential targets in teachers' and administrators' negotiations to achieve increased participation in settings that are underrepresented.

The matrix can be used to identify specific settings that require greater social support, that is, those in which the degree of utilization of opportunities is low. Finally, the matrix can be used to identify settings that are relatively impoverished or enriched in natural opportunities for interaction.

There are several methods for determining the degree of utilization of a setting. One method is to examine the data from each opportunity created within a setting and determine the proportion of those opportunities in which the student spontaneously initiated or responded without external prompts from teachers or peers. A second method is to consider both prompted and unprompted episodes as opportunities that are appropriately utilized. For highly interactive students, the first method provides a meaningful assessment, and for students who require social support from others to participate in the settings, the second method provides a more meaningful assessment of the interactions that occur.

Figure 11.2 shows a Setting Utilization Matrix for a student with severe disabilities in a special education program in a high school setting. First, it is important to document that the student has access to an appropriately full range of school and community settings. In this case, the student attends a regular class, participates in integrated break and lunch settings, receives shopping training in a community store, has a supported work site, takes breaks at the work site, and has access to a community recreational leisure site. The next concern is to determine how rich those settings are in providing opportunities for interactions. In Figure 11.2, this is seen in the row labeled "Mean Number of Opportunities." As described earlier, these data reflect the number of times within that setting that it would have been conventionally appropriate to have a social interaction. Finally, the degree of "Percent Utilization" is important to consider. These data reflect the number of opportunities that actually result in an interaction with nondisabled peers. In Figure 11.2 it can be seen by the percentage of opportunities actually utilized in the regular class, in the break time at the vocational site, and in the recreational leisure set-

SCHOOL

	REGULAR CLASS	INTEGRATED BREAK AREA	LUNCH SETTING	OTHER
PERCENT UTILIZATION	56.25%	75.0%	75.0%	91.75
MEAN # OF OPPORTUNITIES	2.75	4.0	1.5	2.75
ACCESS	P. E.	Breaks Between Classes	Lunchroom	School Kitchen (Work Experience)
TYPE OF SETTING	REGULAR CLASS	INTEGRATED BREAK AREA	LUNCH SETTING	OTHER

COMMUNITY

	COMMUNITY STORES	VOCATIONAL SITE	BREAK AREA AT VOC SITE	REC/LEISURE
PERCENT UTILIZATION	72.5%	93.75%	50%	54%
MEAN # OF OPPORTUNITIES	3.7	2.7	3.25	2.0
ACCESS	Vons	Cottage Hosp	Employee's Lounge	YMCA (Locker Room)
TYPE OF SETTING	COMMUNITY STORES	VOCATIONAL SITE	BREAK AREA AT VOC SITE	REC/LEISURE

FIGURE 11.2 Example of a setting utilization matrix showing the settings to which a student has routine access, the mean number of opportunities for interaction, and the percentage of those opportunities that are used.

ting in the community, that the opportunities may be underutilized. If follow-up observation and interviews with people in these settings support this assessment, that these settings are socially underutilized, support people in these settings can be encouraged to prompt greater numbers of interactions or to make other changes to increase more active social participation.

Assessment of Social Relationships

The following types of assessments reflect current beliefs about the desired effects of social interaction intervention for students with severe disabilities: (1) assessment of friendship and (2) assessment of social participation.

Assessment of Friendship. Although direct observation data of actual social interactions will yield more valid and reliable data as to the friendship patterns of students, another major way to assess friendship patterns is through the use of peer nomination measures. An advantage of peer nomination measures is that an enormous amount of data can be rapidly collected by having nondisabled peers fill out simple questionnaires. In conducting such assessments, nondisabled students within a class are asked individually to nominate those within their class (including mainstreamed students with disabilities and students with disabilities who participate in integrated activities with that class) with whom they would participate in various activities or who, in their perception, fit various criteria. For older students, the patterns of friendship groups and cliques within regular education can be determined by having each member fill out a class list in which they tell who their closest friends are. For example, Hiroshige (1990) asked elementary-aged children the following questions in order to assess the friendship networks of students with severe physical disabilities who were mainstreamed:

1. Whom do you like to play with?
2. Who are your friends?
3. Whom would you invite to your birthday party?

In the survey, students are asked to list at least three children for each question. An advantage of using peer nomination scales is that it is possible to "map" the interrelationships between students in order to determine structural relationships between and within peer groups or cliques. For example, some students can be described as "stars," in that they have the highest rates of nominations by others and tend to form nodal points within such peer nomination networks. Some students are nominated occasionally and are located on the periphery of a group. Other students are rarely nominated, and when they are, it is not clear that they fit into any one peer group or clique. By analyzing the existing patterns of friendships within a class, it is possible to identify key students who might be included in structured friendship programs. Including higher-status children in friendship programs is likely to cause a "spillover" in social interactions to other nondisabled peers (Sasso & Rude, 1987).

Social Participation. The purpose of assessing social participation is to document the degree to which a student is engaged in activities with nondisabled friends and acquaintances in school and in community environments, as well as to document the validity of peer nomination reports in terms of the placement of a student in a peer group. Thus, social events and activities, such as going on a shopping trip, eating lunch, participating in an activity in a mainstreamed class, or attending a sporting event, would be recorded if certain preset criteria for participation had been met—most important, engaging in the activity with a nondisabled person. In determining a profile of student social participation, one would measure the number of different social contexts in which the student was involved, as well as the frequency with which the student engaged in these activities. The development of a system to record social participation would include recording data such as the names of the participants, the types of activities in which they are engaged, the relationship of the participants to each other (e.g., best friends, acquaintances, or siblings), and the level of support within the environment (Kennedy, Horner, & Newton, 1989). The use of preexisting listings of activities, such as the "Activities Catalog" (Wilcox & Bellamy, 1987), can facilitate the development of a coding system to document the quantity of social participation for students in supported education settings. To conduct an assessment of this kind, the teacher should keep a daily log of the key social activities that are engaged in with peers.

Intervention Procedures

Although a great deal of information is available on intervention procedures that are effective with students with severe disabilities, several components of effective intervention are particularly relevant in providing instruction on social interaction skills and structuring situations that are conducive to practicing those skills and building relationships. These aspects of effective intervention are discussed in the paragraphs that follow.

Natural Situations for Direct Instruction. Individuals with severe disabilities can learn complex social and communicative skills, but have difficulty in knowing when and where to use those skills (Gaylord-Ross & Holvoet, 1985). Knowing when and where to use skills is critical, considering the number and types of social interactions that could be deemed inappropriate if demonstrated in settings that differ significantly from those settings in which the interaction skills were first taught. For instance, there are subtle situational cues that indicate when and where it is appropriate to interact socially with another person, as well as cues that indicate specific people with whom it is appropriate to interact. Think about the manner in which you approached your best friend in the hallways of your high school, then compare that with the way you approached a new student in the building, or your math teacher, or a person you used to date. Further, consider how these interactions might change if you saw these same people

as you entered class late, or met them at a shopping mall. Each of these situations projects subtle cues that require different social interactions.

To ensure that individuals with severe disabilities are able to use interaction skills effectively in their appropriate criterion settings, intervention must incorporate the variables that are critical to each setting. The most effective method of incorporating these variables is to teach directly in natural environments. Instructional contexts that can be identified as naturally occurring include: (1) activities that include opportunities to interact, (2) times at which those opportunities arise, (3) locations of those opportunities, (4) individuals who are present during those opportunities, (5) age-appropriate materials that are available in the situation and may or may not be required for the completion of the activity, (6) cues that indicate that it is appropriate to interact socially and with whom that interaction should occur, (7) social interactions that are acceptable, (8) consequences for appropriate social interactions, and (9) cues that indicate the termination of the opportunity to socially interact.

Figure 11.3 provides a work sheet that may be helpful in determining these situations and identifying the social interaction skills for which intervention will occur in that situation. It should be noted that when intervention occurs during naturally occurring situations, the situations themselves dictate the direct instructional cues, acceptable behaviors, and consequences used for intervention. Figure 11.3 can be used as an observation data collection form. Naturally occurring social interaction settings are first identified. These might include unstructured times before class begins, specific activity sites on the playground during recess (e.g., foursquare or the basketball court), or waiting for the school bus after school on the sidewalk. Teachers and other personnel should observe interactions between nondisabled students and record the range of cues for interacting, acceptable types of interaction, possible consequences of interactions, and what cues the termination of interactions. Consideration of these observation data across several natu-

Activity: Time:

Location: Age-Appropriate
                                                   Materials:

People Present	Cues for Interacting	Acceptable Social Interactions	Consequences	Cues for Termination of Interactions

Social Interaction Skills Targetted for Intervention:

Objective(s):

Intervention:

Generalization Situations:

FIGURE 11.3 Example of a planning sheet to use in a natural context to record people present, cues for interaction, acceptable types of social interactions, natural consequences, and cues for terminating interactions.

rally occurring interaction settings is helpful in the identification of both general (skills used across settings) and specific social interaction skills for intervention.

Including Social Skills on a Task Analysis. Task analysis is the most widely used instructional model for students with severe disabilities (e.g., Snell, 1987; Gaylord-Ross & Holvoet, 1985; Sailor

& Guess, 1983). A task analysis specifies the series of responses that are needed for a student to interact appropriately within a specific setting. Therefore, the types of skills that are included within a task analysis determine the resultant skills that will be acquired by a student. For example, if a task analysis for completing a purchase in a fast-food restaurant does not include steps for greeting the cashier or appropriately terminating an interaction, it is extremely unlikely that students will acquire these skills through other means once functional skills instruction is completed. In a critique of task analytic instruction, Brown, Evans, Weed, and Owen (1987) point out that most examples of task analyses are too limited in scope and that social interaction skills and communicative skills are generally missing from a task analysis. In addition, skills necessary to solve a problem if something is wrong in a situation are frequently omitted from task analyses. For example, if a student is being taught a vocational skill, such as washing windows, the student should also be taught a strategy to use if something goes wrong, such as running out of window cleaner. This strategy might be to show the supervisor the empty sprayer. In many cases problem-solving skills involve learning a social interaction response such as asking someone for help or drawing the attention of a supervisor to a problem.

Because task analysis is the predominant mode of instruction for learners with severe disabilities, it is critical to modify task analysis to include the full range of social interaction responses that are routinely associated with a skill, as well as the rarer social responses that are critical to independence. Haring and Kennedy (1988) suggested that task analysis be produced to indicate which responses are critical to task completion, and which responses are optional (such as social responses), but very desirable to learn. The inclusion of social responses on the task analysis ensures, at a minimum, that these responses are not ignored during instruction.

Generalization Training. Generalization is a critically important component of social interaction training. In general, the social responses identified

for training should be those that are maximally generalizable across settings and people. Conducting social skill training directly in the natural environment (as opposed to classroom settings) is one important means to facilitate generalization. However, training in the natural environment alone is rarely sufficient to ensure generalization.

To ensure generalized responding, it is critical to consider first the range of events, stimuli, or people to which the student should generalize. After a list of critical situations is produced, training should be conducted to sample the range of people, stimuli, or events that are needed. Training should continue until generalization to all important situations is documented.

There are two basic procedures to promote generalization of social behavior in students who have severe disabilities. One strategy is to use sequential multiple example training (also referred to as training with sufficient exemplars, or multiple exemplar training [Stokes & Baer, 1977]). In sequential multiple example training, the range of critical examples is first identified. If a greeting response to co-workers on a job site is being taught, the range of co-workers that a student directly works with might constitute the critical set of examples. Training is begun with one co-worker and continues until the student reliably greets that one person. Generalization to the other workers is then assessed. If generalization to some or all of the other co-workers is not observed, training with a second co-worker is initiated. After training with the second co-worker is completed, a generalization assessment is again conducted, and training with a third co-worker is initiated. The cycle of teaching one example at a time, then assessing generalization, is continued until the student greets all of the critical members of the set.

An alternative to sequential multiple example training is concurrent multiple example training. This strategy is the same as sequential training, except that training is initiated simultaneously with a larger set of examples. For example, instead of training one example (one co-worker) at a time, three or four co-workers participate in the training simultaneously. As in the first procedure, training with sub-sets of co-workers is continued until generalization to all critical members of the set is observed. There are other generalization strategies that are useful in social skill training, such as general case programming (Horner, McDonnell, & Bellamy, 1986).

Self-Monitoring. Self-monitoring is a process that includes: (1) discriminating correct from incorrect examples of a target behavior (i.e., establishing a performance standard), (2) observing one's own behavior or the results of a performance, (3) evaluating one's behavior against the standard, (4) self-recording the performance, and (5) self-reinforcement (Koegel & Koegel, 1988). Self-monitoring itself consists of a series of responses. Once these responses are taught, they mediate the performance of other responses. For example, students can be taught to self-monitor their own initiation of social responses. A standard of performance can be created, such as a goal to initiate five conversations per school day. Students can subsequently record each instance of social initiation and receive feedback and reinforcement from others when the successful attainment of this performance standard is reported. Self-monitoring has been widely shown to be teachable to students with moderate and severe disabilities. One area in which it has been widely applied is in increasing work productivity (e.g., Ackerman & Shapiro, 1984).

Liberty (1985) investigated the use of a self-monitoring procedure to increase question answering in students with severe disabilities. In this study, students with severe disabilities used hand counters and wrist counters to self-record two-word answers to questions. The results indicated that wearing the self-monitoring devices controlled responsiveness. Case studies of the application of self-monitoring to increase responsiveness to questions from others have also been reported by Koegel and Koegel (1988).

A major issue in self-monitoring for students with severe disabilities is the probability that it is possible to self-monitor only one response at a time, rather than multiple responses. Therefore, it is important that the response selected for self-monitoring be as pivotal as possible so that broader changes in socialization can be promoted. Another issue with self-monitoring systems is whether they can be faded, with the level of social responding remaining reasonably high. There are relatively few examples of studies in which self-monitoring procedures were systematically faded. Indeed, most demonstrations of self-monitoring show that the self-monitoring system controls responding. This means that when the systems are withdrawn, the behavior typically returns to baseline levels. Finally, the overall success of self-monitoring is dependent on the reinforcement that the student receives for engaging in the self-monitored behaviors. This can occur in two ways, which are not mutually exclusive. First, behaviors should be selected that others in the student's environment would naturally reinforce, or would reinforce more strongly if prompted to do so. A second approach is to reward the students for reporting the self-monitored responses at periodic intervals; however, if students are dependent on this type of reinforcement rather than the former, the probability of successfully fading the self-monitoring program will be lower.

Teaching Generative Scripts. Teaching students to follow scripted interaction patterns is another instructional strategy that is widely employed in social interaction training. Many students fail to respond to the social initiations of others, or fail to initiate interactions themselves, because they do not know what to say or do. *Social scripts* are defined as routine social interaction patterns that can be repeated many times in a variety of contexts. A simple social script may be the following: Seeing a friend; saying, "Hi"; asking, "How are you doing?" Another simple interactional script—approach a friend, greet, offer interactive object, and terminate the interaction—can be taught and used with a variety of settings and materials. Such scripts are *generative*, because an almost infinite number of objects (e,g., hand-held video games, picture communication books, or cups of coffee) can be inserted within the script in various contexts. Once the students have learned this sequence of behaviors across multiple examples and within multiple settings, new objects that can structure interactions will frequently be spontaneously introduced by students. This type of social initiation strategy was employed within the studies by Gaylord-Ross et al. (1984) and Breen et al. (1985).

CRITICAL ISSUES IN SOCIAL SKILL TRAINING AND SUPPORTING RELATIONSHIPS

The creation of social relationships needs to be viewed as a main effect of instruction, not as a side effect. As instruction is planned in community settings, integrated classrooms, and school settings, the creation and support of relationships should be considered as important as the teaching of functional skills. Students with severe disabilities should have the right both to instruction of relevant skills needed for more independent living and to support in developing and maintaining social relationships. There are a number of critical issues that require further research and demonstration to fully implement the goals of socially integrated instruction.

Social Interventions for Students with the Most Severe Disabilities

As students with the most severe disabilities are increasingly served on regular public school campuses, it will be critical to develop intervention procedures to promote social skill learning and social interaction. In particular, increased research in areas such as augmentative communication systems with peers as interactants is particularly needed (e.g., Wacker, Wiggins, Fowler, & Berg, 1988).

Stronger Documentation of the Effects of Intervention on Relationships

As reviewed in the discussion of assessment in this chapter, there is a sufficient assessment methodol-

ogy to assess social networks, acceptance, and relationships. Its tools should be employed periodically to assess the impact of intervention on peers. In addition, once data collection systems are more fully developed, experimental research can focus on the effectiveness of collecting, sharing, and analyzing these data in teachers' efforts to create opportunities for interactions. Teacher and administrative evaluations should include these data as important aspects of performance evaluation.

Increased Participation by Peers in Intervention Design

Reports of peers participating in designing interventions, targeting responses for instruction, or assisting in conducting interventions should be increased. Student support networks can be used to increase the quality and frequency of social interactions. We should also examine the use of student support networks to provide encouragement to students with disabilities within mainstreamed classes. In gauging the success or failure of educational support services, we should increasingly turn to peer feedback and reports of integrated activities that were mutually enjoyable.

Focus on Pivotal Behaviors

Although there are effective intervention strategies to increase highly specific social responses, for example, eye contact, and answering common questions such as "How are you?" (e.g., Tara, Matson, & Leary, 1988), there should be a greater focus on teaching social skills that increase social participation and that are more pivotal to social development. Self-monitoring, hanging out, initiating interactions, and generative scripts are examples of more pivotal responses for interventions.

Identification of Richer Contexts for Interaction

Contextual variation is an important variable in promoting social development. Both physical and social parameters affect social interchanges. Peers are the primary determiners of the social contexts within natural settings. Thus, interventions focused on changing peer responsiveness, peer initiation, and peer participation within natural school contexts are important in an overall strategy. As contexts are identified for interaction, teachers should analyze the activities taking place within those contexts to teach skills needed for participation. In particular, we need to develop strategies for increasing the frequency and quality of social interaction during after-school hours and on weekends.

CURRICULUM MODELS: OVERVIEW OF BEST PRACTICES

Although curriculum packages are enormously popular because of the perceived time savings, as compared with developing more individualized interventions, there are no validated prepackaged curricula in the area of teaching social skills and support of friendships for students with severe disabilities. Instead, the development of curricular packages has proceeded through the development of validated strategies. A strategy is an organizing framework for designing a certain type of instruction for an activity. Fortunately, past research and curriculum development efforts have yielded a fairly extensive catalog of validated curriculum models and strategies for teaching social interaction skills. An advantage of curricular models and strategies as opposed to a packaged curriculum is that a strategy, such as peer initiation training, is sufficiently generic to be used across a wide age range and wide range of abilities. Another advantage of curriculum strategies is that to implement a strategy, the teacher must carefully consider the unique needs of the school, the students to be included in the intervention, and the materials that would be most appropriate to that school or subculture.

Strategies Within Preschool and Kindergarten Programs

Public Law 99-457 ensures that educational programs will be developed to include children with disabilities between 3 and 5 years of age. Like PL 94-142, PL 99-457 is designed with specific language to encourage the maximal social integration of children. In the case of most young children with severe disabilities, the concept of *mainstreaming* describes the organizational arrangement best suited for their developmental needs (Sailor et al., 1990). The developmental tasks of normally developing young children are comparable in terms of content to the developmental tasks needed by young children with severe disabilities. At no other point in development are skills and intervention objectives so closely matched as they are in the early developmental period. Mainstreaming is defined as the primary placement of students with disabilities in the same classroom as children who are not disabled, but with the appropriate level of specialized instruction and support to allow participation in that environment. The primary social settings for young children with severe disabilities should be determined by their ages and by the existing types of programs for nondisabled children of the same age: daycare (18 months to 3 or 4 years of age), preschool (from 3 or 4 through 5 years of age), and kindergarten (from 5 to 6 years of age).

The goal of early childhood programming for children with severe disabilities should be keyed to the skills needed for entry into regular kindergarten (Vincent et al., 1980). By and large, these skills are social and communicative in nature: following directions, attending to the teacher and other students, playing appropriately, and being able to communicate basic requests for objects, attention, and affection. These basic social interaction and communication skills are far more central to future development than the specific skills learned in typical preschool tasks such as drawing or stacking blocks.

Developmental Strategy.   The development of curricular objectives for preschool programs can be guided to some extent by patterns of normal social and communicative development. However, it is important to note that normal social developmental milestones should be used only to develop general goals as to the types of social functions needed by children, and not as a prescriptive series of objectives that must be followed in "lockstep" order. Instead, the teacher should be aware of the social developmental milestones that are important at a given level of development, reinforce strongly instances of more advanced social behavior, and set up tasks and activities that provide opportunities for practicing key social interaction milestones. A brief review of basic developmental milestones is given in Table 11.1.

As Table 11.1 indicates, many of the social developmental milestones involve the development of play skills. Opportunities to play—with appropriate levels of support from adults—form a basic part of all preschool programs. In addition, much of the more formal social and communicative instruction should take place within the context of interactive play, either with peers or with adults. In particular, playing with toys and interacting with other materials is central to programming for children at this age (e.g., Haring, 1985). Hanson and Hanline (1989) give three principles for increasing social interaction in programming for young children:

1. Limit the number of children participating in an activity (e.g., three or four children), the size of the play area, and the amount of materials available. This is an important principle, because the limitation of materials encourages more sharing and requesting of materials from peers. Limiting the number of playmates available creates a need for students to play together. In larger groups of nondisabled peers, students with disabilities run a greater risk of being excluded from play as more developmentally advanced students seek each other out.

2. Form small instructional and play groups with consideration of the preferences and skills of each child. Forming groups by considerations of toy preferences can facilitate interaction. In addition, keeping play groups relatively intact for several days or weeks can allow students to develop roles or subspecialties within a group. For example, in a group formed around playing with Legos®, a stu-

dent with severe disabilities might specialize in finding blocks of a certain type to contribute to a jointly constructed edifice.

3. Determine the optimal size of groups and the degree of developmental match needed for individual students. One advantage of early education programs is that a wide range of developmental levels and ages are evidenced by both students with disabilities and their peers. Some students interact better with more similarly matched students, whereas others may have greater social support from children who are developmentally more sophisticated.

Peer Initiation Strategy. Peer initiation interventions have an extensive history of effectiveness in promoting increased social interaction of young children with disabilities (e.g., Hendrickson, Strain, Trembly, & Shores, 1982). With this strategy, nondisabled peers are trained to initiate interactions with children with disabilities. Research has documented that this strategy results in increases in the social interactions between students with disabilities and their peers. These effects have been robust in children with autism (Strain, Kerr, & Ragland, 1979; Odom & Strain, 1986), behavior disorders (Strain & Fox, 1981), mental retardation (Lancioni, 1982), and severe disabilities (Young & Kerr, 1979). Peer initiation procedures can be applied within school settings or within home settings by siblings (James & Egel, 1986).

The major focus of peer initiation strategies is to teach nondisabled preschoolers to organize play episodes, share toys, respond positively to social responses, and engage in play. The ability to organize play episodes is a skill many nondisabled children display with friends. A child may organize a play episode by saying, "Let's play trains. I'll put the tracks together, you set up the town, and you put the trains on the track." The play organizer thus serves as a social facilitator for the student with disabilities, as well as for other students, by assigning roles and organizing the play context. Sharing toys is one of the most frequently used strategies by all children to enter and participate in

TABLE 11.1   Social Development Milestones

Birth–6 months

Recognizes familiar persons

Reaches out, gazes at others

Maintains eye contact during interaction

Smiles

Makes social response to self in mirror

6–12 months

Cooperates in interactive "games" with adult

Imitates actions and sounds

24–36 months

Demands attention from significant others

Explores environment constantly

Plays contentedly if near adults

Begins to initiate play activities

24–36 months

Watches other children play and engages in parallel play

Briefly joins in play of others

Begins to engage in simple dramatic play (e.g., plays house)

Engages in symbolic play with objects

Participates in simple group activities such as story telling

36–48 months

Shares toys

Exchanges toys in a game-like fashion

Takes turns with assistance

Spontaneously joins in play with other children

Engages in more complex dramatic play (e.g., acting out a trip to the store)

Plays interactive games such as tag

Creates imaginary characters

Enjoys puppet play and singing

48–60 Months

Participates in socially interactive play

Shows concern for playmates in distress

Prefers playing with other children to playing alone

Follows rules when playing games

Adapted from Hanson, M. J., & Hanline, M. F. (1989). Integration options for the very young child. In R. Gaylord-Ross (Ed.), *Integration strategies for students with handicaps* (pp. 177–193). Baltimore: Paul H. Brookes Publishing Co.

play or social interactions. Through modeling and reinforcement, a peer is taught to recognize play situations in which a child with disabilities is playing alone or is not engaged in an activity. The peer is taught to approach that child and use a specific strategy to include the child in his or her play. For example, if a peer initiator is playing with vehicles, with a small group of other children, and notices that the student with disabilities is not playing, the peer would approach the student, share a toy car, and encourage the student to play in proximity to his or her play.

In some cases, peer initiation interventions have not only resulted in increases for targeted students, but have also produced "spillover" effects for nontargeted students (Strain, Shores, & Kerr, 1976). Sasso and Rude (1987) showed that the status of the peers engaged within the intervention influenced other peers to interact with the student who was disabled. Sasso, Hughes, Swanson, and Novak (1987) investigated a technique by which nondisabled peers were trained to reinforce untrained nondisabled peers for initiating interactions with students who were disabled. The results indicated that the procedure was effective in increasing the level of interaction and that teacher prompting of interaction was largely unnecessary.

Organized Play Activities.   A critical principle in planning social interaction interventions is that all participants must enjoy the interaction. Therefore, in planning interventions for young children with severe disabilities, it is important to create social interaction contexts that are playlike and highly enjoyable. For example, Hanson and Hanline (1989) described a preschool social integration activity that centered on an obstacle course. Actions on the obstacle course could include crawling under a table, sitting on a chair, stepping over pillows, crawling through a tunnel, throwing a bean bag at a target, walking on a balance beam, rocking in a rocking boat, and bouncing balls. Social interaction was facilitated by having the students complete the course in pairs (e.g., one student with disabilities and one nondisabled peer) and having

the teacher prompt students to describe the actions they were performing or to offer encouragement to their partners.

Goldstein, Wickstrom, Hoyson, Jamieson, and Odom (1988) investigated sociodramatic script training to promote interaction. Examples of scripted sociodramatic activities that these authors have investigated include a shoe store activity and a magic show. In these interventions, scripts are provided that include roles for three students. For example, in the magic show script there are the roles of magician, magician's assistant, and volunteer from the audience. The teacher supplies all needed props for carrying out the play and teaches the participants to recite lines that correspond to each role. In addition, the teacher encourages elaboration of scripted lines and spontaneous changes in the play. The data indicate that the level of social interaction and language use increases dramatically under these conditions. This kind of intervention may be effective not only because of the facilitative effects of teacher direction and structure, but because of the familiarity of the scripted context over time, the reinforcement for elaboration, and the overall enjoyment and reinforcing quality of putting on a play.

Strategies and Instruction at the Elementary Level

As summarized by Sailor and colleagues (1986), there are three major quality indicators of social integration programming at the elementary level: (1) instruction of students with severe disabilities occurs across all campus environments that are regularly used by nondisabled students, including extracurricular activities; (2) students with severe disabilities participate on an ongoing, individualized basis in academic and nonacademic school settings as specified in each student's IEP; and (3) consistent opportunities for interaction with nondisabled students are organized through structured interventions designed to create opportunities for social interaction as well as promote the development of social interaction skills. In the following paragraphs, we review three strategies to promote social skill use: functional skill activities, peer tutor programs, and friendship programs.

Interactions During Functional Activities.   There are a number of situations in which students with severe disabilities must learn to initiate, complete, and terminate activities that lead to meaningful outcomes in their lives. The nature of activities for teaching functional skills will vary throughout the years for each student. During the elementary years, functional activities can include: (1) self-management activities (e.g., eating in the cafeteria, mobility within the classroom and school, hand washing); (2) community access activities (e.g., purchasing age-appropriate items at a store, street crossing); and (3) work activities (e.g., completing in-class or in-school jobs). One method of maximizing contact with nondisabled peers is to pair students during functional activities. A key objective, however, is to ensure that the instructional time is beneficial to both students, thus creating a cooperative learning activity.

For example, a fourth-grade student with severe disabilities for whom an intervention goal includes the purchasing of a school lunch might have the following goals: (1) identify the items that are wanted; (2) develop a communication card to indicate wanted items; (3) obtain the card and money prior to entering cafeteria; (4) go to the cafeteria; (5) purchase lunch; (6) consume lunch; and (7) go to the next activity. When pairing this student with a classmate from a regular class, the teacher can match the skills that will be addressed with students who can benefit from additional practice in those skills. For instance, there may be students who can benefit from additional practice in math or money skills, or in generating lists on a computer, or simply in completing multiple-step instructions independently. Figure 11.4 provides a work sheet for matching students by functional activity and skill practice needs. Identified students may then rotate as matched partners during this functional activity.

Although this matching of partners only creates

opportunities for interactions to occur, it may then be possible to build intervention for social interaction skills into the functional activity. For instance, the student with severe disabilities might be required to correctly greet his or partner, to politely and correctly indicate item selections at the cafeteria, or to make three initiations during the walk to and from the lunchroom.

The partner may also be provided the information necessary to provide corrective feedback when needed and instructions to respond to the initiations as well as possible. Information relevant to social interaction skill intervention during functional activities with peer partners can easily be included on the work sheet found in Figure 11.4.

Peer Tutor Programs.   Peer tutoring programs are designed to teach nondisabled peers to use systematic instructional procedures (i.e., cueing, prompting, error correction strategies, and reinforcement strategies) to teach social or independent-living skills to students with disabilities. Although peer tutor programs are among the most widely used integration strategies, it should be noted that these programs run the risk of creating the impression that students with disabilities have greater skill differences and power differences than would otherwise be apparent. Sailor and colleagues (1990) refer to this as a "hierarchical" (or vertical) relationship that places the nondisabled student in a more powerful position than the student with disabilities, that is, as the teacher in a teacher-student relationship. Voeltz (1982) warns that these status or power differences between the tutor and the learner may inhibit friendship formation, positive social interaction, and positive attitudes. Clearly, then, if a teacher decides to develop a peer tutor program, he or she must take care to stress the benefits of developing a friendship, in addition to the tutorial aspect of the program.

In setting up a peer tutor program, the initial step must be to obtain the support of the school principal. The next step is to introduce the program to the school faculty through a presentation

```
Functional Activity:   Student Match and Intervention
Student:                      | Student:

Functional Activity Goal:     | Skill Practice Goal:

Intervention:                 | Practice:

Generalization Situations:    | Feedback:

Activity:                     | Time:

                              | Location:
```

```
Functional Activity:   Social Interaction Skill Intervention

Social Interaction Skills Objective(s):
```

People Present	Cues for Interacting	Acceptable Social Interactions	Consequences	Cues for Termination of Interactions

```
Generalization Situations:
```

FIGURE 11.4   Example of a planning form to match students with disabilities and nondisabled peers in functional activities.

that stresses the importance of integration and the need for cooperation between special and regular classes to implement the idea successfully. The third step is to meet with the smaller group of regular class teachers whose students are most appropriately matched with the students receiving special services. The most important agenda item at this meeting is a discussion of times and schedules to determine when, during the day, students could participate as peer tutors. Generally, a small number of students (two or three at a time) should be scheduled. In some cases, teachers schedule peer tutoring time as a privilege that is earned if regularly scheduled work is completed in less than the allowed time. In other cases, a teacher may provide alternative times to complete class work that may be missed by a student participating as a tutor.

Once the teachers of the targeted classrooms have arrived at a suitable arrangement for scheduling, presentations are made to the participating classes. These presentations should stress the importance of integration; the interests, strengths, and learning goals of the students with disabilities; the types of activities that participants might engage in as peer tutors; and why students like them have enjoyed being tutors in the past. Many teachers have found it helpful to develop a slide show that demonstrates the activities and goals of the program. Students who may be interested are asked to sign up and are then requested to visit the special education class to see whether they are still interested. During the subsequent class visits, the special education teacher can talk with the potential tutors and determine the strength of interest, as well as the potential capability, of each tutor. When students have visited at least once, a follow-up meeting with the regular teacher is scheduled to discuss the potential candidates for the program and solicit feedback about the possibility of scheduling specific students at specific times. After the peer tutors have been selected, the teacher schedules a meeting with the tutors to discuss scheduling and activities of special interest to them, and to pass out parent permission slips.

The training of peer tutors is most often done through modeling the specific activities in which they will be engaged. Each peer tutor then demonstrates the activity and receives feedback from the teacher. Additional modeling and feedback are offered until a criterion for successful performance is reached. The teacher should then gradually withdraw from the two students and let the activity proceed without interruption. In conducting peer tutor programs, it is important to touch bases with the tutors before and after participation

in each activity. It is essential to reinforce tutors highly and to develop ongoing supportive relationships with them. It is also critical to help in problem solving and to change activities on an ongoing basis to keep interest levels high.

An important component of any peer tutoring program is the maintenance of a high interest level in both students. Choosing activities that are at least partially of a recreational or leisure-time nature is an important consideration. In recent research on peer tutor relationships, we have used instruction in microcomputer games as an effective context for both tutoring and social interaction (Breen & Haring, 1991).

Friendship   Programs. Friendship programs stress more purely social leisure activities. Meyer and Putnam (1987) suggest that special friend relationships be set up on the basis of age, gender, proximity of residence, shared hobbies and preferences, and students' mutual interest in each other. In elementary schools it is frequently possible to implement friendship programs as part of regular recess times. Recruiting students for participation in a friendship program can follow the basic guidelines given for peer tutor programs. In some ways, setting up a friendship program can be easier, because regular instructional time is not used.

The most important component in setting up a friendship program is determining the activities that can be developed to structure the interactions. For each student receiving special services, a list of activities is generated, which includes activities he or she enjoys and can engage in without a great deal of prompting. The list can include activities such as games, looking at magazines, playing with toys, or interacting with electronic entertainment devices (e.g., computers or music). Once students have been paired, the students with disabilities and the nondisabled students should be prompted to choose activities that they would want to engage in during specifically scheduled times. As with peer tutors, the teacher should make an active effort to talk with the nondisabled friend before or after each interaction. As the relationship develops between the special friend and the student with disabilities, suggestions can be made to extend the interactions to other less structured times, such as eating lunch together or meeting after school. In all cases, the teacher should facilitate and guide these interactions as appropriate. For example, if playing after school is an appropriate extension of the relationship, the teacher could facilitate this activity by calling the parents of both students to obtain permission and help arrange times and transportation if needed.

As friendships develop, the support of these relationships can become one of the most rewarding activities of a special education teacher. It is particularly important to continue to develop a supportive adult-student relationship with the nondisabled peers and to be constantly on the lookout for social interaction skills that can be taught or new activities that can be developed to continue support for friendships.

Strategies and Instruction at the Secondary Level

Many of the strategies that have been described for younger students can also be used for high school students with appropriate adaptations. For example, many nondisabled students at the high school level are interested in participation because they are contemplating a career in teaching and this is an opportunity to learn teaching skills in a supportive relationship with a special education teacher. In addition, at the high school level it is frequently possible to arrange class credit for a participating peer tutor. The most important point to stress to peers at the high school level is that they must keep their interactions with students natural and age appropriate. We frequently remind students to talk and act with their friends who are disabled in the same way they would with any other friends.

Junior and senior high schools offer rich opportunities for promoting social interaction and relationships. At perhaps no other level of schooling are so many diverse opportunities available. In school programs in which social integration programs are well established, there are both structured and un-

structured social interactions happening in regular classes, in the community with peers, during after-school clubs, at formal social events such as school dances, and during the myriad of events that occur during a regular school day as students walk to classes and "hang out." In addition to some of those previously described, the following strategies can be used effectively at the secondary level.

Partners at Lunch Club. "Hanging out" is a pivotal response class for adolescents with severe disabilities. Although the responses needed to appropriately hang out are minimal, an active effort is needed to integrate students with disabilities into existing peer groups. Simply sending students into a typical school lunchroom or courtyard and expecting integration and inclusion to occur is unlikely to result in successful interactions. A major reason for social behavior intervention is not only to teach a social interaction skill, but to set the occasion for ongoing social interactions. Ultimately, it is hoped that teaching pivotal skills, increasing the frequency and quality of interactions, and increasing the rate of social contacts will result in attainment of friendships.

An innovative friendship program is described by Breen, Lovinger, and Haring (1989). At La Colina Junior High School in Santa Barbara, students with severe disabilities are assigned to a special education classroom, but attend regular classes such as art and physical education, as well as all noncurricular activities (e.g., lunch and breaks between classes). In addition to these efforts to include the students with severe disabilities in the mainstream of the school, there is also a program designed to create supported friendships. Within this program, nondisabled students are recruited every school year for participation in a supported friendship program, the Partners at Lunch (PAL) Club. A primary purpose of the PAL Club is to provide a mechanism for planning lunchtime opportunities for students with severe disabilities to hang out with nondisabled peer groups. Another major purpose of the club is to plan and implement schoolwide activities. For example, PAL Club has organized events such as

1950s days and lunchtime assemblies at which members put on skits. The planning of such schoolwide activities sets the agenda for many of the weekly PAL Club meetings.

The friendship program is structured with several unique characteristics. First, the nondisabled students are asked to make a commitment of time, which is purposely kept at a minimum. For example, a student may commit to a minimum of one, two, or three lunch periods per week to be spent with a student with disabilities. Students may exceed the minimum commitment at any time; however, a procedure to limit their initial commitment was instituted because many students overcommitted to the program and became dissatisfied after a month or so of participation. Because the initial commitment is kept low, the majority of the students have successfully maintained friendship interactions for at least a year.

A second unique aspect of the program is that entire peer groups are recruited for participation, not just individuals. As the program typically functions, the student with severe disabilities spends the lunch period with a peer group and follows that group throughout its normal social interaction patterns. A third special feature is that peer groups meet with the students who are disabled and the teacher one afternoon each week after school for social and leisure interactions.

The PAL Club is a recognized after-school club that is formally sanctioned by the student council, as are other school clubs such as the Chess Club or French Club. During PAL Club meeting times, the teacher informally interviews the peer groups to determine how the nonmonitored lunchtime interactions are proceeding. This gives the teacher an opportunity to identify potential problems and provide specific suggestions on how to handle problems in the future. In addition, it provides an opportunity to identify training objectives for social skills or critical skills that are perceived by the peers as requiring intervention.

Student Support Networks.   Support networks to facilitate the integration of students with moderate and severe disabilities are effective means to increase social interaction and support relationships at the junior high and high school levels (Haring & Breen, 1990). Such interventions are based on the formation of support groups that meet on a weekly basis to allow members to listen to each other's concerns and offer suggestions for solving problems. Within the procedure developed by Haring and Breen (1990), peer groups of four nondisabled students and one student with disabilities meet on a weekly basis to discuss ways to increase the social participation of the student with disabilities throughout the school. The group is managed by an adult who helps to organize the discussion and set goals for the group. The intervention follows these steps:

1. *Establish a prenetwork baseline.* The purpose of the prenetwork baseline is to assess the students' current levels of interaction as they go through their school days in the integrated environment. No prompting or intervention of any kind is conducted. Assessment is made as follows: (1) the frequency of interactions between the student with disabilities and others during a school day is recorded, and (2) within this total frequency, the number of initiations by nondisabled students, the number of initiations by the student with disabilities, the number of peers with whom interaction occurs, and the number of multiple-turn interactions are recorded.

2. *Construct social networks.* The purpose of this phase of the investigation is to recruit extant cliques of nondisabled students to participate in the investigation. In the study by Haring and Breen (1990), peers were recruited from the mainstreamed class of the student with disabilities and from the existing peer interaction program that was in place in this school, the PAL Club.

3. *Initiate social network meetings.* The content of the social network meetings is as follows:

Meeting 1. The purpose of the first meeting is to present the goals of the group: to establish friendship, to better integrate students into the mainstream of school, to provide support for a student with disabilities, to model acceptance and willingness for friendships to others.

The adult discussion leader explains how the group will work:

- Each student is responsible for at least one time per day to meet with the student with disabilities and interact with him or her in some way, including greeting the student, including him or her in an activity for a brief period, and terminating the interaction in a friendly manner.
- Each student is responsible for recording when he or she met with the student with disabilities (self-monitoring), who initiated, whether the student with disabilities responded appropriately, and whether the interaction was positive, neutral, or negative.
- The students will attend a meeting once a week to talk about their experiences of the previous week, graph their data, and discuss ways to increase or improve interactions.
- Honesty and openness are of paramount importance in discussing any problems students may experience (e.g., peer pressure not to interact with disabled students).
- All students will map out their daily activities and schedule of courses in order to plan locations for social interactions throughout the school day.

Group leader follow-up to first group meeting. After the first meeting, the group leader develops a matrix of contexts indicating the overlap of locations between the student with disabilities and his or her peers in the peer support network. The leader then develops student assignments for all the students in the group, including the student with disabilities. This information is put together in student binders. The nondisabled students use the binders to hold their schoolwork and to serve as a prompt that specifically gives times and objectives for interactions with the students with disabilities as they go through their school day.

Meeting 2. The purpose of this meeting is to introduce the students to the binder system and implement the peer support network. The group leader provides the students with their schedules for the week, teaches them how to use the self-monitoring system, and encourages verbal partici-

pation by all students, including the student with disabilities. The group leader also verbally reinforces group members for stating goals of the group, prompts the student with disabilities to discuss concerns, and ends the meeting by having group members complete a form for evaluation of the group process.

Meeting 3. The purpose of the third meeting and all subsequent meetings is to reinforce and maintain the operation of the peer support network. During each meeting the group reviews the data collected by group members, assesses the possibility of interaction at times when there may be "holes" in the schedule of the student with disabilities, provides reinforcement or feedback to each student as to the success or failure in meeting his or her commitments, and discusses concerns and positive experiences as a result of participating in the group and socially supporting a student with disabilities.

Starting with the third meeting, the agenda for the group meetings may also include a discussion of social skill interventions that can be conducted to better facilitate the inclusion of the student with disabilities into the group's network and within the school. That is, the students themselves discuss and plan targets for social skill intervention for the student with disabilities so that he or she might better participate in social interactions throughout the school.

Data records were kept by each nondisabled peer, indicating the presence of an interaction, initiator of the interaction, appropriate responding, length of the interaction, and overall rating of the interaction. These data were then summarized in terms of (1) the number of opportunities for interaction with network members, (2) the frequency of initiations, and (3) the number of interactions that included appropriate responding by the student with severe disabilities. Figure 11.5 is an example of the data sheets that peers filled out to monitor the social interactions in which they participated.

The results of testing this program in a junior high school indicated that the peer social support network was a highly effective way to increase

Monday Date:_____

Assigned time: **3rd-4th** Assigned place: **Locker C**

Was there an interaction:	Yes	No
Was there an attempt to interact:	Yes	No
Who started the interaction:	Me	_____
Did ____ respond appropriately:	Yes	No
Did ____ leave appropriately:	Yes	No
Were there other people around:	Yes	No
Did other people react o.k.:	Yes	No
Interaction was:	Good O.k.	Not good

Assigned time: **After school** Assigned place: **Class**

Was there an interaction:	Yes	No
Was there an attempt to interact:	Yes	No
Who started the interaction:	Me	_____
Did ____ respond appropriately:	Yes	No
Did ____ leave appropriately:	Yes	No
Were there other people around:	Yes	No
Did other people react o.k.:	Yes	No
Interaction was:	Good O.k.	Not good

Other times:

When_____Where_____Bad O.K. Good

When_____Where_____Bad O.K. Good

When_____Where_____Bad O.K. Good

Comments:_____

_____

_____

FIGURE 11.5 Example of data collection sheet for use by nondisabled peers to monitor social interactions that occur on campus.

interactions. In two peer support networks that were extensively studied, the frequency of social interaction during a school day increased more than fourfold. Students with disabilities interacted in a more natural way with members of their support group (e.g., between classes, during lunch, in mainstreamed classes, and after school) more than 10 times a day. Baseline rates of interaction with peers prior to initiation of the peer support group were less than four interactions per day.

Strategies in Postsecondary Programs

People with developmental disabilities have experienced significant changes in the quality and location of services over the past decade. Hill and Bruininks (1984), of the Center for Residential and Community Services, state that through continuing program development efforts, total desegregation of people with developmental disabilities will occur by the end of the century. The clear trend has been a progressive movement from isolated and segregated services toward services that are delivered in integrated vocational, home, community, and school settings (Sailor et al., 1986). This change has been facilitated by a variety of important factors: legal mandates for integrated services, a rising philosophical commitment by agencies serving young adults with severe disabilities toward providing integrated community services, and the development of research and demonstration models that have identified organizational features and intervention strategies that maximize the potential for social integration (e.g., Bruininks, Kudla, Hauber, Hill, & Weick, 1981).

Supported Employment. Supported employment is emerging as the most desirable vocational option for adults with severe disabilities. It is, therefore, important to determine the social interaction behaviors that are most valued by employers in nonsheltered settings. It is also important to recognize that not all jobs in competitive employment or enclave settings have the same requirements for social interaction skills. Some jobs are by nature more socially isolating (e.g., night jani-

tor in a large business building), whereas others entail a higher expectation for interaction with co-workers (e.g., food-service jobs). Because there are fewer instructional resources for conducting interventions during the postsecondary years (as compared with secondary school years), it is critical to assess the social skills expectations across job sites and match students to sites and job types that will best accommodate their unique abilities.

A major reason for the job termination of some workers with severe disabilities is the occurrence of problems in the area of social interaction (Goldstein, 1964; Hanley-Maxwell, Rusch, Chadsey-Rusch & Renzaglia, 1986; Wehman et al., 1982). A number of surveys have been conducted to identify the social skills most valued by employers (e.g., Salzberg, 1987). In a summary of past research in this area, Chadsey-Rusch (1990) identified these as the following: asking for assistance, responding to criticism, following directions, offering help to co-workers, providing information about the job, answering questions, greetings, conversing with others, using social amenities, and giving positive comments. The instruction of these skills throughout the school years (throughout school, community, and vocational training sites), as well as in specific job sites during postsecondary job training, should be key features of programming.

Systematic instruction of social interaction skills can be conducted within vocational sites. In a procedure developed by Breen, Haring, Pitts-Conway, and Gaylord-Ross (1985), four youth with autism and other disabilities were taught a break-time script of social behavior. The students were taught to make coffee, through task-analytic instruction, and to approach co-workers in a normal break-time area and offer a cup of coffee. The training was conducted with nondisabled high school students who posed as co-workers within the natural break-time area. Once the social interaction skills were learned, generalization to the interactions with nondisabled workers during natural break times was assessed. When generalization did not occur, training with additional co-workers was added. All four youth learned the skills and generalized the social responses to nondisabled co-workers.

Supported Living.   Living in community-based programs is the predominant arrangement for young adults with severe disabilities. Increasingly, this is being defined as *supported living.* Supported living means providing the necessary physical and social supports to allow persons with disabilities to experience as normal and integrated a life-style as possible. For example, this concept translates into living arrangements with fewer than five people with disabilities sharing an ordinary home or apartment. The transition from living with one's family and going to school, to living away from family and working, is a major life change for all people. People with disabilities are at particular risk for disruption in the pattern of friendships and family relationships. It is therefore important to provide strategies and interventions to support existing relationships and develop new relationships with nondisabled people.

Fortunately, there is one validated strategy that has been implemented with success to support relationships in community residences. This system uses an interactive measurement approach referred to as the Valued Outcome Information System (VOIS) (Newton et al., 1988). The VOIS is an information-gathering system for monitoring and evaluating the quality of social life for residents in community placements. This system provides a means to record the number of socially integrated activities in which residents participate. Each time a resident engages in an integrated activity, a staff member fills out an "activity tag" that records the date, type of activity, names of the people engaged in the activity, relationship of the people to the resident (e.g., acquaintance, family member, or best friend), and the location of the activity. Data are summarized weekly by residential support staff. The purpose of the weekly summary is to ensure that each resident demonstrates a pattern of integrated participation in community activities. If such participation is absent or occurs at too low a frequency, it becomes the responsibility of the staff to develop ways of increasing the occurrence of integrated activities. This may mean contacting family members, friends, or acquaintances to help schedule times for interactions. It may also mean staff members' including the resident in their own circle of friends. If the data from the VOIS indicate that a resident has restricted access to a fuller range of activities (e.g., engaging in only the same one or two activities each week), the staff may contact the people participating in the interaction and suggest a greater diversity of activities. The benefit of this system in assessing and evaluating social contacts has been validated (e.g., Kennedy, Horner, & Newton, 1989).

CONCLUSION

Instruction of social skills is a potentially important means to support integration. However, the conceptualization and implementation of social skills instruction, as well as the focus of research, must shift to a greater concern with behavior within natural contexts and with the use of skills in social relationships so that they become more relevant to social integration as a primary outcome. Because the perceptions and behavior of peers and characteristics of natural contexts are the keys to this process, ultimately, this means that teachers themselves need to be better integrated into the social fabric of the schools, more careful observers of contexts, and more attentive to nondisabled peers, their social support needs, and their perceptions of intervention efforts.

The instruction of social interaction skills and the support of relationships are critical components of programming in special education. Increasingly, intervention in this area is being viewed as the major means of meeting the current federal and state mandates for integration. Fortunately, a sufficient body of assessment and intervention procedures is emerging to allow us to proceed with fuller integration models. Clearly, the success of these goals will be dependent on teacher preparation efforts that directly target strategies and procedures for students' achieving socially integrated life-styles. We hope that this chapter serves as a useful map to the procedures that are currently validated through research as well as practice.

REFERENCES

Ackerman, A. M., & Shapiro, E. S. (1984). Self-monitoring and work productivity with mentally retarded adults. *Journal of Applied Behavior Analysis, 17,* 403–407.

Bates, E. (1976). *Language and pragmatics: The acquisition of pragmatics.* New York: Academic Press.

Brady, M. P., & McEvoy, M. A. (1989). Social skills training as an integration strategy. In R. Gaylord-Ross (Ed.), *Integration strategies for students with handicaps* (pp. 213–232). Baltimore: Paul H. Brookes Publishing Co.

Brady, M. P., Shores, R. E., McEvoy, M. A., Ellis, D., & Fox, J. J. (1987). Increasing social interactions of severely handicapped autistic children. *Journal of Autism and Developmental Disabilities, 17,* 375–391.

Breen, C., Haring, T. G., Pitts-Conway, V., & Gaylord-Ross, R. (1985). The training and generalization of social interaction during breaktime at two job sites in the natural environment. *The Journal of The Association for Persons with Severe Handicaps, 10,* 41–50.

Breen, C. G., & Haring, T. G. (1991). Effects of contextual competence on social initiations. *Journal of Applied Behavior Analysis, 24,* 337–347.

Breen, C. G., Lovinger, L., & Haring, T. G. (1989). Effects of friendship-based and instructional aide experiences on attitudes of junior high school students. Manuscript in preparation.

Brown, F., Evans, I. M., Weed, K. A., & Owen, V. (1987). Delineating functional competencies: A component model. *The Journal of The Association for Persons with Severe Handicaps, 12,* 117–123.

Bruininks, R. H., Kudla, M. J., Hauber, F. A., Hill, B. K., & Weick, C. A. (1985). Recent growth and status of community-based residential alternatives. In R. H. Bruininks, C. E. Meyers, B. B. Sigford, & K. C. Lakin (Eds.), *Deinstitutionalization and community adjustment of mentally retarded people* (pp. 14–27). Washington, DC: Monograph of the American Association on Mental Deficiency.

Chadsey-Rusch, J. (1990). Teaching social skills on the job. In F. R. Rusch (Ed.), *Supported employment: Models, methods, and issues* (pp. 161–180). Sycamore, IL: Sycamore Publishing Co.

Cairns, R. B. (1980). *Social development: The origins and plasticity of interchanges.* San Francisco: W. H. Freeman.

Falvey, M. A. (1989). *Community-based curriculum: Instructional strategies for students with severe handicaps* (2nd ed). Baltimore: Paul H. Brookes Publishing Co.

Forest, M. (1991). It's about relationships. In L. H. Meyer, C. A. Peck, & L. Brown (Eds.), *Critical issues in the lives of people with severe disabilities* (pp. 399–407). Baltimore: Paul H. Brookes Publishing Co.

Fox, J., Shores, R., Lindeman, D., & Strain, P. (1986). Maintaining social initiations of withdrawn handicapped and nonhandicapped preschoolers through a response-dependent fading tactic. *Journal of Abnormal Child Psychology, 14,* 387–396.

Gartner, A., & Lipsky, D. K. (1987). Beyond special education: Toward a quality system for all students. *Harvard Educational Review, 57,* 367–395.

Gaylord-Ross, R. J. (1989) *Integration strategies for students with handicaps.* Baltimore: Paul H. Brookes Publishing Co.

Gaylord-Ross, R. J., Haring, T. G., Breen, C., & Pitts-Conway, V. (1984). The training and generalization of social interaction skills with autistic youth. *Journal of Applied Behavior Analysis, 17,* 229–247.

Gaylord-Ross, R., & Holvoet, J. F. (1985). *Strategies for educating students with severe handicaps.* Boston: Little, Brown & Company.

Goldstein, H. (1964). Social and occupational adjustment. In H. A. Stevens & R. Heber (Eds.), *Mental retardation: A review of research* (pp. 214–258). Chicago: University of Chicago Press.

Goldstein, H., & Wickstrom, S. (1986). Peer intervention effects on communicative interaction among handicapped and nonhandicapped preschoolers. *Journal of Applied Behavior Analysis, 19,* 209–214.

Hanley-Maxwell, C., Rusch, F., Chadsey-Rusch, J., & Renzaglia, A. (1986). Reported factors contributing to job terminations of individuals with severe disabilities. *The Journal of The Association for Persons with Severe Handicaps, 11,* 45–52.

Hanson, M. J., & Hanline, M. F. (1989). Integration options for the very young child. In R. Gaylord-Ross (Ed.), *Integration strategies for students with handi-*

caps (pp. 177–193). Baltimore: Paul H. Brookes Publishing Co.

Haring, T. G. (1985). Teaching between-class generalization of toy play behavior to handicapped children. *Journal of Applied Behavior Analysis, 18,* 127–139.

Haring, T. G., & Breen, C. G. (1990, May). *A peer mediated social network to enhance social integration for persons with severe disabilities.* Paper presented at the 16th Annual Convention of the Association for Behavior Analysis. Nashville, Tennessee.

Haring, T. G., & Kennedy, C. H. (1988). Units of analysis in task-analytic research. *Journal of Applied Behavior Analysis, 21,* 207–215.

Haring, T. G., & Lovinger, L. (1989). Promoting social interaction through teaching generalized play initiation responses to preschool children with autism. *The Journal of The Association for Persons with Severe Handicaps, 14,* 58–67.

Haring, T. G., Roger, B., Lee, M., Breen, C., & Gaylord-Ross, R. (1986). Teaching social language to moderately handicapped students. *Journal of Applied Behavior Analysis, 19,* 159–171.

Hendrickson, J. M., Strain, P. S., Trembly, A., & Shores, R. E. (1982). Interactions of behaviorally handicapped children: Functional effects of peer social initiations. *Behavior Modification, 6,* 323–353.

Hill, B. K., & Bruininks, R. H. (1984). Maladaptive behavior of mentally retarded individuals in residential facilities. *American Journal of Mental Deficiency, 88,* 380–387.

Hiroshige, J. A. (1989). The effects of direct instruction of social skills & peer facilitation on free play at recess of students with physical disabilities. Unpublished Ph.D. diss., University of California, Santa Barbara.

Horner, R. H., McDonnell, J. J., & Bellamy, G. T. (1986). Teaching generalized skills: General case instruction in simulation and community settings. In R. H. Horner, L. H. Meyer, & H. D. Fredericks (Eds.), *Education of learners with severe handicaps: Exemplary service strategies* (pp. 289–314). Baltimore: Paul H. Brookes Publishing Co.

Hunt, P., Alwell, M., & Goetz, L. (1988). Acquisition of conversation skills and the reduction of inappropriate social interaction behaviors. *The Journal of The Association for Persons with Severe Handicaps, 13,* 20–27.

James, S. D., & Egel, A. L. (1986). A direct prompting

strategy for increasing reciprocal interactions between handicapped and nonhandicapped siblings. *Journal of Applied Behavior Analysis, 19,* 173–186.

Kennedy, C. H., Horner, R. H., & Newton, J. S. (1989). Social contacts of adults with severe disabilities living in the community: A descriptive analysis of relationship patterns. *The Journal of The Association for Persons with Severe Handicaps, 14,* 190–196.

Koegel, R. L., & Koegel, L. K. (1988). Generalized responsivity and pivotal behaviors. In R. H. Horner, G. Dunlap, & R. L. Koegel (Eds.), *Generalization and maintenance: Life-style changes in applied settings* (pp. 41–66). Baltimore: Paul H. Brookes Publishing Co.

Lancioni, G. E. (1982). Normal children as tutors to teach social responses to withdrawn mentally retarded schoolmates: Training, maintenance, and generalization. *Journal of Applied Behavior Analysis, 15,* 17–40.

Liberty, K. (1985). Teaching retarded students to reinforce their own behavior: A review of process and operation in the current literature. In N. G. Haring (Ed.), *Investigating the problem of skill generalization* (pp. 88–106). Seattle, WA: Washington Research Organization.

McEvoy, M. A., Nordquist, V. M., Twardosz, S., Heckaman, K., Wehby, J., & Denny, K. R. (1988). Promoting autistic children's peer interaction in an integrated early childhood setting using affection activities. *Journal of Applied Behavior Analysis, 21,* 193–200.

Meyer, L., & Putnam, J. (1988). Social integration. In V. B. Van Hasselt, P. Strain, & M. Hersen (Eds.), *Handbook of developmental and physical disabilities* (pp. 107–133). New York: Pergamon.

Newton, J. S., Stoner, S. K., Bellamy, G. T., Boles, S. M., Horner, R. H., LeBaron, N. J., Moskowitz, D., Romer, L., Romer, M., & Schlesinger, D. (1988). *Valued outcomes information system (VOIS) manual.* Eugene: University of Oregon, Center on Human Development.

Odom, S. C., Hoyson, M., Jamieson, B., & Strain, P. S. (1985). Increasing handicapped preschoolers' peer social interactions: Cross setting and component analysis. *Journal of Applied Behavior Analysis, 18,* 3–17.

Odom, S. L., & Strain, P. S. (1986). A comparison of

peer-initiation and teacher antecedent interventions for promoting reciprocal interactions of autistic preschoolers. *Journal of Applied Behavior Analysis, 19,* 59–72.

Prutting, C. (1982). Pragmatics as social competence. *Journal of Speech and Hearing Disorders, 47,* 123–134.

Romer, D., & Heller, T. (1983). Social adaptation of mentally retarded adults in community settings: A social-ecological approach. *Applied Research in Mental Retardation, 4,* 303–314.

Sailor, W., Anderson, J. L., Halvorson, A. T., Doering, K., Filler, J., & Goetz, L. (1990). *The comprehensive local school: Regular education for all students with disabilities.* Baltimore: Paul H. Brookes Publishing Co.

Sailor, W., & Guess, D. (1983). *Severely handicapped students: An instructional design.* Boston: Houghton Mifflin Co.

Sailor, W., Halvorsen, A., Anderson, J., Goetz, L., Gee, K., Doering, K., & Hunt, P. (1986). Community intensive instruction. In R. H. Horner, L. H. Meyer, & D. B. Fredericks (Eds.), *Education of learners with severe handicaps: Exemplary service strategies* (pp. 251–288). Baltimore: Paul H. Brookes Publishing Co.

Salzberg, C. L., McConaughy, K., Lignugaris-Kraft, B., Agran, M., & Stowitscheck, J. J. (1987). Behaviors of distinction: The transition from acceptable to highly-valued worker. *The Journal for Vocational Special Needs Education, 10,* 23–28.

Sasso, G. M., Hughes, C. G., Swanson, H. L., & Novak, C. G. (1987). A comparison of peer initiation interactions in promoting multiple peer initiators. *Education and Training in Mental Retardation, 22,* 150–155.

Sasso, G. M., & Rude, H. A. (1987). Unprogrammed effects of training high-status peers to interact with severely handicapped children. *Journal of Applied Behavior Analysis, 20,* 35–44.

Sisson, L. A., Babeo, T. J., & Van Hasselt, V. B. (1988). Group training to increase social behaviors in young multihandicapped children. *Behavior Modification, 12,* 497–524.

Snell, M. E. (1987). *Systematic instruction of persons with severe handicaps* (3rd ed.). Columbus, OH: Charles E. Merrill.

Stainback, W., & Stainback, S. (1984). A rationale for the merger of special and regular education. *Exceptional Children, 5,* 102–111.

Strain, P. S., & Fox, J. J. (1981). Peer social interactions and the modification of social withdrawal: A review and future perspective. *Journal of Pediatric Psychology, 6,* 417–433.

Strain, P. S., Kerr, M. M., & Ragland, E. V. (1979). Effects of peer-mediated social initiations and prompting/reinforcement procedures on the social behavior of autistic children. *Journal of Autism and Developmental Disorders, 9,* 41–54.

Strain, P. S., Shores, R. E., & Kerr, M. M. (1976). An experimental analysis of "spillover" effects on the social interaction of behaviorally handicapped preschool children. *Journal of Applied Behavior Analysis, 9,* 31–40.

Tara, M. E., Matson, J. L., & Leary, C. (1988). Training social interpersonal skills in two autistic children. *Journal of Behavior Therapy and Experimental Psychiatry, 19,* 275–280.

Vincent, L. J., Salisbury, C., Walter, G., Gruenwald, L. J., & Powers, M. (1980). Program evaluation and curriculum development in early childhood special education: Criteria of the next environment. In W. Sailor, B. Wilcox, & L. Brown (Eds.), *Methods of instruction for severely handicapped students* (pp. 303–328). Baltimore: Paul H. Brookes Publishing Co.

Voeltz, L. M. (1982). Effects of structured interactions with severely handicapped peers on children's attitudes. *American Journal of Mental Deficiency, 86,* 380–390.

Wacker, D. P., Wiggins, B., Fowler, M., & Berg, W. K. (1988). Training students with profound or multiple handicaps to make requests via microswitches. *Journal of Applied Behavior Analysis, 21,* 331–344.

Warren, S. F., Baer, D. M., & Rogers-Warren, A. (1979). Teaching children to praise: A problem in stimulus and response generalization. *Child Behavior Therapy, 1,* 123–137.

Wehman, P., Hill, J., Soodall, R., Cleveland, R., Brooke, V., & Pentecost, J. (1982). Job placement and follow-up of moderately and severely handicapped individuals after three years. *The Journal of The Association for Persons with Severe Handicaps, 7,* 5–16.

Wilcox, B., & Bellamy, G. T. (1987). *A comprehensive guide to the activities catalog: An alternative cur-*

riculum for youth with severe disabilities. Baltimore: Paul H. Brookes Publishing Co.

Will, M. (1986). Educating children with learning problems: A shared responsibility. *Exceptional Children, 52,* 411–416.

Young, C. C., & Kerr, M. (1979). The effect of a retarded child's initiations on the behavior of severely retarded school-aged peers. *Education and Treatment of the Mentally Retarded, 14,* 185–190.

CHAPTER 12

A FUNCTIONAL APPROACH TO ACADEMICS INSTRUCTION

DEBORAH BOTT SLATON
JOHN SCHUSTER
BELVA COLLINS
University of Kentucky

DOUGLAS CARNINE
University of Oregon

HISTORICAL OVERVIEW

Historically, academic skills have been the focus of instruction for students with and without disabilities. Teaching students to read, write, and solve mathematical problems was thought to prepare them for the adult world. This approach resulted in educational programs for students with severe disabilities that featured a modified regular education curriculum with a *developmental* or "bottom-up" approach. A developmental curriculum assumes that all learners acquire skills in a predetermined sequence, and skills are taught to individuals with severe disabilities in the same order as they would be taught to people without disabilities, without concern for a learner's chronological age (Gast & Schuster, 1993).

In a bottom-up approach, students learn advanced skills after prerequisites are acquired. For example, reading whole words is taught after a student masters numerous prerequisite skills, which include identifying all upper- and lower-case letters and the regular sound-symbol relationships of all letters. When such an approach is used with students without disabilities, most learn basic skills in the elementary grades. When such an approach is used with students with severe disabilities, basic skills are typically not mastered during the elementary years, and teenagers and young adults continue working on preacademic skills of questionable use and age-appropriateness. Students with severe disabilities who spent their years in school learning traditional academic skills within a developmental framework usually did not learn skills that led to greater independence in the "real" world.

During the last decade, educators have voiced opposition to using the developmental approach for teaching persons with severe disabilities (Brown et al., 1979; Browder, 1987; Ford, Davern, Schnorr, Black, & Kaiser, 1989; Neel & Billingsley, 1989; Snell, 1987). Students with severe disabilities have learning and performance characteristics that call for a nontraditional approach to teaching selected academic skills. These individuals require more instructional trials to acquire skills, have difficulty generalizing and synthesizing skills, and exhibit forgetting-recoupment problems (Brown et al., 1983). When these learning and performance characteristics are considered, the inappropriateness of a developmental curriculum becomes evident.

A Functional Approach to Academic Content Curriculum

The developmental approach to curriculum for students with severe disabilities has been replaced by a *functional* or top-down approach during the last decade. This approach is based on the belief of the *criterion of ultimate functioning* (Brown, Nietupski, & Hamre-Nietupski, 1976), which means that students should learn skills that will make them as independent and productive as possible in a variety of community environments. In using this functional approach, skills are targeted for instruction, based not on the developmental age of a student with severe disabilities but on other more pertinent factors such as chronological age of the student, the immediate usefulness of the skill, and the degree of independence the targeted skill, once acquired, will allow the individual. The traditional scope and sequence charts used with students in regular education do not guide instruction when a functional approach is used. For example, sight-reading words (e.g., grocery words, community words) are targeted for instruction regardless of whether a student possesses the traditional prerequisite skills of naming letters and identifying sound-symbol relationships.

In using a functional approach to teach academic behaviors, the function of the behavior is considered more important than the form of the targeted behavior (White, 1980). For example, what is the purpose or function of teaching money skills to an individual with severe disabilities? One function is to enable the person to purchase items. A student can purchase items using a variety of forms, including counting out the necessary number of bills and coins, giving the cashier a credit card, asking the cashier to send a bill to a parent, or using a check. If a student does not know how to make a purchase with dollars and coins, the same function may be obtained by the student's using the next-dollar strategy to make the purchase. When using the next-dollar strategy, rather than counting out the correct combination of bills and coins to pay for a $6.72 purchase, a student would simply count out six one dollar bills, give one more bill to cover the change, and wait for change. This strategy requires far fewer prerequisite academic skills than using money in combinations. As this strategy exemplifies, when the function of the behavior is considered, students may be able to complete many tasks inde-pendently with the skills they already possess, or there may be a way to complete a task in a simpler manner than traditionally performed.

Importance of Partial Participation

In teaching academic skills to individuals with severe disabilities, the principle of partial participation (Baumgart et al., 1982) must also be considered. In the past, there were many skills that students were not taught, because professionals held erroneous assumptions about instruction including the "all or nothing hypothesis" (Baumgart et al., 1982). When teachers held this philosophy, a skill was not targeted for instruction unless the teacher was reasonably sure that the student could learn all steps of the skill. For example, even though a student could select groceries from a picture list, grocery shopping was not taught unless the student could read a shopping list, select groceries, pay a cashier, and exhibit the correct social behaviors in the natural environment. This resulted in the exclusion of many skills from a student's curriculum.

The principle of *partial participation* (Baumgart et al., 1982) states that individuals with severe disabilities "can acquire many skills that will allow them to function, at least in part, in a wide variety of least restrictive . . . environments and activities" (p. 19). Individuals with severe disabilities should be taught to maximize their participation in a variety of skills and activities even when some or all of the following apply: (1) the learner does not exhibit all the necessary prerequisite skills, (2) the learner will not be able to acquire all components of a skill, (3) the learner may not complete the entire activity or skill independently, and (4) the learner's developmental age is lower than his or her corresponding chronological age.

Baumgart and colleagues (1982) delineate the following five types of adaptations that can be used to maximize a student's participation in activities:

1. Using materials and devices that make a skill easier (e.g., use of a calculator when subtracting for price comparison)

2. Adapting skill sequences (e.g., use of the next-dollar strategy to pay for purchases)
3. Using personal assistance (e.g., asking the grocery clerk to obtain a product)
4. Adapting rules (e.g., allowing students more time to complete a skill that is usually time limited)
5. Using social-attitudinal adaptations (e.g., getting store personnel to consequate inappropriate behavior)

These five types of adaptations are extremely important, especially when teaching academic behaviors.

Role of Functional Academic Skills

The focus of this chapter is on *functional academics*. The term *functional* used in this context refers to skills that meet the following conditions: (1) are immediately useful, (2) are demanded in everyday activities and environments both inside and outside of the school setting, (3) result in greater student independence and less dependence on caregivers, and (4) allow a student access to less restrictive environments. Only academic skills that meet the requirements of the term *functional* should be targeted for instruction for students with severe disabilities.

Functional academics are not a separate curricular domain. When targeting academic skills it is imperative that teachers embed these functional academic skills throughout the instruction of skills from the community, social, leisure and recreation, and vocational domains. So-called normal adults rarely, if ever, perform academic skills in isolation. Rather, these skills are performed in conjunction with other skills from other curricular areas. For example, recognizing your own name is never performed in isolation. This skill is used within vocational settings (e.g., selecting your time card), in social situations (e.g., selecting your name tag at a covered dish dinner at church), during leisure activities (e.g., placing your bowling score on the line next to your name), and in community environ-

ments (e.g., finding the appropriate line at the credit counter at the department store based on the beginning letter of your last name).

Consideration of functional academics does not imply that academic skills represent a domain that is separate from the rest of the student's curriculum. In fact, the opposite is true. The teacher should never lose sight of the relative importance of academic skills: they are important only when they allow students to perform activities throughout other curriculum domains. Any academic skill that is truly functional for a student will be performed only as part of an activity stemming from another curriculum domain (e.g., vocational, community, domestic, leisure and recreational). Therefore, it is important to synthesize the information presented in this chapter with information contained in other chapters of this book.

SELECTING, ASSESSING, AND TEACHING FUNCTIONAL ACADEMIC SKILLS

The teaching behaviors required for effective instruction of functional academic skills are not distinct from those required for effective instruction of skills for any other curricular domain. Teachers must do a thorough job of assessment, instruction, and problem solving to promote maximum learning and independence for their students with severe disabilities.

Selecting Relevant Academic Behaviors

Considering that students with severe disabilities acquire "fewer skills than 99% of their chronological age peers" (Brown et al., 1983, p. 93), only the most important tasks should be selected. Because academic skills should not be taught separately, these skills should not be targeted for selection separately either. Selecting academic skills should occur only within a community-referenced context and after a thorough assessment has been conducted. Community-referenced instruction refers to teaching skills that are used across a wide range of school and nonschool, current and future environments. Figure 12.1 presents a summary of steps teachers may follow to select relevant academic behaviors.

Assessment of Relevant Academic Behaviors

To determine what academic skills will be targeted for instruction, it is first necessary to determine what activities are relevant to the student. After the activities are determined, the academic skills required for participation within these activities can then be identified. Because students with severe disabilities need to learn skills that will allow them access to and independence in a variety of current and future community environments, assessing the academic demands of those environments is imperative. Ecological inventories and community catalogs are useful tools for assessing the demands of various environments in terms of the skills needed to function independently in those environments. (See Chapter 2 for more detailed information on assessment procedures.)

An ecological inventory allows a teacher to individualize a curriculum for a student by delineating the necessary skills and activities required in a student's current and future environments. In conducting an ecological inventory, a teacher completes a six-step process (Brown et al., 1979). Although an ecological inventory results in a valuable, individualized curriculum, the process is both time-consuming and complex (Gast & Schuster, 1993). A similar but more convenient approach is to develop what is referred to as a community catalog, or a curriculum catalog (Wilcox & Bellamy, 1982).

Community catalogs are similar to ecological inventories in that both are community referenced. However, a community catalog results in a curriculum that is unique to each school or school district (Kirk & Gallagher, 1989). The catalog, usually developed by a group of teachers, serves as the curriculum for all students with severe disabilities within a school district or community. The final product is a local community-referenced "master list of settings, activities, and skills for students . . . thus precluding the need to repeatedly survey the same environment for each student" (Gast & Schuster, 1993, p. 17). The curriculum is then individualized according to student needs and parent input, among other factors. Parents may use the catalogs to select the places where they most frequently shop, work, and engage in leisure activities. Instruction on targeted skills can then occur in the actual environments where the students will be expected to perform. A portion of a curricular catalog is shown in Figure 12.2. As can be seen in that example, a curricular catalog is specific to the community in which a student lives.

In summary, only those academic skills that relate to independence in the home, school, commu-

---

1. Determine the activities most relevant to the student in home, school, community, and workplace.

2. Assess the demands of the environments in which relevant activities take place, and identify specific skills required to participate in activities.

3. Prioritize skills required by relevant activities according to the following criteria:

   a. Frequently demanded,

   b. Immediately useful,

   c. Results in access to less restrictive settings, and

   d. Decreases dependence on caregivers.

4. Identify academic components within priority skills.

FIGURE 12.1   Four steps in selecting a relevant academic behavior.

+   do
o   cannot do
v   teach
x   taught/mastered

STUDENT: _____

DOMAIN: COMMUNITY

ACTIVITY:	SETTINGS: (Determine w. Parents)	Score/Date:	Score/Date:	Score/Date:	SKILL CLUSTER Curric. No.	Skill:
Grocery Shopping					C06.01	Pushes a grocery cart
					C06.02	Matches item/picture
					C06.03	Reads grocery list
					C06.04	Finds correct brand/size of items
					C06.05	Asks for help
					C06.06	Budgets nontaxable items
					C06.07	Budgets taxable items
					C06.08	Finds cheapest items
					C06.09	Purchases items
					C06.10	Displays appropriate shopping behavior
Shopping in discount/specialty store					C07.01	Purchases items less than $5
					C07.02	Purchases items less than $10
					C07.03	Purchases items lesser than $20
					C07.04	Finds clothing size
					C07.05	Tries on clothing
					C07.06	Locates item
					C07.07	Identifies types of items found in store
					C07.08	Budgets money
					C07.09	Displays appropriate shopping behavior
					C07.10	Exchanges items
					C07.11	Finds cheapest item
					C07.12	Pays for item
Using vending machines					C08.01	Carries change in wallet/purse/pocket
					C08.02	Uses quarters only
					C08.03	Uses exact change
					C08.04	Selects item
					C08.05	Uses coin return
					C08.06	Asks for change
					C08.07	Gets change from machine change slot
					C08.08	Responds to "Out of Order" sign

FIGURE 12.2   Portion of a curricular catalog.

nity, and workplace should be considered part of the educational program for students with severe disabilities. These skills may be identified through ecological inventories or community catalogs; setting instructional priorities is the next step.

Prioritizing Skills for Instruction

It is likely that the majority of students with severe disabilities will not possess most of the skills required for independent performance in their natural environments, so teachers and parents will need to prioritize the skills to be targeted for instruction. Skills that should receive high priority for instruction include those that are frequently demanded, immediately useful, result in immediate access to less restrictive settings, and decrease dependence on caregivers. It could be that many of the skills included in an ecological inventory or community catalog fit this description. Therefore, a teacher will have to reexamine the inventory or catalog and find those skills that are listed repeatedly across different environments and activities. If an activity or skill is listed several times, then it is reasonable to assume that it is very important for a student to learn. Noting frequency of listing is one way to target key skills; teachers, parents, and students may also identify preferences for skill priorities. For example, bed making may appear only one time in the home inventory, but it may be a priority among family members.

Teachers target specific academic skills for instruction only after goals for the overall educational program have been prioritized. An analysis of the prioritized activities and skills leads to identification of any academic components necessary to complete the activities. For example, if grocery shopping has been identified as a high priority behavior, a teacher would analyze the academic skills necessary to complete this activity (e.g., paying for groceries, making discriminations in selecting items, etc.). By so doing, a teacher ensures that only functional academic skills are targeted for instruction. In addition, by identifying the places where the academic skills will be performed, instructional programs can be designed that reflect those environments.

Discrepancy Analysis

Once academic behaviors have been identified as part of a high-priority behavior, a discrepancy analysis should be conducted (Browder, 1987). This assessment strategy allows a teacher to evaluate the student's ability to complete each skill. The teacher indicates whether the student can perform the task, what type of prompting, if any, is needed to complete the task, and possible adaptations that could be used in teaching that skill (Gast & Schuster, 1993). For example, when assessing whether a student can make the necessary discriminations for selecting grocery items, the teacher would evaluate a student's ability to select items from a written grocery list. Based on assessment data and the student's functioning level, a teacher may decide that an adaptation will be necessary for the student to perform the skill independently (e.g., pictures of items, rather than a written shopping list). This is the time when teachers should begin to consider partial participation as well as the critical function of the behavior.

It should be evident from the preceding discussion that academic skill instruction is by no means a separate category of instruction for students with severe disabilities. Only academic behaviors that occur as part of functional life routines in a variety of current and future school and nonschool environments should be targeted for instruction. After activities are selected and prioritized and the necessary academic skills are targeted for instruction, teachers are faced with decisions concerning how to teach these behaviors.

CRITICAL ISSUES: TEACHING STUDENTS TO ACQUIRE, MAINTAIN, AND GENERALIZE FLUENT ACADEMIC SKILLS

Academic behaviors, like all other behaviors, can be divided into two categories: discrete responses and chained responses. Discrete behaviors need involve only a single behavior for the response to be considered complete. Examples of discrete academic behaviors include sight word recognition, identifying coins, and pointing to objects when requested. Chained responses are skills that contain many behaviors that when sequenced together form a complete response. Chained academic behaviors include the use of a calculator, writing personal information, and selecting lower-priced groceries. Whether behaviors are chained or discrete, they are taught in basically the same ways and require a teacher to consider the four phases of learning when targeting these skills for instruction.

The first phase of learning is acquisition. In this phase, a student learns to perform a behavior that was not previously in his or her repertoire. The second phase of learning is fluency. Fluency focuses on the quality or the proficiency of a response (Wolery, Bailey, & Sugai, 1988). The final phases of learning are concerned with maintenance (performing a skill after instruction has ceased) and generalization (performing a skill in different settings, with different people and materials, etc.) of the targeted response. One phase of learning is not necessarily more important than another. However, each phase of learning needs to be addressed so that students learn functional skills that they can exhibit in a variety of environments and activities. Each phase of learning requires specific instructional programming guidelines.

Considerations During the Acquisition Phase

When teaching the acquisition of academic behaviors to students with severe disabilities, teachers must consider several variables (see Figure 12.3). First, when a student is learning any new behavior, the desired response should be reinforced every time it occurs. Second, location of instruction is a key decision. For the most part, priority skills should be taught in the environments where the student will be expected to perform them. For example, selecting groceries from a pictorial shopping list should occur in the grocery store. Third,

- Provide continuous reinforcement for new behaviors.
- When possible, teach new behaviors in the environments in which they will be performed.
- If training in the natural environment does not provide sufficient practice opportunities, then use simulated environments that feature cues very similar to the natural environment.
- Teach new behaviors during naturally occurring times or opportunities.
- Use a distributed trial format for teaching and practice opportunities.

FIGURE 12.3 Instructional considerations during acquisition phase.

the time when instruction should occur is another important decision. It is most appropriate to teach academic skills at naturally occurring times. For example, teaching students to use the next-dollar strategy should occur at the same time that making grocery purchases, fast-food restaurant purchases, and other buying behaviors are taught.

In addition, academic skills should be taught with the use of a distributed trial format (Mulligan, Guess, Holvoet, & Brown, 1980). When a distributed trial format is used, the academic skills are embedded in the instruction of functional tasks and activities throughout the school day, rather than each taught separately (Gast & Schuster, 1993). The result is that academic skills are taught through a skill cluster approach (Holvoet, Guess, Mulligan, & Brown, 1980). For example, when using this approach a teacher would teach a student how to write a grocery list or to select pictures for a grocery list (an academic behavior), navigate curbs, doors, and aisles on the way to and in the grocery store (a motor skill), select items while in the store (an independent living skill), pay for the selected items (an academic behavior), put the items away after returning to the classroom (a vocational skill), wash hands (a self-help skill) before making a snack (an independent living skill that often requires academic skills such as measuring) with the groceries just purchased, set the table (a vocational and domestic skill), eat the snack (a self-help skill), and clean up the area after eating (a vocational and independent living skill). As can be seen in this example, the use of skill clusters will help students to learn "the interrelationships between skills being taught" while learning each skill itself (Mulligan, Guess, Holvoet, & Brown, 1980, p. 326).

Although academic skills should be taught in the natural settings where the students are expected to perform the behaviors and at naturally occurring times within a skill cluster approach, this is not always feasible. For example, if a student is learning how to make purchases using the next-dollar strategy, it is not practical to do this within a grocery store when five other people are waiting in line behind the teacher and the student. In addition, this approach allows only one instructional trial of the next-dollar strategy, which is probably insufficient practice. Therefore, the use of simulations and massed trials are sometimes appropriate for teaching students during the acquisition and fluency phases of instruction.

When simulations are used (i.e., teaching skills within the classroom or "not real" setting), several guidelines should be followed (Nietupski, Hamre-Nietupski, Clancy, & Veerhusen, 1986). First, the teacher should inventory the community settings in which the skills will be needed. The teacher should assess the physical layouts of the settings, as well as the cues and the materials that are used there. Then the teacher should try to make the classroom as similar to those settings as possible. For example, when paying for purchases, the cashier may say, "Three dollars and forty-nine cents, please" or "That will be three-forty-nine." Teachers need to use this information when designing instructional programs in the classroom setting (Gast & Schuster, 1993).

Another way to make simulated settings more conducive to learning generalized skills is to vary the materials, settings, and cues during training so that they match the variety found in the natural environment. Nietupski and colleagues (1986) suggest that simulated settings be used for the intensified practice of skills and that teachers should provide practice in both simulated and natural environments. Based on student performance in the natural environments, the instruction in simulated settings should be modified.

During acquisition and fluency training of academic skills, teachers often rely on massed trials. Massed trials provide students with numerous, repeated opportunities to learn a skill (e.g., reading a set of five sight words five times each within one instructional session). Researchers have examined several near-errorless learning strategies for teaching both chained and discrete academic behaviors to students with severe disabilities (Wolery, Ault, Doyle, & Gast, 1986). Two of the most commonly used instructional strategies for teaching academic tasks include the system of least prompts and the time delay procedure.

System of Least Prompts. The system of least prompts (Doyle, Wolery, Ault, & Gast, 1988) has often been used to teach a variety of chained responses to students with severe disabilities. With this procedure, a teacher uses a hierarchy of prompts arranged from less intrusive to more intrusive. A student has an opportunity to make a response independently; however, if the student makes no response or if an error occurs, a prompt is provided. Again, the student has an opportunity to respond. If the student does not respond or makes an error, the teacher provides an additional, more intrusive prompt (i.e., a prompt that contains more assistance). This continues until a student makes the targeted response. When the system of least prompts is used with chained tasks, the prompt hierarchy is applied to each step in the task analysis. The system of least prompts has been used to teach a variety of academic tasks, including counting money (Bellamy & Buttars, 1975), verbal labeling

(Bates & Renzaglia, 1982), shopping skills (Gaule, Nietupski, & Certo, 1985; McDonnell, Horner, & Williams, 1984; Nietupski, Welch, & Wacker, 1983; Storey, Bates, & Hanson, 1984), concept development (Hupp & Mervis, 1981), calculator use (Koller & Mulheen, 1977), discrimination learning (O'Brien, 1978; Schriebman, 1975), and telling time (Smeets, Lancioni, & VonLieshout, 1985). Figure 12.4 contains a lesson plan for using the system of least prompts in teaching a student how to write a check.

Time Delay Procedure.   Another effective instructional strategy in teaching students with severe disabilities is the time delay procedure. Although it has been used to teach both chained and discrete tasks, the majority of experimental investigations have used the time delay procedure to teach discrete tasks (Wolery, Ault, Doyle, & Gast, 1986). The time delay procedure is considered a near-errorless learning procedure that transfers stimulus control from a teacher's prompt to a natural stimulus (Schuster & Griffen, 1990). During initial sessions, the teacher does not allow the student an opportunity to respond before the prompt. During these "zero-second" delay trials, the teacher provides a task request (e.g., "What word?") and immediately provides a controlling prompt (e.g., "Orange juice"). Over subsequent sessions, the controlling prompt is systematically delayed. That is, the teacher waits a predetermined number of seconds before providing the controlling prompt. This allows the student to respond independently if he or she knows the answer or to wait for assistance if the response is not known. Time delay procedures have been effective in teaching many academic behaviors, including sight word reading (Ault, Gast, & Wolery, 1988; Gast, Ault, Wolery, Doyle, & Belanger, 1988; Kowry & Browder, 1986), symbol identification (Johnson, 1977; Zane, Handen, Mason, & Geffin, 1984), object identification (Barrera & Sulzer-Azaroff, 1983; Godby, Gast, & Wolery, 1987), coin equivalences (McDonagh, McIlvane, & Stoddard, 1984), and visual discriminations (Touchette & Howard, 1984).

Figure 12.5 presents a lesson plan for using a constant time delay procedure in teaching a student expressive sight word reading.

Considerations During the Fluency Phase

In some instances, fluency training will have to occur after a student has acquired a skill. Instructional considerations during the fluency phase include selecting a criterion level, structuring practice sessions, and manipulating the schedule of reinforcement.

A teacher must first decide how fluent a student must be when performing a particular skill. How fast does the student need to write a check when standing in line in a department store? How many errors should the student be allowed when reading grocery words? How often will errors be tolerated when the student is counting change? A teacher can determine the necessary levels of proficiency in numerous ways (Wolery, Bailey, & Sugai, 1988). First, published guidelines can be consulted, which give the "normal" rates established for many academic behaviors, including reading, writing, and spelling (e.g., Mercer & Mercer, 1989). Second, other people can be interviewed. For example, the manager of a department store can be asked how long it takes most people to sign their names on their credit card receipts. Third, a discrepancy analysis can be performed. This involves the teacher's "comparing the student's performance to the performance of others doing the same skill in similar situations" (Wolery et al., 1988, p. 287). For example, the teacher could record the length of time a student takes to use the next-dollar strategy in the grocery store and then record the amount of time it takes several patrons without disabilities to pay for their purchases.

Once a fluency criterion has been established, there are two basic strategies for increasing fluency: structuring practice sessions and manipulating reinforcers (Wolery et al., 1988). Practice sessions should be short, provided several times throughout the school day, and allow the student as many opportunities as possible to perform the

SAMPLE LESSON PLAN

Skill: Writing a Check   **Student:** Andrew

Time: 10:00 A.M. each day when practicing grocery shopping skills.

Materials Needed: Pen, Checkbook and Register, and Calculator
(Two of each - necessary for modeled prompts).
Data sheet and pencil.

Objective: Given the task request "That will be $—.—," the student will write a check completing all steps of the task analysis (10/10) independently for 20 consecutive trials. Prices will vary each trial from $5.00 to $20.00.

Plan of Implementation:

During each session, provide the task request and for each step in the task analysis:

1. Wait 5 seconds for a student response.
2. If the student initiates a response correctly within 5 seconds and completes the step within 30 seconds, record a "+" for that step in the task analysis and reinforce the student.
3. If the student makes no response within 5 seconds or begins to make an error, interrupt the error and provide a verbal prompt (e.g., "Fill in the amount," "Write the date," etc.). If the student responds correctly within 5 seconds and completes the step within 30 seconds, record a "V" for that step of the task analysis and reinforce the student.
4. If the student makes no response within 5 seconds or begins to make an error, interrupt the error and provide a model prompt (e.g., perform the step on the second set of materials). If the student responds correctly within 5 seconds and completes the step within 30 seconds, record an "M" for that step of the task analysis and reinforce the student.
5. If the student makes no response within 5 seconds or begins to make an error, interrupt the error and provide a physical prompt (e.g., hand over hand physical assistance to complete the step). When the student responds correctly within 5 seconds and completes the step within 30 seconds, record a "P" for that step of the task analysis and reinforce the student.
6. After a student is praised, wait 5 seconds for the student to independently initiate the next step of the task analysis (go back to step #1).

Generalization and Maintenance:

1. Use a variety of task requests with varying price amounts from $5.00 to $20.00.
2. Both the classroom assistant and teacher should provide training.
3. Have the student complete the sequence in the natural environment on an intermittent basis.
4. When the student completes the sequence with 100% independent responses for three trials, fade the verbal praise to every other step and continue to fade until the student is praised only at the end of the entire skill.

FIGURE 12.4   Sample lesson plan for using the system of least prompts for teaching a student to write a check.

SAMPLE LESSON PLAN

Skill: Reading Sight Words   **Student:**   Mary Allen

Time: 11:00 A.M. each day before going to the mall for lunch.

Materials Needed: Words written on flash cards, data sheet, pencil

Objective: When presented the words WOMEN, MEN, INFORMATION, and EXIT three times each randomly intermixed with the task request, "What word?" the student will read each word within 4 seconds with 100% correct before the prompt responses for five consecutive sessions.

Plan for Implementation:

Prior to each session, shuffle the word cards and fill out the data sheet.

During the first four sessions a "zero" second delay interval will be used. For each trial:

1. Obtain an attentional response from the student.

2. Present the word card and say, "What word?"

3. Immediately provide the controlling prompt (i.e., the teacher says the word that appears on the card).

4. Record student responses:

   a. Correct after the prompt: Student repeats the verbal label of the word within 4 seconds. Praise the student and place a "+" in the A (after) column for that word.

   b. Incorrect after the prompt: Student says wrong word label or makes no response within 4 seconds after the prompt. Ignore the response and place a "–" in the A (after) column for that word.

5. Repeat for all subsequent words listed on the data sheet.

All subsequent sessions utilize a "four" second delay interval (4 seconds occur between the task request and the teacher providing the prompt). For each trial:

1. Obtain an attentional response from the student.

2. Present the word card and say, "What word?"

3. Wait 4 seconds. If a student makes no response, provide the controlling prompt (i.e., the teacher says the word that appears on the card).

4. Record responses as follows:

   a. Correct before the prompt: A student says the correct word before the teacher provides the prompt. Praise the student and record a "+" in the B (before) column for that word.

   b. Incorrect before the prompt: A student says an incorrect word before the teacher prompt. Correct the student (i.e., "No, the word is _____; if you do not know wait for me to tell you"). Record a "–" in the B (before) column for that word.

FIGURE 12.5   Sample lesson plan for using constant time-delay procedures for teaching expressive sight word reading.

a. Correct after the prompt: Students repeats the verbal label of the word within 4 seconds. Praise the student and place a "+" in the A (after) column for that word.

b. Incorrect after the prompt: Student says wrong word label or makes no response within 4 seconds after the prompt. Ignore the response and place a "–" in the A (after) column for that word.

Generalization and Maintenance:

1. Assess the student's ability to read the words when found in the natural environment at the mall, McDonald's, etc. If students do not respond correctly, teach in natural environment.

2. Use a variety of task requests (e.g., "Read this," "What does this word say?" etc.).

3. When the student obtains 100% corrects before the prompt for one session, fade the praise statements to every other correct response and continue to fade the praise.

4. After acquisition, use a variety of word cards (e.g., uppercase only, upper- and lowercase letters, different color cards, different color print, etc.).

FIGURE 12.5   Continued

target behavior. For example, rather than have a student practice writing his or her name quickly 50 times during one 20-minute practice session each morning, the teacher should provide five sessions throughout the day when the student is required to write his or her name as many times as possible within 4 minutes. Reinforcement should be delivered only when a student has met the criterion established (e.g., writes his or her name within 30 seconds) and after, rather than during, practice sessions (Wolery et al., 1988).

Teaching students to exhibit fluent responses can often be programmed into acquisition training. Sometimes teachers build a fluency criterion into acquisition programming by adding time limitations or other quality requirements to the behavior during acquisition training sessions. These requirements must be met before reinforcement is provided for a correct response. For example, a student is required to read the sight word within 3 seconds; the student must sign his or her name within 30 seconds; the student must use the next-dollar strategy within 15 seconds. By using a fluency criterion during acquisition, the need for separate fluency training often can be avoided.

Teaching Students to Maintain and Generalize Academic Skills

Once a student has acquired a fluent skill, teachers should make sure that the student will maintain the skill after direct instruction has stopped and that the skill will generalize or transfer to the appropriate settings, activities, persons, and materials. The ultimate goal of teaching any behavior is the functional use of that behavior within the environments where it is expected to be performed. Therefore, training should never stop until that goal is reached. Teachers should not assume that acquired and fluent skills will maintain and generalize. The maintenance and generalization of skills must be directly programmed (see Figure 12.6).

The following programming guidelines are designed to assist teachers in establishing behaviors that will maintain and generalize:

1. The schedules of reinforcement and the reinforcers used during acquisition training should be faded to reflect what occurs within the natural environment where the behavior is to be performed. During acquisition training, it is not uncommon, for example, for students to receive some type of

1. Fade reinforcement to the forms and levels typically found in natural environments.

2. Provide instruction in ways that promote overlearning of target skills.

3. Use a variety of training environments throughout instruction.

4. Train the learner to respond to a variety of natural antecedents and cues.

5. Use a variety of real materials during instruction, and select those materials most likely to appear in natural environments.

6. Fade instructional suppports as much as possible.

FIGURE 12.6 Teaching procedures that promote generalization and maintenance.

reinforcer each time they pay for a purchase correctly (e.g., verbal praise and a token). However, after the behavior is learned and the student is expected to buy personal items independently, the cashier in the store will not verbally praise the student or provide a token when he or she completes a purchase correctly.

2. The use of overlearning can encourage maintenance and generalization of a behavior after training has stopped. Rather than a criterion for a student that reads "Writes name correctly with 100 percent accuracy for 1 day," a more conservative criterion can be used (e.g., "Writes name correctly 100 percent of the time over 2 weeks in a minimum of three settings").

3. The teacher should make sure that a variety of training environments are used. Just because a student can order and pay for lunch at McDonald's, it does not necessarily mean that he or she will perform these behaviors at Burger King, a pizza parlor, or a local restaurant.

4. The teacher should make sure that the student can respond to a variety of natural antecedents and cues. During acquisition training, it is not uncommon for teachers, when teaching a student to provide personal information, always to say "What is your name?" However, in the natural environment, students will be expected to respond correctly to "What is your name?" "I need your name, please," "Tell me your name," "Please state your name," and many other cues. Teachers should ensure that a student can respond correctly when given any one of the antecedents found in the environments where the behavior is expected to be performed.

5. A variety of materials should also be provided so that students learn to respond correctly to whatever types of materials are found in natural environments. When a student learns to tell time, it is important that he or she be able to tell time on digital and nondigital clocks, on clocks that have all 12 numbers shown on the face, and on clocks that have no numbers or just a few numbers (e.g., 12, 3, 6, and 9) shown on the face. The use of general case programming (Albin & Horner, 1988) is helpful in deciding how many examples to use during training. General case programming involves selecting and sequencing examples from a stimulus class (e.g., vending machines) in ways that promote generalization across all members of that stimulus class. Albin and Horner listed the following steps for successful general case programming:

a. Define the instructional universe.

b. Define the range of relevant stimulus and response variation within that universe.

c. Select examples from the instructional universe for use in teaching and probe testing.

d. Sequence teaching examples.

e. Teach the examples.

f. Test with nontrained probe examples.

(pp. 103–104)

6. Instructional supports should be faded as much as possible. Some students with severe disabilities may always require some type of instructional support (e.g., a prompt, a prosthetic device, etc.). However, teachers should attempt to remove as many of these supports as possible so that skill maintenance and generalization is encouraged.

Evaluation of Academic Skill Instruction

It is extremely important that teachers monitor student performance with formative evaluation strategies. Because students with severe disabilities require more time to acquire skills, as compared with their nondisabled peers, and because they acquire only a small fraction of the number of skills acquired by their nondisabled peers, effectiveness and efficiency are vital. Data should be collected not only to evaluate student progress and justify teaching attempts, but to make decisions regarding programming. If data reflect a lack of student progress, teachers should manipulate and modify the current instructional program to help "set the student up" for success. Teachers should remember that programs fail, not students. The importance of data collection for instructional decision making cannot be overstated. Figures 12.7 and 12.8 contain data sheets that can be used with the lesson plans found in Figures 12.4 and 12.5. Not only is it important to collect data during instructional programs conducted within the classroom setting, but teachers should also collect data within generalization settings. The data collected in these settings will allow teachers to make judgments concerning whether a student has definitely learned a functional, generalized academic skill.

CURRICULAR CONTENT AREAS FOR FUNCTIONAL ACADEMICS: READING, WRITING, AND ARITHMETIC

Functional academics are synonymous in many ways with the familiar basic skill areas of reading, writing, and arithmetic. As discussed earlier, the teacher working with students with severe disabilities must take a nontraditional approach to teaching these basic skills. Not only is the typical

Skill: _____ Student: _____

1. Print date in appropriate space
2. Print payee in appropriate space
3. Fill in amount (in numbers)
4. Print out amount (in words)
5. Fill in the "for" space
6. Sign name
7. Enter number of check in register
8. Enter payee in register
9. Enter amount in register
10. Subtract amount from balance

+ = independent | Total # of + / V's
V = verbal | Total # of M / P's
M = model | Trainer
P = physical | Date

Comments:

FIGURE 12.7 Training Data Sheet for system of least prompts.

developmental approach inappropriate, but many of the familiar tools of teaching—basal readers, math work sheets, and spelling lists—are also of questionable utility. The assessment process that leads to identifying functional academic skills appropriate for an individual with severe disabilities rarely leads the teacher to a commercial curriculum or materials. Because the assessment process is highly individualized and community based, prepackaged instructional materials will hit some skills and miss others. Components of commercial

STUDENT: _____

Date:	A	B
1. MEN		
2. INFORMATION		
3. WOMEN		
4. MEN		
5. EXIT		
6. WOMEN		
7. INFORMATION		
8. EXIT		
9. INFORMATION		
10. MEN		
11. WOMEN		
12. EXIT		
% Correct		
% Incorrect		

Date:	A	B
1. WOMEN		
2. EXIT		
3. INFORMATION		
4. WOMEN		
5. EXIT		
6. MEN		
7. INFORMATION		
8. MEN		
9. WOMEN		
10. EXIT		
11. INFORMATION		
12. MEN		
% Correct		
% Incorrect		

Trainer: _____   Trainer: _____

FIGURE 12.8   Constant Time Delay Data Sheet.

materials may be adapted and fitted within simulated or community-based teaching sessions, but, more typically, instructional materials will be derived from real objects present in the student's natural environments. The following paragraphs describe the three basic skill areas, as well as a "related skills" category, and offer further suggestions for teaching functional academic skills to students with severe disabilities.

Reading Instruction

Learning to read is difficult for many people, but the task demands of decoding and comprehension are especially difficult for persons with moderate and severe mental disabilities. Making fine discriminations between letters and strings of letters, acquiring sound-symbol relationships (many of which are irregular in the English language), and responding to abstract stimuli are aspects of reading that challenge many persons with disabilities (Hoogeveen, Smeets, & Lancioni, 1989). There is general agreement that many persons with moderate to severe mental disabilities can and should be taught to read a basic, functional sight vocabulary, and there is increasing evidence that given long-term intensive reading instruction, some persons with moderate mental retardation can be taught textual reading at a functional level (Ford, Schnorr, Davern, Black, & Kaiser, 1989). A minimum developmental level is required to master even the most basic of sight word reading skills, and it is important to note that the research evidence for reading skills among persons with mental retardation is thus far limited to populations with mild and moderate mental disabilities. Associating printed symbols with spoken words and their accompanying meanings apparently requires a developmental level beyond that of many persons with severe mental retardation.

Purposes of Reading Instruction. Reading should be part of a student's educational program if any or all of the following purposes are relevant to the individual: reading to gain information, reading to complete tasks, reading for leisure, or reading to locate and keep a job (Grenot-Scheyer & Falvey, 1986). In part, the purpose for reading will dictate selection of vocabulary and preferred location of instruction. For example, if a young adult has demonstrated the ability to decode and comprehend individual words and short phrases and if this individual's workplace features several warning signs, then it would be appropriate to teach directly the vocabulary featured on the signs and to deliver the reading instruction in the workplace. The purposes for reading instruction should also be matched with activities appropriate for the student's chronological age.

Teaching for Independent Performance: Sight Word Reading. Words should be targeted for instruction as sight words if they meet the following two criteria: (1) they occur frequently in the student's environment and (2) reading the words

assists with completion of a priority task. There are many words that occur frequently in an environment that are essentially nonfunctional for an individual with disabilities. Examples include traffic signs that are relevant only to persons who drive. Many words on "sight word" lists found in basic skills curricula are also nonfunctional for some individuals with disabilities; these include color words (i.e., "red" and "black") and many abstract concepts such as "every" and "after." When sight words targeted for instruction occur frequently in the learner's environment and are useful in completing tasks, then the reading skills are more likely to be maintained and generalized after direct instruction.

Time delay instruction has proven to be an effective and efficient procedure for teaching sight word reading to students with moderate mental retardation. In a comparison of progressive and constant time delay procedures used to teach the reading of signs found in the community, both procedures were effective and resulted in rapid acquisition of the words (Ault, Gast, & Wolery, 1988). Because the constant delay procedure involves fewer procedural changes and is easier to administer, it is the more parsimonious and thus the most often preferred of the two delay procedure (Ault et al., 1988; Koury & Browder, 1986).

The simplicity of the time delay procedure allows it to work well as a peer tutoring technique. Koury and Browder (1986) demonstrated that intermediate students with moderate mental retardation could not only master small sets (i.e., five words) of sight vocabulary when taught with the use of time delay, but they could learn to deliver time delay instruction within a peer tutoring setting. Each of the intermediate students used the constant delay procedure to teach primary-level students with moderate mental retardation the five one-syllable sight words these tutors had learned previously. Peer tutoring approaches not only enhance social interaction opportunities among students, but they also free the teacher for more sophisticated problem-solving tasks.

Incidental teaching procedures, frequently used for expressive language instruction, may also hold promise for acquisition of some sight word reading skills (McGee, Krantz, & McClannahan, 1986). McGee and colleagues used a play activity to teach students the labels for preferred toys. When a student gave a verbal or gestural initiation for a target item, the teacher placed five word cards (one target and four distractors) between the child and the item and asked the child to select the word representing the item. A prompting hierarchy was used to promote correct responses. When the student selected the correct word card, he or she was allowed access to the toy. Through this procedure, two students identified as autistic (one of whom was also identified as having moderate mental retardation) were able to master the required discriminations and also to generalize the reading skills to locating toys stored in labeled boxes. Although the functionality of reading names of toys may be questioned (toys would typically be readily available in a child's environment), this strategy could have applications for certain shopping, daily living, and vocational tasks.

The number of different words taught at any one time may be an important instructional variable. Conners (1990) suggests that students with moderate mental retardation who can quickly discriminate printed stimuli may learn more efficiently when words are presented in sets of four rather than two. Certainly the difficulty of the words involved could play a role in optimal set size, and teachers should make data-based instructional decisions on this factor. If a student is dealing with a small set of words (e.g., two words) and learning quickly, the teacher may try increasing the number of words included in a set until the performance data reflect a decline in efficiency or effectiveness.

Computer-assisted instruction (CAI) may be a useful tool for the initial stages of sight word reading instruction for some learners. Speech synthesis technology allows the computer to deliver verbal models and prompts paired with printed words and graphics that appear on the screen. Baumgart and Van Walleghem (1987) compared a CAI program with synthesized speech with teacher-delivered lessons for sight word instruction for three adults with moderate mental retardation. They found CAI to be equally effective for two subjects and ineffective for the third individual. In addition, all subjects exhibited some off-task behavior with the CAI instruction and none with the teacher-delivered lessons. At present, microcomputer technology does not stand alone as a complete instructional program for sight word instruction, and generalization to reading in the natural environment requires teacher-directed interventions. Some commercial software is presently available for teaching recognition of signs featuring safety, information, and job-related messages (Attainment, Inc., 1990).

Authoring systems that allow teachers to create software without learning computer programming hold some promise for developing CAI lessons appropriate for learners who need high levels of repetition and small chunks of content. The Multisensory Authoring Computing System (MACS) is a public-domain package developed at Johns Hopkins University (1985); it features sound, graphics, and text with design options aimed at learners with special needs. This system is especially well suited for teaching sight word recognition and vocabulary. Teachers select content and presentation features to create individualized CAI lessons. MACS uses a match-to-sample format, and design options available to teachers include selection of target words, number of trials per target, number of targets per lesson, reinforcement schedule, and presence or absence of voiced messages. Teachers experienced in using the MACS can create new CAI lessons in less than 5 minutes.

Teaching for Independent Performance: Textual Reading. Some authors maintain that an intensive, comprehensive, and well-designed reading program started in the primary grades can result in independent text reading by individuals with moderate mental disabilities (Ford, Schnorr, Davern, Black, & Kaiser, 1989). If a student's mental abilities are within the moderate range, if language skills are relatively well developed, and if the student learns sight word reading relatively quickly, parents and teachers may decide to include instruction in textual reading as part of the educational program. This decision could represent a departure from the functional approach to instruction. A comprehensive, developmental approach to reading instruction equips learners with several decoding strategies, including use of phonics, contextual cues, syntactical cues, word analysis (i.e., prefixes, suffixes, and root words), and sight word strategies (i.e., whole word reading). The decision to spend instructional time on comprehensive reading instruction should be constantly evaluated against performance data indicating the rate and level of the student's progress in acquiring, maintaining, and generalizing textual reading skills.

Although phonics skills are widely recognized as a valuable tool for reading, the complexity of the phonetic system may prohibit use of this approach with some individuals. Nonetheless, there is evidence that individuals with moderate mental disabilities can master aspects of phonics and apply these skills to decoding unknown words. Phonetic rules and relationships may be used as antecedents to decoding, and phonetic cues may be used as a consequence during error correction. Singh and Singh (1988) compared overcorrection with provision of phonetic cues as consequences for miscues during text reading and found that although overcorrection was initially more effective, across 35 sessions phonetic cues resulted in lower error rates. It is important to note that the subjects in this study, three children with moderate mental retardation, entered the study with some textual reading skills.

Commercial reading materials frequently mentioned as appropriate for learners with mental disabilities are the Edmark Reading Program (Bijou, 1977), and DISTAR (Engelmann & Bruner, 1984). Snell (1987) describes these programs as successful for students with mild or moderate mental retardation. The Edmark materials use stimulus shaping procedures to teach a 150-word

sight vocabulary; the instructional package includes lesson plans, storybooks, and computer software. The DISTAR materials teach phonetic word analysis as well as a sight vocabulary, and they feature a direct instruction format.

Designing Adaptations.   There may be some instances in which a student has an immediate need to read material in his or her environment, but well-designed attempts to teach the reading skills have either failed to establish the reading behavior or resulted in progress too slow to meet the immediate need. In these instances, adapted materials may be helpful. Picture cues are a frequent substitute for decoding strings of printed letters. Examples of pictorial substitutions for printed text include picture cards used to compile a shopping list, prompt the next step in a job task, or remind the student of a safety behavior (e.g., unplug equipment). Picture cues require direct instruction if they are to become meaningful prompts for completing tasks.

Assisted Performance and Alternatives to Reading.   On occasion, individuals with mental retardation will appear to have a demonstrated need to read material in the natural environment, but the reading level of those materials may prohibit decoding and comprehension by persons with limited reading skills. In these instances, individuals will need to be assisted with reading or taught alternative skills. Students with severe disabilities who have verbal skills should be taught to ask for help in reading printed material in ways that are socially appropriate (e.g., "Excuse me, please read this to me"). Another alternative to keep in mind is White's (1980) concept of critical function; one application of this concept is in the instance of reading product warning labels found on many nonfood items. After a comprehensive analysis of product warning labels, Fletcher and Abood (1988) concluded that even persons with a reading grade level of approximately 3.9 could only read about 43 percent of the words on product warning labels. Interestingly, these authors also found that the word *poison,* which appears on many functional word lists, appeared only eight times within a set of 169 product warning labels, and the skull and crossbones symbol was found only three times.

In the case of the warning labels, the critical function is that the individual learn to handle the products safely. Fletcher and Abood (1988) suggest that an instructional alternative to teaching reading of product warning labels is to teach students not to eat or drink any packaged substance without the permission of a person who can read the label. They also suggest teaching individuals to distinguish between hazardous and nonhazardous materials found in their home and community environments, how to handle hazardous materials, and how to treat accidental contacts with such materials. In this instance, the ability to read numerous labels featuring a wide variety of complex vocabulary is improbable for many persons with moderate or severe disabilities. The more functional alternative is the ability to discriminate hazardous from nonhazardous material and handle each class of material appropriately. This one example of how seemingly simple reading tasks are actually quite complex demonstrates the need to be alert to situations that call for developing alternatives to reading.

Written Expression

The need to convey or record information in writing may appear within some functional tasks. Analysis of a local curriculum catalog revealed that several skill clusters that required writing included signing a check, writing the date, and completing personal information required on applications. Although little research evidence is available on teaching writing skills to persons with severe disabilities, several authors mention the importance of teaching individuals to write their own names (Ford et al., 1989; Grenot-Scheyer & Falvey, 1986; Snell, 1987). The form of an individual's signature may be either manuscript or cursive, and there is no consistent recommendation as to which style individuals find easiest to learn and use. The flowing movement of cursive writing may be an advantage to some, but the similarities between manuscript and printed letter forms can be an advantage to others. In addition, if completion of applications and forms is the functional task, then printing is the form of choice, as it is almost universally required in these instances. Some individuals have physical disabilities that preclude controlling a pencil or pen, and adaptations must be made if signing a name or providing personal information is necessary (Grenot-Scheyer & Falvey, 1986). In these instances, a printed card similar to a business card may be used to communicate name, address, and telephone number. Another adaptation is achieved by purchasing a signature stamp that replicates the individual's best attempt at a signature or a caregiver's signing of the individual's name. In the case of both these adaptations, the individual must be taught when and where to use the stamp or card appropriately.

Arithmetic: Adaptations, Strategies, Training, Settings, and Materials

Although there is evidence (Baroody, 1987, 1988; Stoddard, Brown, Hurlbert, Manoli, & McIlvane, 1989) that students with moderate to severe disabilities can learn traditional arithmetic skills (e.g., counting, number comparison, computation, coin equivalence) when taught as an independent domain within the context of the classroom, characteristics of this population indicate that the "best practice" is to teach math skills that are functional or that can be used in a generalized manner within the context of daily living skills.

If the goal of a student's education is to function in the least restrictive environment possible, there are certain arithmetic skills that must be performed as independently as possible. A student who will have access to the community will need to manage money. This will include skills for banking, purchasing necessities, and paying for recreation; it will be necessary to identify prices and match them with corresponding amounts of money. A student who will reside in a residence with minimal supervision will participate in domestic skills involving math, such as paying bills, measuring ingredients for cooking, counting the correct number of plates and utensils for setting the table, and sorting pairs when doing laundry. In addition, it will be necessary to know when activities occur if the individual is to arrive on time for meals, appointments, or parties. Finally, the current emphasis on employment for those with moderate to severe disabilities indicates a need for basic math skills specific to job performance, such as measurement, as well as those necessary for maintaining jobs, such as following a time schedule.

Prerequisite Skills.   Bailey and Wolery (1984) identified premath skills appropriate for instruction of young children with disabilities. These include comparing quantity (e.g., recognizing big and little, one-to-one correspondence), labeling quantity (e.g., rote counting, naming how many), using symbols related to quantity (e.g., associating numerals with number names and quantities), and measuring quantity (e.g., working with time, money, measurement). Although these can be viewed as prerequisite skills for higher math computations, they should not be viewed as prerequisite skills for entry to activities and environments requiring such skills. The natural context of activities within natural environments can serve as a basis for teaching premath skills or as a supplement to ongoing instruction within the context of the classroom. For example, Lalli, Mace, Browder, and Brown (1989) taught adults with moderate to severe disabilities to match numbers within the context of instruction in dialing the telephone. A system of least prompts procedure (verbal, then gestural prompt at 5-second intervals) was used with adapted materials. These consisted of a card with a picture of the person to be called and a corresponding color-coded telephone number that could be placed in a slide card so that only one number was apparent at a time, used with a color-coded disk that was placed over the dial of the telephone.

The following paragraphs examine options for teaching math skills involved in money management, time management, and measurement within a functional context across domains. Figure 12.9 lists some of the options available to teachers for consideration in planning arithmetic instruction.

Money Management.   The functional manipulation of money in the student's environment can be broken into a number of skills. Students will have to identify the amount of money needed across a variety of stimuli, including product labels, labels on shelves, tags on items, signs on displays, verbal word of a salesperson, sign or individual labels on a vending machine, instructions on a video game, and a cash register display. Students will need to search for numbers or be able to understand the verbal request of a price stated by a salesperson. Once the amount needed is clear, students will have to match the price with either the correct number of bills or coins and know when to expect change. On the math skill continuum, the student functioning in the high range would be able to perform these skills as would a peer, interpreting a price and counting out the corresponding amount of tender. A student functioning in the midrange of the continuum might benefit from the use of a calculator or coin card in determining the amount of money needed. A student at the lower range of the continuum would be able to use an adaptation (e.g., charge card, prepaid coupon) to accomplish the same function.

The current literature indicates that purchasing skills (Browder, Snell, & Wildonger, 1988; Matson & Long, 1986; McDonnell, 1987; McDonnell, Horner, & Williams, 1984) and banking skills (Shofer, Inge, & Hill, 1986) have been taught to students with moderate to severe mental disabilities through various strategies (e.g., next-dollar strategy), formats (e.g., forward chaining, total task), adaptations (e.g., calculators, coin strips, shopping cards), and procedures (e.g., error correction, system of least prompts, and time delay). Even though skills were sometimes introduced during classroom simulation with replicated materials (e.g., slides, home-constructed replicas of automated equip-

Adaptations:	number lines, coin cards, shopping books, calculators, picture schedules, picture calendars, timers, pre-measured items, adapted recipes, colored coded telephone overlays
Strategies:	next dollar strategy, general rules for shopping selections, cues from the environment, bulk quantity purchases
Formats:	forward chaining, total task, systematic progression
Procedures:	training package, system of least prompts, constant time delay, progressive time delay, prompt and fade, systematic error correction
Settings:	classroom supplement, home supplement, stores, restaurants, banks, vocational site, domestic site
Materials:	natural materials, xeroxed dollars, simulated vending machine, simulated bank machine, variety of simple timepieces, recycled materials

FIGURE 12.9   Possible options for the instruction of math skills.

ment, photocopies of dollars), instruction was not complete until students could perform target skills with real materials within a functional setting.

Adaptations.   Various adaptations can be used to enable individuals to participate in activities involving money. Students may use a number line (Ford, Davern, Schnorr, Black, & Kaiser, 1989) to count money or a number line in conjunction with coins glued to cardboard strips that correspond to the number line in length (Frank & Wacker, 1986). These visual prompts can enable students to identify and count out the correct number of coins when making purchases. In addition, the visual prompts may be systematically faded over time as instruction in coin skills continues, or they may remain as a permanent adaptation.

The use of shopping cards (Ford, Davern, Schnorr, Black, & Kaiser, 1989; McDonnell, 1987) is another adaptation that may aid individuals in making purchases. Used in the context of purchasing food from restaurants or stores, they can enable those who cannot read to identify items by match-

ing pictures or labels. Prices and the amount of money needed for a purchase can be indicated on the card. Like shopping cards and coin strips, coin cards (Browder, Snell, & Wildonger, 1988) can be carried by individuals to aid them in indentifying the coins needed to make routine transactions, such as vending machines or paying bus fare.

Even with adaptations, coin identification appears to be a difficult step to master during instruction within a natural sequence (Browder et al., 1988) and may require some prerequisite or supplemental training within the classroom setting (Stoddard et al., 1989). Prerequisite or supplemental training may also be indicated in the use of a calculator for making purchases (Matson & Long, 1986). Socially validated as an adaptation inasmuch as it is used by nondisabled peers, the calculator can enable individuals to perform math functions if they are able to turn the calculator on and off; enter numbers, functions, and the equals sign; and clear the calculator. Ford, Davern, Schnorr, Black, and Kaiser (1989) recommend that calculators for individuals with severe disabilities have the following features: (1) battery operated, because a power source is not always available; (2) small enough to be easily carried, but not so small that students have difficulty manipulating buttons; (3) buttons that are not so sensitive that they are easy to press unintentionally, although a key guard may help to avoid this; (4) unnecessary functions or keys eliminated or covered; (5) does not automatically shut off after a certain amount of time for a student who may require extra time during use (e.g., hunting for items during shopping); and (6) rechargeable batteries to save on cost.

Strategies.   In addition to adaptations, there are strategies that may be helpful in teaching students with limited cognitive ability to perform the functions involved in monetary transactions. The next-dollar strategy (McDonnell, Horner, & Williams, 1984) enables students to perform the function of purchasing in the absence of several prerequisite math skills. With this strategy, the individual is taught to identify the first number(s) of the price rung up on the cash register, to say the next higher dollar number, and then to count out the corresponding number of dollar bills. Kleinert, Guiltinan, and Sims (1988) describe a method they have found effective in teaching the selection of lower-priced items to students with moderate mental disabilities. Using a descending number line and items similar in size (visually similar or of the same weight), the students are taught to select the lower price when the prices of both items have the same number of digits by comparing the first numbers in sequence that differ. When prices contain a differing number of digits, students are taught to select the one with the least number. In addition, they are taught always to choose prices with a slash mark or the word "for" (sold in multiples). In other words, general rules are devised for enabling students with mental disabilities to make better purchase choices when shopping.

Training.   There also are options for structuring training, with a variety of procedures available to the teacher. Training may consist of several components combined in a training package such as

those used by Matson and Long (1986) in teaching shopping with a calculator (instructions, trainer modeling, feedback on performance, reinforcement, subject modeling, and self-evaluation presented in a forward-chaining format) or by LaCampagne and Cipani (1987) in teaching bill paying skills (model, rehearsal, feedback on performance in a forward-chaining format). In addition, errorless procedures that enable students to perform tasks with a minimal number of mistakes (thus increasing access to reinforcement and decreasing the likelihood of errors becoming part of the repertoire) are "state-of-the-art" approaches that can facilitate the acquisition of money skills. Shofer, Inge, and Hill (1986) used a least-to-most prompt hierarchy to correct errors made by students while teaching them to make deposits in a bank machine. This allowed the students the opportunity to perform the correct response on each step of the chain with the least amount of assistance necessary. Browder, Snell, and Wildonger (1988) taught students to make vending machine purchases using a progressive time delay procedure within a total task format. McDonnell (1987) compared the system of least prompts and the constant time delay procedure in teaching students with severe disabilities to purchase snack food. Although both procedures were effective and easily delivered in the community setting, the constant time delay procedure was more efficient.

Settings and Materials.   To facilitate generalization, training within the natural setting using natural materials is preferred. Yet there are reasons that a certain amount of training within the classroom setting may be desirable. If classroom instruction is chosen, the trainer should consider conducting it concurrently with training in the natural setting or conducting periodic probes with realistic materials to ensure that the target skill has generalized and become functional. For example, Shofer, Inge, and Hill (1986) used a replica of a banking machine in the home setting to teach banking skills to an adult male functioning in the moderate range. Periodic probe trials avoided the problems associated with training on the actual machine and indicated when the skill had generalized to the natural setting and material, thus allowing the cessation of home training. The acquired use of the machine provided the user with more flexibility in fulfilling banking needs. Browder et al. (1988) taught students with moderate disabilities to make vending machine purchases during a classroom simulation involving a vending machine constructed from enlarged photographs and boxes. The skill transferred during training from the classroom simulation to vending machines in natural settings, although all students had difficulty performing the coin identification step.

Time Management.   Like money management, the management of time is a math skill needed in all environments. Management of an individual's personal time schedule enables him or her to achieve a greater amount of independence within any environment. Functional time management skills include identifying times at which activities should begin and end (e.g., jobs, recreational activities, meals), identifying the days on which activities should occur (e.g., doctor's appointments, holidays, trips), and determining the duration of specific activities (e.g., cooking times for recipes, length of physical exercise, interval needed to cross a street before traffic approaches). The current literature indicates that students with moderate to severe disabilities have been taught to perform time management skills isolated within the classroom (Smeets, Van Lieshout, Lancioni, & Striefel, 1986), within the context of a domestic activity (Cox, 1982), and within the framework of a work setting (Martin, Elias-Berger, & Mithaug, 1987). As with money management skills, there are several options for teaching time management skills.

Adaptations.   Charts with pictures or symbols are common adaptations for students in determining the time when activities should begin and end (Ford, Black, Davern, & Schnorr, 1989). Martin et al. (1987) used a system of least prompts in determining the least intrusive adaptation that would

allow individuals with moderate to mild mental disabilities to self-monitor their daily work schedule in a vocational site. When exposed to a hierarchy of schedules, ranging from typed schedules with instructions to printed schedules with visual prompts (i.e., clock face and task to be completed), two students learned to follow the written schedule, and two other students required the picture prompts. This indicates that individuals should be screened for the least intrusive alternative that will result in a functional outcome. Ford, Black, Davern, and Schnorr (1989) suggest that a teacher consider environmental cues such as school bells and factory whistles when constructing schedule charts. To encompass a broad passage of time, daily charts can be expanded by using pictures within the context of a calendar and having individuals mark off days as they pass. In addition to charts and calendars, timers and electronic watches are adaptations used by the general population to manage short periods of time. These can be preset to cue individuals to follow a schedule or to end an activity (e.g., cooking, exercising) in the absence of the ability to interpret the passage of time on a clock.

Strategies.   Environmental cues (visual, auditory, and physical) can be used to teach individuals to manage daily time schedules (Ford, Black, Davern, & Schnorr, 1989). Daylight entering the bedroom is a natural cue to arise and get dressed. School bells and work whistles are auditory cues to attend to and finish specific tasks. Hunger pangs are physical cues to begin meal preparation. When these cues occur, they can be identified and the subsequent occurrence of the target behavior reinforced.

Training.   Like money skills, basic time skills can be taught through the use of a number of systematic procedures. Smeets and colleagues (1986) recommend sequencing the instruction of time skills in the following order: telling time on the hour, half past the hour, 10 and 5 minutes to, 10 and 5 minutes past, quarter to, and quarter past. Although instruction in this sequence may be ongoing, it does not imply that individuals cannot be taught to manage time in a functional manner in the meantime. When teaching the use of time schedules, Martin and colleagues (1987) provided a verbal prompt to check schedules (i.e., turn pages) after a 5-minute interval if the individual had failed to do so. Thus, use of the adaptation was systematically taught. Cox (1982) prepared simple recipe cards for students engaged in cooking lunch. Modeling and fading were used to teach students to measure the duration of the time listed on the recipe card (e.g., wait 3 minutes before removing tea bag from pan).

Setting and Materials.   As stated earlier, time instruction within the classroom (Smeets et al., 1986) may be conducted as a prerequisite to or concurrently with instruction of time management within the sequence of an activity (Cox, 1982) or in the natural environment (Martin et al., 1987). For selecting timepieces for instruction in telling time, Ford et al. (1989) make several suggestions. The numeral representations on the face of the timepiece should be simple and clear (e.g., numbers rather than Roman numerals or other symbols, minimal decoration). In addition, the passage of time on a digital timepiece may be more difficult to comprehend than the passage of time on a traditional clock face. The trainer should bear in mind the type of timepieces that will be available to the student in the natural context and focus on instruction with these to make the skill truly functional.

Measurement.   The ability to measure is a final area of math skills that may enable an individual to function in a more independent manner. Measurement is involved in domestic skills (e.g., preparation of food, sewing tasks, pouring the proper amounts of detergent) and vocational skills (e.g., cutting boards for assembly, filling a container with a set number of ounces, weighing produce for sale).

Adaptations.   In the domestic domain, a variety of adaptations can be identified that will enable an individual with mental disabilities to perform tasks. While cooking, the individual can use recipes with pictures that correspond to the amounts of ingredients that must be used (e.g., number of eggs, line on cup to show amount of milk or flour, size of teaspoon needed). For those who have not mastered measurement skills, items may be premeasured by others and packaged for use (e.g., 1 cup of pancake mix) or prepackaged ingredients may be purchased (e.g., 1 stick of butter for shortening used in lieu of measuring 1/2 cup). Measuring utensils can be premarked, or measurement utensils purchased that are the size of the amount needed (e.g., graduated set of spoons) so that no measurement is required other than filling the utensil until the ingredient is level with the top. Cox (1982) adapted recipes for students with moderate to severe disabilities so that the need for actual measurement was minimal. The emphasis was on cooking foods that could be measured "by eye" for the groups' needs (e.g., amount of hamburger needed to make tacos) or foods for which precision measuring was not necessary (e.g., omelets, stews, chili).

Strategies.   Cox (1982) taught students to plan menus and shopping lists through simple addition and the use of equivalences to determine amounts that needed to be purchased. For example, the number of slices of bread needed for sandwiches and French toast was determined. This amount was then converted to the number of loaves of bread that were required. Thus, students learned to measure amounts needed through bulk purchases, bypassing the need for determining specific amounts.

Training.   While teaching within the context of a domestic activity, Cox (1982) used prompting and fading (e.g., models, verbal directions, visual cues) to teach lunch preparation skills. At first, students were given specific, step-by-step directions with demonstrations. As their competence increased, the prompts were faded over time.

Setting and Materials.   Like all math skills, measurement instruction can be taught in the classroom as a prerequisite to or concurrently with training in natural activities within the natural setting. Regardless of the setting, materials should be the same as those that will be used in the natural context. In the interest of safety and/or economy, materials that are measured may be simulated (e.g., use of colored liquid or placebo in lieu of medication until appropriate time) or recycled (e.g., several trials in measuring flour before mixing ingredients).

Other Related Academic Skills

Reading, writing, and mathematics skills should not be considered the only relevant academic skills that students with severe disabilities should acquire. Other "academic" skills commonly taught to students with severe disabilities include the expressive identification of personal information (e.g., stating one's name, address, phone number, age, and names of parents), general information (e.g., days of the week and months of the year), functions of community agency personnel (e.g., police officers, bank tellers, and store managers), and safety skills, including dialing 911, asking for help, and appropriate behavior in regard to strangers. For example, Gast, Collins, Wolery, and Jones (1993) taught preschoolers with disabilities to say "No" and get their teacher if strangers approached and offered candy and toys. These related academic skills are usually part of an activity that traditionally falls within other curriculum domains. For example, dialing 911 is an independent living skill that requires, at the very least, the academic skill of number matching.

As discussed early in this chapter, academic skills are relevant only when they are required to complete targeted and prioritized activities and skills. Some skills may be embedded within functional activities. When this occurs, these skills should be targeted for instruction and taught accordingly. Several published curricula, including *The Syracuse Community-Referenced Curriculum Guide* (Ford et al., 1989) and *IMPACT* (Neel &

Billingsley, 1989) cite numerous academic behaviors that often are targeted for instruction. In addition, other sources are available that detail how related academic skills should be selected (Falvey, 1986; Wehman, Renzaglia, & Bates, 1985).

SUMMARY

The factors indicating a functional approach to teaching academic skills to individuals with severe disabilities are numerous. The chronological age of a student may indicate that there is a notable discrepancy in ability as compared with that of peers and that the student's past rate of learning does not indicate that he or she will ever be able to "catch up" with academic skills taught in a sequential manner. In an environmental approach, an ecological inventory indicates those skills that are priorities across domains, both current and future. A student's present functioning level in academic skills must be assessed to determine whether there are prerequisite skills that can be used as a basis for building future skills and whether there is time to teach prerequisite skills. The decision may be that it is necessary to find a way to provide the student with a means of performing reading, writing, or arithmetic functions within the immediate environment in the absence of prerequisite skills. Partial participation and adaptations should always be options for enabling a student to access a variety of environments through the performance of necessary functional skills. This does not mean that academic skills should not be taught to students who are capable of mastering them. The emphasis should be on individualizing the approach to each student's curriculum based on his or her ability, while ensuring that the temporary or permanent absence of specific functional academic skills will not limit the environments in which he or she can function. Students with moderate to severe disabilities can be conceptualized as performing functional academic skills on a community-based continuum (Taylor, 1982). This includes the ability to perform at least partially using an adaptation to the ability to perform independently. Although the upper end of the continuum may continue to be the goal of instruction, a plan should be devised for enabling all students to participate to the fullest extent possible. Not every student will reach the upper end of the continuum, but no one should be denied the right to participate in some manner.

REFERENCES

Albin, R. W., & Horner, R. H. (1988). Generalization with precision. In R. H. Horner, G. Dunlap, & R. L. Koegel (Eds.), *Generalization and maintenance: Life-style changes in applied settings* (pp. 99–120). Baltimore: Paul H. Brookes Publishing Co.

Attainment, Inc. (1990). Information words (computer software). Author.

Ault, M. J., Gast, D. L., & Wolery, M. (1988). Comparison of progressive and constant time delay procedures in teaching community-sign reading. *American Journal on Mental Retardation, 93*, 44–56.

Bailey, D. B., & Wolery, M. (1984). *Teaching infants and preschoolers with handicaps* (pp. 201–203). Columbus, OH: Charles E. Merrill.

Baroody, A. J. (1987). Problem size and mentally retarded children's judgment of commutativity. *American Journal of Mental Deficiency, 91*, 439–442.

Baroody, A. J. (1988). Number-comparison learning by children classified as mentally retarded. *American Journal on Mental Retardation, 92*, 461–471.

Barrera, R., & Sulzer-Azaroff, B. (1983). An alternating treatment comparison of oral and total communication training programs with echolalic autistic children. *Journal of Applied Behavior Analysis, 16*, 379–394.

Bates, P., & Renzaglia, A. (1982). Language instruction with a profoundly retarded adolescent: The use of a table game in the acquisition of verbal labeling skills. *Education and Treatment of Children, 5*, 13–22.

Baumgart, D., Brown, L., Pumpian, I., Nisbet, J., Ford, A., Sweet, M., Messina, R., & Schroeder, J. (1982). Principle of partial participation and individualized adaptations in educational programs for severely handicapped students. *Journal of the Association for the Severely Handicapped, 7*(2), 17–27.

Baumgart, D., & Van Walleghem, J. (1987). Teaching sight words: A comparison between computer-assisted and teacher-taught methods. *Education and Training in Mental Retardation, 22*(1), 56–65.

Bellamy, T., & Buttars, K. L. (1975). Teaching trainable level retarded students to count money: Toward personal independence through academic instruction. *Education and Training of the Mentally Retarded, 10*, 18–26.

Bijou, S. W. (1977). *Edmark reading program.* Bellevue, WA: Edmark.

Browder, D. (1987). *Assessment of individuals with severe handicaps.* Baltimore: Paul H. Brookes Publishing Co.

Browder, D. M., Snell, M. E., & Wildonger, B. A. (1988). Simulation and community-based instruction of vending machines with time delay. *Education and Training in Mental Retardation, 23*, 175–185

Brown, L., Branston, M. B., Hamre-Nietupski, S., Pumpian, I., Certo, N., & Gruenewald, L. (1979). A strategy for developing chronological age-appropriate and functional curricular content for severely handicapped adolescents and young adults. *Journal of Special Education, 13*, 81–90.

Brown, L., Nietupski, J., & Hamre-Nietupski, S. (1976). The criterion of ultimate functioning and public school services for severely handicapped children. In M. A. Thomas (Ed.), *Hey, don't forget about me!* Reston, VA: Council for Exceptional Children.

Brown, L., Nisbet, J., Ford, A., Sweet, M., Shiraga, B., York, J., & Loomis, R. (1983). The critical need for nonschool instruction in educational programs for severely handicapped students. *The Journal of The Association for Persons with Severe Handicaps, 8*(3), 71–77.

Conners, F. A. (1990). Aptitude by treatment interactions in computer-assisted word learning by mentally retarded students. *American Journal on Mental Retardation, 94*(4), 387–397.

Cox, D. C. (1982). The lunch bunch. *Teaching Exceptional Children, 15*, 44–48.

Doyle, P. M., Wolery, M., Ault, M. J., & Gast, D. L. (1988). System of least prompts: A review of procedural parameters. *The Journal of The Association for Persons with Severe Handicaps, 12*, 28–40.

Engelmann, S., & Bruner, E. (1984). *Reading mastery:*

DISTAR reading. Chicago: Science Research Associates.

Falvey, M. A. (1986). *Community-based curriculum: Instructional strategies for students with severe handicaps.* Baltimore: Paul H. Brookes Publishing Co.

Fletcher, D., & Albood, D. (1988). An analysis of the readability of product warning labels: Implications for curriculum development for persons with moderate and severe mental retardation. *Education and Training in Mental Retardation, 23*(3), 224–227.

Ford, A., Black, J., Davern, L., & Schnorr, R. (1989). Time management. In A. Ford, R. Schnorr, L. Meyer, L. Davern, J. Black, & P. Dempsey (Eds.), *The Syracuse community-referenced curriculum guide for students with moderate and severe disabilities* (pp. 149–170). Baltimore: Paul H. Brookes Publishing Co.

Ford, A., Davern, L., Schnorr, R. Black, J., & Kaiser, K. (1989). Money handling. In A. Ford, R. Schnorr, L. Meyer, L. Davern, J. Black, & P. Dempsey (Eds.), *The Syracuse community-referenced curriculum guide for students with moderate and severe disabilities* (pp. 117–148). Baltimore: Paul H. Brookes Publishing Co.

Ford, A., Schnorr, R., Davern, L., Black, J., & Kaiser, K. (1989). Reading and writing. In A. Ford, R. Schnorr, L. Meyer, L. Davern, J. Black, & P. Dempsey (Eds.), *The Syracuse community-referenced curriculum guide for students with moderate and severe disabilities* (pp. 93–116). Baltimore: Paul H. Brookes Publishing Co.

Ford, A., Schnorr, R., Meyer, L., Davern, L., Black, J., & Dempsey, P. (1989). *The Syracuse community-referenced curriculum guide.* Baltimore: Paul H. Brookes Publishing Co.

Frank, A. R., & Wacker, D. P. (1986). Analysis of a visual prompting procedure on acquisition and generalization of coin skills by mentally retarded children. *American Journal of Mental Deficiency, 90,* 468–472.

Gast, D. L., Ault, M. J., Wolery, M., Doyle, P. M., & Belanger, S. (1988). Comparison of constant time delay and the system of least prompts in teaching sight word reading to students with moderate retardation. *Education and Training in Mental Retardation, 23,* 117–128.

Gast, D. L., Collins, B. C., Wolery, M., & Jones, R. (1993). Teaching preschool children with developmental delays to respond to the lures of strangers. *Exceptional Children, 59,* 301–311.

Gast, D. L., & Schuster, J. W. (1993). Severe handicaps. In A. E. Blackhurst & W. H. Berdine (Eds.), *An introduction to special education* (3rd ed.). Boston: Little, Brown & Company.

Gaule, K., Nietupski, J., & Certo, N. (1985). Teaching supermarket shopping skills using an adaptive shopping list. *Education and Training of the Mentally Retarded, 20,* 53–59.

Godby, S., Gast, D. L., & Wolery, M. (1987). A comparison of time delay and system of least prompts in teaching object identification. *Research in Developmental Disabilities, 8,* 283–306.

Grenot-Scheyer, M., & Falvey, M. A. (1986). Functional academic skills. In M. A. Falvey (Ed.), *Community based curriculum* (pp. 187–215). Baltimore: Paul H. Brookes Publishing Co.

Holvoet, J., Guess, D., Mulligan, M., & Brown, F. (1980). The individualized curriculum sequencing model: II. A teaching strategy for severely handicapped students. *Journal of the Association for the Severely Handicapped, 5*(4), 337–351.

Hoogeveen, F. R., Smeets, P. M., & Lancioni, G. E. (1989). Teaching moderately mentally retarded children basic reading skills. *Research in Developmental Disabilities, 10*(1), 1–18.

Hupp, S. C., & Mervis, C. B. (1981). Development of generalized concepts by severely handicapped students. *Journal of the Association for the Severely Handicapped, 6*(1), 14–21.

Johns Hopkins University (1985). *Multisensory authoring computer system.* Baltimore: Author.

Johnson, C. M. (1977). Errorless learning in a multihandicapped adolescent. *Education and Treatment of Children, 1,* 25–33.

Kentucky Systems Chage Project. (1989). *Model local catalogs and curriculum process for students with moderate and severe handicaps.* Lexington: University of Kentucky.

Kirk, S. A., & Gallagher, J. J., (Eds.). (1989). *Educating exceptional children* (6th ed.). Boston: Houghton Mifflin Co.

Kleinert, H. L., Guiltinan, S., & Sims, L. (1988). Selecting lower priced items. *Teaching Exceptional Children, 20,* 18–21.

Koller, E. Z., & Mulheen, T. J. (1977). Use of a pocket calculator to train arithmetic skills with trainable adolescents. *Education and Training of the Mentally Retarded, 12* 332–335.

Koury, M., & Browder, D. M. (1986). The use of delay to teach sight words by peer tutors classified as mentally retarded. *Education and Training of the Mentally Retarded, 21*(4), 252–258.

LaCampagne, J., & Cipani, E. (1987). Training adults with mental retardation to pay bills. *Mental Retardation, 25,* 293–303.

Lalli, J. S., Mace, C., Browder, D., & Brown, K. (1989). Comparison of treatments to teach number matching skills to adults with moderate mental retardation. *Mental Retardation, 27,* 75–85.

Martin, J. E., Elias-Burger, S., & Mithaug, D. E. (1987). Acquisition and maintenance of time-based task change sequence. *Education and Training in Mental Retardation, 22,* 250–255.

Matson, J. L., & Long, S. (1986). Teaching computation/shopping skills to mentally retarded adults. *American Journal of Mental Deficiency, 91,* 98–101.

McDonagh, E. C., McIlvane, W. J., & Stoddard, L. T. (1984). Teaching coin equivalences via matching to sample. *Applied Research in Mental Retardation, 5,* 177–197.

McDonnell, J. (1987). The effects of time delay and increasing prompt hierarchy strategies on the acquisition of purchasing skills by students with severe handicaps. *The Journal of The Association for Persons with Severe Handicaps, 12,* 227–236.

McDonnell, J. J., Horner, R. H., & Williams, J. A. (1984). Comparison of three strategies for teaching generalized grocery purchasing to high school students with severe handicaps. *The Journal of The Association for Persons with Severe Handicaps, 9,* 123–133.

McGee, G. G., Krantz, P. J., & McClannahan, L. E. (1986). An extension of incidental teaching procedures to reading instruction for autistic children. *Journal of Applied Behavior Analysis, 19*(2), 147–157.

Mercer, C. D., & Mercer, A. R. (1989). *Teaching students with learning problems* (3rd ed.). Columbus, OH: Charles E. Merrill.

Mulligan, M., Guess, D., Holvoet, J., & Brown, F. (1980). The individualized curriculum sequencing model: I. Implication from research on massed, distributed, or spaced trial training. *Journal of the Asso-*

ciation for the Severely Handicapped, 5(4), 325–336.

Neel, R. S., & Billingsley, F. F. (1989). *IMPACT: A functional curriculum handbook for students with moderate to severe handicaps.* Baltimore: Paul H. Brookes Publishing Co.

Nietupski, J., Hamre-Nietupski, S., Clancy, P., & Veerhusen, K. (1986). Guidelines for making simulation an effective adjunct to in vivo community instruction. *The Journal of The Association for Persons with Severe Handicaps, 11,* 12–18.

Nietupski, J., Welch, J., & Wacker, D. (1983). Acquisition, maintenance, and transfer of grocery item purchasing skills by moderately and severely handicapped students. *Education and Training of the Mentally Retarded, 18,* 279–286.

O'Brien, F. (1978). An error-free, quick, and enjoyed strategy for teaching multiple discriminations to severely delayed students. *Mental Retardation, 16,* 291–294.

Schriebman, L. (1975). Effects of within-stimulus and extra-stimulus prompting on discrimination learning in autistic children. *Journal of Applied Behavior Analysis, 8,* 91–112.

Schuster, J. W., & Griffen, A. K. (1990). Using time delay with task analyses. *Teaching Exceptional Children, 22*(4), 49–54.

Shofer, M. S., Inge, K. J., & Hill, J. (1986). Acquisition, generalization, and maintenance of automated banking skills. *Education and Training in Mental Retardation, 21,* 265–272.

Singh, N. N., & Singh, J. (1988). Increasing oral reading proficiency through overcorrection and phonic analysis. *American Journal on Mental Retardation, 93*(3), 312–319.

Smeets, P. M., Lancioni, G. E., & VonLieshout, R. W. (1985). Teaching mentally retarded children to use an experimental device for telling time and meeting appointments. *Applied Research in Mental Retardation, 6,* 51–70.

Smeets, P. J., Van Lieshout, R. W., Lancioni, G. E., & Striefel, S. (1986). Teaching mentally retarded students to tell time. *Analysis and Intervention in Developmental Disabilities, 6,* 221–238.

Snell, M. E., (Ed.). (1987). *Systematic instruction of persons with severe handicaps* (3rd ed.). Columbus, OH: Charles E. Merrill.

Stoddard, L. T., Brown, J., Hurbert, B., Manoli, C., &

McIlvane, W. J. (1989). Teaching money skills through stimulus class formation, exclusion, and component matching methods: Three case studies. *Research in Developmental Disabilities, 10,* 413–439.

Storey, K., Bates, P., & Hanson, H. B. (1984). Acquisition and generalization of coffee purchasing skills by adults with severe disabilities. *The Journal of The Association for Persons with Severe Handicaps, 9,* 178–185.

Taylor, S. J. (1982). Caught in the continuum: A critical analysis of the principle of the least restrictive environment. *The Journal of The Association for Persons with Severe Handicaps, 7,* 56–63.

Touchette, P. E., & Howard, J. S. (1984). Errorless learning: Reinforcement contingencies. *Journal of Applied Behavior Analysis, 17,* 175–188.

Wehman, P., Renzaglia, A., & Bates, P. (1985). *Functional living skills for moderately and severely handicapped individuals.* Austin, TX: PRO-ED.

White, O. R. (1980). Adaptive performance objectives: Form versus function. In W. Sailor, B. Wilcox, & L. Brown (Eds.), *Methods of instruction for severely handicapped students.* Baltimore: Paul H. Brookes Publishing Co.

Wilcox, B., & Bellamy, G. T. (1982). Curriculum content. In B. Wilcox & G. T. Bellamy (Eds.), *Design of high school programs for severely handicapped students.* Baltimore: Paul H. Brookes Publishing Co.

Wolery, M., Ault, M. J., Doyle, P. M., & Gast, D. L. (1986). *Comparison of instructional strategies: A literature review.* Unpublished manuscript. University of Kentucky, Department of Special Education, Comparison of Instructional Strategies Project, Lexington.

Wolery, M., Bailey, D. B., & Sugai, G. M. (1988). *Effective teaching: Principles and procedures of applied behavior analysis with exceptional students.* Boston: Allyn & Bacon.

Zane, T., Handen, B. L., Mason, S. A., & Geffin, C. (1984). Teaching symbol identification: A comparison between standard prompting and intervening response procedures. *Analysis and Intervention in Developmental Disabilities, 4,* 367–377.

CHAPTER 13

ASSISTIVE TECHNOLOGY

MARY K. DYKES
University of Florida–Gainesville

JULIA M. LEE
Valdosta State College

Students with severe or multiple disabilities may require the use of assistive devices to enhance their ability to complete actions that are carried out independently by their nondisabled peers.

DEFINITION

With the passage of legislation such as the Individuals with Disabilities Education Act (IDEA) and the Americans with Disabilities Act (ADA), assistive technology has been defined as adaptive equipment that is electronic or nonelectronic, high tech or low tech that causes a person with a disability to become more functional in varied environments. A device may enhance a person's mobility, communication, classroom or vocational performance, access to environments and/or resource acquisition (Church & Glennen, 1992; Lewis, 1993).

IMPORTANCE

Traditionally, equipment was used to position a child in as correct a posture as possible in order to enhance respiration and neuromuscularskeletal development. Equipment used in schools today is selected to enhance class participation, interaction with others, efficient movement, and mobility. Assistive devices are evaluated for their dynamic properties, rather than for passive maintenance or restraint. There are currently many more types of assistive devices than in the past. The advent of microchips, sensors, and new light-weight yet strong materials has greatly enhanced the availability of devices to meet the specific needs of the individual.

USES

Adapted equipment includes a diverse range of devices to meet individual needs. Some may be used to help a child to move, communicate, take care of basic needs such as feeding, or use limited sensory abilities. Some children require special equipment to increase their stability while seated for group interaction or individual learning activities in the classroom. Traditionally, the most frequently used equipment has included wheelchairs, braces, and crutches for students who are physically impaired; canes, glasses, braillewriters, and guide dogs for students who are visually impaired; amplification aids for students with hearing impairments; and communication boards or systems for students who are nonvocal. More recently, ventilators, feeding lines, oxygen tanks, suction machines, monitors, and other health maintenance equipment can be found in schoolrooms, to assist students who are severely health impaired. Occupational and physical therapists, special educators, adapted physical educators, school nurses, biomedical engineers, and physicians have developed devices that assist a specific child to participate as a class member as independently and fully as possible.

Adaptive equipment should be individually prescribed to meet the specific needs of each child.

Therapists and educators work together, often with the advice of physicians and school nurses, to determine what the child needs to do that he or she cannot. The team evaluates the type of aid that is needed and whether there is a nonintrusive or minimally intrusive, effective and affordable assistive device that can be used. If such a device is not available, the team considers whether one can be developed to meet the child's needs, either by members of the team or by a specialist in technology, mechanics, or fabrication.

HISTORICAL DEVELOPMENT

Self-help and adaptive equipment and devices have been used by humans since early times, when clubs and arrow points made hunting more efficient. The wheel allowed easier movement to obtain supplies. Today, people use many devices to help them work more efficiently and effectively. Frozen dinners, teletypewriters (TTY), safety razors, rock haulers, and remote control devices are examples of equipment used in contemporary society that help humans in meeting their needs for self-care, mobility, communication, and so forth in contemporary society. For persons with disabling conditions, the earliest adaptive equipment consisted of rolling beds, wheeled chairs, and crutches made from limbs of trees.

The implementation of Public Law 94-142 and related legislation began the systematic inclusion of large numbers of students with severe and multiple disabilities into the public schools. Many of these students had lived in institutions where they were part of the health care model of service delivery. As they began to receive primary daily interventions through the education system, many changes were necessary. Therapy was no longer necessarily provided in a clinical setting or through the use of a clinical one-to-one delivery of services. In the schools, the ratio of care providers to children was reduced. When possible, students are now expected to do for themselves and to take initiative in learning new skills that they need in order to be like their nondisabled peers.

In the schools, therapists and educators began to use support equipment that had been used in the health care settings. Standard wheelchairs that were used in hospitals to take children for short rides down the corridor or for an excursion outdoors were brought into the schools where children were actively engaged with each other in learning and play for 6 hours each day. Because the demands of school tasks and the school environment are different from those of a hospital or long-term care facility, many items of health care equipment were found to be too bulky, cumbersome, or inefficient to be used in school. In school, for instance, a child must make toileting needs known, eat lunch quickly, and be close to peers to share toys. He or she must be able to move in and out of various positions in order to interact with friends. Equipment such as modified high-back chairs with head straps and support wings may have worked to maintain a child in a satisfactory static position, but in the school environment such equipment can prevent the child from participating in the interaction needed for learning and socialization.

Traditional equipment that, perhaps, had been adequate in other environments for specific events often did not help a child to interact or participate in activities at school. Some of the chairs, gurneys, and wheeled recliners that the children had used were impossible to use in classrooms or were unsafe for transporting a child on even the newest, adapted school buses. The size, weight, and lack of flexibility of such equipment made it difficult to include the child in all school activities.

In the last 10 to 15 years, therapists, educators, medical personnel, rehabilitation engineers, design specialists, and architects have worked independently, and in some cases as teams, in an effort to adapt school-based equipment to facilitate movement, communication, interaction, and daily independence for each child, regardless of his or her special needs. Newer dynamic positioning equipment has been designed to help a child to get into a position, maintain stability while in the position, and leave the position as needed for participation in classroom activities. Traditionally, a child would have been situated in as good a therapeutically correct position as could be obtained.

Such positions often prevented the child from using peripheral vision, making eye contact with other students, or reaching out for materials. Newer devices to help in independent feeding, toileting, and grooming are less bulky and look more like those everyone else uses. Newer communication enhancers require less specialized skill on the part of the listener, are less conspicuous, and require less effort of the speaker to make a need known. Electronic speaking aids have a more realistic voice quality; no longer is a female-sounding high pitch the only voice available.

In today's schools, when used inappropriately, an adaptive device may call undue attention to the user, require that major environment adaptations be undertaken, or that the individual have an assistant to operate the equipment. All of these may make the child feel that he or she is not like or equal to others. Other children may not want to interact with the child for fear of awkwardness related to the use of the device. If any of these patterns emerge when adaptive equipment is used, then professionals should consider whether the assistive device is truly helping or is actually working against the child as he or she seeks to be an accepted, regular member of the peer group.

There are questions today about the long-term versus short-term utility and benefit of adaptive equipment. The wheelchair is an example of equipment in use which may or may not enhance long-term functioning. If the chair does not fit properly, and thus contractures or scoliosis develops, the child may actually lose function more quickly or lose skills entirely that would not have been lost at all if he or she had not been in the wheelchair or had been in it for fewer hours a day.

APPROPRIATE IMPLEMENTATION OF ADAPTIVE EQUIPMENT

The general rules to be followed in considering the use of adaptive equipment in schools include: (1) use no equipment unless it is appropriate and specific to the student's needs, (2) have the child and parent assist in defining the needs and actual equipment to be used, (3) select a device that makes the child appear the least different from peers who are nondisabled, (4) select a device that can be modified as the child grows or as skill levels change, (5) when possible, while the child is using the device, assist him or her to develop skills that will make the child no longer dependent on the device.

Reasons to Use Adaptive Equipment

Adaptive equipment may be used by a child to begin a new skill, such as for stability during weight bearing, and can then be discarded as the child gains the autonomy necessary to perform the skill without assistance. Adaptive equipment may be used to compensate for a skill that the child may never develop, owing to a missing or severely deformed limb, paralysis, or dysfunction in muscle tone or synergy. A third reason for use of adaptive equipment is to assist the child to maintain, as long as possible, the functions that are being lost as a result of progressive degenerative conditions or to contractures. A fourth use of adaptive equipment is to provide for recreation, leisure, and personal time so that the child can be active while alone or can participate in group activities.

Goals for the Use of Adaptive Equipment

Adaptive equipment is used by students with severely disabling conditions to enhance their personal lives by providing the following:

* Participation in school, community, and family activity
* Safety and stability
* Efficiency and effectiveness in activities
* Access to and interaction with peers, equipment, groups, and so on, within a variety of environments, including classrooms, playground, cafeteria, and so on
* Flexibility, choice, and control in when and how to participate in activities

The use of equipment is inappropriate when it is prescribed for all children with a certain condition without consideration of variables specific to each child, such as fit, function, home support, maintenance, daily physical environments and routines, and assistance required to use the device. The characteristics of each piece of equipment must be considered for the child. In each case, the following questions must be asked:

- What *specifically* is the goal for the student?
- Will he or she be able to accomplish this goal independently or with minimal human assistance? If not, can the student accomplish this goal with an adaptive device?

- Over the long term, will the use of the equipment be helpful or will it impair the student's own development of skill and ultimately undermine the student's efforts to do things for him- or herself? (*Exceptional Parent*, 1983).

In addition, there are specific decisions to make in matching a child and his or her unique needs to the specific functions of a piece of adaptive equipment. These points are listed in Table 13.1.

TABLE 13.1   Selection Criteria for Adaptive Equipment

Have the specific needs of the student been identified?

Will the student be able to learn to use an adaptive device?

Are there various types of equipment that could be used to enhance the student's function that will not ultimately work against him or her?

Of the choices of available equipment, which one most closely meets the following criteria:

- Durability (Will it hold up over time and use?)
- Flexibility (As the student's skills and needs change, can it be adapted?)
- Repairability (Is local service available? Can a person gain access to the workings of the machine? Are special skills and unique parts required?)
- Maintenance requirements (Can it be cleaned, charged, lubricated, etc., by the student, family member, or assistant?)
- Strength requirements (Is the strength, pressure, rotation, or lift required to use the device practical?)
- Cost (Is the equipment affordable?)
- Speed (Is the speed with which the student interacts, thinks, moves, and communicates compatible with that of the device?)
- Portability (Do the size, weight, number of pieces, etc., allow the device to be easily portable?)

Further considerations:

- Skills required of communicator and of listener in order to use a communication device
- Noise made by a mechanical device (Does use of the equipment disturb other students or the teacher?)
- Storage requirements when not in use
- Quality of vocal output (pitch, male or female sound, etc.)
- Quality, size, and format of print product
- Paper (Is a unique size, texture, etc., required? If so, is it readily available and easy to install in the machine?)

Once the appropriate equipment has been decided on and is made available to the student, a training program must be established. The individual should be taught to use and maintain the equipment. The child should learn to clean, to lubricate, to purchase and replace batteries, and so on, as needed on a regular basis. He or she should be taught signs of malfunction and when to ask for assistance. Parents, siblings, classroom aides, transportation personnel, and anyone else who is in frequent daily contact with the child and the equipment should be taught to operate and maintain the equipment so as to assist if needed. Parents, teachers, and aides need to know what to hold the student responsible for and when to intervene. The student who is indulged or assisted when help is really not needed may become dependent, lack self-sufficiency, or be resentful of being patronized.

Animals as Assistants

Animals may be used to assist students with disabling conditions. Seeing eye dogs, hearing ear dogs, and other service dogs (Mader, Hart, & Bergin, 1989) and monkeys have all been used successfully to assist individuals with disabilities. Not only do the animals assist in task performance, but they help in the acceptance and socialization of students with disabilities by those who are not disabled. If a helping animal attends school with a child, then teachers, classmates, and assistants all need to realize that this is a working animal and not a pet. The student must be seen as the authority in commanding, reprimanding, and caring for the animal. The student or a family member should talk to the class and to adult staff members as to how to interact with the animal.

EQUIPMENT FOR MOBILITY AND WEIGHT BEARING

Devices such as wheelchairs, crutches and braces, scooters, prone boards, parapodiums, and standing tables are examples of equipment to assist in mobility and weight bearing. This chapter addresses devices used in schools to enhance stability and efficiency in seating, controlled movement and ambulation, weight bearing, and standing.

Seating: Classroom Chairs

A chair for a student with hyper, fluctuating or hypotone variation may need to be adapted in order to maintain as functional and secure a position as possible during instruction and interaction. A classic wooden chair that is in good condition (all glides and screws present and secured, no splinters, etc.) may be adapted by placing a wooden case or carton in front of it for a footrest, a small roll or wedge at the hips, and a soft harness or seat belt as needed (see Figure 13.1). Each child should

FIGURE 13.1   An example of adaptations for a typical wooden chair.

be taught that part of getting ready for participation is to get equipment positioned and the chair set up to meet his or her specific needs ("When you go to reading group, Jane, it is your job—not the aide's or the teacher's—to take your special chair, footrest, and cushion, and be ready to begin when everyone else begins").

Chairs should fit securely, providing adequate support while allowing the student to be actively involved in maintaining posture against gravity. Other seating options should be adapted so that the student has adequate support for maintenance of posture in order to facilitate as much controlled independent movement as possible. The amount of support provided should vary, depending on the specific activity the student is performing while seated. If a student's attention is focused on a task, motoric abilities for maintaining stability may decrease, whereas during times when the student is not as actively involved in learning tasks or skills, less support may be given so as to provide the student with opportunities to develop greater neuromuscular control over maintenance of various seating positions. A student should not be expected to focus full attention on a learning task while having to work to maintain balance.

When a student is placed in a sitting position, particular attention should be focused on the trunk and pelvic area. The pelvis should be in a neutral position, and the trunk should be aligned properly. The hips and knees should most typically maintain a flexed position, at a 90° angle (Fraser, Hensinger, & Phelps, 1987). Feet must be solidly on the floor or a footrest; at no time should they be allowed to dangle.

A number of commercially developed alternative seating options are available. Corner chairs with lap trays allow the student to bear weight on his or her arms while facilitating flexion of the hips at a 90° angle (Fraser et al., 1987). This support allows the student to use his or her upper extremities more purposefully (Bigge, 1991). Bolster seats provide support for abduction of the lower extremities, which is often required for students with hypertonicity and accompanying scissoring of the legs (Fraser et al., 1987).

Mobility Equipment: Wheelchairs and Scooters

A wheelchair may be used by a student throughout the day or for transportation between classes and around the school, or when a student who normally walks needs to move quickly between distant points in the school. Whenever possible, a student should transfer to a regular chair for instructional periods and for socialization. Being seated in the same type of chair as others helps the student by:

- Putting him or her at eye level with others
- Calling less attention to the student and his or her differences
- Providing access to shared materials in the middle of a table
- Removing the sight, height, and accessibility barriers that may be present if a wheelchair is used

The student who uses a motorized chair or scooter needs driving lessons and should not be a hazard to other people; these pieces of equipment are heavy and can hurt others if they are hit. The student must have good control of such equipment before being allowed to drive in the halls or classroom. It may not be possible to take power equipment to the playground because of its weight or inability to track over sand, mud, or snow. In addition, its size and weight may make it difficult to transport. A student using power equipment should have a backup nonelectrical mobility system to use when the powered system cannot be used. General considerations for the use of wheelchairs in classrooms include the following:

- The student must be responsible for locking brakes and taking safety precautions each time he or she moves to a new position in the classroom.
- The student should be included in groups, around the same table, and at eye level with peers whenever possible.
- A wheelchair should not obstruct other students' view of the chalkboard or other visuals.
- The student needs to shift weight at least every 20 minutes, doing arm pushups as often as possible, and leaving the chair for at least 30 minutes

out of each 2-hour period. Adding a cushion or varying foot position is also helpful.

• The student should be responsible for storing all adapted equipment and mobility devices *appropriately* when he or she is not using them.

• When possible, if the student must use a wheelchair during instruction and group project times, the back of the wheelchair should be at a 90° angle to the seat. When the chair is tilted back, the student may not be able to see materials, pictures, and so on, or be able to see when the teacher or peers are waiting for his or her response. If an upright seating position cannot be maintained by the child, supported sitting may be required. It is important to allow the student as much head freedom as possible so that the full range of vision is functional. Pads, straps, and so on should not interfere with hearing.

Equipment used to enhance propulsion for the student in a prone, crawling, or creeping position includes crawlers and scooter boards. These are often used with younger children and in physical education programs to provide alternative positions or to enhance the development of reciprocity, reaching, and propulsion skills, especially in the upper body. Care should be taken that the student does not get arms, hands, hair, or feet caught under the equipment or under his or her body. Students who are paralyzed or who lack pressure or pain sensation should be taught to inspect visually for arms or other appendages that may be trapped, each time before moving.

Prone Boards

Prone boards may be used to facilitate weight bearing and to provide alternative positioning for a student during the school day. Problems have been observed in classrooms when the prone board has the student positioned so that he or she is high off the ground, looking down on a work table. In this position the student is a poor candidate for group participation. It is difficult for others to see him or her, and interactions between a seated child and one high on a prone board may be very unnatural.

When prone boards must be used during in-structional classroom time, the following precautions should be taken:

• The base of the board should be broad and weighted so that if the student is bumped or if he or she lists to one side, the student is not in danger of falling.

• The slope of the board should be evaluated carefully. If the slant is too great, the student will bear weight inappropriately through the upper trunk and chest area. If the board is too nearly upright, the student may fear falling backward and attend primarily to maintaining his or her position instead of to the instructional tasks.

Standing Frames

A standing frame or parapodium may be used instead of a chair for a student who needs to bear weight and become more stable in a standing position. Safety is a major consideration when using this equipment in the classroom. If the student's movements may cause him or her to fall backward, it may be necessary to use sandbags—to add additional weight to the base, or to place a protective wedge behind the child (see Figure 13.2). Depending on how tall the student is and how high the straps are on the student, the table or desk may have to be elevated so that the student can reach items or can be supported for writing or reading without leaning forward. The student should not have to put pressure on the strap(s) to try to reach down to the table, nor should the student have to reach up or try to pull him- or herself up to see or reach materials.

Standing Tables

Standing tables may be used in some classrooms. The student must be checked at least each 10 minutes to be sure that an inappropriate weight shift has not occurred or that improper posture is not being maintained. Some students try to hold themselves upright by pushing down on their elbows or hands on the surface of the desk. Not only is this tiring, but it facilitates inappropriate shoulder and

FIGURE 13.2   An example of a standing frame. Such a device allows for simultaneous weight bearing and classroom or tabletop activities.

neck positions and inhibits appropriate weight bearing. The student cannot use hands and arms for writing or manipulating objects when bearing weight through the elbows or hands. Moreover, in a classroom a standing table may isolate a student from group participation and interaction with peers. A standing table takes up a large space and is not easily moved or approached by peers.

Gurneys and Litters

Gurneys may be used in the classroom when a student must be maintained for all or part of the day in a horizontal or tilt position. Some gurneys tilt to enhance circulation and drainage or to enhance the student's visual contact. This equipment is so bulky that the student may not be able to attend a mainstream class, go to the library, or otherwise participate while using it. It is important to protect the student's privacy, especially if he or she is (1) in a body cast, (2) wearing a dress, or (3) catheterized. When a litter is used, special steps must be taken to secure the student, especially while being transported.

Seating for Specific Events

Although in the classroom a student may use a rather routine seating device, adaptation may be required in positioning for feeding, physical activities, and transportation to other parts of the building or on the school bus. The occupational and physical therapist(s) should be consulted for specific positioning requirements during all specialized activity. The adapted physical education teacher, as well as therapists, should be consulted for positioning during exercise, recreation, and activity periods.

Management of Regular Classroom Furniture

Although this chapter is devoted to equipment not traditionally used in general education classroom settings, there are some important points concerning the use or management of standard desks, chairs, and tables. For students who have difficulty with balance, stability, or fluctuating tone, or who are paralyzed, the following guidelines should be considered:

• Chairs should be sturdy and have glide knobs on the end of each leg, which are adjusted so as to prevent wobbling when the student shifts his or her weight, reaches for an object, and so forth.

• Chairs should have secure, tight joints.

• Chairs may have adjustable legs or wooden footrests so that the student has both feet (including heels) firmly on the floor, thus preventing inappropriate weight bearing in the buttocks and upper legs or the footrest. Legs should not dangle.

• Small wedges or towel rolls may be used at the hips between the chair and the student as needed to enhance the student's upright position in a regular chair and to compensate for a misfit in seat depth.

• Tables should have adjustable legs and no skirts or aprons (shield around edge), whether recessed or at the lip of the surface. This design allows a student in a wheelchair to get up close to the table just as other children do.

• Doors must meet fire code safety standards but must also be designed to allow any seated student to open a door to escape if an emergency occurs inside a classroom.

• Mirrors over sinks, pencil sharpeners, protected plugs, and so on should be located in classrooms and self-care areas so that students can have access to them as needed.

• Sinks should be placed so that a student in a wheelchair can reach the water (usually the apron or skirt on the front, as well as the cabinet under the sink, is removed or redesigned) without burning legs on hot water pipes or waste water evacuation pipes beneath a sink.

• Sand tables, art or gardening areas, and so forth may need to be elevated so that all young students have access to them, including students using adaptive seating.

• Classroom floors should be covered with a surface that does not inhibit crutch walking, chair propulsion, or scooter movement.

• Metal grates in sidewalks and in front of doors placed to help with sand, mud, or snow removal may prevent a student in a wheelchair from entering the area. Such grids should be removed, as well as thick mats and upright metal boot scrapers that are too close to the door to allow entry by the student who is seated. Domed threshold plates may have to be replaced with flat ones.

• Curb cuts and ramps should be examined, as they may be dangerous for a specific student. Lack of appropriate slope, smoothness of intersect with gutter, and so on may all cause a student to have an accident or to be unable to use the ramp or cut. It is important to note where ramps end and to ensure that there is a flat area at the beginning and at the end of each ramp. Ramps that slope into parking lots without a sufficient area to slow down and stop at the end are dangerous.

• There should be firm pathways to playground areas; these need to be kept free of debris so that wheelchair riders and crutch walkers may use the facilities. Sandy areas must be avoided; not only is it impossible to push through, but sand can score bearings on standard chairs and interrupt battery function on motored chairs.

When new furniture is ordered, teachers may want to request several sizes of chairs to accommodate variance in the physique and needs of students in the future. Generally, chairs and tables, or chairs and individual desks with adjustable legs, are preferred to arm chairs. Stackable classroom chairs with metal loop or running loop legs may tip or rock forward when a student moves forward before transferring to a wheelchair or to another piece of equipment. Plastic stops can be attached to such legs to prevent tipping.

COMMUNICATION AIDS

Many students with severe disabilities evidence speech and language disorders. These students may be completely nonverbal or unintelligible. Although for nondisabled persons speech is the most efficient avenue for communication, many individuals with severe disabilities are unable to communicate their needs and desires adequately via speech alone. For a more detailed discussion of augmentative and alternative communication, see Chapter 10.

Augmentative communication systems provide students with added and supplemental methods of communicating their needs and desires, as well as facilitate interaction with peers and others. Adaptive materials and equipment involved in developing and implementing augmentative communication systems range from photograph boards to microcomputers. Augmentative communications, as described by Vanderheiden and Lloyd (1986), may be either aided or unaided. Unaided communication systems are those that do not require equipment to communicate. Manual signing is an example of an unaided system.

Aided augmentative communication systems, however, are the focus of this section. Aided communication systems are most often either communication/language boards or electronic systems. Materials that may need to be adapted for nonelectronic communication boards or electronic devices include both symbol set choices and response mode/access opportunities.

Symbols

In general, there are many options for materials/symbol sets that are used with students with severe disabilities in implementing interventions in the area of augmentative communication. These include the use of objects, photographs, individual line drawings, commercial line drawings (e.g., picture communication system), rebus symbols, Bliss symbols, and words.

For higher-functioning students, words are typically the most efficient symbol set to use in communication (Silverman, 1989). However, many students considered to be severely disabled have cognitive impairments in addition to their physical impairments. These cognitive impairments may prevent the student from acquiring sight vocabulary words and thus prohibit the use of words as the unit of communication.

Response Mode Options

Regardless of the type of communication device selected, students must access information in order to effectively interact in communicative situations. Vanderheiden (1976) presented the three most common response mode options for students in accessing communication devices. These options include direct selection, scanning, and encoding.

Direct Selection

Direct selection is usually considered the most efficient method available for students to use with nonelectronic communication boards (Bigge, 1991; Miller & Alliare, 1987). In essence, direct selection requires the student to point directly to the desired communication symbol. This is the most efficient method available, because it is usually more rapid than other procedures. Direct selection systems may be electronic or nonelectronic. A student who types "drink, please" or selects a picture of a cup, on a computer is using a direct selection electronic device. A student who points to an actual cup, signaling a desire for a drink, is using a direct selection nonelectronic method. Students may directly select through index finger pointing (with or without the use of a splint), fist pointing, eye pointing, head pointing with a head pointer, or light pointing with an optical head pointer (Bigge, 1991). The teacher, speech-language pathologist, and physical and occupational therapists should all be involved in selecting the most appropriate material and equipment to use when choosing direct selection as the response mode for a student.

Scanning Systems

Scanning systems may also be electronic or nonelectronic (Miller & Allaire, 1987). They involve a student's selecting a message upon the presentation of choices one at a time. Scanning systems tend to be quite time-consuming for both the speaker and the listener (Bigge, 1991; Silverman, 1989). Nonelectronic scanning systems may involve the presentation of pictures one at a time and asking the student, "Do you want this?" An example of an electronic scanning system might involve the student's activating a light, which scans different pictures, and deactivating the movement of the light when the desired picture is reached.

Scanning has been reported to be the simplest of the three response modes for the student because it requires less of the student motorically than either direct selection or encoding

Encoding

Encoding involves the use of more than one code to express a message (Bigge, 1991). The student chooses the message, finds or remembers the codes for the message, and expresses or displays those codes to the listener. The listener then translates the codes into the message either through memory or through use of a response panel. Nonelectronic encoding typically allows the student an opportunity to express more messages than most other nonelectronic direct selection or scanning systems (Miller & Alliare, 1987). Students may access codes on a response panel through any of the direct selection modes presented previously. For example, the student presses a 1 and produces an electronic voice presentation: "I'd like a drink, please."

Switching Mechanisms

Electronic communication devices include switching mechanisms to interface the student with the device. These mechanisms provide the student with access to the communicative messages he or she wishes to express.

A student with control of any extremity can access a communication system via switching mechanisms. Silverman (1989) thoroughly discusses switching options for consideration in using augmentative communication devices. Among the mechanisms included are push, position, pneumatic, and light-controlled switches. Push switches are activated by pressure applied directly on the switch by any body part. Single pressure switches are common push switches. A student moves a body part and changes orientation in space in order to activate a position switch. A mercury head switch is an example of a position switch. This switch is activated by movement of the head. Students who have very poor or no control over major

body parts may use pneumatic switches that are controlled by breath. Puff and sip switches are activated or deactivated by the student's inhalation and exhalation of air. A lighted controlled head pointer may facilitate communication by pointing the light and fixing on the symbols needed to communicate.

Silverman (1989) identified several criteria to use when choosing switching mechanisms for students with severe disabilities. These include the following: (1) the least complex type of switching mechanism should be selected, (2) switching mechanisms should be selected that require gestures the student can currently perform or learn quickly, (3) switching mechanisms should be selected that require the least amount of energy from the student for activation, and (4) the least bulky mechanisms, which do not interfere with the student's daily activities, should be selected.

In addition to symbol and response mode selection, attention should be focused on the actual physical placement of the symbol set on the screen and any augmentative or interactive responding device. The placement of these materials and pieces of equipment should facilitate normal components of movement and not increase abnormal reflex activity. It is important to evaluate thoroughly the presence of asymmetrical tonic neck reflexes (ATNR), symmetrical tonic neck reflexes (STNR), and other primitive reflex patterns. For example, a student evidencing a strong ATNR to his or her right will frequently require a communication system with all symbols and access modes presented to his or her left so as to inhibit the occurrence of the reflex. Similarly, a student with a STNR may require symbols placed directly at eye level to avoid movement stimuli that occasion the reflex. Physical and occupational therapists should be actively involved in determining the most appropriate placement of symbols and access choices.

Equipment to Enhance Sensory Functioning

Students with limited auditory or visual proficiency may benefit from the use of amplification devices or corrective lenses. In addition, there are numerous special, often electronic, aids that may be used.

Visually impaired students may be taught to use enhancing and enlarging systems, such as the Visualtek. Students who are visually impaired and capable of academic skill acquisition may use a braille system, a talking computer, an optacon, and/or a Kursweil reader.

Students who are auditorily impaired and/or speech-language impaired may use a variety of equipment designed to enhance communication, such as picture/point books or symbol boards, scanning devices, voice or print output hand-held communicators.

ACTIVITIES OF DAILY LIVING

Within a functional and age-appropriate curricular framework, activities of daily living are almost always targeted for intervention for students with severe disabilities (Snell, 1987). Because of the increased physical and sensory involvement of many students in these programs, materials and equipment frequently must be adapted to allow for full or partial participation in tasks. These adaptations vary according to the specific needs of each student.

The most common activities of daily living are basic self-care skills, which include toileting, dressing, and feeding. Specially designed chairs for toileting or grab bars around the toilet may need to be adapted to provide a student with ad-equate support to maintain his or her position during this activity (see the earlier discussion on seating options). Materials may need to be adapted to allow students to reach for tissue, grasp tissue, and/or release the tissue when finished. Some students with severe disabilities will need adapted utensils for self-feeding because of their lack of a volitional grasp-release pattern (Bigge, 1991). Students with severe disabilities may be physically unable to manipulate buttons on clothing and may require adapted clothing with Velcro fasteners or with larger buttons. There are companies that specialize in adapted, "with it" clothing for children and adults who use wheelchairs. Frequently used clothing adaptations include Velcro seams on jeans legs so that toileting is more easily accomplished. Some students need pants with a longer waist-to-crotch measurement in the back so that skin is not exposed between shirt and pants. For some, a Velcro side-seam skirt affords easier dressing than one with a back or front closing.

SUMMARY

Adaptive equipment, when used correctly, may greatly enhance the quality of life, choice selection, and participation by students in their school and home environments. To provide for students' maximum participation in school, students, parents, teachers, and therapists must work together to determine needs and to select the appropriate equipment.

REFERENCES

Bigge, J. L. (1991). *Teaching individuals with physical and multiple disabilities.* New York: Macmillan Publishing Co.

Church, G., & Glennen, S. (1992). *Handbook of assistive technology.* San Diego, CA: Singular Publishing Group, Inc.

Fraser, B. A., Hensinger, R. N., & Phelps, J. A. (1987). *Physical management of multiple handicaps.* Baltimore: Paul H. Brookes Publishing Co.

Lewis, R. A. (1993). *Special education technology.* Pacific Grove, CA: Brooks/Cole Publishing Co.

Mader, B., Hart, L. A., & Bergin, B. (1989). Social acknowledgements for children with disabilities: Effects of service dogs. *Child Development, 60,* 1529–1534.

Miller, J., & Allaire, J. (1987). Augmentative communication. In M. Snell (Ed.), *Systematic instruction of persons with severe handicaps* (3rd ed.). Columbus, OH: Charles E. Merrill.

Silverman, F. H. (1989). *Communication for the speechless* (2nd ed.). Englewood Cliffs, NJ: Prentice Hall.

Snell, M. (1987). Basic self-care instruction for students without motor impairments. In M. Snell (Ed.), *System instruction of persons with severe handicaps* (3rd ed.). Columbus, OH: Charles E. Merrill.

Vanderheiden, G. C. (1976). Providing the child with a means to indicate. In G. C. Vanderheiden & K. Grilley (Eds.), *Nonvocal communication techniques and aids for the severely physically handicapped.* Baltimore: University Park Press.

Vanderheiden, G. C., & Lloyd, L. L. (1986). Communication systems and their components. In S. W. Blackstone & D. M. Bruskin (Eds.), *Augmentative communication: An introduction.* Rockville, MD: ASHA.

SELECTED SOURCES OF EQUIPMENT

AbleNet, Inc.
1081 10th Avenue, SE
Minneapolis, MN 55414-1312

Able Products
325 West 11th Street
New York, NY 10014

adapt Ability
P.O. Box 515
Colchester, CT 06415-0515
1-800-243-9232

American Printing House for the Blind
1839 Frankfort Avenue
P.O. Box 6085
Louisville, KY 40206-0085
1-800-223-1839

Assistive Technoloty Centers, Inc.
119 First Avenue
Pittsburgh, PA 15222

Crestwood Company
6625 North Sidney Place
Milwaukee, WI 53209
1-414-352-5678

Dunamis
3620 Highway 317
Suwanee, GA 30174
1-800-828-2443

Flaghouse
150 North MacQuesten Parkway
Mt. Vernon, NY 10550
1-800-793-7900

Franklin Electronic Publishers, Inc.
122 Burrs Road
Mt. Holly, NJ 08060

Independent Living Arts
27 Eastman
Plainview, NY 11803

Don Johnston
Developmental Equipment
P.O. Box 639
1000 North Rand Road, Building 115
Wauconda, IL 60084-0639
1-800-999-4600

Kaye Products
535 Dimmocks Mill Road
Hillsborough, NC 27278

LS&S Grup
P.O. Box 673
Northbrook, IL 60065

Maddak
Pequannock, NJ 07440-1993

Mulholland
1563 Los Angeles Avenue
Ventura, CA 93003

J. A. Preston
P.O. Box 89
Jackson, MI 49204
1-800-631-7277

Prentke Romich
1022 Heyl Road
Wooster, OH 44691
1-800-262-1984

Rifton
Route 213
Rifton, NY 12471
1-914-658-3141

Fred Sammons
Box 32
Brookfield, IL 60513
1-800-323-5547

Science Products
Box 888
Southeastern, PA 19399
1-800-888-7400

Telesensory Systems, Inc.
3408 Hillview Avenue
P.O. Box 10099
Palo Alto, CA 94304

Therapeutic Toys, Inc.
P.O. Box 418
Moodus, CT 06469
1-800-638-0676

Therapy Skill Builders
(also) Communication Skill Builders
3830 East Bellevue
P.O. Box 42050-C93
Tucson, AZ 85733
1-602-323-7500

Toys for Special Children
385 Warburton Avenue
Hastings-on-Hudson, NY 10706
1-914-478-0960

Visualtek
1610 26th Street
Santa Monica, CA 90404

Zygo
P.O. Box 1008
Portland, OR 97207

PART THREE

ISSUES IN SERVICE DELIVERY

Part III of this book presents three chapters with information on various aspects of educational service delivery and other critical issues for persons with severe disabilities. Chapter 14 provides an overview of early intervention approaches as they relate to toddlers and preschoolers with severe disabilities. It discusses the legislation leading to the current widespread efforts in early intervention. The authors review the efficacy of early intervention for children with severe disabilities and identify best professional practices for personnel working with children from birth to age 5. Methods to deliver services through age-appropriate and functional interventions are stressed.

Chapter 15 provides a framework for delivering consultation to teachers, parents, and care providers, within both classroom and community settings. This chapter addresses a current pressing need in the field, as many more children are mainstreamed into less restrictive settings where instructional personnel may not be as well trained to treat and educate children with severe disabilities. Special education teachers may find themselves more frequently in the role of consultant to other teachers, staff, and parents. The authors of this chapter review a number of consultation models, including behavioral and collaborative consultation models, and then identify a specific program that has application to classrooms, homes, and day program management. The authors' program relies on setting performance stan-

dards, monitoring the program, providing feedback with staff training, and determining outcomes via evaluation.

The last chapter of this book, Chapter 16, presents the reader with helpful information on medication management. Although it is not expected that a teacher would be as competent as a physician in understanding drugs, inasmuch as that is not their role, this chapter, however, does present information that classroom teachers will find helpful in working with children who are taking medication. It is important to note that the provision of such a chapter is not a wholehearted endorsement of a medical model. However, because medication for controlling behavior is a pervasive phenomenon in special education, the knowledgeable teacher can play a vital role in monitoring of the effects of medication and providing more accurate data to the physician in this regard. Once a teacher acquires some knowledge about the types of medication and their proposed behavioral effects, he or she can serve as a better advocate for the child when dealing with the medical profession. It is to this end that this chapter is fitting for our textbook. Prevalence and patterns of drug use are identified, as well as current issues in the use of medication for students with disabilities. Chapter 16 also discusses the effects of various drug types on behavior and learning, prevalence rates, subclasses of drugs within major drug categories, and side effects.

CHAPTER 14

EARLY INTERVENTION

MARY LYNNE CALHOUN
TERRY L. ROSE
University of North Carolina at Charlotte

Early intervention for children with disabilities is a component of America's efforts to provide early education for all children. Therefore, before discussing early intervention efforts for children with severe disabilities, it may be instructive to consider the zeitgeist of early education in America.

Early childhood education has developed in the absence of any consensually agreed-upon vision or policy, resulting in a system that is really a nonsystem characterized by competition, fragmentation, and, in many cases, practice that does not reflect current knowledge about effective programming (Kagan, 1989, 1990; Scarr & Weinberg, 1986). One cause for this disarray may be found by noting that, until relatively recently, day care and early education were viewed as unimportant educationally and as distinctly different enterprises with very different functions. Day care was established as a social service for working or indigent parents, whereas private preschool programs were generally developed to meet the needs of middle-class Americans and provided educational and socialization opportunities for both parents and children (Kagan, 1990).

Even more recently, federal- and state-supported programs were sponsored in response to our increased social conscience to overcome the negative effects of poverty and other social ills. Programs such as Head Start, Title I of the Elementary and Secondary Education Act, and a few state programs were developed to enhance children's cognitive, social, emotional, and physi-

cal needs (Kagan, 1990). Thus, a dual system of private, fee-for-service programs and compensatory, public-support programs developed and was institutionalized.

Compounding this situation is a chronic lack of support for early education efforts. First, salaries and benefits for early education personnel are so low that staff turnover and recruitment of new staff, consistently the most vexing problems facing program directors, have a major impact on the quality of services offered. For example, staff turnover has been estimated to average about 41 percent a year nationally (Whitebrook, Howes, & Phillips, 1989). Second, funding for programs lags far behind the amount that early education programs require to be highly successful. For example, average expenditures in high-quality early education programs average about $4660 per child (U.S. General Accounting Office, 1989), and only $3000 per child is spent annually in all child-care programs (Child Care Action Campaign, 1988).

Despite the formidable policy and fiscal problems, a number of research findings have demonstrated the effectiveness and cost-effectiveness of early intervention for children from disadvantaged situations (e.g., Berrueta-Clement, Schweinhart, Barnett, Epstein, & Weikart, 1984; Lazar & Darlington, 1982).

The development of early intervention services for children with disabilities has paralleled, to a large extent, the development of programs for children without disabilities, with one major difference. Services for children with disabilities, especially those with severe disabilities, have been driven more by the federal government than by the private sector. Legislation was incorporated into the Social Security Act of 1935 to fund state Crippled Children's Services to locate children with disabilities and to diagnose, hospitalize, and provide corrective surgery and postoperative care for these children. By the 1950s, the Maternal and Child Health Services began to provide assistance to children with mental retardation. In the 1960s, the U.S. Office of Education began funding model programs for early intervention. The impetus for these efforts by the government was not only published reports linking mental retardation to premature birth, brain damage, low income, and inadequate prenatal care, but President Kennedy's personal interest.

Throughout the intervening years, a wide variety of programs have been developed to intervene on behalf of children with disabilities. The Early Education Program for Children with Disabilities (EEPCD) is one such program that has had notable success in stimulating the development of educational programs for infants and young children with disabilities. Funded originally by the Handicapped Children's Early Education Act, passed in 1968, EEPCD has provided seed money to develop model demonstration projects as well as a national network of early intervention programs. These programs have been successful at the national, state, and local levels (Swan, 1980). The culmination of the federal commitment may be seen in the passage of Public Law 99-457, the Education of the Handicapped Act Amendments of 1986, along with PL 102-119, its reauthorization in 1991.

As has generally been the case in early childhood educational services, there was little evidence of a pervasive policy or vision to guide these efforts. As a result, even the term *early intervention* means different things to different people: it may involve full-day center-based service provided by a staff of professionals or home-based service provided by parents with minimal contact with professionals; it may mean service provided

from a medical perspective or service with an educational orientation; and it may cost a few hundred dollars a year per child or tens of thousands of dollars per child.

However, as with evidence regarding programs for children without disabilities, abundant evidence began to accrue that early intervention was effective, even despite the programmatic problems. For example, in 1985 the Office of Special Education and Rehabilitative Services reported to Congress that:

> *Studies of the effectiveness of preschool education for the handicapped have demonstrated beyond doubt the economic and educational benefits for programs of young handicapped children. (p. 211)*

Although these findings are certainly encouraging, the majority of the studies mentioned in the preceding quotation were conducted with children with mild to moderate disabling conditions. Until recently, few early intervention programs were developed to provide service to children with severe disabilities. Not until the passage of PL 99-457 and the political action of groups such as the Council for Exceptional Children (CEC) and The Association for Persons with Severe Handicaps (TASH) did infants and preschool children with severe disabilities begin receiving early intervention services with any degree of regularity (Bricker & Kaminski, 1986).

Review of Child Outcome Data

We have progressed considerably from the time when documentation of developmental gains for programs providing early intervention to children with severe disabilities was unnecessary, or even unexpected, because these programs provided some kind of stimulation or enrichment that was superior to custodial care (Weatherford, 1986). Where we accepted these early programs on humanitarian grounds because they had "presumed value" (Ackerman & Moore, 1976), we now require empirical evidence of success.

Unfortunately, much of the early intervention evaluation research reported thus far has been criticized for serious methodological flaws (Bricker, Bailey, & Bruder, 1984; Dunst, 1986; Dunst & Rheingrover, 1981; Odom & Fewell, 1983; Simeonsson, Cooper, & Schiener, 1982; White & Casto, 1984). The causes of these flaws may be many, but apparently two may relate specifically to studies of early intervention with children with severe disabilities. First, social policy dictated that large-scale early intervention programs be established quickly, with an emphasis on program delivery rather than evaluation (Casto, 1988). Second, the variability in program characteristics and the children's disabilities may result in a large number of related lines of research, rather than one global research line that asks the question, "Does early intervention work?" For example, categorizing children by their disabling label (e.g., motor delay, autism) only touches the surface of a clear description of these children. Other descriptors, such as the severity of each primary problem, the extent of associated disabilities, related functional characteristics, and family situations are only a few of the many related variables that describe each child. Therefore, the question of whether early intervention works should be modified to "For whom does it work, under what conditions, and toward what goals and objectives?" (Guralnick, 1988).

In addition, few programs have been designed specifically for children with severe disabilities, and these few programs vary considerably in populations receiving service, service delivery models, and curriculum approaches (Bricker & Kaminski, 1986). For example, Bricker and Kaminski (1986) reported the results of a survey of Handicapped Children's Early Education Programs (HCEEP) that were in existence in 1981–1982 for children with severe disabilities. These programs served between 6 and 39 children whose ages ranged from birth to 9 years. Disabling conditions included multiple disabilities, nonverbal condition, autism, brain damage, and severe retardation. Services were provided primarily in home and center-based combinations. No curricular approach predominated, although some versions of a developmental approach are reported by four of the programs. This variability further supports the notion that we should ask the more specific question regarding early intervention, rather than the more global, "Does it work?"

Given all of these methodological and programmatic difficulties, we should probably view efficacy studies of early intervention for children with severe disabilities as "first-generation" studies. That is, they will probably not be able to answer questions of efficacy in general, but will be able to answer some questions about specific variables that seem to be related to success. As other researchers build upon these first-generation findings, more questions can be answered in more detail.

Global effects.   We may examine the effects of early intervention from a global perspective— "Does it work?" and "For whom does it work?" Casto and Mastropieri (1986) reported the results of a massive review of the research literature on early intervention for children with disabilities. Using sophisticated meta-analysis statistical procedures, these authors reviewed 74 studies of heterogeneous groups of children with disabilities. They reported significant short-term effects that were greatest for cognitive measures, but were also significant for such domains as language and motor skills. We must remember, however, that the studies they reviewed varied greatly in quality and in the characteristics of the children involved. Therefore, we should be careful in drawing conclusions from their review.

Another way to answer these global questions is to focus on studies using children with specific disabilities. For example, following a review of research studies of children with Down syndrome, Guralnick and Bricker (1987) concluded that early intervention was significantly effective in increasing cognitive measures. Longitudinal studies have revealed that the pronounced decline in IQ measures during the first few years of life for children with Down syndrome can be prevented by early and consistent intervention programs (Berry, Gunn, & Andrews, 1984; Connolly, 1978; Melyn & White, 1973; Schnell, 1984). Similar, but weaker, results have been found for children with other biologically based delays, and analyses of other disability groups (e.g., language disorders, autism) have demonstrated mixed results (Guralnick & Bennett, 1987). Thus, we may conclude that the more specific questions—"for whom, under what conditions"—are beginning to be answered positively, at least for some groups of children.

Specific effects. Given the relatively positive findings for the global questions of efficacy, we now turn to the findings regarding more specific findings. Admittedly, there are few definite answers at this time, but we can conclude that several variables seem to be related to success. First, *parent involvement* has been proven to be linked to successful outcomes, although the nature of that involvement seems to be shifting. Early programs used parents as "service providers"; after training by professionals, they became the primary source of educational interventions. Parents have demonstrated success in this role (Bruder & Bricker, 1985; Gross, Eudy, & Drabman, 1982), but have voiced concern over its restrictive nature (e.g., Calhoun, Calhoun, & Rose, 1989). Consequently, more programs have begun to focus on developing social networks for parents (e.g., Bailey & Simeonsson, 1988), implementing a social systems approach in which parents and professionals become partners, or on developing natural, reciprocal relationships between parent and child (Calhoun & Rose, 1988, 1989). (The interested reader is referred to a review by Rosenberg and Robinson [1988].) Although many questions remain, parental involvement is a variable that appears to be closely related to success.

Program intensity is a second variable that appears to be closely related to child performance. Intensity does not mean just the amount of time a child may be receiving services, because most infant and toddler programs average only about 2 to 6 hours per week (Guralnick, 1988). Intensity also includes "engagement time," which is the time spent by a child in active participation in appropriate activities during the time given to early intervention. Data regarding these effects are still few, but it appears that more researchers are beginning to study this variable (Carta, Sainato, & Greenwood, 1988). The intensity of any program will be limited to some degree by the children's ages, disability levels, and the resources available to the program, but current research seems to support intensity as a way to increase children's learning (see reviews by Casto and Mastropieri [1986] and Bryant and Ramey [1987]). Two sets of studies are especially noteworthy for their support of increasing program intensity. In the first, Lovaas (1987) reported the preliminary results of a study in which autistic children received intensive behaviorally based interventions for up to 40 hours per week. Treatment intensity declined as the children made progress. The comparison group of autistic children received similar instruction, but for only 10 hours per week. Substantial improvement was reported for more than 90 percent of the intensive treatment group, whereas virtually all of the children in the less intensive group continued to demonstrate significant developmental delays. In the second group of related studies, Strain and his colleagues (Hoyson, Jamieson, & Strain, 1984; Strain, Jamieson, & Hoyson, 1986) implemented a programmed classroom-based intervention for "autistic-like" young children with severe developmental and behavioral difficulties. The classroom activities occurred 3 hours a day, 5 days a week, with extensive parent involvement in the classroom and at home. By the end of the study, the children's rate of development was double the rate that would have otherwise been expected. Given these and more recent, similar findings (e.g., Rose & Calhoun, 1990), we certainly must begin to consider the effects that increased program intensity may have on children's rates of improvement. We may even be excited about these findings, but much more has to be done before we can answer questions related to intensity for each child with severe disabilities.

Several researchers have found that problems

in *social interactions* are serious and pervasive for children with severe disabilities (e.g., Eaton & Menolascino, 1982; Reiss, Levitan, & McNally, 1982; Thompson, 1984). For example, Watkins (cited in Guralnick [1988]) reported that social and behavioral problems were the only differences between a group of children who had received early intervention and a group who had not received early intervention. Success in developing more appropriate social interactions has been reported (e.g., Rose & Calhoun, 1990; Strain & Kohler, 1988), but much remains to be done before we can answer questions related to "for whom, under what conditions."

Summary of Best Professional Practices

Despite the variability in the conceptualization, implementation, and evaluation of programs for this population, some consistencies are apparent in many programs. For example, most programs seem to be founded on the premise that changes in the children and their families can be attained and, as a result, that indirect, generalized changes will also occur (Bricker & Kaminski, 1986). Given this conceptual foundation, we can subscribe to Gentry and Olson's (1985) description of the elements that successful programs seem to share. These elements include: (1) a philosophical basis for the program, (2) a clearly specified, well-conceived curriculum, (3) staff that have been trained well, (4) parent and family involvement, and (5) a comprehensive, well-conceived evaluation plan. (The interested reader is referred to Bricker [1982] or Gentry and Olson [1985] for more detailed descriptions of these elements.)

OVERVIEW OF FEDERAL LEGISLATION

Access to early intervention services has depended historically on where a person lived and whether he or she had the "right" disability. Although excellent early intervention services have been in existence for a number of years, their accessibility has by no means been universal, and, in general, the younger the child and the more severe the disability, the less available the service (Hayden, 1979; Calhoun & Rose, 1986).

Early intervention services are now increasingly available to infants and young children with severe disabilities as a result of the enactment of PL 99-457 (1986) and its reauthorization PL 10-119 (1991). Congress enacted this legislative program to expand and improve early education efforts. This legislation, which has been called "a new national agenda for young special needs children" (Trohanis, 1987, p. 1), was fueled by the documented benefits of early intervention and preschool services.

The two major programs of PL 99-457 are the Handicapped Infants and Toddlers Program (Part H) and the Preschool Program (Part B). Each state has been asked to develop a statewide delivery system to expand and improve services for infants, toddlers, and preschoolers. As more and more states move toward full compliance, the chances of children who need early intervention services actually receiving them are greatly increased.

The Handicapped Infants and Toddlers Program (Part H) creates a discretionary program to help states implement services for all eligible young children who are handicapped or developmentally delayed in the birth-to-3-years age range. A key feature of Part H programs is the family focus, recognizing families' essential role in facilitating the growth and development of their children with special needs. Infants and toddlers are "uniquely dependent on their families for their survival and nurturance" (Johnson, McGonigel, & Kaufmann, 1989, p. 5). For that reason, early intervention services for this age group necessitate a family-centered approach to early intervention. Family education and counseling can be included in Part H intervention services, and there is a strong emphasis on respecting families' preferences and wishes in the design and implementation of services. Respect for families' autonomy, independence, and decision making is an underlying principle, and early intervention services should be flexible, accessible, and responsive to family needs.

This family focus introduces a new set of initials

to the language of early intervention: *IFSP*. These initials stand for the Individualized Family Service Plan, designed to serve the child within the context of serving the entire family (Turnbull & Turnbull, 1988). The IFSP is analogous to the Individualized education plan (IEP), long used to develop programs for school-aged persons with special needs. The family focus of the IFSP, however, sets it apart from the IEP, its predecessor.

Rather than establishing goals that reflect desired changes in the child's behavior as does the IEP, the IFSP develops outcomes expected to be achieved for the child and family (Johnson, McGonigel, & Kaufmann, 1989). In every step of the IFSP process, families and professionals share information, discuss options for services, then develop outcomes and strategies to achieve those outcomes. The following are examples of IFSP outcomes:

Outcome 1

Pam's mom and dad will get help in locating and using baby-sitting and respite care services.

Outcome 2

Pam's family will get some help with mealtimes in order for Pam to learn how to eat solid food and be less fussy.

Outcome 3

Pam will receive physical therapy to improve head control, balance, and sitting skills.

Guidelines and sample formats for developing IFSPs have been reported by Johnson, McGonigel, and Kaufmann (1989).

The Preschool Program (Part B) of PL 99-457 creates a new mandate for state education agencies to serve all 3-, 4-, and 5-year-old children who have disabilities. This new mandate was achieved by lowering the PL 94-142 mandate to age 3 (Smith, n.d.). PL 94-142, the Education for All Handicapped Children Act of 1975, created a right to education for children with disabilities who were of school age. Although PL 94-142 allowed services to children as young as 3 in certain circumstances, such services have not been universally available. Now this right to education is extended to children beginning at age 3. The Preschool Program thus differs from the Infant and Toddler Program in this crucial way: it is a mandate rather than an incentive.

Children aged 3, 4, and 5 are eligible for services under this new program if they have disabilities according to one or more of the PL 94-142 diagnostic categories: deaf or hard of hearing, deaf-blind, mentally retarded, multiply disabled, orthopedically impaired, otherwise health impaired, seriously emotionally disturbed, having a specific learning disability, speech impaired, or visually disabled. The new law makes an important distinction, however: the documentation of children required by the federal government from the states does not have to be based on diagnostic category for this age group. This allows states to serve 3- to 5-year-olds without labeling them (Smith, n.d.).

The special education and related services and protections that have been available to school-age children—due process, rights, evaluation and placement in the least restrictive environment, and IEPs—are now extended downward to the 3- to 5-year-olds who need them (Trohanis, 1987). There are some new twists, however. Service delivery models need not follow the traditional "school day." Delivery systems may include a variety of models, including home-based, center-based shared enrollment, or other variations. Although the "family focus" is not as clear an emphasis as is reflected in the Infant and Toddler Program, the Preschool Program also recognizes the important role of parents in the lives of their young children. Parental instruction is an allowable cost in this program, rather than only services delivered directly to the child. The least restrictive environment (LRE) provision of PL 99-457 requires that children with disabilities receive educational services to the maximum extent appropriate with typically developing children (McLean & Odom, 1988).

What will this new federal direction mean for young children with severe disabilities? The promise of widely available services, the emphasis on experiences with nondisabled peers, a family focus that supports and respects family needs and preferences—all offer a vision of a hopeful future. The first generations of infants and young children with severe disabilities for whom early intervention services are widely available will likely offer us some surprises and teach us a lot. Their experiences will influence not only early intervention services, but services for persons with severe disabilities across the lifespan.

SERVICE DELIVERY MODELS

Flexible programming within a continuum of services is the early intervention ideal for infants and young children with severe disabilities. A recent study of concerns of parents about early intervention found great variability in readiness to participate and enroll children in programs, as well as great variability in perceptions of desirable program features. Moreover, parents' wishes about early intervention shifted with changing family needs (Calhoun, Calhoun, & Rose, 1989). It seems clear that the features of the "perfect" early intervention program cannot be delineated independently but, rather, must fit well with the needs of families and be flexible enough to change as family needs change. This "goodness-of-fit" concept (Simeonsson, Bailey, Huntington, & Comfort, 1986) asks us to consider the unique characteristics of child and family as they interact with the demands, expectations, and opportunities of the environment and to be flexible in our program offerings. The following paragraphs describe typical service delivery options for children in the range of birth to age 5:

Home-Based Services

Recognizing that parents are the key people in children's early development and that staying at home for the first months or years of life is "age appropriate" and typical for many babies, home-based services provide instruction to parents in developmental or adaptive activities that they can do with their children at home. In a typical home-based program, an early interventionist visits the home every week or two to check on the child's progress and to offer instruction and support. The interventionist can be a teacher, nurse, therapist, social worker, psychologist, or paraprofessional. The intervention plan for the young child will be based on a multidisciplinary team assessment, and the actual home services will be transdisciplinary; that is, the interventionist will offer ideas and instruction from all disciplines, rather than just one specialty area. Home-based programs are more often available for children in the birth to 2 years age range than for older preschoolers.

Classroom-Based Services

More intensive services can be offered in a more school-like classroom setting to which groups of young children come for extended sessions daily or several times a week. Center-based services can offer the advantage of consistent intervention with access to specialists such as early educators and physical, occupational, and speech therapists, as well as to specialized equipment. In addition, the shared responsibility for a child's progress and care offers some respite time to families.

Classroom programs can be available for both very young children (birth to 2 years) and preschoolers (3 to 5 years); their availability is more widespread at the preschool level.

Combination Classroom-Based and Home-Based Program

Some early intervention programs combine the best features of the center-based and home-based models and offer both types of services. Home visits permit the interventionist to see a child in his or her most familiar environment and to share intervention routines with all the important people in the child's life. Classroom services provide the opportunity for group interaction, specialized therapies, and some respite for the primary caregivers. When programs are able to offer services in both settings, communication between parents and interventionists and consistency in intervention routines are enhanced.

Hospital Programs

Home- or classroom-based programs no longer represent the first opportunity for providing early intervention and family support. New models of service delivery are being developed that address the needs of babies with severe disabilities in the first days or weeks of life in the neonatal intensive care unit (NICU) of local hospitals.

The NICU environment is an extraordinary one. The infant born prematurely or with other significant health problems is transferred from the warm, cushioned environment of the amniotic sac in utero to an intensely bright, noisy newborn nursery. (Lawhorn, 1986). Not only are babies exposed to an intense physical environment, but they are also subject to a multitude of medical procedures that involve a high level of handling, which may cause discomfort. Professionals providing care to infants in the NICU must not only attend to survival issues, but must optimize growth and development as well. Transition support to community-based programs will be needed.

Integration Models

The mainstreaming trend, which has been such a powerful force in the education of school-age children, is increasingly important in preschool services as well. Advocacy groups propose that education in the least restricted environment, defined as proximity to normally developing peers, should be the cornerstone of any educational program for young children with disabilities (Division for Early Childhood, 1987; The Association for Persons with Severe Handicaps, 1987). For very young children, of course, the public school mainstream model does not work, because schools do not provide educational programs or day care for all normally developing preschool children, and many normally developing infants and preschoolers attend no educational program until age 5.

Four potential options for integrated early intervention programs have been identified by McLean and Odom (1988): (1) mainstreamed educational programs in preschool programs such as Head Start, (2) mainstreamed noneducational programs in day-care settings, (3) integrated special education programs, also known as reverse mainstreaming, and (4) nonintegrated special education programs located in regular schools. As noted earlier, no single service delivery model will be ideal for all children and families. The availability of several options is the secret of effective, responsive early intervention service delivery.

ISSUES IN SERVICE DELIVERY

The Least Restrictive Environment

A key provision of PL 99-457 is that early intervention be provided for young children with special needs in the least restrictive environment (LRE). LRE can be defined as the place where the child receives appropriate educational services and is educated to the greatest extent possible with children who are not disabled (Division for Early Childhood, 1987). The value of integrated educational experiences has been strongly stated in legal and moral terms (Snell, 1987; Turnbull, 1982; The Association for Persons with Severe Handicaps, 1987); moreover, the hope has been expressed that there may be developmental or educational benefits to placement in mainstreamed settings (Odom & McEvoy, 1988).

The potential benefits of early integrated education are the subject of increasing examination by researchers. Growth, particularly in social skills, has been demonstrated for both typical children and children who are developmentally delayed within mainstreamed settings (Guralnick & Groom, 1988; Odom, Deklyen, & Jenkins, 1984).

Most research, however, has focused on young children with mild to moderate disabilities; when children with severe disabilities are included, the changes in interaction patterns are less apparent (Beckman, 1983; Guralnick, 1981). There is a growing body of literature that concludes that the "proximity test" of social integration—having children with disabilities and those without disabilities in the same physical space—does not promote social growth (Kugelmass, 1989). The assumption that the child with disabilities will learn from, generalize, or make developmental gains as a result of simple proximity to children who are not disabled is also false (Jenkins, Speltz, & Odom, 1985).

For children with disabilities to gain social and developmental benefits from early integrated education, positive programming practices must be developed. It is important to consider a number of factors: the selection of play activities, games, and materials that will facilitate interaction; the use of specific reinforcement principles and procedures to build the observational, imitative, group involvement, and social interaction skills of children with special needs; systematic use of prompting activities by teachers; and flexibility in the design, content, and organization of the curriculum. *Integrated Preschool Curriculum* (Odom et al., 1991) offers specific strategies to promote social integration. This resource provides a large number of play activities and gives specific directions to teachers to prompt imitation of appropriate social and play behavior and to reinforce interaction.

At this point in our understanding of best professional practices for early intervention, the question of what constitutes the least restrictive environment for very young children with severe disabilities has not been fully answered. Although the philosophic and legal arguments for mainstreamed programs are compelling, the question of the availability of intervention services of appropriate intensity and consistency has yet to be explored. Some interventionists have argued that specialized, intensive early intervention in the first months or years of life may be the least restrictive option for young chil-

dren with severe disabilities, because such intervention may accelerate development, open doors to future educational opportunities, and impart greater ability to meet the demands of the environment (Rose & Calhoun, 1990). If we can include subsequent placement in more normalized settings as an important characteristic of an appropriate educational plan, then the persuasiveness of including specialized, intensive early intervention alternatives in any continuum of services is clear. The issues in developing the most effective intervention programs in the least restrictive environment may be different for infants (birth to 2 years) than for preschoolers (3 to 5 years). As children with severe disabilities reach the age when nondisabled peers often attend preschool, opportunities for integration will increase.

As the questions about LRE continue to be explored by early intervention researchers and policymakers, it is important to maintain an ongoing evaluation of the effectiveness of a particular program for each individual child. Changes in program placement and program implementation should be made as soon as changing needs are identified. Sensitivity and responsiveness to the needs of individual children and openness to meaningful opportunities for interaction with nondisabled peers will lead to the discovery of environments that are "least restrictive" for young children with severe disabilities.

Staffing Patterns

Young children with complex, severe, and multiple disabilities need service from many different professional disciplines. Those disciplines involved in early intervention include education, psychology, child development, social work, occupational therapy, physical therapy, speech pathology and audiology, nutrition, medicine, and nursing. When these professionals work smoothly and cooperatively together, along with the child's family, the child is well served and the family is better able to meet the demands of their challenging situation.

How do professionals from a wide variety of disciplines work together to meet the needs of children and families? In describing early intervention staffing patterns, the word *disciplinary,* referring to a particular professional discipline, is often preceded by one of these prefixes: *multi, inter,* or *trans.* Each of these words—multidisciplinary, interdisciplinary, and transdisciplinary—describes a model for professional interaction. Each of these models recognizes the value of participation from and cooperation among the various professional disciplines. Peterson (1987) describes the models in this way: on a *multidisciplinary team,* each professional works in isolation from other specialists but recognizes and appreciates the work of others; on an *interdisciplinary team,* professionals work together in jointly planned programs with goals developed that are specific to each discipline; on a *transdisciplinary team,* there is a pooling and sharing of information, knowledge, and skills, crossing traditional professional boundaries.

The transdisciplinary team model has been identified as the staffing pattern best suited for infants and children with severe disabilities (Brimer, 1990). This approach integrates program goals and objectives from various disciplines beginning in the assessment process and extending through programming. Each team member is responsible for sharing information and skills so that multiple interventions can occur simultaneously. In other words, interventions with a child reflect the knowledge and skills of the team, no matter which professional is working directly with the child. A key ingredient in the transdisciplinary approach is the identification of a team leader, sometimes called a case manager or service coordinator, who is responsible for coordinating and integrating intervention services. This role may be assigned to the interventionist who sees the child most frequently, such as the classroom teacher, for a child enrolled in a center-based program, or the interventionists whose professional expertise is most essential to the child's development and well-being at a particular time, such as the nurse for a child who needs many special procedures to sustain life and health or the speech pathologist for a child with a severe hearing disorder.

It is essential that the interventionists providing direct service have continued support from other members as new questions arise or as routines need fine-tuning to meet a child's changing needs. The essential team elements of common goal (to maximize the developmental potential of each child and family), interdependence, commitment, accountability, and leadership (Robinson, n.d.) will make effective early intervention possible for young children with severe disabilities and their families.

Health and Safety Concerns

All young children deserve environments that promote their health and safety, and children with special needs are no exception. Certain characteristics of infants and young children with severe disabilities may require that early intervention programs pay careful attention to health and safety issues.

An increasing number of children in early intervention programs are described as medically fragile, meaning that they may require special technology, unusual treatment plans, and special feeding devices and diets, as well as cardiac and respiratory monitors for their survival. Many early interventionists will be called upon to provide services that have traditionally been in the realm of health care but are now necessary in early education programs if medically fragile children are to access such programs. There may be a need in educational settings for health-related services such as seizure monitoring, medication administration, skin care, bowel care, nutrition monitoring and supplements, CPR, shunt monitoring, cast care, colostomy or ileostomy care, nasogastric tube feeding, gastrostomy tube feeding, clean intermittent catheterization, and tracheotomy care (Graff, Ault, Guess, Taylor, & Thompson, 1990). In addition to such specialized procedures, children who are medically fragile usually require some modification of the daily schedule, need specialized equipment such as a heart monitor, oxygen, or suctioning unit, and need specific management throughout their environments. Nursing consultation is crucial to early intervention programs (Campbell, Cohen, & Rich, 1987).

Early intervention staff should receive direct instruction from a nurse in the specialized procedures and management strategies that foster the health and development of young children who are medically fragile. In addition, program staff should plan for emergencies with specific instructors and receive permissions from parents and physicians.

In addition to concerns about children who are medically fragile, an early intervention program must attend to health and hygiene issues for the protection of all children and staff in the program. When children are seen in groups or when one staff member works with several children sequentially, steps must be taken to avoid the transmission of communicable diseases.

In general, children who are disabled are not at higher risk than nondisabled children for communicable diseases, but the kind and severity of disabilities may predispose a child to infection. Concerns about infectious diseases can be grouped into four areas (Aronson & Osterholm, 1984). First, there are infections that can cause illness primarily among young children in child-care settings (e.g., heamophilus influenza type B). Second, there are certain infections that equally affect children, staff, and close family members (e.g., viral diarrhea), Third, there are infections that cause few symptoms in young children but can cause serious illness in adults (e.g., hepatitis A). Finally, some infections cause mild or no illness in most children and adults, but are potentially serious to unborn children of pregnant women (e.g., rubella, cytomegalovirus [CMV], and toxoplasmosis). This last set of infectious diseases has particular relevance for programs for children who are severely disabled. The reason some children may need early intervention services is that they contracted these infections prenatally. There may, therefore, be a higher incidence of children with these congenital infections in programs

for children with severe disabilities than in the population as a whole. It is of great importance that hygiene procedures be established to protect the health of children, staff, and family members. Good sources of information about health and hygiene routines are Anderson, Bale, Blackman, and Murph (1986) and Prendergast (1988).

Early intervention programs should develop specific guidelines for cleanliness and disinfection and follow them precisely. Topics that should be addressed include hand-washing procedures, diapering, cleaning and disinfecting the classroom, care of sick children, and special management of children with chronic viral infections.

Transitions

Transitions have been identified as times of vulnerability for children with disabilities and times of stress for their parents (O'Brien, Thiele, & Robinson, 1990). In the preschool years, young children with severe disabilities may undergo many transitions, for example, from an NICU to home, to enrollment in a home-based early intervention program, to enrollment in a special education preschool program, to enrollment in a public school kindergarten.

A change in early intervention services brings possible risks as well as benefits. For example, new services may be delayed; they may be inconsistent with previous service strategies; they may bring hardship for the family, such as more complicated transportation demands or greater expense. When a trusting relationship between a family and an early intervention service provider has been established, it can be disconcerting to the family to leave that relationship and begin new ones in a new program.

Best practices in early intervention suggest that we take the challenges of transitions seriously and support children, families, and service providers in making these changes as comfortable and positive as possible. It has been suggested that transition planning be an ongoing part of early intervention services (Diamond, Spiegel-McGill, & Hanraham,

1988). Among the steps in planning and implementing the transition process are the development of placement options, visits by parents and staff, parent education focusing on due process rights, referral to appropriate programs, and referral to appropriate multidisciplinary teams. It is important to include transition planning in a child's IFSP or IEP. When a transition to an integrated preschool or kindergarten is being considered, characteristics of the classroom organization and instructional environment should be identified. Individualizing family involvement in school transitions should be an early intervention priority. A recent investigation of parents' wishes regarding transition planning found that parents rated as "very important" opportunities to participate in planning, to select the next program, and to receive descriptions of potential programs (Fowler, Chandler, Johnson, & Stella, 1988).

ASSESSMENT

Assessment is a key component in early intervention services because assessment information is used to establish program eligibility, to establish short-range and long-range goals, and to monitor progress. Assessment is, therefore, important not only when a child enters an early intervention program, but throughout the program as well.

Diagnosis of a disability or risk for a disabling condition is often viewed as the first step in entering an early intervention program (Hutinger, 1988). There is usually no question about eligibility for early intervention for babies and young children with severe disabilities, as in all probability such children have an established risk for developmental delay based on a diagnosed medical disorder. The medical diagnosis of a biologic condition associated with severe disabilities will be the starting point in understanding the needs of a child and family, but it certainly does not tell the whole story. The systematic observation and testing of the child is needed to establish areas for intervention and for program planning. A wide range of tests and procedures are used in early intervention programs, and most early childhood

professionals believe that a great deal of work still needs to be done in the area of assessment instrument development (Hutinger, 1988).

For young children with severe cognitive delays and the added complexities of sensory and motor disabilities, most early childhood assessment instruments fail to address their special needs and fail to yield information useful in program planning. Many standardized tests, for example, are norm-referenced; that is, they have been standardized via representative samples of children (most often nondisabled children) in order to establish norms. A child's score can be compared with those of others the same age. These tests are likely to reveal that children with severe disabilities are functioning well below nondisabled same-age peers in all areas of development, but in most cases, this information is already known. Although standardized norm-referenced tests may be helpful as general measures of development and as instruments to measure child progress for program evaluation purposes, their results cannot be easily translated into program goals and are, therefore, not sufficient for early intervention assessment. Two norm-referenced tests that may be useful for such general purposes are the following:

The Bayley Scales of Infant Development (Bayley, 1969)
Available from:
> The Psychological Corporation
> 1372 Peachtree Street N.E.
> Atlanta, GA 30309

This scale is designed for children in the age range of 2 to 30 months and assesses mental and motor development.

The Developmental Profile II (revised edition) (Alpern, Boll, & Shearer, 1980)
Available from:
> Western Psychological Services
> 12031 Wilshire Boulevard
> Los Angeles, CA 90025

This norm-referenced and standardized measure, for the age range of birth to 9.6 years, can be given as a parent interview or as a direct test. Physical, self-help, social, academic, and communication domains are measured.

Curriculum-referenced tests, composed of precisely stated items accompanied by specified instructional strategies, offer a much more functional approach to assessment (Fewell, 1983). Curriculum-based assessment has been described by Notari and Bricker (1990): Only skills that can be taught are included in the assessment instrument and then sequenced in a hierarchical, logical teaching order. Each assessment item is linked to an educational objective. Children are assessed on objectives to be learned and then evaluated on the achievement of the targeted objectives. The individual child's performance is usually measured according to a predetermined standard, rather than to a norm. The following are examples of curriculum-based assessment instruments:

Assessment, Evaluation, and Programming System (AEPS) for Infants and Children (Bricker, 1993)
> Available from:
>> Paul H. Brookes Publishing Co.
>> P.O. Box 10624
>> Baltimore, MD 21285-0624

This criterion-referenced instrument includes functional goals and objectives based on observation, direct testing, and parent reporting. Test domains include gross motor, fine motor, communication, cognition, self-help, and social. Adaptations for sensory and motor impairments are permitted. Age range is from birth to 3 years.

The Callier-Azusa Scale (Stillman, 1978)
> Available from:
>> The University of Texas at Dallas
>> Callier Center for Communication
>>> Disorders
>> 1966 Inwood Road
>> Dallas, TX 75235

This criterion-referenced test was developed for children who are deaf-blind and severely impaired in the age range from birth to 9 years. Eighteen subscales assess behaviors in motor development, perceptual abilities, daily living skills, cognition, communication, and social development.

There is increasing emphasis on making use of the child's natural environments and events in conducting assessments. The role of the family in the assessment process is also a contemporary issue of great importance.

Assessment in early intervention is not restricted, of course, to an evaluation of a child's strengths and needs. The family focus emphasis of PL 99-457 requires that family strengths and needs be assessed as well (Bailey & Simeonsson, 1988). Assessing parent-child interactions, interviewing families to determine how early intervention programs can offer strength and support, and communicating effectively to establish program goals are important responsibilities for members of an early intervention team.

CURRICULUM APPROACHES AND INSTRUCTIONAL STRATEGIES

Curriculum is the "what to teach," the message or the content of education (Mori & Neisworth, 1983), and in early intervention programs for young children with severe disabilities, the "what to teach" covers a broad range indeed. Rather than assuming a narrow academic focus, early intervention curricula draw upon the interdisciplinary team's understanding of the needs of the child and family. The "what to teach" in early intervention may include such diverse areas as self-feeding, imitation, head control, parent-child interactions, reduction of self-injurious behavior, and computer-assisted communication. Early intervention curriculum, then, is the sum total of activities and services that can be carried out to meet the goals of the whole program plan for the child and family (Hutinger, 1988).

Two broad early intervention curriculum models for young children with severe disabilities have been developed. These models, the developmental approach and the functional approach, are sometimes viewed as competing and mutually exclusive. In actuality, distinctions between the models for children in the first months and years of life are somewhat artificial; both perspectives can offer helpful guidance to early intervention programs.

The *developmental curriculum model* assumes that the normal sequence of development provides a logical structure for educational goals (Brimer, 1990). It is argued that children with severe disabilities follow the same developmental sequence as their nondisabled peers, and that as each child is helped to master the next step in the developmental sequence, the child has not only acquired an important skill, but is ready for the next, more sophisticated developmental step. Developmental curricula for the preschool years typically present goals and strategies from these developmental domains: gross motor, fine motor, language and communication, cognitive, self-help, and social-emotional. Some developmental curricula are based on a particular theory of child development. For example, Dunst (1981) developed a curriculum guide based on the Piagetian sensorimotor stages. Developmental models of curriculum have prominence in many preschool programs, including those for children with mild to moderate disabilities and for typically developing children, as well as for children with severe disabilities.

From the literature focusing specifically on meeting the needs of persons with severe disabilities comes the second model, the *functional curriculum*. A functional curriculum emphasizes skills that have practical use to the child now or in the future. For example, self-feeding is considered functional because it increases the child's independence in the current environment. Functional curricula are based on the criterion of ultimate functioning (Brown, Nietupski, & Hamre-Nietupski, 1976), emphasizing the skills adults with severe disabilities will need to function independently in the community. Because adult skills do not seem especially relevant for infants and toddlers with disabilities, focusing on the next educational environment (such as public school kindergarten) has become a preschool modification of the criterion of ultimate functioning.

Both the developmental and functional approaches to curriculum have much to offer early intervention programs. In the first months and years of life, many key skills are both developmental and functional. For example, developing stable head control is an early developmental milestone; it is also an extremely functional skill, as it will enable the child to make eye contact and develop social relations, as well as take in important information from the environment. Curriculum guides that focus on young children with severe disabilities often draw on developmental sequences and then select for emphasis those tasks that have the clearest relevance for the child's life. For example, the *Charlotte Circle Intervention Guide for Parent-Child Interactions* (Calhoun, Rose, & Prendergast, 1991) focuses on parent-child interactions as both developmentally appropriate and functional. Because social relationships are the foundations for later learning and because they improve the quality of life for children and families, goal areas such as increasing smiling, increasing playfulness, and managing and comforting crying are emphasized.

A functional approach to curriculum leads us to look for alternative approaches to problems in daily living, rather than relying exclusively on the typical developmental sequence of skills. For example, rather than waiting for a young child with severe disabilities to talk in order to foster interpersonal communication, alternative communication strategies, such as early signaling systems using gestures or computer-assisted communication systems, may be taught. Because it is relevant to the child's life to be able to express needs and preferences, alternatives such as these are an important aspect of the curriculum.

The "what to teach" in early intervention programs for young children with severe disabilities, then, should emphasize skills that are relevant and useful, skills that help children strengthen their social relationships with others, and skills that will lead to more complex learning in the future. The questions of "what to teach" should be followed by questions of "how to teach." Careful consideration of effective instructional strategies is another important concern of early intervention. Effective instruction for young children with severe disabilities includes an emphasis on increasing engagement, making use of technological adaptations, and conducting instruction within natural routines and environments.

Engagement means the active and prolonged participation by the child in appropriate learning activities (Bailey & Wolery, 1984). The amount of engagement is sometimes seen as the key indicator of the quality of early intervention programs. Because some young children with severe disabilities may tend to be passive and nonresponsive (Calhoun, Rose, & Prendergast, 1991), increasing their engagement is a challenging issue. Guess and his colleagues (1988) suggest that as a starting point, early interventionists tune in to the biobehavioral states of children with profound disabilities. Biobehavioral states range from sleeping, to awake-alert, to crying. The awake-alert state is the one in which children are most receptive to stimulation. Awareness of the child's state and timing educational efforts to match the child's state is the first step toward increasing engagement. Other strategies include making materials and activities appealing, identifying children's preferences for materials and activities, and following the child's lead in interactions.

The child's response needs and preferences can be attended to in many cases with the help of technology. The use of switches and battery-operated toys can open up a world of play for young children and help them begin to understand cause-and-effect relationships. Computers can assist children in responding to the environment more actively than previously possible. The promise of technology in early intervention programs is great. A special curriculum, *Activating Children Through Technology* (ACTT), offers guidance in computer-assisted functional activities by young children (Hutinger, Perry, Robinson, Weaver, & Whitaker, 1986).

Finally, it should be noted that the best instruction for young children with severe disabilities occurs within natural environments and routines. Sensory integration therapy, for example, designed to help a child organize multisensory stimuli or reduce intolerance to movement, might be more effective in a play situation with a parent or teacher, rather than in a pull-out therapy session, removed from people and environments familiar to the child. If therapeutic routines can be consistent across the child's important environments—home, school, community—learning will take place at a faster rate and generalization will be promoted (Bailey & Wolery, 1984).

SUMMARY

Early intervention for young children with severe disabilities holds great promise for improving the quality of life for children and families. Increasing accessibility of programs, a responsive focus that supports and respects families, and careful attention to effective instruction, curriculum, and service delivery underscore the promise of early intervention.

ANNOTATED BIBLIOGRAPHY

Curriculum Materials for Young Children with Severe Handicaps

Calhoun, M. L., Rose, T. L., & Prendergast, D. P. (1991). *The Charlotte Circle intervention guide for parent-child interactions.* Tucson, AZ: Communication SkillBuilders.

Format: Book
Target age range: 0–3

This data-based, field-tested curriculum guide focuses on key behaviors that strengthen interaction between parents and young children with severe handicaps. Intervention areas include smiling, relaxation, imitation, play, early communication, and comforting crying. Reproducible "Parent Pages" in English and Spanish are included.

Dunst, C. J. (1981). *Infant learning: A cognitive-linguistic intervention strategy.* Allen, TX: DLM Teaching Resources.

Format: Book
Target age range: 0–2

This intervention approach, based on Piagetian theory and focusing on the sensorimotor stage of development, includes qualitative performance assessment and psychoeducational intervention for seven stages of sensorimotor development.

Fredericks, H. D., et al. (1980). *The teaching research curriculum for moderately and severely handicapped* (2nd ed.). Springfield, IL: Charles C. Thomas.

Format: Two volumes, supplemental wall charts
Target age: 0–6

Developmentally sequenced tasks in gross and fine motor, self-help, and cognitive skills are presented.

Furuno, S., Hosaka, C., Zeisloft, B., O'Reilly, K., Inatsuka, T., & Allmon, T. (1979). *Hawaii early learning profile (HELP) and HELP activity guide.* Palo Alto, CA: VORT Corporation.

Format: Book
Target age: 0–36 months

Developmentally sequenced curriculum includes target behaviors and activities in these areas: cognition, expressive language, gross motor, fine motor, social-emotional, and self-help. The home activities are designed to be incorporated into daily family routines.

Hutinger, P. L., Marshall, S., & McCartan, K. (1983). *Macomb 0–3 regional project core curriculum* (3rd ed.).

Available from: Macomb 0–3 Regional Project, Room 27 Horrahim Hall, Western Illinois University, Macomb, IL 61455.

Format: Looseleaf notebook
Target age: 0–36 months

Functional goals are presented in the areas of gross motor, fine motor, cognition, communicational, social, and self-care skills. Auditory, visual, and motor adaptations are provided.

Johnson-Martin, N., Jens, K. G., & Attermeier, S. M. (1986). *The Carolina curriculum for handicapped infants and infants at risk.* Baltimore: Paul H. Brookes Publishing Co.

Format: Book
Target age: 0–24 months

Sequenced curriculum, developed for use with infants and toddlers with severe disabilities, is a developmentally sequenced curriculum based on Piagetian theory. Examples of areas are gestured communication, tactile integration, and auditory localization. Visual and motor adaptations are included. An assessment log is available.

Mahoney, G., & Powell, A. (1984). *Transactional intervention program.*

Available from: High/Scope Educational Research Foundation, 600 N. River Street, Ypsilanti, MI 48198.

Format: Book
Target age: 0–3 years

An interactional approach to early development. Strategies are presented to help caregivers match children's activities by either imitating or elaborating slightly the activity in which the child is engaged. The transactional intervention program helps children develop a sense of efficacy and strengthens the parent-child relationship.

Odom, S. L., Bender, M., Stein, M., Doran, L., Houden, P., McInnes, M., Gilbert M., Deklyen, M., Speltz, M., & Jenkins, J. (1991). *The integrated preschool curriculum.* Seattle: University of Washington Press.

Format: Looseleaf notebook
Target age: 2–5 years

Designed to promote the social integration of both children who are disabled and children who are developing normally in integrated preschool programs. Social integration activities, assessment, and direct instruction of social skills are included. Play activities are heavily emphasized. Although the guide was developed primarily for children with mild to moderate disabilities, the authors note that children with severe disabilities can benefit from the program if the preschool class also contains children with less severe disabling conditions.

REFERENCES

Ackerman, P. R., & Moore, M. (1976). Delivery of educational services to preschool handicapped children. In T. D. Tjossem (Ed.), *Intervention strategies for high risk infants and young children* (pp. 669–688). Baltimore: University Park Press.

Alpern, G., Boll, T., & Shearer, M. (1980). *The developmental profile II.* Los Angeles: Western Psychological Services.

Anderson, R. D., Bale, J.F ., Blackman, J. A., & Murph, J. R. (1986). *Infections in children: A source book for educators and childcare providers.* Rockville, MD: Aspen.

Aronson, S. S., & Osterholm, M. T. (1984). Prevention and management of infectious diseases in child care. *Child Care Information Exchange,* (December), 8–10.

Bailey, D. B., & Simeonsson, R. J. (1988). *Family assessments in early intervention.* Columbus, OH: Charles E. Merrill.

Bailey, D. B., & Wolery, M. (1984). *Teaching infants and preschoolers with handicaps.* Columbus, OH: Charles E. Merrill.

Bayley, N. (1969). *Scales of infant development.* New York: Psychological Corporation.

Beckman, P. J. (1983). The relationship between behavioral characteristics of children and social interaction in an integrated setting. *Journal of the Division for Early Childhood, 7,* 69–77.

Berrueta-Clement, J. R., Schweinhart, L. J., Barnett, W. S., Epstein, A. S., & Weikart, D. P. (1984). *Changed lives: The effects of the Perry Preschool Program on youths through age 19.* Ypsilanti, MI: The High/Scope Press.

Berry, P., Gunn, V. P., & Andrews, R. J. (1984). Development of Down's syndrome children from birth to five years. In J. M. Berg (Ed.), *Perspectives and progress in mental retardation: Social, psychological, and educational aspects* (vol. 1, pp. 167–177). Baltimore: University Park Press.

Bricker, D. (1982). Program planning for at-risk and handicapped infants. In C. Ramey & P. Trohanis (Eds.), *Finding and educating high-risk and handicapped infants.* Austin, TX: PRO-ED.

Bricker, D., Bailey, D., & Bruder, M. (1984). The efficacy of early intervention and the handicapped infant: A wise or wasted resource. *Advances in Developmental and Behavioral Pediatrics, 5.*

Bricker, D. D., Gentry, D., & Bailey, E. J. (1985). *The evaluation and programming system: For infants and young children.* Assessment level I: Developmentally 1 month to 3 years. Eugene: University of Oregon.

Bricker, D., & Kaminski, R. (1986). Intervention programs for severely handicapped infants and children. In L. Bickman & D. L. Weatherford (Eds.), *Evaluating early intervention programs for severely handicapped children and their families* (pp. 51–75). Austin, TX: PRO-ED.

Brimer, R.W. (1990). *Students with severe disabilities: Current perspectives and practices.* Mountain View, CA: Mayfield Publishing Company.

Brown, L., Nietupski, J., & Hamre-Nietupski, S. (1976). The criterion of ultimate functioning. In M. Thomas (Ed.), *Hey, don't forget about me! Education is investment in the severely and profoundly handicapped.* Reston, VA: Council for Exceptional Children.

Bruder, M. B., & Bricker, D. (1985). Parents as teachers of their children and other parents. *Journal of the Division for Early Childhood, 9,* 136–150.

Bryant, D. M., & Ramey, C. T. (1987). An analysis of the effectiveness of early intervention programs for environmentally at-risk children. In M. J. Guralnick & F. C. Bennett (Eds.), *The effectiveness of early intervention for at-risk and handicapped children* (pp. 33–78). New York: Academic Press.

Calhoun, M. L., Calhoun, L. G., & Rose, T. L. (1989). Parents of babies with severe handicaps: Concerns about early intervention. *Journal of Early Intervention, 13,* 146–152.

Calhoun, M. L., & Rose, T. L. (1989). Special focus–serving young children with severe handicaps: Promoting positive parent-child interactions. *Teaching Exceptional Children, 21* (4), 44–53.

Calhoun, M. L., & Rose, T. L. (1988). Early social reciprocity interventions with infants with severe retardation: Current findings and implications for the future. *Education and Training of the Mentally Retarded, 23,* 340–343.

Calhoun, M. L., & Rose, T. L. (1986). *Social reciprocity: Early intervention for young children with severe/profound handicaps.* Charlotte: The University of North Carolina at Charlotte. (ERIC Document Reproduction Service No. ED 294 362).

Calhoun, M. L., Rose, T. L., & Prendergast, D. E. (1991). *The Charlotte circle intervention guide for parent-child interactions.* Tucson, AZ: Communication Skill Builders.

Campbell, M. S., Cohen, S. L., & Rich, M. (1987). *Guidelines for the management of health impaired students.* Portland, OR: Providence Child Center. (ERIC Document Reproduction Service No. ED 182 465).

Carta, J. J., Sainato, D. M., & Greenwood, C. R. (1988). Advances in the ecological assessment of classroom instruction for young children with handicaps. In S. L. Odom & M. B. Karnes (Eds.), *Early intervention for infants and children with handicaps: An empirical base* (pp. 217–240). Baltimore: Paul H. Brookes Publishing Co.

Casto, G. (1988). Research and program evaluation in

early childhood special education. In S. L. Odom & M. B. Karnes (Eds.), *Early intervention for infants and children with handicaps: An empirical base* (pp. 51–62). Baltimore: Paul H. Brookes Publishing Co.

Casto, G., & Mastropieri, M. A. (1986). The efficacy of early intervention programs: A meta-analysis. *Exceptional Children, 52,* 417–424.

Child Care Action Campaign. (1988). *Child care: The bottom line.* New York: Author.

Connolly, J. A. (1978). Intelligence levels of Down's syndrome children. *American Journal of Mental Deficiency, 83,* 193–196.

Diamond, K. E., Spiegel-McGill, P., & Hanraham, P. (1988). Planning for school transition: An ecological-developmental approach. *Journal of the Division for Early Childhood, 12,* 245–252.

Division for Early Childhood. (1987). *DEC position statements and recommendations.* Reston, VA: Council for Exceptional Children.

Dunst, C. J. (1986). Overview of the efficacy of early intervention programs. In L. Bickman & D. L. Weatherford (Eds.), *Evaluating early intervention programs for severely handicapped children and their families* (pp. 79–148). Austin, TX: PRO-ED.

Dunst, C. J. (1981). *Infant learning: A cognitive-linguistic intervention strategy.* Hingham, MA: Teaching Resources.

Dunst, C. J., & Rheingrover, R. M. (1981). An analysis of the efficacy of infant intervention programs with organically handicapped children. *Evaluation and Program Planning, 4,* 287–323.

Eaton, L. F., & Menolascino, F. J. (1982). Psychiatric disorders in the mentally retarded: Types, problems, and challenges. *American Journal of Psychiatry, 139,* 1297–1303.

Fewell, R. (1983). Assessing handicapped infants. In S. G. Garwood & R. R. Fewell (Eds.), *Educating handicapped infants: Issues in development and intervention* (pp. 257–297). Rockville, MD: Aspen.

Fowler, S. A., Chandler, L. K., Johnson, T. E., & Stella, M. E. (1988). Individualizing family involvement in school transitions: Gathering information and choosing the next program. *Journal of the Division for Early Childhood, 12,* 208–216.

Gentry, D., & Olson, J. (1985). Severely mentally retarded young children. In D. Bricker & J. Filler (Eds.), *Severe mental retardation: From theory to practice.* Lancaster, PA: Lancaster Press.

Graff, J. C., Ault, M. M., Guess, D., Taylor, M., &

Thompson, B. (1990). *Health care for students with disabilities.* Baltimore: Paul H. Brookes Publishing Co.

Gross, A. M., Eudy, C., & Drabman, R. S. (1982). Training parents to be physical therapists with their physically handicapped child. *Journal of Behavioral Medicine, 5,* 321–327.

Guess, D., Mulligan-Ault, M., Roberts, S., Struth, J., Siegel-Causey, E., Thompson, B., Bronicki, G. J. B., & Gray, B. (1988). Implications of biobehavioral states for the education and treatment of students with the most profoundly handicapping conditions. *The Journal of The Association for Persons with Severe Handicaps, 13,* 163–174.

Guralnick, M. J. (1988). Efficacy research in early childhood intervention programs. In S. L. Odom & M. B. Karnes (Eds.), *Early intervention for infants and children with handicaps: An empirical base* (pp. 75–88). Baltimore: Paul H. Brookes Publishing Co.

Guralnick, M. J. (1981). Social interaction among preschool handicapped children. *Exceptional Children, 46,* 248–253.

Guralnick, M. J., & Bennett, F. C. (Eds.). (1987). *The effectiveness of early intervention for at-risk and handicapped children.* New York: Academic Press.

Guralnick, M. J., & Bricker, D. (1987). The effectiveness of early intervention for children with cognitive and general developmental delays. In M. J. Guralnick & F. C. Bennett (Eds.), *The effectiveness of early intervention for at-risk and handicapped children* (pp. 115–173). New York: Academic Press.

Guralnick, M. J., & Groom, J. J. (1988). Peer interactions in mainstreamed and specialized classrooms: A comparative analysis. *Exceptional Children, 54,* 415–425.

Hayden, A. H. (1979). Handicapped children, birth to age 3. *Exceptional Children, 45,* 510–516.

Hoyson, M., Jamieson, B., & Strain, P. S. (1984). Individualized group instruction of normally developing and autistic-like children: The LEAP curriculum model. *Journal of the Division for Early Childhood, 8,* 157–172.

Hutinger, P. L. (1988). Linking screening, identification, and assessment with curriculum. In J. Jordan (Ed.), *Early childhood special education: Birth to three.* Reston, VA: Council for Exceptional Children.

Hutinger, P., Perry, L., Robinson, L., Weaver, K., &

Whitaker, K. (1986). *ACTT Curriculum*. Macomb, IL: Project ACTT, Western Illinois University.

Jenkins, J. R., Speltz, J. L., & Odom, S. L. (1985). Integrating normal and handicapped preschoolers: Effects on child development and social interaction. *Exceptional Children, 52*, 7–17.

Johnson, B. H., McGonigel, M. J., & Kaufmann, R. K., (Eds.). (1989). *Guidelines and recommended practices for the individualized family service plan*. Washington, DC: Association for the Care of Children's Health.

Kagan, S. L. (1990). *Excellence in early childhood education: Defining characteristics and next-decade strategies*. Washington, DC: U.S. Department of Education.

Kagan, S. L. (1989). Early care and education: Tackling the tough issues. *Phi Delta Kappan, 70*, 441–445.

Kugelmass, J. W. (1989). The "shared classroom": A case study of interactions between early childhood and special education staff and children. *Journal of Early Intervention, 13*, 36–44.

Lawhorn, G. (1986). Management of stress in premature infants. In D. J. Angelini, C. M. Whelan-Knapp, & R. M. Gibes (Eds.), *Perinatal/neonatal nursing: A clinical handbook*. Boston: Blackwell Scientific Publications.

Lazar, I., & Darlington, R. (1982). Lasting effects of early education: A report from the Consortium for Longitudinal Studies. *Monographs of the Society for Research in Child Development, 47* (2–3, Serial No. 195).

Lovaas, O. I. (1987). Behavioral treatment and normal educational and intellectual functioning in young autistic children. *Journal of Consulting and Clinical Psychology, 55*, 3–9.

McLean, M., & Odom, S. (1988). *Least restrictive environment and social integration*. (Available from the Division for Early Childhood, The Council for Exceptional Children, 1920 Association Drive, Reston, VA 22091.)

Melyn, M. A., & White, D. T. (1973). Mental and developmental milestones of noninstitutionalized Down's syndrome children. *Pediatrics, 52*, 542–545.

Mori, A. A., & Neisworth, J. T. (1983). Curricula in early childhood education: Some generic and special considerations. *Topics in Early Childhood Special Education, 2*, 1–8.

Notari, A. R., & Bricker, D. D. (1990). The utility of a curriculum-based assessment instrument in the development of individualized education plans for infants and young children. *Journal of Early Intervention, 14*, 117–132.

O'Brien, M., Thiele, J., & Robinson, P. (1990, October). *Transitions: Longitudinal study*. Paper presented at the annual conference of the Division for Early Childhood. Albuquerque, New Mexico.

Odom, S. L., Bender, M., Stein, M., Doran, L., Houden, P., McInnes, M., Gilbert, M., Deklyen, M., Speltz, M., & Jenkins, J. (1991). *Integrated preschool curriculum*. Seattle: University of Washington Press.

Odom, S. L., & Fewell, R. R. (1983). Program evaluation in early childhood special education: A meta-evaluation. *Educational Evaluation and Policy Analysis, 5*, 445–460.

Odom, S., Deklyen, M., & Jenkins, J. R. (1984). Integrating handicapped preschoolers: Developmental impact on nonhandicapped children. *Exceptional Children, 51*, 41–48.

Odom, S. L., & McEvoy, M. A. (1988). Integration of young children with handicaps and normally-developing children. In S. L. Odom & M. B. Karnes (Eds.), *Early intervention for infants and children with handicaps*. Baltimore: Paul H. Brookes Publishing Co.

Office of Special Education and Rehabilitative Services (1985). *Seventh annual report to Congress on the implementation of the education of the handicapped act*. Washington, DC: U.S. Department of Education.

Peterson, N. L. (1987). *Early intervention for handicapped and at-risk children*. Denver: Love Publishing Company.

Prendergast, D. (1988). *Health and hygiene issues*. (Available from: Charlotte Circle Outreach, Dept. of Teaching Specialties, UNC-Charlotte, Charlotte, NC 28233.)

Reiss, S., Levitan, G. W., & McNally, R. J. (1982). Emotionally disturbed mentally retarded people: An underserved population. *American Psychologist, 37*, 361–367.

Robinson, C., (Ed.). (n.d.). *Getting started together*. (Available from: Media Resource Center, Meyer Rehabilitation Institute, University of Nebraska Medical Center, 444 South 44th Street, Omaha, NE 68131-3795.)

Rose, T. L., & Calhoun, M. L. (1990). The Charlotte Circle Project: A program for infants and toddlers with severe/profound disabilities. *Journal of Early Intervention, 14*, 175–185.

Rosenberg, S. A., & Robinson, C. C. (1988). Interactions of parents with their young handicapped children. In S. L. Odom & M. B. Karnes (Eds.), *Early intervention for infants and children with handicaps: An empirical base* (pp. 159–178). Baltimore: Paul H. Brookes Publishing Co.

Scarr, S., & Weinberg, R. (1986). The early childhood enterprise: Care and education of the young. *American Psychologist, 41,* 1140–1146.

Schnell, R. R. (1984). Psychomotor development. In S. M. Puleschel (Ed.), *The young child with Down syndrome* (pp. 207–226). New York: Human Sciences Press.

Simeonsson, R. J., Bailey, D. B., Huntington, G. S., & Comfort, M. (1986). Toward the concept of goodness of fit in early intervention. *Infant Mental Health Journal, 7,* 81–94.

Simeonsson, R. J., Cooper, D. H., & Schiener, A. P. (1982). A review and analysis of the effectiveness of early intervention programs. *Pediatrics, 69,* 635.

Smith, B. J. (n.d.). PL 99-457—The new law. *In PL 99-457: Resources for the implementation of Public Law 99-457, the Education of the Handicapped Act Amendments of 1986.* Chapel Hill, NC: Resource Access Project for Head Start Handicap Services.

Snell, M. E. (1987). Serving young children with special needs and their families and P.L. 99-457. *TASH Newsletter, 13*(9), 1–2.

Stillman, R. (Ed.). (1978). *Callier-Azusa scale.* Dallas, TX: Callier Center for Communication Disorders, The University of Texas at Dallas.

Strain, P. S., Jamieson, B., & Hoyson, M. (1986). Learning experiences. An alternative program for preschoolers and parents: A comprehensive service system for the mainstreaming of autistic-like preschoolers. In C. J. Meisel (Ed.), *Mainstreamed handicapped children: Outcomes, controversies, and new directions* (pp. 251–269). Hillsdale, NJ: Lawrence Erlbaum Associates.

Strain, P. S., & Kohler, F. W. (1988). Social skill intervention with young children with handicaps: Some new conceptualizations and directions. In S. L. Odom & M. B. Karnes (Eds.), *Early intervention for*

infants and children with handicaps: An empirical base (pp. 129–144). Baltimore: Paul H. Brookes Publishing Co.

Swan, W. (1980). The handicapped children's early education program. *Exceptional Children, 47,* 12–16.

The Association for Persons with Severe Handicaps (1987). *Reauthorization of the Education of the Handicapped Amendments of 1986: Committee paper.* Seattle, WA: TASH.

Thompson, R. J. (1984). Behavior problems in developmentally disabled children. In M. Wolraich & D. K. Routh (Eds.), *Advances in developmental and behavioral pediatrics* (vol. 5, pp. 265–330). Greenwich, CT: JAI Press.

Trohanis, P. (1987). A brief introduction to P.L. 99-457. *Early Childhood Update, 3,* 1, 7. Denver: University of Colorado, Health Sciences Center.

Turnbull, A., & Turnbull, R. (1988). The IFSP: what does it mean for families? *OSERS News in Print, 1* (4), 4, 6.

Turnbull, A. P. (1982). Preschool mainstreaming: A policy and implementation analysis. *Educational Evaluation and Policy Analysis, 4,* 281–291.

U.S. General Accounting Office. (1989, July). *Early childhood education: Information on costs and services at high-quality centers.* Washington, DC: Author.

Weatherford, D. L. (1986). The challenge of evaluating early intervention programs for severely handicapped children and their families. In L. Bickman & D. L. Weatherford (Eds.), *Evaluating early intervention programs for severely handicapped children and their families* (pp. 1–18). Austin, TX: PRO-ED.

White, K. R., & Casto, G. (1984). An integrative review of early intervention efficacy studies with at-risk children: Implications for the handicapped. *Analysis and Intervention in Developmental Disabilities, 5,* 7–31.

Whitebrook, M., Howes, C., & Phillips, D. (1989). *National child care staffing study.* Oakland, CA: Child Care Employee Project. R.M. Douglas, Gilbarco Inc., P.O. Box 22087, 7300 W. Friendly Road, Greensboro, NC 27420.

CHAPTER 15

EFFECTIVE CONSULTATION FOR CLASSROOM AND COMMUNITY SETTINGS

GARY W. LAVIGNA
THOMAS J. WILLIS
JULIA F. SHAULL
MARYAM ABEDI
MELISSA SWEITZER
Institute for Applied Behavior Analysis

Because of their specialized training and skills, experienced special education teachers are often thrust into the role of consultant. They are asked to provide consultation services to their newer, less experienced colleagues in special education, as well as to teachers of regular education who increasingly face the challenge of instructing students with special needs. Very often referrals are made to consulting teachers on an informal basis.

A teacher having a difficult time ameliorating the behavior of one child or several children in her class may ask the special education teacher for "advice." At other times the role of consultant may be more formalized, either as a part of the teacher's regular duties or as a member of the student success team (SST), a regular education function in the effort to solve learning or behavior problems before a change of placement is considered.

Most preservice personnel who will or do become special education teachers do not initially see themselves in the role of consulting with other school personnel on problems and issues that are not directly related to their classrooms. In point of fact, each teacher's own classroom is considered his or her own "castle." Yet in today's educational system, the education of persons with severe handi-

caps often occurs in many different environments, both within the school system (e.g., the person is provided instruction in more than one class), as well as throughout the periods of the day (e.g., at home and in the community). It is the infrequent circumstance when a teacher in special education would not have to be concerned with how other people are educating and caring for the child or adolescent with severe learning difficulties.

The position taken in this book is that changing a child's education placement, that is, to a more restrictive educational setting, is not the sole solution to any learning or behavioral problem. As children with severe disabilities increasingly become part of the regular educational system, personnel working in such a system will have to rely even more on consultation with teachers who have greater expertise with this clientele. Consultation skills must be a requisite for teachers in special education; they are, therefore, included in this teacher training text.

There are a number of consultation models available to guide teachers as they take on this role. The emphasis of these models includes developing and providing in-service training programs (Harris, 1980), providing consultation within a behavioral framework (Bergan, 1977; Cipani, 1985), and collaboration between the teacher-consultant and university faculty, based on a formal effort to prepare consulting teachers as part of a teacher training program (Paolucci-Whitcomb & Nevin, 1985).

Most often, consultation or technical assistance is provided in a teacher in-service session. In this approach, an expert is brought to speak to a number of teachers and other instructional and related personnel. Frequently, the in-service session does not address specific problems in particular classes, but rather provides a cursory treatment of a general topic (e.g., discipline methods). Although this approach is the most prevalent (because of its low cost when computed for a large number of attendees), owing to its nonspecific nature, it often does not provide adequate or effective technical assistance to teachers with specific problems that must be addressed.

A behavioral approach to consultation incorporates a specific problem(s) identification-resolution focus. Evaluation of the effectiveness of the consultation is based on how well the additional skills acquired by the professional (teacher, aide, or therapist) resulted in the change of the targeted problem behavior. The consultation may focus on problems considered to be behavioral excesses (i.e., a child exhibits a certain behavior in greater frequency than desired, which may be disruptive behavior) or behavioral deficits (i.e., a child does not exhibit the desired behavior, such as an appropriate greeting response), or does not perform the behavior often enough or at a fluent level, or under enough circumstances. Usually, a consultant must consider both excess and deficit problems in the same consultative effort. Specific procedures for addressing such needs have been delineated and are replicable across different consultants (Bergan, 1977; Cipani, 1985).

A collaborative consultation model (Idol-Maestras, 1983; Paolucci-Whitcomb & Nevin, 1985) encourages the sharing of expertise of both the consultant and the consultee. It can incorporate a procedural format similar to that of a behavioral consultation model or can be less directive in fo-

cus. Certainly, all professionals and members of an interdisciplinary team can offer useful information and data. However, at some point, we feel consultants (and the consultation model) must "pin down" the specific objectives of the consultation and identify the most effective plan for achieving those objectives. Some professionals may have greater expertise in problem resolution than others, but all plans are subjected to the judgment of their efficacy in ameliorating the problem or reaching the designated objective.

A CONSULTATION MODEL FOR SPECIAL EDUCATION

Among the major challenges all consultants face, regardless of the model being utilized, is to get those personnel receiving consultation assistance to follow through and fully implement the recommendations that are made and agreed to. This chapter describes a system that increases the likelihood of successful implementation of instructional and behavioral plans. This system was designed at the Institute for Applied Behavior Analysis (IABA) with the hope that it may help the new consultant to be more effective in that role. Although we believe the system could be adapted to any content, the focus here is on the provision of behavioral consultation in classroom and community settings (Bergan, 1977; Cipani, 1985).

A review of the literature provides an understanding that the frustration of consultants in seeing that recommendations are implemented reflects the more ubiquitous problem of poor organization and management of available resources. Reid and Whitman (1983) observed that where "performance has been less than adequate, it is a primary reflection of the ineffectiveness of the management currently operating." Christian and Reitz (1986) say that "management practice is the number one reason why there is a discrepancy between the development and implementation of treatment programs" (p. 24). It seems that classroom programs and other service settings are often plagued with inconsistency and poor follow-through. This is not just a problem for consultants' recommendations.

Typical problems include data that are not kept or not kept accurately, behavior intervention and instructional programs that are not in operation or not implemented as designed, schedules that are not followed, progress reports that are not completed, and so on.

A consultant's recommendations may be made in situations in which the teacher or supervisor is struggling to follow through with his or her own plans and objectives. Therefore, effective consultation may be enhanced by helping to improve the organization and management of the classroom or other setting. This chapter describes the system that we offer to teachers and supervisors to better organize and manage their resources. This enables us to be more effective consultants. We believe that the consulting teacher will find this system comfortable for two important reasons. First, it is explicitly designed as a two-way system: it puts the teacher or supervisor in control of staff, and it is also designed as a bottom-up system that gives staff a large measure of influence. This collaborative spirit is modeled by the consultant. Second, the strategies for improving organization and management are built strictly on the principles of positive reinforcement. These contribute to the development of a positive, nonthreatening relationship between the consulting teachers and those to whom they provide their services.

Elements of Effective Management

Reid, Parsons, and Green (1989) reviewed the research literature and identified a number of essential elements for effective organization and management. These include defining performance responsibilities and expectations, monitoring performance, changing performance, and teaching skills to staff (see Table 15.1).

Program Status Report: Classroom Application

The Program Status Report (PSR) is both an instrument and a system. It is an instrument to assess consistency in implementing a consultant's recom-

TABLE 15.1 Essential Elements of Effective Management

- Define performance responsibilities and expectations.
- Monitor performance.
- Change performance when needed.
- Teach instructional skills to staff.

mendations regarding individual student programming. It is also a system to improve classroom and program performance generally. A PSR incorporates the findings of research by including the previously mentioned elements (Reid et al., 1989) and has also been designed to fill the gaps. It efficiently addresses the challenge of consistency at the molar (i.e., the overall program) level and can assess performance at the classroom level, precluding the need to improve consistency through the molecular process of addressing each separate teacher and aide responsibility, for each student. Further, the PSR has proven to be effective in maintaining lasting change and improvement.

As an instrument, the PSR is easy to understand. It involves a score sheet on which an individual student's program is scored and given points, depending on whether objectively defined criteria have been met for each of the standards that have been adopted. A sample score sheet developed for a classroom program is shown in Table 15.2. Each standard listed on the score sheet was operationally defined. Samples of these operational definitions appear in Table 15.3.

Figure 15.1 shows the effects of the PSR system in a classroom setting during its first year of application. The performance standards against which a program is evaluated are a function of the population served, the resources available, and the program's philosophy and design. They are also a function of the consultant's recommendations in collaboration and discussion with the classroom teacher. In this case, the classroom served adolescents with the problems associated with autism and similar disabilities. As can be seen, by the end

TABLE 15.2   Sample Program Status Report for Classroom Use

Date: _____   Teacher: _____

	1/O	COMMENTS

A. GENERAL COMPONENTS
   1. Philosophy
   2. Age-Appropriate/Functional Curriculum		

B. ADMINISTRATIVE
   1. Student Notebooks
   2. Medical Records		

C. INDIVIDUAL SKILL PROGRAM
   1. Working Notebooks
   2. Schedule
   3. IEP
   4. ITP
   5. Lesson Plan
   6. Data
   7. Data Summaries/Graphs
   8. Progress Reports
   9. Emergency Procedures
   10. Reliability Checks
       a. Interobserver
       b. Procedural		

D. INDIVIDUAL BEHAVIOR PROGRAM
   1. Assessment Reports/Intervention Plans
   2. Behavior Protocol/Checklist
   3. Raw Data
   4. Reinforcement Charts
   5. Program Implementation
   6. Competing Contingencies Not Present
   7. Data Summaries
       a. Charts
       b. Graphs
   8. Reliability Check
   9. Emergency Procedures
   10. Reliability Check
       a Interobserver
       b. Procedural		

E. INSTRUCTION
   1. Individualized
   2. Methods
   3. Environments
   4. Community Instruction
   5. Communication		

F. STAFF DEVELOPMENT
   1. Workshops
   2. Scheduled Staff Meetings
   3. In-Service
   4. Team Input		

TABLE 15.2   Continued

	1/O	COMMENTS
5. Classroom Team Meetings 6. Mainstream Staff 7. Mainstream Students 8. Specialist		

G. FAMILY INVOLVEMENT
   1. PPT
   2. Communication
   3. Meetings
   4. Parent Committee		

H. COORDINATION OF PROGRAM
   1. Roles
   2. Responsibilities
   3. Team		

I. STATUS REPORT DOCUMENT		

TOTAL _____

TOTAL POSSIBLE _____

PERCENTAGE SCORE _____

REPORT COMPLETED BY: _____

of the year this classroom was performing quite well against a comprehensive set of very rigorous standards.

The program status reports that we design can have 40 or more standards. It is not likely that a consulting teacher will find it necessary to develop such elaborate documents; however, we believe that the development of more limited but similar systems can lead to greater effectiveness. In contrast to the PSR *instrument,* the PSR *system* is made up of four carefully integrated elements: performance standards, monitoring, feedback, and training. These are illustrated in Table 15.4, and each is described in the following sections.

Performance Standards

Performance standards are defined as the specification and the operationalized definition of staff (teacher, aide, itinerant teacher) responsibilities. The rationale for developing operationalized performance standards is that they then provide the basis for training, monitoring, performance evaluation, and teacher (or supervisor) and consultant action to improve and maintain staff performance.

There are two major kinds of performance standards, product standards and process standards. Product standards provide the basis for *outcome evaluation,* that is, measure a classroom team's success in meeting goals and objectives, whereas process standards hold a classroom team accountable for doing those things necessary to reach their goals and objectives (Christian & Romanczyk, 1986). There are three key sources for both product and process standards that a consulting teacher might recommend. These include student needs, administrative requirements, and externally imposed rules and regulations (e.g., the requirements of Public

TABLE 15.3   Sample Standards for Classroom Program Status Report

A. General Component

PHILOSOPHY: The philosophy of the program is stated in the students' notebooks. The basis of the program is preparation for living, working, and enjoying life in an integrated environment.

B. Administrative

STUDENT NOTEBOOKS: For each student there is an up-to-date notebook that includes pertinent forms, schedules, current individualized education plans (IEPs) and Individual Transition Plans (ITPs), data forms, graphs, lesson plans, progress reports, behavior programs, emergency information, home-school communication, and a table of contents.

C. Individual Skill Programs

WORKING NOTEBOOKS: For each student there is a working notebook located in the classroom and used by staff daily. It includes the following information: daily schedule, current IEP, lesson plans, data sheets, and current behavior plan.

D. Individual Behavior Programs

ASSESSMENT REPORTS AND INTERVENTION PLANS: For any existing program, there is a written assessment report and intervention plan following district protocols. Copies are located in student notebooks within 30 days of the start of the school year, the end of the quarter, or upon the students' enrollment. No aversives will be written into the plan.

E. Instruction

COMMUNITY INSTRUCTION: For each student there is a minimum of five community-based objectives.

F. Staff Development

WORKSHOPS: Staff attends workshops and professional meetings pertinent to job duties, which take place within the school system and out of district (a minimum of two per year).

G. Family Involvement

COMMUNICATION: At least weekly communication between staff and families via phone, notes, etc., as documented in the working notebooks.

H. Coordination of Program

ROLE: There is a written definition of each team member's role. Copies are located in the central office and in the classroom.

I. Program Status Report Document

EFFECTIVENESS: There is an annual check and review of the effectiveness of this document.

TABLE 15.4   Integrated Elements for Classroom Program Status Report

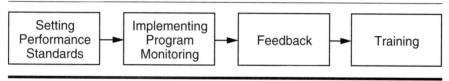

Law 94-142). The most important among these is, of course, student needs. Table 15.5 gives an example of a process standard based on student needs, and Table 15.6 provides an example of a product or outcome standard.

These examples illustrate how both process and product standards are important. It would be an empty accomplishment to be carrying out a process, if that process did not lead us to some meaningful goals. At the same time, we cannot expect to reach our goals without designing and carrying out a process. In summary, PSRs may

include both process and product standards generated by student goals and objectives, by administrative requirements, and by the rules and regulations of external authorities. There are four basic principles to follow in developing performance standards, as listed in Table 15.7.

Emphasis on Essentials.   The first principle to follow in developing performance standards for a PSR is to emphasize the essential, critical elements of a program. It would be overwhelming and unfeasible for a consulting teacher to try to be

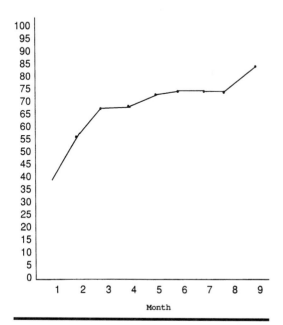

FIGURE 15.1   An example of progress per month with the PSR within the first year of application.

TABLE 15.5   Sample Process Standard: Direct Instruction in Self-Care

Student records indicate that each has received at least 10 minutes of direct instruction each day on at least one self-care skill (e.g., hand washing, brushing teeth, etc.). To receive credit on the weekly PSR, 80 percent of students in a class need to have received this level of instruction.

TABLE 15.6   Sample Product Standard: Skill Acquisition

Quarterly progress reports show that students are meeting the skill acquisition objectives established for them on their annual IEPs. To receive credit on the weekly PSR, the last quarterly progress report must be in the student's file and show that a prorated proportion of the annual objectives have been met.

TABLE 15.7   Basic Principles for Developing
Performance Standards

- Emphasize essentials
- Realistic standards
- Explicit criteria
- Verifiability

all-inclusive. To make the system manageable and feasible, it is important to identify and develop key standards. There are a number of strategies that help in developing an efficient PSR that includes critical standards. One is to organize a program into a series of response chains. A standard developed to address the last link in the chain would then implicitly measure performance around the earlier links. For example, we may define a chain of responses concerning behavior intervention. This chain of standards may say that behavior intervention should be based on: (1) baseline data, (2) direct observation, (3) staff and parent interviews, (4) a review of records, and (5) an assessment report by the school psychologist or behavior specialist that summarizes the foregoing information. Given this chain of behavior, we do not have to include a standard on our PSR for each of the elements, just for the last link. Specifically, we would hold ourselves accountable as addressed on our PSR for having a current (within 1 year) assessment report in the file, available to classroom staff, that meets 85 percent of the criteria that we might provide on a checklist to guide the school psychologist or behavioral specialist. If this standard is met, there is reason to believe that the other standards are being met as well, given the way they have been organized.

Another strategy for developing a PSR that emphasizes the pivotal elements of a program is to include standards for different categories of classroom personnel (Christian & Hannah, 1983). This strategy reflects the respective contributions from different members of the interdisciplinary team. In addition to teachers and aides, standards should

also reflect (i.e., be the responsibility of) the professionals who serve on the team, as well as the supervisors, consulting teacher, and perhaps even the school administration. The responsibility of providing a good program of educational services is not solely that of direct instructional staff. The PSR should reflect this multidisciplinary process.

Realistic Standards. It is important that the standards recommended by a consulting teacher for a PSR be realistic (Christian & Hannah, 1983). It should reasonably be possible within the resource capability of the school or agency to meet the standards, with proper consideration of budget, staffing, materials, and so on. This is a particular responsibility of an external consulting teacher. The purpose of a PSR is not to establish a set of idealized standards that leave the classroom team constantly unable to meet their goals, bemoaning the fact that they simply do not have the resources to do a good job, but rather to establish a set of standards that will allow a program to provide the best education possible, given the available resources.

There are different ways to go about this. One is to base standards on average past performance. Obviously, if a classroom has performed at a certain level in the past, it is realistic to aim for that level in the future. This strategy, however, will simply maintain the status quo and will not effect program improvement. Another approach is to base standards on best past performance. One way to judge a program's best past performance is to determine how well it was doing when it was prepared for an outside evaluation. The point is that if a program can perform up to a certain level for "visitors," it should be realistic to expect that level of performance on an ongoing basis. Actually, we recommend a third approach to the consulting teacher, which looks at neither average past performance nor best past performance. Rather, based on the available resources, we recommend standards be established as objectives to strive toward. We feel this is the most powerful way to maximize a program in the classroom (or in other settings). The risk here is that in establishing such objectives, we may overshoot our resource capability. There is a discussion later in this chapter about what corrective action can be taken if, after a period of time, the consultant and the teacher conclude that the reason standards are not being met is that there are insufficient resources.

Explicit Criteria.   A third principle in developing standards is to base them on explicit criteria (Christian & Hannah, 1983). This requires both operational definitions and time lines. The goal is to remove subjectivity from the monitoring process. For example, to establish a standard that says, "Every student in a classroom has a schedule" leaves too much room for interpretation. If we operationalize this standard, however, to say that each student in a classroom has his or her own daily schedule, listing the educational activity for each 15-minute period, including when the student is to have his or her data-based instructional sessions, and when interobserver and procedural reliability checks are to be carried out, we leave little room for opinion as to whether the standard has been met. We may even further operationalize the standard to say that the listed educational activity cannot be generic (e.g., recreation or leisure) but must be specific (e.g., shooting baskets or knitting). If the activity is to be the student's choice, we may require that the schedule refer to the set of educational activities from which the choice will be made. Finally, we would expect that this schedule be available for review at all times. Time line requirements are important to our explicit criteria. For example, it is not enough to say that instructional data should be summarized on a graph. We must also establish in our standard when this is to be done. For example, we might establish that it be done within the last instructional session, weekly, daily, or at other intervals.

Verifiability.   Finally, we need to specify how we will verify that a standard has been met (Christian & Hannah, 1983). This can be done only by a review of permanent products or by direct observa-tion. For example, a review of a behavioral assessment report in a student's file can determine whether the appropriate information is included and whether it is current, that is, dated within 1 year. Similarly, logs, summary graphs, posted schedules, student notebooks, reinforcement charts, and so on can be reviewed to verify whether a variety of standards are being met. On the other hand, a whole host of important standards that might be included in a PSR may be verifiable only by direct observation. These may include, for example, reliability checks to determine whether data are accurate, fidelity checks to determine whether lesson plans are being properly followed, or observations to verify the quality of student interactions. However, to make the PSR process itself an efficient one, we recommend that the results of direct observations be documented in a permanent form. Thus, in performing a PSR review, each standard is scored on the basis of permanent product evaluation, including the permanent records that document the results of previously carried out direct observations. If designed correctly, a weekly PSR review should take no more than a half hour.

IMPLEMENTING PROGRAM MONITORING

Program monitoring is defined as the ongoing verification that assigned responsibilities have been carried out. It forms the second element of the strategy to assure effective consultation. In fact, monitoring can be the *key* difference in assuring follow-through with a consulting teacher's recommendations. In one study, performance monitoring was found to be different in comparing effective and ineffective supervisors, whereas no differences were found in the time they spent in providing performance feedback (Komaki, 1986). This makes perfect sense, since *meaningful* (i.e., contingent) feedback could not be provided without observation, that is, without performance monitoring.

Many consulting teachers report to us, however, that they are uncomfortable with the idea that they have to monitor the performance of other classroom staff. Teachers who are asked to monitor the performance of their own aides also report discomfort. This is probably because, for most people, monitoring has set the occasion for punishment in the past. However, it is interesting to note that people being interviewed for employment say that they welcome the frequent monitoring and feedback by those employers who provide it. They often say that in their previous jobs nobody ever told them how they were doing. The fear of resistance to a monitoring system is perhaps more relevant to an existing staff. However, we feel monitoring can work effectively in classroom situations without undue discomfort to the recipient instructional staff if the monitoring incorporates some critical elements. The guidelines described in the following paragraphs may be helpful in achieving staff acceptance of monitoring systems (see Table 15.8).

Positive Payoffs

The consulting teacher should use the results of the PSR monitoring system for positive purposes only (Christian & Hannah, 1983). Regardless of the results of the PSR review, the consulting teacher can provide three kinds of positive feedback. The first is positive feedback about the visibility the monitoring system provides. It can be emphasized that no classroom program (or other program) can improve unless the team knows its present status. A teacher can be shown that the PSR system provides this information. Second,

TABLE 15.8   Guidelines for Increasing Staff Acceptance of a Monitoring System

1. Positive payoffs
2. Staff participation
3. Shared responsibility
4. Initial self-monitoring
5. Emphasis on professionalism
6. Staff commentary

the consultant should focus on those standards that are being met and acknowledge the effort and good work this represents. For example, a teacher might be praised heavily when initiating the summary behavioral data on a graph. Third, those standards that are not being met should be discussed after the first two instances of feedback, and such situations should *not* be characterized as failures, deficiencies, or problems. Rather, they should be characterized as opportunities for improvement. The little circles entered onto a PSR score sheet are not zeros, they are "O's," which stand for *opportunities*. A program cannot improve unless its staff knows where the opportunities lie. Discovering these opportunities is, therefore, portrayed as a positive process, not a negative one.

Staff Participation

A second strategy for increasing acceptance of a monitoring process is to arrange for active participation by the teacher and other classroom staff at every step in the program. This includes their participation in setting the standards and developing the Program Status Report, participation in the monitoring process, and participation in setting each week's objectives for improvement. Contrary to most expectations, given the opportunity, instructional staff will set rigorous, relevant, and feasible performance standards (Christian & Hannah, 1983). Further, operationalized performance standards eliminate subjective judgment from the monitoring process, enabling staff to participate in the PSR review without compromising the results. Finally, giving classroom staff the opportunity to identify the opportunities they want to take advantage of, for the coming week, emphasizes the bottom-up, two-way nature of the system and contributes to staff members' sense of ownership.

Shared Responsibility

A third strategy for increasing acceptance of a monitoring system is to construct it to include standards that reflect the contributions of as many members of the interdisciplinary team as possible (Christian & Hannah, 1983). If it were used to monitor only the performance of the teacher and aides, the system would make them particularly visible and vulnerable. As a shared responsibility, the PSR keeps the focus on the interdisciplinary process and does not make any one or two job categories subject to scrutiny.

Initial Self-Monitoring

Another recommended strategy is to schedule a period for self-monitoring (each person collects data on his or her own performance) 2 to 3 months after the development of a PSR. During this period, no formal monitoring takes place, but the whole team, knowing the standards that have been established, have this time to get organized and, it is hoped, to meet their respective responsibilities to assure the best initial result when formal monitoring actually begins. Although people rarely take advantage of this period of self-monitoring, their knowing that it will be available facilitates the acceptance of a monitoring system.

Emphasis on Professionalism

Consulting teachers should *not* characterize the PSR system as one that is necessary because they expect instructional staff to do nothing unless someone is looking over their shoulders. Rather, they should communicate the expectation that if given the necessary information and support, staff

will perform at professional levels. The PSR is portrayed as a system that provides this assistance, and consultants are rarely disappointed in the response of staff in meeting the most rigorous standards.

Staff Commentary

The final strategy we recommend to increase acceptance of the monitoring system is to provide space on the PSR score sheet for instructional staff to record any explanations they would like to provide as to why an opportunity may exist. This is where explanations of factors such as illness, behavioral crises, and lack of funds are documented. An opportunity to improve is an opportunity to improve, but staff feel better if their explanations are acknowledged (Christian & Hannah, 1983).

Using positive feedback, arranging for participation by instructional staff, monitoring across different job categories on a single PSR, scheduling a period for self-monitoring, emphasizing the professionalism of staff, and treating staff explanations with respect are very useful as guidelines to increase acceptance of a monitoring system. The following paragraphs discuss the basic principles to follow in the actual monitoring process, which are shown in Table 15.9.

Sampling

It is probably not practical to look at every student's program every time a PSR review is done. For those standards that require the review of specific programs, it is best to use a sampling

TABLE 15.9   Basic Principles of Monitoring

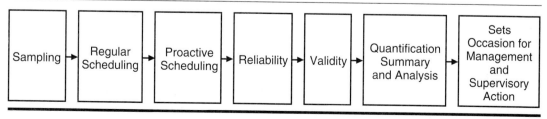

process. For example, in a classroom with eight students, for a standard that requires the summary of instructional data on a graph and keeping such summaries up-to-date within one instructional session, we would not recommend looking at every student's records but only the one that had been randomly selected for that review. Furthermore, that student's name will be back in the "hat" next week and could be selected for 2 (or more) weeks in a row, just by chance. Such sampling procedures guard against neglecting a person's program just because it is assumed that it will not be the one reviewed that week (i.e., they protect us from our own fixed interval performance) (Ferster & Skinner, 1957).

Regular Scheduling

In many settings monitoring is traditionally done annually or perhaps even quarterly. It is important for monitoring to be done frequently and regularly if it is to be an active part of a system to increase staff follow-through with program design and the consulting teacher's recommendations. Ideally, a PSR should be performed weekly to be most effective, especially at the beginning of the process. If this is not possible, at least monthly checks are recommended.

Proactive Scheduling

The PSR is designed as an ongoing system. If it is used just to bring program performance up to a given level and then discontinued, performance will deteriorate. Monitoring must be continued by the teacher or other school staff to maintain a high level of performance, even after the consulting teacher is no longer involved.

Reliability

Monitoring should produce consistent results regardless of who does the monitoring. By basing the PSR on operationalized standards, we assure a reliable monitoring system. A PSR can be checked

for reliability by having different teams or people evaluate the same program using the same documentation. If the PSR outcome is the same, the monitoring system is reliable.

Validity

A monitoring system should address important and relevant standards for the program. By recommending process and product standards for meeting student needs, which also address critical administrative and outside authority requirements, and by including staff participation in PSR development, we assure that the PSR has validity.

Quantification, Summary, and Analysis

A monitoring system is most useful to teachers and consultants if it can be quantified, summarized, and analyzed. The PSR provides for this by requiring binary scoring summarized as a percentage score that is then graphed and analyzed. This analysis can include a review of staff commentary to provide additional insight as to why an opportunity may exist.

Setting the Occasion for Action

Perhaps most important, monitoring should set the occasion and form the basis for action by the teacher, the consulting teacher, and supervisory staff. The following section of this chapter discusses the nature of such action.

THE FEEDBACK LOOP

The feedback loop is defined as teacher, consulting teacher, and supervisory action based on program monitoring. The purpose of such action is to improve and maintain staff performance and to maximize the school's implementation of the consulting teacher's recommendations. Providing feedback to staff, like monitoring, is another one of those important functions that some may shy away from because of its past association with punishment. When a person hears a supervisor

TABLE 15.10   Elements of Feedback

- Visual feedback
- Positive reinforcement
- Clarification and training
- Mutual and realistic goals

say, "Will you come into my office at 4:30 this afternoon? There is some feedback I want to give you," it is likely he or she will think that the feedback is going to be negative. In fact, because people often precede criticism with a compliment, compliments themselves have become conditioned aversive stimuli for many. When the boss starts a compliment, an employee may cringe, waiting for the other shoe to drop. Punitive feedback characterizes the typical work setting and contributes to hostility, resistance, absenteeism, turnover, low morale, and other staff problems (Hogan, 1990). To avoid these problems, it is wise to adhere to certain principles in providing feedback, as listed in Table 15.10.

Visual Feedback

A primary feedback strategy that has helped assure effective consultation has been the visual feedback of the PSR graphs themselves. The effectiveness of visual feedback in changing staff behavior is well documented in the literature (Quilitch, 1975; Kreitner, Reif, & Morris, 1977; Hutchison, Jarman, & Bailey, 1980; Welsch, Ludwig, Radiker, & Krapfl, 1973). Updating and posting the PSR graphs for each classroom, group home, or other program unit is a key strategy for motivating program staff to follow through with recommendations and to perform at the highest levels.

In providing such weekly feedback to staff, there are some considerations to keep in mind. In a system in which there is more than one program unit, such as a school with several classrooms or an agency with several group homes, competition between units should not be encouraged. Experi-

ence has shown that such competition quickly becomes aversive by holding the "poor performers" up to public exposure. The posting of a PSR graph should be limited to the setting of the program unit (e.g., the classroom or group home), with copies transmitted to the relevant supervisors. For example, individual classroom units should be informed of the school's performance as a whole, but not of the performance of other classrooms. This can be accomplished through the production of a summary PSR graph reflecting the average PSR results for the entire school. In this way, the individual classroom unit can be encouraged to compete against the mean or, preferably, against its own individual score. Such graphs summarized by program category, school, or other organizational unit also give upper management ample access to hard information concerning daily program operations at the service delivery level.

Positive Reinforcement

As mentioned earlier, the consultant should make a point of being only positive with the PSR results. For instance, the consulting teacher can be positive about the visibility the system provides—a person can *see* where he or she is on the feedback graph, about the score already achieved and the high standards of performance it represents, and about the opportunities for improvement that have been uncovered. The consulting teacher should be positive in these three ways during the monitoring and feedback session itself and should train the teachers and supervisory staff to act in like manner.

Clarification and Training

One of the ways a consulting teacher might respond to an identified opportunity is to use it as an occasion to provide further clarification and training. The spirit to communicate is that the opportunity may exist because the consulting teacher may not have provided sufficient information or training and that he or she is willing to assume some ownership for the opportunity. Such an approach also prevents staff defensiveness and helps to keep the system positive.

Mutual and Realistic Goals

Finally, the PSR review and feedback session ends with joint decisions about what opportunities people plan to take advantage of for the coming week. The consulting teacher's role here is to keep staff realistic about what they plan to accomplish. It is better for them to establish a modest goal and to be successful than to be overambitious about what they want to do and to fail. Small goals accumulate, and the feedback graph helps keep the team on track to the ultimate goal of 85 percent to 90 percent performance.

Constructive Corrective Action

Occasionally, following implementation of the strategies described earlier, a PSR graph levels off and reaches a plateau or drops before it rises to the 85 percent level. In such cases, constructive changes such as additional training, reassignment of resources, or other modifications may be necessary for continued improvement.

STAFF TRAINING

Staff training is a necessary element of any system that works at maximizing program follow-through, inasmuch as teachers and other class-room staff may not always have the training and experience to perform many of the recommended tasks. We define *staff training* as instruction to establish competence of staff members to perform their responsibilities. Given that definition, a 1-day workshop or even a 2-week in-service training program, organized around a comprehensive list of topics, would not qualify as training if all that was documented were hours of attendance. To qualify as training under this definition, the objectives of training must be stated in terms of operationalized competencies as evaluated against a set of objective criteria. At IABA, we approach

staff training as an element of the PSR system at two different levels, general and specific.

General Skills

A general skills training program, utilized by IABA, is organized around a comprehensive list of topics (See Table 15.11). However, for each topic area, we have specified both the general skills and the competencies that we want our staff to have and the criteria against which the mastery of those competencies will be measured. Sample competencies are provided in Table 15.12.

Although a school might want to develop a general training program such as that described earlier for certain categories of staff, the PSR system itself can be used as a needs assessment strategy to help identify training objectives. That is, the identified opportunities might very well be opportunities to provide more focused or better training.

TABLE 15.11   Training Topics

1. Orientation
2. Administrative Requirements
3. Philosophy of Normalization
4. Ethical Issues
5. Public Relations
6. Basic Principles of Behavior
7. Identifying and Using Positive Reinforcement
8. Measurement
9. Assessment Report and Intervention Plan
10. Positive Programming
11. Teaching Strategies
12. Reducing Behavior Problems
13. Methods of Evaluation
14. Planning for Generalization and Maintenance
15. Organization and Management
16. Supported Work Model

TABLE 15.12   Sample Competencies

A. Administrative Requirements

Competency: Identifies job description, chain of command, and general program policies.

Criteria:

1. Given a written or verbal test, trainee can state three aspects of his or her job duties.

2. Given a written or verbal test, trainee correctly describes program's grievance procedures.

B. Ethical Issues

Competency: Understands that the client has the right to be informed, and should be, of all aspects of treatment, including goals, methods, procedures, and possible benefits and drawbacks associated with the program.

Criterion: Given three vignettes, the trainee is able to identify the particular ethical issue being addressed, and can describe whether the client's rights are being violated.

C. Teaching Strategies

Competency: Defines *chaining* as a strategy to develop a new behavior.

Criterion: Definition includes the variations of behavioral chaining, forward chaining, and whole-task presentation, and at least one example of how each could be applied to client behavior.

D. Basic Principles of Behavior

Competency: The trainee is able to describe the three-part contingency and label each element.

Criteria: Given five written or videotaped vignettes, the trainee is able to describe each, using the three-part contingency. Each should include:

    a. Antecedent stimulus

    b. Behavior

    c. Consequences

Specific Skills

Assuming instructional and support staff have the necessary general skills, attention can then be turned to their mastering the specifics of individual student programs. Both instructional programs and behavior intervention programs should be operationalized and task analyzed on detailed protocols and checklists (Cipani, 1985). After staff members read and review a protocol, it can be explained by the consulting teacher, teacher, or supervisor. All questions should be answered. One can then assess mastery. We recommend that this be done at three different levels: verbal competence (Can the trainee describe each step in the protocol or checklist?); analog or role-play competence (Can the trainee demonstrate each step in the protocol or checklist?); and in vivo competence (Can the trainee actually carry out each step in the protocol or checklist when working with the student?). As simple as this three-tiered method of training may seem, it is surprisingly powerful as a training strategy, for which staff are invariably appreciative. After staff have been trained to the in vivo level of competence, ongoing fidelity should be monitored through a regular schedule of procedural reliability checks to protect against procedural drift (Billingsley, White, & Munson, 1980).

CONCLUSION

This chapter has described a strategy for ensuring effective consultation for the consulting teacher. The system consists of four key elements: performance standards, performance monitoring, staff feedback, and staff training. Our experience is that many settings have one or more of these features in place, incorporating to a greater or lesser extent the basic principles described in the preceding sections. Our experience is equally, however, that it is the use of the whole system that makes it work and that the implementation of isolated parts does not create a productive context for ensuring effective consultation.

This system might seem quite daunting to someone considering its introduction into a typical classroom setting. We therefore suggest following the steps for developing and implementing a PSR system listed in Table 15.13.

The system is sufficiently powerful and effective to support itself with ongoing expansion and

TABLE 15.13 Strategies for Initiating a Program Status Report Process

1. Develop a draft set of standards, based on your previous interviews with staff, that you feel represent a major step in the right direction for the setting to which you are providing consultation services. Make sure the standards address contributions from more than one job category. They should also include some responsibilities of your own.

2. At a staff meeting, introduce the spirit and framework of a PSR system. Present your draft PSR as a set of starting points for staff discussion. Be open to suggestions for changes and revisions. Ownership is important.

3. Revise the PSR based on input from those who will be most directly affected.

4. Schedule a period of self-monitoring, which you have described at the orientation meeting. Staff should be informed that they will have time to prepare for monitoring once standards have been agreed upon. This is everyone's opportunity to gear up for the formal monitoring process.

5. Start formal monitoring and feedback, weekly if possible, but no less frequently than monthly, using all of the principles described in this chapter.

revisions. It is important not to allow administration to expand this as a top-down system. It will work best if everyone involved keeps a focus on its bottom-up qualities.

REFERENCES

Bergan, J. R. (1977). *Behavioral consultation.* Columbus, OH: Charles E. Merrill.

Billingsley, F. F., White, O. R., & Munson, R. (1980). Procedural reliability: A rationale and an example. *Behavioral Assessment, 2,* 247–256.

Christian, W. P., & Hannah, G. T. (1983). *Effective management in human services.* Englewood Cliffs, NJ: Prentice Hall.

Christian, W. P., & Reitz, A. (1986). Administration. In F. J. Fuoco & W. P. Christian (Eds.), *Behavior analysis and therapy in residential programs* (pp. 24–49). New York: Van Nostrand Reinhold.

Christian, W. P., & Romanczyk, R. G. (1986). Evaluation. In F. J. Fuoco & W. P. Christian (Eds.), *Behavior analysis and therapy in residential programs* (pp. 145–193). New York: Van Nostrand Reinhold.

Cipani, E. (1985). The three phases of behavioral consultation: Objectives, intervention and quality assurance. *Teacher Education and Special Education, 8* (3), 144–152.

Ferster, C. B., & Skinner, B. F. (1957). *Schedules of reinforcement*. New York: Appleton-Century-Crofts.

Harris, B. (1980). *Improving staff performance through in-service education*. Boston: Allyn & Bacon.

Hogan, R., Curphy, G., & Hogan, J. (in press). Leadership effectiveness. *American Psychologist*.

Hutchinson, J. M., Jarman, P. H., & Bailey, J. S. (1980). Public posting with a habilitation team: Effects on attendance and performance. *Behavior Modification, 4*, 57–70.

Idol-Maestas, L. (1983). *Special educator's consultation handbook*. Rockville, MD: Aspen.

Komaki, J. L. (1986). Toward effective supervision: An operant analysis and comparison of managers at work. *Journal of Applied Psychology, 71*, 270–279.

Kreitner, R., Reif, W. E., & Morris, M. (1977). Measuring the impact of feedback on the performance of mental health technicians. *Journal of Organizational Behavior Management, 1*, 105–109.

Paolucci-Whitcomb, P., & Nevin, A. (1985). Preparing consulting teachers through a collaborative approach between university faculty and field-based consulting teachers. *Teacher Education and Special Education, 8(3)*, 132–143.

Quilitch, M. R. (1975). A comparison of their staff management procedures. *Journal of Applied Behavior Analysis, 8*, 59–66.

Reid, D. H., Parsons, M. B., & Green, C. W. (1989). Treating aberrant behavior through effective staff management: A developing technology. In E. Cipani (Ed.), *The treatment of severe disorders: Behavior analysis approach* (pp. 175–190). New York: AAMR Monographs.

Reid, D. H., & Whitman, T. L. (1983). Behavioral staff management in institutions: A critical review of effectiveness and acceptability. *Analysis and Intervention in Developmental Disabilities, 3*, 131–149.

Welsh, W. V., Ludwig, C., Radiker, J. E., & Krapfl, J. E. (1973). Effects of feedback on daily completion of behavior modification projects. *Mental Retardation, 11*, 24–26.

CHAPTER 16

MEDICATION MANAGEMENT

NIRBHAY N. SINGH
CYNTHIA R. ELLIS
YADHU N. SINGH
Virginia Treatment Center for Children

For at least 35 years drugs have been used to control the behavior of students with severe disabilities. Historically, they have been used somewhat indiscriminately with this population, often at very high dosages to achieve a sedative effect. Use of medication is particularly common if the student exhibits violent, explosive behavior or engages in life-threatening behaviors such as self-injury and rumination (Aman & Singh, 1988). In these circumstances, drugs are often used as chemical restraints and as a substitute for appropriate services. This was and is unfortunate, because research has demonstrated that drugs can impair learning, cognitive performance, and adaptive behavior (Aman & Singh, 1980).

Fortunately, major legal and social changes during the last 20 years have had a profound impact on the way drugs are now prescribed for students with severe disabilities. What will probably stand out as the turning point in the history of drug therapy for all individuals with developmental disabilities is the *Wyatt v. Sticknev* (1972) decision mandating that drugs cannot be used as punishment, for the convenience of staff, or in amounts that affect the student's ability to respond to habilitative programs. This decision was followed by another, equally important, judicial decision, *Welsch v. Likins* (1974), requiring institutions to monitor and empirically evaluate the effects of all behavior-controlling drugs in a careful, systematic manner. Further, in *Price v. Sheppard* (1976), the courts accepted the concept that drugs are more intrusive than alternative treatments, such as positive reinforcement programs, making it mandatory to have procedural safeguards designed to ensure that the need for drug treatment is balanced against its intrusiveness.

Before progressing further, some explanation of terms is in order. In this chapter, we use the term *psychotropic drug* to refer to any pharmacological agent that is prescribed for the explicit purpose of bringing about behavioral, cognitive, or emotional changes in a student. The term *psychoactive drug* is used in a more general sense to refer to any agent that may have these effects, regardless of a doctor's intent in prescribing this drug. *Behavioral effects* refer to the effects of a medication on the target problem behavior, such as aggression, disruption, and self-injury.

WHY LEARN ABOUT THE EFFECTS OF DRUGS?

Given that persons with developmental disabilities are probably the most medicated group in our society, it behooves all of us to have some basic knowledge about the effects of drugs on their behavior. Indeed, it is very likely that up to a third of all students with severe disabilities will be taking either psychotropic or anticonvulsant medication. For a teacher, this means that possibly 3 of the 10 children in his or her class are taking medication.

Given the impact of medication on many aspects of a child's life, teachers must have an increasing knowledge base about medication, such as types of medication, dosages, the desired effects, and side effects. As noted by Gadow (1986), "the very behaviors that are altered by drugs are often inter-related with the educational, habilitative, and parenting process" (p. xix).

Another important reason for teachers to be knowledgeable is that drugs do not affect all students in the same manner. For example, although the majority of hyperactive children apparently benefit from a titrated dose of methylphenidate (Ritalin), some children do not. It is helpful for teachers to know that Ritalin can have this differential effect, especially if the behavior of a student worsens when taking this medication, so that they can bring it to the attention of the parents and the prescribing physician. In addition, some drugs have a number of serious side effects, such as uncontrollable motor movements, that may impair a child's adaptive behavior or affect a child's performance in academic and physical activities.

If teachers are knowledgeable about the effects and side effects of various medications, they can be relied upon to monitor and provide feedback to the prescribing physician. Studies have shown that informed teacher feedback greatly enhances treatment-related decisions (Sprague & Gadow, 1976). Indeed, recent models of assessment, diagnosis, and treatment of childhood disorders rely heavily on informed feedback from teachers and parents to enhance clinical decision making in multi-disciplinary teams (Singh, Parmelee, Sood, & Katz, 1993; Singh, Sood, Sonenklar, & Ellis, 1991).

This chapter first discusses how and when drugs are most often prescribed for students with severe disabilities. It then provides a brief outline of the effects and side effects of the various classes of drugs that are prescribed by medical personnel for students with severe handicaps. It will also cover the following issues related to medication management: (1) the roles of teachers, family members, and direct care staff in delivering and monitoring the effects of drugs, (2) coordination between doctor, parents, and teachers, (3) what the teacher needs to know or do with regard to the use of medication, (4) the teacher's responsibilities and liabilities in this area, (5) how medication should be delivered, and (6) establishing or improving educator-medical relations.

PREVALENCE AND PATTERNS OF DRUG USE

Although litigation regarding the use of drugs has had a major impact on programming for students with severe disabilities, drugs are still used with a substantial number of individuals who are developmentally disabled (Aman & Singh, 1988).

Institutions

Surveys of psychotropic drug usage in institutions for individuals with developmental disabilities range from a low of 19 percent to a high of 86 percent, with most studies reporting rates between about 30 percent and 50 percent. Medication that is used for controlling epileptic seizures ranges from a low of 24 percent to a high of 56 percent, although it is typically between 25 percent and 45 percent. In general, the use of psychotropic and antiepileptic medication ranges from 50 percent to 70 percent, with both types being prescribed concurrently for some individuals.

Community

In community-based surveys, the reported use of psychotropic medication with children who have developmental disabilities ranges from 2 percent to 7 percent; for adults, the range is 14 percent to 36 percent. The use of medication for controlling epileptic seizures is between 12 percent and 31 percent for children, and 18 percent and 24 percent for adults. The combined prevalence of psychotropic and antiepileptic medication in the community is between 19 percent and 33 percent for children, and 36 percent and 48 percent for adults.

Factors Influencing Drug Use

Various factors influence psychotropic drug use by individuals with developmental disabilities. Increasing dosage has been found to correlate highly with increasing age and decreasing intellectual impairment. There is also a strong relationship between the type of residential facility and the use of medication, with more medication being prescribed in larger facilities and in facilities with very restrictive environments. Further, there is a strong positive correlation between the number and severity of a student's behavioral and psychiatric problems and the use of medication (Aman & Singh, 1988). For example, students who exhibit aggression, hyperactivity, self-injury, screaming, or anxiety are more likely to receive drug treatment than those with milder and less disruptive problems (e.g., noncompliance).

EFFECTS OF DRUGS ON BEHAVIOR AND LEARNING

Drugs can be classified according to their chemical structure, mechanism of action, behavioral effects, or therapeutic usage. The most common classification is based on therapeutic usage, with the drugs that are prescribed for the treatment of given clinical diagnoses being grouped together. Drug groups that are commonly used in students with severe disabilities include the antipsychotics, stimulants, antidepressants, antimanics, and anxiolytics. The antiepileptics, especially carbamazepine (Tegretol), are also occasionally used for their psychotropic effects and are included in our discussion of the effects of psychotropic drugs. Table 16.1 presents psychoactive and psychotropic drugs by classification, generic name, and trade name.

Antipsychotics

Antipsychotics, the most frequently used drugs with persons who have severe disabilities, include four major classes of compounds: phenothiazines (e.g.,

thioridazine, chlorpromazine), butyrophenones (e.g., haloperidol), thioxanthenes (e.g., thiothixene), and rauwolfia alkaloids (e.g., reserpine). Of these, the phenothiazines and butyrophenones are of prime importance, because they are the most widely used in students with severe disabilities.

Effects on Behavior. The antipsychotics are most frequently prescribed to students who are aggressive, destructive, self-injurious, hyperactive, and antisocial in an attempt to control the level of these behaviors. However, our current state of knowledge of the behavioral effects of these drugs is rather limited, because there are so few well-controlled studies from which we can draw firm conclusions.

Some of the early studies with chlorpromazine (Thorazine) indicated that the drug was effective in reducing a number of problem behaviors, such as self-injury and stereotypy, in persons with severe disabilities (Aman & Singh, 1988). Unfortunately, these studies were methodologically flawed in several respects and their conclusions regarding the efficacy of Thorazine on problem behaviors are open to criticism. Indeed, more recent and better controlled studies suggest that chlorpromazine may actually have a detrimental effect on some appropriate behaviors in some persons (Schroeder, 1988). Other studies have found that although problem behaviors (e.g., stereotypy) are suppressed, some appropriate behaviors (e.g., conditioning tasks) are worsened (Aman & Singh, 1988).

Thioridazine (Mellaril) is a popular drug used to treat problem behavior in students with severe disabilities. However, the scientific basis for this usage is weak owing to the fact that only a quarter of all published studies are methodologically adequate (Aman & Singh, 1980). The studies that meet scientific standards of rigor suggest that thioridazine decreases hyperactivity, aggression, and stereotypy in persons with severe disabilities. There have been at least five recent studies with this drug, and all have shown similar positive results. In addition, one study showed that a low dose of thioridazine was as effective as a higher

TABLE 16.1   Psychoactive and Psychotropic Drugs Classified by Therapeutic Effect

DRUG CLASS/SUBCLASS	GENERIC NAME	TRADE NAME
Antipsychotics		
Phenothiazines		
	chlorpromazine	Thorazine
	fluphenazine	Prolixin
	mesoridazine	Serentil
	perphenazine	Trilafon
	thioridazine	Mellaril
	trifluoperazine	Stelazine
Thioxanthenes		
	chlorprothixene	Taractan
	thiothixene	Navane
Butyrophenones		
	haloperidol	Haldol
	pipamperon	Dipiperon
Rauwolfia alkaloids		
	reserpine	Rauloydin, Reserpoid, Sandril
Antidepressants		
Tricyclics		
	amitriptyline	Elavil, Amitril
	imipramine	Tofranil
	desipramine	Norpramin
	doxepin	Sinequan
	nortriptyline	Pamelor, Nortab
Monoamine oxidase inhibitors		
	isocarboxazid	Marplan
	phenelzine	Nardil
	tranylcypromine	Parnate
Antimanics		
	lithium carbonate	Eskalith, Lithane, Lithobid
Anxiolytics		
Benzodiazepines		
	alprazolam	Xanax
	chlordiazepoxide	Librium
	diazepam	Valium
	lorazepam	Ativan
	oxazepam	Serax
	prazepam	Verstran
	temazepam	Restoril
	triazolam	Halcion

(continued)

TABLE 16.1   Continued

DRUG CLASS/SUBCLASS	GENERIC NAME	TRADE NAME
Anxiolytics (cont.)		
Antihistamines		
	diphenhydramine	Benadryl
	hydroxyzine	Atarax
	promethazine	Phenergan
Stimulants		
	amphetamine sulfate	Benzedrine
	dextroamphetamine	Dexedrine
	methylphenidate	Ritalin
	pemoline	Cylert
Antiepileptics		
	carbamazepine	Tegretol
	clonazepam	Clonopin
	diazepam	Valium
	ethosuximide	Zarontin
	phenobarbital	Luminal, Gardenal
	phenytoin	Dilantin
	primidone	Mysoline
	sodium valproate	Depakene, Epilim
	sulthiame	Ospolot
Others		
Beta-adrenergic blocker		
	propranolol	Inderal
Opiate antagonist		
	naloxone	Narcan
	naltrexone	Trexan
Sympathomimetic amine		
	fenfluramine	Pondimin

dose in controlling stereotypy (Singh & Aman, 1981). In general, we believe there is fairly good evidence that thioridazine is more effective than chlorpromazine in controlling the problem behaviors of persons with severe disabilities.

Haloperidol (Haldol) is often used because it has a much lower sedative effect than thioridazine or chlorpromazine. It is typically used to suppress hyperactivity, aggression, hostility, and impulsivity in persons with severe disabilities. However, there are very few well-controlled studies attesting to the efficacy of this drug with this population (Aman & Singh, 1991).

Even fewer data are available on some of the

other antipsychotics, and no conclusions regarding their efficacy can be drawn at this time. These studies have been reviewed by Schroeder (1988). In summary, one must use caution in assuming the efficacy of the antipsychotics in controlling the problem behavior of students with severe disabilities because of the paucity of methodologically sound studies.

Effects on Learning.   The majority of the studies on the effects of antipsychotics have been concerned with the reduction of problem behaviors in persons with severe disabilities rather than on their effects on learning and performance. Those who did study the effects on learning and performance used either IQ or achievement tests to assess drug effects on learning. In all the studies using chlorpromazine and thioridazine, considered together, about a third demonstrated that the individuals' learning and performance improved while taking these drugs (Aman, 1984). Of the remaining studies, one showed a deterioration in learning, and the other reported no change in the learning of the students (Aman, 1984). The studies showing an improvement in learning used relatively low doses of the drugs (about 75 mg to 100 mg/day), suggesting that low doses of antipsychotics may actually facilitate learning and performance in some persons with severe disabilities, probably by suppressing incompatible behaviors.

Side Effects.   Antipsychotics tend to produce side effects that range from mild to severe. The more common and milder side effects include dry mouth, constipation, difficulty with urination, blurred vision, weight gain, and an increased sensitivity of the skin to the effects of sunlight. They can also cause an increase in heart rate, as well as a lowering of blood pressure. In addition, certain abnormal muscle and movement disorders have resulted from antipsychotic drug usage, including acute dystonic reactions (muscle spasms, usually of the face and neck), tardive dyskinesia (involuntary movements of the face, mouth, tongue, trunk, or extremities, which usually appear after prolonged usage or immediately following discontinuation of the medica-

tion), and parkinsonian symptoms (such as muscle rigidity, hand tremor, and a mask-like facial appearance). Finally, teachers must be aware that a student's alertness may decrease because of the nonspecific sedative nature of most antipsychotic medications.

Antidepressants and Antimanics

The monoamine oxidase inhibitors (MAOIs) and the tri- and quadricyclic antidepressants are the major subgroups of antidepressant drugs used in the treatment of clinical depression. Typically, antidepressants are not used to any great extent with persons who are severely disabled. The MAOIs, which are rarely used with children, do not appear to have much effect on problem behaviors of persons with severe disabilities. The role of tricyclics in controlling problem behaviors is not very clear, given that few studies on their effects are available. In the two most recent and well-controlled studies, it was reported that imipramine caused an increase in food consumption, decreased screaming and crying, and stabilized sleep patterns in one study (Field, Aman, White, & Vaithianathan, 1986), and a significant increase in irritability, lethargy and social withdrawal, and hyperactivity in the other study (Aman, White, Vaithianathan, & Teehan, 1986).

The antidepressants are probably most commonly prescribed for the treatment of enuresis in persons with severe disabilities, as they are for children in the general population. However, the response of persons with severe disabilities to the antidepressants is typically associated with a less favorable outcome when compared with that of nondisabled peers. Enuresis in these individuals has not responded well to antidepressants (Aman & Singh, 1988).

Lithium carbonate is the only important antimanic drug that is used with students with severe disabilities. It appears to be the drug of choice for treating bipolar or recurrent unipolar depression in this population (Chandler, Gualtieri, & Fahs, 1988). Students diagnosed as having bipolar depression exhibit one or more manic episodes (elevated or irritable mood) and major depressive episodes. The few well-controlled studies available indicate that lithium may have a modest but clinically significant effect on affective symptoms (i.e., manic and depressive episodes). Further, several case reports and a small number of studies have found lithium to increase "adaptability" and reduce aggression, motor activity, restlessness, excitability, and self-injury.

Effects on Learning.   We do not know what effects antidepressant and antimanic drugs have on the learning, cognition, and adaptive behavior of persons with severe disabilities. What little is known about the effects of lithium on these functions has been extrapolated from studies with nondisabled persons.

Side Effects.   The antidepressants have several side effects similar to those reported for the antipsychotics, including dry mouth, constipation, difficulty with urination, and blurred vision. Tricyclics may also cause a decrease in blood pressure, a rapid heart rate, and occasionally, more serious changes in heart function. The most serious side effect of lithium carbonate is the potential for a central nervous system confusional state, including sluggishness, tremor, ataxia, coma, and seizures (which, in rare cases, have resulted in death).

Anxiolytics

The anxiolytics, or antianxiety drugs, such as diazepam (Valium) and chlordiazepoxide (Librium), are used fairly extensively in persons with severe disabilities. In addition to the treatment for anxiety, these drugs also are used as hypnotics or anticonvulsants (e.g., diazepam) or for their psychotropic effects in controlling such behaviors as hyperactivity, agitation, aggression, and disruption. There are no empirical studies evaluating the effects of anxiolytics on anxiety in persons with severe disabilities. The two best-controlled studies evaluated the effects on acting-out and hyper-

active behaviors and showed that anxiolytics significantly worsened these behaviors in persons with severe disabilities (La Veck & Buckley, 1961; Walters, Singh, & Beale, 1977). At present there is little indication for the use of anxiolytics to control specific problem behaviors in persons with severe disabilities; indeed, they may actually increase the occurrence of these behaviors.

Effects on Learning.   No empirical data are available on the effects that anxiolytic drugs may have on the learning or cognition of persons with severe disabilities.

Side Effects.   In the short term, the most frequent side effect of anxiolytics involves the sedative actions of these drugs; other short-term effects include headaches, nausea, skin rashes, and impaired sexual performance. Even at low doses they may induce aggressiveness and irritability. At higher doses there is increased activity, psychotic-like behavior, and suicidal actions. The long-term effects include a continuation of some of the short-term effects, along with physical and psychological dependence.

Stimulants

The stimulants, such as dextroamphetamine (Dexedrine), methylphenidate (Ritalin), and magnesium pemoline (Cylert), are the drugs of choice for treating hyperactivity in children; however, they are not widely used in persons with severe disabilities. The early, usually uncontrolled, studies on the effects of these drugs in persons with severe disabilities showed that they had few positive effects on a variety of problem behaviors. More recent studies, particularly those with persons who have mild to moderate levels of disability, have shown a modest but statistically significant decrease in hyperactivity and other behavior problems with the use of stimulant drug therapy (e.g., Varley & Trupin, 1982). However, studies show that the stimulants do not improve the hyperactive behavior (i.e., decrease such behavior) of persons with severe disabilities (Aman & Singh, 1982). What we can conclude from the results of the better-controlled studies is that the effects of stimulants decrease as the functional level of the person decreases.

Effects on Learning.   The cognitive effects of the stimulant drugs have not been well studied in persons with severe disabilities. The general finding from the few studies available suggests that they may worsen intellectual performance, as measured on the Weschler Adult Intelligence Scale (see Aman & Singh, 1991). No classroom-based studies have been conducted with students who have severe disabilities.

Side Effects.   Insomnia, decreased appetite, weight loss, abdominal pain, and headaches are the most frequently reported side effects of the stimulant drugs. Less common side effects include drowsiness, sadness, increased talkativeness, and dizziness. There is a temporary suppression of growth with chronic administration of methylphenidate and the amphetamines.

Antiepileptics

The antiepileptics are used to manage a variety of convulsive disorders, collectively known as epilepsy. A typical episode of epilepsy involves the disturbance or loss of consciousness, abnormal and excessive EEG discharge, convulsions or repetitive body movements in a characteristic pattern, and an increase in autonomic activity. Although there are over a dozen distinguishable forms of epilepsy, the three most common forms include the generalized tonic-clonic (grand mal), generalized absence (petit mal), and complex partial focal (psychomotor) epilepsy. Generalized tonic-clonic seizures are characterized by the person's losing consciousness without any premonitory symptoms (Gadow & Poling, 1988). Generalized absence seizures are characterized by a sudden onset, interruption of ongoing activities, a blank stare, and possibly a brief upward rotation of the eyes (Gadow & Poling, 1988). Partial sei-

zures are classified as simple if the person does not lose consciousness, and complex if he or she does lose consciousness during a seizure.

The primary mode of treatment for epilepsy is drug treatment, and such treatment is usually very effective (Stores, 1988). Seizure activity is fairly common among students with severe disabilities, and it is certain that many will be taking antiepileptic medication.

In the case of a student actually having a seizure while at school, teachers need to provide care for the student, particularly if he or she has a tonic-clonic seizure. Various, often contradictory, advice has been given to teachers on the procedures to be followed in such cases. The best advice we know comes from Gadow and Poling (1988, pp. 188–189), who recommend that the steps outlined in Table 16.2 be followed during the course of a seizure.

Psychotropic Effects of the Antiepileptics.
Antiepileptic drugs are thought to have useful psychotropic properties and are often prescribed specifically for the control of problem behaviors. In addition, even when prescribed for the control of epilepsy, a number of antiepileptic drugs appear to have effects on problem behavior and cognition.

Early studies strongly suggested that phenytoin (Dilantin) may have some behavioral effects on students with severe disabilities, but these claims have not been validated in subsequent well-controlled investigations (see Aman and Singh, 1991). More recently, attention has been directed at carbamazepine (Tegretol) as having useful behavioral effects, but, again, the empirical literature is not supportive of this notion regarding children (Evans, Clay, & Gualtieri, 1987; Reid, Naylor, & Kay, 1981; Singh & Winton, 1984), although the drug may be effective for treating certain psychiatric disorders in adults (Post & Uhde, 1986). Although some clinicians advocate the use of antiepileptic medication for their psychotropic effects, this is truly a case in which clinical enthusiasm far exceeds the scientific evidence for its purported effects.

TABLE 16.2   Guidelines for Managing a
Student Who Has an Epileptic Seizure

1. Remove any objects that the person may
   strike during the clonic phase (jerking
   movements) of the seizure.

2. Loosen restrictive clothing.

3. Turn the person on his or her side. This will
   allow saliva and vomitus to flow out of the
   mouth instead of being aspirated.

4. Do *not* try to restrain the person's movements
   during the active (tonic-clonic) phase of the
   seizure.

5. Do *not* try to move the person during the
   active phase of the seizure.

6. Do *not* insert any objects into the person's
   mouth. In the rare case that a doctor has
   recommended that an object be placed in the
   student's mouth to prevent self-injury, follow
   the specific directions of the doctor.

7. If the student lapses into a deep sleep
   following a seizure, do not awaken him or her.
   The student may be somewhat confused,
   afraid, and upset upon awakening.
   Appropriate explanation and supportive
   counseling by the teacher will help the student
   to continue with schoolwork.

Adapted from Gadow, K. D., & Poling, A. G. (1988).
Pharmacotherapy and mental retardation (p. 188).
Boston: College-Hill.

Unintended Behavioral Effects.   As noted earlier, antiepileptics are usually prescribed for the
management of seizure disorders. There is some
concern that long-term administration of these
drugs may cause untoward behavioral, cognitive,
or motoric effects. At high drug concentrations,
the long-term administration of phenobarbital
(Luminal), phenytoin (Dilantin), or primidone
(Mysoline) is associated with psychomotor deterioration. Deterioration of learning following administration of antiepileptics has been noted on
tests of intelligence, specialized tests of learning
and cognitive style, neuropsychological tests, ret-
rospective clinical judgments, and rating scales

(Gay, 1984). Although some studies actually indicated an improvement on some of these measures,
judging the research as a whole, the studies show a
consistent pattern of worsening performance following medication (Trimble & Corbett, 1980).

Phenobarbital has been noted to elicit hyperactivity and aggression in persons with severe disabilities,
especially children (Schain, 1979). Primidone also
has been noted to elicit hyperactivity in children.
However, there is little evidence in the literature to
suggest that carbamazepine (Tegretol) causes a deterioration in psychomotor functions. Indeed, the opposite is true, with some studies reporting cognitive
enhancement with this drug. Similar effects have
been noted with some other antiepileptics, such as
ethosuximide (Zarontin). Minimal adverse effects
have been noted with other drugs, such as valproic
acid (Depakene).

Toxic or Side Effects.   At high doses, the antiepileptics occasionally have toxic effects that may
become confused with the developmental disability
of a student with severe disabilities. These include
mental confusion, disturbances of coordination and
vision, lethargy, and slurred speech. Especially
with the drug phenytoin, these and other adverse
effects resulting in behavioral abnormalities, reduction in IQ, and other neurological symptoms
may seem to represent a progressive deterioration
in the student's neurological status. Blood abnormalities, gastrointestinal distress, and skin rashes
are additional potential adverse reactions.

Novel Agents

A number of novel psychoactive agents are being
used with persons who are severely disabled. The
rationale for their use has been the discovery of
biochemical abnormalities associated with cognitive, behavioral, or motor problems that may be
amenable to treatment with specific drugs.

Fenfluramine.   Elevated levels of the neuro-
transmitter serotonin, a chemical active in the
brain, has been hypothesized as a causal factor in
certain behavioral, cognitive, and motor problems

in persons with severe disabilities. For example, about 30 percent of persons with autism have been reported to have elevated serotonin levels. It has been suggested that a powerful serotonin antagonist drug, such as fenfluramine (Pondimin, Ponderax), may be useful in treating their problem behaviors by decreasing these individuals' serotonin levels to within the normal range.

Early studies, particularly those by Ritvo and his colleagues (1986), reported enhancement of IQ with fenfluramine, but this has not been confirmed in later studies. Although the data are mixed, there is a consistent pattern of results that show enhanced social relatedness, reduction in stereotypic and overactive behavior, and improved attention span in children with autism (Aman & Kern, 1989). Only further research will establish how well students with severe disabilities will respond to this drug.

Naloxone and Naltrexone.   Recently, a number of studies have reported that opiate antagonists (Naloxone, Naltrexone) may provide an effective treatment for self-injury in persons with severe disabilities on the basis of the purported role of endogenous opioids in the attenuation of pain (Singh, Singh, & Ellis, 1992). Thus far, the overall results are unclear, because some studies report the effectiveness of the drugs in reducing severe self-injury whereas others do not (Singh et al., 1992). However, there is enough theoretical interest in this pharmacological model of self-injury that further elucidation of the effects of opiate antagonists will be forthcoming in the near future.

Propranolol.   Propranolol (Inderal), usually prescribed for hypertension, angina pectoris, cardiac arrthymias, and essential tremor, has been found to control violent, explosive, and aggressive behaviors in persons with severe disabilities (Singh & Winton, 1989). Our knowledge of the effects of this drug on the behavior of persons with severe disabilities derives from several case reports and uncontrolled studies. However, there is intense interest in this drug because it promises control over a range of serious problem behaviors that of-ten prove intractable to both behavioral and psychopharmacological treatment.

Minerals, Diets, and Vitamins

Teachers and parents should be aware that various minerals, diets, and vitamins have been purported to have some beneficial effect on the behavior of persons with disabilities. At one time or another, a number of different treatments have been proposed, including glutamic acid, several vitamins, pituitary extract, sicca cell, and thyroid therapies. Based on the extant research literature, we can state with considerable confidence that none of these substances have a major effect on the behavior of persons with severe disabilities (Singh, 1987).

Some mention should be made of the Feingold diet, although it is typically used with nondisabled hyperactive children. Only about 5 percent of hyperactive children benefit (Singh, 1987), but the enthusiasm of some family physicians and parents for this diet has not diminished since it was first introduced. Studies conducted with persons who are mentally retarded show little effect of the diet on their behavior. Given the current lack of empirical verification, the Feingold diet does *not* present a viable alternative to other proven treatments.

MANAGEMENT ISSUES

There are a number of management issues that teachers of students with severe disabilities need to be aware of. First and foremost, teachers should be familiar with the general effects and side effects of drugs because it is more than likely that some students in each class will be receiving medication (see Table 16.3). Teachers are probably the prime sources of information with regard to the possible effects of medication on a student's behavior and learning during school hours. It is therefore imperative that teachers fully participate in any clinical decision making regarding the pharmacotherapy of their students; otherwise, decisions will be made that may not be responsive to a student's needs in the classroom.

TABLE 16.3 Recommended Doses for the Various Classes of Drugs

Drugs	Dose (mg)		
	CHILDREN	**ADOLESCENTS**	**ADULTS**
Antipsychotics			
chlorpromazine (>6 mos of age)*	10–200	10–200+ (max. 2 mg/kg)	100–800
thioridazine (>2 yrs of age)*	10–200	10–200+ (max. 3 mg/kg)	<800
trifluoperazine (>6 yrs of age)*	1–15	1–15+	15–40
thiothixene (>12 yrs of age)*		5–40 (av. 15)	20–60
haloperidol (>3 yrs of age)*	.05–8	2–16 (.02–.2 mg/kg)	2–16(+)
reserpine	.02–.25	.1–1.0	.1–1.0
Antidepressants			
amitriptyline** (>12 yrs of age)*		25–50	75–150
desipramine** (>12 yrs of age)*		25–150	100–200
imipramine** (>6 yrs of age)*	25–75	25–100 (max. 5 mg)	75–200
nortriptyline** (>12 yrs of age)*		75–150 (0.5–2 mg/kg)	75–150
phenelzine (>16 yrs of age)*			45–90
Antimanics			
lithium carbonate** (>12 yrs of age)*		900–1200	900–1200
Anxiolytics			
alprazolam (>18 yrs of age)*	.25–4	.75–8	.75–8
chlordiazepoxide (6 yrs of age)*	10–30	20–60	20–100
diazepam (>6 mos of age)*	1–15	2–30 (max. 0.8 mg)	4–40
lorazepam (12 yrs of age)*	.25–4	.5–9	1–10

TABLE 16.3   Continued

Drugs	Dose (mg)		
	CHILDREN	**ADOLESCENTS**	**ADULTS**
Anxiolytics (cont.)			
diphenhydramine	25–200	50–300 (max. 5 mg/kg)	50–400
hydroxyzine	25–200	50–300 (max. 5 mg/kg)	100–400
Stimulants			
dextroamphetamine (>3 yrs of age)*	1.25	5–40 (.15–.5mg/kg)	10–40
methylphenidate (>6 yrs of age)*	2.5–30	10–60 (.3–1mg/kg)	20–60
pemoline (>6 yrs of age)*	18–75	37–112	37–112
Antiepileptics (when used to control seizures)			
carbamazepine** (>6 yrs of age)*	200–1000	400–1000	400–1200
ethosuximide**	250–800	500–1500 (av. 20–30 mg/kg)	500–1500
phenobarbitol**	<250	150–250 (av. 4–6 mg/kg)	150–250
phenytoin**	<300	300–750 (av. 4–8 mg/kg)	300–750
sodium valproate**	250–500	500–1000	750–1250
primidone	450–750	750–2000	750–2000
Others			
fenfluramine (dose for weight loss) (>12 yrs of age)*		60–120	60–120
propranolol (dose for hypertension)	5–80	20–140 (max. 2 mg/kg)	80–480
naloxone naltrexone	0.5–1.5 mg/kg	0.5–1.5 mg/kg	0.5–1.5mg/kg

*Recommended FDA guidelines
**Dosage titrated using serum levels

Role of Medication

There is some confusion among teachers about the role of medication in the behavior management and learning of students with severe disabilities. Medication is typically used as one component of a broad therapeutic approach to help students control their behavior and learn alternative but acceptable forms of behavior (Singh et al., 1993). Medication does *not* teach the student any new skills; it merely acts as a setting event for the occurrence of appropriate behavior by reducing maladaptive behaviors. When problem behaviors are reduced, the classroom environment is more conducive to students' learning appropriate social and academic skills. For psychiatric problems (such as anxiety or depression), medication provides symptomatic relief, allowing a student to function more fully at school and at home. Furthermore, it must be remembered that medication may relieve a student's symptoms of psychiatric illness, but it does not remove the vulnerability to its recurrence, because the environmental and constitutional stresses that gave rise to the illness are not affected by medication.

Teachers' Knowledge and Perceptions of Psychotropic Drugs

Given that drug therapy is a fairly common treatment modality for students with severe behavior disorders, it is essential that teachers be well informed about the effects and side effects of drugs. However, in two recent studies teachers reported that their preservice training had provided them with insufficient information on the use of medication (Epstein, Singh, Leubke, & Stout, 1991; Singh, Epstein, Leubke, & Singh, 1990). Moreover, these teachers also reported that they had minimal in-service training on this topic. They suggested that the major effects of drugs, alternatives to medication, and the assessment of drug effects would be high on their priority list for future in-service training. Similar findings have been reported from a study with direct care staff

who work with persons with severe disabilities (Aman, Singh, & White, 1987).

Professional Roles and Drug Decisions

Recent studies on clinical decision making regarding drug therapy for students with severe disabilities indicate that the unit director and, to a lesser extent, the student's doctor are perceived as the prime movers in either starting or stopping medication for a student's behavior problems (Aman et al., 1987). School personnel are seen as having relatively little influence in the decision-making process. This is an interesting finding, given that teachers are in contact with the students for the better part of a school day and are in a unique position to provide reliable evaluation of drug effects. The extent to which teachers' lack of knowledge and technical language necessary to communicate properly with school personnel has led to this situation remains to be explored (Gadow & Kane, 1983).

We see the establishment of an interdisciplinary case committee as the best route to take in clinical decision making involving drug or alternative therapies (see Singh et al., 1993). Members of this committee should include parents, teachers, school psychologists, physician, school nurse, and school principal. The current literature indicates that, as compared with the traditional model—the physician alone making the treatment decision—an interdisciplinary team decision-making model results in far fewer students receiving medication (Briggs, 1989; Findholt & Emmett, 1990).

Evaluation of Drug Effects

Teachers are in an ideal position to evaluate the effects of drugs on the behavior and learning of their students. They can inform the physician and the interdisciplinary team if the side effects of a drug are impairing a student's school performance, or if the drug is in fact having any effect at all. The doctor can use this information to either change the dosage (see Table 16.4), change the medication, or alter the mode of treatment.

Teachers of students with learning disabilities or serious emotional disturbance have reported that they are willing to use assessment strategies that require additional time and effort in order to evaluate the effects of medication on their students (Epstein et al., 1991; Singh et al., 1990). This is in contrast to the preference of direct care workers and nurses working with persons with severe disabilities, which is to use assessment instruments that can be incorporated into their routine duties rather than take additional time to use more formal approaches of assessment (Aman et al., 1987). A number of well-validated instruments are currently available for assessing the effects of medication on students with severe disabilities, but teachers may need continuing education in order to incorporate these strategies into their current practices.

Teachers' Views on Alternatives to Medication

Given that psychotropic medication is typically prescribed for controlling problem behaviors, teachers tend to view behavior modification as a suitable alternative treatment, especially for behaviors such as acting out and aggression (Singh et al., 1990). This is probably a reflection of their background training toward psychological treatment for problem behaviors that are usually externally motivated, and their observation of the sometimes limited effects of drugs in controlling such behaviors. However, behavior modification is not seen as a suitable alternative for the more internalized disorders (e.g., depression, delusions, hallucinations) that traditionally have been treated with medication.

Medication Practices and Policies at School

Teachers of students with severe disabilities are often required to administer medication at school. For example, in one study, 42 percent of teachers in classes for students with moderate to severe

mental retardation, as well as all teachers in early childhood special education classes, administered medication at school (Gadow, 1982). It is likely that the school nurse also is involved in much of the medication administration at school. Yet this is an added burden: the teacher not only has to evaluate the effects of medication, but also has to make sure that the students actually receive their medication while at school.

Given the high prevalence of medication usage at school, it is imperative that each school district have a drug policy (Singh et al., 1990). However, in one study it was reported that only 32 percent of a random sample of 159 school districts in the United States had policies concerning the administration and storage of prescribed medication in their schools (Kinnison & Nimmer, 1979). Further, in a study of state policies, Courtnage (1982) found that the majority of the states do not have legislation or regulations concerning the use of medication in schools. It is essential that school districts serving students with severe disabilities use a multidisciplinary team approach to develop comprehensive drug policies.

Role of Family Members and Direct Care Staff

Family members and direct care staff can play a role similar to that of the teacher in administering medication and evaluating its effects on the student. They are also seen as being an important part of the multidisciplinary treatment team that decides on the nature of treatment required and the manner in which it should be carried out. The family members and direct care staff are able to provide information on the student's behavior in his or her natural environment. Given that medication may have contextual effects (see Singh & Aman, 1990), it is important that the behavior of students receiving medication be assessed in different environmental conditions. For example, in one study it was found that medication reduced undesirable behaviors in the classroom, but not in the dayroom (Schroeder & Gualtieri, 1985).

TABLE 16.4   Effects and Side Effects of Various Classes of Drugs

---

DRUG CLASS

Antipsychotics

Indications: Psychotic states; schizophrenia (exacerbations and maintenance); mania (in conjunction with lithium); agitation, aggressivity, self-injury, and stereotypical behaviors in mental retardation and pervasive developmental disorders; dyskinetic movement disorders (e.g., Tourette's disorder and Juvenile Huntington's disease); and severe behavioral dyscontrol/intractable aggressivity

Side effects: Anticholinergic effects, including dry mouth, constipation, blurred vision, and urinary retention; parkinsonian symptoms, including acute dystonia, malignant neuroleptic syndrome, akathesia, tardive dyskinesia, and perioral tremor; other central nervous system effects, including sedation, fatigue, cognitive blunting, psychotic symptoms, confusion, and excitement; orthostatic hypotension and cardiac conduction abnormalities; endocrine disturbances (e.g., menstrual irregularities and weight gain); gastrointestinal distress; skin photosensitivity; and allergic reactions

---

Antidepressants

Indications: Enuresis; attention-deficit hyperactive disorder; major depressive disorder; phobic disorders (including school phobia); separation anxiety disorder; panic disorder; and obsessive-compulsive disorder

Side effects: Anticholinergic effects, including dry mouth, constipation, blurred vision, and urinary retention; cardiac conduction slowing, increased and/or irregular pulse rate and decreased or increased blood pressure; confusion or the induction of psychosis; seizures; rash; and endocrine abnormalities

---

Antimanics

Indications: Manic episodes of manic-depressive illness, unipolar depression

Effects: Normalization of the symptoms of mania, which may include pressure of speech, hyperactivity, grandiosity, elation, poor judgment, reduced need for sleep, flight of ideas, aggressiveness, irritability, and hostility

Side effects: Kidney abnormalities leading to increased urination and thirst; gastrointestinal distress; fine hand tremor, weakness and ataxia; thyroid abnormalities, weight gain, and electrolyte imbalances; sedation, confusion, slurred speech, irritability, headache, and subtle cogwheel rigidity; orthostatic hypotension and pulse rate irregularities; and allergic reactions

TABLE 16.4   Continued

DRUG CLASS

Anxiolytics

Indications: Anxiety disorders; seizure control; night terrors; sleepwalking; insomnia and acute management of agitation and impulsivity

Side effects: Headache, sedation, and decreased cognitive performance; behavioral disinhibition, including overexcitement, hyperactivity, increased aggressivity, and irritability; gastrointestinal distress; central nervous system disinhibition resulting in hallucinations, psychotic-like behavior, and suicidal actions; physical and psychological dependence; blood abnormalities; and allergic reactions

Stimulants

Indications: Attention-deficit hyperactive disorder in children, adolescents, and adults (including those with mental retardation, fragile X syndrome, Tourette's disorder, head trauma, and pervasive developmental disorders)

Effects: Decreased hyperactivity, distractibility, and impulsivity; improved motivation, attention, and short-term memory; reduced oppositionality and aggressivity

Side effects: Decreased appetite, weight loss; abdominal pain; headaches, insomnia, irritability, sadness and depression, and increased excitability and talkativeness; increases in pulse rate and blood pressure; and temporary suppression of growth

Antiepileptics

Indications: Seizure control; severe behavior problems (e.g., aggression, self-injury)

Side effects: Sedation, weakness, dizziness, disturbances of coordination and vision, hallucinations, confusion, abnormal movements, nystagmus, slurred speech, and depression; blood abnormalities; gastrointestinal distress; skin rashes, alterations in pigmentation and photosensitivity reactions; increased or decreased blood pressure and congestive heart failure; abnormalities of liver functions: genitourinary tract dysfunction; and coarsening of facial features, enlargement of the lips, gingival hyperplasia, and excessive hair growth (phenytoin)

(continued)

TABLE 16.4   Continued

DRUG CLASS

Others

Fenfluramine

Indications: Management of obesity; control of some behavior problems

Side effects: Drowsiness, dizziness, confusion, headache, incoordination, mood alterations, anxiety, insomnia, weakness, agitation, and slurred speech; gastrointestinal distress; increased or decreased blood pressure and palpitations; skin rashes; dry mouth; eye irritation; and muscle aches

Naloxone and Naltrexone

Indications: Reversal of narcotic depression; control of self-injurious behavior

Side effects: Drowsiness, dizziness, dry mouth, sweating, nausea, abdominal pain, and loss of energy

Propranolol

Indications: Hypertension, angina pectoris, and cardiac arrhythmias; psychiatric disorders, especially those manifesting explosive and violent behavior

Side effects: Decreased heart rate, peripheral circulation and blood pressure; fatigue, weakness, insomnia, nightmares, dizziness, hallucinations, and mild symptoms of depression; shortness of breath and wheezing (especially in patients with asthma); and gastrointestinal distress

At a more basic level, parents have the responsibility of making sure that the student actually takes the medication each day as specified by the doctor. Medication compliance is a problem with all children, but particularly so in students with severe disabilities. Parents also have to make certain that the school authorities are alerted to the fact that their child is receiving medication and, if the medication is to be taken at school, the dosage that is to be administered.

Parents need to provide their permission and written instructions to the teacher or school nurse for giving the medication to the child as directed by the doctor. It is probably best if each school district has a standard form designed specifically for this purpose, which parents are requested to complete and sign. The completed form should be filed at the school together with the student's permanent records.

Furthermore, parents should inform the teacher of any changes in dosage or drug, and of any side effects that may interfere with school performance. Teachers should make sure that the medication is properly labeled (with the student's name, name of the drug, dosage schedule, and who is authorized to administer the medication) and stored appropriately (but not in the classroom) and that precise records of drug administration are kept.

Guidelines for Teachers

A number of professionals have provided guidelines for teachers and other school personnel regarding medication management. In Table 16.5,

TABLE 16.5 Guidelines for Teachers on Medication Management

1. Learn about the commonly used therapeutic drugs, their indications and contra-indications, and possible side effects.

2. Become better informed about the effects that various drugs may have on the behavior and learning of students with severe disabilities.

3. Familiarize yourself with and closely follow your school's policy regarding the administration of prescribed drugs to students at school. (School districts and states lacking such a policy should develop one in order to legally protect personnel who must administer medication).

4. Actively engage in communication with the doctor and the interdisciplinary committee regarding each student's medication.

5. Collect data on target behaviors before, during, and after drug treatment. It is also useful to collect data on other behaviors that may change as a consequence of taking medication (e.g., learning).

6. Collect data on anticipated side effects of the drugs. A prior knowledge of the side effects of different drugs will help.

7. Discuss the anticipated effects of the drug, and possible side effects, with the student.

8. Discuss the anticipated effects of the drug, and possible side effects, with the parent. Also explain to the parent why it is essential that the student take his or her medication as prescribed by the doctor.

9. Continue to provide the best educational program possible and provide related services where indicated. Remember that drugs do not teach new skills, teachers do.

Adapted and extended from Epstein, M. H., & Olinger, E. (1987). Use of medication in school programs for behaviorally disordered pupils. *Behavioral Disorders, 12,* 138–145.

we present one set of guidelines, adapted from Epstein and Olinger (1987). It is the responsibility of the school personnel and the parent to initiate and maintain good communication between members of the school-parent-doctor-interdisciplinary treatment team whenever medication therapy is started for a student. Studies have shown that if there is a breakdown in communication between any of these persons, it is usually due to the absence of a plan for the exchange of information rather than to a lack of concern (Sprague & Ullman, 1981). The school's medication policy should have established procedures for initiating and maintaining such communication. Schools may adapt and use the data collection and communication form proposed by Brulle, Barton, and Foskett (1983).

CONCLUSION

Increasingly, students with severe disabilities are placed in special and regular education classes in the community, and often they are treated with medication. Although teachers are not expected to be experts, some knowledge of the various therapeutic drugs, the indications for their use, and common side effects will assist them not only in understanding the student better but also in being able to liaise with the doctor and the interdisciplinary treatment team regarding the student's treatment. Such knowledge should help the teacher in evaluating the effects of medication on the student's behavior and learning. This chapter's presentation of the issues involved in the management of medication for students with severe disabilities is brief by design; however, for a more extensive coverage of this topic, teachers may consult the textbook *Psychopharmacology for the Developmental Disabilities* (Aman & Singh, 1988).

REFERENCES

Aman, M. G. (1984). Drugs and learning in mentally retarded persons. *Advances in Human Psychopharmacology, 3,* 121–163.

Aman, M. G., & Kern, R. A. (1989). Review of fenfluramine in the treatment of the developmental disabilities. *Journal of the American Academy of Child and Adolescent Psychiatry, 28,* 549–565.

Aman, M. G., & Singh, N. N. (1991). Psychopharmacological intervention: An update. In J. L. Matson & J. A. Mulick (Eds.), *Handbook of mental retardation* (2nd ed., pp. 347–372). New York: Pergamon Press.

Aman, M. G., & Singh, N. N. (1988). *Psychopharmacology of the developmental disabilities.* New York: Springer-Verlag.

Aman, M. G., & Singh, N. N. (1982). Methylphenidate in severely retarded residents and the clinical significance of stereotypic behavior. *Applied Research in Mental Retardation, 3,* 1–14.

Aman, M. G., & Singh, N. N. (1980). The usefulness of thioridazine for treating childhood disorders: Fact or folklore? *American Journal of Mental Deficiency, 84,* 331–338.

Aman, M. G., Singh, N. N., & White, A. J. (1987). Caregiver perceptions of psychotropic medication in residential facilities. *Research in Developmental Disabilities, 8,* 449–465.

Aman, M. G., White, A. J., Vaithianathan, C., & Teehan, C. J. (1986). Preliminary study of imipramine in profoundly retarded residents. *Journal of Autism and Developmental Disorders, 16,* 263–273.

Briggs, R. (1989). Monitoring and evaluating psychotropic drug use for persons with mental retardation: A follow-up report. *American Journal of Mental Retardation, 93,* 633–639.

Brulle, A. R., Barton, L. E., & Foskett, J. J. (1983). Educator/physician interchanges: A survey and suggestions. *Education and Training of the Mentally Retarded, 18,* 313–317.

Chandler, M., Gualtieri, C. T., & Fahs, J. J. (1988). Other psychotropic drugs. In M. G. Aman & N. N. Singh (Eds.), *Psychopharmacology of the developmental disabilities* (pp. 119–145). New York: Springer-Verlag.

Courtnage, L. (1982). A survey of state policies on the use of medication in schools. *Exceptional Children, 49,* 75–77.

Epstein, M. H., & Olinger, E. (1987). Use of medication in school programs for behaviorally disordered pupils. *Behavioral Disorders, 12,* 138–145.

Epstein, M. H., Singh, N. N., Leubke, J., & Stout, C. E. (1991). Psychopharmacological intervention: II. Teacher perceptions of psychotropic medication for students with learning disabilities. *Journal of Learning Disabilities, 24,* 477–483.

Evans, R. W., Clay, T. H., & Gualtieri, T. (1987). Carbamazepine in pediatric psychiatry. *Journal of the American Academy of Child and Adolescent Psychiatry, 26,* 2–8.

Field, C. J., Aman, M. G., White, A. J., & Vaithianathan, C. (1986). A single-subject study of imipramine in a mentally retarded woman with depressive symptoms. *Journal of Mental Deficiency Research, 30,* 191–198.

Findholt, N. E., & Emmett, C. G. (1990). Impact of interdisciplinary team review on psychotropic drug use with persons who have mental retardation. *Mental Retardation, 25,* 41–46.

Gadow, K. D. (1986). *Children on medication.* Boston: College-Hill.

Gadow, K. D. (1982). School involvement in the treatment of seizure disorders. *Epilepsia, 23,* 215–224.

Gadow, K. D., & Kane, K. M. (1983). Administration of medication by school personnel. *Journal of School Health, 53,* 178–183.

Gadow, K. D., & Poling, A. G. (1988). *Pharmacotherapy and mental retardation.* Boston: College-Hill.

Gay, P. E. (1984). Effects of antiepileptic drugs and seizure type on operant responding in mentally retarded persons. *Epilepsia, 25,* 377–386.

Kinnison, L., & Nimmer, D. (1979). An analysis of policies regulating medication in the schools. *Journal of School Health, 49,* 280–283.

LaVeck, G. D., & Buckley, P. (1961). The use of psychopharmacologic agents in retarded children with behavior disorders. *Journal of Chronic Diseases, 13,* 174–183.

Post, R. M., & Uhde, T. W. (1986). Anticonvulsants in non-epileptic psychosis. In M. R. Trimble & T. G. Bolwig (Eds.), *Aspects of epilepsy and psychiatry* (pp. 177–212). New York: John Wiley & Sons.

Price v. Sheppard, Minnesota Supreme Court, 239 N.W. 2d 905 (1976).

Reid, A. H., Naylor, G. J., & Kay, D. S. G. (1981). A double-blind placebo controlled, crossover trial of carbamazepine in overactive, severely mentally handicapped patients. *Psychological Medicine, 11,* 109–113.

Ritvo, E. R., Freeman, B. J., Yuwiler, A., Geller, E., Schroth, P., & Yokota, A. (1986). Fenfluramine treatment of autism: UCLA collaborative study of 81 patients at nine medical centers. *Psychopharmacology Bulletin, 22,* 133–147.

Schain, R. J. (1979). Problems with the use of conventional anticonvulsant drugs in mentally retarded individuals. *Brain and Development, 1,* 77–82.

Schroeder, S. R. (1988). Neuroleptic medications for persons with developmental disabilities. In M. G. Aman & N. N. Singh (Eds.), *Psychopharmacology of the developmental disabilities* (pp. 82–100). New York: Springer-Verlag.

Schroeder, S. R., & Gualtieri, C. T. (1985). Behavioral interactions induced by chronic neuroleptic therapy in persons with mental retardation. *Psychopharmacology Bulletin, 21,* 310–315.

Singh, N. N. (1987). Diet and childhood behavior disorders. In J. Birkbeck (Ed.), *Are we really what we eat?* (pp. 35–45). Auckland, New Zealand: Dairy Advisory Bureau.

Singh, N. N., & Aman, M. G. (1981). Effects of thioridazine dosage on the behavior of severely mentally retarded persons. *American Journal of Mental Deficiency, 85,* 580–587.

Singh, N. N., & Aman, N. N. (1990). Ecobehavioral assessment of pharmacotherapy. In S. Schroeder (Ed.), *Ecobehavioral analysis in developmental disabilities* (pp. 182–200). New York: Springer-Verlag.

Singh, N. N., Epstein, M. H., Luebke, J., & Singh, Y. N. (1990). Psychopharmacological intervention: I. Teacher perceptions of psychotropic medication for seriously emotionally disturbed students. *The Journal of Special Education, 24,* 283–295.

Singh, N. N., Parmelee, D. X., Sood, A., & Katz, R. C. (1993). Collaboration of disciplines. In J. L. Matson (Ed.), *Handbook of hyperactivity in children* (pp. 305–322). Boston: Allyn & Bacon.

Singh, N. N., Singh, Y. N., & Ellis, C. R. (1992). Psychopharmacology of self-injury. In J. K. Luiselli, J. L. Matson, & N. N. Singh (Eds.), *Self-injury: Assessment, analysis, and treatment* (pp. 307–351). New York: Springer-Verlag.

Singh, N. N., Sood, A., Sonenklar, N., & Ellis, C. R. (1991). Assessment and diagnosis of mental illness in persons with mental retardation: Methods and measures. *Behavior Modification, 15,* 419–443.

Singh, N. N., & Winton, A. S. W. (1989). Behavioral pharmacology. In J. K. Luiselli (Ed.), *Behavioral medicine and developmental disabilities* (pp. 152–179). New York: Springer-Verlag.

Singh, N. N., & Winton, A. S. W. (1984). Behavioral monitoring of pharmacological interventions for self-injury. *Applied Research in Mental Retardation, 5,* 161–170.

Sprague, R. L., & Gadow, K. D. (1976). The role of the teacher in drug treatment. *School Review, 85,* 109–140.

Sprague, R. L., & Ullman, R. K. (1981). Psychoactive drugs and child management. In J. M. Kauffman & D. P. Hallahan (Eds.), *Handbook of special education* (pp. 749–766). Englewood Cliffs, NJ: Prentice Hall.

Stores, G. (1988). Antiepileptic drugs. In M. G. Aman & N. N. Singh (Eds.), *Psychopharmacology of the developmental disabilities* (pp. 101–118). New York: Springer-Verlag.

Trimble, M. R., & Corbett, J. A. (1980). Behavioral and cognitive disturbances in epileptic children. *Irish Medical Journal, 73,* 21–28.

Varley, C. K., & Trupin, E. W. (1982). Double-blind administration of methylphenidate to mentally retarded children with attention deficit disorder: A preliminary study. *American Journal of Mental Deficiency, 86,* 560–566.

Walters, A., Singh, N. N., & Beale, I. L. (1977). Effects of lorazepam on hyperactivity in retarded children. *New Zealand Medical Journal, 86,* 473–475.

Welsch v. Likins, 375 F. Supp. 487 (D. Minn., 1974).

Wyatt v. Stickney, 503 F. 2d 1305 (1972).

INDEX